**Do you want to become a stronger reader?**
**Do you want to track your progress in your reading course?**
**Do you want to get a better grade?**

**MyReadingLab has helped students all over the country improve as readers and succeed in college. MyReadingLab will help you become a better reader and help you get a better grade too!**

---

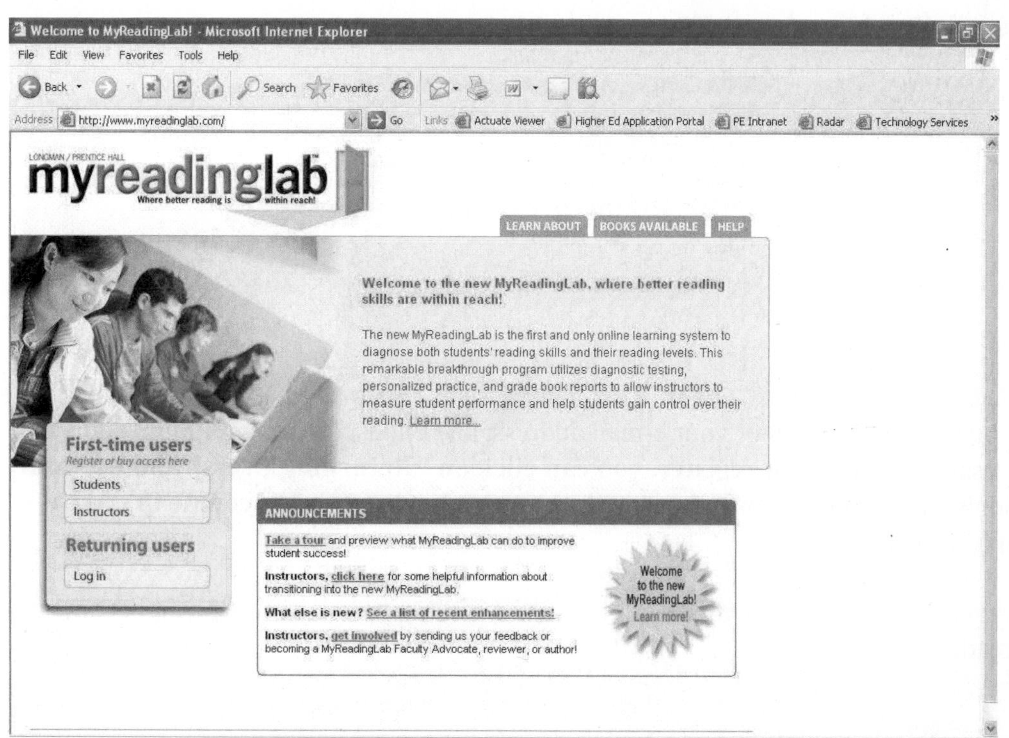


**www.myreadinglab.com**

# REGISTER …

It is easy to get started! Simply follow these easy steps to get into your MyReadingLab course.

1) **Find Your Access Code** (it is either packaged with your textbook, or you purchased it separately in the bookstore or at www.myreadinglab.com). You will need this access code and your COURSEID to log into your MyReadingLab course. Your instructor already has your COURSEID, so make sure you have that before logging in.

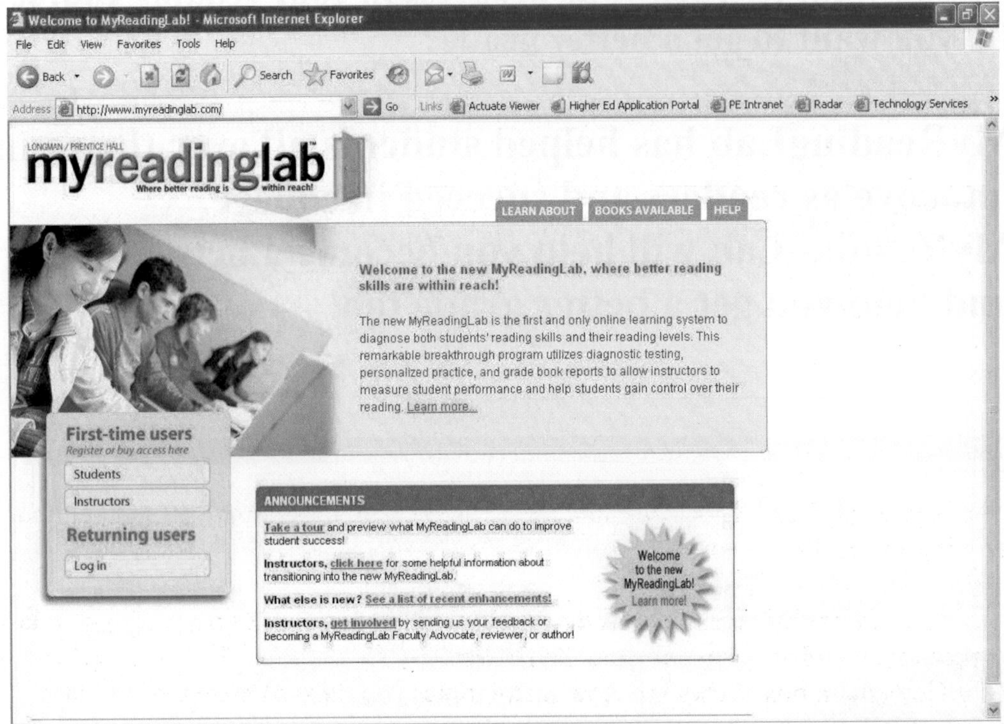


2) Click on "Students" under "First-Time Users." Here you will be prompted to enter your access code, enter your e-mail address, and choose your own Login Name and Password. **Once you register, you can click on "Returning Users" and use your new login name and password every time you go back into your course in MyReadingLab.**

After logging in, you will see all the ways MyReadingLab can help you become a better reader.

**www.myreadinglab.com**

# HOME PAGE ...

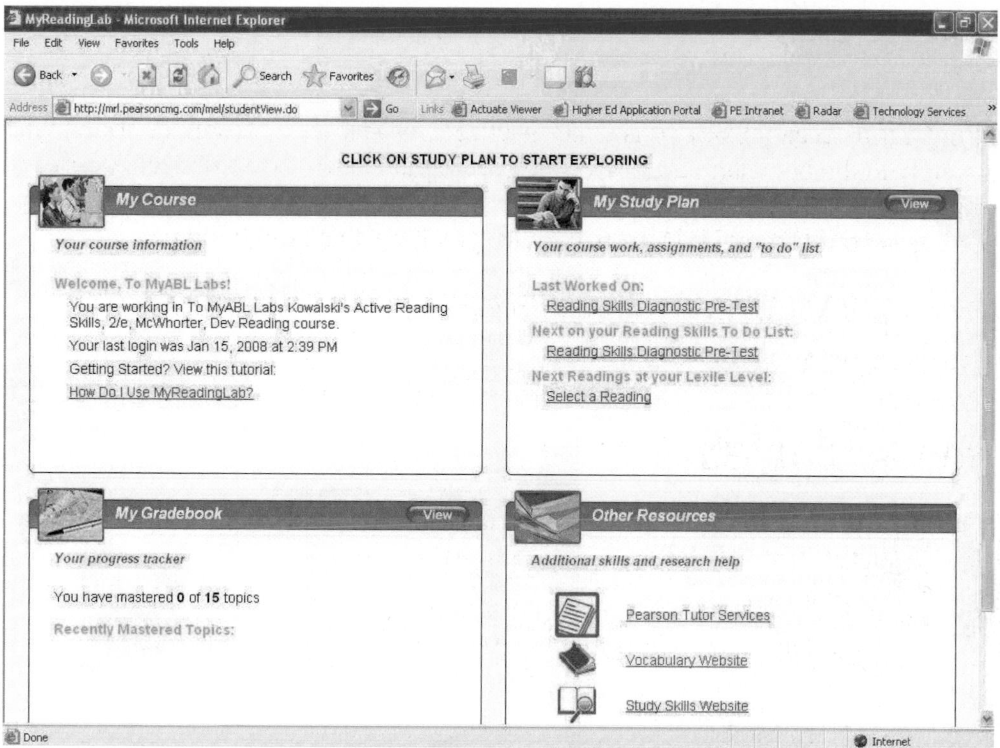


Here is your MyReadingLab Home Page. You get a quick summary of your course standing(s) every time you log in.

Your course box displays the class details. Your Study Plan box shows what you last worked on and what is next on your To Do list.
Your Gradebook box shows you how many topics you have mastered in the class.
Your Other Resources box supplies you with amazing tools such as:

- Pearson Tutor Services – click here and see how you can get help on your papers by qualified tutors ... before handing them in!
- Vocabulary Website – this site provides additional support with definitions of key words, quizzes, and more to help you develop your vocabulary skills.
- Study Skills – extra help that includes tips, and quizzes on how to improve your study skills.
- Research Navigator – click here and see how this resembles your library with access to online journals to research paper assignments.

---------------------------------------------

Now, let's start practicing to become better readers. Click on the Study Plan tab. This is where you will do all your course work.

# STUDY PLAN …

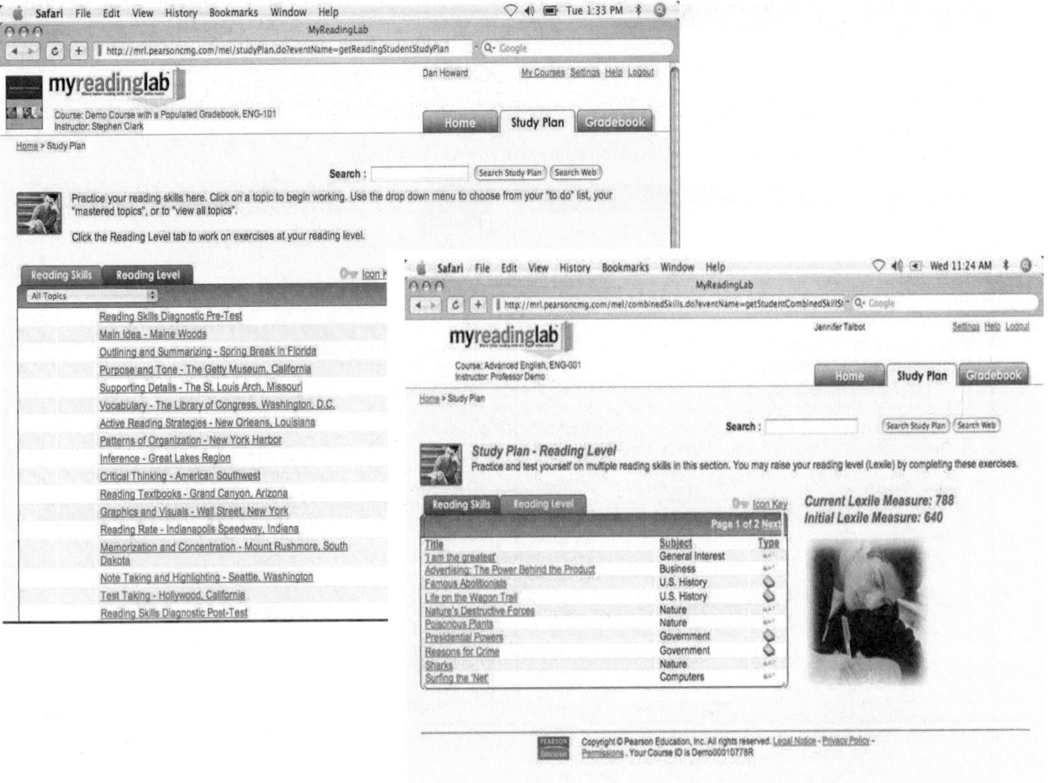


The extensive practice in *MyReadingLab* was designed to make you a better reader. Practice opportunities come in two formats:

- practice with the individual skills to improve you **reading skill** mastery.
- practice reading comprehension skills to improve your **reading level.** Your instructor can choose to offer this section to you, so you may or may not see this in your MyReadingLab course.

MyReadingLab allows you to practice reading skills through a mastery-based format in which you get an overview of the skill, see models of the skill at work, go through an abundance of practice exercises to apply what you have learned, and then take a mastery test.

# DIAGNOSTIC PRE-TESTS …

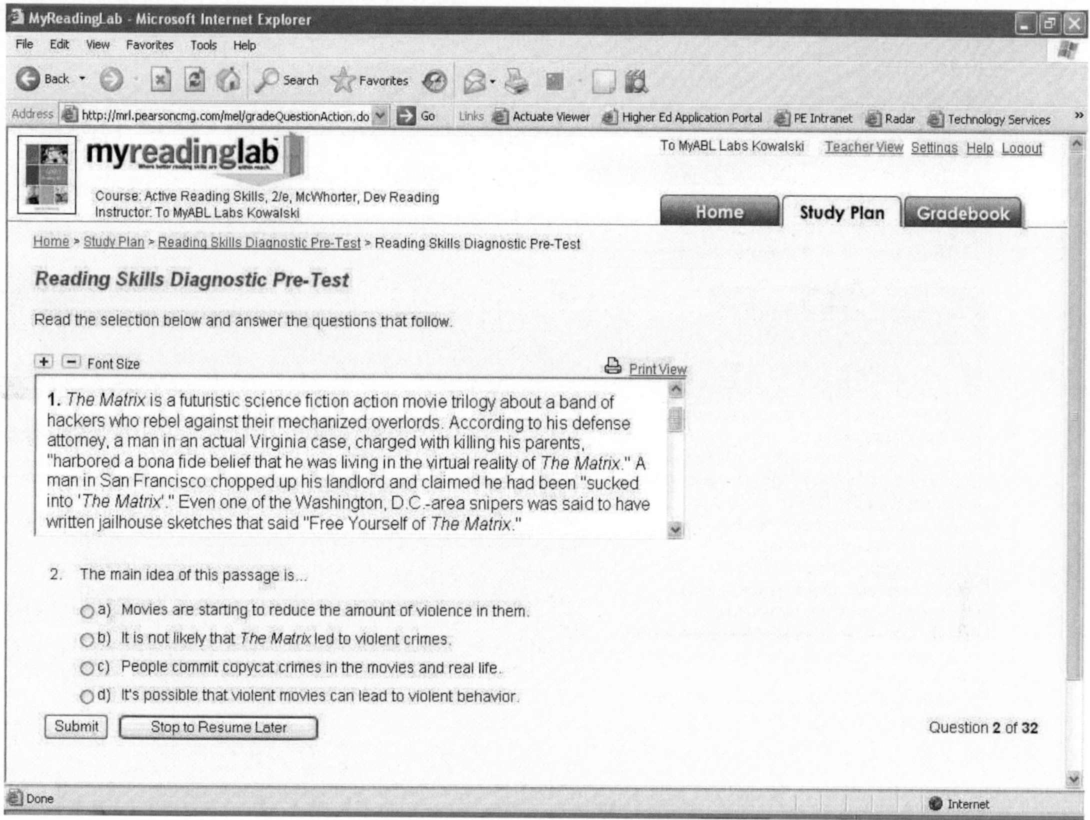


Your instructor may assign the Reading Skill diagnostic pre-test to assess your strengths at the individual skill level. The Reading Level diagnostic provides you with an initial "Lexile" measurement, which you and your instructor can use to measure reading level progress through the semester.

After completing the diagnostic pre-test, you can return to your study plan and work on any concepts that you have yet to master.

# GRADEBOOK …

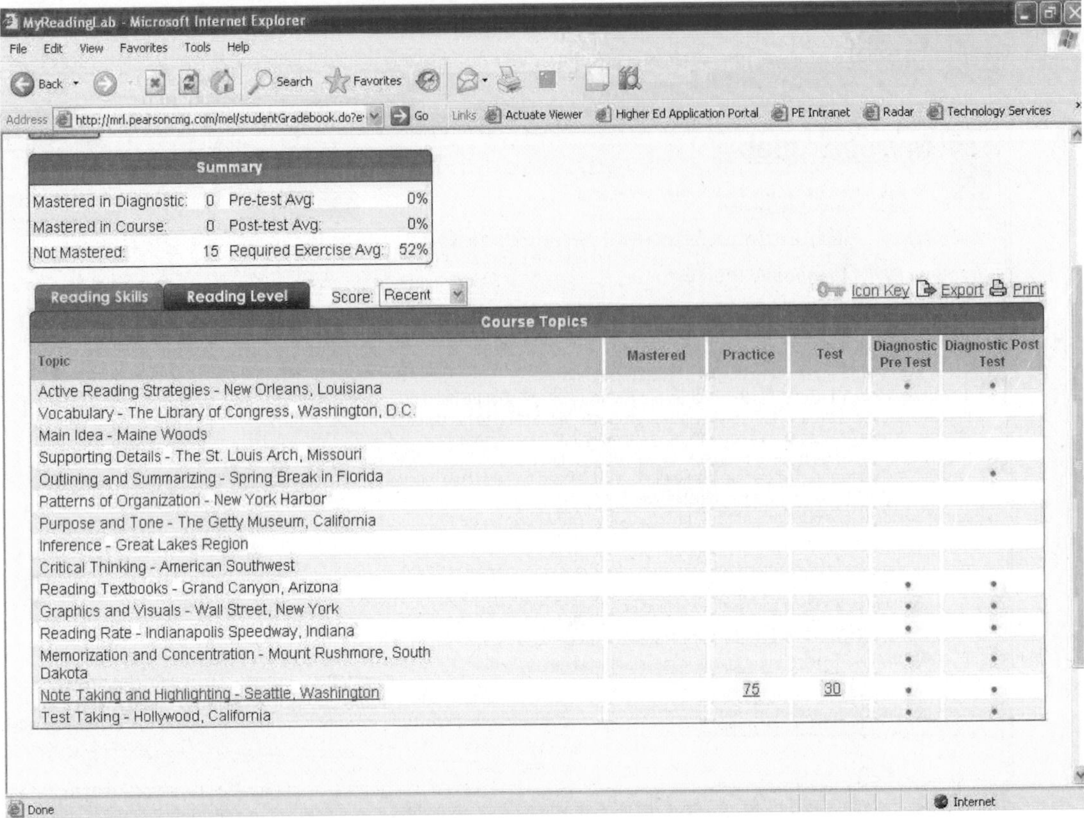


Let's look at how your MyReadingLab gradebook will help you track your progress.

Click on the "Gradebook" tab and the "Student Detail" report

Here you are able to see how you are doing in each area. If you feel you need to go back and review, simply click on any score and your score sheet will appear.

You also have a Diagnostic Detail report so you can go back and review your diagnostic pretest and see how much MyReadingLab has helped you improve!

# HERE TO HELP YOU …

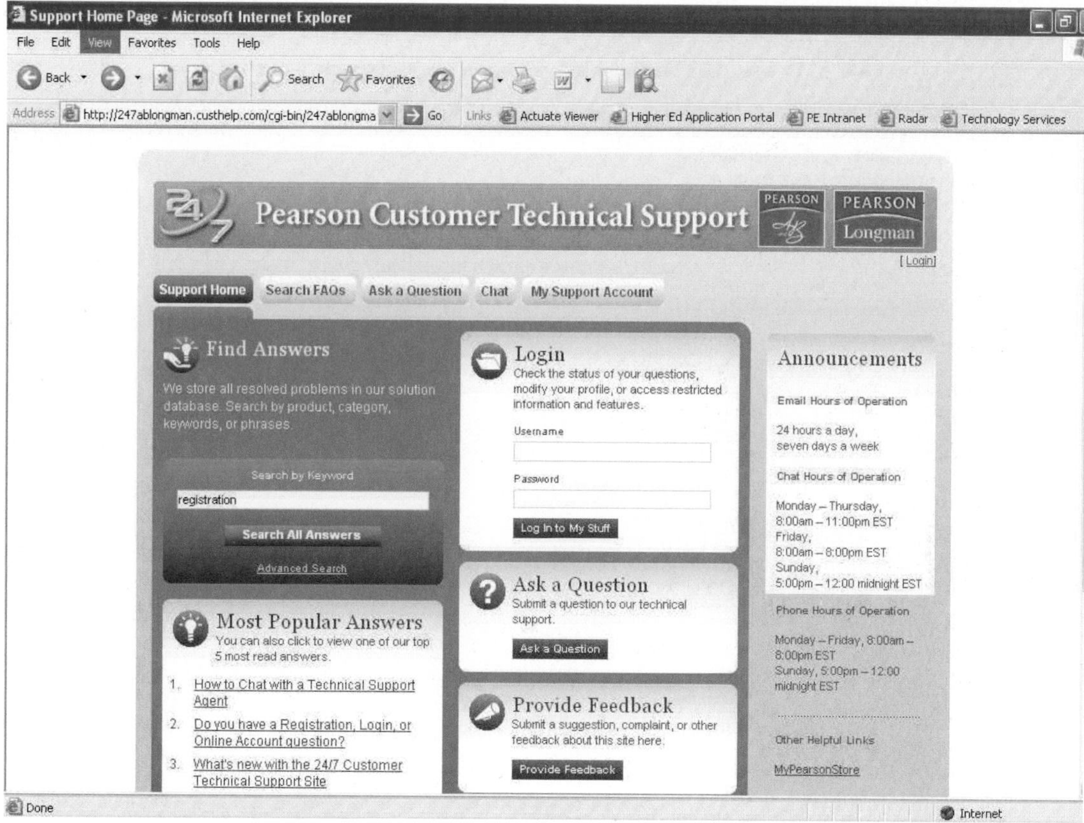


**Our goal is to provide answers to your MyReadingLab questions as quickly as possible and deliver the highest level of support. By visiting www.myreadinglab.com/help.html, many questions can be resolved in just a few minutes or less. Here you will find help on:**

- System Requirements
- How to Register for MyReadingLab
- How to Use MyReadingLab

**Contact Support.** We also invite you to contact Pearson Product Support (above). You can contact our Support Representatives online at http://247.pearsoned.com. Here you can:

- Search Frequently Asked Questions about MyReadingLab
- E-mail a Question to our Support Team
- Chat with a Support Representative

# The Effective Reader

Second Edition

**D. J. Henry**

*Daytona State College*

New York Boston San Francisco
London Toronto Sydney Tokyo Singapore Madrid
Mexico City Munich Paris Cape Town Hong Kong Montreal

Acquisitions Editor: Kate Edwards
Development Editor: Janice Wiggins-Clarke
Marketing Manager: Thomas DeMarco
Senior Supplements Editor: Donna Campion
Media Supplements Editor: Nancy Garcia
Production Manager: Ellen MacElree
Project Coordination, Text Design, and Electronic Page Makeup: Nesbitt Graphics, Inc.
Cover Design Manager: Wendy Ann Fredericks
Cover Designer: Nancy Sacks
Cover Photo: Courtesy of www.istockphoto.com/Matte Falko
Photo Researcher: Jody Potter
Manufacturing Manager: Dennis J. Para
Printer and Binder: Quebecor World–Taunton
Cover Printer: Phoenix Color Corps



Library of Congress Cataloging-in-Publication Data on file with the Library of Congress



Please visit us at http://www.ablongman.com/henry

ISBN 13: 978-0-205-57319-6 (student ed.)
ISBN 10: 0-205-57319-3 (student ed.) 4 5 6 7 8 9 10—WCT—10 09 SE
ISBN 13: 978-0-205-56699-0 (instructor's ed.)
ISBN 10: 0-205-56699-5 (instructor's ed.) 3 4 5 6 7 8 9 10—WCT—10 09 IE

# Brief Contents

# Detailed Contents

WE WANT TO HELP YOU, NOT
LET'S STOP FRIVOLOUS LAWSUITS

## PART TWO
## Additional Readings 655



## PART THREE
## Combined-Skills Tests 741

## PART FOUR
## Reading Enrichment 773

# Preface

Dear Colleagues:

The story of Annie Sullivan and Helen Keller is one of my favorite success stories. Annie patiently, lovingly tapped thousands of words into Helen's palm knowing that Helen's stubborn rebellion would melt once the flame of knowledge was ignited. These two remarkable women and their teaching and learning relationship serve as reminders of two ideals: reading empowers an individual life, and our work as instructors is of great and urgent importance. Many of our students come to us needing to reinforce the basic skills that make effective reading and clear thinking possible. Too often they struggle with text structure and feel uncertain about their comprehension. However with solid instruction and guided practice, these students can discover the power and pleasure of reading. *The Effective Reader,* Second Edition, has been designed to address these challenges.

## New to This Edition

The following changes have been made to *The Effective Reader*, Second Edition, to help students become effective readers and critical thinkers.

- Twenty-five percent of the short and long reading selections and accompanying pedagogy in the book have been revised, giving students even more lively, thought-provoking reading material. The new topics honor cultural diversity by offering high-interest readings about the people, traditions, and values of Hispanic, Asian, and African American cultures. In addition, a significant number of new readings deal with interpersonal communication and relationships, science, health, literature, and history.
- Coverage of SQ3R in Chapter 1, "A Reading System for Effective Readers," has been enhanced with graphics that illustrate the reading process. Throughout the book, SQ3R prompts have been revised to better activate reading strategies.

- Chapter 2, "Vocabulary and Dictionary Skills," has been expanded with material on how to use a dictionary as well as additional coverage of common word parts.
- Additional practice exercises have been added to Chapter 6, "Transitions and Thought Patterns" and Chapter 7, "More Thought Patterns," giving students even more practice in the various organizational patterns.
- Visual Vocabulary exercises in each chapter have been revised, providing students with new opportunities to interact with photographs and graphics by completing captions and answering skill-based questions.

## Guiding Principles

*The Effective Reader,* Second Edition, was written to develop in students the essential abilities that will enable them to become effective readers and critical thinkers.

### Practice and Feedback

The best way *to learn* is *to do.* Thus, one of the primary aims of this text is to give students plentiful opportunities to practice, practice, practice! Every concept introduced in the book is accompanied by an explanation of the concept, an example with explanation of the example, and one or more practice exercises. Each chapter also contains a chapter review, brief skill applications, four review tests, and six mastery tests. Two more review tests and two more mastery tests are on the book's website. For ease of teacher feedback, scoring sheets are provided for the review and mastery tests.

### High-Interest Reading Selections

For many, enthusiasm for reading is stimulated by material that offers high-interest topics written in a fast-paced style. Every effort has been made to provide reading passages in examples, reviews, and tests that students will find lively and engaging. Topics are taken from issues arising out of popular culture and textbooks—some examples are gangs, movies, weight loss, sports figures, depression, interpersonal relationships, drug use, nutrition, inspirational and success stories, role models, stress management and exercise—all written in active language using short, lively sentences. A special effort was made to include a variety of passages from textbooks across the curriculum.

## Integration of the Reading Process and Reading Skills

Effective readers blend individual reading skills into a reading process such as SQ3R. Before reading, effective readers skim for new or key vocabulary or main ideas. They create study questions and make connections to their prior knowledge. During reading, effective readers check their comprehension. For example, they annotate the text. They notice thought patterns and the relationship between ideas. They read for the answers to the questions they created before reading. After reading, effective readers use outlines, concept maps, and summaries to review what they have read and deepen their understanding. Students are taught to integrate each skill into a reading process in Part One.

In Chapter 1, "A Reading System for Effective Readers," students are introduced to SQ3R. In every other Part One chapter, students actively apply SQ3R strategies in "Before Reading About" and "After Reading About" activities. "Before Reading About" activities are pre-reading exercises that appear at the beginning of each chapter. These activities guide the student to review important concepts studied in earlier chapters, build on prior knowledge, and preview upcoming material. "After Reading About" activities are review activities that appear after the review tests in each chapter. These activities guide the student to reflect upon his or her achievements and assume responsibility for learning. Since many students are visual learners, the "Before Reading About" and "After Reading About" activities are signaled with reading process icons.

## Comprehensive Approach

*The Effective Reader,* Second Edition, offers several levels of learning. First, students are given an abundance of practice. They are able to focus on individual reading skills through a chapter-by-chapter workbook approach. In each chapter of Part One, Review Test 4 offers a multiparagraph passage with items on all the skills taught up to that point. In addition, Chapter 1, "A Reading System for Effective Readers," teaches students how to apply their reading skills to the reading process before, during, and after reading by using SQ3R. Students also learn to apply all skills in combination in Part Two, "Additional Readings," and Part Three, "Combined-Skills Tests." The aim is to provide our students with varied and rich opportunities to learn and practice reading skills and to apply reading processes.

## Textbook Structure

To help students become effective readers and critical thinkers, *The Effective Reader,* Second Edition, introduces the most important basic reading skills in Part One and then provides additional readings in Part Two, and combined-skills tests in Part Three.

### Part One, Becoming an Effective Reader

Essential reading skills are introduced sequentially in Part One. Each chapter focuses on a particular skill.

- Chapter 1, "A Reading System for Effective Readers," guides students through the reading process. Stages of the SQ3R process are explained thoroughly, with ample opportunities for practice, review, and mastery. The aim is to show students how to apply the skills they acquire in each of the chapters to reading before, during, and after reading.
- Chapter 2, "Vocabulary and Dictionary Skills," fosters vocabulary acquisition during reading by using a mnemonic technique: SAGE stands for **S**ynonyms, **A**ntonyms, **G**eneral context, and **E**xample. The chapter also develops language skills by demonstrating how to determine word meanings from prefixes, roots, and suffixes. Finally, the chapter offers instruction in dictionary skills.
- Chapter 3, "Stated Main Ideas," offers both verbal and visual strategies to enable students to see the building-block relationship among topics, main ideas, and supporting details and explains strategies to identify main ideas along with extensive practice in doing so. In addition, this chapter teaches students to identify the central idea of multiparagraph passages.
- Chapter 4, "Supporting Details," identifies the differences between major and minor details.
- Chapter 5, "Outlines and Concept Maps," reinforces the skills of locating main ideas and identifying major and minor supporting details. The chapter teaches the students the structure of a text by offering instruction and practice in the applications of outlines and concept maps.
- Chapter 6, "Transitions and Thought Patterns," introduces the fundamental thought patterns and the words that signal those patterns. Students are given numerous opportunities to practice identifying the signal words and their relationships to the thought patterns they establish. The chapter includes the time order, space order, listing, and classification patterns.

- Chapter 7, "More Thought Patterns," introduces more complex thought patterns and the words that signal those patterns. Just as in Chapter 6, students are given extensive practice opportunities. Chapter 7 introduces the comparison-and-contrast, cause-and-effect, generalization-and-example, and definition patterns.
- Chapter 8, "Implied Main Ideas and Implied Central Ideas," furthers students' understanding about the central idea of longer passages and the main idea by explaining unstated main ideas and unstated central ideas. The chapter offers extensive practice.
- Chapter 9, "Fact and Opinion," explains the differences between fact and opinion and develops the higher-level thinking skills that enable students to separate fact from opinion through extensive practice.
- Chapter 10, "Tone and Purpose," continues the students' study of the importance of word choice and the author's purpose. Detailed instruction and extensive practice develop the students' ability to determine whether the author's purpose is to entertain, to inform, or to persuade.
- Chapter 11, "Inferences," carefully addresses the advanced skill of making inferences by dividing the necessary mental processes into units of activity. Students are taught the basic skills necessary to evaluate an author's purpose and choice of words.
- Chapter 12, "The Basics of Argument," teaches the fundamental logical thought process used to examine the author's claim and supports. Students learn to recognize the author's claim and to evaluate supports as adequate and relevant.
- Chapter 13, "Advanced Argument: Persuasive Techniques," offers extensive explanations and practice of several common biased arguments that use logical fallacies and propaganda techniques. The logical fallacies include personal attack, straw man, begging the question, either-or, false comparison, and false cause. The propaganda techniques covered are name-calling, testimonials, bandwagon, plain folks, card stacking, transfer, and glittering generalities.

## Part Two, Additional Readings

Part Two is a collection of ten reading selections followed by skills questions designed to give students real reading opportunities and the opportunity to gauge their growth. This part begins with a key discussion about the relationship between reading and writing, and offers a few pointers on basic writing skills. The readings, which include magazine articles and textbook excerpts, were chosen based on each one's likelihood to engage, encourage, and motivate readers. Each selection is followed by skills questions so that students can practice all the skills taught in Part One. The skills questions are followed by discussion and writing topics so that students can practice making connections among listening, speaking, reading, and writing.

### Part Three, Combined-Skills Tests

Part Three is a set of 15 reading passages and combined-skills tests. The purpose of this part is to offer students ample opportunities to apply reading skills and strategies and to become more familiar with standardized testing formats to help prepare them for exit exams, standardized reading tests, and future content course quizzes, tests, and exams.

### Part Four, Reading Enrichment

Supplementary material is provided here for students to learn a process for reading informational graphics. Appendix A, "Reading Graphics in Textbooks," offers basic guidelines for reading and analyzing graphics, followed by specific examples and explanations of tables, line graphs, bar graphs, pie charts, diagrams, and pictograms.

## Chapter Features

Each chapter in Part One has several important features that help students become effective readers.

**"Before Reading About . . .":** "Before Reading About" activities appear at the beginning of Chapters 2–13 in Part One. These activities are pre-reading exercises based on SQ3R: they review important concepts studied in earlier chapters, build on prior knowledge, and preview the chapter. For example, students may be asked to create study questions based on the chapter preview and then record the answers to those questions as they read the chapter. Or, students may review relevant information from previous chapters. Sometimes these pre-reading activities direct students to skim the chapter and create a skeleton outline that they complete as they study the chapter. The purpose of "Before Reading About . . ." is to actively teach students to develop a reading process that applies individual reading skills as they study.

**"After Reading About . . .":** "After Reading About . . ." activities appear after Review Test 4 in Chapters 2–13 of Part One. Based on SQ3R, "After Reading About . . ." activities teach students to reflect on their achievements and assume responsibility for their own learning. These activities ask students reflective questions to check their comprehension of the skill taught in the chapter. Students learn to integrate individual reading skills into a reading process; they learn the value of reviewing material; and finally, students create a learning journal that enables them to see patterns in their behaviors and record their growth as readers.

**Instruction, example, explanation, and practice:** The chapter skill is broken down into components, and each component is introduced and explained. Instruction is followed by an example, an explanation of the example, and a practice. For example, Chapter 2, "Vocabulary and Dictionary Skills," is broken into three parts: Context Clues, Word Parts, and Dictionary Skills. Each section has its own instruction, example, explanation, and practice exercises.

Textbook Skills

**Textbook Skills:** In the last section in each chapter, students are shown the ways in which the skills they are learning apply to reading textbooks. These activities, signaled by the icon to the left, present material from a textbook reading and direct students to apply the chapter's skill to the passage or visual. In a concerted effort to prepare students to be effective readers in their content courses, activities that foster textbook skills across the curriculum are also carefully woven throughout the entire textbook. The Textbook Skills icon signals these activities.

**Visual Vocabulary:** The influence of technology and the media on reading is evident in the widespread use of graphics in newspapers, magazines, and textbooks. The Textbook Skill on page 76 zeroes in on the much-needed skill of blending information in visuals (such as photographs, charts, and graphs) with text for full comprehension. Throughout this textbook, visual vocabulary is presented as part of the reading process, and students interact with these visuals by completing captions or answering skill-based questions. The aim is to teach students to value photos, graphs, illustrations, and maps as important sources of information.

**Chapter Review:** Every chapter includes a fill-in review of the information about a particular reading skill. Students complete statements with words from a word box. The Chapter Review serves as a comprehension check for the reading concepts being taught.

**Applications:** Immediately following the Chapter Review, brief applications give students a chance to apply each component of the reading skill as a strategy.

**Review Tests:** Each chapter has six Review Tests, four in the book and two on the book's website. Review Tests 1 through 3 are designed to give ample opportunity for practice with the specific skill taught in the chapter; Review Test 4 offers a multiparagraph passage with combined-skills questions based on all the skills taught up to and including that particular chapter. Review Test 4 also gives discussion and writing topics so that teachers have the opportunity to guide students as they develop critical thinking skills.

**Mastery Tests:** Each chapter includes eight Mastery Tests, six in the book and two on the website. Most of the Mastery Tests are based on excerpts from science, history, psychology, social science, and literature textbooks.

Review Tests 5 and 6 and Mastery Tests 7 and 8 are available on the book's website. To access these tests, go to **http://www.ablongman.com/henry**. Click on *The Effective Reader,* then select "More Review and Mastery Tests." These tests can be electronically scored and the scores entered into the instructor's gradebook, if desired.

## The Longman Teaching and Learning Package

*The Effective Reader,* Second Edition, is supported by a series of innovative teaching and learning supplements.

The **Annotated Instructor's Edition** (**AIE**) is a replica of the student text, with all answers included. Ask your Longman sales representative for ISBN 0-205-56699-5.

**The Instructor's Manual,** prepared by Mary Dubbé of Thomas Nelson Community College, features teaching strategies for each textbook chapter, plus additional readings that engage students with a variety of learning styles and encourage active learning through class, group, and independent practices. Each chapter includes an introduction designed to hook the students, reproducible handouts, and study-strategy cards. Also included are a 10-item quiz for each chapter and a summary of corresponding activities in the Companion Website. A supplemental section provides a sample syllabus, readability calculations for each reading in *The Effective Reader,* Second Edition, five book quizzes to encourage independent reading and the creation of book groups, sample THEA and Florida State Exit Exams, and a scaffolded book review form. ISBN 0-205-57370-3.

The **Test Bank,** prepared by Mary Dubbé of Thomas Nelson Community College, features four preformatted quizzes/tests per chapter, plus a midterm exam and a final exam. It is available both in electronic format and printed format. Ask your Longman sales representative for a copy, or download the content at **http://www.ablongman.com/henry** (Instructor Resources section). Your sales representative will provide you with the username and password to access these materials. ISBN 0-205-57055-0.

**PowerPoint Presentations** for each chapter can be downloaded from the Instructor's Resource Center.

The **Companion Website** offers additional review tests and mastery tests for students as well as sample THEA and Florida State Exit Exams.

The **Lab Manual,** prepared by Mary Dubbé of Thomas Nelson Community College, is designed as a student workbook and provides a collection of 65 activities that provide additional practice, enrichment, and assessment for the skills presented in *The Effective Reader*. The activities for each chapter include practice exercises, one review test, and two mastery tests that mirror the design of *The Effective Reader* and emphasize the reading skills and applications students need in order to succeed in college. The lab activities give students realistic practice, encourage them to use the strategies they have learned, and offer an opportunity for students to continue to build a base of general, background knowledge. This lab manual can be used to strengthen students' reading skills, to allow them to assess their own progress, and to measure their success and readiness for college level reading. The lab manual is available packaged with *The Effective Reader* for an additional cost. ISBN 0-205-57660-5.

## Developmental Reading Student Supplements

**Longman Annotated Literature Series** Now, timeless texts are complemented by engaging pedagogy and illuminating content. Essay and review questions, activities, and discussion journals allow students to directly engage the story and gain a fuller sense of the material. In addition to utilizing reading skills, students will sharpen their vocabulary, critical thinking, and writing skills. Please visit **www.ablongman.com/devenglish** for more information.

**Longman Literature for College Readers Series** Literature anthologies, edited by Yvonne Sisko, help students maximize their reading and writing abilities with supportive pedagogy and experience literature like never before. Please visit **www.ablongman.com/devenglish** for a list of the anthologies and additional information.

**Vocabulary Skills Study Card (Student / 0-321-31802-1)** Colorful, affordable, and packed with useful information, Longman's Vocabulary Study Card is a concise, 8-page reference guide to developing key vocabulary skills, such as learning to recognize context clues, reading a dictionary entry, and recognizing key root words, suffixes, and prefixes. Laminated for durability, students can keep this Study Card for years to come and pull it out whenever they need a quick review.

**Reading Skills Study Card (Student / 0-321-33833-2)** Colorful, affordable, and packed with useful information, Longman's Reading Skills Study Card is a concise, 8-page reference guide to help students develop basic reading skills, such as concept skills, structural skills, language skills, and reasoning skills. Laminated for durability, students can keep this Study Card for years to come and pull it out whenever they need a quick review.

**The Longman Textbook Reader, 2nd Edition (with answers: Student / 0-321-48629-3 or without answers: Student / 0-205-51924-5)** Offers six complete chapters from our textbooks: psychology, mathematics, biology, history, literature, and business. Each chapter includes additional comprehension quizzes, critical thinking questions, and group activities.

**The Longman Reader's Portfolio and Student Planner (Student/0-321-29610-9)** This unique supplement provides students with a space to plan, think about, and present their work. The portfolio includes a diagnostic area (including a learning style questionnaire), a working area (including calendars, vocabulary logs, reading response sheets, book club tips, and other valuable materials), and a display area (including a progress chart, a final table of contents, and a final assessment), as well as a daily planner for students including daily, weekly, and monthly calendars.

**The Longman Reader's Journal, by Kathleen McWhorter (Student/0-321-08843-3)** The first journal for readers, The Longman Reader's Journal offers a place for students to record their reactions to and questions about any reading.

**The Longman Planner (Student/0-321-04573-4)** Ideal for organizing a busy college life! Included are hour-by-hour schedules, monthly and weekly calendars, an address book, and an almanac of tips and useful information.

**What Every Student Should Know About Study Skills (Student/0-321-44736-0).** This supplement teaches students the study skills they need to master for college success. The strategy-development activities throughout the book allow students to assess their learning styles, improve time management and stress management, and become active learners.

***Newsweek* Discount Subscription Coupon (12 weeks) (Student/0-321-08895-6)** *Newsweek* gets students reading, writing, and thinking about what's going on in the world around them. The price of the subscription is added to the cost of the book. Instructors receive weekly lesson plans, quizzes, and curriculum guides as well as a complimentary *Newsweek* subscription. *Package item only.*

**Interactive Guide to *Newsweek* (Student/0-321-05528-4)** Available with the 12-week subscription to *Newsweek*, this guide serves as a workbook for students who are using the magazine.

**Research Navigator Guide for English, H. Eric Branscomb and Michelle D. Trim (Student/0-321-49601-9)** Designed to teach students how to conduct high-quality online research and to document it properly, Research Navigator guides provide discipline-specific academic resources; in addition to helpful tips on the writing process, online research, and finding and citing valid sources. Research Navigator guides include an access code to Research Navigator™-providing access to thousands of academic journals and periodicals, the *New York Times* Search by Subject Archive, Link Library, Library Guides, and more.

**The Oxford American Desk Dictionary and Thesaurus, Second Edition (ISBN 0-425-18068-9)** From the Oxford University Press and Berkley Publishing

Group comes this one-of-a-kind reference book that combines both of the essential language tools—dictionary and thesaurus—in a single, integrated A-to-Z volume. The 1,024-page book offers more than 150,000 entries, definitions, and synonyms so you can find the right word every time, as well as appendices of valuable quick-reference information including signs and symbols, weights and measures, presidents of the United States, U.S. states and capitals, and more.

**The Oxford Essential Thesaurus (ISBN 0-425-16421-7)** From Oxford University Press, renowned for quality educational and reference works, comes this concise, easy-to-use thesaurus—the essential tool for finding just the right word for every occasion. The 528-page book includes 175,000 synonyms in a simple A-to-Z format, more than 10,000 entries, extensive word choices, example sentences and phrases, and guidance on usage, punctuation, and more in the exclusive "Writers Toolkit."

**Penguin Discount Novel Program** In cooperation with Penguin Putnam, Inc., Longman is proud to offer a variety of Penguin paperbacks at a significant discount when packaged with any Longman title. Excellent additions to any developmental reading course, Penguin titles give students the opportunity to explore contemporary and classical fiction and drama. The available titles include works by authors as diverse as Toni Morrison, Julia Alvarez, Mary Shelley, and Shakespeare. To review the complete list of titles available, visit the Longman-Penguin-Putnam website at **http://www.ablongman.com/penguin.**

### *Multimedia Offerings*

Interested in incorporating online materials into your course? Longman is happy to help. Our regional technology specialists provide training on all of our multimedia offerings.

**MyReadingLab (www.myreadinglab.com)** MyReadingLab is the first and only online learning system to diagnose both students' reading skills and reading levels. This remarkable program utilizes diagnostic testing, personalized practice, and gradebook reports to allow instructors to measure student performance and help students gain control over their reading. Specifically created for developmental students, MyReadingLab is a website that provides diagnostics, practice, tests, and reporting on student reading skills and student reading levels. Student reading skills are improved through a mastery-based format of exercises and tests. Exercises include objective-based questions, open-ended questions, short answer questions, combined skills exercises and more. Student reading level is assessed through a Lexile framework (developed by Metametrics™, an educational measurement expert). Once diagnosed, students are assigned a Lexile number, which indicates their reading comprehension skills, and throughout the program, the Lexile number rises as the students' reading level improves. The result of this skills and level combination is a personalized student study plan to address individual needs and quantifiable data that measures individual student reading level advancement.

**The Longman Vocabulary Web Site (http://www.ablongman.com/vocabulary)** This unique website features hundreds of exercises in ten topic areas to strengthen vocabulary skills. Students will also benefit from "100 Words That All High School Graduates Should Know," a useful resource that provides definitions for each of the words on this list, vocabulary flashcards, and audio clips to help facilitate pronunciation skills.

**Longman Study Skills Website (http://www.ablongman.com/studyskills)** This site offers hundreds of review strategies for college success, time and stress management skills, study strategies, and more. Students can take a variety of assessment tests to learn about their organizational skills and learning styles, with follow-up quizzes to reinforce the strategies they have learned.

## Developmental Reading Instructor Resources

**Printed Test Bank for Developmental Reading (Instructor / 0-321-08596-5)** Offers more than 3,000 questions in all areas of reading, including vocabulary, main idea, supporting details, patterns of organization, critical thinking, analytical reasoning, inference, point of view, visual aides, and textbook reading. (Electronic also available; see CDs.)

**Electronic Test Bank for Developmental Reading (Instructor / CD 0-321-08179-X)** Offers more than 3,000 questions in all areas of reading, including vocabulary, main idea, supporting details, patterns of organization, critical thinking, analytical reasoning, inference, point of view, visual aides, and textbook reading. Instructors simply choose questions, then print out the completed test for distribution OR offer the test online.

**The Longman Guide to Classroom Management (Instructor / 0-321-09246-5)** This guide is designed as a helpful resource for instructors who have classroom management problems. It includes helpful strategies for dealing with disruptive students in the classroom and the "do's and don'ts" of discipline.

**The Longman Guide to Community Service-Learning in the English Classroom and Beyond (Instructor / 0-321-12749-8)** Written by Elizabeth Rodriguez Kessler of California State University–Northridge, this monograph provides a definition and history of service-learning, as well as an overview of how service-learning can be integrated effectively into the college classroom.

**The Longman Instructor's Planner (Instructor / 0-321-09247-3)** This planner includes weekly and monthly calendars, student attendance and grading rosters, space for contact information, Web references, an almanac, and blank pages for notes.

## State-Specific Supplements

*For Florida Adopters*

**Thinking Through the Test: A Study Guide for the Florida College Basic Skills Exit Test, by D. J. Henry.** This workbook helps students strengthen their reading skills in preparation for the Florida College Basic Skills Exit Test. It features both diagnostic tests to help assess areas that may need improvement and exit tests to help test skill mastery. Detailed explanatory answers have been provided for almost all of the questions.

**Reading Skills Summary for the Florida State Exit Exam, by D. J. Henry (Student / 0-321-08478-0)** An excellent study tool for students preparing to take the Florida College Basic Skills Exit Test for Reading, this laminated reading grid summarizes all the skills tested on the Exit Exam.

*For Texas Adopters*

**The Longman THEA Study Guide, by Jeannette Harris (Student / 0-321-27240-0)** Created specifically for students in Texas, this study guide includes straightforward explanations and numerous practice exercises to help students prepare for the reading and writing sections of THEA Test.

**TASP Test Package, Third Edition (Instructor / Print ISBN 0-321-01959-8)** These 12 practice pre-tests and post-tests assess the same reading and writing skills covered in the Texas TASP examination.

*For New York/CUNY Adopters*

**Preparing for the CUNY-ACT Reading and Writing Test, edited by Patricia Licklider (Student / 0-321-19608-2)** This booklet, prepared by reading and writing faculty from across the CUNY system, is designed to help students prepare for the CUNY-ACT exit test. It includes test-taking tips, reading passages, typical exam questions, and sample writing prompts to help students become familiar with each portion of the test.

**CLAST Test Package, Fourth Edition (Instructor / Print ISBN 0-321-01950-4)** These two, 40-item objective tests evaluate students' readiness for the Florida CLAST exams. Strategies for teaching CLAST preparedness are included.

## Acknowledgments

As I worked on the second edition of this reading series, I felt an overwhelming sense of gratitude and humility for the opportunity to serve the learning community as a textbook author. I would like to thank the entire Longman team for their dedication to providing the best possible materials to foster literacy. To every person, from the editorial team to the representatives in the field, all demonstrate a passion for students, teachers, and learning. It is a joy to be part of such a team. Special thanks are due to the following: Kate Edwards, Acquisitions Editor, and Janice Wiggins-Clarke, Developmental Editor, for their guidance and support; Kathy Smith with Nesbitt Graphics, Inc. for her tireless devotion to excellence; Ellen MacElree and the entire production team for their work ethic and gracious attitudes, including Katherine Grimaldi and Genevieve Coyne. I would also like to thank Mary Dubbé for authoring the Lab Manual and the Instructor's Manual that supplement this reading series.

For nearly twenty-five years, I worked with the most amazing group of faculty from across the State of Florida as an item-writer, reviewer, or scorer of state-wide assessment exams for student learning and professional certification. The work that we accomplished together continues to inform me as a teacher, writer, and consultant. I owe a debt of gratitude to this group who sacrificed much for the good of our students. In particular, I owe thanks to the following for their mentorship: Dr. Dan Kelly, University of Florida; Don Tighe, Valencia Community College; Dr. Willa Wolcott, University of Florida; and Pat Hare, Brevard Community College.

I would also like to acknowledge several of my colleagues at Daytona Beach Community College: Dustin Weeks, Librarian; Dr. Rhodella Brown, Dean of the Virtual College; and Sandra Offiah-Hawkins, reading professor. As Tennyson extols in "Ulysses," these are the "souls that have toiled, and wrought, and thought with me." Their influence and support has made me a better person, teacher, and writer.

Finally, I would like to gratefully recognize the invaluable insights provided by the following colleagues and reviewers. I deeply appreciate their investment of time and energy: Danette W. Foster, Central Carolina Community College; Richard A. Gair, Valencia Community College; Irene Lindgren, Valencia Community College; Debbie McCarty, Metropolitan Community College; Acquelnetta Yvette Myrick, Community College of Baltimore County; Gwen Parsons, Howard College; Sandra Thomson, Northwest Vista College; Jacquelyn Warmsley, Tarrant County College; and Quakish Williams, Miami Dade College.

**D.J. Henry**
*Daytona Beach, Florida*

# Introduction

Congratulations! If you are reading this textbook, then you have come face to face with a life-changing fact: reading is a vital tool for success.

Reading is one of the most important skills we can gain. Good reading skills give us access to better paying jobs. Reading well makes everyday life easier and more interesting. As effective readers, we can earn a living wage. We can understand contracts and help our children with their homework. As effective readers, we also find joy in a well-told story or a well-made point.

A few semesters ago, Jamie, a former reading student of mine who had struggled with math for years, burst into my office beaming with pride. "I am doing great in math," she boasted with a wide grin. "Did you know that there are words—not just numbers, but words, too—in a math textbook? Once I learn the vocabulary for each chapter, the formulas begin to make sense. And everything I learned in reading class works in my math class." Jamie passed her math course with one of the highest grade point averages in her class. She had become an effective reader.

## What Is an Effective Reader?

Just what is an effective reader? An effective reader is one who has a positive attitude, who wants to learn, who finds good reasons to read, and who stays focused. This textbook is designed to teach you how to become such a reader. Here are some quick pointers to get you started.

## How to Stay Focused

- Create a place for studying. Study in that one place as often as you can, and don't play, sleep, or watch TV there.
- Manage your time. Make a plan for how you will spend your time, and then stick to it. Create a weekly plan. Once you see how much you can accomplish in a week, change your next weekly plan so that it is even more realistic.

- Let go of distractions. If you find your mind wandering when you are trying to study, start a list. Jot down the reminders on a separate piece of paper. Store them on paper, not in your mind.
- Set goals, and remember the times you have met your goals. In order to reach your goals, you have to set them. For example, you probably want to graduate from college. What are your other goals? To help you reach your goals, think back to times when you have reached goals you have set, and give yourself positive feedback for your success.

## How to Succeed in College

- Attend class. To get the most out of college and to learn from your courses, you need to go to class. And your instructors will expect you to know what has been covered in class.
- Read assignments before class. Do the reading assignment so that you will have some basic understanding of the subject before the lecture and class discussion. Think about questions you'd like to ask about the reading.
- Review your lecture notes after class. Within a day after a class, review your notes and fill in the blanks while the lecture is still fresh in your mind. If you didn't understand part of the discussion, ask your instructor or a classmate for help.
- Learn about the campus. Find out where the library is and what hours it is open. Become familiar with the college offices so you will know how to get things done.

## Previewing This Text

This textbook is designed to help you become an effective reader. Knowing how the book is set up and what features it has will help you make the most of your studies.

### Reading Skills and Practice Materials

Each chapter addresses a specific reading skill. For example, Chapter 1 deals with the reading process. Take a moment to look over the table of contents, which is on pages iv–x. Answer the following questions:

1. How many reading skills (chapters) are in Part One? ____________________
2. What skill is taught in Chapter 10? ______________________________

In each chapter, the skill is explained and examples are given. Practice exercises follow to help you practice each skill. In addition, each chapter includes review tests and mastery tests (with scorecards) so that you and your instructor can track your progress.

The tests have been designed to give you lots of opportunities to practice test-taking skills in preparation for the standardized tests you will face in your academic career. Look in Chapters 4 and 5 at the review tests and mastery tests, and answer the following questions:

**3.** How many review tests does each chapter have? ____________________

**4.** How many mastery tests does each chapter have? ____________________

## Textbook Skills

Textbook Skills

One of the main goals of a reading course is to prepare you for college-level textbook reading; therefore, "textbook skills" have been included in every chapter for your benefit. Passages are taken from college textbooks that are used in business courses, the humanities, the social sciences, and the physical sciences. Textbook skills are marked with an icon as seen at left:

**5.** Look through Chapter 6. What are three pages that include the Textbook Skills icon? ____________________________________________

____________________________________________

**6.** In Chapter 2, does Review Test 4 deal with textbook skills? ____________

## Additional Readings

Part Two of the book contains ten additional readings. Each reading is preceded by a brief introduction, and a list of vocabulary words and definitions. After each reading are questions to help you test your vocabulary and your understanding of the reading. Discussion questions are also given to help get a conversation about the reading started.

**7.** Look at a reading in Part Two. What is the list of vocabulary words before the reading called? ____________________________________

**8.** What is the title of Reading Selection 1? ______________________________

## Combined Skills Tests

Part Three consists of fifteen tests that combine all the skills you are learning. Most of the tests have a short reading selection and questions that follow them.

**9.** Look at Test 3. What is the title of the reading selection? ______________

**10.** How many questions does Test 7 have? ______________

### Visual Vocabulary

More and more academic and everyday readings include photographs, charts, graphs, or some other visual or graphic aid to help make a point clear. Thus each chapter of this textbook also teaches visual literacy skills, asking you to study photographs or graphics and answer questions about them.

**11.** Look at the photo on page 24. What does the photo show? ______________

______________________________________________

## Reading as Power

Reading is a great source of power and joy. It is my sincere hope that your semester is both productive and rewarding as you discover the joyful power of reading. Here is to your success as an effective reader both now and in your future coursework.

**D. J. Henry**

PART ONE

# Becoming an Effective Reader

CHAPTER

1

# A Reading System for Effective Readers

**CHAPTER PREVIEW**



Many people think that reading involves simply passing our eyes over the words in the order that they appear on the page. But reading is much more than that. Once we understand the **reading process**, we can follow specific steps and apply strategies that will make us effective readers. The most important aspect of being an effective reader is being an active reader.

Reading is an active process during which you draw information from the text to create meaning. When you understand what you've read, you've achieved **comprehension** of the material.

**Comprehension** is an understanding of what has been read.

Active reading means that you ask questions, find answers, and react to the author's ideas. Before we examine the reading process in detail, it is important to talk about the role of prior knowledge.

## Prior Knowledge

We all have a large body of information that we have learned through a lifetime of experience. This body of information is called **prior knowledge**.

Knowledge is gained from experience and stored in memory. Every day, our prior knowledge is expanded by what we experience. For example, a small child hears the word *hot* as her father blows on a spoonful of steaming soup. The hungry child grabs for the bowl and cries as some of the hot liquid spills on her hand. The child has learned and will remember the meaning of *hot*.

**Prior knowledge** is the large body of information that is learned throughout a lifetime of experience.

The following graphic illustrates specific ways to connect to prior knowledge in each phase of the reading process. Connecting to prior knowledge increases comprehension.

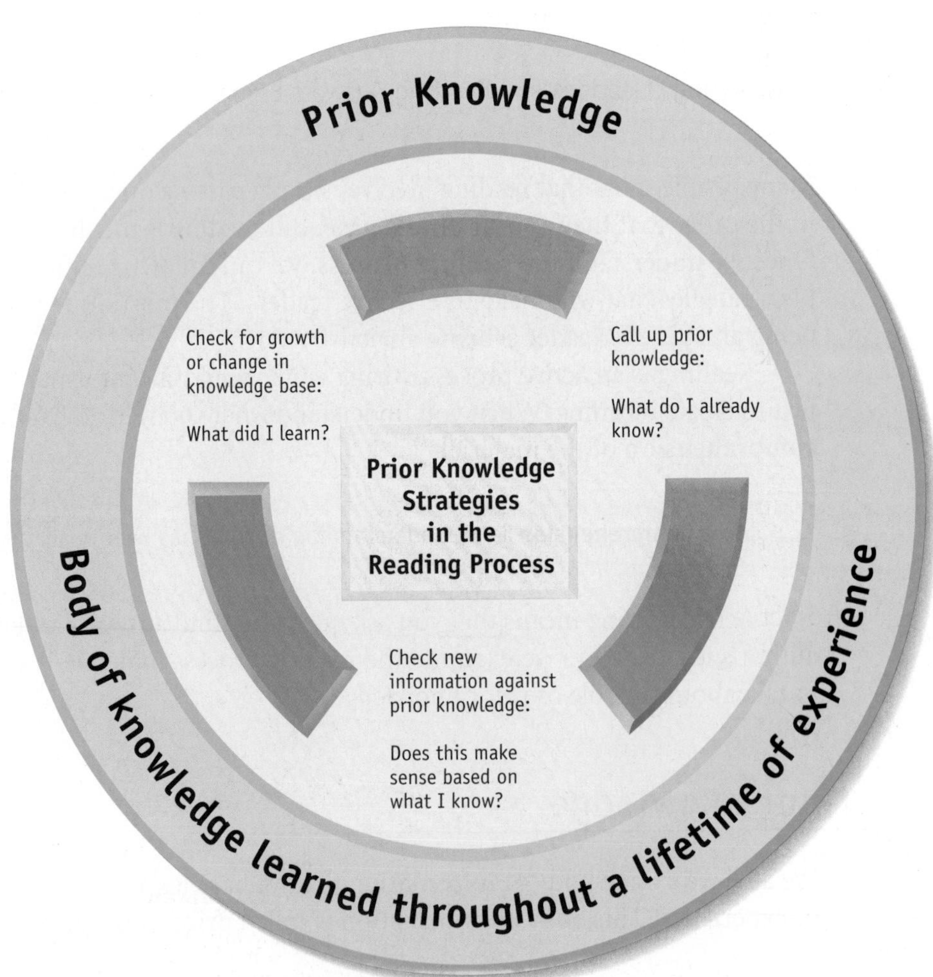

**EXAMPLE** Read the following paragraph. In the space provided, list any topics from the paragraph about which you already have prior knowledge.

**Physical and Mental Fitness**

Just as physical exercise builds up the body, mental exercise builds the mind. None of us expects to be able to suddenly run a marathon or lift heavy weights without training. And our bodies rarely take on that lean, toned look without physical effort. However, as we exercise our bodies, they become stronger and leaner. Likewise, as we exercise our minds through reading and writing, our mental abilities become stronger and more efficient.

______________________________________________

______________________________________________

**EXPLANATION** If you know about psychology and the issues linked to mental well-being, then this paragraph makes more sense to you than to someone who does not understand the complexity suggested by the expression "mental fitness." However, even if you do not know much about psychology, you may have helpful prior knowledge about some of the other ideas in the passage. For example, most of us have seen the effects of working out on the human body. Either we know someone who is dedicated to physical fitness, or we have that goal ourselves. We understand that physical fitness comes from hard work and commitment. People who stay in shape work out on a regular basis. Our prior knowledge about physical fitness helps us understand the kind of commitment we must make to our own mental fitness.

The more prior knowledge we have about a topic, the more likely we are to understand that topic. The more you know, the easier it is to learn. This is why effective readers build their knowledge base by reading often!

Active readers call up prior knowledge by using questions. The following practice will prepare you to use questions before you read. You will study this skill in more depth in the next section.



## PRACTICE 1

Read the following paragraph from a college health textbook. Then answer the questions that follow it.

Textbook Skills

**Toxic Fumes: Cigarette Smoke**

[1]Most of the compounds in cigarette smoke are gaseous, and many of them are toxic. [2]By far the most hazardous of these gases is carbon monoxide,

the same gas that is emitted from the exhaust pipe of a car. [3]The difference is that there are community or statewide standards to keep carbon monoxide auto emissions within a safe level, whereas no standards exist for cigarette smoke. [4]The amount of carbon monoxide that stays in a smoker's blood is related to activity levels. [5]During the day, carbon monoxide remains in the blood for two to four hours; during sleep, however, it remains for up to eight hours.

—Adapted from Pruitt & Stein, *Health Styles*, 2nd ed., p. 185.

**1.** What did you already know about carbon monoxide? That is, what was your prior knowledge? ____________________

______________________________

**2.** What did you already know about cigarette smoke? ________________

______________________________

**3.** When you think of carbon monoxide, what do you think of? Describe ideas and experiences that come to mind. ________________

______________________________

**4.** When you think of cigarette smoke, what do you think of? Describe ideas and experiences that come to mind. ________________

______________________________

**5.** Was this an easy passage to understand? How does your prior knowledge affect your understanding of this passage? ________________

______________________________

**6.** List any parts of the passage you had no prior knowledge of: ________

______________________________

## The Reading Process

Triggering prior knowledge is a reading skill that you as an active reader can turn into a reading strategy by using it as you read. **Reading** is best described as a process defined by three distinct phases. Each phase has its own thinking steps.

SQ3R is a reading system that connects to prior knowledge and offers strategies for each phase of the reading process. The following graphic illustrates the phases of the reading process through SQ3R. Effective readers repeat or move among phases as needed to repair comprehension.

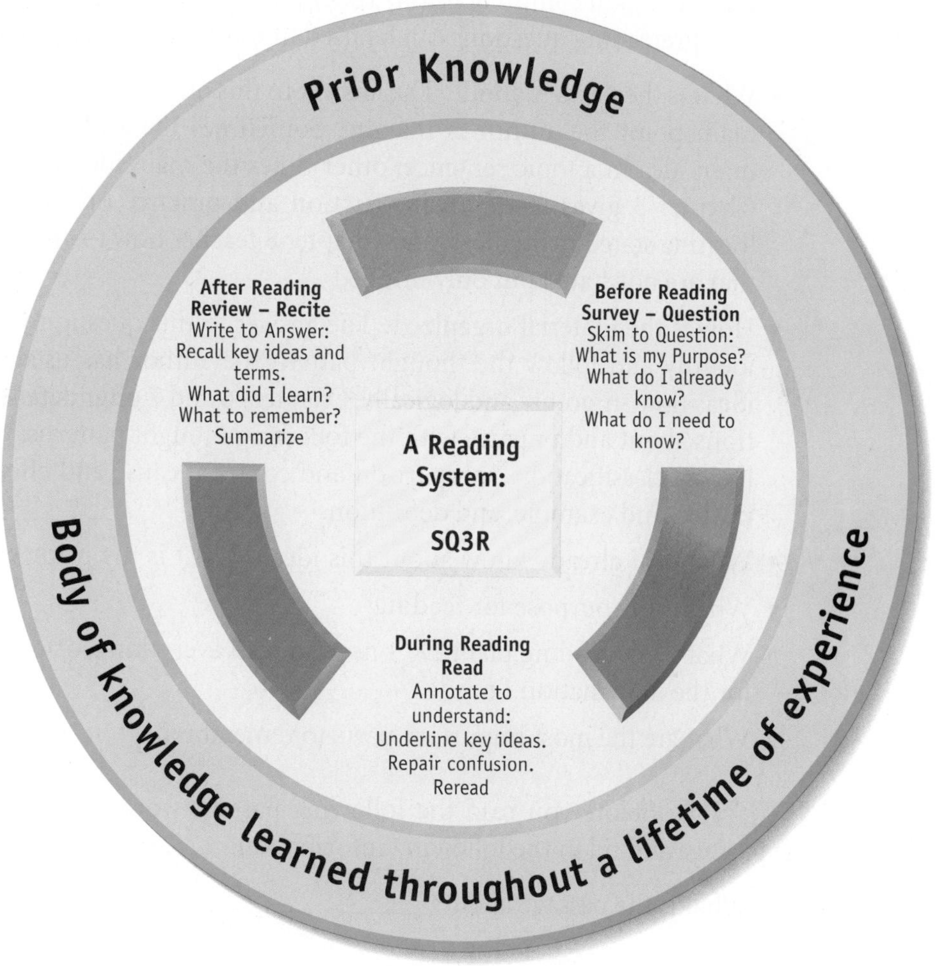

Prior Knowledge

**After Reading**
**Review – Recite**
Write to Answer:
Recall key ideas and terms.
What did I learn?
What to remember?
Summarize

**Before Reading**
**Survey – Question**
Skim to Question:
What is my Purpose?
What do I already know?
What do I need to know?

**A Reading System:**

**SQ3R**

**During Reading**
**Read**
Annotate to understand:
Underline key ideas.
Repair confusion.
Reread

Body of knowledge learned throughout a lifetime of experience

**SQ3R** stands for Survey, Question, Read, Recite, and Review.

## Before Reading: Survey and Question

**A. Survey:** Quickly look over, or **skim,** the reading passage for clues about how it is organized and what it is going to talk about or teach you.

To skim effectively, look at *italic* and **bold** type, and take note of titles, the introduction, and headings. Also look at pictures and graphs. Finally, read the first paragraph, summaries, and questions. Each of these clues provides important information.

B. **Question:** To aid in comprehension, ask questions before you read. The following list of prereading questions can be used in most reading situations:

- What is the passage about? The answer to this question will lead you to the main point the author is making. Sometimes the author will state the main idea in a topic sentence; other times the main idea will be implied. Chapter 3 gives in-depth instruction and practice on identifying and locating stated main ideas, and Chapter 8 teaches how to grasp main ideas that are not stated but only implied.
- How is the material organized? The answer to this question will help you identify and follow the thought pattern the author has used so that the ideas flow smoothly and logically. Chapters 6 and 7 offer detailed explanations about and practice with the following thought patterns: time, space, listing, classification, comparison and contrast, cause and effect, generalization and example, and definition.
- What do I already know about this idea? (What is my prior knowledge?)
- What is my purpose for reading?
- What is my reading plan? Do I need to read everything, or can I just skim for the information I need?
- What are the most important parts to remember?

**EXAMPLE** Before you read the following passage word for word, look over the passage and fill in the following information.

**1.** What is the passage about? ______________________________

______________________________________________

What do I already know about this topic? ______________________

______________________________________________

**2.** What is my purpose for reading? That is, why am I reading this? What do I need to remember? ______________________________

______________________________________________

______________________________________________

3. What ideas in the passage are in *italics* or in **bold** type? ______________

______________________________________________

______________________________________________

Textbook Skills

### The Problems of Designer Drugs

**Designer drugs** are produced in chemical laboratories or made in homes and sold illegally. These drugs are easy to produce from available raw material. The drugs themselves were once technically legal because the law had to specify the exact chemical structure of an illegal drug. However, there is now a law in place that bans all chemical cousins of illegal drugs.

Collectively known as **club drugs**, these dangerous substances include *Ecstasy*, *Special K*, and *Rohypnol*. Although users may think of them as harmless, research has shown that club drugs can produce a range of unwanted effects. Some of these effects include hallucinations, paranoia, amnesia, and in some cases, death. Some club drugs work on the same brain mechanisms as alcohol and therefore can dangerously boost the effects of both substances. Because the drugs are odorless and tasteless, people can easily slip them into drinks. Some of them have been associated with sexual assaults and for that reason are referred to as *date rape drugs*.

—Adapted from Donatelle, *Health*, 5th ed., pp. 181–82.

**EXPLANATION**

1. What is the passage about? The title of the passage gives us a clue: "The Problems of Designer Drugs." So does the first paragraph. By quickly looking at the terms in *italic* and **bold** print, you can see that this passage is about the dangers of designer drugs, also known as club drugs.

2. What do I already know about this topic? This answer will vary for each of you. Some of you may know someone who has used or been a victim of designer drugs; thus you already know a great deal that will help you understand the details in this passage. Others may not have any experience with illegal drugs. Yet most of you probably know someone who has struggled with alcoholism or misuse of legal drugs. So you can connect your experience to the information in the passage.

3. What is my purpose for reading? I need to know what is so dangerous about designer drugs.

4. What are the words in *italic* and **bold** type? *Designer drugs, club drugs, Ecstasy, Special K, Rohypnol,* and *date rape drugs.* Simply by writing the highlighted words in a list, you have begun to summarize the author's main point (for more on summarizing, see pages 660–661).

## Before Reading

To support the connection between reading skills and the reading process, Chapters 2 to 13 begin with activities to do before reading the chapter, called **Before Reading About . . . .** These activities apply a variety of surveying and questioning strategies. Sometimes, the activity directs you to review skills taught in previous chapters to trigger your memory for prior knowledge and to help you consider the relationship between individual skills. Other times, the activity asks you to skim the chapter and create questions that you can answer as you read about the skill. For example, in Chapter 3, "Before Reading About Stated Main Ideas" asks you to create several questions based on the chapter preview. (Every chapter begins with a list of the main topics in the chapter, called the "Chapter Preview.")

## During Reading: Read and Recite

After you have surveyed and asked questions about the text, it's time to read the entire passage.

**A. Read:** As you read, think about the importance of the information by continuing to ask questions:

- Does this new information agree with what I already knew?
- Do I need to change what I thought I knew?
- What is the significance of this information? Do I need to remember this?

In addition to asking questions while you read, acknowledge and resolve any confusion as it occurs.

- Create questions based on the headings, subheadings, and words in **bold** type and *italics*.

- Reread the parts you don't understand.
- Reread when your mind drifts during reading.
- Read ahead to see if the idea becomes clearer.
- Determine the meaning of words from the context.
- Look up new or difficult words.
- Think about ideas even when they differ from your own.

**B. Recite:** Make the material your own. Make sure you understand it by repeating the information.

- Create a picture in your mind or on paper.
- Restate the ideas in your own words.
- Write out answers to the questions you created based on the headings and subheadings.

**EXAMPLE**

**A.** Before you read the following passage from a college science textbook, survey the passage and answer the following questions.

**1.** What is the passage about? ______________________________

**2.** What do I already know about this passage? What is my prior knowledge?

______________________________

______________________________

**3.** What is important about this passage? What do I need to remember?

______________________________

______________________________

**4.** What words in **bold** type will help me remember what I need to know?

______________________________

______________________________

Textbook Skills

**B.** Once you have surveyed the information, read the passage. During reading, check your understanding by writing answers to the questions based on the ideas in **bold** print.

**5.** What new or difficult words do I need to look up?

______________________

______________________

**6.** What is color resemblance?

______________________

**7.** What are some examples of color resemblance?

______________________

**8.** What is countershading?

______________________

**9.** What is an example of countershading?

______________________

### Hiding to Live: Animal Camouflage

[1]Animals in danger of being hunted and killed have evolved ways to camouflage themselves. [2]Perhaps the simplest type of camouflage is **color resemblance**, in which an animal's color matches the color of its background. [3]Color resemblance is illustrated by green aphids that live on vegetation, gray-brown lizards inhabiting sandy areas, and black beetles that cling to the bark of trees.

[4]Another type of camouflage is **countershading**. [5]Without markings, an object will reflect more light—and appear lighter—on its top surface than on its bottom surface. [6]This difference makes an animal stand out against its background. [7]Countershading, or the placement of darker markings on the top of the animal, reduces the reflection and allows the animal to blend into its background. [8]For example, most fish are darkest on their top sides and consequently less visible when alive than when dead and floating belly up.

—Adapted from Maier, *Comparative Animal Behavior: An Evolutionary and Ecological Approach*, pp. 148–49.

**EXPLANATION**

## A. Before Reading: Survey and Question

1. What is the passage about? Types of camouflage used by animals
2. What do I already know about this passage? What is my prior knowledge? Answers will vary.
3. What is important about this passage? What do I need to remember? Wording will vary: the ways in which camouflaging helps an animal survive
4. What words are in **bold** type? Color resemblance and countershading

## B. During Reading: Read and Recite

5. What are the new or difficult words I need to look up? Answers will vary.
6. What is color resemblance? A type of camouflage in which an animal's color matches the color of its background
7. What are some examples of color resemblance? Green aphids, gray-brown lizards, and black beetles

**8.** What is countershading? Markings on the top of the animal that are darker than those on the bottom

**9.** What is an example of countershading? Most fish

**10.** Identify any ideas you needed to reread to understand. Answers will vary.

## After Reading: Review

Once you have read the entire selection, go back over the material to review it.

- Summarize the most important parts (for more information about how to summarize, see pages 660–661).
- Revisit and answer the questions raised by headings and subheadings.
- Review new words and their meanings based on the way they were used in the passage.

As part of your review, take time to think and write about what you have read.

- Connect new information to your prior knowledge about the topic.
- Form opinions about the material and the author.
- Notice changes in your opinions based on the new information.
- Write about what you have read.

### PRACTICE 2

Now that you have learned about each of the three phases of the reading process, practice putting all three together. Think before, during, and after reading. Apply SQ3R to the following passage. Remember the steps:

- **Survey:** Look over the whole passage.
- **Question:** Ask questions about the content. Predict how the new information fits in with what you already know about the topic.
- **Read:** Continue to question, look up new words, reread, and create pictures in your mind.
- **Recite:** Take notes: write out questions and answers, definitions of words, and new knowledge.
- **Review:** Think about what you have read and written. Use writing to capture your opinions and feelings about what you have read.

**A. Before Reading: Survey and Question.** Skim the passage from a college history textbook, and answer the following questions:

1. What is this passage about? ______________________________

______________________________

______________________________

2. What do I already know about this information? ______________________________

______________________________

3. What do I need to remember? ______________________________

______________________________

4. What ideas are in *italics* and **bold** type? ______________________________

______________________________

*Before you go on:* Use the words you listed in item 4 to create questions. Write the questions in the boxes beside the textbook passage. You will write your answers in these same boxes during reading.

Textbook Skills

**B. During Reading: Read and Recite.** As you read, answer the questions you created from the ideas in **bold** and *italic* type.

5. ______________________________

______________________________

______________________________

______________________________

______________________________

6. ______________________________

______________________________

______________________________

______________________________

### Age and Opinion in American Politics and Public Opinion

[1]Age group differences in politics and public opinion are sometimes referred to as the **generation gap**. [2]In many cases, older people seem to be more conservative than younger people. [3]For example, older people are less likely to be in favor of legalizing marijuana. [4]Younger people in general seem to be less interested in politics than their elders. [5]For example, younger people are less likely to keep up with political news. [6]They are also less likely to vote.

[7]How can we explain this generation gap in politics and public opinion? [8]The generation gap may be a product of **generational effects.** [9]This term describes the effect of historical events on the views of the people

**7.** ____________________

____________________

____________________

**8.** ____________________

____________________

____________________

who lived through them. [10]For example, the *Great Depression generation,* who grew up in the 1930s, may give greater support to Social Security because of this experience. [11]The *baby boomers* were born in the high-birthrate years following World War II (1946–1964); they lived through the civil rights movement, the Vietnam War, and changes in sexual morality. [12]These events may affect their views on many social issues.

—Adapted from Dye, *Politics in America,* 5th ed., pp. 148–49.

**C. After Reading: Review**

**9.** What other political and public opinion differences do you think may be based on age differences? ____________________

____________________

**10.** What are some of the historical events that could shape the views of young people today? ____________________

____________________

## After Reading

To reinforce the connection between reading skills and the reading process, Chapters 2 to 13 include sections called **"After Reading About . . ."** as a final comprehension check before the Mastery Tests. After you have completed the review tests, you will be asked questions that focus your studies. Your written answers to these questions can become an important learning log or journal that tracks your increasing strengths.

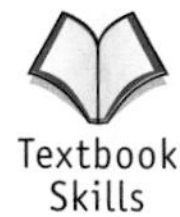


## Asking Questions and Reciting Answers Before, During, and After Reading

A vast number of textbooks use titles, headings, **bold** print, and *italics* to organize ideas. An effective reader applies the questioning and reciting steps to these pieces of information. For example, before reading, notice titles and headings. Use titles and headings to create questions. Write these questions out. During or after reading, write out the answers to these questions. After reading, use the questions and answers as a review quiz.

**EXAMPLE** Before you read the following passage from a college communications textbook, skim the information and write out five questions based on the title and words in **bold** print. After you read, answer the questions you created before you read.

Textbook Skills

### Three Ways to Organize Perception

[1]**Perception** is the process by which you become aware of objects, events, and, especially, people through your *senses*: sight, smell, taste, touch, and hearing. [2]Perception is an active, not passive, process. [3]Your perceptions result from what exists in the outside world and from your own experiences, desires, needs and wants, loves and hatreds. [4]Three interesting ways in which people organize their perceptions are by rules, by schemata, and by scripts.

#### *Organization by Rules*

[5]One often used rule is that of *proximity*, or physical closeness. [6]The **rule,** simply stated, says that things that are physically close together make up a *unit*. [7]Thus, using this rule, you would perceive people who are often together, or messages sent one right after the other, as units, as belonging together. [8]For example, when you see a person nod her head and at the same time say yes, you think of the two messages (the nod and the yes) as one unit.

#### *Organization by Schemata*

[9]Another way you organize material is by creating schemata. [10]**Schemata** are mental patterns or structures. [11]These *patterns of thought* help you sort out and make sense of the millions of items of information you come into contact with every day as well as those you already have in memory. [12]Schemata may thus be viewed as general ideas about people, yourself, or social roles. [13]You develop schemata from your own experiences. [14]These experiences include actual as well as vicarious experience gained from television, reading, and hearsay. [15]For example, you may have developed schemata about college athletes, and this might include that they are strong and ambitious.

*Organization by Scripts*

[16]A **script** is really a type of schema. [17]Like a schema, a script is an organized body of information about some action, event, or procedure. [18]It's a general idea of how some event should play out or unfold; it's the rules governing the events and their sequence. [19]For example, you probably have a script for how you do laundry.

—DeVito, *Essentials of Human Communication,* 4th ed., pp. 55–57.

**1.** Question: ______________________________

______________________________

Answer: ______________________________

______________________________

**2.** Question: ______________________________

______________________________

Answer: ______________________________

______________________________

**3.** Question: ______________________________

______________________________

Answer: ______________________________

______________________________

**4.** Question: ______________________________

______________________________

Answer: ______________________________

______________________________

**5.** Question: ______________________________

______________________________

Answer: ______________________________

______________________________

**EXPLANATION** Compare your questions and answers to the ones given here.

1. Question: What are the three ways to organize perception?

   Answer: Three interesting ways in which people organize their perceptions are by rules, by schemata, and by scripts. (Note that this sentence is the main idea of the passage.)

2. Question: What is perception, and what is an example of it?

   Answer:

   Definition: Perception is an active process by which you become aware of objects, events, and, especially, people through your *senses*: sight, smell, taste, touch, and hearing.

   Example: Ways in which people organize their perceptions are by rules, by schemata, and by scripts

3. Question: What is proximity, and what is an example of it?

   Answer:

   Definition: Proximity means physical closeness.

   Example: Words and gestures that follow closely such as nodding the head and saying yes are seen as one unit

4. Question: What are schemata, and what is an example of them?

   Answer:

   Definition: Schemata are mental patterns or structures; patterns of thought.

   Example: general ideas about what athletes are like

5. Question: What is a script, and what is an example of it?

   Answer:

   Definition: A script is a general idea of how some event should play out; the rules governing the events and their sequence.

   Example: how one does laundry

The phrase "three ways" suggests a list. And the list includes special terms, definitions of the terms, and examples of the terms. Thus the questions about the passage were created based on the terms in **bold** print and their definitions and examples, and then the answers were stated using the same pattern. By writing out the questions and answers in this way, you create an excellent study outline for later review. Not all passages give as much detail as the one used in this example; therefore, you must adapt your questions to the information in the passage.

## PRACTICE 3

Before you read the following passage from a college ecology textbook, skim the information and write out four questions based on the title and words in **bold** print. After you read, answer the questions you created before you read.

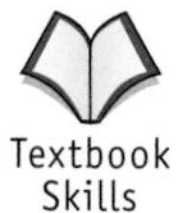
Textbook Skills

### Water Erosion

[1]Stripped of its protective vegetation and litter by plowing, logging, grazing, road building, and construction, soil is highly vulnerable to soil erosion. [2]**Soil erosion** is the carrying away of particles by wind and water faster than new soil can form.

[3]Rain falling on bare ground hammers the soil's surface, removing lightweight organic matter, breaking the soil down, and forming a seal on the surface. [4]Unable to soak into the soil, the water moves across the surface as runoff, carrying soil particles with it. [5]The least obvious type of soil erosion is **sheet erosion**. [6]Sheet erosion is a more or less even removal of soil over a field. [7]Soil compaction can increase sheet erosion. [8]**Rill erosion** occurs when runoff concentrates in small channels or rills instead of moving evenly over a sloping land, its cutting force increased. [9]Rill erosion channels water rapidly downslope. [10]On areas where concentrated water cuts the same rill long enough or where runoff develops in large enough amounts to cut deeply into the soil, highly destructive **gully erosion** results. [11]Gully erosion often begins in wheel ruts made by off-road vehicles in fields and forests, on logging roads and skid trails, and on livestock and hiking trails.

—Smith & Smith, *Elements of Ecology*, 4th ed., p. 120.

**1.** Question: ______________________________

Answer: ______________________________

______________________________

**2.** Question: ______________________________

Answer: ______________________________

______________________________

3. Question: ______________________________

   Answer: ______________________________

   ______________________________

4. Question: ______________________________

   Answer: ______________________________

   ______________________________

**VISUAL VOCABULARY**

This piece of land shows the devastating effects of ____________ erosion.

## Chapter Review

Test your understanding of what you have read in this chapter by filling in the blank with an expression from the box. Use each term only once.

| after reading | comprehension | prior knowledge | review | survey |
|---|---|---|---|---|

1. ____________ is the body of information that is learned throughout a lifetime of experience.
2. ____________ is an understanding of information.

**3.** Effective readers divide the reading process into the following three phases:

a. Before reading

b. During reading

c. _______________

**4.** SQ3R stands for _______________, Question, Read, Recite, and _______________.

## Applications

### Application 1: Before, During, and After Reading

This activity is designed to give you an opportunity to apply the entire reading process to a short selection from a college social science textbook. Survey the paragraph and answer the "Before Reading" question. Read the paragraph and answer the questions.

Textbook Skills

**Culture and Listening**

[1]Speakers from different cultures have different **cultural rules** that govern nonverbal behaviors in public settings. [2]As you listen to another person, you should also listen to their nonverbal messages. [3]For example, some Western cultures favor **direct speech**, which makes the speaker's intentions clear. [4]For example, people of Western Europe and the United States might advise you to "say what you mean and mean what you say." [5]Other cultures value **indirect speech**, which hides the speaker's true intentions. [6]For example, many Asian cultures focus on politeness and a positive public image rather than absolute truth. [7]When listening to someone, consider that the meanings the speaker wishes to send with indirectness may be very different from the meanings you would send with indirectness.

—Adapted from DeVito, *The Interpersonal Communication Book*, 10th ed., p. 129.

### Before Reading

**1.** What is your prior knowledge about cultural rules? _______________

_______________

_______________

_______________

## During and After Reading

2. What does the term *cultural rules* mean? ______________________

______________________

______________________

3. What is *direct speech* and what is an example of it?

   Definition: ______________________

   Example: ______________________

______________________

4. What is *indirect speech* and what is an example of it?

   Definition: ______________________

   Example: ______________________

______________________

## After Reading

5. Write a one- or two-sentence summary. ______________________

______________________

______________________

______________________

6. Write a paragraph that states your personal views about what you have read. Use these questions as a guide: What do you think about cultural rules? What do you think about direct speech? Indirect speech?

______________________

______________________

______________________

______________________

______________________

**VISUAL VOCABULARY**

The person in this photograph is using ________________ speech.

## REVIEW Test 1

### Before Reading

Survey the following paragraph. Then, using the words in **bold** print, create at least five questions to guide your reading.

Textbook Skills

**Types of Knowledge**

[1]**Knowledge** is the outcome of learning. [2]When we learn a name, the history of a nation, or the rules of tennis, we know something new. [3]However, knowledge is more than the end product of previous learning; it also guides new learning. [4]Several types of knowledge exist. [5]One type is domain-specific knowledge. [6]**Domain-specific knowledge** relates to a particular task or subject. [7]For example, knowing that the shortstop plays between second and third base is specific to the domain of baseball. [8]In contrast, another type is **general knowledge**, which applies to many different situations. [9]For example, general knowledge about how to read or write or use a word processor is useful in and out of school. [10]A third type is **declarative knowledge.** [11]This is knowledge that can be stated, usually in words, through lectures, books, writing, conversation, sign language, and so on.

—Adapted from Woolfolk, *Educational Psychology,* 8th ed., pp. 241–42.

1. ______________________

2. ______________________

3. ______________________

4. ______________________

5. ______________________

## REVIEW Test 2

### During Reading

Read the following passage from a college science textbook. As you read, answer the questions in the box.

Textbook Skills

**Important and Unique Properties of Water**

[1]Water has a number of unique properties related to its hydrogen bonds; three of these traits are high specific heat, high latent heat, and high viscosity.

> **1.** What are the three traits of water? ______________, ______________, and ______________
>
> **2.** What is **specific heat?** ______________ ______________ ______________

[2]First, water has the property of high specific heat. [3]**Specific heat** is the number of calories necessary to raise one gram of water one degree Celsius. [4]The specific heat of water is defined as a value of 1, and other substances are given a value relative to water. [5]Water can store great amounts of heat energy with a small rise in temperature. [6]Because of the high specific heat of water, large quantities of heat energy must be removed before water can change from a liquid to a solid. [7]Conversely, large amounts of heat must be absorbed for ice to turn to water. [8]Collectively, the energy released or absorbed when water changes from one state to another is called **latent heat**.

**3.** What is **latent heat?**

______________________________

______________________________

______________________________

**4.** What is **viscosity?**

______________________________

______________________________

______________________________

**5.** What is **surface tension?**

______________________________

______________________________

______________________________

______________________________

[9]A third trait of water is high viscosity. [10]**Viscosity** is the resistance of a liquid to flow. [11]Because of the energy in hydrogen bonds, the viscosity of water is high. [12]Imagine liquid flowing through a glass tube. [13]The liquid behaves as if it lays in layers that flow over one another. [14]The rate of flow is greatest at the center; because of internal friction between layers, the flow decreases toward the side of the tube. [15]Viscosity is the source of frictional resistance to objects moving through water.

[16]Within all substances similar molecules are attracted to one another. [17]Water is no exception. [18]Molecules of water below the surface are surrounded by other molecules. [19]The forces of attraction are the same on all sides. [20]At the water's surface, there is a different set of conditions. [21]Below the surface, molecules of water are strongly attracted to one another. [22]Above the water, air molecules and water molecules have a much weaker attraction to each other. [23]Therefore, molecules on the surface are drawn downward; thus the surface becomes taut like an inflated balloon. [24]This condition is called **surface tension,** and it is important in the lives of aquatic organisms.

[25]The surface of water is able to support small objects and animals, such as the water strider (Gerridae) and water spiders (*Dolomedes* spp.) that run across the pond's surface. [26]To other small organisms, surface tension is a barrier, whether they wish to penetrate the water below or escape into the air above. [27]For some the surface tension is too great to break. [28]For others, it is a trap to avoid while skimming the surface to feed or to lay eggs. [29]If caught in the surface tension, a small insect may flounder on the surface. [30]Surface tension hinders the efforts of the nymphs of mayflies *(Ephemeroptera)* and caddisflies *(Trichoptera)* in their efforts to emerge from the water as winged adults. [31]Slowed down at the surface, these insects become easy prey for fish.

[32]Surface tension is associated with *capillary action,* or capillarity—the rise and fall of liquids within narrow tubes. [33]Capillarity affects the movement of water in soil and the transport of water to all parts of plants.

—Adapted from Smith & Smith, *Elements of Ecology,* 4th ed. pp. 73–74.

# REVIEW Test 3

## Before, During, and After Reading

Textbook Skills

**A.** Before you read, survey the following passage from a college health textbook, and then answer the questions given here.

**1.** What is the passage about? ______________________________

______________________________

**2.** What are the ideas in *italics* or in **bold** print? ______________________________

______________________________

**3.** What do I already know about this idea? ______________________________

______________________________

**4.** What do I need to remember? ______________________________

______________________________

______________________________

**B.** Read the passage. As you read, answer the questions in the left margin.

**5.** What does **physiological** mean? ______________________________

______________________________

______________________________

______________________________

**6.** What are some of the effects of aging on the *skin?*

______________________________

______________________________

______________________________

______________________________

______________________________

### Aging: Physical Changes

[1]Although the **physiological** consequences of aging can differ in severity and timing, certain typical changes occur as a result of the aging process. [2]The changes that occur to skin and bones illustrate what can be expected.

#### *Skin*

[3]As a normal consequence of aging, the skin becomes thinner and loses elasticity. [4]This loss occurs most in the outer surfaces. [5]Fat deposits, which add to the soft lines and shape of the skin, diminish. [6]Starting at age 30, lines develop on the forehead as a result of smiling, squinting, and other facial expressions. [7]These lines become more obvious, with added "crow's feet" around the eyes, during the 40s. [8]During a person's 50s and 60s, the skin begins to sag and lose

**7.** What are some of the effects of aging on *bones?*

______________________________

______________________________

______________________________

**8.** What is *osteoporosis?*

______________________________

______________________________

______________________________

______________________________

color, leading to pallor in the 70s. [9]Body fat in underlying layers of skin tends to shift away from limbs and into the trunk region of the body. [10]Age spots become more numerous because of patches of excessive pigments under the skin.

### *Bones*

[11]Throughout the life span, bones are continually changing because of the accumulation and loss of minerals. [12]By the third or fourth decade of life, mineral loss from bones becomes more prevalent than mineral accumulation. [13]The result is weakness and porosity (diminishing density) of bony tissue. [14]This loss of minerals, such as calcium, occurs in both sexes. [15]However, it is much more common in females. [16]Loss of calcium can lead to **osteoporosis,** a disease marked by low bone density and structural deterioration of bone tissue. [17]These fragile, porous bones are prone to fracture. [18]This condition, however, can occur at any age.

—Adapted from Donatelle, *Health: The Basics,* 5th ed., p. 387.

## VISUAL VOCABULARY

_____ The best meaning of the word **melanin** as used in the caption below is_____.

a. a vitamin
b. a natural sunscreen
c. dark skin color

▶ Melanin is a pigment that offers protection against UV rays for dark-skinned people. In contrast, fair-skinned people are much less protected and more susceptible to aging and diseases of the skin.

C. After reading, answer the following questions.

**9.** How can sun and diet affect the aging process for skin and bones?

______________________________________________

______________________________________________

______________________________________________

**10.** What could a person do to minimize the impact of aging on skin and bones?

______________________________________________

______________________________________________

______________________________________________

## REVIEW Test 4

**Before reading:** Survey the following passage from a college psychology textbook. Study the words in the Vocabulary Preview; then skim the passage, noting the words in bold print. Answer the **Before Reading** questions that follow the passage. Then **read** the passage and answer the **After Reading** question that follows.

### Vocabulary Preview

*debilitating* (1): devastating
*neurons* (11): nerve cells
*neurotransmitter* (12): a substance that transmits or carries nerve impulses

Textbook Skills

### Parkinson's Disease

[1]The connection between the brain and behavior is seen in the **debilitating** effects of Parkinson's disease, a brain disorder. [2]Parkinson's afflicts about half a million Americans from every slice of life—from celebrity Michael J. Fox to the lady next door.

[3]The physical effects are obvious. [4]The hands of people with Parkinson's disease shake; they may move slowly, *lethargically,* with a stooped posture and shuffling walk; their limbs often seem frozen in position and resist attempts to bend them. [5]Along with the physical effects, Parkinson's disease also takes an emotional and social toll.

[6]A piano tuner named John had to stop working because he developed Parkinson's disease. [7]He had difficulty controlling his movements, and his behavior changed as well. [8]He became so listless that he rarely left his house. [9]He missed meals. [10]And he started to contract various minor illnesses, which worsened his other symptoms.

[11]All these changes, physical and behavioral, were caused directly or indirectly by the death of certain **neurons** in John's brain. [12]In the brains of people with Parkinson's disease, cells that produce the **neurotransmitter** dopamine have died. [13]Dopamine plays a key role in the areas of the brain that are involved in planning movements. [14]When patients take a drug that helps produce dopamine, symptoms decrease, often for a long period of time.

[15]When John's neurons no longer produced enough dopamine, the working of his brain was affected, and his muscle control was impaired. [16]His shaky hands made it almost impossible for him to tune pianos, so John had to retire. [17]After he gave up the work he loved, he became depressed. [18]He began to think of himself as diseased. [19]As a consequence, he lost interest in going out. [20]He stopped seeing many people, who in turn stopped seeing, and helping, him. [21]The events in his brain influenced his feelings about himself and his relationships with other people.

—Adapted from Kosslyn & Rosenberg, *Psychology: The Brain, The Person, The World,* p. 52.

## Before Reading Questions

Complete the following sentence by filling in the blanks with the title of the passage and the words in the Vocabulary Preview:

The (**1**) ______________ symptoms of (**2**) ______________ are caused by the death of (**3**) ______________ in the brain that produce the (**4**) ______________ dopamine.

## After Reading Question

**5.** What are the physical, emotional, and social effects of Parkinson's disease?

________________________________________

________________________________________

________________________________________

## EFFECTIVE READER Scorecard

### A Reading System for Effective Readers

| Test | Number Correct | | Points | | Score |
|---|---|---|---|---|---|
| Review Test 1 | ________ | × | 20 | = | ________ |
| Review Test 2 | ________ | × | 25 | = | ________ |
| Review Test 3 | ________ | × | 10 | = | ________ |
| Review Test 4 | ________ | × | 20 | = | ________ |
| Review Test 5 (website) | ________ | × | 20 | = | ________ |
| Review Test 6 (website) | ________ | × | 20 | = | ________ |

Enter your scores on the Effective Reader Scorecard: Chapter 1 Review Tests inside the back cover.

Name ______________________ Section ____________

# MASTERY Test 1

Date ____________ **Score** (number correct) ______ × 20 = ______%

Before you read the following passage from a college zoology textbook, skim the information and write out five questions based on the words in **bold** print. After you read, answer the questions you created before you read.

## African Elephants

[1]African elephant social groups are strongly matriarchal and have a system of social units. [2]The smallest unit is known as the **family** and consists of 10 to 20 females and their young offspring. [3]The oldest female, known as the **matriarch,** is usually the leader of the family group. [4]Because elephants continue to grow throughout their lives, the oldest female is also the largest.

[5]In contrast to wildebeest groups, which are somewhat temporary, elephant family groups are extremely stable and are likely to include both daughters and granddaughters of the matriarch. [6]The matriarch leads the other members of the group and takes the forward position when danger threatens.

[7]The second level of social organization in the system is the **kinship group**. [8]Kinship groups consist of family groups that remain fairly close to one another and include relatives that split off when the family group becomes too large.

[9]When migrating, elephants often form still another level of social organization known as a **clan**, which may contain as many as 250 elephants. [10]However, the clan is not well organized above the level of the kinship group.

—Adapted from Maier, *Comparative Animal Behavior: An Evolutionary and Ecological Approach,* p. 332.

**1.** Question: ______________________________

Answer: ______________________________

______________________________

**2.** Question: ______________________________

Answer: ______________________________

______________________________

**3.** Question: ______________________________

Answer: ______________________________

______________________________

**4.** Question: ______________________________

Answer: ______________________________

______________________________

**5.** Question: ______________________________

Answer: ______________________________

______________________________

**MASTERY Test 2**

Name ______________________ Section ______________

Date ______________ **Score** (number correct) ______ × 20 = ______%

Using SQ3R, read the following passage from a college health textbook. Then complete the outline.

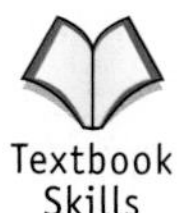

Textbook Skills

### What to Do in the Event of a Heart Attack

[1]Because heart attacks are so serious and so frightening, we would prefer not to think about them. [2]However, knowing how to act in an emergency could save your life or that of somebody else.

[3]*Know the warning signs of a heart attack.* [4]Be aware of uncomfortable pressure, fullness, squeezing, or pain in the center of the chest, lasting two minutes or longer. [5]Jaw pain and/or shortness of breath are also signs of a heart attack. [6]So is pain spreading to the shoulders, neck, or arms. [7]Finally, be aware that heart attacks are also signaled by dizziness, fatigue, fainting, sweating, and/or nausea.

[8]*Know what to do in an emergency.* [9]Find out which hospitals in your area have 24-hour emergency cardiac care. [10]Determine in advance the hospital or medical facility that's nearest your home and office, and tell your family and friends to call this facility in an emergency. [11]Keep a list of emergency rescue service numbers next to your telephone and in your pocket, wallet, or purse. [12]If you have chest or jaw discomfort that lasts more than two minutes, call the emergency rescue service. [13]Finally, if you can get to a hospital faster by not waiting for an ambulance, have someone drive you there. [14]Don't drive yourself.

—Donatelle, *Health,* 5th ed., p. 319.

**Main idea:** Knowing how to act in an emergency could save your life or that of somebody else.

A. Warning Signs of a Heart Attack

**1.** ______________________________________________

______________________________________________

**2.** ______________________________________________

______________________________________________

3. Pain spreading to the shoulders, neck, or arms
4. Dizziness, fatigue, fainting, sweating, and/or nausea

B. What to Do in an Emergency

1. Find out what hospitals in your area have 24-hour emergency cardiac care.
2. Determine in advance the hospital or medical facility that's nearest your home and office, and tell your family and friends to call this facility in an emergency.
3. ______________________________

______________________________

4. ______________________________

______________________________

5. ______________________________

______________________________

MASTERY **Test 3**

Name ______________________ Section ____________

Date ____________ **Score** (number correct) ______ × 20 = ______%

Using SQ3R, read the following passage from a first-year college English course outline.

### First-Year Writing Syllabus

**Course Purpose and Content:** The purpose of this course is to develop academic writing skills. You will learn a variety of rhetorical modes or patterns of organization, you will explore topics and themes through reading and writing, and you will learn to use the full writing process. By using teacher feedback, peer feedback, and self-assessment, you will document strengths and needs, progress, and mastery.

**Rhetorical Modes:** Essays vary in length from 500 to 1,500 words. The research project will require note and bibliography cards and must be at least 1,500 words in length. Essays will use the following patterns of organization:

- Narrative or description
- Process
- Cause and effect
- Classification
- Comparison and contrast
- Definition
- Argumentation
- Research

**1.** What is the course's purpose? ______________________

______________________

**2.** What are rhetorical modes? ______________________

______________________

**3–4.** What are two examples of a rhetorical mode? ______________________

______________________

______________________

**5.** What is the total number of types of essays that will be studied? ____________

______________________

MASTERY **Test 4**

Name ______________________ Section ____________

Date ____________ Score (number correct) ______ × 20 = ______%

Using SQ3R, read the following passage from a personal finance textbook.

Textbook Skills

## Advantages and Disadvantages of Credit

### *Background on Credit*

[1]Credit represents funds a creditor provides to a borrower that the borrower will repay in the future with interest. [2]The funds borrowed are sometimes referred to as the principal, so we segment repayment of credit into interest and principal payments. [3]Credit is frequently extended to borrowers as a loan with set terms such as the amount of credit provided and the maturity date when the credit will be repaid. [4]For most types of loans, interest payments are made periodically (such as every quarter or year), and the principal payment is made at the maturity date, when the loan is to be terminated.

### *Advantages of Using Credit*

[5]Individuals borrow funds when the dollar amount of their purchases exceeds the amount of their available cash. [6]Many individuals use borrowed funds to purchase a home or car or to pay their tuition fees. [7]In contrast, others use credit (such as a credit card) for convenience when making day-to-day purchases.

### *Disadvantages of Using Credit*

[8]There can be a high cost to using credit. [9]If you borrow too much money, you may have difficulty making your credit card payments. [10]It is easier to obtain credit than to pay it back. [11]And having a credit line can tempt you to make impulse purchases that you cannot afford. [12]College students are carrying credit cards in record numbers. [13]Eighty-three percent of all students have at least one credit card, and the average credit card balance is $2,327. [14]Many students make minimum payments on their credit cards while in school with the expectation that they will be able to pay off their balance once they graduate and are working full-time. [15]Yet the accumulating interest fees catch many by surprise, and the debt can quickly become difficult to manage. [16]Today's graduating students have an average of $20,402 in combined education loan and credit card balances. [17]If you are unable to repay the credit you receive, you may not be able to obtain credit again or will

have to pay a very high interest rate to obtain it. [18]Your ability to save money will also be reduced if you have large credit payments. [19]If spending and credit card payments exceed your net cash flows, you will need to withdraw savings to cover the deficiency.

[20]Warren Buffett, a successful billionaire investor, recently offered financial advice to some students. [21]He told them that they will not make financial progress if they are borrowing money at 18 percent (a typical interest rate on credit cards). [22]In recent years, more than 1 million people in the United States have filed for bankruptcy each year. [23]A primary reason for these bankruptcies is that the individuals obtained more credit than they could repay. [24]Even if obtaining credit at a high interest rate does not cause personal bankruptcy, it limits the potential increase in personal wealth.

—Adapted from Madura, *Personal Finance*, 2nd ed., pp. 186–187.

**1.** What is this passage about? ______________________________

______________________________________________________

Complete the following concept map with information from the passage.

**Impact of Credit Payments on Saving**

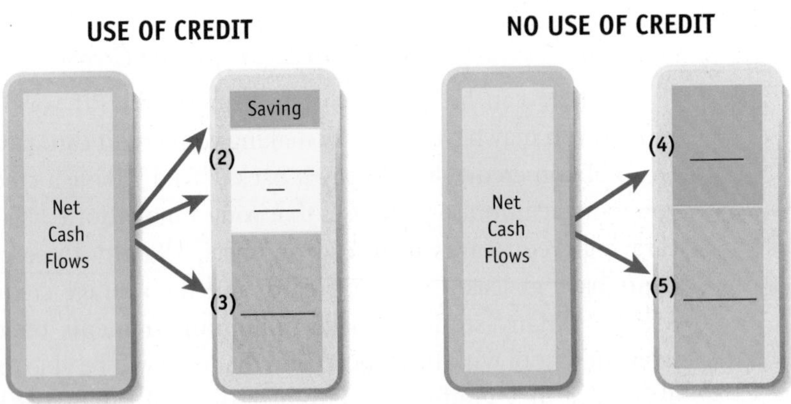

MASTERY **Test 5**

Name ______________________ Section ______________

Date ______________ **Score** (number correct) ______ × 20 = ______%

Using SQ3R, read the following paragraph taken from a college literature textbook.

Textbook Skills

## Hyperbole and Overstatement

[1]Most of us, from time to time, emphasize a point with a statement containing an exaggeration: "Faster than greased lightning," "I've told him a thousand times." [2]We speak, then, not literal truth but use a figure of speech called **overstatement** or **hyperbole**. [3]Poets, too, being fond of emphasis, often exaggerate for effect. [4]Instances are Marvell's claim of a love that should grow "vaster than empires and more slow." [5]Another is John Burgon's description of Petra: "A rose-red city, half as old as time." [6]Overstatement can also be used for humor. [7]Take, for instance, the fat woman's boast (from a blues song): "Every time I shake, some skinny gal loses her home." [8]The opposite is **understatement**, which is a figure of speech that implies more than is said. [9]For example, Robert Frost's line "One could do worse than be a swinger of birches" uses understatement. [10]All through the poem, he has suggested that to swing on a birch tree is one of the most deeply satisfying activities in the world.

—Adapted from Kennedy & Gioia, *Literature*, 8th ed., p. 867.

**1.** What is this passage about? ____________________________________

____________________________________________

Complete the concept map with information from the paragraph.

| Figure of Speech | Definition | Example |
|---|---|---|
| Overstatement or hyperbole | **2.** ____________ | "Vaster than empires and more slow," Marvell "Every time I shake, some skinny gal loses her home," blues song |
| **3.** ____________ | **4.** ____________ | **5.** ____________ |

MASTERY **Test 6** Name ______________________ Section ____________

Date ____________ **Score** (number correct) ______ × 20 = ______%

Using SQ3R, read the following passage from a college psychology textbook. Answer the questions in the left margin.

1. What are mnemonic devices?

______________________________

______________________________

______________________________

2. What are interactive images?

______________________________

______________________________

______________________________

3. What are acronyms?

______________________________

______________________________

______________________________

______________________________

4. What are initialisms?

______________________________

______________________________

______________________________

## Mnemonic Devices

[1]**Mnemonic devices** are strategies that improve memory. [2]Mnemonics can easily double your recall and are well worth the effort of learning. [3]Mnemonic devices not only help you learn something in the first place, but should you forget it, you will be able to relearn it more effectively.

[4]Probably the single most effective mnemonic device is the use of **interactive images.** [5]Forming images of objects interacting will improve memory even without any effort to learn the material. [6]For example, if you want to learn someone's first name, visualize someone else you already know who has the same first name. [7]Then imagine that person interacting with your new acquaintance in some way. [8]You might envision them fighting or hugging.

[9]Another effective mnemonic device is the use of acronyms. [10]**Acronyms** are words made from the first letters of the important words in a phrase. [11]Acronyms can be pronounced. [12]One example is NOW, for the National Organization for Women. [13]**Initialisms** are simply the initial letters of words in a phrase that probably do not combine to make a word, such as DNA for deoxyribonucleic acid. [14]Initialisms may be easier to make up. [15]The idea of using both acronyms and initialisms is to create a single unit that can be "unpacked" as a set of cues for something more complicated.

—Adapted from Kosslyn & Rosenberg, *Psychology: The Brain, The Person, The World,* pp. 228–29.

## VISUAL VOCABULARY

______ The best meaning of the word **loci** is

a. locals.
b. places.
c. imaginations.

▲ To use the "method of loci" mnemonic device, pick out a set of locations in your house, and visualize each to-be-remembered object in a different location as you mentally walk through the house. To recall, later repeat this mental walk and "see" what's in each location.

CHAPTER

2

# Vocabulary and Dictionary Skills

## CHAPTER PREVIEW

## Before Reading About Vocabulary Skills

Chapter 1 taught you the importance of surveying material before you begin reading by skimming the information for **bold** or *italic* type. Throughout this textbook, key ideas are emphasized in bold or italic print where they appear in the passage; often they are also set apart visually in a box that gives the definition or examples of the term. Skim the chapter for key ideas in boxes that will help you understand vocabulary skills. Refer to these boxes and create at least six questions that you can answer as you read the chapter. Write your questions in the following spaces (record the page number for the key term in each question):

________________________________________ (page______)

________________________________________ (page______)

________________________________________ (page______)

________________________________________ (page______)

________________________________________ (page______)

Compare the questions you created with the following questions. Then write the ones that seem most helpful in your notebook, leaving enough space between each question to record the answers as you read and study the chapter.

What is vocabulary? (page 48) What is a context clue? (page 49) What are word parts? (page 58) What kind of information does a dictionary provide? (page 69) What is a glossary? (page 55) How will each of these skills help me develop my vocabulary? (pages 48 and 58)

## Words Are Building Blocks

Words are the building blocks of meaning. Have you ever watched a child with a set of building blocks such as Legos? Hundreds of separate pieces can be joined together to create buildings, planes, cars, or even spaceships. Words are like that, too. A word is the smallest unit of thought. Words properly joined create meaning.

**Vocabulary** is all the words used or understood by a person.

How many words do you have in your **vocabulary**? If you are like most people, by the time you are 18 years old, you know about 60,000 words. During your college studies, you will most likely learn an additional 20,000 words. Each subject you study will have its own set of words. There are several ways to study vocabulary.

## Context Clues : A SAGE Approach

Effective readers interact with new words in a number of ways. One way is to use **context clues**. The meaning of a word is shaped by its context. The word *context* means "surroundings." The meaning of a word is shaped by the words surrounding it—its context. Effective readers use context clues to learn new words.

A **context clue** is the information that surrounds a new word, and is used to understand its meaning.

There are four types of context clues:

- Synonyms
- Antonyms
- General context
- Examples

Notice that, put together, the first letter of each context clue spells the word SAGE. The word *sage* means "wise." Using context clues is a wise—a SAGE—reading strategy.

## Synonyms

A **synonym** is a word that has the same or nearly the same meaning as another word. Many times, an author will place a synonym near a new or difficult word as a context clue to the word's meaning. Usually, a synonym is set off with a pair of commas, a pair of dashes, or a pair of parentheses before and after it.

| **Synonym Signal Words** | |
|---|---|
| *or* | *that is* |

**EXAMPLES** Each of the following sentences has a key word in **bold** type. In each sentence, underline the signal word and then circle the synonym for the word in **bold**.

1. The dentist gave me laughing gas to **alleviate** (or ease) the pain of cutting out my wisdom teeth.
2. Being **nocturnal**, that is, active at night, owls are rarely seen during the day.

**EXPLANATIONS**

1. The signal word *or* clues the reader that the synonym for alleviate is *ease.*
2. The signal words *that is* clue the reader that the synonym for nocturnal is *active at night.*

**VISUAL VOCABULARY**

Owls are ______________ animals who feed mostly on rabbits, mice, skunks, raccoons, and snakes.

## PRACTICE 1

Each of the following sentences contains a word that is a synonym for the word in **bold** type. Underline the signal words and circle the synonym in each sentence.

1. The government should not **infringe on** or violate a person's right to free speech.
2. Jermaine was so **engrossed**, that is, involved, in the football game on television that he did not hear his wife's question.
3. Endangered species such as manatees need a **sanctuary**, or haven, so they can begin to thrive again.

**VISUAL VOCABULARY**

The National Elk Refuge, in Wyoming, is a ______________ for large elk.

## Antonyms

An **antonym** is a word that has the opposite meaning of another word. Antonyms help you see the shade of a word's meaning by showing you what the original word is *not*. The following contrast words often act as signals that an antonym is being used.

| **Antonym Signal Words** | | |
|---|---|---|
| *but* | *instead* | *unlike* |
| *however* | *not* | *yet* |
| *in contrast* | *on the other hand* | |

Sometimes antonyms can be found next to the new word. In those cases, commas, dashes, or parentheses set them off. At other times, antonyms are placed in other parts of the sentence to emphasize the contrast between the ideas.

**EXAMPLES** In each sentence, underline the signal word and circle the antonym for the word in **bold** type. In the blank, write the letter of the word that best defines the word in **bold**.

_____ **1.** During dinner, Anne Marie let out a long, loud burp that **mortified** her mother but amused her friends.

a. embarrassed
b. killed
c. silenced
d. delighted

_____ **2.** Suzanne's tone was surprisingly **flippant**, in contrast to her usual respectful manner.

a. polite
b. sassy
c. funny
d. loud

**EXPLANATIONS**

**1.** The signal word *but* clues the reader that the antonym is *amused*. The best definition of the word *mortified* is (a) *embarrassed*.

**2.** The signal words *in contrast* clue the reader that the antonym is *respectful*. The best definition of the word *flippant* is (b) *sassy*.

## PRACTICE 2

In each sentence, underline the signal word and circle the antonym for the word in **bold** type. In the blank, write the letter of the word that best defines the word in **bold**.

_____ **1.** Please leave the kitchen **immaculate**, not filthy, when you finish your meal preparations.

a. messy
b. well-stocked
c. spotless
d. cool

_____ **2.** Maxine acted **smug** when instead she should have been humble.

a. joyful
b. depressed
c. calm
d. conceited

_____ **3.** At the beginning of Dickens's novel *A Christmas Carol,* the character Scrooge has a **mercenary** nature, but by the story's end, he has become a generous spirit.

a. carefree
b. angry
c. greedy
d. curious

## General Context

Often you will find that the author has not provided a synonym clue or an antonym clue. In that case, you will have to rely on the general context of the passage to figure out the meaning of the unfamiliar word. This requires you to read the entire sentence, or to read ahead for a few sentences, for information that will help you understand the new word.

Information about the word can be included in the passage in several ways. Sometimes a definition of the word may be provided. Vivid word pictures or descriptions of a situation can provide a sense of the word's meaning. Sometimes you may need to figure out the meaning of an unknown word by using logic and reasoning skills.

**EXAMPLES** In the blank, write the letter of the word that best defines the word in **bold** type.

_____ **1.** To ensure safety, written and road tests should be **mandatory** for everyone who seeks a driver's license for the first time; no exceptions should be allowed.

a. optional
b. difficult
c. required
d. debated

_____ **2.** Instead of being placed in adult prisons, where they often become more antisocial by mixing with hardened criminals, youth who have been convicted of crimes should be placed in programs that **rehabilitate** them.

a. restore to useful life
b. punish for good reason
c. exhaust in order to break the spirit
d. entertain

**EXPLANATIONS**

1. The best meaning of the word *mandatory* is (c) *required.* Clues from the sentence are the words *ensure* and *no exceptions should be allowed.*

2. The best meaning of the word *rehabilitate* is (a) *restore to useful life.* The passage suggests that placing young people in adult prisons just makes them tougher, so the word *rehabilitate* must mean something different, because of the contrast word *instead.*

## PRACTICE 3

Each of the following sentences has a word in **bold** type. In the blank, write the letter of the word that best defines the word in **bold**.

_____ **1.** Jamie **speculated** about how much weight he wanted to gain during the three-month bodybuilding program he was beginning.

a. knew  c. worried
b. wondered  d. celebrated

_____ **2.** Losing weight too quickly—more than a pound or two a week—can be **detrimental** to long-term weight control and good health.

a. helpful  c. harmful
b. odd  d. pleasing

_____ **3.** Many employers use yearly bonuses and raises as **incentives** to encourage work habits that go beyond expectations.

a. dreams  c. barriers
b. tricks  d. motivators

## Examples

Many times an author will show the meaning of a new or difficult word by providing an example. Signal words indicate that an example is coming.

**Example Signal Words**

*for instance* *for example* *such as* *including* *consists of*

Colons and dashes can also indicate examples.

**EXAMPLES** Using example clues, choose the correct meaning of the words in **bold** type.

_____ **1.** The American presidency has suffered **infamous** events such as the Watergate scandal of Richard Nixon and the impeachment of Bill Clinton by the House of Representatives.
a. exciting, little-known
b. boring, well-known
c. tarnishing, well-known
d. frightening, little-known

_____ **2.** Some authors use **pseudonyms**; for example, famous American author Mark Twain's real name was Samuel Clemens.
a. typists
b. mental tricks
c. ghost writers
d. pen names

**EXPLANATIONS**

**1.** The best meaning of the word *infamous* is (c) *tarnishing, well-known.*

**2.** The best meaning of the word *pseudonyms* is (d) *pen names.*

## PRACTICE 4

Using example clues, choose the correct meaning of the word in **bold** type.

_____ **1.** Baseball figure Yogi Berra's humor was based on using **malapropisms**; for instance, one of his most famous is "If you see a fork in the road, take it."
a. misuses of words
b. personal attacks
c. social situations
d. nature jokes

_____ **2.** **Rigorous** programs, such as boot camps and outward-bound programs, help develop character in the individuals who take part.
a. required
b. lengthy
c. difficult
d. abusive

Textbook Skills

# Textbook Skills: Using a Glossary

Each subject or content area, such as science, mathematics, or English, has its own specialized vocabulary. Therefore, some textbooks provide an extra section in the back of the book called a *glossary* that alphabetically lists all the specialized terms with their definitions as they were used throughout the textbook. Other textbooks may provide short glossaries within each chapter; in these cases, the glossaries may appear in the margins or in highlighted boxes, listing the words in the order that they appear on the page. The meanings given in a glossary are limited to the way in which the word or term is used in that content area.

> A **glossary** is a list of selected terms with their definitions as used in a specific area of study.

Glossaries provide excellent opportunities to use strategies before and after reading. Before reading, skim the section for specialized terms (usually these words are in **bold** or *italic* print). Checking the words and their meanings triggers prior knowledge or establishes meaning that will deepen your comprehension. In addition, you can create vocabulary review lists using glossary terms by paraphrasing or restating the definition in your own words. These vocabulary lists can be used after reading to review and test your recall of the material.

Textbook Skills

**EXAMPLE** The following selection is from a college psychology textbook. Before reading, use the glossary to complete the vocabulary review list. Then read the passage. After reading, answer the questions.

**Glossary**

**algorithm** a set of steps that, if followed methodically, will guarantee the solution to a problem.

**heuristic** a rule of thumb that does not guarantee the correct answer to a problem but offers a likely shortcut to it.

### Algorithms and Heuristics: Getting From Here to There

[1]To solve a problem you need a **strategy,** an approach to solving a problem determined by the type of **representation** used and the processing steps to be tried. [2]There are two types of strategies: algorithms and heuristics. [3]Let's say you heard about a fantastic price being offered on a hit alternative music CD by an independent record store, but you don't know the name of the store. [4]You could try to find it by calling every relevant listing in the yellow pages. [5]This process involves using an **algorithm,** a set of steps that if followed methodically will guarantee the right answer. [6]But you may not have time to call every store. [7]Instead, you

might guess that the record store is in a part of town where many students live. [8]In this case, having reduced the list of candidates to those located near the campus, you might find the store after calling only a few. [9]This process reflects use of a **heuristic,** a rule of thumb that does not guarantee the correct answer but offers a likely shortcut to it. [10]One common heuristic is to divide a big problem into parts and solve them one at a time.

—Adapted from Kosslyn and Rosenberg, *Psychology: The Brain, The Person, The World,* p. 206.

**Glossary**

**representation** a way of looking at a problem.

**strategy** an approach to solving a problem, determined by the type of representation used and the processing steps to be tried.

## BEFORE READING

**1.** ______________ an approach to solving a problem based on a way of looking at a problem and the steps taken to solve the problem

**2.** ______________ a series of systematic steps that assures the right answer

**3.** heuristic ______________________________________________

______________________________________________

## AFTER READING

______ **4.** Which sentence uses most of the words listed in the glossary?

______ **5.** Which problem-solving strategy is described in the following example? Kimberly couldn't find the rice, but started in aisle 3 first, because she thought it might be with the pasta. Then she tried aisle 10, because she thought it might be with the international foods.

—Kosslyn & Rosenberg, p. 236.

a. algorithm    b. heuristic

**EXPLANATION**

**1.** A *strategy* is an approach to solving a problem based on a way of looking at a problem and the steps taken to solve the problem. Note that the paraphrase (restatement) of the definition for strategy draws on information given in the definition for *representation.*

**2.** *Algorithm* is a series of systematic steps that assures the right answer.

**3.** Compare your paraphrase of the definition for *heuristic* with the following: *use of prior knowledge or experience that is likely to lead to the solution more quickly.*

4. Sentence 1 uses most of the words listed in the glossary. Sentence 1 also states the main idea of the paragraph, the point the author is making.

5. Kimberly used (b), the heuristic approach. This approach is an experimental, trial-and-error approach in contrast to the algorithm, which approaches problem solving using proven formulas. The importance of glossaries is evident when you consider that this question about Kimberly came directly from the psychology textbook's chapter review. Textbook reviews and course tests often include questions about the key terms listed in glossaries.

## PRACTICE 5

Textbook Skills

The following selection is from a college psychology textbook. Before reading, use the glossary to complete your vocabulary review list. Then read the passage. After reading, answer the questions.

### Incentives, Rewards, Needs, Wants

[1]When an activity is inherently rewarding, it is said to provide **intrinsic motivation:** The activity is desirable for its own sake. [2]An activity that is attractive for other reasons, such as a favorable response from other people or satisfactory payment, is said to provide **extrinsic motivation.** [3]Some research has shown that rewarding children for activities they already enjoy can make them less likely to engage in the activity when they are no longer reinforced for doing so (Deci et al., 1999; Lepper et al., 1999).

[4]Different things motivate different people: A monk is not motivated to make money; an entrepreneur is not motivated to give away all earthly possessions and seek enlightenment on a mountaintop. [5]Moreover, you are not motivated by the same forces day in and day out; rather, motivations may shift over the course of the day (or year, or life span). [6]A particular motivation comes to the fore when you have a *need* or *want.* [7]A **need** is a condition that arises from the lack of a requirement. [8]Needs give rise to drives, which push you to a particular goal that will reduce the need. [9]Lacking nutrients is a need; being hungry is a drive. [10]In contrast, a **want** is a condition that arises when you have an unmet goal that will not fill a requirement. [11]A want causes the goal to act as an incentive. [12]You might need to eat, but you don't need a fancier wristwatch, although you might desperately want one—and the promise of a Rolex as a reward for getting good grades would be an incentive for you to work hard.

—Adapted from Kosslyn & Rosenberg, *Psychology: The Brain, The Person, The World,* p. 254.

#### Glossary

**extrinsic motivation** motivation that leads a person to want to engage in an activity for external reasons.

**incentive** a stimulus that draws a person toward a particular goal, in anticipation of a reward.

**intrinsic motivation** motivation that leads a person to want to engage in an activity for its own sake.

**need** a condition that arises from the lack of a requirement; needs give rise to drives.

**want** a condition that arises when an animal has an unmet goal that will not fill a requirement; wants turn goals into incentives.

### Before Reading

1. ______________ the desire to engage in an activity for external reasons such as a favorable response from others or payment

2. ______________ the desire to engage in an activity for its own reward

3. ______________ arises from the lack of a requirement; gives rise to drives

4. ______________ arises from an unmet goal that will not meet a requirement; goals based on wants become incentives

### After Reading

_____ **5.** Thirst is a good example of a
a. drive.
b. want.
c. need.

_____ **6.** If you play the piano because you get paid to do so, you are _____ motivated.
a. intrinsically
b. extrinsically
c. inherently
d. expectantly

_____ **7.** Lacking nutrients is an example of
a. a need.
b. a want.
c. an incentive.
d. a motive.

## Word Parts

Just as ideas are made up of words, words are also made up of smaller parts. *Word parts* can help you learn vocabulary more easily and quickly. In addition, knowing the meaning of the parts of words helps you understand a new word when you see it in context.

Many words are divided into the following three parts: *roots*, *prefixes*, and *suffixes*.

**Root** The basic or main part of a word. Prefixes and suffixes are added to roots to make a new word.
Example: *press* means "press."

**Prefix** A group of letters with a specific meaning added to the beginning of a word (root) to make a new word.
Example: ***com***press means "press together."

**Suffix** A group of letters with a specific meaning added to the end of a word (root) to make a new word.

Example: *press**ure*** means "act of pressing."

Effective readers understand how the three word parts join together to make additional words. The following chart lists a few of the most common prefixes, roots, and suffixes in the English language. To improve your vocabulary, memorize these word parts.

**Commonly Used Word Parts**

| Word Part: | Meaning | Sample Word |
|---|---|---|
| **Prefix** | | |
| anti- | against | antisocial |
| de- | opposite | defrost |
| in-, im- | in | inside |
| pre- | before | predawn |
| sub- | under | subgroup |
| un- | not | unheard |
| **Root** | | |
| capere-, cep-, cip, ceipt- | to seize, take, contain | intercept |
| dic-, dit-, dict- | to say | dictation |
| ducere-, duct-, duc- | to draw or lead | conduct |
| graph-, graf- | to write, draw | graph |
| mittere-, mit-, mis-, mise- | to put or send | remit |
| scribe-, script- | to write | scripture |
| stare-, stat- | to stand | stature |
| **Suffix** | | |
| -able, -ible | can be done | capable |
| -ate | cause to be | graduate |
| -al | having traits of | practical |
| -er | comparative | higher |
| -ic | having the traits of | simplistic |
| -less | without | effortless |
| -ous, -eous, -ious | possessing qualities of | joyous |
| -y | characterized by | honestly |

**EXAMPLES** Look at the following root, prefix, and suffix. Make two new words by combining the word parts. The meaning of each part is in parentheses. You don't have to use all the parts to make a word.

| | | |
|---|---|---|
| Prefix: | *in-* | (not) |
| Root: | *vis* | (see) |
| Suffix: | *-ible* | (capable of) |

1. ______________________________
2. ______________________________

**EXPLANATIONS**

1. The root and suffix combine to form the word *visible,* which means "capable of being seen," as in the following sentence: *Carmen's joy was visible in her smile.*
2. All three word parts combine to form the word *invisible,* which means "not capable of being seen," as in the following sentence: *Josie was so embarrassed that she wished she were invisible.*

## PRACTICE 6

**A.** Study the word parts. Using the meanings of the prefix, the root, the suffixes, and context clues, put each word into the sentence that best fits its meaning. Use each word once.

| Prefix | Meaning | Root | Meaning | Suffixes | Meaning |
|---|---|---|---|---|---|
| *a-* | not | *type* | model, image | *-ical* | possessing or expressing a quality |
| | | | | *-ify* | make, form into |
| | | | | *-ly* | in such a manner |

| ***type* = model, image** | | |
|---|---|---|
| atypical | typically | typify |

**1.** The main characters in Shakespeare's play *Romeo and Juliet* ______________ the beauty and pain of young love.

**2.** Americans ______________ celebrate the Fourth of July watching the evening sky sparkle with fireworks.

**3.** Jeremy's depressed behavior is ______________; he is usually cheerful and confident.

**B.** Study the following word parts. Create four new words by combining word parts. Write a sentence using each word you create.

| Prefix | Meaning | Root | Meaning | Suffix | Meaning |
|---|---|---|---|---|---|
| *de-* | opposite, to take away from | *duct-* | to draw or lead | *-ive* *-ic* | condition of, like, related to, being |
| | | *miss-, mit-* | to put or send | | |
| *sub-* | under | *stat-* | to stand | | |

**4.** Word 1: ______________

**5.** Sentence for Word 1: ______________

**6.** Word 2: ______________

Sentence for Word 2: ______________

**7.** Word 3: ______________

**8.** Sentence for Word 3: ______________

**9.** Word 4: ______________

**10.** Sentence for Word 4: ______________

## Roots

The **root** is the basic or main part of a word. Many times a root combined with other word parts will create a whole family of closely related words. Even when the root word is joined with other word parts to form new words, the meaning of the root does not change. Knowing the commonly used roots will help you master many new and difficult words.

**EXAMPLES** The root *fact* means "make" or "do." Study the following words. Using the meaning of the root *fact* and the context of each sentence, put each word into the sentence that best fits its meaning. Use each word once.

| Root | Meaning | Suffixes | Meaning |
|---|---|---|---|
| fact | make, do | *-oid*<br>*-ion* | resembling a thing<br>act |

| *fact* = make, do | |
|---|---|
| faction | factoid |

1. In 2003, a writer for the *New York Times* was fired because he used ____________, not the truth, in his stories.
2. A significant ____________ of the population took to the streets in protest.

**EXPLANATIONS** Both words contain the root *fact* ("make" or "do"), and each word uses the meaning differently. The additional word parts—in this case, suffixes—created the different meanings. However, the meaning of the root word and the context of the sentence should have helped you choose the correct word for each sentence.

1. A *factoid* is a fact that has been made up or invented but is believed because it is in print. The *New York Times* writer was fired because he made up facts for his stories.
2. A *faction* is a group of people working together in a common cause against another group or the larger group. In this sentence, the faction has been formed to create a protest.

## PRACTICE 7

**A.** Study the following words. The root *quir* means "ask." Using the meaning of the root *quir* and context clues, put each word into the sentence that best fits its meaning. Use each word once. Slight changes in spelling may be necessary.

| Prefix | Meaning | Root | Meaning | Suffixes | Meaning |
|---|---|---|---|---|---|
| *in-* | in, into | *quir* | ask | *-ition* | result, means, action, |
| *re-* | again | | | *-ment* | action, state, process |

| ***quir* = ask** | | |
|---|---|---|
| inquire | inquisition | requirement |

**1.** I would like to ______________ at the bank about taking out a small business loan.

**2.** Tomás de Torquemada led a reign of terror during the Spanish ______________, searching out and punishing anyone who did not follow the Catholic faith.

**3.** The minimum ______________ for a two-year associate of arts degree is 60 hours of coursework.

**B.** Study the following word parts. Create four new words by combining the root with the prefixes and suffixes. Write a sentence for each word you create.

| Prefix | Meaning | Root | Meaning | Suffix | Meaning |
|---|---|---|---|---|---|
| *in-* | in, into | *dic-, dit-, dict-* | to say | *-ate* | cause to be |
| *pre-* | before | | | *-able* | capable of |

**4.** Word 1: ______________________________

**5.** Sentence for Word 1: ______________________________

______________________________

**6.** Word 2: ________________________________

Sentence for Word 2: ________________________________

________________________________

**7.** Word 3: ________________________________

**8.** Sentence for Word 3: ________________________________

________________________________

**9.** Word 4: ________________________________

**10.** Sentence for Word 4: ________________________________

________________________________

## Prefixes

A **prefix** is a group of letters with a specific meaning added to the beginning of a word or root to make a new word. Though the basic meaning of a root is not changed, a prefix changes the meaning of the word as a whole. For example, the prefix *ex-* means "out of" or "from." When placed in front of the root *tract* (which means "pull" or "drag"), the word *extract* is formed. *Extract* means "pull or drag out." The same root *tract* joined with the prefix *con-* (which means "with" or "together") creates the word *contract*. A *contract* legally pulls people together to accomplish something.

The importance of prefixes can be seen in the family of words that comes from the root *ject*, which means "throw." Look over the following examples of prefixes and their meanings. Note the change in the meaning of the whole word based on the meaning of the prefix.

| Prefix | Meaning | Root | Meaning | Example |
|---|---|---|---|---|
| *e-* | out of, from | *ject* | throw | *eject* |
| *in-* | in, into | | | *inject* |
| *re-* | back, again | | | *reject* |

**EXAMPLES** Using the meanings of the prefixes, root, and context clues, put each word into the sentence that best fits its meaning. Use each word once.

| Prefix | Meaning | Root | Meaning |
|---|---|---|---|
| *ex-* | out of, from | *pel* | push, drive |
| *pro-* | forward, in favor of | | |

| ***pel* = push, drive** | |
|---|---|
| expel | propel |

1. The sorority threatened to ______________ Danielle because she would not join in hazing new members.
2. Len Watson used his family's name and fortune to ______________ him into a seat in the Senate.

**EXPLANATIONS**

1. The sorority wanted to "drive out" Danielle because she refused to conform.
2. Len used his family's success to push him forward into becoming a senator.

## PRACTICE 8

**A.** Study the meaning of each of the following prefixes and roots.

| Prefix | Meaning | Root | Meaning |
|---|---|---|---|
| *in-* | not | *somn* | sleep |
| *retro-* | backward | *sect* | cut |
| *dis-* | apart | *spect* | look |

Create at least three words by joining these prefixes and roots.

1. ______________________________
2. ______________________________
3. ______________________________

**B.** Study the following word parts. Create four new words by combining the root with the prefixes and suffixes. Write a sentence using each word you create.

| Prefix | Meaning | Root | Meaning | Suffix | Meaning |
|---|---|---|---|---|---|
| *in-* | in, into | *scrib- script-* | write | *-le* | cause to be |
| *de-* | to take away from | | | | |
| *pre-* | before | | | | |

**4.** Word 1: ______

**5.** Sentence for Word 1: ______

______

**6.** Word 2: ______

Sentence for Word 2: ______

______

**7.** Word 3: ______

**8.** Sentence for Word 3: ______

______

**9.** Word 4: ______

**10.** Sentence for Word 4: ______

______

## Suffixes

A **suffix** is a group of letters with a specific meaning added to the end of a word or root to make a new word. Though the basic meaning of a root does not change, a suffix can change the type of word and the way a word is used. Look at the following set of examples:

| Root | Meaning | Suffix | Meaning | Word |
|---|---|---|---|---|
| *psych* | mind | *-ology* | study | *psychology* |
| | | *-ist* | person | *psychologist* |
| | | *-ical* | possessing or expressing a quality | *psychological* |

**EXAMPLES** Using the meanings of the root, suffixes, and context clues, put each of the words in the box into the sentence that best fits its meaning. Use each word once.

| Root | Meaning | Suffix | Meaning |
|---|---|---|---|
| *tact* | touch | *-ile* | of, like, related to, being |
| | | *-ful* | full of |
| | | *-ly* | in such a manner |
| | | *-less* | without |

| ***tact* = touch** | |
|---|---|
| tactfully | tactile |

1. Many blind people rely on their ______________ sense to read braille.
2. I don't know how to tell you this ______________, but your zipper is down.

**EXPLANATIONS**

1. Many blind people use the tips of their fingers to feel words written in braille; they are using their *tactile* sense, their sense of touch.
2. The speaker would like to have a gentle touch and deliver the embarrassing news about the zipper *tactfully.*

## PRACTICE 9

A. Using the meanings of the roots, suffixes, and context clues, put each word in the box into the sentence that best fits its meaning. Use each word once. Slight changes in spelling may be necessary.

| Root | Meaning | Suffix | Meaning |
|---|---|---|---|
| *homo* | human | *-cide* | kill |
| *crypt* | secret | *-ic* | of, like, related to, being |
| *log* | speech, science | *-al* | of, like, related to, being |

| homicide | cryptic | logical |
|---|---|---|

1. Problem solving requires ______________ thinking.
2. During my childhood, my friends and I would use a secret code to send ______________ messages to one another.

3. A favorite plot for prime-time television shows is the ______________ that detectives must solve by finding the murderer.

**B.** Study the following word parts. Create four new words by combining the roots with the prefix and suffixes. Write a sentence using each word you create.

| Prefix | Meaning | Root | Meaning | Suffix | Meaning |
|---|---|---|---|---|---|
| *im-* | not | *ped-* | foot | *-al* | having traits of |
| | | *ment-* | mind | *-ion* | condition or action |

4. Word 1: ______________________________
5. Sentence for Word 1: ______________________________

______________________________

6. Word 2: ______________________________

Sentence for Word 2: ______________________________

______________________________

7. Word 3: ______________________________
8. Sentence for Word 3: ______________________________

______________________________

9. Word 4: ______________________________
10. Sentence for Word 4: ______________________________

______________________________

## Reading the Dictionary

Experts believe that most English-speaking adults know and use between 25,000 and 50,000 words. That seems like a large number, yet the English language has over a million words. Effective readers use a dictionary to understand new or difficult words.

Most dictionaries provide the following information:

- Guide words (the words at the top of each page)
- Spelling (how the word and its different forms are spelled)
- Pronunciation (how to say the word)
- Part of speech (the function of the word)
- Definition (the meaning of the word)
- Synonyms (words that have similar meanings)
- Etymology (the history of the word)

All dictionaries have guide words at the top of each page. However, dictionaries differ from each other in the way they give other information about words. Some dictionaries give more information about the origin of the word; other dictionaries give long lists of synonyms. Each dictionary will explain how to use its resources in the first few pages of the book.

## How to Read a Dictionary Entry

The following entry from *Merriam-Webster's Collegiate Dictionary,* 11th edition, will be used as an example for the discussions about the kinds of information a dictionary provides.

> **her·bi·cide** \ˈ(h)ər-bə-ˌsīd*n* [L *herba* + ISV =*cide*] (1899) : an agent used to destroy or inhibit plant growth — **her·bi·cid·al** \ˌ(h)ər-bə-ˈsī-d$^{ə}$l*adj* — **her·bi·cid·al·ly** \-d$^{ə}$l-ē\ *adv*

## Spelling and Syllables

The spelling of the main word is given first in **bold** type. The word is also divided into syllables. The word *herbicide* has three syllables: *her-bi-cide.* Spellings of words based on this word are given at the end of the entry. This listing is especially helpful when letters are dropped or added to create a new word. The word *herbicide* changes form and spelling to become *herbicidal,* which has four syllables, *her-bi-cid-al,* and *herbicidally,* which has five syllables, *her-bi-cid-al-ly.*

**EXAMPLES** Use a dictionary to break the following words into syllables. Place a dot ( · ) between the syllables.

**1.** intermit ________________________________________

**2.** pedagogy ______________________________________

**EXPLANATIONS**

1. *Intermit* has three syllables: *in-ter-mit.*
2. *Pedagogy* has four syllables: *ped-a-go-gy.*

## PRACTICE 10

Place a dot ( · ) between the syllables.

1. scavenger ______________________________
2. tundra ______________________________

**Pronunciation symbols** indicate the sounds of consonants and vowels. Dictionaries provide pronunciation keys so that you will understand the symbols used in the pronunciation guide to a word. Below is a sample pronunciation key.

**Pronunciation Key**

\ə\abut \$^{ə}$\ kitten, F table \ər\further \a\ash \ā\ace \ä\\mop, mar
\au̇\out \ch\chin \e\bet \ē\easy \g\go \i\hit \ ī\ice \j\job
\n \sing \ō\go \ȯ\law \ȯi\boy \th\thin \th\the \ü\loot \u̇\foot
\y\yet \zh\vision, beige \k,$^{n}$, œ, ue, $^{y}$\

Note that each letter and symbol is followed by a sample word. The sample word tells you how that letter and symbol sounds. For example, the long *a* sounds like *a* in *ace.* And the short *i* has the sound of the *i* in *bit.* The symbol that looks like an upside down *e* (ə) is called a schwa. The schwa has a sound like *uh*, as in *about.*

Different dictionaries use different symbols in their pronunciation keys, so be sure to check the key of the dictionary you are using.

**EXAMPLES** Use the pronunciation key reprinted in this book to answer questions about the following words.

______ 1. con·sign (kən-'sīn)

The *i* in *consign* sounds like the *i* in

a. sit
b. sigh

_____ **2.** de·vi·ate·(ˈdē-vē-āt)

The *a* in *deviate* sounds like the *a* in

a. mat

b. day

## PRACTICE 11

Using your dictionary, find and write in the pronunciation symbols and accent marks for each of the following words.

**1.** ouster ________________________________

**2.** papyrus ________________________________

## Parts of Speech

Parts of speech indicate how a word functions in a sentence. Dictionary entries tell you what part of speech a word is—noun, verb, adjective, and so on. The part of speech is abbreviated and printed in italics. Your dictionary provides a full list of abbreviations. The following are the most common abbreviations for the parts of speech:

**Parts of Speech**

| | | | |
|---|---|---|---|
| *adj* | adjective | *n* | noun |
| *adv* | adverb | *prep* | preposition |
| *conj* | conjunction | *pron* | pronoun |
| *interj* | interjection | *v, vi, vt* | verb |

Read again the sample dictionary entry for herbicide.

**her·bi·cide** \ˈ(h)ər-bə-ˌsīd\ *n* [L *herba* + ISV =*cide*] (1899) : an agent used to destroy or inhibit plant growth — **her·bi·cid·al** \ˌ(h)ər-bə-ˈsī-dᵊl\ *adj* — **her·bi·cid·al·ly** \-dᵊl-ē\ *adv*

As the entry shows, the word *herbicide* is a noun. Two other forms of the word are identified as an adjective (*herbicidal*) and an adverb (*herbicidally*).

**EXAMPLES** Use your dictionary to identify the parts of speech for each of the following words. A word may be used as more than one part of speech.

1. complement ______________________
2. before ______________________
3. fly ______________________

## PRACTICE 12

Use your dictionary to identify the parts of speech for each of the following words. A word may be used as more than one part of speech.

1. graph ______________________
2. angle ______________________
3. degree ______________________

## Definitions

Most words have more than one meaning. When there is more than one definition, each meaning is numbered. Many times the dictionary will also provide examples of sentences in which the word is used.

**EXAMPLES** Three definitions are given for the word *degree.* In the spaces provided, write the number of the definition that best fits its meaning in each sentence.

1. A step or stage in a process
2. A unit of measurement for angles and curves
3. A title conferred on students by a college, university, or professional school upon completion of a program of study

_____ **A.** Joanne changed her physical fitness activities by degrees; she began with short 5-minute walks and built up to 30-minute walks every day of the week.

_____ **B.** John received his associate of arts degree from a community college and his bachelor of arts degree from a four-year university.

_____ **C.** If two triangles are similar, their corresponding angles have the same number of degrees.

## PRACTICE 13

Here are two words, their definitions, and sentences using the words based on their various definitions. In the spaces provided, write the number of the definition that best fits each sentence. Note that one definition is not used.

**A.** **factor: 1** something that brings about a result, ingredient **2** one who acts or transacts the business of another **3** a number that will divide into another number exactly

**B.** **plot : 1** *n* a small area of planted ground **2** *n* the plan or main story of a literary work **3** *v* to mark or note on as if on a map or chart

_____ **1.** The *factors* of 10 are 1, 2, and 5.

_____ **2.** The doctor discovered that pollen was a *factor* in Justine's sinus condition.

_____ **3.** I love to read a novel with a fast-paced *plot.*

_____ **4.** The graph of an equation is a drawing that *plots* all its solutions.

_____ **5.** Grandmother worked in the vegetable *plot* all morning.

## Textbook Aids for Learning Content Words

### Content Words

Many students think they should be able to pick up a textbook and simply read it. However, a textbook is written for a content or subject area, such as math, history, or English. Each content area has its own vocabulary. For example, a history textbook takes a different approach from that of a literature textbook. Different courses may use the same words, but the words often take on a new or different meaning in the context of the content area.

**EXAMPLES** The following sentences all use the word *parallel.* Write the letter of the course that would use the word in the context in which it appears.

_____ **1.** The brain appears to be a parallel processor, in which many different groups of neuron circuits work on different tasks at the same time.

a. mathematics
b. English
c. history
d. psychology

_____ **2.** Some writers use parallel structure of words and phrases for a balanced and smooth flow of ideas.

a. mathematics c. history
b. English d. psychology

_____ **3.** Parallel lines never intersect.

a. mathematics c. history
b. English d. psychology

**EXPLANATIONS** Use context clues to determine your answers.

1. The word *parallel* in this sentence is used in the study of the mind. So this term is used in a psychology class (d).
2. The word *parallel* in this sentence is used in an English class (b). Parallel structure refers to the repetition of words and phrases that are equal in their forms.
3. The word *parallel* in this sentence is used in a mathematics class (a). Parallel lines can run side by side without meeting.

## Textbook Definitions

You do not always need to use the dictionary to find the meaning of a word. In fact, many textbooks contain words or word groups that you cannot find in a dictionary. The content word is usually typed in bold or italic print. The definition follows, and many times an example is given. Context clues are helpful.

**EXAMPLES** Read the following passage from a psychology textbook. Then answer the questions that follow it.

Textbook Skills

**Disconfirmation** is a communication pattern in which you ignore a person's presence as well as that person's communications. You say, in effect, that the person and what she or he has to say aren't worth serious attention. Disconfirming responses often lead to loss of self-esteem. Note that disconfirmation is not the same as rejection. In **rejection**, you disagree with the person; you indicate your unwillingness to accept something the other person says or does. In disconfirming someone, however, you deny that person's significance; you claim that what this person says or does simply does not count.

—DeVito, *The Interpersonal Communication Book*, 10th ed., p. 171.

**1.** A communication pattern in which you ignore a person's presence as well as that person's communications is ______________________.

**2.** An unwillingness to accept something the other person says or does is ______________________.

**EXPLANATIONS** The author knows that these words, or the specific uses of these words, may be new for many students, so the words are set in **bold** print and definitions are given.

**1.** disconfirmation **2.** rejection

## PRACTICE 14

Read each of the following textbook passages. Then write the definition for each of the words in **bold** print.

Textbook Skills

**1.** To say that $x + 4 <$ (is less than) 10 and $x <$ (is less than) 6 are **equivalent** is to say that they have the same solution set. For example, the number 3 is a solution to $x + 4 < 10$. It is also a solution for $x < 6$. The number $-2$ is a solution of $x < 6$. It is also a solution of $x + 4 < 10$. Any solution of one is a solution of the other; they are equivalent.

—Bittinger & Beecher, *Introductory and Intermediate Algebra,* 2nd ed., p. 143.

______________________________________________.

**2.** To borrow the useful terms of the English novelist E. M. Forster, characters may seem **flat** or round. A **flat** character has only one outstanding trait or feature: for example, the stock character of the mad scientist, with his lust for absolute power and his crazily gleaming eyes.

—Adapted from Kennedy & Gioia, *Literature,* 8th ed., p. 78.

______________________________________________.

**3.** **Codependence** refers to a self-defeating relationship pattern in which a person is "addicted to the addict."

—Donatelle, *Access to Health,* 7th ed., p. 321.

______________________________________________

______________________________________________

Textbook Skills

## Visual Vocabulary

Textbooks often make information clearer by providing a visual image such as a graph, chart, or photograph. Take time to study these visual images and their captions to figure out how each one ties in to the information given in words.

**EXAMPLES** Study the following visual image and its caption, which were used in a college business textbook.

"It says, all our accounts have been frozen!"

______ What does **frozen** mean?

a. icy
b. made inactive
c. cold
d. hard

**EXPLANATION** In this example, the word *frozen* has two meanings. It can indicate that something is so cold that it is solid like ice. Another meaning of *frozen* is that something cannot move or is inactive. In the example, the context of the sentence gives *frozen* the meaning of (b) *made inactive*. The humor of this cartoon is that it uses both meanings. In banking, a *frozen account* is an account that has been inactivated so that the customer cannot withdraw any funds from it.

## PRACTICE 15

Study the following visual image and its caption, which were used in a college psychology textbook.

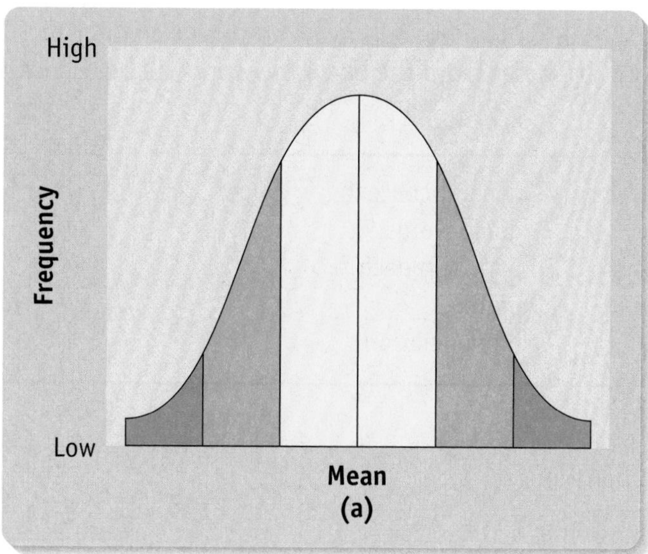


◀ Curve showing the **mean** of IQ scores of 850 children $2^1/_2$ years of age.

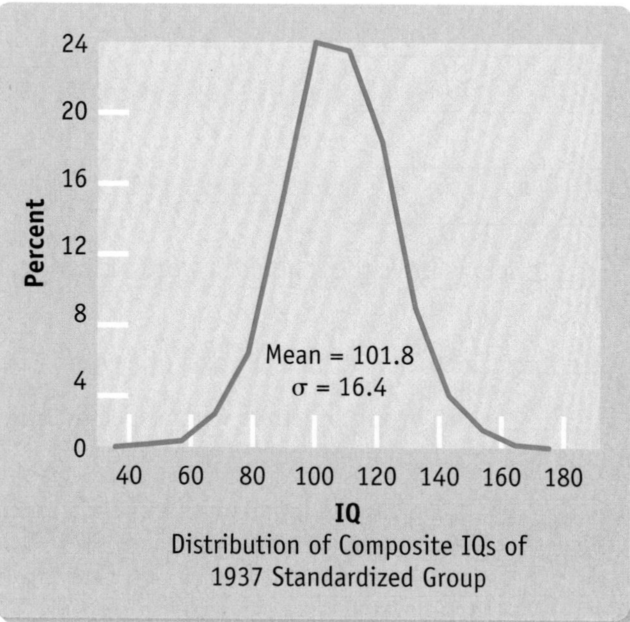


 Reprinted from Fig. 11.2 Carlson, Neil R. and William Buskist, *Psychology: The Science of Behavior,* 5th ed., Allyn & Bacon 1997, p. 343.

_____ What is the best meaning of the word **mean** in the graph?

a. middle score
b. most frequent score
c. smallest score
d. largest score

## Chapter Review

Test your understanding of what you have read in this chapter by filling in the blank with a word or phrase from the box. One word will be used twice.

| | | |
|---|---|---|
| antonyms | general context | root |
| content | guide words | SAGE |
| context clues | part of speech | suffix |
| etymology | prefix | synonyms |
| examples | pronunciation | |

1. There are four types of _______________.
2. Using context clues is a wise, or _______________, reading strategy.

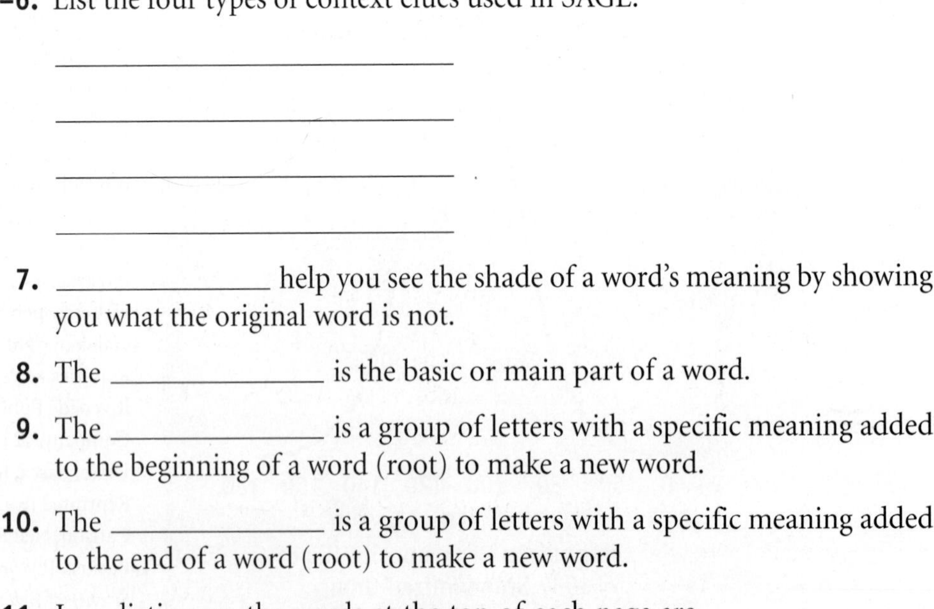

3–6. List the four types of context clues used in SAGE:

_____________________________

_____________________________

_____________________________

_____________________________

7. _______________ help you see the shade of a word's meaning by showing you what the original word is not.
8. The _______________ is the basic or main part of a word.
9. The _______________ is a group of letters with a specific meaning added to the beginning of a word (root) to make a new word.
10. The _______________ is a group of letters with a specific meaning added to the end of a word (root) to make a new word.
11. In a dictionary, the words at the top of each page are _______________.

12. The sounds of consonants and vowels are indicated by _______________ symbols.

13. A dictionary entry describes the function of a word by identifying its _______________.

14. A dictionary entry may also provide the _______________, the history of the word.

15. Each subject matter has its own _______________ vocabulary.

## Applications

### Application 1: Synonyms and Antonyms

**A.** (1–3.) The following paragraph uses synonyms as context clues for three words. Underline the signal words and circle the synonym given for each of the words in **bold** type.

Textbook Skills

**Liquidity**

Liquidity refers to your ability to cover any short-term cash **deficiencies** or shortages. Some people rely on a credit card as a source of liquidity rather than keeping liquid investments. Many credit cards provide short-term or **temporary** free financing from the time you make purchases until the date when your payment is due. If you have **insufficient funds**—that is, not enough money to pay the entire credit card balance when the bill is due—you may pay only a portion of your balance. You can then finance the rest of the payment. The interest rate is commonly quite high, ranging from 8 to 20 percent.

—Madura, *Personal Finance,* 2nd ed., p. 160.

**B.** In the sentence, underline the signal word and circle the antonym for the word in **bold** type. In the blank, write the letter of the best definition for the word in **bold.**

4. A **hypothesis** is not a factual statement: it is a tentative idea that might explain a set of facts or actions.

______ 5. The best definition for **hypothesis** is
a. an educated guess.
b. a well-thought-out lie.
c. a set of facts or actions.

## Application 2: Context Clues

Read the following paragraph, and then answer the questions.

### Empathy

[1]To **empathize** with someone is to feel as that person feels. [2]When you feel empathy for another, you're able to experience what the other is experiencing from that person's point of view. [3]**Empathy** is not a lack of concern, but neither does it mean that you agree with what the other person says or does. [4]You never lose your own identity or your own attitudes or beliefs. [5]To **sympathize**, on the other hand, is to feel for the individual—to feel sorry for the person, for example.

—DeVito, *Messages: Building Interpersonal Communication Skills,* 4th ed., p. 221.

______ **1.** The synonym for the term **empathize** in sentence 1 is
a. think.
b. feel.
c. agree.

______ **2.** The antonym for **empathy** in sentence 3 is
a. agreement.
b. feeling.
c. concern.
d. lack of concern.

**3.** What example of **sympathize** is given in sentence 5? Fill in the blank:

*Sympathize* means to feel ______________ for another person.

## Application 3: Word Parts

Study the chart of word parts and their meanings. Below the chart are three words made from the word parts in the chart. Answer the questions in sections A and B based on this chart.

| Prefix | Meaning | Root | Meaning | Suffix | Meaning |
|---|---|---|---|---|---|
| *bi-* | two | *ocul* | eye | *-ar* | relating to, being |
| *mono-* | one | *primus* | leader, of first rank | *-ate* | quality, state |

| binocular | monocular | primate |
|---|---|---|

**A.** Fill in the blanks to match each word to its definition.

**1.** _______________ means "two-eyed."

**2.** _______________ means "any of an order of mammals that includes humans, apes, and monkeys."

**3.** _______________ means "one-eyed."

**B.** (**4–6.**) Using word meanings and context clues, put each word into the sentence that best fits its meaning. Use each word once.

| binocular | monocular | primates |
|---|---|---|

Textbook Skills

**Depth Perception**

Depth perception requires that we perceive the distance of objects in the environment from us and from each other. We do so by means of two kinds of cues: binocular and monocular. _______________ cues arise from the fact that the visual fields of both eyes overlap. Only animals that have eyes on the front of the head (such as _______________, cats, and some birds) can obtain binocular cues. Animals that have eyes on the sides of their heads (such as rabbits and fish) can obtain only _______________ cues.

—Carlson & Buskist, *Psychology: The Science of Behavior,* p. 217.

## Application 4: Dictionary Skills

To expand your vocabulary, use a Dictionary Log. Before you read, identify one or two new or difficult words to add to your working vocabulary. Look up the words in a dictionary and record key information to remember. Then read. After reading, create a sentence using the word. Do this to expand your prior knowledge. A log like this is an excellent vocabulary building technique.

Read the following series of sentences. Use your dictionary to complete the following log based on words used in the sentences.

An **acrimonious** dispute about money divided the family. **Caustic** words spoken in anger left deep emotional wounds. An **arbitrator** had to be brought in to settle the dispute. Even once the money issue was **equitably** decided, certain family members could not forgive or forget the hurt.

**A Dictionary Log**

| Word | Part of Speech | Pronunciation and Syllables | Definition |
|---|---|---|---|
| 1. acrimonious | adj | \ˌa-krə–ˈmō-nē-əs\ | biting, sharp in feelings, language, or manner |
| Use in new sentence: | | | |
| 2. caustic | | | |
| Use in new sentence: | | | |
| 3. arbitrator | | | |
| Use in new sentence: | | | |
| 4. equitably | | | |
| Use in new sentence: | | | |

# REVIEW Test 1

## Context Clues

**A.** Use context clues. Select the letter of the best meaning for each word in **bold** type. Then identify the context clue you used.

_____ **1.** Manny's attendance **dwindled**, until he finally stopped coming altogether.

a. lessened c. enhanced
b. improved d. ended

_____ **2.** The context clue used for the word *dwindled* in sentence 1:

a. synonym c. general context
b. antonym d. example

_____ **3.** Researchers have learned to control or eliminate many **blights** such as smallpox and the bubonic plague.

a. barriers c. diseases
b. tests d. mysteries

_____ **4.** The context clue used for the word *blights* in sentence 3:

a. synonym
b. antonym
c. general context
d. example

**B.** Using context clues, write the definition for each word in **bold** type. Choose definitions from the box. Use each definition once.

| complicated | illnesses | disagreement |
|---|---|---|
| range | environment | smooth-talking |

**5.** Few singers can boast of a musical **repertoire** like that of Elvis Presley, who easily mastered gospel, ballads, and rock and roll.

_______________

**6.** In a democratic society, individuals who disagree with government are allowed to voice their **dissent** by writing, speaking, and even marching in the streets.

_______________

**7.** Washing hands with warm, sudsy water is an important step in the fight against **infirmities** caused by unseen germs.

_______________

**8.** Con artists cheat countless numbers of us with their **glib** promises and high-pressure sales tactics.

_______________

**9.** The handmade lacework on the tablecloth has a beautiful and **intricate** design of roses and scallops.

_______________

**10.** Central Florida alligators enjoy a **habitat** of spring-fed waterways, sandy beaches with fallen logs, and shallow wetlands for hunting and nesting.

_______________

# REVIEW Test 2

## Dictionary and Glossary Skills

Textbook Skills

**A.** Look over the following entry from *Merriam-Webster's Collegiate Dictionary* 11th edition. Then mark the numbered items **T** if it is true or **F** if it is false based on the entry.

> **my·o·pia** \mī-'ō-pē-ə*n* [NL, fr. GK *myōpia,* fr. *myōp-, myōps*] (ca.1752)
> **1** : a condition in which the visual images come to a focus in front of the retina of the eye resulting esp. in defective vision of distant objects
> **2** : a lack of foresight or discernment: a narrow view of something — **my·o·pic** \-'ō-pik, -'ä*adj* — **my·o·pi·cal·ly** \-pi-k(ə-)lē\ *adv*

______ **1.** The entry gives three forms of the word *myopia.*

______ **2.** *Myopia* can be a way of thinking about a topic.

______ **3.** *Myopia* has three syllables.

______ **4.** The *y* in *myopia* sounds like the *y* in *yard.*

______ **5.** *Myopic* is a noun.

Textbook Skills

**B.** Look over the following list of words from the glossary of the college textbook *Access to Health.* Based on the definition of each word and the context of each sentence, label each statement **T** if it is true or **F** if it is false.

**Glossary**

- **Stress** Mental and physical responses to change.
- **Stressor** A physical, social, or psychological event or condition that requires adjustment.
- **Adjustment** The attempt to cope with a given situation.
- **Strain** The wear-and-tear sustained by the body and mind in adjusting to or resisting a stressor.

______ **6.** **Stress** is usually the result of an internal state of emotional tension that occurs in response to the various demands of living.

______ **7.** An angry parent is an example of a **stressor.**

______ **8.** Adjustments are used as a last resort in response to **stress.**

______ **9.** **Strain** is always a physical problem.

_____ **10.** Binge eating may be an unhealthy adjustment to the **stress** caused by low self-esteem.

# REVIEW Test 3

## Word Parts

**A.** Using the information in the chart and the context of each sentence, select the word that best fits the meaning of the sentence. Use each word once.

| Prefix | Meaning | Root | Meaning | Suffixes | Meaning |
|---|---|---|---|---|---|
| *dys-* | bad, impaired | *ent* | intestines | *-ery* | state, condition |
| *omni-* | all | *nocturn* | night | *-al* | possessing or expressing a quality |
| *carni-* | flesh | *function* | perform | *-ous* | possessing the qualities of |
| | | *vor* | devour, feed | | |

| dysentery | nocturnal | dysfunctional | carnivorous | omnivores |
|---|---|---|---|---|

**1.** Some birds such as eagles and ospreys are _______________, with diets consisting of fish and small animals.

**2.** Julia is suffering with _______________ because of water she drank in the jungle.

**3.** Just like a bat, my son Chip is a _______________ creature who prefers to sleep during the day.

**4.** Most _______________ have two types of teeth: sharp, tearing teeth for eating meat and flat, grinding teeth for eating plants.

**5.** If I don't get enough sleep, I become completely _______________.

**B.** Using the information from the chart and the context of each sentence, select the word that best fits the meaning of the sentence. Use each word once.

| Prefix | Meaning | Root | Meaning | Suffix | Meaning |
|---|---|---|---|---|---|
| *pro-* | forward, in favor of | *ject* | throw | *-ile* | capability |
| *e-* | out of, from | *pellere* | to drive | *-ion* | action, state |

| propel | ejects | projects | projectile | ejection |
|---|---|---|---|---|

6. Because mother _______________ her fears into action, she taught all of us the Heimlich maneuver as a safety precaution.

7. The Heimlich maneuver is an emergency procedure that _______________ foreign objects from a choking victim's airway.

8. The maneuver causes the _______________ of the foreign object by forcing quick bursts of air up from the abdomen.

9. Sometimes a strong burst of air turns the object that is blocking the air passage into a _______________ as it shoots out of the victim's mouth.

10. Place a clenched fist and hands together just below the sternum; use inward and upward thrusts to _______________ the object from the air passage.

**VISUAL VOCABULARY**

This diagram shows the proper way to perform the _______________ _______________.

# REVIEW Test 4

## Vocabulary Skills

**Before reading:** Survey the following passage adapted from the college textbook *American Government: Continuity and Change.* Study words in the Vocabulary Preview; then skim the passage, noting the words in bold print. Answer the

**Before Reading** questions that follow the passage. Then read the passage. Finally, **after reading,** check the answers you gave before reading to make sure they are accurate. Use the discussion and writing topics as activities to do after reading.

## Vocabulary Preview

*random* (1): without a definite plan, purpose, or pattern
*outraged* (4): very angry
*informed* (8): told
*violated* (9): infringed on, failed to honor
*effective* (13): producing the desired result
*zero-tolerance* (17): accepting nothing

Textbook Skills

### Civil Liberties

[1]In spring 2000, the principal of Highland Springs High School in Virginia entered Liz Armstrong's tenth-grade biology class to **announce** or declare a "**random** search." [2]In spite of the cry that went up from the class, the **administrators**, including the principal, forced students to empty their pockets, pocketbooks, and backpacks. [3]No weapons or drugs were found.

[4]Armstrong, a nine-year **veteran** of the classroom, was **outraged.** [5]She promised her students that she would find out more about the public school district's search policy. [6]She also promised to contact the American Civil Liberties Union (ACLU) on her students' behalf. [7]The next day she received a letter from the president of the Virginia ACLU. [8]The letter **informed** her that the search was "clearly illegal." [9]The search **violated** the students' Fourth Amendment right to be free from unlawful and **unwarranted** or unnecessary searches and seizures. [10]In addition, the search did not follow the guidelines for student searches as set out by the Virginia Board of Education. [11]Upon receipt of the letter, Armstrong sent a letter to her principal informing him about the unlawfulness of the search; she also suggested how a legal policy could be implemented.

[12]Armstrong was **suspended** a few days later. [13]She wasn't charged with speaking up for her students; instead, she was charged with failing to make "**effective** use of instructional time." [14]How did Armstrong do that? [15]She talked to her students about the search. [16]In May, she was **dismissed** from her position.

[17]In the wake of the 1999 shootings at Columbine High School in Littleton, Colorado, many school boards put in place **zero-tolerance** weapons policies for students and teachers. [18]In spite of federal rulings to the contrary, students often fall prey to **overzealous** administrators who turn from reason to keep order in their schools. [19]In this case, the students lost their rights to be free from unreasonable searches; they also lost the right to privacy for their

persons and their belongings. [20]These rights were balanced against the right of the community to be free from violence and harm. [21]Although these students were victims of an unlawful search, unless they wish to sue, they have little other recourse.

—Adapted from O'Connor, Sabato, Haag, & Keith, *American Government: Continuity and Change, 2004 Texas Edition,* p. 139.

## BEFORE READING

**A.** Use context clues to answer the following questions.

_____ **1.** In sentence 1, the word **announce** means
a. make known. c. force.
b. cover up. d. silence.

_____ **2.** Identify the context clue used for the word **announce** in sentence 1.
a. synonym c. general context
b. antonym d. example

_____ **3.** In sentence 2, the word **administrators** means
a. workers. c. officials.
b. assistants. d. police officers.

_____ **4.** Identify the context clue used for the word **administrators** in sentence 2.
a. synonym c. general context
b. antonym d. example

_____ **5.** In sentence 9, the word **unwarranted** means
a. promised. c. necessary.
b. unreasonable. d. unsure.

_____ **6.** In sentence 18, the word **overzealous** means
a. logical. c. mild.
b. overly enthusiastic. d. fair.

_____ **7.** The context clue used for the word **overzealous** in sentence 18 is
a. synonym. c. general context.
b. antonym. d. example.

**B.** Study the following chart of word parts. Use context clues and the word parts to answer the questions that follow.

| Prefix | Meaning | Root | Meaning | Suffix | Meaning |
|---|---|---|---|---|---|
| *dis-* | apart, in different directions | *veter* | old | *-an* | person |
| | | *miss* | send | *-ed* | in the past |
| *sus-* | up | *pend* | hang | | |

_____ **8.** Armstrong, a nine-year **veteran** of the classroom, was outraged. (sentence 4)

The word **veteran** in sentence 4 means

a. beginner.
b. old hand.
c. soldier.
d. student.

_____ **9.** Armstrong was **suspended** a few days later. (sentence 12)

The word **suspended** in sentence 12 means

a. given a warning.
b. rewarded with a raise.
c. placed in prison.
d. placed on leave.

_____ **10.** In May, she was **dismissed** from her position. (sentence 16)

The word **dismissed** in sentence 16 means

a. praised.
b. promoted.
c. fired.
d. mistreated.

Use context clues to choose the best word below to complete the caption in the Visual Vocabulary box.

| veteran | effective | random |
|---|---|---|

**VISUAL VOCABULARY**

Dogs that are trained to detect drugs are often used in _____________ searches in public schools.

## AFTER READING

### Discussion Topics

1. What could be another reason for Armstrong's dismissal?
2. Which should have the greater weight: the students' rights to privacy and freedom from searches or the community's right to safety? Why?
3. Why is the Fourth Amendment so important?

### Writing Topics

1. Write a letter to the editor of a newspaper for or against Liz Armstrong's actions.
2. Write a paragraph to explain why Liz Armstrong should have been or should not have been fired.

## EFFECTIVE READER Scorecard

**Vocabulary Skills**

| Test | Number Correct | | Points | | Score |
|---|---|---|---|---|---|
| Review Test 1 | ________ | × | 10 | = | ________ |
| Review Test 2 | ________ | × | 10 | = | ________ |
| Review Test 3 | ________ | × | 10 | = | ________ |
| Review Test 4 | ________ | × | 10 | = | ________ |
| Review Test 5 (website) | ________ | × | 10 | = | ________ |
| Review Test 6 (website) | ________ | × | 10 | = | ________ |

Enter your scores on the Effective Reader Scorecard: Chapter 2 Review Tests inside the back cover.

## After Reading About Vocabulary and Dictionary Skills

The reading system you learned in Chapter 1 is an excellent study system that will help you comprehend and retain large sections of information, such as this textbook chapter about vocabulary skills. Now that you have studied the chapter, take time to reflect on what you have learned before you begin the mastery tests. Stop and think about your learning and performance by answering the following questions. Write your answers in your notebook.

What did I learn?

What do I need to remember?

How has my knowledge base or prior knowledge changed?

## More Review and Mastery Tests

For more practice, go to the book's website at **http://www.ablongman.com/henry** and click on *The Effective Reader.* Then select "More Review and Mastery Tests." The tests are organized by chapter.

Name ______________________ Section ____________

# MASTERY Test 1

Date ____________ **Score** (number correct) ______ × 10 = ______%

**A.** Using context clues, write the definition for each word in **bold** type. Choose definitions from the box. Use each definition once.

| | | |
|---|---|---|
| in confusion | a polite term | thorough |
| basic | mission | vary |

**1.** Marion used a **euphemism** when she described herself as "full-figured" when she was 50 pounds overweight.

**Euphemism** means ______________.

**2.** The movie *Lorenzo's Oil* tells the story of a mother's **quest** to find a cure for a disease that was slowly robbing her son of his ability to speak or move.

**Quest** means ______________.

**3.** Roxanne was so surprised and excited by Sam's marriage proposal that she babbled **incoherently** before she came to her senses and said yes.

**Incoherently** means ______________.

**4.** Manny is an excellent study partner; he will not let you get away with incomplete information but demands an **exhaustive** review.

**Exhaustive** means ______________.

**5.** Humor and laughter seem to be **intrinsic** or central human traits that are present in almost all cultures.

**Intrinsic** means ______________.

**6.** Some winter days in Florida can bring temperatures that **fluctuate** from the 30s and 40s in the mornings to the 70s in the afternoons.

**Fluctuate** means ______________.

**B.** Using the information in the chart and the context of each sentence, select the word that best fits the meaning of the sentence. Use each word once.

| Prefix | Meaning | Root | Meaning | Suffix | Meaning |
|---|---|---|---|---|---|
| *in-* | not | *somn* | sleep | *-ology* | study |
| | | *theo* | God | *-ic* | of, like, related to, being |
| | | *psych* | mind | *-ia* | condition |

| theology | insomnia | psychology | psychic |
|---|---|---|---|

7. Unlike people who suffer from ______________, Justine can fall asleep anytime and anyplace.
8. People who have some understanding of ______________ are better able to deal with issues like conflict, stress, anger, and depression.
9. A serious ______________ student may want to study the Koran, the Torah, and the New Testament to compare and contrast Islam, Judaism, and Christianity.
10. Some people seem to be gifted with ______________ abilities, such as the ability to predict events that will happen in the future.

MASTERY **Test 2**

Name ______________________ Section ______________

Date ______________ **Score** (number correct) ______ × 10 = ______%

**A.** Read the following passage adapted from a college business textbook. Using context clues, write the definition for each word in **bold** type. Choose definitions from the box. You will not use all the definitions.

Textbook Skills

### Financial Planning for a Vacation

[1]Imagine that you are taking a vacation next year. [2]This is a major event for you, and you wish to plan **thoroughly,** leaving nothing to chance, so that nothing goes wrong. [3]You have many choices to make.

[4]Should you drive or should you fly and rent a car at the **destination** of your journey? [5]Which hotel will suit you best? [6]Where will you eat? [7]What clothes will you take with you? [8]Do you schedule every minute of your time or build in free time in case something of interest presents itself? [9]How big is your vacation budget, and how do you want to **allocate** or dole it out? [10]Will the weather affect your plans? [11]When do you want to arrive back home? [12]All of this requires detailed planning. [13]You choose your **itinerary**, carefully save your money and vacation time, and have the time of your life. [14]A **fantasy**? [15]No, these dreams are realized by millions of people every year.

—Adapted from Madura, *Personal Finance,* 2nd ed., p. 1.

| | | |
|---|---|---|
| distribute | save | place |
| hastily | route | time |
| dream | thoughts | carefully |

**1.** In sentence 2, **thoroughly** means ______________.

**2.** In sentence 4, **destination** means ______________.

**3.** In sentence 9, **allocate** means ______________.

**4.** In sentence 13, **itinerary** means ______________.

**5.** In sentence 14, **fantasy** means ______________.

**B.** Read the following paragraph adapted from a college science textbook. Using context clues, write the definition for each word in **bold** type. Choose definitions from the box. You will not use all the definitions.

Textbook Skills

## Plagiarism

[1]**Plagiarism** is the use of someone else's words or ideas without giving proper credit. [2]Such intellectual theft is not tolerated in science. [3]There are many ways to plagiarize. [4]Some cases of plagiarism are **obvious** and clear. [5]But many are **subjective**, or judgment calls that scientists must learn to make. [6]Using someone else's wording can be done only if it is presented as a quote and the original work is **cited**. [7]The original work must also be cited if it is **paraphrased** or rephrased. [8]If some part of another work (data, results, methods, etc.) is used, even if the wording is significantly different, the source must be cited. [9]Citations are not necessary, however, if ideas are widely known. [10]For example, if "the earth revolves around the sun" is used in a paper, it is not necessary to cite the work of the scientist Copernicus. [11]Everyone who reads the paper can be expected to know that the earth revolves around the sun. [12]However, if new findings about the details of how the earth revolves around the sun are used in a paper, the source of that new information should be cited.

—Adapted from Lee, *The Scientific Endeavor: A Primer on Scientific Principles and Practice,* p. 69.

| | | |
|---|---|---|
| easy to see | difficult | based on personal opinion |
| reworded | written | stolen |
| the act of stealing words or ideas | new | mentioned |

**6.** In sentence 1, **plagiarism** means ______________________.

**7.** In sentence 4, **obvious** means ______________________.

**8.** In sentence 5, **subjective** means ______________________.

**9.** In sentence 6, **cited** means ______________________.

**10.** In sentence 7, **paraphrased** means ______________________.

# MASTERY Test 3

Name ______________________ Section ____________

Date ____________ **Score** (number correct) ______ × 10 = ______%

**A.** Read the following short passages adapted from a college psychology textbook. Answer the questions that follow each passage.

Textbook Skills

### Distress or Disability

[1]A person who suffers from distress is **disabled.** [2]Distress creates a risk of physical or **psychological** deterioration or loss of freedom of action. [3]An example of **distress** is a man who cannot leave his home without weeping and therefore cannot pursue everyday life goals.

—Adapted from Gerrig & Zimbardo, *Psychology and Life,* 16th ed., p. 468.

_____ **1.** The best meaning of the word **disabled** in sentence 1 is
- a. not able to function fully.
- b. powerful.
- c. upset.
- d. disturbed.

_____ **2.** The context clue used for **disabled** in sentence 1 is
- a. synonym.
- b. antonym.
- c. general context.
- d. example.

_____ **3.** The best meaning of the word **distress** in sentence 3 is
- a. weakness.
- b. mental suffering.
- c. peacefulness.
- d. fear.

_____ **4.** The context clue used for **distress** in sentence 3 is
- a. synonym.
- b. antonym.
- c. general context.
- d. example.

_____ **5.** Using context clues and word parts, choose the best definition of the word **psychological** as it is used in sentence 2.

| Root | Meaning | Suffix | Meaning |
|---|---|---|---|
| *psych* | mind | *-ology* | study of |
| | | *-al* | of, like, related to, being |

- a. head
- b. mental
- c. thoughts
- d. active

**B.**

Textbook Skills

## Irrationality

[1]An **irrational** person acts or talks in ways that are not logical to others. [2]For example, a man who responds to voices that do not exist is behaving **irrationally**.

—Adapted from Gerrig & Zimbardo, *Psychology and Life,* 16th ed., p. 468.

_____ **6.** Using context clues and word parts, choose the best definition of the word **irrational** as it is used in sentence 1.

| Prefix | Meaning | Root | Meaning | Suffix | Meaning |
|---|---|---|---|---|---|
| *ir-* | not | *ratio* | reason | *-al* | of, like, related to |

a. stupid
b. hurtful
c. sick
d. unreasonable

_____ **7.** The context clue for **irrational** in sentence 1 is
a. synonym.
b. antonym.
c. general context.
d. example.

_____ **8.** The context clue for **irrationally** in sentence 2 is
a. synonym.
b. antonym.
c. general context.
d. example.

**C.**

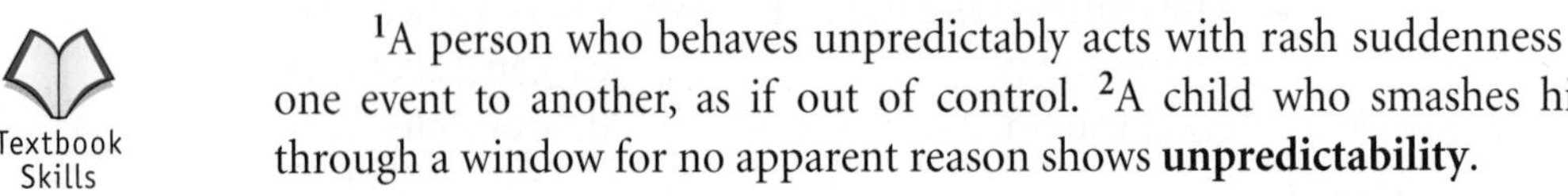

Textbook Skills

## Unpredictability

[1]A person who behaves unpredictably acts with rash suddenness from one event to another, as if out of control. [2]A child who smashes his fist through a window for no apparent reason shows **unpredictability**.

—Adapted from Gerrig & Zimbardo, *Psychology and Life,* 16th ed., p. 468.

_____ **9.** The best meaning of the word **unpredictability** in this passage is
a. being selfish.
b. acting reasonably.
c. doing unexpected things.
d. giving pleasure to others.

_____ **10.** The context clue used for **unpredictability** in sentence 2 is
a. synonym.
b. antonym.
c. general context.
d. example.

MASTERY **Test 4**

Name ______________________ Section ____________

Date ____________ **Score** (number correct) ______ × 10 = ______%

---

**A.** Look over the following entry from *Merriam-Webster's Collegiate Dictionary*, 11th edition. Then mark each item **T** if it is true or **F** if it is false, based on the entry.

> [1]**myr·i·ad** \'mir-ē-əd\ *n* [GK *myriad-, myrias*, fr. *myrioi* countless, ten thousand] (1555) **1** : ten thousand **2** : a great number ⟨a ~ of ideas⟩
> [2]**myriad** *adj* (1765) **1** : INNUMERABLE ⟨those ~ problems⟩; also : both numerous and diverse ⟨~ topics⟩ **2** : having innumerable aspects or elements ⟨the ~ activity of the new land—Meridel Le Sueur⟩

______ **1.** The noun *myriad* comes from a Greek word meaning "ten thousand."

______ **2.** The word *myriad* can be used as a noun or as an adjective.

______ **3.** The word *myriad* has four syllables.

______ **4.** The *i* in *myriad* sounds like the *i* in sigh.

**B.** Look over the following list of words from the glossary of an ecology textbook. Based on the definition of each word and the context of each sentence, label each statement **T** if it is true or **F** if it is false.

**Glossary**

- **Alluvial** A water-carved canyon
- **Arroyo** Related to material deposited by running water
- **Playa** A natural, low water basin
- **Topography** The physical structure of the landscape

______ **5.** The **topography** of a desert is made up of lush vegetation.

______ **6.** **Playas** can receive water that rushes down a hill.

______ **7.** After a violent storm, **alluvial** fans carved in the soil stretch across the desert.

Textbook Skills

**C.** Look over the following list of words from the glossary of an English handbook. Based on the definition of each word and the context of each sentence, label each statement **T** if it is true or **F** if it is false.

**Glossary of Usage and Terms**

- **Annotation** A brief note you write about a text while reading it by making marks such as underlining, circling, and highlighting. Notes can be words, phrases, questions, or statements.
- **Paraphrase** A restatement in your own words of the author's ideas and structure. A paraphrase closely follows the original source, pulls in many details, and may be as long as the original text.
- **Summary** A condensed version of a text in which you explain the author's meaning fairly and accurately in your own words. A summary focuses on the author's main idea and is shorter than the original text.

_____ **8.** **Annotations** are written directly on the pages of a textbook.

_____ **9.** A **summary** is longer than a **paraphrase.**

_____ **10.** **Paraphrasing** is an effective reading and writing skill when the order of the author's ideas is important for emphasis.

Name ______________________ Section ____________

MASTERY **Test 5** Date ____________ **Score** (number correct) ______ × 10 = ______%

Read the following passage, adapted from a college mathematics textbook. Use context clues and the graphs to write the definitions for each word in **bold** type. Choose definitions from the box. One answer will be used twice.

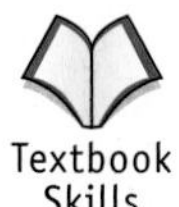


## Integers and the Real World

[1]A **set** is a collection of objects. [2]For our purposes, we will most often be considering sets of numbers. [3]The set of **natural numbers** are those numbers to the right of zero. [4]The **whole numbers** are the natural numbers with 0 included. [5]We can represent these two sets of numbers on a visual called a **number line.**

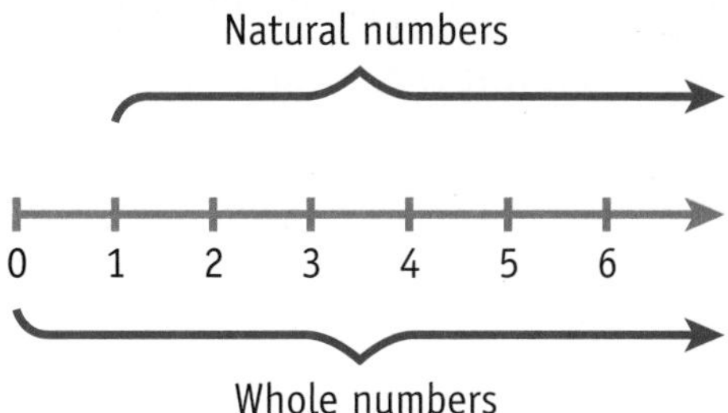


[6]We create a new set of numbers called *integers* by starting with the whole numbers, 0, 1, 2, 3, and so on. [7]For each natural number 1, 2, 3, and so on, we obtain a new number to the left of the zero on the number line: [8]For the number 1, there will be an opposite number –1 (negative 1); for the number 2, there will be an opposite number –2 (negative 2); and so on. [9]We call these new numbers to the left of zero **negative integers.** [10]The natural numbers are also called **positive integers.** [11]The set of **integers** equals {. . . –5, –4, –3, –2, –1, 0, 1, 2, 3, 4, 5 . . .}.

[12]Integers relate to many real-world problems and situations. [13]The following example will help you get ready to turn problem situations that use integers into mathematical language.

| group | {. . . −5, −4, −3, −2, −1} | {1, 2, 3, 4, 5 . . .} |
|---|---|---|
| {0, 1, 2, 3, 4, 5 . . .} | graph | natural numbers |
| {1, 2, 3, 4, 5 . . .} | natural numbers, zero, and the opposites of natural numbers | |

1. In sentence 1, **set** means ________________________.
2. In sentence 3, **natural numbers** means ________________________.
3. In sentence 4, **whole numbers** means ________________________.
4. In sentence 5, a **number line** is a ________________________ of sets of numbers.
5. In sentence 9, **negative integers** means ________________________.
6. In sentence 10, **positive integers** means ________________________.
7. In sentence 10, a synonym for **positive integers** is ________________.
8. In sentence 11, **integers** means ________________________________________.

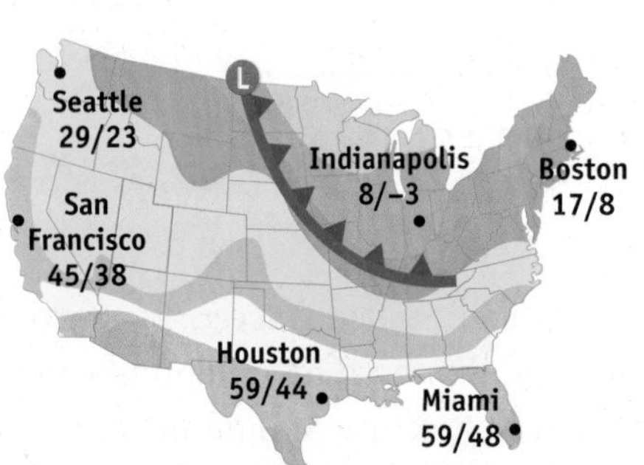


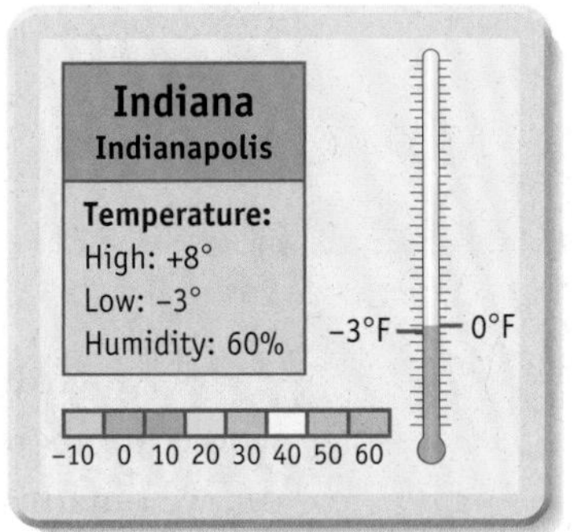


—Adapted from Bittinger & Beecher, *Introductory and Intermediate Algebra,* 2nd ed., p. 13. Copyright © 2003 Pearson Education, Inc. Reprinted by permission of Pearson Education, Inc. Publishing as Pearson Addison Wesley.

**9–10.** Use the temperature map to answer the following questions.

**9.** The low temperature in Indianapolis is 3 degrees below zero. Which integer co-responds to this situation? ________________

**10.** The high temperature in Indianapolis is 8 degrees above zero. Which integer co-responds to this situation? ________________

MASTERY **Test 6**

Name ______________________ Section ____________

Date ____________ **Score** (number correct) ______ × 10 = ______%

**A.** Read the following passage, adapted from a college psychology textbook. Use context clues to write the definition for each word in **bold** type. Choose definitions from the box. You will not use all of the definitions.

Textbook Skills

### Personality Types and Traits

[1]It has long been clear that people differ in personality. [2]The earliest known reason given for these individual differences is the humoral theory. [3]This **premise** was first put forth by the Greek physician Galen in the second century. [4]He based his beliefs on the then-current medical beliefs that had **originated** with the ancient Greeks. [5]The body was thought to contain four humors, or fluids: yellow bile, black bile, phlegm, and blood. [6]People were classified according to the disposition caused by the **predominance** or power of one of those humors in the body. [7]Choleric people, who had an excess of yellow bile, were bad-tempered and **irritable**. [8]Melancholic people, who had an excess of black bile, had gloomy and pessimistic natures. [9]Phlegmatic people, whose bodies had large amounts of phlegm, were sluggish, calm, and unexcitable. [10]Sanguine people had a **preponderance** of blood, which made them cheerful and passionate.

—Adapted from Carlson & Buskist, *Psychology,* 5th ed., p. 449.

| | | |
|---|---|---|
| begun | idea | weakness |
| stopped | great amount | good-natured |
| influence | offered | easily angered |

**1.** In sentence 3, **premise** means ________________.

**2.** In sentence 4, **originated** means ________________.

**3.** In sentence 6, **predominance** means ________________.

**4.** In sentence 7, **irritable** means ________________.

**5.** In sentence 10, **preponderance** means ________________.

**B.** Read the following passage, adapted from a college health textbook. Use context clues and word parts to write the definition for each word in **bold** type. Choose definitions from the box. Use each definition once.

Textbook Skills

### The Pathogens: Routes of Transmission

[1]**Pathogens** enter the body in several ways. [2]They may be **transmitted** by direct contact between infected persons, such as by kissing, or by indirect contact such as by touching the object an infected person has had contact with. [3]The hands are probably the greatest source of infectious disease transmission. [4]You may also **autoinoculate** yourself, or transmit a pathogen from one part of your body to another. [5]For example, you may touch a sore on your lip that is teeming with viral herpes and then transmit the virus to your eye when you scratch your itchy eyelid.

[6]Pathogens are also transmitted by airborne contact; you can breathe in air that carries a particular pathogen. [7]Pathogens are also passed through foodborne infection if you eat something **contaminated** by **microorganisms**.

—Donatelle, *Health*, 5th ed., p. 348.

| Prefix | Meaning | Root | Meaning | Suffix | Meaning |
|---|---|---|---|---|---|
| *trans-* | across | *path* | disease | *-gen* | cause |
| *auto-* | self | *mit* | send | *-ate* | make, do, cause |
| *in-* | into | *ocul* | eye, bud | *-ism* | being |
| *con-* | with | *tamin* | spoil | | |
| *micro-* | small | *organ* | work | | |

| | | |
|---|---|---|
| to infect another part of one's body | germs | life forms too small to be seen by the naked eye |
| spread | poisoned | |

**6.** In sentence 1, **pathogens** means ______________.

**7.** In sentence 2, **transmitted** means ______________.

**8.** In sentence 4, **autoinoculate** means ______________.

**9.** In sentence 7, **contaminated** means ______________.

**10.** In sentence 7, **microorganisms** means ______________.

CHAPTER

3

# Stated Main Ideas

## CHAPTER PREVIEW

## Before Reading About Stated Main Ideas

Effective use of the reading process relies on developing questions about the material that will guide you as you read. Using the chapter preview above, create at least five questions that you can answer as you study the chapter. Write your questions in the following spaces:

________________________________________ (page_____)

________________________________________ (page_____)

________________________________________ (page_____)

________________________________________ (page_____)

________________________________________ (page_____)

Compare the questions you created based on the chapter preview with the following questions. Then write the ones that seem the most helpful in your notebook, leaving enough space between each question to record the answers as you read and study the chapter.

What are the traits of a main idea? (p. 106) What is the difference between a topic and a topic sentence? (p. 112) How is the flow of ideas related to the placement of topic sentences? (p. 119) What is the central idea? (p. 128) What is the difference between the central idea and a topic sentence? (p. 128)

## The Traits of a Main Idea

A **main idea** is the author's controlling point about the topic. It usually includes the topic and the author's attitude or opinion about the topic, or the author's approach to the topic.

To identify the main idea, ask yourself two questions:

- Who or what is the paragraph about? The answer is the *topic*. The topic can be stated in just a few words.
- What is the author's controlling point about the topic? The answer is the *main idea*. The main idea is stated in one sentence.

Consider these questions as you read the following paragraph from a health textbook.

Textbook Skills

### The Cool-Down Period

The cool-down period is an important part of an exercise workout for several reasons. The cool-down involves reducing the intensity of exercise to allow the body to recover from the workout. During vigorous exercise such as jogging, a lot of blood is pumped to the legs, and there may not be enough to supply the heart and brain; failure to cool down properly may result in dizziness, fainting, and, in rare instances, a heart attack. By gradually reducing the level of physical activity, blood flow is directed back to the heart and brain.

—Adapted from Pruitt & Stein, *Health Styles*, 2nd ed., p. 169.

- Who or what is the paragraph about? The topic of the paragraph is "the cool-down period of an exercise workout."

- What is the author's controlling point about the topic? The controlling point is that it "is an important part." Putting topic and controlling point together, the main idea is "The cool-down period is an important part of an exercise workout for several reasons."

To better understand the traits of a main idea, compare a passage to a well-planned house of ideas. The *topic* or general subject matter is the roof. The roof covers all the rooms of the house. The *main idea* is the frame of the house, and the supporting details are the different rooms. The following diagram shows the relationship of the ideas:

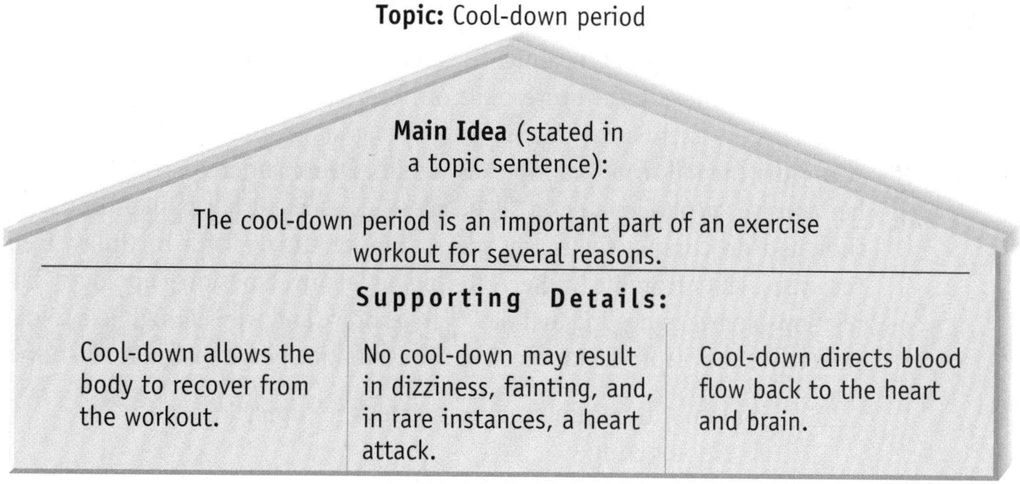

**Topic:** Cool-down period

**Main Idea** (stated in a topic sentence):

The cool-down period is an important part of an exercise workout for several reasons.

**Supporting Details:**

| Cool-down allows the body to recover from the workout. | No cool-down may result in dizziness, fainting, and, in rare instances, a heart attack. | Cool-down directs blood flow back to the heart and brain. |
|---|---|---|

Each of the supporting details explains why the cool-down period is an important part of an exercise workout.

## Identifying the Topic of a Paragraph

When you ask the question "Who or what is the paragraph about?" you must be sure that your answer is neither too general nor too specific. A general subject needs specific ideas to support or explain it. However, no single paragraph can discuss all the specific ideas linked to a general idea. So an author narrows the general subject to a topic that needs a specific set of ideas to support it. For example, the very general subject "music" can be narrowed to "hip-hop music." And the specific details related to hip-hop music might include the different rappers, ranging from Eminem to Ludacris to Akon. In fact, a piece of writing dealing with the general topic "music" will include a very different set of specific ideas than the narrower topic of "hip-hop music." The more general category of music might include classical music and country music, for example. Or it might include symphonies, marching bands, and barber shop quartets.

Often an author shows the relationship between the topic and the specific details by repeating the topic throughout the paragraph as new pieces of information about the topic are introduced. To identify the topic, an effective reader often skims the material for this recurring idea. Skimming for the topic allows you to grasp the relationship among a general subject, the topic, and specific details.

**EXAMPLE** Skim the following paragraph. Circle the topic as it recurs throughout the paragraph. Answer the question that follows.

### A Sincere Apology

[1]A sincere apology is a powerful human experience. [2]A sincere apology is a peace offering that honors the importance of the wronged one's feelings. [3]It defuses anger and fosters healing. [4]A genuine apology offers closure to a painful past and openness to a future built on forgiveness and empathy. [5]A genuine "I'm sorry" accepts the blame for wrongdoing and the painful results. [6]Consider the following example: as a child, Debra suffered greatly because of her abusive, alcoholic father. [7]At the age of 17, she left her father's house, and they had no contact for many years. [8]On her thirty-fifth birthday, Debra received a letter from her father, offering her a long, emotional apology. [9]Their relationship began healing that day. [10]To be brave and wise enough to apologize sincerely is to accept a lesson from life and a unique peace based on self-respect.

_____ Which of the following best states the topic?

a. Apologizing
b. A sincere apology
c. The importance of the wronged one's feelings

**EXPLANATION** "Apologizing" is too general, for it could cover insincere apologies, how to apologize, or what to do if someone will not accept an apology. "The importance of the wronged one's feelings" is too narrow. This idea is a supporting detail, just one of the reasons an apology is so powerful. The topic of this paragraph is (b), *a sincere apology*. You should have circled the following phrases: "sincere apology" (sentence 1), "sincere apology" (sentence 2), "genuine apology" (sentence 4), "genuine 'I'm sorry'" (sentence 5), and "apologize sincerely" (sentence 10). Note that the author used the synonym "genuine" to vary the wording of the topic. Note that the title of the paragraph also stated the topic. Authors often use titles to relay the topic of the material.

## PRACTICE 1

Skim each of the following paragraphs and circle the topic as it recurs throughout the paragraph. Then, identify the idea that correctly states the topic. (Hint: one idea is too general to be the topic; another idea is too specific.)

_____ **1.** [1]Many myths exist about the causes of acne. [2]Chocolate and greasy foods are often blamed, but foods seem to have little effect on the development and course of acne in most people. [3]Another common myth is that dirty skin causes acne; however, blackheads and other acne lesions are not caused by dirt. [5]Finally, stress does not cause acne.

—Adapted from National Institute of Arthritis and Musculoskeletal and Skin Diseases, "Questions and Answers about Acne."

a. Dirty skin
b. Causes of acne
c. Myths about what causes acne

_____ **2.** [1]Playing rigorous sports in the heat can lead to several types of heat injuries. [2]The first type of heat-related illness is dehydration, which is a lack of body fluids. [3]The second type is heat exhaustion. [4]Heat exhaustion has numerous effects, including nausea, dizziness, weakness, headache, pale and moist skin, heavy perspiration, normal or low body temperature, weak pulse, dilated pupils, disorientation, and fainting spells. [5]A third type of heat injury is heat stroke. [6]Heat stroke can lead to headaches, dizziness, confusion, and hot dry skin, possibly leading to vascular collapse, coma, and death. [7]Each of these heat injuries can be prevented.

—Adapted from National Institute of Arthritis and Musculoskeletal and Skin Diseases, "Childhood Sports Injuries and Their Prevention."

a. Types of heat injuries
b. Injuries
c. Heatstroke

_____ **3.** [1]Older people benefit from volunteer work in several ways. [2]First, being a volunteer improves the overall quality of an older person's life; it gives meaning and purpose to their lives. [3]Second, older persons who volunteer have fewer medical problems than other people their age who are not as active. [4]Older persons stay physically active when they volunteer; thus they do not suffer as often from heart disease and diabetes. [5]Finally, volunteer work helps keep the brain active, and an active brain helps protect the memory as people age.

—Adapted from Administration on Aging, "Older Volunteers Leading the Way."

a. Volunteer work
b. Benefits of volunteer work for older people
c. Fewer medical problems

Textbook Skills

______ **4.** [1]The barriers to women's advancement to top positions in the workforce are often very subtle, giving rise to the phrase ***glass ceiling***. [2]In explaining "why women aren't getting to the top," one observer argues that "at senior management levels, competence is assumed. [3]What you are looking for is someone who fits, someone who gets along, someone you trust. [4]Now that's subtle stuff. [5]How does a group of men feel that a woman is going to fit in? [6]I think it's very hard." [7]Or as a woman bank executive says, "The men just don't feel comfortable." [8]There are many explanations for the glass ceiling, all controversial. [9]For example, some say that women choose staff assignments rather than fast-track, operating-head assignments. [10]Others claim that women are cautious and unaggressive in corporate politics. [11]Finally, some believe that women have lower expectations about peak earnings and positions, and these expectations become self-fulfilling.

—Dye, *Politics in America*, 5th ed., p. 589.

a. Working women
b. Women's low expectations about earnings
c. The glass ceiling for women

**VISUAL VOCABULARY**

A "glass ceiling" is

______ an invisible barrier preventing women from rising to the highest positions in the workforce.

______ the sexual harassment a woman faces on the job.

______ a popular architectural design for large office complexes.

_____ **5.** [1]Intellectual blocks involve obstacles to knowledge. [2]You may find yourself unable to solve a problem for two reasons. [3]First, you may be blocked because you lack information. [4]Second, you may be blocked because you have incorrect or incomplete information. [5]When you buy a car, for example, you can be blocked by being unaware of various cars' performance ratings, repair records, or safety features. [6]Or you may be blocked because you have only one-sided information—the information given by the salesperson. [7]Or maybe you simply don't know enough about cars to buy one with confidence.

—Adapted from Di Yanni and Hoy, *The Scribner Handbook for Writers*, 3rd ed., p. 65.

a. Intellectual blocks
b. Incorrect information
c. Problem solving

## Identifying a Topic Sentence

Most paragraphs have three parts:

- A topic (the general idea or subject)
- A main idea (the controlling point the author is making about the topic, often stated in a topic sentence)
- Supporting details (the specific ideas to support the main idea)

Think again of the house of ideas that a writer builds. Remember, the main idea *frames* the specific ideas. Think of all the different rooms in a house: the kitchen, bedroom, bathroom, living room. Each room is a different part of the house. The frame determines the space for each room and the flow of traffic between rooms. Similarly, the main idea determines how much detail is given and how one detail flows into the next. The main idea of a paragraph is usually stated in a single sentence called the **topic sentence**. The topic sentence—the stated main idea—is unique in two ways.

First, the topic sentence contains two types of information: the topic and the author's controlling point, which restricts or qualifies the topic. At times, the controlling point may be expressed as the author's opinion using biased words. (For more information on biased words see Chapter 9, "Fact and Opinion.") For example, in the topic sentence "A sincere apology is a powerful human experience," the biased words "sincere" and "powerful" limit and control the topic "apology."

Other times, the controlling point may express the author's thought pattern, the way in which the thoughts are going to be organized. (For more information on words that indicate thought patterns, see Chapters 6 and 7.) For example, the topic sentence, "Playing rigorous sports in the heat can lead to several types of heat injuries," uses the phrase "several types" to reveal that the author will control the topic by classifying or dividing the topic into types.

Often, an author will use both biased words and a thought pattern to qualify or limit the topic. For example, the topic sentence, "Older people benefit from volunteer work in several ways," combines the biased word "benefit" and the phrase "several ways" to indicate a list of positive examples and explanations will follow.

These qualifiers—words that convey the author's bias or thought pattern—helped you correctly identify the topic in the previous section. An important difference between the topic and the topic sentence is that the topic sentence states the author's main idea in a complete sentence.

A **topic sentence** is a single sentence that states the topic and words that qualify the topic by revealing the author's opinion about the topic or the author's approach to the topic.

The second unique trait of the topic sentence is its scope: the topic sentence is a general statement that all the other sentences in the paragraph explain or support. A topic sentence states an author's opinion or thought process, which must be explained further with specific supporting details. For example, in the paragraph about the cool-down period after a workout, the topic and the author's controlling point about the topic are stated in the first sentence. Each of the other sentences in the paragraph gives a different reason to explain why the cool-down period is an important part of an exercise workout:

Topic ↓ Author's attitude ↓ Author's thought pattern ↓

The *cool-down period* is an *important part* of an exercise workout for *several reasons.*

| First reason | Second reason | Third reason |
|---|---|---|
| Cool-down allows the body to recover from the workout. | No cool-down may result in dizziness, fainting, and, in rare instances, a heart attack. | Cool-down directs blood flow back to the heart and brain. |

> **Supporting details** are specific ideas that *develop, explain,* or *support* the main idea.

The supporting details of a paragraph are framed by the main idea, and all work together to explain or support the author's view of the topic. As an effective reader, you will see that every paragraph has a topic, a main idea, and supporting details. It is much easier to tell the difference between these three parts of a passage once you understand how each part works. A topic, as the general subject of the paragraph, can be expressed in a word or phrase. The main idea contains both the topic and the author's controlling point about the topic and can be stated in one sentence called the topic sentence. The supporting details are all the sentences that state reasons and explanations for the main idea. To locate the topic sentence of a paragraph ask yourself two questions:

- Which sentence contains qualifiers that reveal the author's controlling point—that is, the author's attitude about the topic or approach to the topic?
- Do all the specific details in the passage support this statement?

**EXAMPLES**

**A.** The following group of ideas contains a topic, a main idea, and two supporting details. Circle the topic and underline the author's controlling point. Then, answer the questions.

a. Many headaches occur for two reasons.
b. Poor posture that tenses the muscles in the neck and back can trigger a headache.
c. Headaches are sometimes the result of stress, anxiety, and depression that cause the muscles in the neck, face, and scalp to become tense.

_____ **1.** Which of the following best states the topic?
a. headaches    b. poor posture    c. anxiety

_____ **2.** Which sentence is the stated main idea?

**B.** Read the following paragraph. Circle the topic and underline the author's controlling point. Then answer the two questions that follow it.

### Shopaholics

[1]Shopaholics, people who suffer from an uncontrollable urge to shop, struggle with a serious problem. [2]Experts believe that one in every five people has a problem keeping his or her spending habits under control. [3]Shopaholics use shopping as a way to fill an emotional void in their lives. [4]They buy compulsively; they hide their purchases and their bills. [5]They fill their closets, their garages, and even their living spaces with unopened packages bought on a whim. [6]They continue to spend despite the destructive effects of their habit. [7]Shopaholics shop until they bankrupt their bank accounts and destroy their relationships with loved ones.

**1.** What is the topic of the paragraph? ______________________________

**2.** Which sentence is the topic sentence stating the main idea? __________

**C.** Read the following paragraph. Circle the topic and underline the author's controlling point. Then answer the two questions that follow it.

### Who Are the Chicanos?

[1]Mexican Americans have redefined "Chicano" from a racial slur to a word synonymous with ethnic pride. [2]"Chicano" is a shortened, slang form of the Spanish word *Mexicano*. According to some historians, the word originally had two purposes. [4]In the 19th century, wealthy Mexicans and Anglos used the term "Chicano" to refer to low-income, unskilled Mexicans. [5]However, the term was also used as a deliberate ethnic slur against recent Mexican immigrants into the United States. [6]Eventually, "Chicano" became a label applied to most Mexcian Americans, even after generations of residency or citizenship. [7]Fortunately, Mexican Americans have redefined the term from an insulting pejorative expression into a statement of respect to honor their unique culture. [8]During the Civil Rights era of the 1960s, the Brown Power movement celebrated *la raza*, the people. [9]And inspired leaders such as Cesar Chavez stood up for dignity, equality, and justice. [10]In a show of self-respect and independence, Mexican Americans began referring to themsleves with pride as "Chicano."

—Adapted from Novas, Himilce. *Everything You Need to Know about Latino History*. Plum: NY, 2003, p. 52.

**3.** What is the topic of the paragraph? ______________________________.

**4.** Which sentence states the author's main idea? __________________

**VISUAL VOCABULARY**

Based on the picture, write the definition of solidarity.

______________

▲ People come together during difficult times in a show of solidarity.

**EXPLANATIONS**

**A.** The topic is (a) "headaches." Note that the topic is stated with just a few words—a phrase, not a complete sentence. The first item (a) is the main idea. Note that the main idea is stated as a topic sentence. The main idea contains both the topic, "headaches," and the author's controlling point about the topic, "two reasons." The main idea is always stated as a complete sentence. The second and third items (b and c) give details that support the main idea.

**B.** The word "shopaholics" recurs in sentences 1, 3, and 7; "shopaholics" is the topic of the paragraph. The main idea stated as a topic sentence is sentence 1. This sentence contains the topic and the author's opinion about the topic expressed with the biased words "suffer," "uncontrollable," "struggle," and "serious problem." All the other sentences in the paragraph offer explanations for these qualifiers.

**C.** As you read, it becomes clear that every idea in the paragraph has to do with the word "Chicano." Remember, to identify the topic of a passage, ask "Who or what is this passage about?" You should be able to answer this question in just a few words. Sentence 1 states the main idea as a topic sentence: "Mexican Americans have redefined 'Chicano' from a racial slur to a word synonymous with ethnic pride." The topic sentence also states the author's controlling point about the topic. In this case, the author's point is about the word "redefined . . . from a racial slur to a word synonymous with ethnic pride."



## PRACTICE 2

**A.** Each of the following groups of ideas contains a topic, a main idea, and two supporting details. In each group, first identify the topic. Then identify the stated main idea. (Hint: circle the topic and underline the author's controlling point in each group.)

### Group 1

a. A successful sales approach is sincere, optimistic, and confident.
b. Use a sincere smile and an optimistic attitude to attract a potential customer.
c. Look your customer directly in the eye and speak confidently and clearly at an easy-to-listen-to pace.

______ **1.** Which of the following best states the topic?
a. a successful sales approach
b. sales
c. optimism

______ **2.** Which sentence is the stated main idea?

### Group 2

a. Head Start recruits children from age 3 to school entry age.
b. Head Start is a federal program designed to break the cycle of poverty.
c. The program offers children of low-income families a range of services to meet their emotional, social, health, nutritional, and psychological needs.

______ **3.** Which of the following best states the topic?
a. preschool children
b. Head Start
c. cycle of poverty

______ **4.** Which sentence is the stated main idea?

### Group 3

a. Malcolm X was a controversial African American activist during the civil rights era.
b. Malcolm X, born Malcolm Little, changed his name to protest bigotry.
c. Malcolm X, the son of a Baptist minister, became a member of the Black Muslim organization.

______ **5.** Which of the following best states the topic?
a. Malcolm X
b. bigotry
c. Civil Rights era

______ **6.** Which sentence is the stated main idea?

### Group 4

a. The collapse sinkhole is a common type of sinkhole in Florida.
b. It forms with little warning and leaves a deep, steep-sided hole.
c. Collapse sinkholes occur because of the weakening of the rock of the aquifer by erosion.

_____ **7.** Which of the following best states the topic?
a. a deep, steep hole
b. sinkholes
c. a collapse sinkhole

_____ **8.** Which sentence is the stated main idea?

**VISUAL VOCABULARY**

_____ The aquifer is

a. a naturally occurring deep well of water.
b. a body of porous sediment or rock, consisting of sand, shell, or limestone, that allows water to move underground.

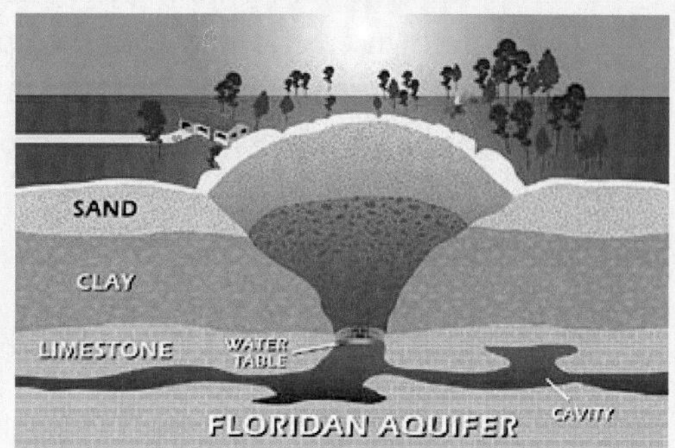


▲ Sinkholes form in a natural process of dissolving and eroding limestone that makes up the aquifer system.

Source: "Low Ground Waters Can Lead to Sinkholes." *Streamlines*, Fall 2000. Used by permission of the St. Johns River Water Management District. State of Florida.

**B.** Read the following paragraphs from college textbooks. Then answer the questions that follow them.

Textbook Skills

### Paragraph from a Communications Textbook

[1]Lifelong learning has now become a necessity. [2]The more you know, the better prepared you will be to understand new ideas and adjust to the changes around you. [3]"I must be getting old" is no longer an excuse—for anyone. [4]When new computer systems are introduced, you need to understand how they operate. [5]When your doctor suggests a battery of new tests, insist that he or she explain their purposes and potential risks. [6]When you listen to the media, make sure you identify and understand the facts.

—Brownell, *Listening: Attitudes, Principles, and Skills,* 2nd ed., p. 10.

______ **9.** The topic of the paragraph is

a. getting older.
b. computer systems.
c. the media.
d. lifelong learning.

______ **10.** Which sentence states the author's main idea about the topic?

Textbook Skills

**Paragraph from a Psychology Textbook**

[1]Creativity is a person's ability to generate ideas or products that are both *novel* and *appropriate* to the circumstances in which they were created. [2]Consider the creation of the wheel. [3]The device was novel because no one before its unknown creator had seen the application of rolling objects. [4]It was appropriate because the use to which the novel object could be put was very clear. [5]Without appropriateness, new ideas or objects are often thought of as strange or useless.

—Adapted from Gerrig & Zimbardo, *Psychology and Life,* 16th ed., p. 311.

______ **11.** The topic of the paragraph is

a. the wheel.
b. creativity.
c. appropriateness.
d. novel objects.

______ **12.** Which sentence states the author's main idea about that topic?

Textbook Skills

**Paragraph from an Accounting Textbook**

[1]Money management involves decisions regarding how much money to retain in liquid form and how to allot the funds among short-term investments. [2]If you do not have access to money to cover cash needs, you may have insufficient liquidity. [3]That is, you have the assets to cover your expenses, but the money is not easily available. [4]Funding an effective liquidity level involves deciding how to invest your money so that you can earn a return but also have easy access to cash if needed. [5]At times, you may be unable to avoid cash shortages because of unexpected expenses.

—Adapted from Madura, *Personal Finance,* 2nd ed., p. 5.

______ **13.** The topic of the passage is

a. money management.
b. liquidity.
c. investments.
d. assets.

______ **14.** Which sentence states the author's main idea about the topic?

Textbook Skills

**Paragraph from a Social Science Textbook**

[1]Today Hispanics are the nation's largest minority. [2]The term *Hispanic* generally refers to people who are of Spanish-speaking origin. [3]The group

includes Mexican Americans, Cuban Americans, and Puerto Ricans. [4]Today, around 36 million Hispanics live in the United States. [5]The largest subgroup is Mexican Americans. [6]Some of these are offspring of citizens who lived in the Mexican territory that became part of the United States in 1848. [7]But most have come to the United States in recent years. [8]The largest Mexican American groups live in Texas, Arizona, New Mexico, and California. [9]The second-largest subgroup is Puerto Ricans. [10]Many Puerto Ricans move back and forth from the island to the mainland, largely in New York City. [11]The third-largest subgroup is Cubans who have fled from Castro's Cuba. [12]They live mainly in Miami, Florida.

—Adapted from Dye, *Politics in America,* 5th ed., p. 40.

______ **15.** The topic of the passage is
a. Mexican Americans.
b. Puerto Ricans.
c. Hispanics living in America.
d. immigrants.

______ **16.** Which sentence states the author's main idea about the topic?

## The Flow of Ideas and Placement of Topic Sentences

So far, many of the paragraphs you have worked with in this textbook have placed the topic sentence/main idea as the first sentence in the paragraph. The three parts of a paragraph have flowed from general to specific ideas: the topic, the main idea stated in a topic sentence, and the supporting details. However, not all paragraphs put the main idea first. In fact, a topic sentence can be placed at the **beginning** of a paragraph, **within** a paragraph, or at the **end** of a paragraph. The placement of the topic sentence controls the flow of ideas. In a sense, when a writer builds a house of ideas, the floor plan—the flow of ideas—changes based on the location of the topic sentence. One of the first things an effective reader looks for is the location of the topic sentence.

### Topic Sentence at the Beginning of a Paragraph

Remember that the topic sentence is the one sentence that is general enough to include all the ideas in the paragraph. So a topic sentence that begins a paragraph signals a move from general ideas to specific ideas. This flow from general to specific, in which an author begins with a general statement and moves to specific reasons and supports, is also known as deductive reasoning. Articles in encyclopedias and news stories in magazines and newspapers typically use the deductive flow of ideas. The chart on page 120 shows this flow from general to specific ideas.

Main idea: topic sentence
Supporting detail
Supporting detail
Supporting detail
Supporting detail

**EXAMPLE** Read the following paragraph, and identify its topic sentence. Remember to ask, "Does this sentence cover all the ideas in the paragraph?"

**The Painful, Pesky Fire Ant**

[1]Fire ants are painful and destructive pests. [2]The fire ant earned its name because of its venom. [3]The insect uses a wasplike stinger to inject the venom, which causes a painful burning sensation and leaves tiny, itching pustules. [4]The ants will swarm over anyone or anything that disturbs their nests. [5]In addition to causing pain, fire ants damage many crops by eating the plants and by protecting other insects that damage crops. [6]Fire ants are attracted to soybeans, eggplant, corn, okra, strawberries, and potatoes.

Topic sentence: _____

**VISUAL VOCABULARY**

*Swarm* can be used as a verb and as a noun. Write a definition for each use. Use your dictionary if you want to.

Verb: ____________________

Noun: ____________________

____________________

**EXPLANATION** The topic sentence of this paragraph is sentence 1: "Fire ants are painful and destructive pests." All the other sentences explain the ways in which fire ants are painful and destructive. Notice how the passage first presents the general idea of fire ants as "painful and destructive." Next the details focus on the pain they cause, and then on the harm they do.

## Topic Sentence Within a Paragraph

Topic sentences within a paragraph can be near the beginning or in the middle of the paragraph.

### Near the Beginning

A paragraph does not always start with the topic sentence. Instead, it may begin with a sentence or two that give a general overview of the topic. These introductory sentences are used to get the reader interested in the topic. They also lead the reader to the topic sentence. Sometimes introductory sentences tell how the ideas in one paragraph tie in to the ideas of earlier paragraphs. At other times, the introductory sentences give background information about the topic.

The flow of ideas remains deductive as it moves from general ideas (the introduction) and main idea (topic sentence) to specific ideas (supporting details). Human interest stories and editorials in magazines and newspapers, as well as academic papers, often rely on this flow of ideas. The following diagram shows this flow from general to specific ideas:

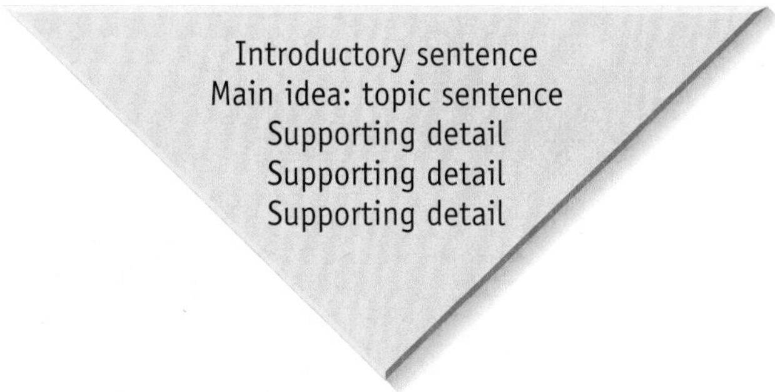

Introductory sentence
Main idea: topic sentence
Supporting detail
Supporting detail
Supporting detail

**EXAMPLE** Read the following paragraph, and identify its topic sentence. Remember to ask, "Does this sentence cover all the ideas in the passage?"

**Ice Cream Myths**

[1]Ice cream reigns as a rich, delicious treat enjoyed by the majority of Americans. [2]Many myths exist about the origin of this well-loved concoction of sugar and ice. [3]The three most common myths involve an explorer and

two members of royalty. [4]One popular legend has the famous explorer Marco Polo bringing water ices from China to Italy. [5]Another myth claims that Catherine de Medici of Florence took her sorbetto recipes with her when she married Henry II and became queen of France in 1533. [6]The third popular myth credits Charles I of England with a formula for "frozen milk" he bought from a French chef in the 17th century.

Topic sentence: ______

**EXPLANATION** Sentence 3 is the topic sentence of this paragraph. Sentence 1 offers a simple but true background statement about the topic. The purpose of this sentence is to get the reader's attention. Sentence 2 introduces the topic "myths about the origin of ice cream." Sentences 4–6 are the supporting details that discuss the three myths.

### In the Middle

At times, an author begins a paragraph with a few attention-grabbing details. These details are placed first to stir the reader's interest in the topic. The flow of ideas no longer follows the deductive pattern of thinking because the material now moves from specific ideas (supporting details) to a general idea (the topic sentence) to specific ideas (additional supporting details). Creative essays and special interest stories that strive to excite reader interest often employ this approach. Often television news stories begin with shocking details to hook the viewer and prevent channel surfing. The following diagram shows this flow of ideas:

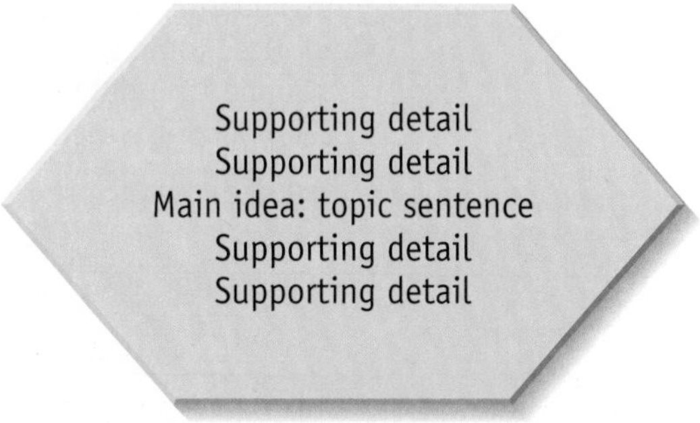

Supporting detail
Supporting detail
Main idea: topic sentence
Supporting detail
Supporting detail

**EXAMPLE** Read the following paragraph, and identify its topic sentence. Remember to ask, "Does this sentence cover all the ideas in the passage?"

**Calculating Life**

[1]What if we could predict how long we might live? [2]What if we could know for sure that certain behaviors could lengthen our lives? [3]Shorten our lives? [4]Would we choose a healthful lifestyle—giving up smoking, overeating,

stressing out? [5]Of course, none of us can with certainty predict the length of a life. [6]Life is too unpredictable and full of events outside our control, such as those accidents that are bound to occur. [7]However, the more scientists learn about our bodies, the more we understand the strong connection between our lifestyles and our longevity. [8]A special online longevity calculator offers us estimation about how long we will live. [9]Tom Peris, M.D., developed the calculator based on a formula based on lifestyle factors. [10]We input information about our good and bad habits. [11]We input how often we exercise, drink alcohol, smoke, eat healthfully, and handle stress. [12]Naturally, the calculator can't take into account genetic factors. [13]Still, it offers powerful motivation for improvement. [14]The calculator shows that we can take control of factors that affect how long we will live. [15]And we can use the calculator to track our improvement. [16]Try it out! [17]If you are under 50, use the longevity calculator at LivingTo100.com. [18]If you are over 50, use the calculator at eons.com.

—McCafferty, Dennis. "How Long Will You Live?"
*USAWEEKEND.* 2 March 2007. pp. 6–8.

Topic sentence: ______

**EXPLANATION** Sentences 1 through 4 are a series of questions that act to introduce the general topic of the desire to live for a long time. These questions are meant to engage the reader's interest. Sentences 5 through 7 narrow the topic to focus on the connection between lifestyles and longevity. The author's purpose is to direct the reader to the online longevity calculator so that the reader can learn more about his or her lifestyle and longevity connection. Sentence 8 states this main idea. Sentences 9 through 18 explain how the reader can use the calculator.

## Topic Sentence at the End of a Paragraph

Sometimes an author waits until the end of the paragraph to state the topic sentence and main idea. This approach can be very effective, for it allows the details to build up to the main idea. The pattern is sometimes called climactic order.

The flow of ideas is known as inductive as the author's thoughts move from specific (supporting details) to general (the topic sentence). Inductive reasoning is often used in math and science to generate hypotheses and theories, and to discover relationships between details. In addition, inductive reasoning is often used in argument (for more about argument, see Chapters 12 and 13). Politicians and advertisers use this approach to convince people to agree with their ideas or to buy their products. If a politician begins with a general statement such as "Taxes must be raised," the audience may strongly disagree. Then they may not listen to the specific reasons about why taxes must be raised. However, if the politician begins with the details and leads up to the main idea, people are more likely to listen. For example, people are more likely to agree that roads need to be repaired. Once they hear the specific details, they may then agree to raise taxes. Inductive reasoning is the process of arriving at a general understanding based on specific details. The following diagram shows the ideas moving from specific to general.

Supporting detail
Supporting detail
Supporting detail
Supporting detail
Main idea: topic sentence

**EXAMPLE** Read the following paragraph, and identify its topic sentence. Remember to ask, "Does this sentence cover all the ideas in the passage?"

**A Personal Journey**

[1]Every summer, my mother and I journeyed from our home in Florida to the farm in Mississippi on which she was raised. [2]However, the summer of my twenty-second year, we began our trip from Alabama instead of Florida. [3]The entire Mississippi clan had traveled over to witness my graduation from Judson College. [4]As a first-generation college graduate, I just knew I knew more than any of them, especially my mother. [5]Relief, joy, and a sense of freedom flooded me as Mother suggested I drive her car and she ride with Aunt Kaye. [6]Every so often, I purposefully lagged behind the caravan, lit up a cigarette, and smoked as I pleased—no matter that smoking was absolutely forbidden in Mother's car. [7]The cross-breeze from the rolled-down windows and my flicking the butts out the front window guaranteed she would never know. [8]Late that evening, as we unloaded the back seat, we both came upon a startling discovery at the same time: a deep burn hole the size of a knuckle. [9]One of the butts had blown back in and lodged in the back seat. [10]Silence loomed. [11]Then Mother said, "People are more important than things; I will not let this ruin this special time for us." [12]In a blink, I traveled from pride to shame to redemption. [13]Mother's one moment of mercy taught me more than four years of college.

Topic sentence: ______

**EXPLANATION** Sentences 1 through 11 tell the story of the author's journey to her mother's birthplace. The details of the story show the author's immaturity. In sentence 12, the author makes a statement that connects the physical trip and her journey of personal growth. Sentence 13 is the topic sentence. It clearly states the point the author is making, and it sums up the lesson of the story. Starting the passage with the details of the author's journey makes the idea much more interesting. Ending the passage with the main idea is very powerful.

## Topic Sentence at the Beginning and the End of a Paragraph

A paragraph may start and end by stating one main idea in two different sentences. Even though these two sentences state the same idea, they usually word the idea in different ways. A topic sentence presents the main idea at the beginning of the paragraph. Then, at the end of the paragraph, the main idea is stated again, this time using different words. This flow of ideas is based on the age-old advice given to writers to "tell the reader what you are going to say; say it; then tell the reader what you said." Many essays written by college students rely on this presentation of ideas. The following diagram shows this flow of ideas:

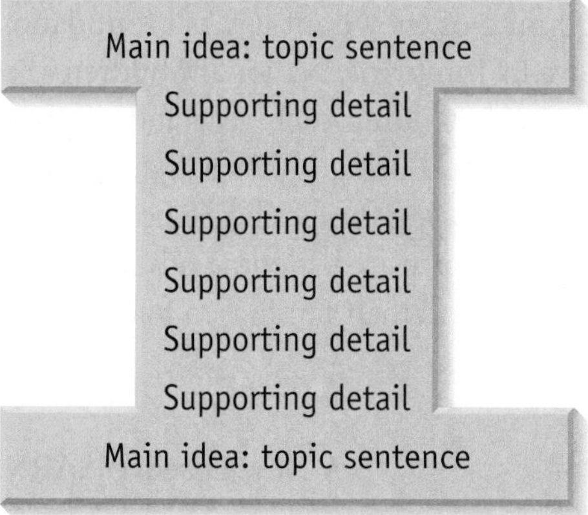


**EXAMPLE** Read the following paragraph, and identify its topic sentences. Remember to ask, "Do these sentences cover all the ideas in the passage?"

> [1]Using art as a form of therapy calls for a level of concentration that allows a person to relieve the pain of mental or emotional stress. [2]Art therapy is not limited to painting or drawing but can include dance, photography, music, writing, or any other art form. [3]The main goal of art therapy is healing through self-expression. [4]It allows a person to use visual means to explore feelings and emotions, to make the unseen seen, to discover how the mind works. [5]Art therapy does not require artistic ability, nor does it demand high artistic products. [6]Indeed, art therapy focuses on the process, not the product. [7]Art is therapy; art heals.
>
> Topic sentences: ______

**EXPLANATION** Sentences 1 and 7 both state the main idea of the passage: Art therapy is healing. Notice how the wording changes at the end of the passage. Repeating the main idea makes the point much stronger and more likely to be remembered.

## PRACTICE 3

Read the following paragraphs, and identify the topic sentence(s). Remember to ask, "Do these sentences cover all the ideas in the paragraph?"

### Believe in Tomorrow

[1]If you had one wish, what would it be? [2]Would you wish for fame or for fortune? [3]The organization known as Believe in Tomorrow strives to grant the wishes and improve the quality of the lives of thousands of critically ill children and their families. [4]Just what are the wishes of these children? [5]One little girl in 1982 had just one wish as she faced a life-threatening illness: a pair of green roller skates. [6]Brian Morrison met that wish, and his simple act of compassion was the beginning of the Grant-a-Wish foundation. [7]That foundation is now named Believe in Tomorrow National Children's Foundation. [8]The foundation serves over 38,000 children each year and offers services that help ease pain, reduce loneliness, and bring joy over the course of their treatment. [9]Services include hospital housing for families, emotional support and networking, pain management, and once-in-a-lifetime adventures. [10]Each program is designed to inspire children and their families to focus on the promise of the future.

**1.** Topic sentence: ______

### A New Disease: SARS

[1]Severe acute respiratory syndrome (SARS) is a new and serious disease. [2]The disease, first noticed in 2003, developed in China and then spread to North America and Europe. [3]It usually begins with a fever that is higher than 100.4 degrees Fahrenheit. [4]Other signs may include a headache, an overall feeling of discomfort, and body aches. [5]After two to seven days, SARS patients may develop a dry cough, and they may have trouble breathing. [6]SARS has led to death in some cases.

**2.** Topic sentence: ______

### A Movie to Remember

[1]Although many of the reviews for the movie *A Walk to Remember* dubbed the movie a sweet teen drama that fails to understand modern teenage life, the film offers a refreshing change from the run-of-the-mill Hollywood

fare. [2]*A Walk to Remember* is worth the moviegoer's time and money. [3]Based on a best-selling novel by Nicholas Sparks, the basic plot does follow countless other teen movies: a bad boy falls for a good girl with a deep, dark secret. [4]Peer pressure, parental disapproval, and her secret keep the couple apart until their true love overcomes all obstacles. [5]The main character, Jamie, never betrays her strongly held religious beliefs, and she doesn't go through a makeover to become acceptable. [6]Her unswerving faith brings a passion to her life that changes the course of boyfriend Landon's life. [7]The message of being yourself and the power of faith make *A Walk to Remember* a movie well worth seeing.

**3.** Topic sentences: _____

**You've Got Spam: How to "Can" Unwanted E-Mail**

[1]Do you receive lots of junk e-mail messages from people you don't know? [2]It's no surprise if you do. [3]As more people use e-mail, marketers are increasingly using e-mail messages to pitch their products and services. [4]Some consumers find unsolicited commercial e-mail, also known as spam, annoying and time consuming; others have lost money to bogus offers that arrived in their e-mail in-box. [5]An e-mail spammer buys a list of e-mail addresses from a list broker, who compiles it by "harvesting" addresses from the Internet. [6]Following are five simple suggestions to help reduce the amount of spam you receive. [7]First, try not to display your e-mail address in public. [8]This includes newsgroup postings, chat rooms, websites, or in an online service's membership directory. [9]Second, check the privacy policy when you submit your address to a website. [10]Third, read and understand the entire form before you send personal information through a website. [11]Fourth, use two e-mail addresses: one for personal messages and one for newsgroups and chat rooms. [12]Finally, use an e-mail filter; your e-mail account may provide a tool to block potential spam.

—Adapted from Federal Trade Commission, "You've Got Spam: How to 'Can' Unwanted E-Mail."

**4.** Topic sentence: _____

**One Harmless Lie**

[1]Fourteen-year-old Laura Cantrell thought she was being a good friend when she lied for 15-year-old Rebecca Anderson. [2]Rebecca told Laura that her parents were trying to control her life because they wouldn't let her date Sam Larson, who was 27 years old. [3]Rebecca begged Laura to help her come up with a way to get out of the house so she could be with Sam one more time, just to tell him good-bye. [4]So Laura covered for her by telling Rebecca's parents that Rebecca was spending the night with her. [5]That night, Rebecca

ran away from home. [6]By the time the truth was discovered, Rebecca and Sam had vanished without a trace. [7]Laura felt shocked, horrified, and betrayed. [8]Laura's parents were ashamed of their daughter's part in Rebecca's disappearance. [9]And Mr. and Mrs. Anderson struggled with grief, guilt, and fear. [10]A lie that seems harmless can have devastating results.

**5.** Topic sentence: _____

## The Central Idea and the Thesis Statement

Just as a single paragraph has a main idea, longer passages made up of two or more paragraphs also have a main idea. You encounter these longer passages in articles, essays, and textbooks. In longer passages, the main idea is called the **central idea**. Often the author will state the central idea in a single sentence called the **thesis statement**.

> The **central idea** is the main idea of a passage made up of two or more paragraphs.
> The **thesis statement** is a sentence that states the topic and the author's controlling point about the topic for a passage of two or more paragraphs.

You find the central idea of longer passages the same way you locate the main idea or topic sentence of a paragraph. The thesis statement is the one sentence that is general enough to include all the ideas in the passage.

**EXAMPLE** Read the following passage from a college communications textbook, and identify the thesis statement, which states the central idea.

Textbook Skills

**Supportive Responses**

[1]Listening stops when you feel threatened. [2]No one likes to be proven wrong in front of others, criticized, or ignored. [3]Defensive individuals are usually more concerned with protecting their self-concept and saving face than promoting communication. [4]The more defensive a person becomes, the less able he is to perceive his partner's motives, values, and emotions.

[5]Your goal is to create situations that foster open communication in a supportive climate. [6]Supportive responses are based on several behaviors that encourage problem solving and build healthy relationships. [7]First, be aware of the use of "I" and "you." [8]Instead of saying, "You're never around when I need you," a supportive response says, "I felt frustrated and needed your help." [9]Second, focus on solving problems instead of placing blame. [10]Third,

show empathy instead of indifference. [11]And finally, be open-minded to the views of others instead of asserting your own view as the only or correct one.

—Adapted from Brownell, *Listening: Attitudes, Principles, and Skills,* 2nd ed., p. 284.

Thesis statement: ______

**EXPLANATION** The first four sentences introduce the need to know about the topic "supportive responses." These sentences are designed to hook the reader's interest in the topic. Sentence 5 is a link between the need to know and the author's central idea, which is stated in the next sentence. Sentence 6 is the central idea of the passage. It is the only sentence general enough to include most of the details in the passage. Note that sentence 6 includes the topic "supportive responses" and the author's controlling point about the topic; they are "behaviors that encourage problem solving and build healthy relationships." Sentences 7 through 11 are supporting details that list the supportive responses.

## PRACTICE 4

Read the following passage from a college writing handbook, and identify the thesis statement, which states the central idea.

Textbook Skills

### Creative Thinking: Shifting Attention

[1]Sometimes in writing you come to a dead end or run out of ideas because you focus too sharply on a single aspect of your topic. [2]As you think about what you are going to write, thoughtfully shifting attention away from the chief element of your topic can lead you to additional ideas. [3]For example, in writing a paper about the effects of excessive drinking, you may be concentrating on an individual drinker. [4]Shifting your focus to the effects of alcohol on the drinker's family and friends will stimulate further thought and additional ideas. [5]So will a different kind of shift, one to a consideration of the broader social effects of alcoholism. [6]You might find yourself refocusing your paper; you may even revise your initial purpose, point, and emphasis.

[7]The following example shows how a shift of attention can lead to the solution of a problem.

[8]As a man is driving home from work, his car comes to a halt. [9]Lifting up the hood, he notices that he has a broken fan belt. [10]His solution? [11]He takes off his necktie and ties it tightly in the fan belt position. [12]He drives a quarter of a mile to the nearest service station and replaces his fan belt. [13]With the money he saved on a towing charge, he buys a new tie.

—Adapted from Di Yanni & Hoy, *The Scribner Handbook for Writers,* 3rd ed., pp. 59–60.

Thesis statement: ______

Textbook Skills

## Topics, Main Ideas, and Central Ideas in Textbooks

Textbooks identify topics in the title of each chapter. An excellent study strategy is to read a textbook's table of contents, a listing of all the chapters' titles, which are the general topics covered in the textbook. In addition to providing topics in chapter titles, textbooks also identify topics within each chapter. Other publications, such as newspapers and magazines, also use titles and headings to point out topics.

Textbook authors often state the topic of a passage or paragraph in a heading. For example, titles of graphs often help readers identify the main idea of the graph by stating the topic. Identifying the topic in a heading makes it easier to find the main idea and supporting details.

**EXAMPLE** Read the following paragraph from an ecology textbook. Then answer the questions that follow it.

**Environmental Tolerance**

[1]A stable population of an organism is possible only within a limited range of conditions in the environment. [2]The graph shows this range. [3]Let the *x* axis represent a trait of the physical environment. [4]Because it is so closely linked to the survival of an organism, we will use temperature. [5]Axis *y* tracks the response of the organism. [6]The response of an organism falls along a bell-shaped curve describing performance (which in this case is survival). [7]The point along the *x* axis where the response of the organism is highest is called the *optimum*. [8]As conditions vary from this optimum, the chances of survival lessen. [9]The two points (minimum and maximum) at which the curve meets the *x* axis show the conditions under which the organism cannot survive. [10]Within these two points is the range of conditions under which an organism can live but perhaps not grow or reproduce. [11]The minimum and maximum values of the environment are known as the *environmental tolerance* of the organism.

—Adapted from Smith & Smith, *Elements of Ecology*, 4th ed., p. 12.

**1.** The topic of the paragraph is ______________________________.

______ **2.** Sentence 11 is

a. the topic sentence.　　b. a supporting detail.

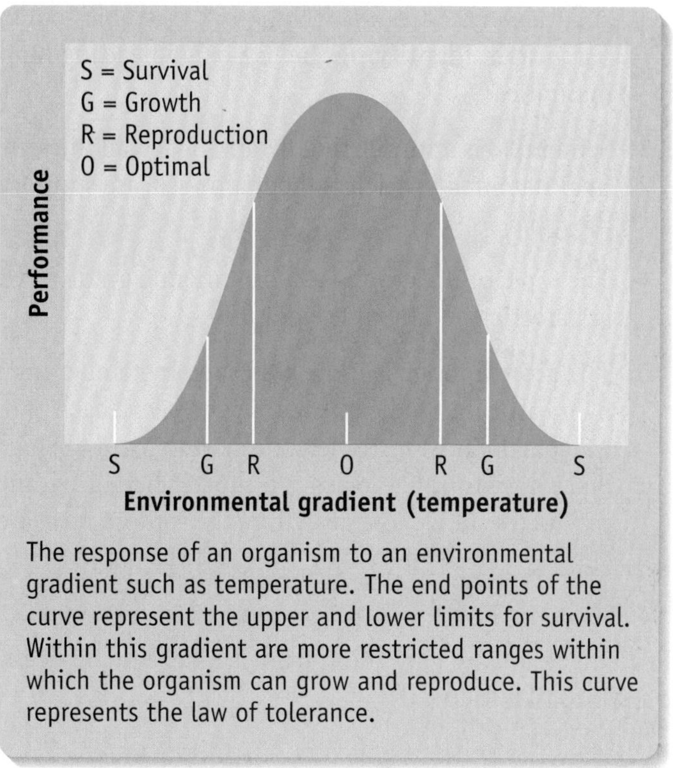


The response of an organism to an environmental gradient such as temperature. The end points of the curve represent the upper and lower limits for survival. Within this gradient are more restricted ranges within which the organism can grow and reproduce. This curve represents the law of tolerance.

—Smith, Robert, and Smith, Thomas. *Elements of Ecology,* 4th ed., p. 12.


_____ **3.** Sentence 8 is
a. the topic sentence. b. a supporting detail.

**4.** The topic of the graph is ______________________________.

**5.** Which range in the gradient is more restricted?

_____ The growth range

_____ The reproduction range

**EXPLANATION**

**1.** The topic of the paragraph is environmental tolerance. The topic is stated in the heading.

**2.** Sentence 11 is the topic sentence; it states the topic and the author's controlling point about the topic, which is a definition of the term *environmental tolerance.* Note that the topic sentence is at the end of this paragraph. Identifying the topic in a heading helps the reader locate the main idea.

3. Sentence 8 is a supporting detail. In fact, all the sentences leading up to the final statement, which is the main idea, are supporting details that explain the topic.

4. The topic of the graph is environmental gradient (temperature). The topic is stated in the title of the graph.

5. The growth range is more restricted by temperature levels. We can see this by measuring the height within the curve each range attains. The optimal range is the least restricted and rises to form the highest point on the curve. Since growth range reaches a shorter height within the curve than the reproductive range, the growth range is more restricted by temperature.

## PRACTICE 5

**A.** Read the following paragraph from a college finance textbook. Then answer the questions that follow it.

Textbook Skills

**Interest Rates**

[1]Interest rates can affect economic growth and therefore have an indirect impact on stock prices. [2]In general, stocks perform better when interest rates are low because firms can obtain financing at relatively low rates. [3]Firms tend to be more willing to expand when interest rates are low, and their expansions stimulate the economy. [4]When interest rates are low, investors also tend to shift more of their funds into stocks because the interest earned on money market securities is relatively low. [5]The general shift into stocks increases the demand for stocks, which places upward pressure on stock prices.

—Madura, *Personal Finance*, 2nd ed., p. 403.

1. The topic of the paragraph is ______________________________.

______ 2. Sentence 1 is
a. the topic sentence. b. a supporting detail.

______ 3. Sentence 2 is
a. the topic sentence. b. a supporting detail.

______ 4. Sentence 3 is
a. the topic sentence. b. a supporting detail.

______ **5.** Sentence 4 is
a. the topic sentence. b. a supporting detail.

______ **6.** Sentence 5 is
a. the topic sentence. b. a supporting detail.

**B.** Read the following passage from a college textbook. In the space provided, write the letter of the sentence that best states the central idea of the passage.

Textbook Skills

**The Spiral of Silence**

[1]The spiral of silence theory argues that you're more likely to voice agreement than disagreement. [2]The theory claims that when a controversial issue arises, you guess about public opinion. [3]By paying attention to the media, you figure out which views are popular and which are not. [4]You also think about the punishments you're likely to get for expressing minority views. [5]You then adapt your expression of opinion.

[6]Generally, you're more likely to voice your opinions when you agree with the majority than when you disagree. [7]You may do this to avoid being isolated from the majority or being proven wrong. [8]Or you may simply assume that the majority—because they're a majority—must be right.

[9]As people with minority views remain silent, the media position gets stronger (because those who agree with it are the ones speaking). [10]As the media's position grows stronger, the silence of the opposition also grows. [11]And the situation becomes a growing spiral. [12]So when you hear opinions from the media, you're likely to think that nearly everyone is in agreement. [13]After all, those who do disagree are not voicing their opinions.

—Adapted from DeVito, *The Interpersonal Communication Book*, 10th ed., p. 193.

______ **7.** Which sentence best states the central idea of the passage?
a. Sentence 1 c. Sentence 9
b. Sentence 2 d. Sentence 13

## Chapter Review

Test your understanding of what you have read in this chapter by filling in the blank with a word from the box.

| | | |
|---|---|---|
| beginning | specific | topic sentence |
| central idea | supporting details | words |
| main idea | thesis statement | |
| questions | topic | |

1. The _______________ is the author's controlling point about a topic.
2. The _______________ is a single sentence in a paragraph that states the author's main idea.
3. The _______________ is the general subject matter of a reading passage.
4. The topic can be stated in just a few _______________.
5. To identify the main idea ask yourself two _______________: "What is the topic?" and "What is the author's controlling point about the topic?"
6. When you ask the question "Who or what is the paragraph about?" you must be sure that your answer is neither too general nor too _________.
7. _______________ are specific ideas that develop, explain, or support the main idea.
8. The topic sentence can be placed at the _______________ of a paragraph, within a paragraph, or at the end of a paragraph.
9. The _______________ is the main idea of a passage made up of two or more paragraphs.
10. The _______________ is a sentence that states a longer passage's central idea.

## Applications

### Application 1: Identifying Topics

Read the following paragraphs. Circle the topic as it recurs in each paragraph. Then answer the question that follows each paragraph.

[1]Dipping and chewing tobacco has several harmful results. [2]Dipping and chewing can cause your gums to pull away from your teeth in the place where the tobacco is held. [3]The gums do not grow back. [4]In addition, the

sugar in the tobacco may cause decay in exposed tooth roots. [5]Leathery white patches, called *leukoplakia*, and red sores are common in the mouths of dippers and chewers and can turn into cancer.

—National Institute of Dental and Craniofacial Research, "Welcome to Spit Tobacco: A Guide for Quitting."

_____ **1.** Which of the following best states the topic?
a. Tobacco
b. Dipping and chewing tobacco
c. Leathery white patches called leukoplakia

[1]Pollution, sun, rain, and salt air can cause serious damage to your car's finish. [2]Waxing your car a few times a year will provide it with much-needed protection. [3]Occasional waxing not only keeps your car looking good but also extends its life and maintains the car's resale value. [4]Although you should be sure to wax your car at least twice a year, feel free to wax anytime the finish looks dull or water fails to bead on its surface. [5]When you wax, wash and dry your car first to avoid grinding dirt into the finish, and wax in the shade for best results.

_____ **2.** Which of the following best states the topic?
a. Water beading up
b. Waxing your car
c. Waxing your car in the shade

## Application 2: Topics and the Main Idea

Read the following paragraph. Then answer the questions that follow it.

**What Creates a Childhood Bully?**

[1]The typical childhood bully is not the independent leader his peers think he is. [2]The bully is actually the product of his surroundings. [3]A bully thrives in a social climate that favors one group over another, where the "I am better than you" attitude is allowed to thrive. [4]This climate arises out of an intolerance toward anyone who is different and derives its power from the bystanders who say nothing while the bully torments his victim. [5]Most often the bully is simply a kid who needs to be accepted and liked by his peers.

_____ **1.** What is the topic of the paragraph?
a. A bully
b. A childhood bully
c. A kid who needs to be accepted and liked by his peers

_____ **2.** Which sentence states the author's main idea?
a. Sentence 1
b. Sentence 2
c. Sentence 4

## Application 3: Topics, Main Ideas, and Supporting Details

Each of the following groups of ideas has a topic, one main idea, and two supporting details. In each group, first identify the topic. Then identify the stated main idea. (Hint: circle the topic and underline the author's controlling point in each group.)

### Group 1

a. American Idol's faithful fans vote each week and ultimately determine the winner.
b. Simon Cowell, Randy Jackson, and Paula Abdul have all at one time or another ridiculed a contestant.
c. The television show American Idol is a smash hit based on challenging competition, brutal ridicule, and audience interaction.

_____ **1.** Which of the following best states the topic?
a. The Cruelty of American Idol
b. The Audience Wins with American Idol
c. American Idol the Smash Hit

_____ **2.** Which sentence is the stated main idea?

### Group 2

a. Sit up straight, pull your shoulders down to form a gentle V, and with your mouth closed, breathe deeply, pushing air in and out with your abdomen.
b. Take a break from your computer by standing up, lacing your fingers behind your back, bending forward, and pulling your hands up behind you as far as you can.
c. Two simple stretches can help you relieve workday stress.

_____ **3.** Which of the following best states the topic?
a. two stretches
b. workday stress
c. a gentle V

_____ **4.** Which sentence is the stated main idea?

### Group 3

a. Home safety is a simple matter of common sense.
b. Use slip-proof mats in showers and tubs, and use rubberized mats to secure scatter rugs to the floor so they won't slip.

c. Keep clutter picked up and train pets to stay out from under your feet to avoid stumbling or tripping.

_____ **5.** Which of the following best states the topic?
a. safety
b. eliminating clutter
c. safety in the home

_____ **6.** Which sentence is the stated main idea?

## Application 4: Location of Topic Sentences

Read the following paragraph from a college health textbook and identify its topic sentence or sentences. Remember to ask, "Does this sentence (Do these sentences) cover all the ideas in the passage?"

**Sharing Feelings**

[1]Although men tend to talk about intimate issues with women more often than with men, women still complain that men do not communicate enough about what is really on their minds. [2]This conflict is the result of the contrast in communication styles that comes from the different socializing processes experienced by women and men. [3]Throughout their lives, females are encouraged to share their thoughts and feelings with others. [4]In contrast, males receive strong messages to withhold their feelings. [5]The classic example of this training in very young males is the familiar saying, "big boys don't cry." [6]Males learn very early that certain emotions are not to be shared. [7]The result is that they are more information-focused and businesslike in discussions with females than females are. [8]Such differences in communication styles contribute to misunderstandings and conflict between the sexes.

—Adapted from Donatelle, *Access to Health,* 7th ed., p. 136.

Topic sentence(s): _____

# REVIEW Test 1

## Identifying Topics and Main Ideas

**A.** Skim each paragraph and circle the topic as it recurs throughout the paragraph. Then identify the idea that correctly states the topic. (Hint: one idea is too general to be the topic; another idea is too specific.)

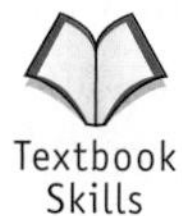


_____ **1.** [1]Food additives serve a number of functions. [2]They make foods more attractive. [3]They enhance the taste and quality of foods, and they help food last longer in storage. [4]The term *food additive* is defined as any substance that results or may be reasonably expected to result in its becoming a part or affecting the characteristics of any food. [5]Anything used in producing, processing, treating, packaging, transporting, or storing food is considered a food additive. [6]Five broad types of additives exist: nutrients, preservatives, processing aids, flavorings, and colorings.

—Adapted from Pruitt & Stein, *Health Styles, Decisions for Living Well,* 2nd ed., p. 107.

a. Food additives
b. Five types of food additives
c. Foods

_____ **2.** [1]Charlton Heston enjoyed a long public career. [2]In 2003, his career ended because of failing health. [3]His last public role was as a spokesperson for the National Rifle Association. [4]However, Heston enjoyed a long and successful career as an actor. [5]He began his career in the 1940s, and he acted in over a hundred films. [6]Many people remember him for his strong performance as Moses in *The Ten Commandments.* [7]During a recorded farewell speech, Heston told the public that he most likely has Alzheimer's disease.

a. Alzheimer's disease
b. Charlton Heston as Moses in *The Ten Commandments*
c. Charlton Heston

_____ **3.** [1]Some people have no fear of hurricanes. [2]When a hurricane threatens their area, they are the ones who refuse to leave for higher ground. [3]These people are very foolish because hurricanes pose several types of threats. [4]Hurricanes bring with them storm surges, strong winds, tornadoes, and floods. [5]According to some experts, storm surges can raise the sea level by 15 feet and are a great threat to human life. [6]Hurricanes can and do kill.

a. People who are very foolish
b. Hurricanes and tornadoes
c. Hurricanes

**B.** Read the following paragraph, and identify the sentence (or sentences) that states the main idea.

[1]Parents, educators, and students all have their own opinions about what should be taught in public schools. [2]The debate seems to be most heated when discussing elementary education. [3]Everyone seems to agree that

reading, writing, and arithmetic are as important as ever, but agreement seems to end there. [4]However, real-world needs should play a major role in early education. [5]For example, keyboard skills are basic and necessary. [6]Students who can master basic typing skills will be much more successful in school and on the job. [7]Research and writing can be accomplished at higher levels of proficiency when students know how to use the Internet and word processing programs. [8]Many jobs require personal computers, and the retail industry relies on complicated keypads to enter orders and track stock. [9]Public elementary schools should examine real-world needs when considering what to teach their students.

**4.** Topic sentence(s): _____

# REVIEW Test 2

## Topics, Main Ideas, and Supporting Details

**A.** Each of the following groups of ideas includes one topic, one main idea, and two supporting details. In each group, first identify the topic. Then identify the stated main idea. (Hint: circle the topic and underline the author's controlling point in each group.)

### Group 1

a. Procrastination has two possible causes.
b. Many people may procrastinate because they have a fear of failure, and if they don't begin a task or project, they can't fail at it.
c. Others may procrastinate out of laziness; these careless workers have not yet developed a strong work ethic.

_____ **1.** Which of the following best states the topic?
a. laziness
b. procrastination
c. a strong work ethic

_____ **2.** Which sentence best states the main idea?

Textbook Skills

### Group 2

a. A snake can control its body temperature in two ways.
b. First, a snake can darken its skin to absorb higher levels of solar heat; once its body reaches a suitable temperature, the snake can lighten its skin color.
c. A snake also spreads and flattens its body as it lies at a right angle to the sun's rays to expose more of its body and raise its temperature; to reduce its

body temperature, a snake lies parallel to the sun's rays or moves into the shade.

—Adapted from Smith & Smith, *Elements of Ecology*, 4th ed., p. 11-A.

_____ **3.** Which of the following best states the topic?
a. body temperature
b. snakes
c. a snake's body temperature

_____ **4.** Which sentence best states the main idea?

**B.** Read the paragraph. Then answer the question.

[1]First Monday, Mississippi's largest flea market, and one of the nation's oldest, is a long-standing success that offers something for everybody. [2]Established in 1893, this open market was originally located on Ripley's downtown court square, but it is now stationed south of the city limits across from the county fairgrounds. [3]First Monday sits on over 50 acres and offers hundreds of booths that house vendors and assorted items for sale. [4]The variety of goods ranges from unique and hard-to-find items to new and used products, antiques, crafts, and much more, including pets. [5]First Monday is open the Saturday and Sunday preceding the first Monday of each month, and buyers travel hundreds of miles to trade there. [6]Admission is free, and the grounds provide dining facilities, electrical hookups, showers, a laundry room, table rental, cable TV hookup, and early-morning church services.

_____ **5.** Which sentence states the main idea of the paragraph?
a. Sentence 1
b. Sentence 2
c. Sentence 5
d. Sentence 6

## REVIEW Test 3

### Topics, Main Ideas, and Supporting Details

**A.** Each of the following groups of ideas includes one topic, one main idea, and two supporting details. In each group, first identify the topic. Then identify the stated main idea. (Hint: circle the topic and underline the author's controlling point in each group.)

**Group 1**

a. Gardening has emotional and physical benefits.
b. Pulling weeds, raking, digging, and planting while gardening strengthen all of the major muscle groups.

c. The sense of accomplishment and the enjoyment of beautiful surroundings bring many gardeners emotional satisfaction.

______ **1.** Which of the following best states the topic?
a. pulling weeds
b. emotional satisfaction
c. gardening

______ **2.** Which sentence best states the main idea?

## Group 2

a. Also, surprise a child with an unexpected reward, such as a day trip to a special place, for a job well done.
b. Positive reinforcement teaches children the satisfaction and reward of good behavior.
c. One way to offer positive reinforcement is to give sincere praise when it is well deserved; children need to hear statements like "I'm proud of you" or "The way you mow and trim makes the yard look neat and healthy."

______ **3.** Which of the following best states the topic?
a. parenting
b. positive reinforcement
c. good behavior

______ **4.** Which sentence best states the main idea?

**B.** Read the following paragraph. Then answer the questions that follow it.

### Co-Parenting Adult Children

[1]Protecting your marriage from the rigors of parenting adult children requires a bit of strategy. [2]Consider these four pointers: First, you and your mate don't have to agree. [3]Your kids are mature enough now to handle differing points of view. [4]Second, don't argue over how to help your child. [5]Ask her directly, "How can I be helpful to you in this situation?" [6]You may or may not be able to give what's requested, but that should be an individual decision made by each parent. [7]Third, get out of the middle. [8]Don't be the messenger. [9]Encourage family members to talk directly to one another about their grievances. [10]It doesn't help your marriage for you to be the bearer of unpleasant news. [11]Fourth, choose the well-being of your marriage. [12]If your practice of giving unlimited financial help or unlimited counseling on the telephone is putting a strain on your marriage, set limits. [13]Your mate needs love and support too!

—Adapted from Sills, "Co-Parenting Adult Children," p. 44.

______ **5.** Which sentence states the main idea of the paragraph?
a. Sentence 1
b. Sentence 2
c. Sentence 6
d. Sentence 13

# REVIEW Test 4

## Topics and Main Ideas

**Before reading:** Survey the following passage adapted from the college textbook *Psychology and Life*. Skim the passage, noting the words in bold print. Answer the **Before Reading** questions that follow the passage. Then read the passage. Next, answer the **After Reading** questions. Use the discussion and writing topics as activities to do after reading.

### Vocabulary Preview

*consistent* (1): constant, regular
*appreciation* (6): admiration, enjoyment, understanding
*philosophy* (6): viewpoint, way of life
*deteriorated* (14): declined
*maturation* (21): growth

Textbook Skills

### WHAT IS LEARNING?

[1]Learning is a process that results in a relatively **consistent** change in behavior or behavior potential and is based on experience. [2]The three critical parts of this definition deserve careful study.

#### A Change in Behavior or Behavior Potential

[3]It is obvious that learning has taken place when you are able to demonstrate the results, such as when you drive a car or use a microwave oven. [4]You can't directly observe learning itself, but learning is **apparent** from improvements in your performance. [5]Often, however, your performance doesn't show everything that you have learned. [6]Sometimes, too, you have **acquired** general attitudes, such as an **appreciation** of modern art or an understanding of Eastern **philosophy**, that may not be apparent in your measurable actions. [7]In such cases, you have achieved a potential for behavior change. [8]You have learned attitudes and values that can influence the kinds of books you read or the way you spend your leisure time. [9]This is an example of learning performance distinction; it is the difference between what has been learned and what is expressed, or performed, in **overt** behavior.

#### A Relatively Consistent Change

[10]To qualify as learned, a change in behavior or behavior potential must be relatively consistent over different occasions. [11]Thus once you learn to

swim, you will probably always be able to do so. [12]Note that consistent changes are not always permanent changes. [13]You may, for example, have become quite a consistent dart thrower when you practiced every day. [14]If you gave up the sport, however, your skills might have **deteriorated** toward their original level. [15]But if you have learned once to be a championship dart thrower, it ought to be easier for you to learn a second time. [16]Something has been "saved" from your prior experience. [17]In that sense, the change may be permanent.

### A Process Based on Experience

[18]Learning can take place only through experience. [19]Experience includes taking in information and making responses that affect the environment. [20]Learning is made up of a response affected by the lessons of memory. [21]Learned behavior does not include changes that come about because of physical **maturation**, nor does it simply rely on brain development as the organism ages. [22]Some learning requires a combination of experience and **maturity**. [23]For example, think about the timetable that controls when an infant is ready to crawl, stand, walk, run, and be toilet trained. [24]No amount of training or practice will produce those behaviors before the child is mature enough to be ready to learn.

—Adapted from Gerrig & Zimbardo, *Psychology and Life,* 16th ed., p. 181.

## BEFORE READING

### Vocabulary in Context

_____ **1.** The word **apparent** in sentence 4 means
a. unseen.
b. obvious.
c. reinforced.
d. encouraged.

_____ **2.** The word **acquired** in sentence 6 means
a. rated.
b. overcome.
c. rejected.
d. gained.

_____ **3.** The word **overt** in sentence 9 means
a. hidden.
b. wise.
c. visible.
d. concerned.

_____ **4.** The word **maturity** in sentence 22 means
a. fully developed.
b. understanding.
c. passion.
d. inexperience.

## Topics and Main Ideas

_____ **5.** What is the topic of the passage?
a. Demonstrating results
b. Learning
c. Consistent change
d. Change in behavior

## AFTER READING

_____ **6.** Which sentence states the central idea of the passage?
a. Sentence 1
b. Sentence 3
c. Sentence 10
d. Sentence 24

_____ **7.** What is the topic of the third paragraph (sentences 10–17)?
a. A change in behavior or behavior potential
b. A relatively consistent change in behavior or behavior potential
c. Permanent changes in behavior potential
d. Prior experiences of behavior change

_____ **8.** Which sentence states the main idea of the third paragraph?
a. Sentence 10
b. Sentence 11
c. Sentence 12
d. Sentence 16

**9–10.** Label each of the following two sentences from the fourth paragraph (sentences 18–24). Use **A** if it states the main idea or **B** if it supplies a supporting detail.

_____ **9.** Learning can take place only through experience.

_____ **10.** Learning is made up of a response affected by the lessons of memory.

## Discussion Topics

1. Discuss some examples of "learning performance distinction," the difference between what has been learned and what can be expressed. When have you experienced this distinction?
2. What is the connection between learning and the "lessons of memory"?
3. Are there times when one can learn something without experience?

## Writing Topics

1. Describe a learning experience that resulted in a change in your behavior or the behavior of someone you know.
2. Write a paragraph or two discussing the ways prior knowledge or experience affects learning.

3. Explore the relationship between physical maturity and learning. Do certain topics or tasks require a certain level of maturity or age to be fully learned? Give examples to support your point of view.

## EFFECTIVE READER Scorecard

**Stated Main Ideas**

| Test | Number Correct | | Points | | Score |
|---|---|---|---|---|---|
| Review Test 1 | ______ | × | 25 | = | ______ |
| Review Test 2 | ______ | × | 20 | = | ______ |
| Review Test 3 | ______ | × | 20 | = | ______ |
| Review Test 4 | ______ | × | 10 | = | ______ |
| Review Test 5 (website) | ______ | × | 25 | = | ______ |
| Review Test 6 (website) | ______ | × | 20 | = | ______ |

Enter your scores on the Effective Reader Scorecard: Chapter 3 Review Tests inside the back cover.

## After Reading About Stated Main Ideas

A crucial step in the reading process occurs during the after reading phase when you take time to reflect on what you have learned. Before you move on to the mastery tests on stated main ideas, take time to reflect on your learning and performance by answering the following questions. Write your answers in your notebook.

What did I learn?

What do I need to remember?

How has my knowledge base or prior knowledge changed?

### More Review and Mastery Tests

For more practice, go to the book's website at **http://ablongman.com/henry/** and click on *The Effective Reader*. Then select "More Review and Mastery Tests." The tests are organized by chapter.

# MASTERY Test 1

Name ______________________ Section ____________

Date ____________ **Score** (number correct) ______ × 20 = ______%

**A.** Skim each of the following paragraphs and circle the topic as it recurs throughout the paragraph. Then, identify the idea that correctly states the topic. (Hint: one idea is too general to be the topic; another idea is too specific.)

______ **1.** [1]Did you know that May is Foot Health Awareness Month? [2]The foot is often the most ignored part of our bodies. [3]Yet with its 28 bones, 33 joints, and 19 muscles, the foot deserves year-round pampering. [4]Good foot care begins with shoes that fit properly. [5]Ill-fitting shoes cause many problems, including poor circulation, injury due to lack of proper support, corns, bunions, and calluses. [6]Good foot care also entails keeping the feet clean. [7]Plantar warts are caused by a virus that enters the foot through an open sore or cut. [8]The best activity for the feet is walking. [9]Walking stimulates circulation and keeps the feet strong and limber.

a. Feet
b. Foot Health Awareness Month
c. Proper foot care

______ **2.** [1]"Hispanic" is a widely used term for a person of Spanish-language heritage living in the United States. [2]The term was first coined by the government for census-taking purposes. [3]Hispanic, from the Latin word for "Spain," refers generally to all Spanish-speaking peoples. [4]The term emphasizes the common factor of a shared language among groups that may have little else in common. [5]Hispanic can be used in referring to Spain and its history and culture. [6]A native of Spain residing in the United States is a Hispanic. [7]Hispanics are persons of Cuban, Mexican, Puerto Rican, South or Central-American, or other Spanish culture or origin, regardless of race. [8]The federal government considers race and Hispanic origin to be two separate and distinct concepts. [9]Hispanic Americans may be any race. [10]According to the 2000 U.S. Census, Hispanics of all races represent 13.3 percent of the U.S. population, which is about 37.4 million individuals. [11]The Census Bureau projects that by the year 2040 there will be 87.5 million Hispanic individuals, making up 22.3 percent of the population. [12]Though they share many aspects of a common heritage such as language and emphasis on extended family, Hispanic cultures vary greatly by country of origin.

[13]Therefore, the broad term "Hispanic" is not an appropriate title for such a diverse people.

—Adapted from United States Centers for Disease Control.
"Hispanic or Latino Populations." Office of Minority Health. 15 August 2007.
<http://www.cdc.gov/omh/Populations/HL/HL.htm>.

a. The origin of the term "Hispanic"
b. Latin Americans
c. The limitations of the term "Hispanic"

**B.** Read the following group of ideas from a college psychology textbook. Answer the questions that follow.

a. Basic emotions can combine to produce more complex and subtle ones.
b. For example, joy and acceptance, which are closely related, can combine to produce love; joy and fear, which are not closely related, can join to produce guilt.
c. When distant emotions mix, a person typically feels conflicted.

_____ **3.** Statement (a) is
a. the main idea. b. a supporting detail.

_____ **4.** Statement (b) is
a. the main idea. b. a supporting detail.

_____ **5.** Statement (c) is
a. the main idea. b. a supporting detail.

**VISUAL VOCABULARY**

What emotion does Plutchik's palette suggest will be the result of mixing fear and surprise?

_______________

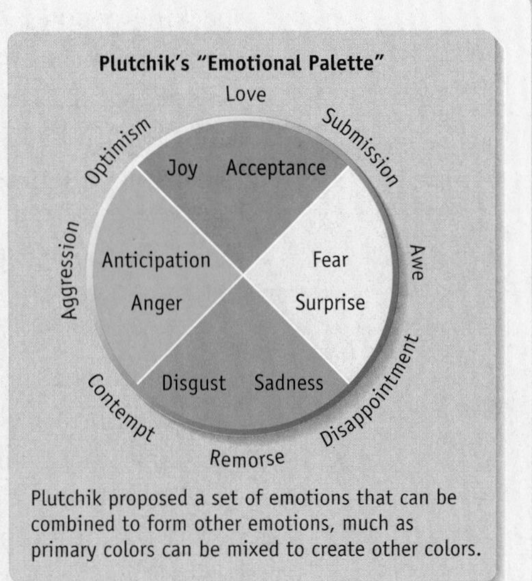


Plutchik proposed a set of emotions that can be combined to form other emotions, much as primary colors can be mixed to create other colors.

—From Robert Plutchik, *Emotion*, © 1980. Published by Allyn & Bacon, Boston, MA. Copyright © 1980 by Pearson Education. Adapted by permission of the publisher.

MASTERY **Test 2**

Name ______________________ Section ____________

Date ____________ **Score** (number correct) ______ × 20 = ______%

---

**A.** Skim each of the following paragraphs and circle the topic as it recurs throughout the paragraph. Then identify the idea that correctly states the topic. (Hint: one idea is too general to be the topic; another idea is too specific.)

______ **1.** [1]Adolescence is a bridge between childhood and adulthood. [2]This stage of development is a time of transition and adjustment that is often not easy. [3]Still young and inexperienced, adolescents do not have the maturity to understand some of the decisions they make or the feelings they have. [4]Yet at the same time, they are by nature risk takers who need to learn by trial and error. [5]For many, the hormones that are working to change the body from that of a child to that of an adult can cause extreme mood swings, and adolescents can become moody, depressed, and easily emotional.

a. Growing up
b. Adolescence
c. Hormone changes

______ **2.** [1]Many of us have memories of chasing fireflies in the early evening as dusk closed in. [2]These amazing creatures (which are actually beetles, not flies) use their flashing lights for two reasons. [3]First, it is thought that fireflies glow as a warning to their predators. [4]The light signals that they don't taste very good because they are full of defensive chemicals. [5]Second, fireflies most likely use their lights to attract a mate. [6]Their ability to flash each other is their own special brand of courtship.

a. Attracting a mate
b. Fireflies' flashing lights
c. Memories of fireflies

**B.** Read the following group of ideas and then answer the questions that follow.

a. Having someone to talk to about problems can reduce anxiety and fear.
b. People who have healthy relationships with family and friends tend to live longer, healthier lives.
c. A strong support system helps lessen the negative effects of stress.

______ **3.** Statement (a) is
a. the main idea.
b. a supporting detail.

_____ **4.** Statement (b) is
a. the main idea.
b. a supporting detail.

_____ **5.** Statement (c) is
a. the main idea.
b. a supporting detail.

MASTERY **Test 3**

Name ______________________ Section ______________

Date ______________ **Score** (number correct) ______ × 10 = ______%

**A.** Read each group of ideas and answer the questions that follow.

**Group 1**

a. Becoming environmentally friendly doesn't have to take much time, effort, or money—it just requires awareness and creativity.
b. Brush your hair outside, and place the hair from your brush under a tree or bush so that birds can gather it as material for their nests.
c. For example, birds benefit greatly from a few thoughtful human actions, such as helping female birds build up calcium for egg laying by putting egg shells out for them to eat.

______ **1.** Statement (a) is
a. the main idea. b. a supporting detail.

______ **2.** Statement (b) is
a. the main idea. b. a supporting detail.

______ **3.** Statement (c) is
a. the main idea. b. a supporting detail.

**4.** What is the topic? ______________________

**Group 2**

a. To say "Belinda smiled, and the whole world smiled with her" is to use hyperbole.
b. Hyperbole is a figure of speech that makes an exaggeration.
c. Another example of hyperbole is "James has a pimple the size of a watermelon."

______ **5.** Statement (a) is
a. the main idea. b. a supporting detail.

______ **6.** Statement (b) is
a. the main idea. b. a supporting detail.

______ **7.** Statement (c) is
a. the main idea. b. a supporting detail.

**8.** What is the topic? ______________________

**B.** Read the following passage from a college communications textbook. Then answer the questions that follow it.

Textbook Skills

### Communication Framework

[1]Consider the following communication situation. [2]Two men meet in a city park. [3]One man has a dog on a leash. [4]Looking over at the dog, the first man asks, "Does your dog bite?" [5]The second man assures him that his dog does not bite. [6]The first man then reaches down to pet the dog and is immediately bitten. [7]"I thought you said your dog didn't bite," the man shouts, holding his injured hand. [8]"This isn't my dog," the second man calmly replies.

[9]The conversation is an example of the impact of a communication framework. [10]A communication framework is the large image of a situation that you use to make sense of what is going on. [11]This "framing" is dynamic and often has such a strong influence on the way you see the world that your understanding of what you hear becomes very limited. [12]In the conversation about the dog, the communication framework resulted in a misunderstanding.

—Adapted from Brownell, *Listening: Attitudes, Principles, and Skills,* 2nd ed., p. 47.

______ **9.** What is the topic of the passage?
a. Misunderstanding
b. A conversation about a dog
c. Communication framework
d. Two men talking

______ **10.** Which sentence states the central idea of the passage?
a. Sentence 1
b. Sentence 9
c. Sentence 10
d. Sentence 12

MASTERY **Test 4**

Name ______________________ Section ____________

Date ____________ **Score** (number correct) ______ × 20 = ______%

Identify the topic sentence of each of the following paragraphs from college textbooks.

**A.** Paragraph from a college psychology textbook

### Types of Personality Tests

[1]Think of all the ways in which you differ from your best friend. [2]Psychologists use personality tests to identify the different traits that characterize an individual. [3]They think about what sets one person apart from another; they want to know what distinguishes people in one group from another. [4]For example, certain traits seem to separate shy people from outgoing people. [5]Two beliefs are basic to these attempts to understand and describe human personality. [6]The first is that personal traits of individuals give logic to their behavior. [7]The second belief is that those traits can be measured. [8]Personality tests that represent these two beliefs are known as either *objective* or *projective.*

—Adapted from Gerrig & Zimbardo, *Psychology and Life,* 16th ed., p. 460.

Topic sentence(s): _____

**B.** Paragraph from a college health textbook

### Determining What Triggers an Eating Disorder

[1]Before you can change a behavior, you must first determine what causes it. [2]Many people have found it helpful to keep a chart of their eating patterns: when they feel like eating, the amount of time they spend eating, where they are when they decide to eat, other activities they engage in during the meal (watching television or reading), whether they eat alone or with others, what and how much they consume, and how they felt before they took their first bite. [3]If you keep a detailed daily log of eating triggers for at least a week, you will discover useful clues about what in your environment or emotional makeup causes you to want food. [4]Typically, these dietary triggers center on problems in everyday living rather than on real hunger pangs. [5]Many people find that they eat when stressed or when they have problems in their relationships. [6]For other people, the same circumstances diminish their appetite, causing them to lose weight.

—Adapted from Donatelle, *Health: the Basics,* 5th ed., p. 270.

Topic sentence(s): _____

**C.** Paragraph from a college accounting textbook

### Cash Advances

[1]Many credit cards allow cash advances at automated teller machines (ATMs). [2]Since a cash advance represents credit extended by the sponsoring financial institution, interest

is charged on this transaction. [3]A transaction fee of 1 to 2 percent of the advance may also be charged. [4]Credit card companies also provide checks that you can use to make purchases that cannot be made by credit card. [5]The interest rate applied to cash advances is often higher than the interest rate charged on credit extended for specific credit card purchases. [6]The interest rate is applied at the time of the cash advance; the grace period that applies to purchases with a credit card does not apply to cash advances. [7]So, although cash advances are convenient, they can also be extremely costly.

—Madura, *Personal Finance*, 2nd ed., p. 196.

Topic sentence(s): ______

**D.** Paragraph from a college history textbook

Textbook Skills

**The First Lady**

[1]From Martha Washington to Laura Bush, first ladies have acted as informal advisers to the presidents. [2]In addition, they have made other important contributions to American society. [3]However, until recently, the only formal national recognition given to first ladies was a display of inaugural ball gowns at the Smithsonian Institution. [4]Not any more. [5]Most likely, the highly visible role Hillary Rodham Clinton played in the Clinton administration sharpened interest in first ladies. [6]Now the Smithsonian has an exhibit of the activities of all the first ladies. [7]The new exhibit is built around three themes. [8]First, the exhibit records the political role of the first ladies. [9]This includes how they were depicted in the media and how they were seen by the public. [10]Second, the exhibit notes their contributions to society, with a focus on their personal causes. [11]And third, of course, their inaugural gowns are still displayed.

—Adapted from O'Connor, Sabato, Haag, & Keith, *American Government: Continuity and Change, 2004 Texas Edition,* pp. 291–92.

Topic sentence(s): ______

**E.** Paragraph from a college communications textbook

Textbook Skills

[1]*USA Today* has had an intense effect on American newspaper publishing. [2]First, the paper uses much color and many graphics. [3]And it stresses a concise writing style; it uses short main stories and many summaries. [4]The paper also has a detailed and up-to-the-minute sports page. [5]It has a unique editorial opinion policy, and it offers a full-color weather page. [6]The paper is designed for an audience that is used to the color and quickness of television news stories. [7]Right away, editors of other newspapers began to imitate its color charts, weather layout, and other features.

—Adapted from Agee, Ault, & Emery, *Introduction to Mass Communications,* 12th ed., p. 139.

Topic sentence(s): ______

MASTERY **Test 5**

Name ______________ Section ______________

Date ______________ **Score** (number correct) ______ × 20 = ______%

Identify the topic sentence in each of the following paragraphs.

**A.** Paragraph from a college accounting textbook

### Cash Flow and Type of Job

[1]Income varies by job type. [2]Jobs that require specialized skills tend to pay higher salaries than those that require skills that can be obtained very quickly and easily. [3]The income level associated with specific skills is also affected by the demand for those skills. [4]The demand for people with a nursing license has been very high in recent years, so hospitals have been forced to pay high salaries to outbid other hospitals for nurses. [5]In contrast, the demand for people with a history or English literature degree is low because more students major in these area than there are jobs.

—Madura, *Personal Finance,* 2nd ed., p. 31.

Topic sentence(s): ______

**B.** Paragraph from a college health textbook

### Trust and a Healthy Relationship

[1]Relationships that are satisfying and stable share certain traits. [2]A key ingredient is *trust,* the degree of confidence partners feel in a relationship. [3]Without trust, intimacy will not develop, and the relationship could fail. [4]Trust includes three fundamental elements. [5]First, trust means predictability. [6]You can predict that your partner will act consistently in positive ways. [7]Second, trust means dependability. [8]You can rely on your partner to give support in all situations. [9]You know you can depend on him or her when you feel threatened with hurt or rejection. [10]Finally, trust means faith. [11]You feel absolutely certain about your partner's intentions and behaviors.

—Adapted from Donatelle, *Health: The Basics,* 5th ed., p. 113.

Topic sentence(s): ______

**C.** Paragraph from a college psychology textbook

### Brain Structure

[1]The brain is the most important component of your central nervous system. [2]The human brain has three interconnected layers: the brain stem and cerebellum, the limbic system, and the cerebrum. [3]The brain stem largely sustains basic life functions such as breathing, heart rate, and digestion. [4]The cerebellum coordinates bodily movement, and it affects some forms of learning. [5]The limbic system plays an important role in

motivation, emotion, and memory. [6]The cerebrum controls the higher processes of language and thought.

—Adapted from Gerrig & Zimbardo, *Psychology and Life,* 16th ed., p. 71.

Topic sentence(s): ______

**D.** Paragraph from a college education textbook

[1]Building expectations for student success means encouraging students to see that success can be reached through their own efforts. [2]Helping students realize that they control their fortunes in school by the amount of time and effort they are willing to put into their work is an important task. [3]This control principle can be impressed on students by having them keep track of the time they spend on a unit or project. [4]In addition, students can be shown how to evaluate their work using criteria developed by the teacher or the class. [5]Making students aware of their progress through the use of charts and graphs helps them see that they have control over their achievement. [6]They realize that the grades they receive are not given by the teacher but rather are the result of their own efforts.

—Wilen, Ishler, Hutchison, & Kindsvatter, *Dynamics of Effective Teaching,* 4th ed., p. 41.

Topic sentence(s): ______

**E.** Paragraph from a college English handbook

**Discussing Your Reading with Others**

[1]One of the pleasures of reading comes from discussing what you have read with others. [2]Although reading is usually thought of as a private affair (just you and the text existing quietly together), it is also a social act. [3]Reading has a social dynamic not only because you bring to your reading a wide range of social experiences but also because in reading you communicate with another person—the author. [4]You may also find yourself bringing your reading into everyday social situations. [5]When you discuss what you have read with others, you discover different ideas in the reading. [6]Other people's responses to texts reflect their social histories and backgrounds, just as your responses do. [7]Hearing what someone else thinks about the material deepens your understanding of it.

—Adapted from DiYanni & Hoy, *The Scribner Handbook for Writers,* 3rd ed., p. 45.

Topic sentence(s): ______

MASTERY **Test 6**

Name ______________ Section ______
Date ________ **Score** (number correct) ______ × 25 = ______%

Read the passage. Then answer the questions that follow it.

Textbook Skills

**Tone in a Poem**

[1]In old Western movies, when one hombre taunts another, it is customary for the second to drawl, "Smile when you say that, pardner" or "Mister, I don't like your tone of voice." [2]Sometimes in reading a poem, although we can neither see a face nor hear a voice, we can infer the poet's attitude from other evidence.

[3]Like tone of voice, tone in literature often conveys an attitude toward the person addressed. [4]Like the manner of a person, the manner of a poem may be friendly or belligerent toward its reader. [5]Again like tone of voice, the tone of a poem may tell us how the speaker feels about himself or herself: cocksure or humble, sad or glad. [6]But usually when we ask, "What is the tone of a poem?" we mean "What attitude does the poet take toward a theme or subject?" [7]Is the poet being affectionate, hostile, earnest, playful, sarcastic, or what? [8]We may never be able to know, of course, the poet's personal feelings. [9]All we need know is how to feel when we read the poem.

[10]Strictly speaking, tone isn't an attitude; it is whatever in the poem makes an attitude clear to us: the choice of certain words instead of others, the picking out of certain details. [11]In A. E. Houseman's "Loveliest of Trees," for example, the poet communicates his admiration for a cherry tree's beauty by singling out for attention its white blossoms; had he wanted to show his dislike for the tree, he might have concentrated on its broken branches, birdlime, or snails. [12]To perceive the tone of a poem correctly, we need to read the poem carefully, paying attention to whatever suggestions we find in it.

—Kennedy & Gioia, *Literature: An Introduction to Fiction, Poetry, and Drama*, 8th ed., p. 757.

______ **1.** What is the topic of the passage?
- a. Old Western movies
- b. The tone of a poem
- c. Tone
- d. A. E. Houseman's "Loveliest of Trees"

______ **2.** Which sentence or sentences state the central idea of the passage?
- a. Sentences 1 and 8
- b. Sentence 2
- c. Sentence 9
- d. Sentence 11

______ **3.** Which sentence states the main idea of the second paragraph?
- a. Sentence 3
- b. Sentence 5
- c. Sentence 8
- d. Sentence 9

_____ **4.** Which sentence or sentences state the main idea of the third paragraph?

a. Sentences 10 and 12
b. Sentence 10
c. Sentence 11
d. Sentence 12

### VISUAL VOCABULARY

_____ The tone or attitude of the parent portrayed in this photo is

a. compassionate.
b. angry.
c. joyful.

CHAPTER

4

# Supporting Details

## CHAPTER PREVIEW

## Before Reading About Supporting Details

In Chapter 3, you learned several important ideas that will help you as you work through this chapter. Use the following questions to call up your prior knowledge about supporting details.

What is a main idea? (page 106.) ______________________________

______________________________

______________________________

What are the three parts of most paragraphs? (page 111.) ______________________________,

______________________________, and ______________________________.

Define supporting details. (page 113.) ______________________________

______________________________

What are the different possible locations of topic sentences? (pages 119–128.)

______________________________

______________________________

What is a central idea? (page 128.) ____________________

____________________

## Questions for Locating Supporting Details

To locate supporting details, an effective reader turns the main idea into a question by asking one of the following reporter's questions: *who, what, when, where, why,* or *how.* The answer to this question will yield a specific set of supporting details. For example, the question *why* is often answered by listing and explaining reasons or causes. The question *how* is answered by explaining a process. The answer to the question *when* is based on time order. An author strives to answer some or all of these questions with the details in the paragraph. You may want to try out several of the reporter's questions as you turn the main idea into a question. Experiment to discover which question is best answered by the details.

**Supporting details** explain, develop, and illustrate the main idea.

Take, for example, the topic "dog bites." An author might choose to write about a few of the reasons a dog might bite someone. The main idea of such a paragraph may read as follows:

**Main idea:** In certain situations a dog's natural aggression will make it more likely to bite.

Using the word *when* turns the main idea into the following question: "When is a dog likely to bite?" Read the following paragraph for the answers to this question.

**A Dog's Natural Aggression**

[1]In certain situations, a dog's natural aggression will make it more likely to bite. [2]For example, a dog may react aggressively if its personal space is invaded. [3]Therefore, a dog that is sleeping, eating, or nurturing its puppies may very well react with violence to defend itself, its food, or its offspring. [4]Aggression may also occur when a dog has been fenced in or tethered outside. [5]In these cases, the dog may feel easily frustrated or threatened and thus feel the urge to protect itself or its territory by biting. [6]A final situation that arouses the dog's animal aggression occurs when a person runs away in fear from a dog. [7]A dog's natural desire is to pursue prey; therefore, running past or away from a dog will almost always incite the animal to give chase and perhaps bite.

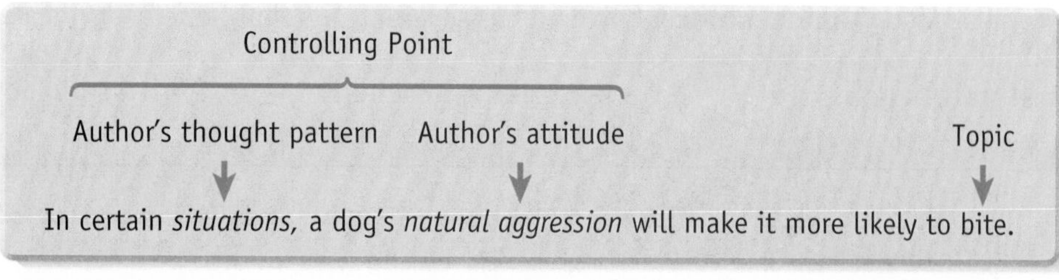


| **First situation** | **Second situation** | **Third situation** |
|---|---|---|
| A dog may react aggressively if its personal space is invaded. | Aggression may also occur when a dog has been fenced in or tethered outside. | Animal aggression occurs when a person runs away in fear from a dog. |

The supporting details for this main idea answer the question "when?" by listing the situations that are likely to arouse a dog's aggression and lead to biting. Then the paragraph discusses why the dog behaves this way.

Note the relationship between the author's controlling point and the supporting details.

Notice also that the details about situations directly explain the main idea. However, additional supporting details were given in the paragraph that are not listed. Each of the main supporting details needed further explanation. This paragraph shows us that there are two kinds of supporting details: details that explain the main idea and details that explain other details.

**EXAMPLE** Read the paragraph. Turn the topic sentence into a question using one of the reporter's questions (Who? What? When? Where? Why? How?). Write the question in the space provided. Fill in the graph with the answers to the question you have created.

**The Healthful Traits of Olive Oil**

[1]Olive oil has several traits that benefit our health. [2]First, olive oil is a monounsaturated fat. [3]Monounsaturated fats lower blood cholesterol levels; they keep arteries free of blockages, and they reduce the chances of heart attacks and strokes. [4]Second, olive oil contains antioxidants. [5]Just like rust on a car, oxidation damages our cells. [6]Antioxidants help prevent oxidation. [7]They also may help increase immune function; thus they may decrease risk of infection and cancer. [8]Third, olive oil also has polyphenols. [9]Polyphenols also strengthen the immune system and protect the body from infection. [10]They have been linked to preventing cancer and heart disease.

**Question based on topic sentence:** ______________________________

______________________________________________________________

**Topic sentence:** Olive oil has several traits that benefit our health.

| **First trait/benefit** | **Second trait/benefit** | **Third trait/benefit** |
|---|---|---|
| (1) ______ | (2) ______ | (3) ______ |
| ______ | ______ | ______ |
| ______ | ______ | ______ |
| ______ | ______ | ______ |
| ______ | ______ | ______ |
| ______ | ______ | |
| ______ | | |

**EXPLANATION** Using the reporter's question *What?*, you should have turned the topic sentence into the following question: *What are the several traits of olive oil that benefit our health?* The answer to this question yields the supporting details. Compare your answers to the following: (1) Monounsaturated fat, (2) Antioxidant, and (3) Polyphenol.

## PRACTICE 1

Read the paragraph. Turn the topic sentence into a question using one of the reporter's questions (Who? What? When? Where? Why? How?). Write the question in the space provided. Fill in the graph with the answers to the question you have created.

### Halitosis

[1]Halitosis, more commonly known as bad breath, occurs due to several specific circumstances. [2]As certain foods are digested, they result in bad breath. [3]Foods such as garlic and onions are absorbed into the bloodstream, carried to the lungs and expelled as bad breath through the mouth. [4]When dry mouth occurs and the flow of saliva decreases, bad breath occurs because saliva cleanses the mouth. [5]When oral hygiene is poor, bad breath is the result. [6]Improper brushing and flossing leaves food particles in the mouth. [7]In these instances, bacteria grows and creates sulfur compounds that also result in bad breath. [8]Finally, bad breath occurs when a medical disorder is present. [9]Bad breath may be a warning sign of infections of the sinuses or respiratory tract, liver or kidney problems, and diabetes.

**Question based on topic sentence:** ______

**Topic sentence:** Halitosis, more commonly known as bad breath, occurs due to several specific circumstances.

| First circumstance | Second circumstance | Third circumstance | Fourth circumstance |
|---|---|---|---|
| (1) ______________ | (2) When dry mouth occurs | (3) ______________ | (4) When a medical disorder is present |

## Major and Minor Details

A supporting detail will always be one of two types:

> A **major detail** directly explains, develops, or illustrates the *main idea.*
> A **minor detail** explains, develops, or illustrates a *major detail.*

A **major detail** is directly tied to the main idea. Without the major details, the author's main idea would not be clear because the major details are the principal points the author is making about the topic.

In contrast, a **minor detail** explains a major detail. The minor details could be left out, and the main idea would still be clear. Thus minor details are not as important as major details. Minor details are used to add interest and to give further descriptions, examples, testimonies, analysis, illustrations, and reasons for the major details. To better understand the flow of ideas, study the following diagram:

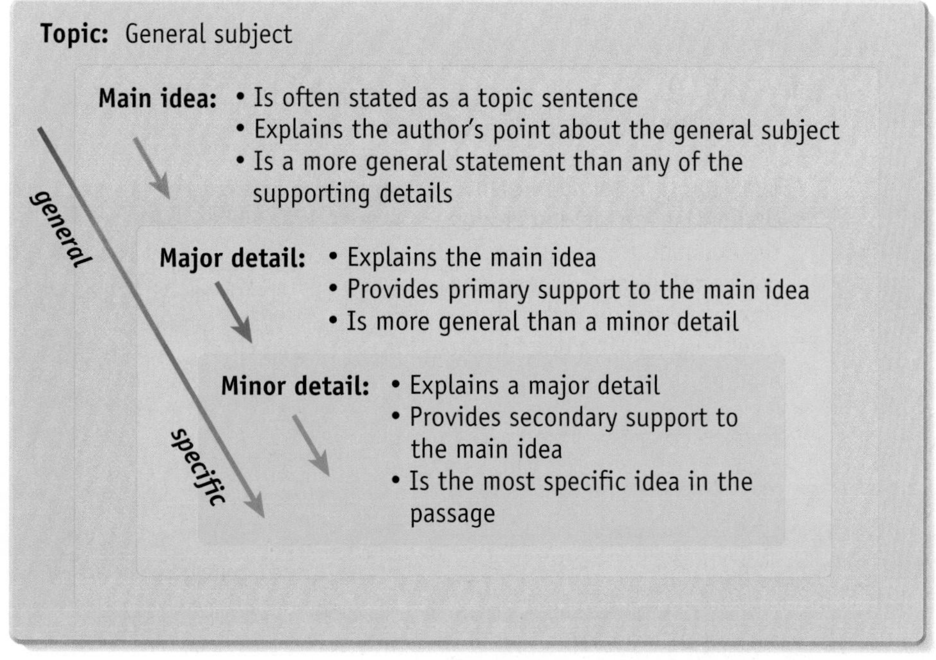

As ideas move from general to specific details, the author often uses signal words to introduce a new detail. These signal words—such as *first*, *second*, *next*, *in addition*, or *finally*—can help you identify major and minor details.

**EXAMPLE** See if you can tell the difference between major and minor details. Read the following paragraph. The second sentence is the topic sentence, which states the main idea.

### The Differences Between Porpoises and Dolphins

[1]Porpoises and dolphins are so similar in general appearance that many people mistake one for the other. [2]However, these two sea mammals do have distinct differences. [3]One difference is their shape. [4]Porpoises are smaller and plumper than dolphins, which have long, streamlined bodies. [5]In addition, the porpoise has a rounded head and a blunt snout, in contrast to the dolphin's beaklike nose. [6]A second difference can be seen in their size. [7]Porpoises rarely grow to be more than 6 feet in length or weigh more than 300 pounds. [8]In contrast, dolphins can be 4 to 26 feet long, and they can weigh 70 to 1,500 pounds. [9]The animals' fins also differ significantly. [10]Porpoises have a small, triangular dorsal fin, whereas dolphins have a prominent dorsal fin that curves toward the animal's tail. [11]Finally, the teeth of these marine mammals have very different shapes. [12]A dolphin's teeth are sharp and conelike; in contrast, the porpoise's teeth are flatter and spade-shaped.

**VISUAL VOCABULARY**

The Vaquita is found only in shallow lagoons in and around the Colorado River delta in the northern Gulf of California and Mexico. Based on this picture, would you call it a dolphin or a porpoise?

______________ Why?

______________

______________

Complete the following outline of the paragraph.

Stated main idea: These two sea mammals possess distinct differences.

A. ______________________________

1. ______________________________

______________________________

2. The porpoise has a rounded head and a blunt snout, in contrast to the dolphin's beaklike nose.

B. ______________________________

1. Porpoises rarely grow to be more than 6 feet in length or weigh more than 300 pounds.

2. ______________________________

C. The animals' fins also differ significantly.

1. Porpoises have a small, triangular dorsal fin.

2. ______________________________

D. The teeth of these marine mammals have very different shapes.

1. A dolphin's teeth are sharp and conelike.

2. The porpoise's teeth are flatter and spade-shaped.

**EXPLANATION** Every detail in the paragraph supports the main idea, which states that porpoises and dolphins are different. The author supplies four major supporting details that directly explain the main idea. In addition, the author gives further information by supplying two minor supporting details for each of the major supporting details.

The first major supporting detail that explains the main idea is sentence 3: "One difference is their shape." This first major supporting detail is signaled by the words *one difference*. However, this detail raises another question: the reader needs to know how their shapes differ. Therefore, the author supplies the explanation with two minor details. Sentence 4, "Porpoises are smaller and plumper than dolphins, which have long, streamlined bodies," is a minor detail that explains the major detail about the differences in shape.

Sentence 5 is a minor detail that explains how the shape of the porpoise's nose differs from that of the dolphin. The second major detail directly related to the main idea is sentence 6, "A second difference can be seen in their size." Note that this major detail has been introduced using the signal words *a second difference*. This major detail also needs additional information, and the author supplies two minor details: one to note the size of porpoises and the second to state the size of dolphins. Note that in sentence 8, "In contrast, dolphins can be 4 to 26 feet long, and they can weigh 70 to 1,500 pounds," the second minor detail is introduced with the signal words *in contrast*.

The third major supporting detail that explains the differences between these two animals focuses on their fins. The minor details for this point are combined in one sentence. In sentence 10, the phrase "dolphins have a prominent dorsal fin that curves toward the animal's tail," is the second part of the sentence that contains the two minor supporting details. This particular minor detail is introduced with the signal word *whereas*, which points out a detail of difference.

The fourth major supporting detail is in sentence 11, "Finally, the teeth of these marine mammals have very different shapes." The signal word *finally* alerts the reader to the last major supporting detail. Sentence 12 is the minor detail that explains the differences in the tooth shape of each animal.

## PRACTICE 2

Read the following paragraph. Then identify the major and minor details by completing the outline that follows it.

### Safety Tips for Meeting People Online

[1]Following a few basic safety tips makes it more likely that you will enjoy a safe and fun date with someone you meet online. [2]First, use caution, and start out slowly. [3]Start by communicating only through e-mail. [4]Don't respond to anyone who is rude or offensive or makes you feel uncomfortable. [5]Trust your instincts. [6]Second, protect your anonymity. [7]Never give your home address or phone number to anybody. [8]If you decide to communicate directly with someone you have met online, you be the one to make the phone call. [9]Third, ask for a photograph. [10]A photo can give you important additional information about the person. [11]Ask for several photos in different circumstances, featuring casual to formal dress. [12]An unwillingness to share photographs should be a warning that the person has something to hide. [13]Finally, if you decide to meet in person, choose a public place. [14]Never arrange for your date to pick you up at your home. [15]Be sure to leave word with a friend or family member about where you are going and whom you are meeting.

**Stated main idea:** Following a few basic safety tips makes it more likely that you will enjoy a safe and fun date with someone you meet online.

**A.** ______________________________

1. Start by communicating only through e-mail.
2. ______________________________
3. Trust your instincts.

**B.** ______________________________

1. Never give your home address or phone number to anybody.
2. If you decide to communicate directly with someone you have met online, you be the one to make the phone call.

**C.** ______________________________

1. A photo can give you important additional information about the person.
2. Ask for several photos in different circumstances, featuring casual to formal dress.
3. An unwillingness to share photographs should be a warning that the person has something to hide.

**D.** Finally, if you decide to meet in person, choose a public place.

1. Never arrange for your date to pick you up at your home.
2. ______________________________

## Creating a Summary from Annotations

Reading for main ideas and major supporting details is an excellent study technique. After you read, writing down main ideas and major supporting details in a summary is an effective strategy to deepen your understanding and provide you with study notes for review. (For more reading strategies see Chapter 1.) A **summary** condenses a paragraph or passage to only its primary points by restating the main idea, major supporting details, and important examples. Often you will want to paraphrase, that is, restate the ideas in your own words. Other times, you may need to use the exact language of the text to ensure accuracy. For example, scientific or medical terms have precise meanings that must be memorized; thus your summaries of these types of ideas would include the original language of the text.

A **summary** is a brief, clear restatement of the most important points of a paragraph or passage.

Different lengths of text require different lengths of summaries. For example, a paragraph can be summarized in one sentence or a few sentences. A passage of several paragraphs can be reduced to one paragraph, and a much longer selection such as a chapter in a textbook may require a summary of a page or two in length.

To create a summary after reading, you can **annotate**, or mark, your text during reading. For example, as you read, circle the main idea and underline the major supporting details and important examples. To learn more about annotating a text see page 659 in Part Two.

**EXAMPLE** Read the following paragraph from a college accounting textbook. Circle the main idea, and underline the major supporting details. Then complete the summary.

Textbook Skills

**Liquid Assets**

[1]**Liquid assets** are financial assets that can be easily sold without a loss in value. [2]They are especially useful for covering upcoming expenses. [3]Some of the more common liquid assets are cash, checking accounts, and savings accounts. [4]Cash is handy to cover small purchases, while a checking account is convenient for large purchases. [5]Savings accounts are desirable because they pay interest on the money that is deposited. [6]For example, if your savings account offers an interest rate of 4 percent, you earn annual interest of $4 for every $100 deposited in your account.

—Madura, *Personal Finance,* 2nd ed., p. 40.

**Summary:** Liquid assets are ______________________________

______________________________________________;

For example, three types are ______________________________

______________________________________________

**EXPLANATION** The main idea about the topic "liquid assets" is stated in the first sentence, which is the topic sentence of the paragraph: "Liquid assets are financial assets that can be easily sold without a loss in value." The paragraph goes on to list the following examples: cash, checking accounts, and savings accounts. To create a summary of the information, combine the main idea and major supporting details. Compare your summary to the following: Liquid assets are financial assets that can be easily sold without a loss in value. For example, three types are cash, checking accounts, and savings accounts.

## PRACTICE 3

Read the following paragraph from a college health textbook. Circle the main idea, and underline the major supporting details. Complete the summary by filling in the blanks with information from the passage.

### The Body's Response to Stress

[1]Whenever we are surprised by a sudden stressor, such as someone swerving into our lane of traffic, the adrenal glands jump into action. [2]These two almond-shaped glands sitting atop the kidneys secrete adrenaline and other hormones into the bloodstream. [3]As a result, the heart speeds up, breathing rate increases, blood pressure elevates, and the flow of blood to the muscles increases. [4]This sudden burst of energy and strength is believed to provide the extra edge that has helped generations of humans survive during adversity. [5]This response is believed to be one of our most basic, innate survival instincts. [6]Known as the **fight or flight response**, this physiological reaction prepares the body to combat a real or perceived threat. [7]It is a point at which our bodies go on the alert to either fight or escape.

—Donatelle, *Health: the Basics,* 5th ed., p. 54.

**Summary:** The **fight or flight response** is a ______________ reaction that prepares the body to combat a real or perceived threat. For example, someone swerving into our lane of traffic triggers the ______________ glands to speed up the ______________, increase ______________ rate, elevate blood pressure, and increase the flow of blood to the ______________.

## Textbook Skills: Chapter-End Questions in a Textbook

Textbooks often provide questions at the end of a chapter or section to help you identify and remember the most important points. In addition, the answers to questions at the end of a section summarize its main idea and major supporting details. Often, to deepen learning, the chapter-end questions will also ask you to give some examples of minor details. As you read, annotate your text by marking content words, main ideas, and major supporting details. These key ideas will help you answer the chapter-end questions. Some students look at the chapter-end questions before they read as a guide to what is most important. These students use chapter-end questions before, during, and after reading.

**EXAMPLE** Read the following section from the college textbook *Introduction to Mass Communication,* 12th ed. Turn the heading into a question. Annotate the text as you read by underlining main ideas, circling content words, and underlining their definitions. Then, answer the questions.

### What Communication Means

[1]Each of us communicates with another person by directing a message to one or more of the person's senses—sight, sound, touch, taste, or smell. [2]This is known as *interpersonal communication,* in contrast to *intrapersonal communication,* in which one "talks to oneself." [3]When we smile, we communicate a desire for friendliness; the tone in which we say "good morning" can indicate feelings all the way from surliness to warm pleasure; and the words we choose in speaking or writing convey a message we want to "put across" to the other person. [4]The more effectively we select and deliver these words, the better the communication.

[5]In today's complex society, one-to-one communication frequently is inadequate. [6]To be effective, our important messages must reach numerous people at one time. [7]The next step is *group communication,* such as when a homeowner couple invite their neighbors for coffee in order to propose a neighborhood improvement plan. [8]If the sponsoring couple convinces a local television news program to air a story about the project, thousands of people learn about it. [9]This is *mass communication.*

[10]The success of the message, in all phases of communication, depends on the *frame of reference,* that is, the life experience and mind-set of both the sender and receiver of the message. [11]The more these frames of reference overlap, the more likely there will be understanding and possible acceptance of the message. [12]One-to-one communication has heavy overlap when people are close friends or agree wholeheartedly on the subject of interpersonal discussion. [13]As the size of the receiving audience grows, these attributes decline. [14]So does the degree of interpersonal success.

[15]For example, a news story about plans by Congress to increase unemployment benefits raises hope in the mind of a person who fears being laid off a job; the same dispatch may disturb a struggling entrepreneur who sees in it the possibility of higher taxes.

[16]Similarly, when a presidential candidate appears on a national TV talk show he reaches millions of voters, vastly more than he could through

handshaking tours. [17]His use of mass communication may be a comparative failure, however, if he is unable to project over the air the same feeling of sincerity and ability that he displays through a handshake and a smile in personal contacts.

[18]The art of mass communication, then, is much more difficult than that of face-to-face discussion.[19] The communicator who is addressing thousands of different personalities simultaneously cannot adjust an appeal to meet their individual reactions. [20]An approach that convinces one part of the audience may alienate another part. [21]The successful mass communicator is one who finds the right method of expression to establish empathy with the largest possible number of individuals in the audience. [22]Psychological research and knowledge of communication theory help the speaker to "push the right buttons."

—Agee, Ault, and Emery. *Introduction to Mass Communication*, 12th ed., pp. 64–65.

**1.** What is interpersonal communication? ______________________

______________________________________________

______________________________________________

**2.** What is intrapersonal communication? ______________________

______________________________________________

**3.** When does group communication occur? ______________________

______________________________________________

**4.** When does mass communication occur? ______________________

______________________________________________

**5.** How and why does "frame of reference" affect communication? ________

______________________________________________

______________________________________________

______________________________________________

**EXPLANATION** To answer these questions, you should have circled the following terms and underlined their definitions: *interpersonal communication, intrapersonal communication, group communication, mass communication,* and *frame of reference.* Compare your answers to the chapter-end question to the following:

1. What is interpersonal communication? Interpersonal communication is directing a message to one or more of another person's senses—sight, sound, touch, taste, or smell.

2. What is intrapersonal communication? Intrapersonal communication occurs when one talks to oneself.

3. When does group communication occur? Group communication occurs when a message must reach numerous people at one time.

4. When does mass communication occur? Mass communication occurs when a message must reach thousands of people.

5. How and why does "frame of reference" affect communication? Frame of reference is made up of the life experiences and mind-sets of the people communicating. Understanding and accepting a message is more likely if the message is based on a shared frame of reference.

## PRACTICE 3

Read the following section from the college textbook *Introduction to Mass Communication,* 12th ed. Annotate the text as you read by underlining the main ideas, circling the content words, and underlining their definitions. Then answer the questions.

### The Language Used to Research Communication

[1]Researchers identify four basic elements in the communication process. [2]To be precise in their findings, they use specialized terms to describe them. [3]These elements are:

[4]The *communicator,* called the *encoder.*

[5]The *message.* The words, pictures, or sounds comprising the message are called *codes or symbols.*

[6]The *channel.* In mass communication, this is one of the media, such as newspapers, magazines, radio, or television.

[7]The *audience.* A person in the audience is known as a *decoder.*

[8]The communicator understands the characteristics of the channel to be used and studies the varying comprehension levels of the groups of people comprising the total audience. [9]The message is molded to the requirements of each channel—pictures on television against only words on radio, for example—and to the characteristics of the audience being sought.

[10]Before a message enters our mass communication system, it must be approved by someone of authority within the medium. [11]These men and

women, known to researchers as *gatekeepers,* include the responsible editor on a newspaper or magazine staff, the news editor of a radio or television station, and an advertising director or the equivalent for commercial messages. [12]These people judge the messages for public interest, effectiveness, taste, and legality. [13]Since more candidates for publication exist than limited newspaper space and air time can absorb, news stories and entertainment offerings must be weighed against others in the same category—certainly not an exact science. [14]The lack of such gatekeepers in most computer communication services, such as online databases and the Internet, differentiates them from traditional mass media.

[15]Exerting pressure on the gatekeepers, in attempts to influence their decisions as to what will or won't be published, are organizations and individuals known to researchers as *regulators.* [16]These include public pressure groups, government agencies, advertisers, consumers, courts, and legislatures. [17]Such pressures, sometimes applied publicly and sometimes behind the scenes, do affect media content and performance.

—Adapted from Agee, Ault, and Emery. *Introduction to Mass Communication, 12th ed.,* pp. 65–66.

**1.** Who is the encoder? ______________________________

**2.** What makes up the message? ______________________________

______________________________

**3.** Who is the decoder? ______________________________

**4.** Who are gatekeepers and what is their role? ______________________________

______________________________

**5.** Who are regulators and what is their role? ______________________________

______________________________

______________________________

## Chapter Review

Test your understanding of what you have read in this chapter by filling in the blank with a word from the box. Use each word once.

| after reading | minor detail | summary |
|---|---|---|
| annotate | paraphrase | supporting details |
| during reading | question | why |
| major detail | specific | |

1. ______________ explain, develop, and illustrate a main idea.
2. To locate supporting details, an effective reader turns the main idea into a ______________.
3. One helpful question for locating a main idea is ______________.
4. A ______________ directly explains, develops, or illustrates the main idea.
5. A ______________ explains, develops, or illustrates the major detail.
6. In a paragraph or passage, ideas usually flow from general to ______________ ideas.
7. Creating a summary is an effective ______________ activity.
8. A ______________ is a brief, clear restatement of the most important points of a paragraph or passage.
9. To ______________ means to restate the ideas in your own words.
10. To create a summary after reading, you can ______________ or mark your text ______________ by underlining main ideas and important supporting details and examples.

## Applications

### Application 1: Main Ideas, Major Supporting Details, and Minor Supporting Details

Read the following paragraph from a government website. Answer the questions.

**Mother's Drinking Puts Baby at Risk**

[1]Mothers who drank alcohol heavily during pregnancy gave birth to children who had damage to the nerves in the arms and legs, according to a study by researchers at the National Institute of Child Health and Human Development. [2]The study was conducted in partnership with researchers at the University

of Chile. [3]Adults who drink excessive amounts of alcohol can experience peripheral neuropathy; this is a condition that occurs when nerves involved in carrying messages between the central nervous system (the brain and spinal cord) and the rest of the body are damaged. [4]This can lead to tingling sensations, numbness, pain, or weakness. [5]"Heavy drinking" is defined as having four standard drinks per day (one standard drink is equivalent to one can of beer, one glass of wine, or one mixed drink).[6]The children exposed to alcohol before they were born faced significant problems in conducting a message through the nerves—both at one month and at one year of age. [7]The alcohol-exposed children did not show any improvement in nerve function by the time they reached their first birthday. [8]The study suggests that heavy alcohol consumption by the mother may cause permanent nerve damage to her child.

—Adapted from "New Study Finds Babies Born to Mothers Who Drink Alcohol Heavily May Suffer Permanent Nerve Damage." NIH News. National Institute of Health. 8 March 2004. 13 June 2004.

_____ **1.** Sentence 1 is a
- a. main idea.
- b. major supporting detail.
- c. minor supporting detail.

_____ **2.** Sentence 5 is a
- a. main idea.
- b. major supporting detail.
- c. minor supporting detail.

_____ **3.** Sentence 8 is a
- a. main idea.
- b. major supporting detail.
- c. minor supporting detail.

## Application 2: Using the Main Idea and Supporting Details to Summarize

Read the following passage from a college sociology textbook. Annotate the passage by circling the main idea and underlining the major supporting details. Then complete the summary with information from the passage.

Textbook Skills

### Biological Aging

[1]Biologists and physiologists study aging in everything from one-celled animals to human populations. [2]They identify two causes of aging. [3]First, **intrinsic** aging is due to normal physical function. [4]Second, **extrinsic** aging is due to life style, environment, and disease. [5]Intrinsic aging includes decreases in lung capacity, loss of brain cells, and hardened arteries. [6]Extrinsic aging includes changes in the body due to sunlight, smoking, or noise. [7]Scientists try to separate out the effects of these two causes of aging.

[8]Experts list four criteria, or rules, for intrinsic (or true) aging. [9]First, true aging is universal. [10]It occurs in all members of a species if they live long enough. [11]Wrinkled skin in humans fits this definition. [12]Second, true aging is basic to the organism. [13]A person cannot undo it or stop it. [14]Decreased lung elasticity falls into this category. [15]Third, true aging is progressive. [16]Debris builds up in the cell over time until the cell stops working. [17]Fourth, true aging is deleterious. [18]It leads to decline in physical function. [19]This puts the person at risk of illness and leads to death.

—Adapted from Novak, *Issues in Aging: An Introduction to Gerontology*, 1997, p. 96.

**VISUAL VOCABULARY**

Kudzu has a **deleterious** effect on other plants; the fast-growing vine climbs over other plants (including natives) and kills them.

The best synonym for the word *deleterious* is ____________

a. valuable.
b. harmful.
c. immediate.

**Summary:** Scientists identify two causes of biological (**1**) ____________. First, (**2**) ____________ aging is due to normal physical function. Second, (**3**) ____________ aging is due to (**4**) ____________, environment, and disease. Intrinsic (or true) aging has four criteria: true aging is universal; it is basic to the organism; it is (**5**) ____________; and it is deleterious.

# REVIEW Test 1

## Main Ideas, Major and Minor Supporting Details

Read the paragraph, and answer the questions.

## Job Outlook for Physical Therapists

[1]Employment of physical therapists is expected to grow faster than the average for all occupations through 2012. [2]Future Federal legislation may impose limits on payment for therapy services, which may have a negative effect on the short-term job outlook for physical therapists. [3]However, over the long run, the demand for physical therapists should continue to rise as growth in the number of individuals with disabilities or limited function spurs demand for therapy services. [4]First, as people age, they are more likely to need physical therapy. [5]The growing elderly population is particularly vulnerable to chronic and debilitating conditions that require therapeutic services. [6]Also, the baby-boom generation is entering the prime age for heart attacks and strokes, increasing the demand for cardiac and physical rehabilitation. [7]Second, medical and technological advances will create a greater demand for physical therapy. [8]Young people will need physical therapy as technological advances save the lives of a larger number of newborns with severe birth defects. [9]Future medical developments also should permit a higher percentage of trauma victims to survive; many of these individuals will likely need physical therapy. [10]In addition, growth may result from advances in medical technology that could permit the treatment of more disabling conditions. [11]Finally, widespread interest in promoting health also should increase demand for physical therapy services. [12]A growing number of employers are using physical therapists to evaluate worksites, develop exercise programs, and teach safe work habits to employees in the hope of reducing injuries.

—Adapted from Bureau of Labor Statistics, U.S. Department of Labor, *Occupational Outlook Handbook, 2004–05 Edition*, Physical Therapists.

______ **1.** Sentence 3 is a
a. main idea.
b. major supporting detail.
c. minor supporting detail.

______ **2.** Sentence 4 is a
a. main idea.
b. major supporting detail.
c. minor supporting detail.

______ **3.** Sentence 6 is a
a. main idea.
b. major supporting detail.
c. minor supporting detail.

______ **4.** Sentence 7 is a
a. main idea.
b. major supporting detail.
c. minor supporting detail.

______ 5. Sentence 12 is a
a. main idea.
b. major supporting detail.
c. minor supporting detail.

## REVIEW Test 2

### Main Ideas, Major and Minor Supporting Details

Read the paragraph and answer the questions.

**West Nile Virus: What You Need to Know**

[1]West Nile Virus (WNV) is a potentially serious illness. [2]Experts believe WNV is a seasonal epidemic in North America that flares up in the summer and continues into the fall. [3]The general public must understand symptoms of WNV and how it is transmitted. [4]WNV affects the central nervous system, and its symptoms vary. [5]Nearly 80 percent of people who are infected will not show any symptoms at all. [6]Up to 20 percent of the people who become infected will display mild symptoms. [7]Mild symptoms include fever, headache, and body aches, nausea, vomiting, and sometimes swollen lymph glands or a skin rash on the chest, stomach, and back. [8]Symptoms usually last a few days. [9]About one in 150 people infected with WNV will develop severe illness. [10]The severe symptoms can include high fever, headache, neck stiffness, stupor, disorientation, coma, tremors, convulsions, muscle weakness, vision loss, numbness, and paralysis. [11]These symptoms may last several weeks, and neurological effects may be permanent. [12]WNV is transmitted several ways. [13]Generally, WNV is spread by the bite of an infected mosquito. [14]Mosquitoes become infected when they feed on infected birds. [15]Infected mosquitoes can then spread WNV to humans and other animals when they bite. [16]In a very small number of cases, it also has spread through blood transfusions, organ transplants, breastfeeding, and even during pregnancy from mother to baby. [17]WNV is not spread through casual contact such as touching or kissing a person with the virus. [18]People are better able to protect themselves once they understand the symptoms of West Nile Virus and how it is spread.

—Adapted from "West Nile Virus: What You Need To Know CDC Factsheet," Centers for Disease Control and Prevention. 9 June 2004.

______ 1. Which sentence is the topic sentence that states both the topic and the author's controlling point about the topic?
a. Sentence 1
b. Sentence 2
c. Sentence 3

_____ **2.** Sentence 4 is a
a. main idea.
b. major supporting detail.
c. minor supporting detail.

_____ **3.** Sentence 8 is a
a. main idea.
b. major supporting detail.
c. minor supporting detail.

_____ **4.** Sentence 12 is a
a. main idea.
b. major supporting detail.
c. minor supporting detail.

_____ **5.** Sentence 18 is a
a. main idea.
b. major supporting detail.
c. minor supporting detail.

# REVIEW Test 3

## Main Ideas, Supporting Details, and Summarizing

Read the following news release published by the Federal Trade Commission. Answer the questions, and complete the summary.

### Cigars: No Such Thing As a Safe Smoke

[1]Since 2000, cigar packages and ads have been required to warn smokers about the serious health risks of cigar smoking. [2]Whether you buy Coronas or Churchills, Panatelas, Robustos, Lonsdales, or any other kind of cigar, you will see five new federally mandated health warnings. [3]The messages should sound familiar: Cigarette companies have been required to give similar health warnings since the mid-1960's and smokeless tobacco manufacturers since the mid-1980's.

[4]The warnings came about as a result of a report by the National Cancer Institute detailing the health risks of cigar smoking. [5]Specifically, cigar smoking can cause cancers of the mouth, esophagus, pharynx, larynx, and lungs. [6]For smokers who inhale, the health risks increase dramatically. [7]Cigar smoking also can cause heart disease and emphysema.

[8]The warnings, which cigar companies are required to rotate, include:

| | |
|---|---|
| **SURGEON GENERAL WARNING:** | Cigar Smoking Can Cause Cancers Of The Mouth And Throat, Even If You Do Not Inhale. |
| **SURGEON GENERAL WARNING:** | Cigar Smoking Can Cause Lung Cancer And Heart Disease. |
| **SURGEON GENERAL WARNING:** | Tobacco Use Increases The Risk Of Infertility, Stillbirth And Low Birth Weight. |
| **SURGEON GENERAL WARNING:** | Cigars Are Not A Safe Alternative To Cigarettes. |
| **SURGEON GENERAL WARNING:** | Tobacco Smoke Increases The Risk Of Lung Cancer And Heart Disease, Even In Nonsmokers. |

[9]Cigar companies must display these warnings clearly and prominently on packages, in print ads, on audio and video ads, on the Internet, and on point-of-purchase displays. [10]The point, say federal consumer protection and health officials, is to make sure that companies disclose the health risks of cigar smoking and that consumers understand that there's no such thing as a safe smoke.

—Adapted from "Cigars: No Such Thing As a Safe Smoke."
Federal Trade Commission. June 2000. 11 July 2004
http://www.ftc.gov/bcp/conline/pubs/alerts/cigaralrt.htm

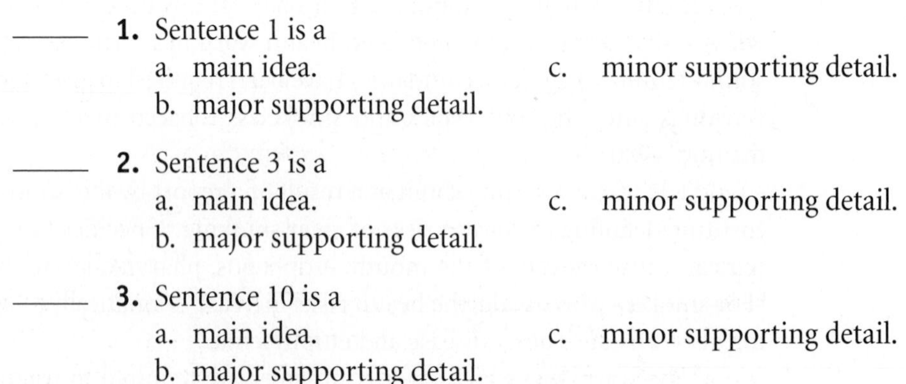

_____ **1.** Sentence 1 is a
a. main idea.
b. major supporting detail.
c. minor supporting detail.

_____ **2.** Sentence 3 is a
a. main idea.
b. major supporting detail.
c. minor supporting detail.

_____ **3.** Sentence 10 is a
a. main idea.
b. major supporting detail.
c. minor supporting detail.

**4–5.** Complete the summary.

Cigar packages and advertisements are required to include warnings to smokers about the serious health risks of cigar smoking. The _____________ warnings which the cigar companies are required to rotate caution that cigar smoking can cause cancers of the mouth, throat, esophagus, pharynx, larynx, and lungs; heart disease; the risk of _____________; stillbirth; and low birth weight.

## REVIEW Test 4

### Main Ideas, Major and Minor Supporting Details

Before you read the following passage from a college sociology textbook, skim the material and answer the **Before Reading** questions. Read the passage. Then answer the **After Reading** questions.

**Vocabulary Preview**

*subtly* (2) indirectly
*cohesion* (3) unity
*autonomy* (5) independence, self-reliance
*regulation* (8) control
*enmeshed* (9) entangled, tangled

### Family Cohesion

[1]From the moment you were born, you have been learning how to handle distance or closeness within your family system. [2]You were taught directly or **subtly** how to be connected to, or separated from, other family members. [3]**Cohesion** occurs on two levels. [4]First, cohesion deals with the levels of emotional bonding between family members. [5]In addition, cohesion considers the amount of **autonomy** a person achieves within the family system. [6]In other words, every family attempts to deal with the level of closeness that is encouraged or discouraged.

[7]Although different terms are used, cohesion has been identified by scholars from various fields as central to the understanding of family life. [8]Family researchers Kantor and Lehr (1976) view "distance **regulation**" as a major family function. [9]Family therapist Minuchin et al. (1967) talks about "**enmeshed** and disengaged" families. [10]Sociologists Hess and Handel (1959)

describe the family's need to "establish a pattern of separateness and connectedness." [11]There are four levels of cohesion ranging from extremely low cohesion to extremely high cohesion. [12]These levels are as follows:

> [13]**Disengaged:** Family members maintain extreme separateness and little family belonging or loyalty.
> [14]**Separated:** Family members are emotionally independent with some joint involvement and belonging.
> [15]**Connected:** Family members strive for emotional closeness, loyalty, and joint involvement with some individuality.
> [16]**Enmeshed:** Family members are extremely close and loyal, and they express almost no individuality (Carnes, 1989).

[17]It is through communication that family members are able to develop and maintain or change their patterns of cohesion. [18]A father may decide that it is inappropriate to continue the physical closeness he has experienced with his daughter now that she has become a teenager, and he may limit his touching or playful roughhousing. [19]These nonverbal messages may be confusing or hurtful to his daughter. [20]She may become angry, find new ways of being close, develop more outside friendships, or attempt to force her father back into the old patterns. [21]A husband may demand more intimacy from his wife as he ages. [22]He asks for more serious conversation, makes more sexual advances, or shares more of his feelings. [23]His wife may ignore this new behavior or engage in more intimate behaviors herself.

[24]Families with extremely high cohesion are often referred to as "enmeshed." [25]Members are so closely bonded and over-involved that individuals experience little autonomy or fulfillment of personal needs and goals. [26]Family members appear fused or joined so tightly that personal identities do not develop appropriately. [27]Enmeshed persons do not experience life as individuals, as indicated by the following example:

> [28]*My mother and I are the same person.* [29]*She was always protective of me, knew everything about me, told me how to act, and how to answer questions.* [30]*None of this was done in a bad way or had* **detrimental** *effects, but the reality is that she was and still is somewhat overbearing.* [31]*If someone asked me a question, I typically answered, "Please direct all questions to my mother.* [32]*She knows what to say."*

[33]"Disengaged" refers to families at the other end of the continuum in which members experience very little closeness or family **solidarity**, yet each member has high autonomy and individuality. [34]There is a strong sense of emotional separation or divorce. [35]Members experience little or no sense of connectedness to each other.

[36]As you examine cohesion in families, you may want to look at factors such as "emotional bonding, independence, boundaries, time, space, friends, decision making, and interests and recreation" (Olson, Sprenkle, & Russell, p. 6). [37]Families do not remain permanently at one point on the cohesion scale. [38]Members do not come together and stay the same, as is evident from the previous examples. [39]Because there are widely varying cultural norms, what seems balanced for one family may be quite distant for another. [40]For example, Latino families may find balanced cohesion at a point that is too close for families with a Northern European background.

—Adapted from Galvin & Brommel, *Family Communication: Cohesion and Change*, 5th ed., 2000, pp. 31–32.

## BEFORE READING

### Vocabulary in Context

_____ **1.** In sentence 30 of the passage, the word **detrimental** means
a. helpful.
b. injurious.
c. long lasting.
d. short term.

_____ **2.** In sentence 33 of the passage, the word **solidarity** means
a. disengagement.
b. independence.
c. understanding.
d. unity.

## AFTER READING

### Main Ideas

_____ **3.** Which of the following best states the topic and the author's controlling point about the topic?
a. Levels of family cohesion
b. Causes of family cohesion
c. Ways to achieve family cohesion
d. Dangers of family cohesion

_____ **4.** Which sentence is the thesis statement for the passage?
a. Sentence 1
b. Sentence 6
c. Sentence 11
d. Sentence 40

### Supporting Details

_____ **5.** Sentences 13 through 16 are
a. major supporting details.
b. minor supporting details.

_____ **6.** Sentences 28 through 32 are
a. major supporting details.
b. minor supporting details.

**7–10.** Complete the summary notes with information from the passage.

The four levels of family cohesion, which range from extremely low to high, include the following: ____________ (family members are separate with little loyalty or sense of belonging), ____________ (family members are independent with some involvement and sense of belonging), ____________ (family members work to remain close, loyal, involved with some individuality), and ____________ (members are extremely close, loyal, with almost no individuality).

## Discussion Topics

1. Which of the four levels of family cohesion seems the most ideal? Why? Which level seems to be the least ideal? Why?
2. In what ways can a family directly or subtly teach members to be connected to or separated from other family members?
3. What are some of the situations that can occur to cause a family to change its level of cohesion?

## Writing Topics

1. Use your own words to define a disengaged family and an enmeshed family. Give three examples of behavior that might characterize each type of family.
2. Write a short story about a day in the life of a "connected" family.

## EFFECTIVE READER Scorecard

**Supporting Details**

| Test | Number Correct | | Points | | Score |
|---|---|---|---|---|---|
| Review Test 1 | ________ | × | 20 | = | ________ |
| Review Test 2 | ________ | × | 20 | = | ________ |
| Review Test 3 | ________ | × | 20 | = | ________ |
| Review Test 4 | ________ | × | 10 | = | ________ |
| Review Test 5 (website) | ________ | × | 20 | = | ________ |
| Review Test 6 (website) | ________ | × | 20 | = | ________ |

Enter your scores on the Effective Reader Scorecard: Chapter 4 Review Tests inside the back cover.

## After Reading About Supporting Details

Before you move on to the mastery tests on supporting details, take time to reflect on your learning and performance by answering the following questions. Write your answers in your notebook.

What did I learn about supporting details?
What do I need to remember about supporting details?
How has my knowledge base or prior knowledge about supporting details changed?

### More Reviews and Mastery Tests

For more practice, go to the book's website at **http://ablongman.com/henry/** and click on *The Effective Reader*. Then select "More Review and Mastery Tests." The tests are organized by chapter.

MASTERY **Test 1**

Name ______________ Section ______

Date ______ **Score** (number correct) ______ × 20 = ______%

Read the following paragraph from a college literature textbook and answer the questions.

Textbook Skills

### Character in Fiction

[1]A character is presumably an imagined person who inhabits a story. [2]However, that simple definition may admit to a few exceptions. [3]In George Stewart's novel *Storm,* the central character is the wind; in Richard Adams's *Watership Down,* the main characters are rabbits. [4]But usually we recognize, in the main characters of a story, human personalities that become familiar to us. [5]If the story seems "true to life," we generally find that its characters act in a reasonably consistent manner, and that the author has provided them with motivation. [6]The author gives the characters sufficient reason to behave as they do. [7]Should a character behave in a sudden and unexpected way, we trust that he had a reason, and sooner or later we will discover it. [8]Characters may seem flat or round, depending on whether a writer sketches or sculpts them.

[9]A **flat** character has only one outstanding trait or feature, or at most a few distinguishing marks. [10]For example, one familiar stock character is the mad scientist, with his lust for absolute power and his crazily gleaming eyes. [11]Flat characters, however, need not be stock characters. [12]For instance, in all of literature there is probably only one Tiny Tim, though his functions in *A Christmas Carol* are mainly to invoke blessings and to remind others of their Christian duties. [13]Some writers try to distinguish the flat ones by giving each a single odd physical feature or mannerism—a nervous twitch, a piercing gaze, an obsessive fondness for oysters. [14]**Round** characters, however, present us with more facets—that is, their authors portray them in greater depth and in more generous detail. [15]Such a round character may appear to us only as he appears to the other characters in the story. [16]If their views of him differ, we will see him from more than one side. [17]In other stories, we enter a character's mind and come to know him through his own thoughts, feelings, and perceptions. [18]By the time we finish reading Katherine Mansfield's "Miss Brill," we are well acquainted with the central character and find her amply three-dimensional.

[19]Flat characters tend to stay the same throughout a story, but round characters often change—learn or become enlightened, grow or deteriorate. [20]In William Faulkner's "Barn Burning," the boy Sarty Snopes, driven to defy his proud and violent father, becomes at the story's end more knowing and more mature. [21](Some critics call a fixed character **static;** a changing one, **dynamic**.) [22]This is not to damn a flat character as an inferior work of art. [23]In most fiction—even the greatest—minor characters tend to be flat instead of round. [24]Why? [25]Rounding them would cost time and space; and so enlarged, they might only distract us from the main characters.

—Adapted from Kennedy & Gioia, *Literature: An Introduction to Fiction, Poetry, and Drama*, 3rd Compact Ed., p. 61.

_____ **1.** Which sentence is the thesis sentence that states the topic and the author's controlling point about the topic?
a. Sentence 1
b. Sentence 2
c. Sentence 8

_____ **2.** Sentence 9 is a _______________ of the paragraph.
a. main idea
b. major supporting detail
c. minor supporting detail

_____ 3. Sentence 19 is a _______________ of the paragraph.
a. main idea
b. major supporting detail
c. minor supporting detail

_____ **4.** Sentence 20 is a _______________ of the paragraph.
a. main idea
b. major supporting detail
c. minor supporting detail

_____ **5.** Sentence 21 is a _______________ of the paragraph.
a. main idea
b. major supporting detail
c. minor supporting detail

MASTERY **Test 2**

Name ______________________ Section ____________

Date ____________ **Score** (number correct) ______ × 25 = ______%

Read the following passage from a college literature textbook. Answer the questions.

Textbook Skills

### Psychological Criticism

[1]Modern psychology has had a vast effect on both literature and literary criticism. [2]Sigmund Freud's theories of psychoanalysis changed our ideas about human behavior. [3]His work explored wish-fulfillment, sexuality, the unconscious, and repression. [4]He also showed how language and symbols reflect unconscious fears or desires. [5]According to Freud, he learned a great deal about psychology from the study of literature. [6]Reading classical literature was as important as his clinical studies to the development of his ideas. [7]Some of Freud's most important writings could be seen as literary criticism. [8]One of the most famous examples of his work is his analysis of Sophocles' Oedipus. [9](Written in the 5th century B.C.E., the play *Oedipus* depicts the rise and fall of the hero Oedipus the King; Oedipus unwittingly kills his father and marries his mother.) [10]Freud believed that great literature truthfully reflects life.

[11]Psychological criticism is a varied category. [12]However, it often takes three approaches. [13]First, it looks into the creative process of the artist. [14]What is the nature of literary genius? [15]How does it relate to normal mental functions? [16]The second major area for this type of criticism is the psychological study of a particular artist. [17]Most modern literary biographies rely on psychology to understand their subject's motivations and behavior. [18]One recent book stands as an example of this approach. [19]In her book *Anne Sexton: A Biography,* Diane Middlebrook actually used tapes of the poet's sessions with her psychiatrist as material for her study of the poet. [20]The third common area of psychological criticism is the analysis of fictional characters. [21]Freud's study of Oedipus is the model for this approach. [22]Freud tried to bring modern insights about human behavior into the study of how fictional people act.

—Adapted from Kennedy & Gioia, *Literature: An Introduction to Fiction, Poetry, and Drama*, 3rd Compact Ed., p. 1477.

______ **1.** Which sentence is the thesis statement that states the topic and the author's controlling point about the topic?

a. Sentence 1

b. Sentence 2

c. Sentence 3

_____ **2.** In the second paragraph, sentence 12 serves as a _____ for the paragraph.
a. main idea
b. major supporting detail
c. minor supporting detail

_____ **3.** In the second paragraph, sentence 16 serves as a _____ for the paragraph.
a. main idea
b. major supporting detail
c. minor supporting detail

_____ **4.** Sentence 19 is a
a. main idea.
b. major supporting detail.
c. minor supporting detail.

MASTERY **Test 3**

Name ______________________ Section __________

Date __________ **Score** (number correct) ______ × 20 = ______%

Read the following passage from a college humanities textbook. Then answer the questions and complete the summary.

### Displaying Emotions

[1]Facial expressions that convey emotions are largely shared across cultures. [2]However, questions have remained about facial expressions and emotions. [3]How widespread or common are emotional facial expressions? [4]Are these expressions accurately recognized by others? [4]Research in New Guinea, Brazil, Chile, Argentina, Japan, and the United States speaks to these questions. [5]According to the research, people are highly accurate in recognizing the meaning of facial expressions. [6]This research has yielded some additional interesting conclusions.

- [7]Apparently some emotions are "universal": enjoyment, sadness, anger, disgust, surprise, and fear (Ekman, Sorenson, & Friesen, 1969).
- [8]Joy and surprise are consistently recognized, but interest and shame are the least often identified (Izard, 1979).
- [9]Sadness is more identifiable in collectivist cultures (Matsumoto, 1989). [10] A comparison was made of Japanese and Americans regarding emotion recognition. [11]Americans were better at identifying anger, disgust, fear, and sadness. [12]Both groups recognized happiness and surprise. [13]The Japanese have difficulty identifying negative emotions. [14]Expressing such emotions is socially less desirable in Japan than in the United States (Smith & Bond, 1994, p. 61).
- [15]Friesen (1972, cited in Smith & Bond, 1994), offered an unpublished but often discussed study. [16]The study compared Japanese and American students' reactions as they watched two films. [17]One was a short film about body mutilation, and the other was an emotionally neutral film. [18]At first Japanese and American students alike showed disgust while they watched the film. [19]But when a "scientist" in a white coat (an apparent authority figure) was present, the Japanese displayed a slightly *smiling* expression.

[20]Emotions are expressed with similar expressions across cultures. [21]However, social correctness varies. [22]The ways, timing, and exchanges of emotional expression vary greatly from culture to culture. [23]What is appropriate in one country may appear uncouth in another.

—Adapted from Kelly, Marylin S. *Communication@ Work*, pp. 127–28.

_____ **1.** Sentence 6 is a
a. main idea.
b. major supporting detail.
c. minor supporting detail.

_____ **2.** Sentence 7 is a
a. main idea.
b. major supporting detail.
c. minor supporting detail.

_____ **3.** Sentence 12 is a
a. main idea.
b. major supporting detail.
c. minor supporting detail.

**4–5.** Complete the summary with information from the passage.

Research in New Guinea, Brazil, Chile, Argentina, Japan, and the United States has yielded several interesting conclusions about _______________ that convey emotions. Emotions are expressed with similar expressions across cultures. In addition, people are highly accurate in recognizing the meaning of facial expressions. However, the social __________ of facial expressions of emotions varies from culture to culture.

# MASTERY Test 4

Name ______________________ Section ____________

Date ____________ **Score** (number correct) ______ × 25 = ______%

Read the following passage from a college history textbook. Answer the questions.

Textbook Skills

## Obscenity

[1]In *The Brethren*, a gossipy portrayal of the Supreme Court, Bob Woodward and Scott Armstrong recount the tale of Justice Thurgood Marshall's lunch with some law clerks. [2]Glancing at his watch at about 1:50 P.M., the story goes, Marshall exclaimed, "My God, I almost forgot. [3]It's movie day, we've got to get back." [4]Movie day at the Court was an annual event when movies brought before the Court on obscenity charges were shown in a basement storeroom.

[5]Several justices have boycotted these showings, arguing that obscenity should never be banned and thus that how "dirty" a movie is has no relevance. [6]In 1957, however, the majority held that "obscenity is not within the area of constitutionally protected speech or press" (*Roth v. United States*). [7]The doctrine set forth in this case still prevails. [8]Deciding what is obscene, though, has never been an easy matter. [9]In a line that would haunt him for the rest of his life, Justice Potter Stewart once remarked that although he could not define obscenity, "I know it when I see it."

[10]Efforts to define obscenity have perplexed the courts for years. [11]Obviously, public standards vary from time to time, place to place, and person to person. [12]Much of today's MTV would have been banned a decade or two ago. [13]At one time or another, the works of Aristophanes, those of Mark Twain, and even the "Tarzan" stories of Edgar Rice Burroughs were banned. [14]The state of Georgia banned the acclaimed film *Carnal Knowledge*—a ban the Supreme Court struck down in 1974.

[15]The Court tried to clarify its doctrine by spelling out what could be classified as obscene and thus outside First Amendment protection in the 1973 case of *Miller v. California*.[16] Then Chief Justice Warren Burger wrote that materials were obscene if

- [17]The work, taken as a whole, appealed "to a prurient interest in sex."
- [18]The work showed "patently offensive" sexual conduct that was specifically defined by an obscenity law.
- [19]The work, taken as a whole, lacked "serious literary, artistic, political, or scientific value."

[20]Decisions regarding whether material was obscene, said the Court, should be based on average people (in other words, juries) applying the standards of their local communities.

[21]Cities throughout the country copied the language of *Miller* in their obscenity laws. [22]The difficulty remains in deciding what is *lewd* or *offensive.* [23]Laws must satisfy these terms to avoid banning anatomy texts, for example, as obscene.

[24]Guilty verdicts for obscenity can be difficult to win. [25]There is no nationwide consensus that offensive material that is limited to adults should be banned. [26]In many areas, the laws are relaxed regarding pornography. [27]Prosecutors know that they may not get a jury to convict. [28]Thus, obscene material is widely available in adult bookstores, video stores, and movie theaters.

—Adapted from Edwards, Wattenburg, & Lineberry, *Government in America: People, Politics, and Policy*, 5th ed., pp. 89–90.

_____ **1.** The thesis statement is
a. sentence 1.
b. sentence 10.
c. sentence 15.

_____ **2.** In the second paragraph, sentence 9 serves as a _____ for the paragraph.
a. main idea
b. major supporting detail
c. minor supporting detail

_____ **3.** In the third paragraph, sentence 11 serves as a _____ for the paragraph.
a. main idea
b. major supporting detail
c. minor supporting detail

_____ **4.** In the final paragraph, sentence 24 serves as a _____ for the paragraph.
a. main idea
b. major supporting detail
c. minor supporting detail

**MASTERY Test 5**

Name _______________ Section _______________
Date _______________ Score (number correct) _______ × 20 = _______%

Read the following passage from a college communications textbook. Then complete the summary.

Textbook Skills

### Touch Communication

[1]Touch communication (known technically as **haptics**) is perhaps the most primitive form of communication. [2]Touch develops before the other senses; even in the womb the child is stimulated by touch. [3]Soon after birth the child is fondled, caressed, patted, and stroked. [4]In turn, the child explores its world through touch and quickly learns to communicate a variety of meanings through touch. [5]Nonverbal researchers have identified the major meanings of touch:

- [6]**Positive emotion:** Touch may communicate such positive feelings as support, appreciation, inclusion, sexual interest or intent, and affection.
- [7]**Playfulness:** Touch often speaks of our intention to play. [8]This kind of touch can be either affectionate or aggressive.
- [9]**Control:** Touch may also direct the behaviors, attitudes, or feelings of the other person. [10]In attention-getting, for example, you touch the person to gain his or her attention. [11]This kind of touch says "look at me" or "look over here."
- [12]**Ritual:** Ritualistic touching centers on greetings and departures. [13]For example, shaking hands to say "hello" or "goodbye" or hugging, kissing, or putting your arm around another's shoulder when greeting or saying farewell are rituals.
- [14]**Task-relatedness:** Task-related touching occurs while you're performing some function. [15]Removing a speck of dust from another person's face or helping someone out of a car are two examples.

[16]Different cultures will view these types of touching differently. [17]For example, some task-related touching is viewed as acceptable in much of the United States. [18]However, this same touch would be viewed negatively in some cultures. [19]Among Koreans, for example, it's considered rude for a store owner to touch a customer while handing back change. [20]It's considered too intimate a gesture. [21]Members of other cultures, expecting some touching, may consider the Korean's behavior cold and insulting.

—Adapted from DeVito, *Messages: Building Interpersonal Communication Skills*, 4th ed., pp. 152–53.

**VISUAL VOCABULARY**

The people in this picture illustrate ______________ touch.

a. playful
b. task-related
c. ritualistic

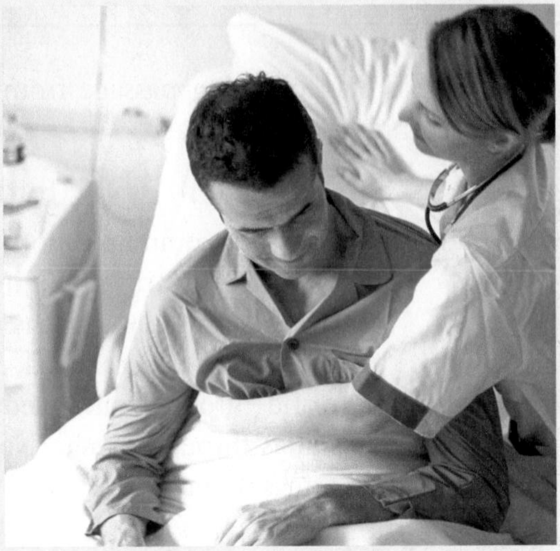

**1–5.** Complete the summary with information from the paragraph.

Researchers of touch communication, which is also known as (**1**) ________, have identified several major meanings of touch. Touch can convey positive emotion, (**2**) ______________, (**3**) ______________, (**4**) ______________, and task-relatedness. Different (**5**) ______________ view these types of touch differently.

**MASTERY Test 6**

Name ______________________ Section __________

Date __________ **Score** (number correct) ______ × 20 = ______%

Read the following passage from a college communications textbook. Then complete the summary.

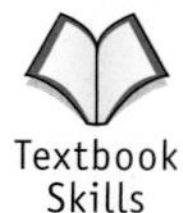


### Social Penetration Theory

[1]*Social penetration* theory is not so much a theory of why relationships develop as what happens when they do develop. [2]It describes relationships in terms of the number of topics that people talk about and their degree of personal closeness. [3]The *breadth* of a relationship refers to the number of topics you and your partner talk about. [4]The *depth* of a relationship refers to the degree to which you penetrate the inner personality or the core of your individual.

[5]When a relationship begins to deteriorate, the breadth and depth will, in many ways, reverse themselves, a process called *depenetration*. [6]For example, while ending a relationship, you might cut out certain topics from your interpersonal communications. [7]At the same time you might discuss the remaining topics in less depth. [8]In some instances of relational deterioration, however, both the breadth and the depth of interaction increase. [9]For example, when a couple breaks up and each is finally free from an oppressive relationship, they may—after some time—begin to discuss problems and feelings they would never have discussed when they were together. [10]In fact, they may become extremely close friends and come to like each other more than when they were together. [11]In these cases the breadth and depth of their relationship may increase rather than decrease.

—Adapted from DeVito, *Messages: Building Interpersonal Communication Skills*, 4th ed., pp. 276–77.

**1-5.** Complete the summary with information from the paragraph.

(**1**) ______________ theory describes relationships based on the number of topics discussed and the degree of (**2**) __________ closeness between people. The (**3**) __________ of social penetration refers to the number of topics partners discuss, and the (**4**) __________ of social penetration refers to the degree to which the inner or core individual is accessed. (**5**) ______________ occurs when the breadth and depth of a relationship reverses.

CHAPTER

5

# Outlines and Concept Maps

## CHAPTER PREVIEW

## Before Reading About Outlines and Concept Maps

In Chapter 4, you learned several important ideas that will help you use outlines and concept maps effectively. To review, reread the diagram about the flow of ideas on page 163 in Chapter 4. Next, skim this chapter for key ideas in boxes about outlines, concept maps, and the table of contents in a textbook. Refer to the diagrams and boxes and create at least three questions that you can answer as you read the chapter. Write your questions in the following spaces (record the page number for the key term in each question):

______________________________________________________________________

__________________________________________________________ (page ______)?

______________________________________________________________________

__________________________________________________________ (page ______)?

______________________________________________________________________

__________________________________________________________ (page ______)?

Compare the questions you created with the following questions. Then write the ones that seem most helpful in your notebook, leaving enough space between each question to record the answers as you read and study the chapter.

How does an outline show the relationship among the main idea, major supporting details, and minor supporting details? Where are main ideas used in an outline, concept map, and table of contents? Where are major supporting details used in an outline, concept map, and table of contents? Where are minor supporting details used in an outline, concept map, and table of contents? What is the difference between a formal and an informal outline?

## Outlines

An outline shows how a paragraph moves from a general idea to specific supporting details; thus it helps you make sense of the ways ideas relate to one another. An effective reader uses an outline to see the main idea, major supporting details, and minor supporting details.

An **outline** shows the relationship among the main idea, major supporting details, and minor supporting details.

An author often uses signal words or phrases such as *a few causes, a number of reasons, several steps*, or *several kinds of* to introduce a main idea; in addition, an author often uses signal words such as *first, second, furthermore, moreover, next,* or *finally* to indicate that a supporting detail is coming. You will learn more about signal words, also called transitions, and their relationship to ideas in Chapters 6 and 7.

Outlines can be formal or informal. A **formal** or **traditional outline** uses Roman numerals to indicate the main idea, capital letters to indicate the major details, and Arabic numbers to indicate minor details. A formal outline is particularly useful for studying complex reading material. Sometimes, you may choose to use an **informal outline** and record only the main ideas and the major supporting details. Because these outlines are informal, their format may vary according to each student's notetaking style. Elements may or may not be capitalized. One person might label the main idea with the number 1 and the major supporting details with letters *a, b, c, d*, and so on. Another person might not label the main idea at all and label each major supporting detail with letters or numbers.

**EXAMPLE** Read the following paragraph. Fill in the details to complete the outline. Then answer the questions that follow it.

**Antlers: Distinct, Unique, and Purposeful**

[1]Certain male mammals such as deer, moose, elk, and caribou grow antlers. [2]Antlers are distinct and unique for several reasons. [3]First, antlers have distinct traits. [4]They are outgrowths of the animal's skull and are made of bone tissue; they are nourished by blood vessels and covered with a soft, skin-like tissue with short, fine hair known as velvet. [5]The first set of antlers on young deer is often made up of short spikes; as the deer matures, the antlers grow longer into branches or points. [6]Second, antlers develop through a unique growth cycle. [7]Antlers are deciduous, which means they are shed every year. [8]They begin as soft bumps on the animal's head and are fully grown by August or September. [9]Antlers usually drop off the animal at the end of the breeding cycle between January and April. [10]Immediately after dropping off, the antler begins to regenerate or grow back. [11]Finally, antlers serve several purposes. [12]They play an important role in the mating ritual as males lock horns to assert their dominance over rivals. [13]An animal may also use its antlers to forage for food and protect its young.

## Outline

Main idea: ______________________________

A. Antlers have distinct traits.

B. ______________________________

C. Antlers serve several purposes.

## Questions

**1.** What word or phrase in the topic sentence signals that a list of details will follow? ______________________________

______ **2.** Sentence 10 is a

a. major supporting detail. b. minor supporting detail.

**3–5.** What word or phrase introduces each major detail?

Major detail 1: ______________________________

Major detail 2: ______________________________

Major detail 3: ______________________________

______ **6.** The outline used in this activity is an example of

a. an informal outline. b. a formal outline.

**EXPLANATION** The main idea of this passage is located near the beginning of the passage and is stated in sentence 2, "Antlers are distinct and unique for several reasons." The author indicates that a list of several major supporting details will be presented and explained with the phrase "several reasons." The first major detail is in sentence 3, "First, antlers have distinct traits." The second major supporting detail is sentence 6, "Second, antlers develop through a unique growth cycle." Both major supporting details are introduced with signal words: "first" and "second." Sentence 10 is a minor supporting detail that illustrates the second major supporting detail. This outline is an example of an informal outline that includes only the main idea and the major supporting details.

Notice how an outline of the main idea and the major supporting details—without the minor supporting details—condenses the material into a summary of the author's primary points.

A formal outline of the information looks like the following:

Stated main idea: Antlers are distinct and unique for several reasons.

I. Antlers have distinct traits.
   A. They are outgrowths of the animal's skull and are made of bone tissue; they are nourished by blood vessels and covered with a soft, skin-like tissue with short, fine hair known as velvet.
   B. The first set of antlers on young deer is often made up of short spikes; as the deer matures, the antlers grow longer into branches or points.

II. Antlers develop through a unique growth cycle.
   A. Antlers are deciduous, which means they are shed every year.
   B. They begin as soft bumps on the animal's head and are fully grown by August or September.
   C. Antlers usually drop off the animal at the end of the breeding cycle between January and April.
   D. Immediately after dropping off, the antler begins to regenerate or grow back.

III. Antlers serve several purposes.
   A. They play an important role in the mating ritual as males lock horns to assert their dominance over rivals.
   B. An animal may also use its antlers to forage for food and protect its young.

Note that in a formal outline of one paragraph, the first major supporting detail is labeled with the Roman numeral I, and the minor supporting details are labeled A and B. This pattern continues: the second and third major supporting details are labeled Roman numerals II and III, and each of the minor supporting details is labeled A, B, C, and so on.

## PRACTICE 1

Read the following paragraph from a college communications textbook. Then answer the questions that follow it.

Textbook Skills

### Eye Contact

[1]You use eye contact to serve several important functions. [2]First, you can use eye contact to monitor feedback. [3]For example, when you talk with someone, you look at the person intently as if to say, "Well, what do you think?" or "React to what I have just said." [4]You also look at speakers to let them know you are listening. [5]Another important use of eye contact is to gain the attention and interest of your listeners. [6]When someone fails to pay the attention you want, you may increase your eye contact, hoping your focus on this person will increase attention. [7]When making an especially important point, maintaining close eye contact with your listeners may prevent them from giving attention to anything but what you are saying. [8]A third important function of eye contact is control of the conversation. [9]Eye movements inform the other person that the channel of communication is open and that she or he should now speak. [10]A clear example of controlling the conversation occurs in the college classroom, where the instructor asks a question and then locks eyes with a student. [11]Without any verbal message, it is known that the student should answer the question.

—Adapted from DeVito, *The Interpersonal Communication Book,* 10th ed., p. 187.

**1–5.** Complete the following outline.

Stated main idea: You use eye contact to serve several important functions.

I. ______________________________

A. ______________________________

B. Eye contact also lets speakers know you are listening.

II. ______________________________

______________________________

A. Increased eye contact will increase attention.

B. Close eye contact prevents listeners from giving attention to anything but what you are saying.

III. ______________________________

A. Eye movements inform the other person that the channel of communication is open.

B. ______________________________

______________________________

**6.** What word or phrase in the topic sentence signals that a list of details will follow? ______________________________

______ **7.** Sentence 3, "For example, when you talk with someone, you look at the person intently as if to say, 'Well, what do you think?' or 'React to what I have just said,' " is a

a. major supporting detail. b. minor supporting detail.

**8–10.** What word or phrase introduces the first, second, and third major detail?

Major detail 1: ______________________________

Major detail 2: ______________________________

Major detail 3: ______________________________

**VISUAL VOCABULARY**

______ The best synonym for **dominance** is

a. superiority.
b. arrogance.
c. humility.

▲ Visual dominance is the use of your eyes to maintain a powerful position.

## Concept Maps

An outline is one way to see the details that support a main idea. Another way to see details is through the use of a concept map. A **concept map** is a diagram that shows the flow of ideas from the main idea to the supporting details. Think of what you already know about a map. Someone can tell you how to get somewhere, but it is much easier to understand the directions if you can see how each road connects to the other by studying a map. Likewise, a concept map shows how ideas connect to one another.

A **concept map** is a diagram that shows the flow of ideas from the main idea to the supporting details.

To make a concept map, an effective reader places the main idea in a box or circle as a heading and then places the major supporting details in boxes or circles beneath the main idea. Often arrows or lines are used to show the flow of ideas.

**EXAMPLE** Read the following paragraph. Then complete the concept map by filling in the four major supporting details from the paragraph.

### A Brief History of Armor

[1]From the earliest civilizations to current times, humans have used armor to protect themselves from injury. [2]The earliest armor was most likely a shield made of wood and animal hide used to deflect rocks and spears during the Neolithic era. [3]Eventually, the Greeks fashioned a set of armor that consisted of a large round shield, a bronze helmet, and shin guards. [4]Later, body armor advanced with the development of scale armor, made of metal plates that overlap each other and chain mail, made up of thousands of iron rings that interlocked to form an entire suit. [5]Currently, armor is still used to protect soldiers in combat, but its use has been expanded to include athletes and workers. [6]Modern soldiers still use helmets and now have flak jackets or bullet proof vests made of Kevlar. [7]In addition, athletes use helmets, pads, and shin guards to protect themselves as they compete in various sports such as football and baseball. [8]Similarly, construction workers don hard hats and boots with reinforced steel toes to protect themselves from on-the-job injuries.

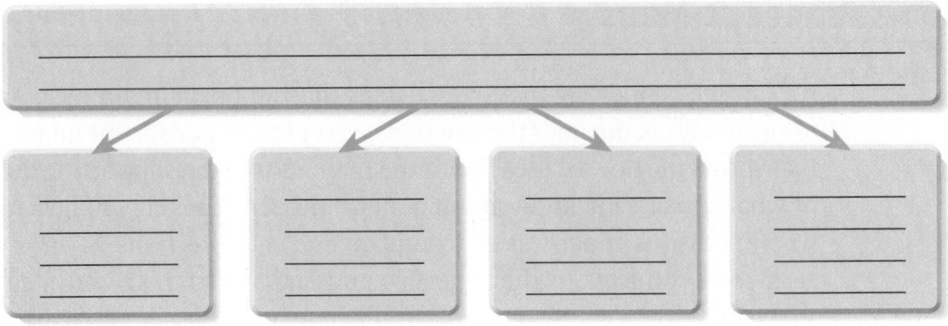

**EXPLANATION** Note that the main idea is in the top box. The phrase "From the earliest civilizations to current times" in the topic sentence indicates that the major details follow a time order. The signal words "earliest," "eventually," "later," and "currently" indicate the major supporting details. As you can see, a concept map presents ideas in a highly visual manner, making it easy for the reader to grasp the author's primary points. This particular concept map includes only the major supporting details. However, mapping can include the minor supporting details as well. Look at the concept map below that follows the flow of ideas for the third major supporting detail, "Currently, armor is still used . . . " Concept maps, like outlines, can show all three levels of thought: the main idea, the major supporting details, and the minor supporting details.

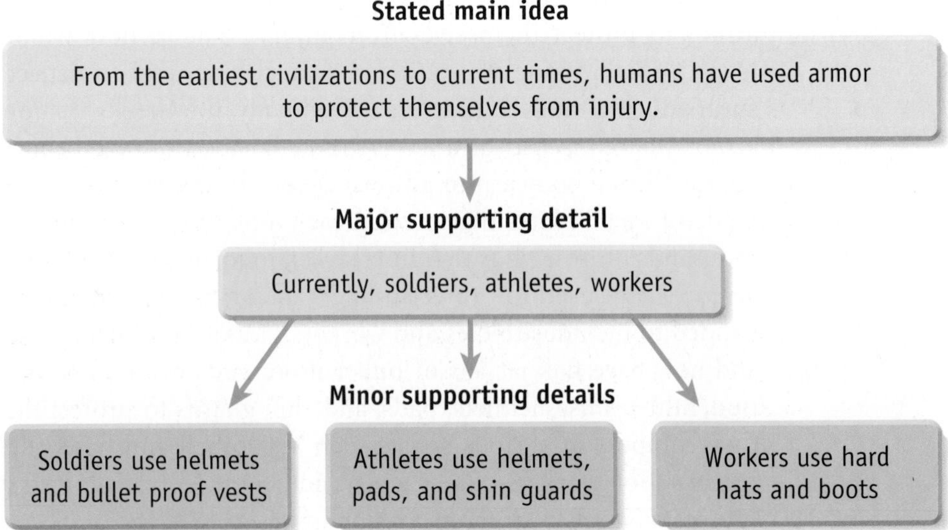

## PRACTICE 2

Read the following paragraphs. Fill in the concept maps with the missing information from each paragraph.

### Paragraph A

**Keeping a Personal Journal**

[1]Many people find that keeping a personal journal has several benefits. [2]The first benefit of a personal journal is the opportunity the act of writing gives to vent emotions in private; instead of allowing them to build up over time and then explode, writing acts as a release. [3]The second benefit of keeping a journal is the level of self-reflection it demands; the act of putting experiences and emotions into words forces one to think about what is and what is not important enough to record. [4]Another benefit is the personal historical record the writer compiles over time; instead of fading away, memories are in a lasting record that can be revisited at any time.

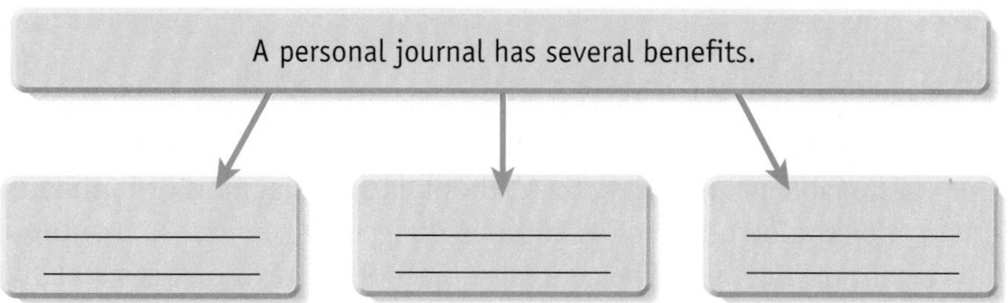


### Paragraph B from a College English Handbook

**Syllogism: A Type of Argument**

[1]A syllogism is an argument arranged in three parts: a major premise, a minor premise, and a conclusion. [2]First, a major premise or idea stipulates a general principle. [3]One example of a major premise is "that all spiders have eight legs." [4]Next, a minor premise reflects a specific instance. [5]For example, "the creature crawling across your desk has six legs" is a minor premise. [6]Finally, a conclusion is the idea that follows logically from the major and minor premises. [7]For example, your conclusion "that the creature crawling across your desk is not a spider" is logical, for it can be supported by the evidence.

—Adapted from DiYanni and Hoy, *The Scribner Handbook for Writers*, 3rd ed., p. 69.

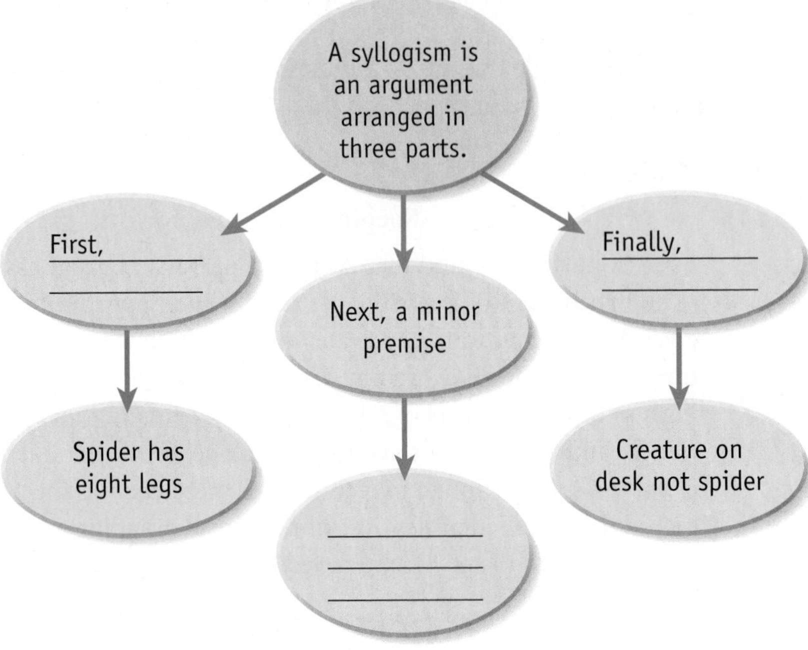


Textbook Skills

## The Table of Contents

The table of contents of a textbook is a special kind of outline that is based on topics and subtopics. A **topic** is the *general subject*, so a **subtopic** is a *smaller part* of the topic. The general subject of the textbook is stated in the textbook's title. For example, the title *Health in America: A Multicultural Perspective* tells us that the book is about health concerns from the view of different cultures.

Textbooks divide the general subject into smaller sections or subtopics. These subtopics form the chapters of the textbook. Because a textbook looks deeply into the general subject, a large amount of information is found in each chapter. Thus, a chapter is further divided into smaller parts or subtopics, and each subtopic is labeled with a heading.

The table of contents lists the general subjects and subtopics of each chapter. Most textbooks provide a brief table of contents which divides the textbook into sections and lists the chapter titles for each section. A separate detailed table of contents may also be provided which lists the subtopics for each chapter. An effective reader examines the table of contents of a textbook to understand how the author has organized the information and where specific information can be found.

**EXAMPLE** Survey, or look over, the following brief table of contents of the first three units in a college textbook. Then answer the questions.

**Biology: Concepts & Connections, 5th ed.**

BRIEF CONTENTS



—Campbell, *Biology: Concepts & Connections*, 5th ed., p. xv.

**1.** What is the general topic of this textbook? ______________________

______________________________________________

**2.** How many chapters did the author use to divide Unit I ? ____________

**3.** What is the topic of Unit I? ______________________

What is the approximate length of Chapter 2? ______________ pages.

**4.** Create two questions based on two of the chapter titles.

______________________________________________

______________________________________________

**EXPLANATION** The general topic of this textbook is stated in its title: *Biology: Concepts & Connections.* The author divides the first part of this general topic into three units: "The Life of the Cell," "Cellular Reproduction and Genetics," and "Concepts of Evolution." Each unit is divided into chapters. Knowing the length of each chapter helps you set aside the proper amount of time needed to read and study. In this textbook, each chapter is about twenty pages in length. One way to get a general sense of the ideas in a chapter or unit is by creating questions from the titles. Compare your questions to the following: "What is the chemical basis of life?" (Chapter 2) "How do cells harvest chemical energy?" (Chapter 6).

## PRACTICE 3

Study the following detailed table of contents for Chapter 2 of *Biology: Concepts & Connections,* 5th ed.

UNIT I

### The Life of the Cell

#### 2 THE CHEMICAL BASIS OF LIFE 16

1. What is the topic of the chapter? ____________________

2. How many subtopics are listed for the section "Water's Life-Supporting Properties"? ____________________

3. On what page does the discussion about atoms and their protons, neutrons, and electrons begin? ____________________

4. What are the major supporting details of this chapter? ____________________

____________________

____________________

## Chapter Review

Test your understanding of what you have read in this chapter by filling in the blank with a word or term from the box. Use each word or term once.

| concept map | outline | supporting detail |
|---|---|---|
| formal outline | signal words | |

1. An ____________ shows the relationships among the main idea, major supporting details, and minor supporting details.

2. An author often uses ____________ such as *a few causes, a number of reasons, several steps,* or *several kinds of* to introduce a main idea.

3. An author often uses signal words such as *first, second, furthermore, moreover, next,* or *finally* to indicate that a ____________ is coming.

4. A ____________ uses Roman numerals to indicate the main idea, capital letters to indicate the major details, and Arabic numbers to indicate the minor details.

5. A ____________ is a diagram that shows the flow of ideas from the main idea to the supporting details.

## Applications

### Application 1: Major Supporting Details and Outlines

Read the following paragraph from a college health textbook.

Textbook Skills

**Spirituality**

[1]Spirituality refers to the ability to develop spiritual nature to its fullest potential and fosters three convictions: faith, hope, and love. [2]Faith is the belief that helps us realize our purpose in life. [3]Hope is the belief that allows us to look confidently and courageously to the future. [4]And love involves accepting, affirming, and respecting self and others regardless of who they are. [5]Love also encompasses caring for and cherishing our environment.

—Adapted from Donatelle, *Access to Health,* 7th ed., p. 43.

**1–4.** Outline the paragraph by filling in the blanks.

Stated main idea: ______________________________________________

______________________________________________

a. ______________________________________________

b. ______________________________________________

c. ______________________________________________

______ **5.** This is an example of
a. an informal outline.
b. a formal outline.

### Application 2: Major Details, Minor Supporting Details, and Outlines

Read the following paragraph from a college communications textbook.

Textbook Skills

**Organizing Information: Schemata**

[1]One important way you organize information is by creating *schemata.* [2]You build mental structures that help you organize the millions of items of information you come into contact with every day as well as those you already have in memory. [3](*Schemata* is the plural of *schema.*) [4]Thus, **schemata** may be viewed as general ideas about people, yourself, or social roles. [5]You develop schemata from your own experience. [6]Your experiences may be firsthand, or they may be from television, reading, and hearsay. [7]You might have a schema for college athletes, for example, and this might include that they're

strong, ambitious, academically weak, and self-centered. [8]In contrast, another person who has had a different experience may have a schema that includes college athletes who are giving and successful students.

—Adapted from DeVito, *The Interpersonal Communication Book,* 10th ed., p. 92.

**1–4.** Outline the paragraph by filling in the blanks.

Stated main idea: ______________________________________________

______________________________________________

**A.** Mental structures organize information.

**B.** ______________________________________________

**C.** ______________________________________________

**1.** Experiences may be firsthand.

**2.** ______________________________________________

**3.** One schema of college athletes might be that they're strong, ambitious, academically weak, and self-centered.

**4.** Another schema might include college athletes who are giving and successful students.

______ **5.** Sentence 6 is a
a. major supporting detail.
b. minor supporting detail.

## Application 3: Concept Maps and Signal Words

Read the following paragraph. Then complete the concept map with the missing information from the paragraph.

### Famous Dominican Americans

[1]During the last half of the twentieth century, many Dominican Americans immigrated to the United States due to civil war and economic depression in the Dominican Republic. [2]These new Americans combined talent and hard work to become famous for their contributions to American culture. [3]For example, Julia Alvarez is the daughter of immigrants from the Dominican Republic. [4]Although she was born in New York City, her parents returned to the Dominican Republic when she was three years old and did not come back until she was ten. [5]She evolved from knowing very little

English into a world-renowned literary author. [6]Her work such as *In the Time of the Butterflies* has won her numerous awards and critical acclaim. [7]Another famous Dominican American is Oscar de La Renta, who has received worldwide recognition for his fashion designs. [8]He left the Dominican Republic when he was 18 years old to study painting in Madrid, Spain, where he quickly became interested in clothing design. [9]He built a billion-dollar industry that includes high fashion, ready-to-wear clothing, accessories, and home décor. [10]Also born in the Dominican Republic, Mary Jo Fernandez stormed the tennis world by becoming one the best doubles players, winning two gold medals in the 1992 and 1996 Summer Olympics. [11]In addition, she garnered nineteen career titles, two of which were Grand Slam events. [12]By her retirement, she had thrilled fans and earned millions. [13]Perhaps one of the best known Dominican American sports figures is the legendary baseball player Sammy Sosa. [14]He made sports history in 1998 when he beat Roger Maris's record of sixty-one home runs in a single season. [15]At one point, he signed a contract that earned him $72 million.

—Adapted from Novas, Himilce. *Everything You Need to Know About Latino History*, pp. 226–27.

## Application 4: Annotations and Summary

Read the following paragraph from a college political science textbook. Annotate the paragraph by circling the main idea and underlining the example. Complete the summary by filling in the blanks with information from the paragraph.

Textbook Skills

### Federalism

[1]**Federalism** is a way of organizing a nation so that two or more levels of government have formal authority over the same area and people. [2]It is a system of shared power between units of government. [3]For example, the state

of California has formal authority over those who live there. [4]However, the national government can also pass laws and put policies into place that affect those who live in the state. [5]We are subject to the formal authority of both the state and the national governments.

—Adapted from Edwards, Wattenberg, & Lineberry, *Government in America: People, Politics, and Policy*, 5th ed., p. 55.

Summary:

**Federalism** is ______________________________

______________________________

for example, ______________________________

______________________________

# REVIEW Test 1

## Main Ideas, Major and Minor Supporting Details, and Outlines

A. (1–5) Read the paragraph. Then complete the outline of the paragraph by giving the main idea and inserting the missing major and minor details.

### Types of Strength Training

[1]Building muscle mass has several advantages and can be accomplished through a variety of strength-training activities. [2]First, well-defined muscles give the body a pleasing aesthetic quality. [3]Second, muscle mass increases the body's metabolism, burning more calories than fat, thus making weight control by dieting less of an issue. [4]In addition, strength training builds bone mass, which helps protect against fractures, "shrinking," and osteoporosis. [5]Several types of strength-training exercises bring effective results. [6]One of the most common methods is lifting weights using either free weights or machines. [7]A second method is the use of resistance bands, which are rubberized strips or cables of varying tensions. [8]A third method consists of doing exercises that bear the body's weight, such as push-ups and pull-ups.

Stated main idea: ______________________________

______________________________

I. Muscle mass

A. ______________________________

B. ______________________________

______________________________

C. In addition, strength training builds bone mass, which helps protect against fractures, "shrinking," and osteoporosis.

II. ______________________________

A. One of the most common methods is lifting weights using either free weights or machines.

B. A second method is the use of resistance bands, which are rubberized strips or cables of varying tensions.

C. ______________________________

______________________________

**B.** **(6–10.)** Read the following paragraph. Then complete the outline with major and minor details from the paragraph.

**To Drink or Not to Drink: The Question of Wine**

[1]The research offers conflicting information on whether or not wine is actually good for you. [2]Some research shows that one or two glasses of wine a day may have several benefits. [3]For example, some studies indicate that drinking wine is good for the heart. [4]It lowers the overall level of cholesterol. [5]In women, it also protects against the hardening and thickening of blood vessels. [6]Furthermore, moderate wine consumption seems to reduce the risk of developing macular degeneration. [7]This condition causes the loss of central vision in older people. [8]It is believed that some of the natural agents in wine may prevent bleeding in tiny blood vessels in the eyes. [9]In addition, ongoing studies on aging indicate that moderate use of wine greatly decreases the risk of dementia. [10]However, research also shows that drinking wine does carry some risks. [11]For example, several large-scale studies have shown that one drink per day raises the risk of breast cancer by 10 percent. [12]In addition, drinking even small amounts of alcohol in the early weeks of pregnancy has been linked with fetal alcohol syndrome.

—Adapted from University of Illinois College of Medicine at Rockford, "Research Shows Potential Benefits, Risks of Wine."

Stated main idea: The research offers conflicting information on whether or not wine is actually good for you.

I. ______________________________

______________________________

A. ______________________________

1. It lowers the overall level of cholesterol.

2. In women, it also protects against the hardening and thickening of blood vessels.

B. ______________________________

______________________________

1. This condition causes the loss of central vision in older people.

2. It is believed that some of the natural agents in wine may prevent bleeding in tiny blood vessels in the eyes.

C. ______________________________

______________________________

II. ______________________________

A. For example, several large-scale studies have shown that one drink per day raises the risk of breast cancer by 10 percent.

B. In addition, drinking even small amounts of alcohol in the early weeks of pregnancy has been linked with fetal alcohol syndrome.

# REVIEW Test 2

## Main Ideas, Supporting Details, Signal Words, and Concept Maps

**A.** Read the following paragraph from a college health textbook.

Textbook Skills

### Risks for Depression

[1]Most experts believe that major depressive disorders are caused by several factors. [2]One factor is biology. [3]Biological theories suggest that chemical and genetic processes are the main reasons for depression. [4]Another factor is known as learned behavior. [5]Learning theories suggest that people develop

flawed behaviors, and these behaviors make them prone to depression. [6]Finally, cognitive or thinking factors play a role in depression. [7]Cognitive theories suggest that illogical behaviors and beliefs cause people to use poor coping behaviors.

—Adapted from Donatelle, *Access to Health,* 7th ed., p. 47.

Fill in the concept map with the main idea and the missing major supporting details from the paragraph.

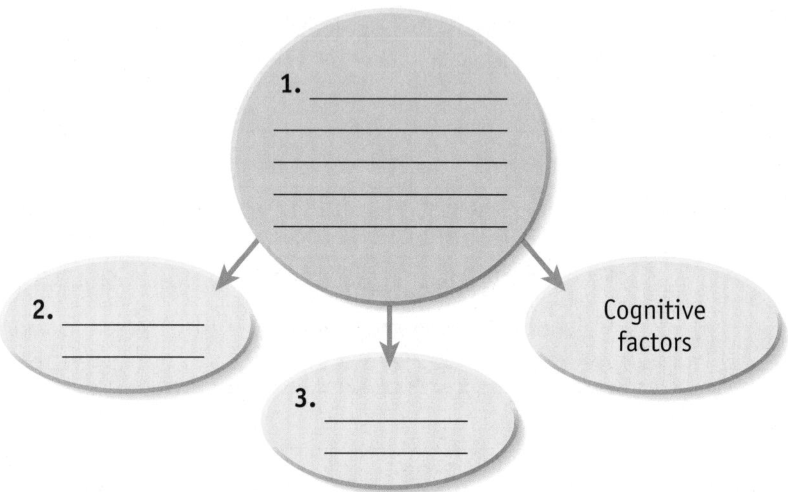


4. What signal word or phrase introduces the third major supporting detail?

______________________________

B. Read the following paragraph from a college political science textbook.

### Traditional Democratic Theory

[1]Democracy depends on a number of key values. [2]The first value is equality in voting. [3]The ideal of "one person, one vote" is basic to democracy. [4]Another principle of a self-ruling people is effective participation. [5]Citizens must be able to express their desires and wishes during the decision-making process. [6]A third value is enlightened understanding. [7]A self-governing society must be a marketplace of ideas with a free press and free speech. [8]Fourth, citizens must control the agenda. [9]Citizens should have the collective right to control the government's policy agenda. [10]Finally, inclusion is key. [11]The government must include, and extend rights to, all who are subject to its laws.

—Adapted from Edwards, Wattenberg, & Lineberry, *Government in America: People, Politics, and Policy,* 5th ed., p. 10.

Fill in the concept map with the main idea and major supporting details from the paragraph.

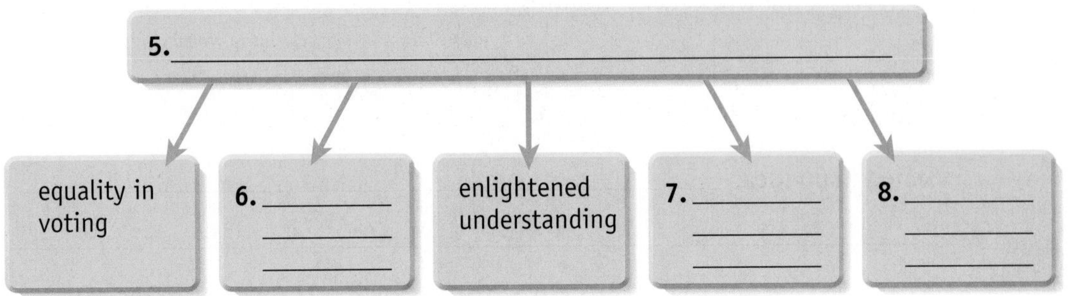


9. What word or phrase in the topic sentence indicates that a list of supporting details will follow? ____

10. What word or phrase introduces the second major supporting detail?

____

# REVIEW Test 3

## Supporting Details, Outlines, and Concept Maps

A. (1–6.) Read the following paragraph from a college communications textbook. Then complete the informal outline by giving the main idea and the major supporting details.

### Stage Two of the Listening Process: Understanding

[1]In stage one of the listening process, you receive the speaker's message; however, in stage two, you must take into consideration the speaker's thoughts and emotional tone. [2]Understanding is the stage in the listening process at which you learn what the speaker means. [3]In the understanding phase, you should adopt several effective listening behaviors. [4]First, you should avoid assuming you understand what the speaker is going to say before he or she actually says it. [5]Second, you should relate new information the speaker is giving to what you already know. [6]Third, you should see the speaker's message from the speaker's point of view; avoid judging the message until you fully understand it as the speaker intended it. [7]Fourth, you

should ask questions for clarification, if necessary; ask for additional details or examples if they are needed. [8]Finally, rephrase the speaker's ideas in your own words. [9]Adopting these listening behaviors should ensure that you understand the speaker's meaning.

—Adapted from DeVito, *The Interpersonal Communication Book*, 10th ed., p. 118.

Stated main idea: ______________________________________________

______________________________________________

______________________________________________

**A.** ______________________________________________

______________________________________________

**B.** ______________________________________________

**C.** ______________________________________________

______________________________________________

**D.** ______________________________________________

______________________________________________

**E.** ______________________________________________

**B.** (7–10.) Read the following paragraph from a college science textbook. Complete the concept map with the main idea and the major supporting details from the paragraph.

Textbook Skills

**Diverse Ecosystems**

[1]A view from the window of a plane reveals the diversity of the world's ecosystems. [2]On a trip of less than eight hours, the airborne ecologist can look down and see a wide range of vegetation that took years to discover. [3]Botanists were the first to note that the world could be divided into several great blocks of vegetation. [4]The first type of vegetation block is the desert. [5]Experts define deserts as lands where less than 10 inches of precipitation falls per year. [6]In addition, all deserts have a wide daily range in temperature from hot by day to cool by night. [7]The second type is made up of the grasslands. [8]All grasslands have in common a climate in which the precipitation is too light to support a heavy forest and too great to result in a desert. [9]They also share a rolling to flat

terrain. [10]A third type of vegetation is the many and varied forests, which range from boreal to tropical. [11]One example is a temperate rain forest that has a mild climate, heavy rainfall, and lush vegetation growth.

—Adapted from Smith & Smith, *Elements of Ecology*, 4th ed., pp. 390, 397, 414, and 549.

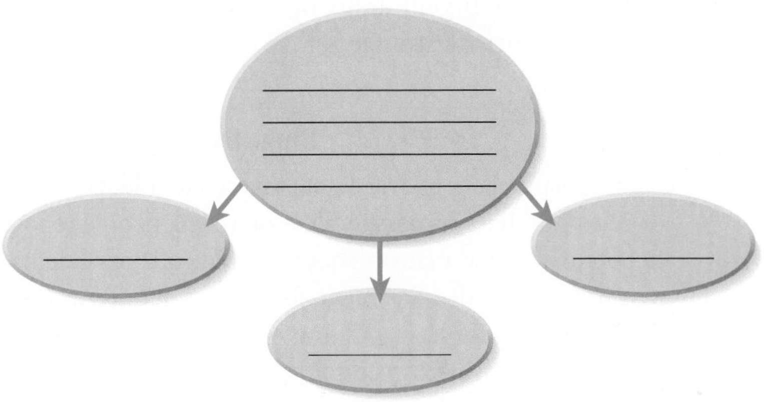

**VISUAL VOCABULARY**

The ecoregion shown in the photo is a type of __________

a. desert.
b. grassland.
c. boreal forest.

# REVIEW Test 4

## Supporting Details and Outlines

Before you read the following passage, skim the material and answer the **Before Reading** questions. Read the passage. Then answer the **After Reading** questions.

### Vocabulary Preview

*prevalence* (4): frequency of occurrence
*adolescence* (5): teenage years
*surveyed* (9): studied, questioned
*symptoms* (16): warning signs
*compulsiveness* (24): urgent desire or driven behavior
*deviant* (24): abnormal, strange

## Binge Drinking

[1]Despite laws in every state that make it illegal for anyone under the age of 21 to purchase or possess alcohol, young people report that alcohol is easy to obtain and that many high school and college students drink with one goal in mind—to get drunk. [2]Binge drinking is defined as consuming five or more drinks in a row for boys and four or more in a row for girls. [3]The alarming aspects of binge drinking cannot be overlooked or underestimated.

[4]One troubling aspect of binge drinking is its **prevalence** among youth and college students. [5]Often starting as young as age 13, these drinkers tend to increase bingeing during **adolescence**. [6]The behavior peaks in young adulthood, which includes the ages from 18 to 22. [7]Then this **perilous** conduct slowly decreases. [8]According to a 1997 national study, among 12- to 20-year-olds, fifteen percent were binge drinkers. [9]A 1995 study found that nearly half of all college students **surveyed** drank four or five drinks in one sitting within a two-week period. [10]In addition, students who live in fraternity and sorority houses are the heaviest drinkers. [11]Over 80 percent of them reported that they take part in binge drinking.

[12]Binge drinking is risky behavior that has serious **consequences**. [13]The most grave effect is **alcohol poisoning**, which is an **acute** physical reaction to an overdose of the alcohol. [14]During bingeing, the brain is deprived of oxygen. [15]This lack of oxygen eventually causes the brain to shut down the heart and lungs. [16]Alcohol poisoning has several **symptoms**. [17]They include vomiting and unconsciousness. [18]In addition, the skin becomes cold, clammy, pale or bluish in color. [19]Breathing becomes slow or irregular.

[20]Binge drinking brings about other disturbing behaviors or effects as well. [21]In schools with high binge drinking rates, binge drinkers are likely to insult, **humiliate**, push, or hit their peers. [22]Frequent binge drinkers were eight times more likely than nonbinge drinkers to miss a class, fall behind in schoolwork, get hurt or injured, and damage property. [23]Binge drinking during college may be linked with mental health disorders. [24]These disorders include **compulsiveness**, depression or anxiety, or early **deviant** behavior.

[25]Alarmingly, nearly one out of every five teenagers has experienced "blackout" spells. [26]During these spells, they could not remember what happened the previous evening because of heavy binge drinking. [27]Finally, many who are frequent binge drinkers also drink and drive.

—Adapted from U.S. Department of Human and Health Services, "Binge Drinking in Adolescents and College Students."

## BEFORE READING

### Vocabulary in Context

_____ **1.** In sentence 7 of the passage, the word **perilous** means
a. adventurous.
b. dangerous.
c. fun-loving.
d. disgusting.

_____ **2.** In sentence 13 of the passage, the word **acute** means
a. unavoidable.
b. short-term.
c. invisible.
d. severe.

## AFTER READING

### Main Ideas

_____ **3.** Which sentence states the central idea of the passage?
a. Sentence 1
b. Sentence 2
c. Sentence 3
d. Sentence 4

_____ **4.** Which sentence is the topic sentence of the fourth paragraph?
a. Sentence 20
b. Sentence 21
c. Sentence 26
d. Sentence 27

### Supporting Details

**5-7.** Complete the summary with information from the passage.

Alcohol poisoning is ______________________________.

Symptoms include vomiting; ______________; cold, clammy, pale or bluish skin; slow or irregular ______________.

**8–10.** Complete the following informal outline of the fourth paragraph by filling in the blanks.

Stated main idea: Binge drinking brings about other disturbing behaviors or effects.

**A.** ______________________________

**B.** Binge drinkers are more likely to do poorly in school, get hurt, cause damage.

**C.** ______________________________

**D.** Binge drinkers may have blackout spells.

**E.** ______________________________

## Discussion Topics

1. Why is binge drinking so prevalent among youth and college students?
2. Why do you think binge drinking is related to mental disorders?
3. What role should colleges play in addressing the problem of binge drinking?

## Writing Topics

1. Write a letter to a college or school newspaper explaining the dangers of binge drinking. Include real-life examples if you know of any.
2. In a paragraph, explore or discuss a way to address the problem of binge drinking.

## EFFECTIVE READER Scorecard

### Outlines and Concept Maps

| Test | Number Correct | | Points | | Score |
|---|---|---|---|---|---|
| Review Test 1 | ________ | × | 10 | = | ________ |
| Review Test 2 | ________ | × | 10 | = | ________ |
| Review Test 3 | ________ | × | 10 | = | ________ |
| Review Test 4 | ________ | × | 10 | = | ________ |
| Review Test 5 (website) | ________ | × | 10 | = | ________ |
| Review Test 6 (website) | ________ | × | 10 | = | ________ |

Enter your scores on the Effective Reader Scorecard: Chapter 5 Review Tests inside the back cover.

## After Reading About Outlines and Concept Maps

Before you move on to the mastery tests on outlines and concept maps, take time to reflect on your learning and performance by answering the following questions. Write your answers in your notebook.

What did I learn about outlines and concept maps?

What do I need to remember about outlines and concept maps?

How has my knowledge base or prior knowledge about outlines and concept maps changed?

### More Review and Mastery Tests

For more practice, go to the book's website at **http://www.ablongman.com/henry/** and click on *The Effective Reader*. Then select "More Review and Mastery Tests." The tests are organized by chapter.

MASTERY **Test 1**

Name ______________________ Section ____________

Date ____________ **Score** (number correct) ______ × 10 = ______%

Read the following passage from a college textbook about gender and communication. Complete the activities that follow with information from the passage.

## Self-Concept

[1]**Self-concept** is comprised of everything one thinks and knows about oneself. [2]It is the relatively stable set of views one attributes to oneself. [3]As a personal assessment of yourself, your self-concept can be summed up by what you think of yourself in relationship to others. [4]Your self-concept didn't form overnight. [5]Like your gender identity, your self-concept developed in early childhood. [6]And, once established, self-concept is fairly resistant to change. [7]The first day you said "I," or "me," you recognized yourself as separate from your surroundings. [8]You distinguished yourself from others around you. [9]The idea *self-concept* is sometimes broken into two components: *self-image* and *self-esteem.*

## Self-Image and Self-Esteem

[10]**Self-image** is the sort of person you believe yourself to be. [11]Self-image is made up of physical and emotional descriptions of the self and the roles you play. [12]**Self-esteem** is a measure of the value you place on the images you have of yourself. [13]Self-esteem includes your attitudes and feelings about yourself including how well you like and value yourself. [14]It is your judgment of how you are doing in life (your perceived self) compared to how you think you should be doing (your ideal self).

[15]According to researcher Chris Mruk, self-esteem is composed of five dimensions:

- [16]*competence* (your beliefs about your ability to be effective),
- [17]*worthiness* (your beliefs about the extent to which others value you),
- [18]*cognition* (your beliefs about your character and personality),
- [19]*affect* (how you evaluate yourself and the feelings generated by this evaluation), and
- [20]*stability* or change (which greatly affects your communication with others).

[21]A number of social forces come together to help create and feed your self-concept. [22]First, the image people have of you guides what they expect of you, how they relate to you, and how they interact with you. [23]Second, as you learn about and understand their images, your self-concept affects the way you think about yourself. [24]For example, if people who are important to you have a positive image of you, they are apt to make you feel accepted, valued, worthwhile, loved, and significant. [25]If, on the other hand, they have a negative image of you, more than likely they will contribute to your feeling small, worthless, unloved, or insignificant. [26]Whatever its nature, you never stop receiving information about yourself.

—Adapted from Teri Kwai Gamble and Michael W. Gamble. (2003) *The Gender Communication Connection,* New York: Longman. pp. 43–44.

**1–5.** Complete the concept map by filling in the main idea and the missing major and minor supporting details. ______________________.

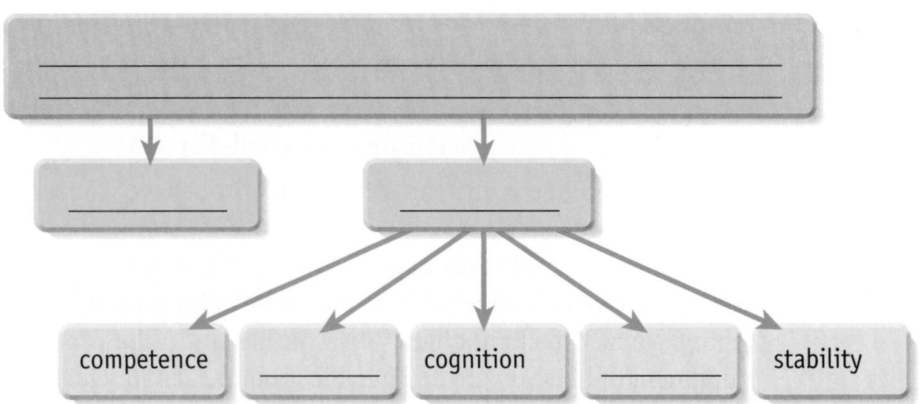


**6–8.** Complete the following outline of the third paragraph with the missing supporting details.

Topic Sentence: ______________________________________.

1. The image people have of you guides what they expect of you, how they relate to you, and how they interact with you.
2. ______________________________________
______________________________________.

a. For example, if people who are important to you have a positive image of you, they are apt to make you feel accepted, valued, worthwhile, loved, and significant.

b. ______________________________________________

______________________________________________.

**9–10.** Complete the following summary with information from the passage. Wording may vary.

**Self-concept** is made up of everything one thinks and knows about oneself. Self-concept is broken into two components: self-image and self-esteem. **Self-image** is ______________________________. **Self-esteem** is ______________________________. Self-esteem is composed of five dimensions: competence, worthiness, cognition, affect, and stability.

MASTERY **Test 2**

Name ______________________ Section __________

Date __________ **Score** (number correct) ______ × 10 = ______%

**A.** Read the following paragraph from a college government textbook.

Textbook Skills

### Prior Restraint

[1]The principle of prior restraint stands out clearly in the history of freedom of expression laws. [2]Time and time again, the Supreme Court has struck down prior restraint on speech and press. [3]**Prior restraint** refers to a government's actions that prevent materials from being published. [4]Prior restraint is censorship. [5]In the United States, the First Amendment ensures that even if the government frowns on certain material, a person's right to publish it is sacred. [6]A landmark case involving prior restraint is *Near* v. *Minnesota* (1931). [7]A blunt newspaper editor called local officials a string of names including "grafters" and "Jewish gangsters." [8]The state closed down his business. [9]But the Supreme Court ordered the paper reopened.

—Adapted from Edwards, Wattenberg, and Lineberry, *Government in America,* p. 87.

**1–8.** Fill in the outline with the main idea, major supporting details, and minor supporting details from the paragraph.

Stated main idea: ______________________________

______________________________

I. ______________________________

II. ______________________________

______________________________

III. ______________________________

IV. ______________________________

A. ______________________________

B. ______________________________

C. ______________________________

**B.** Read the following paragraph from a college literature textbook.

Textbook Skills

### Hamartia and Hubris

[1]In ancient Greek drama, the tragic hero is a person of "high estate," most likely a king or queen or other person of noble birth. [2]However, the tragic hero is not a superman; he is fallible. [3]According to Aristotle, the famous fourth century B.C. philosopher who defined ancient tragedy, the hero's downfall is the result of his **hamartia**—that is, his flaw or weakness of character. [4]Every tragic hero has some type of fatal weakness that brings him to a bad end. [5]In some classical tragedies, the flaw is a weakness the Greeks called **hubris**, or extreme pride.

—Adapted from Kennedy & Gioia, *Literature*, 8th ed., p. 1380.

**9–10.** Complete the summary.

Aristotle defined the tragic hero's fatal flaw in two ways. **Hamartia** is ________________________________, and **hubris** is __________.

MASTERY **Test 3**

Name ______________________ Section ____________

Date ____________ **Score** (number correct) ______ × 20 = ______%

**A.** Read the following paragraph from a college algebra textbook.

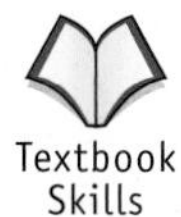
Textbook Skills

### Applications of Slope: Rates of Change

[1]Slope has many real-world applications. [2]For example, numbers like 2%, 3%, and 6% are often used to represent the **grade** of a road, a measure of how steep a road on a hill or mountain is. [3]For example, a 3% grade means that for every horizontal distance of 100 feet, the road rises 3 feet. [4]The concept of grade also occurs in skiing or snowboarding, where a 4% grade is considered very tame but a 40% grade is considered extremely steep. [5]And in cardiology, a physician may change the grade of a treadmill to measure its effect on heartbeat. [6]Architects and carpenters use slope when designing and building stairs, ramps, or roof pitches. [7]Another application occurs in hydrology. [8]When a river flows, the strength or force of the river depends on how far the river falls vertically compared to how far it flows horizontally.

—Bittinger & Beecher, *Introductory and Intermediate Algebra,* 2nd ed., p. 210.

______ **1.** Which sentence states the main idea of the paragraph?
a. Sentence 1
b. Sentence 2
c. Sentence 3
d. Sentence 8

______ **2.** In general, the major details of this paragraph are
a. facts that describe the causes of a slope.
b. ways to measure a slope.
c. definitions of slopes and grades.
d. examples of slopes and grades in everyday situations.

______ **3.** Numbers expressed in percentages are used to
a. measure heartbeat.
b. measure the distance of a road.
c. represent the grade of a road.
d. represent the force of a river.

______ **4.** How many major details does the author give in this paragraph?
a. two
b. three
c. four
d. five

_____ **5.** The first major detail is signaled by the word or phrase

a. first.
b. for example.
c. one.
d. often.

### VISUAL VOCABULARY

Which word or phrase best completes the following sentence?

The ski slope of the Headwall on Mount Washington in New Hampshire has an 80% grade, making it among the ______________ skiable terrains in North America.

a. most tame
b. safest
c. steepest
d. most interesting

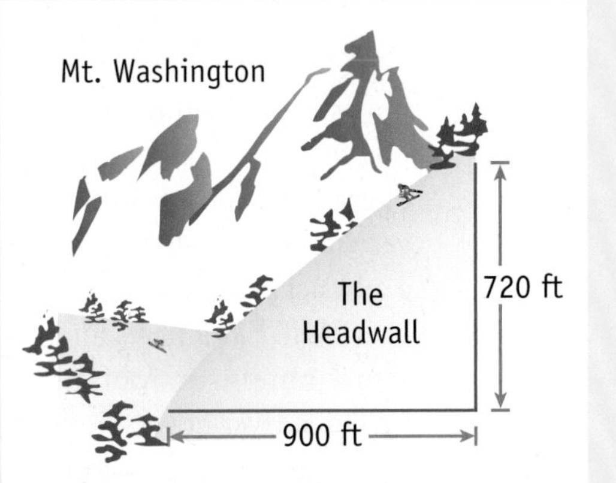


—Bittinger/Beecher, *Introductory and Intermediate Algebra: Combined Approach.* Copyright © 2003 Pearson Education, Inc. Reprinted by permission of Pearson Education, Inc. Publishing as Pearson/Addison Wesley.

# MASTERY Test 4

Name ______________________ Section ____________

Date ____________ **Score** (number correct) ______ × 10 = ______%

**A.** Read the following paragraph from a college government textbook.

### Tasks of Political Parties

[1]Political parties, such as the Democratic, Republican, and Independent parties, are important links between government and the citizens. [2]To work properly, the parties should perform five essential tasks. [3]One primary task of parties is to pick candidates. [4]Almost no one above the local level (and often not even there) gets elected to a public office without winning a party's endorsement. [5]A second task is to run campaigns. [6]On the national, state, and local levels, parties coordinate campaigns. [7]Another important function of parties is that they give cues to voters. [8]Most voters have a party image; that is, they know (or think they know) what each party stands for. [9]Some aspects of a party's image may include liberal, conservative, probusiness, or prolabor views. [10]In addition to the tasks already stated, parties should convey policies. [11]Each political party stands for specific policies. [12]For example, the Democratic party has clearly supported abortion rights; in contrast, the Republican party has often called for limits on abortion. [13]Finally, parties should coordinate policymaking. [14]Parties are vital in the task of bringing together the branches of government. [15]Nearly all major public officials are also members of a party. [16]When they need support to get something done, the first place they look is to their fellow party members.

—Adapted from Edwards, Wattenberg, and Lineberry, *Government in America*, 5th ed., p. 184.

**1–6.** Complete the concept map with the main idea and major supporting details from the paragraph.

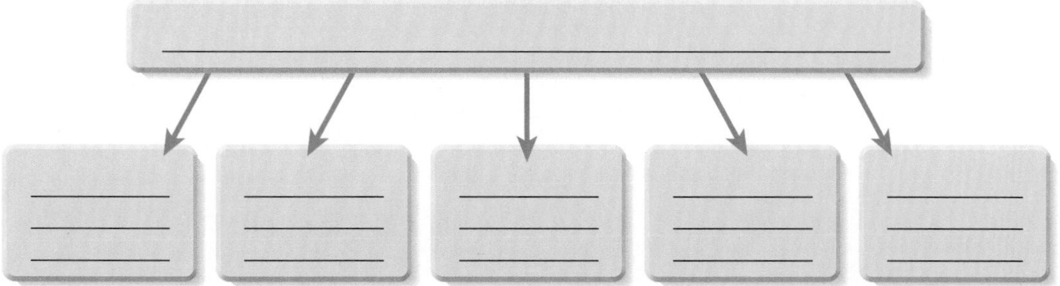

_____ **7.** In general, the major supporting details of this paragraph are
a. examples of political parties.
b. tasks parties should perform.
c. common complaints about political parties.
d. reasons to vote.

_____ **8.** When a party gives its endorsement, it is fulfilling the task of
a. picking candidates.
b. running campaigns.
c. giving voters cues.
d. conveying policies.
e. coordinating policymaking.

_____ **9.** What word or phrase signals the first major supporting detail?
a. for example
b. one
c. first
d. another

_____ **10.** What word or phrase signals the last major supporting detail?
a. nearly
b. in addition
c. also
d. finally

MASTERY **Test 5**

Name ______________________ Section ____________

Date __________ **Score** (number correct) ______ × 10 = ______%

Read the following paragraph. Then complete the items that follow it.

Textbook Skills

### Famine: A Human Tragedy

[1]According to the United States Agency for International Development (USAID), famine is a catastrophic food crisis that results in widespread acute malnutrition and mass mortality. [2]USAID also states that famine is not simply a process, but rather it is an event, with a beginning, middle, and end. [3]Famines have plagued humanity throughout the world over the course of history. [4]For example, Ancient Egypt struggled with famine on occasions due to the Nile River. [5]If the river did not rise, a drought occurred and led to famine; if the river rose too much, flooding caused famine. [6]One of the worst famines in modern European history took place in Ireland from 1845–1849. [7]In 1845, after three weeks of rain, the potato crops became blackened by blight. [8]The next year, the crops failed again, and the winter was unusually severe. [9]In 1849, blight reappeared on a widespread scale. [10]More than 1 million people starved, and 1.6 million left Ireland. [11]In the 1930s, a severe drought caused a famine in part of the United States. [12]The great drought in Oklahoma, Kansas, and eastern Colorado coupled with poor farming techniques caused a famine. [13]The afflicted area became known as the "Dust Bowl." [14]Nearly 250,000 American citizens fled their farms and homes and migrated to California to find jobs. [15]India and China have also struggled with bouts of famine. [16]In some years, heavy rains in these heavily populated countries wash out crops before they can be harvested; at other times, drought makes planting or growing crops impossible.

______ **1.** Sentence 3 is a
a. main idea.
b. major supporting detail.

______ **2.** How many major supporting details are in this paragraph?
a. two
b. three
c. four
d. five

______ **3.** What word or phrase signals the first major supporting detail?
a. first
b. one
c. for example
d. during

_____ **4.** What word or phrase signals the fourth major supporting detail?

a. and
b. next
c. third
d. also

_____ **5.** In general, the supporting details of this paragraph

a. call for better farming techniques.
b. list examples of famines that have occurred.
c. explain the causes of famines.
d. explain the need to send food to areas plagued by famines.

_____ **6.** The "dust bowl" is a name for the famine that

a. occurred in Egypt around 1450.
b. occurred in a part of the United States in the 1930s.
c. occurred in China and India.
d. can be avoided with better farming techniques.

**7–10.** Complete the outline of the paragraph's third major supporting detail and its missing minor supporting details.

Third major supporting detail: ______________________________

______________________________________________

**1.** ______________________________________________

______________________________________________

**2.** ______________________________________________

**3.** ______________________________________________

______________________________________________

# MASTERY Test 6

Name ________________ Section ________

Date ________ **Score** (number correct) ______ × 10 = ______%

Read the following passage.

## Work Addiction

[1]Work addiction is a serious problem for two reasons: lack of understanding about the addiction and the effects of the addiction on the addicts and those around them.

[2]First, in order to understand work addiction, we need to understand the concept of healthy work and how it differs from work addiction. [3]Healthy work provides a sense of identity, helps develop our strengths, and is a means of satisfaction, accomplishment, and mastery of problems. [4]Healthy workers may work for long hours. [5]Although they have occasional projects that keep them away from friends, family, and personal interests for short periods, they generally maintain balance in their lives and are in full control of their schedules. [6]Healthy work does not consume the worker. [7]In contrast, work addiction is the compulsive use of work to fulfill needs of intimacy, power, and success. [8]It is characterized by obsession, rigidity, fear, anxiety, low self-esteem, isolation, and the need to be perfect. [9]Work addiction is more than being unable to relax when not doing something thought of as "productive." [10]It is the pursuit of the "work persona," an image that work addicts wish to project onto others.

[11]In addition to understanding the basic traits of work addiction, we must also understand the dangerous effects it has on individuals and those around them. [12]One area that is deeply affected is family life. [13]Work addiction is a major source of marital problems and family breakups. [14]In fact, most work addicts come from homes that were alcoholic, rigid, violent, or otherwise unhealthy. [15]In addition to harming the family, work addiction takes a toll on people's emotional and physical health. [16]They may become emotionally crippled. [17]They lose the ability to connect with other people. [18]They are often riddled with guilt and fear; they fear failure, and they fear their shortcomings will be discovered. [19]Work addicts may also suffer several physical effects. [20]For example, because they are unable to relax and play, they often suffer from chronic fatigue syndrome. [21]Work addicts suffer as well from digestive problems, and they often report feeling pressure in the chest, difficulty breathing, dizziness, and lightheadedness.

—Adapted from Donatelle, *Access to Health*, 7th ed., p. 318.

______ **1.** In the overall passage, sentence 2 is a

a. thesis statement.
b. major supporting detail.
c. minor supporting detail.

_____ **2.** How many major supporting details support the thesis statement in this passage?
a. two
b. three
c. four
d. five

_____ **3.** What word or phrase signals the first major supporting detail?
a. first
b. one
c. for example
d. during

_____ **4.** What word or phrase signals the second major supporting detail?
a. and
b. next
c. in addition
d. also

_____ **5.** In general, the supporting details of the second paragraph
a. explain the differences between healthy work and work addiction.
b. offer ways to cope with work addiction.
c. explain the term *work persona.*
d. list situations in which workers become addicted to their work.

_____ **6.** Overall, the supporting details of the third paragraph
a. list the physical effects of work addiction.
b. list the emotional effects of work addiction.
c. explain the causes of work addiction.
d. explain the emotional and physical effects of work addiction.

**7–10.** Complete the concept map with supporting details from the second paragraph.

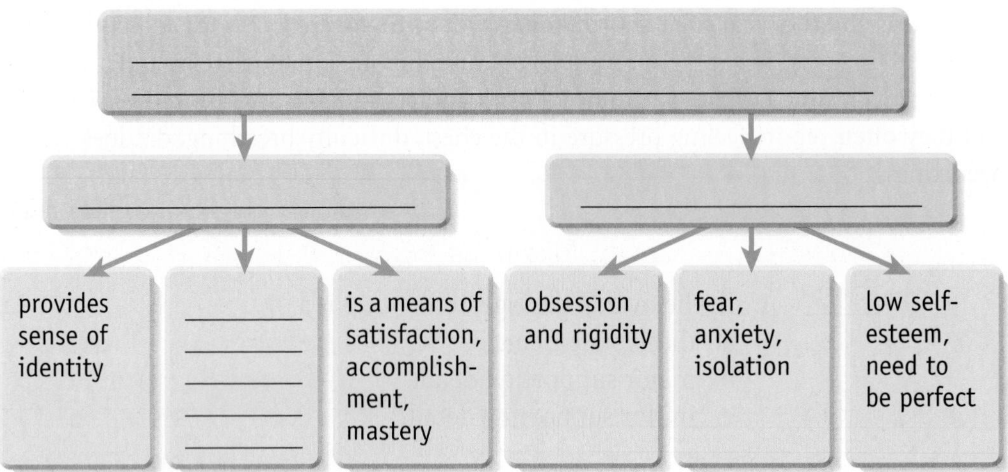

CHAPTER

6

# Transitions and Thought Patterns

## CHAPTER PREVIEW

## Before Reading About Transitions and Thought Patterns

Using the reporter's questions (Who? What? When? Where? Why? and How?), refer to the chapter preview and create at least three questions that you can answer as you study the chapter. Write your questions in the following spaces:

______________________________________________________?

______________________________________________________?

______________________________________________________?

Now take a few minutes to skim the chapter for ideas and terms that you have studied in previous chapters. List those ideas in the following spaces:

______________________________________________________

______________________________________________________

Compare the questions you created based on the chapter preview with the following questions. Then write the ones that seem the most helpful in your notebook, leaving enough space between each question to record the answers as you read and study the chapter.

What are transitions? What are thought patterns? What is the relationship between transition words and thought patterns? How do thought patterns use transition words?

On page 249, the terms main idea, supporting details, and outlines are discussed in relationship to transitions and thought patterns. Consider the following study questions based on these ideas: How can transitions help me understand the author's main idea? How can transitions help me create an outline?

## Transition Words: Relationships Within a Sentence

Read the following set of ideas. Which word makes the relationship between the ideas clear?

> Martha Stewart had achieved remarkable success and enormous wealth by making smart business decisions. ________________, in 2002, she made an unwise decision about a stock market trade that caused her to resign from her position as chair of her company, Martha Stewart Living Omnimedia.
>
> a. Also  b. However  c. For example

The word that makes the relationship between these two ideas clear is (b) *However*. The first sentence describes Martha Stewart as successful and smart. The second sentence offers a stark contrast by stating she made an "unwise" and damaging decision. The word *however* best signals this contrast.

Transitions are key pattern words and phrases that signal the logical relationships within and between sentences. **Transitions** help you make sense of an author's idea in two basic ways. First, transitions join ideas within a sentence. Second, transitions establish **thought patterns** so readers can understand the logical flow of ideas between sentences.

**Transitions** are words and phrases that signal thought patterns by showing the logical relationships within a sentence and between sentences.

A **thought pattern** is established by using transitions to show the logical relationship between ideas in a paragraph or passage.

Read the following sentence. Which word makes the relationship of ideas within the sentence clear?

Fernando deserves to be recognized for his public service _______________ he has worked faithfully for twenty years with the Boy Scouts and the youth soccer league.

a. before b. in addition c. because

All three of these choices are transitions; however, the word that best clarifies the relationship of ideas within this sentence is (c) *because*. Fernando's work with youth is the reason he deserves to be recognized. The relationship is one of cause and effect. Transition (a) *before* reveals time order, and transition (b) *in addition* indicates that the author is adding to the first idea. In the next section, you will learn more about these transitions and thought patterns. First, it is helpful to see how transitions serve a vital function in building ideas within a sentence.

**EXAMPLE** Complete the following with a transition that shows the relationship of ideas within each sentence. Fill in each blank with a word from the box. Use each word once.

| also | as a result | inside | such as |
|---|---|---|---|

1. Not only does academic cheating rob the cheating student of knowledge, it can _______________ severely damage that student's reputation.
2. One kind of effective foot warmer is a soft, lightweight insole that generates its own heat with exposure to air and can be slipped _______________ a shoe or boot.
3. Travis eliminated unhealthy eating habits, diligently worked out at the gym three times a week, and walked vigorously for 30 minutes every day; _______________, after six months he attained his ideal weight.
4. Olivia invests in a variety of financial assets _______________ stocks, bonds, and real estate.

**EXPLANATION**

1. The topic of this sentence is cheating. The author makes two points about cheating. *Also* indicates the addition of the second point.

2. The topic of this sentence is one kind of foot warmer. The author is describing its traits. One trait is where it is used; it is placed *inside* the shoe or boot.

3. This sentence brings two topics or ideas together. The first part of the sentence deals with Travis' healthy lifestyle (this topic is suggested by the list of details). The topic of the second part of the sentence is "ideal weight." The second idea is the result of the first. The correct answer is *as a result.*

4. The topic of this sentence is the variety of Olivia's assets. The phrase *such as* indicates that a list of examples follows.

Note that to determine the correct transition for each of the sentences, you had to rely upon context clues to first determine the relationship of ideas. Understanding relationships and thought patterns is closely related to a clear understanding of vocabulary.

## PRACTICE 1

Complete the following with a transition that shows the relationship of ideas within each sentence. Fill in each blank with a word from the box. Use each word once.

| besides | because | furthermore | such as |
|---|---|---|---|

1. The Internet offers several benefits ______________ instant communication, access to a worldwide market, and access to a variety of sources for personal and educational information.

2. Travis has maintained his ideal weight for over two years ______________ he changed his lifestyle.

3. ______________ being a business owner, president of the Women's Council, a wife, and a mother of three small children, Elizabeth is a regular volunteer for Habitat for Humanity.

4. A group of angry citizens is fighting a development company's plans to build a 1,500-home golf course community on The Loop. The Loop is a 23-mile stretch of roadway that winds through a rare and beautiful patch of old Florida. Increased traffic and the use of golf course chemicals will threaten wildlife; ______________, this project will destroy a majestic canopy of oaks that shrouds the roadway.

**VISUAL VOCABULARY**

______ The word **shrouds** means

a. blocks.
b. beautifies.
c. covers.

Transitions express a variety of relationships between ideas. You must therefore look carefully at the meaning of each transitional word or phrase. Some transition words have similar meanings. For example, *also, too,* and *furthermore* all signal the relationship of addition or listing. Sometimes a single word can serve as two different types of transitions, depending on how it is used. For example, the word *since* can reveal time order, or it can signal a cause. Notice the difference in the following two sentences.

> *Since* I began working, I have saved several thousand dollars.
>
> *Since* you are familiar with the assignment, Janice, please lead the group discussion.

The relationship between the ideas in the first sentence is based on time order. The relationship between the ideas in the second sentence is based on cause and effect.

Effective readers look for transition words, study their meaning in context, and use them as keys to unlock the author's thought patterns.

## PRACTICE 2

Read the following paragraph. Fill in each blank with a transition that shows the relationship between ideas. Choose your answers from the words in the box. Use each word once.

| | | |
|---|---|---|
| although | for example | so |
| and | however | such as |
| because | in addition | |
| but | now | |

### Out of Control

Substance abuse on college campuses is nothing new, (**1**) ____________ it is taking a more extreme and dangerous form. The percentage of students who drink has remained about the same. (**2**) ____________, the intensity of the drinking has radically changed. (**3**) ____________, more students binge drink two or three times a week. (**4**) ____________, more are drinking 10 or more times a month, (**5**) ____________ they get drunk three or more times in a month. (**6**) ____________ more students are abusing prescription drugs (**7**) ____________ Ritalin, alcohol remains the most abused drug. Young adults in general have higher abuse rates, (**8**) ____________ a higher rate for college students is to be expected. This trend must be stopped (**9**) ____________ of the physical and mental health dangers. (**10**) ____________ that we recognize the extreme levels of substance abuse on our college campuses, we must take action.

—Adapted from "College Binge Drinking, Pill Abuse Intensify." MSNBC.com 18 March 2007. <http://www.msnbc.msn.com/id/17613969>.

## Thought Patterns: Relationships Between Sentences

Not only do transitions reveal the relationships of ideas *within* a sentence, they also show the relationship *between* sentences. Read the following sentences and choose the word that best states the relationship between the sentences.

Resistance training, such as weightlifting, offers several benefits. ______________, it tones the muscles and increases bone density.

a. As a result b. However c. For example

The transition that best states the relationship between these sentences is (c) *For example*. The first sentence is a generalization. It contains a topic and a controlling point about the topic. The topic is "resistance training"; the point is "several benefits." The second sentence offers an example as a supporting detail for the general point. Transition (a) *As a result* signals cause and effect. And (b) *However* indicates a contrast. In this chapter and Chapter 7, you will study the ways in which authors use these and other thought patterns in paragraphs and longer passages. First, it is important to learn to find the relationship between sentences.

**EXAMPLE** Complete the following with transitions that make the relationship between the sentences clear. Fill in each blank with a word from the box. Use each word once.

| after | above | furthermore |
|---|---|---|

1. Jennifer Lopez broke off her engagement with Ben Affleck due to excessive media attention. ____________ five months of recovering from her heartbreak, she married Marc Anthony in a private and secret ceremony.
2. A frustrated father overheard talking to his son said, "You are going to make several major changes. You will come home at a decent hour. You will keep your room orderly. You will speak respectfully to your mother and me. ______________, you will get a job."
3. Airplanes offer two storage places for carry-on luggage. Small bags can be placed under the seat in front of a passenger. Larger bags must be stored in compartments located ______________ the seat.

**EXPLANATION**

1. The relationship between the sentences is based on time. The words "five months" serve as a clue that the correct transition is *after*.
2. The father states a list of behaviors he expects from his son. The word *furthermore* signals an additional behavior that is expected.
3. The first sentence establishes the relationship between these sentences as space order with the use of the word "places." The correct transition is *above*.

## PRACTICE 3

Complete the following with transitions. Fill in each blank with a word from the box. Use each word once.

| as a result | before | during | in contrast | when |
|---|---|---|---|---|

Kaleigh learned that equipment makes a significant difference in the success and enjoyment of a sport or exercise when she traded her old bike in for a new comfort bike. Her old bike was equipped with aerodynamic handle bars, a hard, narrow seat, and no shock absorbers. (**1**) ________________, she endured bumpy, uncomfortable rides that left her sore, and she dreaded cycling as an activity. (**2**) ________________, her comfort bike is equipped with upright handle bars, a plush gel seat, and state of the art shock absorbers. Now Kaleigh loves long-distance cycling. Every morning long (**3**) ________________ most people are up, Kaleigh already has on her helmet, pads, and gloves. (**4**) ________________ she first begins a ride, she considers how long the ride will be so that she can set a pace and conserve her energy. (**5**) ________________ the ride, Kaleigh varies her pace to maximize her workout. After a long ride, Kaleigh feels a sense of satisfaction and strength.

## PRACTICE 4

Complete the following paragraph by inserting transitions. Fill in each blank with a word from the box. Use each word once.

| | | |
|---|---|---|
| and | however | when |
| during | thus | |

### Confucius

The name Confucius is the latinized form of the Chinese characters, K′ung Foo-tsze, meaning, "The master, K′ung." The bearer of this name was born of an ancient and distinguished family in the district of Tsow, in the present province of Shen-tung, China, B. C. 551. His father was a soldier of reputation and governor of Tsow, but not a man of wealth. Confucius married at nineteen, (**1**) ________________, in his early manhood held a minor office; but within a few years he became a public teacher, and soon attracted numerous disciples. Rising in reputation, he was invited to the court of Chow. (**2**) ________________ this time, he investigated the traditional ceremonies and maxims of the ruling dynasty; and in the following year visited another state where he studied ancient music. (**3**) ________________ he was nearly fifty, in the year 500 B.C., he again took office, becoming, in turn, chief magistrate of the town of Chung-too, Assistant-Superintendent of

Works to the Ruler of Loo, and finally Minister of Crime. In spite of almost miraculous efficiency, he lost the support of his ruler in 496 B.C.; and until his death in 478 B.C., he wandered from state to state, sometimes well-treated, sometimes enduring severe hardships, always saddened by the refusal of the turbulent potentates to be guided by his beneficent counsels. No sooner was he dead, (**4**) _______________, than his wisdom was recognized by peasant and emperor alike; admiration rose to veneration, veneration to worship. (**5**) _______________ , sacrifices were offered to him, temples built in his honor, and a cult established which has lasted almost two thousand years.

—Adapted from *The Sayings of Confucius.* Vol. XLIV, Part 1. The Harvard Classics. New York: P.F. Collier & Son, 1909–14; Bartleby.com, 2001. www.bartleby.com/44/1/. 15 August 2007.

You will recall that a paragraph is made up of a group of ideas. Major details support the main idea, and minor details support the major details. Transitions make the relationship between these three levels of ideas clear, smooth, and easy to follow.

Before beginning to write, an author must ask, "What thought pattern best expresses these ideas?" or "How should these ideas be organized so that the reader can follow and understand my point?" A **thought pattern** (also called a **pattern of organization**) allows the author to arrange the supporting details in a clear and smooth flow by using transition words.

> **Thought patterns** (or **patterns of organization**) are signalled by using transitions to show the logical relationship between ideas in a paragraph, passage, or textbook chapter.

As you learned in Chapter 3, a main idea is made up of a topic and the author's controlling point about the topic. One way an author controls the topic is by using a specific thought pattern. Read the following paragraph. Identify the topic sentence by circling the topic and underlining the controlling point.

### The Traits of Olfaction

The sense of smell, also known as olfaction, has two interesting traits. First, people have difficulty describing odors in words. Second, odors have a powerful ability to call to mind old memories and feelings, even many years after an event.

—Adapted from Carlson and Buskist. *Psychology: The Science of Behavior,* 5th ed., p. 191.

The topic is the "sense of smell" and the controlling point is the phrase "two interesting traits." The word "interesting" states the author's opinion. The words "two traits" state the author's thought pattern. The author's controlling point limits the supporting details to listing and describing two interesting traits of smell. The transition words *first* and *second* signal each of the supporting details. Authors often introduce supporting details with transition words based on the controlling point. Creating an outline using transition words is an excellent way to grasp an author's thought pattern.

**EXAMPLE** Read the following paragraph. Complete the informal outline, then answer the question.

**The Landscape of Taste**

Moving from front to back, the surface of the tongue is differentially sensitive to taste. The front or tip is most sensitive to sweet and salty substances. Next, the sides are most sensitive to sour substances. Finally, the back of the tongue, the back of the throat, and the soft palate overhanging the back of the tongue are sensitive to bitter substances.

—Adapted from Carlson and Buskist. *Psychology: The Science of Behavior,* 5th ed., p. 190.

**Topic sentence:** ______________________________________________

______________________________________________

a. ______________________________________________

b. ______________________________________________

c. ______________________________________________

______________________________________________

______ What is the author's thought pattern?

a. time order    b. space order

**EXPLANATION** Compare your outline to the following:

**Topic sentence:** Moving from front to back, the surface of the tongue is differentially sensitive to taste.

a. The front or tip is most sensitive to sweet and salty substances.

b. Next, the sides are most sensitive to sour substances.

c. Finally, the back of the tongue, the back of the throat, and the soft palate overhanging the back of the tongue are sensitive to bitter substances.

The topic is "the surface of the tongue." The thought pattern is expressed in the words "moving from front to back" and "differentially sensitive." The transitions clearly carry out the thought pattern by beginning with the *front* of the tongue, next the *sides*, and finally the *back* of the tongue. In this paragraph, the transitions establish the (b) space order thought pattern.

## PRACTICE 5

Read the following paragraph. Then complete the informal outline.

**Taste Versus Flavor**

Taste is different from flavor. On the one hand, taste is the simple ability to sense four sensations: sourness, sweetness, saltiness, and bitterness. On the other hand, the flavor of a food includes its odor as well as its taste. For example, you have probably noticed that the flavors of foods are diminished when you have a head cold. Mucus makes it difficult for odor-laden air to reach your receptors for the sense of smell.

—Adapted from Carlson and Buskist, *Psychology: The Science of Behavior*, 5th ed., p. 189.

**Topic sentence:** ______________________________

a. ______________________________

______________________________

b. ______________________________

1. ______________________________

______________________________

2. Mucus makes it difficult for odor-laden air to reach your receptors for the sense of smell.

Note how the headings for the paragraphs you just read show the close tie between the topic and the author's thought pattern used to present the main idea and organize the supporting details. For example, the title "The Landscape of Taste" uses the word "landscape" to clue the reader to the space order thought pattern. An excellent activity to do before reading is to read the heading and skim ahead for transition words to get the gist of the author's thought pattern.

In this chapter, we discuss four common thought patterns and the transition words and phrases used to signal each:

- The time order pattern
- The space order pattern
- The listing pattern
- The classification pattern

Some additional common thought patterns are covered in Chapter 7.

## The Time Order Pattern

The **time order** thought pattern generally shows a chain of events. The actions or events are listed in the order in which they occur. This is called *chronological order*. Two types of chronological order are narration and process. An author will use narration to tell about the important events in the life of a famous person or a significant event in history. Narration is also used to organize a piece of fiction. The second type of chronological order is process. Process is used to give directions to a task in time order. In summary, there are two basic uses of time order: (1) narration: a chain of events and (2) process: steps, stages, or directions.

### Narration: A Chain of Events

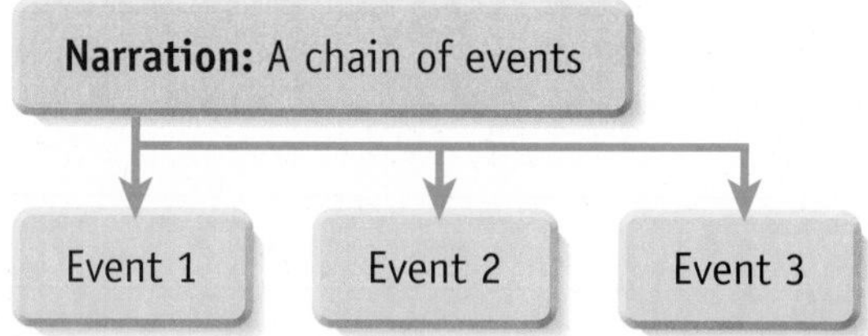


Transitions of **time** signal that the writer is describing *when* things occurred and *in what order*. The writer presents an event and then shows when each of the additional details or events flowed from the first event. Thus the details follow a logical order based on time.

> John Wilkes Booth, who led a very prominent life as an actor in the years before he assassinated Abraham Lincoln, ultimately died a traitor's death.

Notice that this sentence lays out three events. The transition words *before* and *ultimately* tell the order in which the events occurred.

**Transitions Used in the Time Order Pattern for Narration**

| | | | | |
|---|---|---|---|---|
| after | during | later | previously | ultimately |
| afterward | eventually | meanwhile | second | until |
| as | finally | next | since | when |
| before | first | now | soon | while |
| currently | last | often | then | |

**EXAMPLE** Determine the logical order of the following sentences. Write **1** by the sentence that should come first, **2** by the sentence that should come second, **3** by the sentence that should come third, and **4** by the sentence that should come last. (Hint: Circle the time transition words.)

_____ Eventually, his passion for learning earned him a master's degree and a doctorate.

_____ During those early years as a teacher, he found that the more he learned, the more excited he was about teaching, and he loved studying under the guidance of professional teachers.

_____ His first notions of wanting only a four-year bachelor's degree were quickly dispelled.

_____ When Corbin decided to become a teacher, he had no idea that he was also deciding to become a career student.

**EXPLANATION** Compare your answers to the sentences arranged in the proper order in the following paragraph. The transitions are in **bold** print.

> [1]**When** Corbin decided to become a teacher, he had no idea that he was also deciding to become a career student. [2]His **first** notions of wanting only a four-year bachelor's degree were quickly dispelled. [3]**During** those early years as a teacher, he found that the more he learned, the more excited he was about teaching, and he loved studying under the guidance of professional teachers. [4]**Eventually**, his passion for learning earned him a master's degree and a doctorate.

## PRACTICE 6

Determine the logical order for the following sentences. Write **1** by the sentence that should come first, **2** by the sentence that should come second, **3** by the sentence that should come third, **4** by the sentence that should come fourth, and **5** by the sentence that should come fifth. (Hint: Circle the time transition words.)

### Battling Emotional Eating

_____ Clara constantly struggles with the cycle of emotional eating.

_____ At the first sign of a stressor, she resists the urge to eat the foods that bring her comfort, such as fast-food hamburgers and fries, cookies, ice cream, or anything else high in fat and carbohydrates.

_____ Eventually, she gains enough unwanted weight to shock her into self-control.

_____ Then she begins to eat a balanced diet and lose the weight—until the next stressful time.

_____ As the stress stretches into days, she finds her resolve weakened and heads for the junk food.

## Process: Steps, Stages, or Directions

The time order thought pattern for steps, stages, or directions shows actions that can be repeated at any time with similar results. This pattern is used to give steps or directions for completing a task.

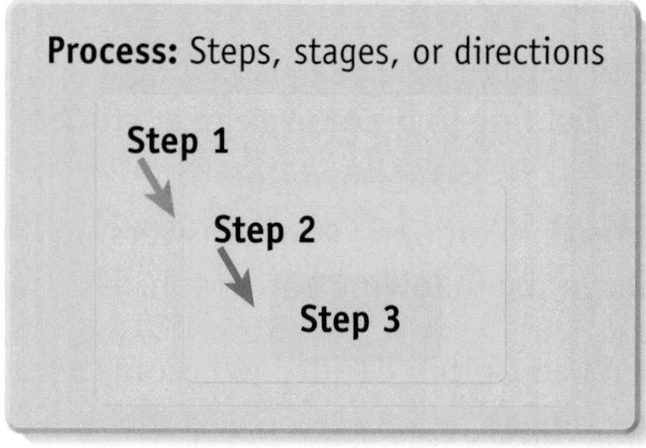


Read the following topic sentences. Underline the words that signal process time order.

1. Follow five simple steps to develop and deepen your friendships.
2. Procrastination recurs in a cycle of self destruction.
3. Grief moves through several stages.

Sentence 1 uses the word *steps* to introduce directions for the reader to follow. Sentence 2 signals that procrastination occurs as part of a pattern of self-destruction with the word *cycle*. Sentence 3 uses the process signal word *stages* to convey the time order of grief. In paragraphs that developed these topic sentences, transitions of time order would likely signal the supporting details.

**Transitions Used in the Time Order Pattern for Process**

| | | | | |
|---|---|---|---|---|
| after | during | later | previously | ultimately |
| afterward | eventually | meanwhile | second | until |
| as | finally | next | since | when |
| before | first | now | soon | while |
| currently | last | often | then | |

**EXAMPLE** The following paragraph uses the time order pattern for process to organize its ideas. Complete the list of steps that follows it by giving the missing details in their proper order. (Hint: Circle the time order transition words.)

### Flossing: Interdental Cleaning

[1]To ensure proper interdental cleaning, floss each day. [2]First, break off about 18 inches of floss and wind most of it around one of your middle fingers. [3]Second, wind the remaining floss around the same finger of the opposite hand. [4]This finger will take up the floss as it becomes dirty. [5]Third, hold the floss tightly between your thumbs and forefingers. [6]Next, guide the floss between your teeth using a gentle rubbing motion; never snap the floss into the gums. [7]When the floss reaches the gum line, curve it into a C shape against one tooth. [8]Then gently slide it into the space between the gum and the tooth. [9]As you hold the floss tightly against the tooth, gently rub the side of the tooth, moving the floss away from the gum with up-and-down motions. [10]Continue this method on the rest of your teeth. [11]Finally, don't forget to floss the back side of your last tooth.

—Adapted from American Dental Association, "Cleaning Your Teeth and Gums."

**VISUAL VOCABULARY**

_____ The word **interdental** means

a. between the teeth.
b. under the gums.
c. in the mouth.

**Flossing: Interdental Cleaning**

Step 1: ______________________________.

Step 2: ______________________________.

Step 3: ______________________________.

Step 4: Guide floss between your teeth.

Step 5: ______________________________.

Step 6: Slide floss into the space between the gum and the tooth.

Step 7: Rub the side of the tooth with up-and-down motions.

Step 8: Floss each tooth.

Step 9: ______________________________.

**EXPLANATION** Compare your answers to the following. Your wording may differ slightly.

**Flossing: Interdental Cleaning**

Step 1: Wind most of 18 inches of floss around a middle finger.

Step 2: Wind the rest of the floss around your other middle finger.

Step 3: Hold the floss tightly between your thumbs and forefingers.

Step 4: Guide floss between your teeth.

Step 5: When at the gum line, curve floss into a C shape against one tooth.

Step 6: Slide floss into the space between the gum and the tooth.

Step 7: Rub the side of the tooth with up-and-down motions.

Step 8: Floss each tooth.

Step 9: Floss the back side of your last tooth.

## PRACTICE 7

The following paragraph uses the time order pattern for process to organize its ideas. Complete the list of steps that follows it by giving the missing details in their proper order. (Hint: Circle the time order transition words.)

**How to Change Your Car's Oil**

[1]First, warm up your car's engine. [2]Next, before getting under your car, turn off the engine, block the wheels, and set the parking brake. [3]Third, remove the drain plug on the bottom of the engine's oil pan, and allow the used oil to drain from your car into a drip pan. [4]Fourth, tightly replace the drain

plug. [5]Fifth, carefully add the new engine oil. [6]Do not overfill. [7]Sixth, with the parking brake still set, and in a well-ventilated area, start the car, and allow the engine to run for a few minutes. [8]Seventh, turn off the engine and check the oil level. [9]Also check around the oil filter and drain plug for leaks. [10]Eighth, so you know when to change your oil next, write down the date, mileage, grade, and brand of the motor oil you installed. [11]Next, carefully pour the used oil from the drip pan into a suitable recycling container. [12]Finally, protect the environment and conserve resources by taking your used oil to the nearest public used-oil collection center, such as a service station or lube center. [13]Also look for the "oil drop." [14]This is a petroleum industry symbol indicating that used oil is collected for recycling or reuse.

—U.S. Environmental Protection Agency,
"Collecting Used Oil for Recycling/Reuse."

**How to Change Your Car's Oil**

Step 1: ______________________________.

Step 2: ______________________________.

Step 3: Remove the drain plug on the bottom of the engine's oil pan, and drain oil into a drip pan.

Step 4: ______________________________.

Step 5: Add the new engine oil.

Step 6: Start the car, and run the engine for a few minutes.

Step 7: Turn off the engine, check the oil level, and check the oil filter and drain plug for leaks.

Step 8: ______________________________.

Step 9: Pour the used oil from the drip pan into a suitable recycling container.

Step 10: ______________________________.

## PRACTICE 8

The following passage uses time order to describe a Mexican American tradition.

Complete the following passage by inserting transitions. Fill in each blank with a word from the box. Use each word once.

| | | | | |
|---|---|---|---|---|
| after | finally | next | then | when |
| before | first | second | third | while |

### How to Make Your Own Cascarones

The egg is the perfect symbol of renewal, befitting spring. (**1**) __________ Easter comes, Latinos add a new twist to Easter—egg decorating and hunting—the Mexican cascaron (eggshell). Mexican American families take care to drain and clean whole eggshells at least a month (**2**) __________ Easter, in order to create *cascarones. Cascarones,* filled with confetti and sealed with brightly colored tissue paper "hats," are meant to be cracked on people's heads. Creating your own *cascarones* takes some advance planning. How many *cascarones* you end up with depends on how many eggs your household regularly uses and how soon you start saving the emptied eggshells. Follow these steps:

(**3**) __________ save your eggshells. Starting at least a month in advance, every time you use an egg, it should be carefully broken from the narrow end, leaving as much of the oval eggshell intact as possible. (Since these eggs are not for decoration but for play, the use of an egg blower, which removes the yolk through a pinhole, is not necessary.) A hole approximately 1/2 inch in diameter is large enough to remove the egg's liquid contents as well as to insert confetti later. (**4**) __________, clean the eggshells. Prepare a soap bath for the empty shells. Swish through the soapy water and allow them to soak for a few minutes. Rinse well. (**5**) __________ they are clean, let them air dry, and store them in egg cartons. (**6**) __________, decorate your eggshells. On the Saturday before Easter (Holy Saturday), your family can decorate the eggs as you would regular eggs—with PAAS Easter egg dye, glitter, paint, etc. Be very careful not to crack the delicate shells (it's a good idea to have a few extra on hand, just in case). (**7**) __________, fill your eggshells. To fill the eggs, use pre-made confetti or make your own confetti by cutting bits of colored construction paper (the second option is the traditional one). Fill half full. (**8**) _______________ seal the eggshells. For egg covers, use brightly colored tissue paper. Cut out circles big enough to cover the open end of the egg. Apply glue around the rim of the egg and attach the tissue top so that it seals the opening without breaking. The seal should leave the egg with a small, flat top. Families can work in teams. One group can color and decorate the shells, (**9**) _______________ the other group prepares the confetti and egg covers. (**10**) _______________, enjoy! Remember, the purpose of making them is to break them on someone's head. Have fun.

—Adapted from Menard, Valerie. (2004) *The Latino Holiday Book*. New York: Marlowe & Company. pp. 12, 15–16.

## The Space Order Pattern

The **space order pattern** allows authors to describe a person, place, or thing based on its location or the way it is arranged in space. In the space order pattern, also known as spatial order, the writer often uses descriptive details to help readers create vivid mental pictures of what the writer is describing. An author may choose to describe an object from top to bottom, from bottom to top, from right to left, from left to right, from near to far, from far to near, from inside to outside, or from outside to inside.

**Space Order: Descriptive Details**

Descriptive detail 1 → Descriptive detail 2 → Descriptive detail 3

Transition words of **space order** signal that the details follow a logical order based on two elements: (1) how the object, place, or person is arranged in space, and (2) the starting point from which the author chooses to begin the description.

**Transition Words Used in the Space Order Pattern**

| | | | | | | |
|---|---|---|---|---|---|---|
| above | at the side | beneath | close to | here | nearby | right |
| across | at the top | beside | down | in | next to | there |
| adjacent | back | beyond | far away | inside | on | under |
| around | behind | by | farther | left | outside | underneath |
| at the bottom | below | center | front | middle | over | within |

**EXAMPLE** Choose a word from the box to fill in each blank with a signal word that shows the relationship between ideas. Use each word once.

| between | back | edges | on top | out | upper |
|---|---|---|---|---|---|

**The Humpback Whale**

From their heads to the tips of their tails, humpback whales bear distinctive markings. (**1**) ______________ of a humpback whale are fleshy knobs called tubercles. A strand of hair with many nerve endings grows (**2**) ______________ of each tubercle; scientists speculate that they may serve some sensory function. Mature humpbacks are dark gray to black on their (**3**) ______________ and side bodies. Humpbacks have the longest pectoral flipper of all the whales—about one third the length of the body (adult males grow to be as much as 45 feet in body length)—which can be mottled white on the (**4**) ______________ and lower surface. Their undersides are mostly dark, although some individuals have splotches of white. The undersides of their tail flukes are as distinctive as our fingerprints, and range from all black to all white, with a whole gamut of splotching and scarring in (**5**) ______________. The trailing (**6**) ______________ of the flukes have a slight "S" curve and many knobby scallops and average 15 feet in width.

—Adapted from Bernard. "Humpback Whales." Hawaiian Islands Humpback Whale National Marine Sanctuaries. 10 March 2003.

**EXPLANATION** Compare your answers to the following: (1) on top, (2) out, (3) back, (4) upper, (5) between, and (6) edges.

## PRACTICE 9

Refer to the picture. Choose a word from the box to fill in each blank with a transition that shows the relationship between ideas. Use each word once.

| at | end | in | inward | surrounded |
|---|---|---|---|---|

### Structure of Skeletal Muscle

Skeletal muscle fiber is a single muscle cell shaped like a tube. An individual skeletal muscle may be made up of hundreds, or even thousands, of muscle fibers bundled together and wrapped (**1**) ____________ a connective tissue covering. Each muscle is (**2**) ____________ by a connective tissue sheath called the epimysium. Portions of the epimysium project (**3**) ____________ to divide the muscle into compartments. Connective tissue outside the epimysium is called fascia, and it surrounds and separates the muscles. Typically a muscle spans a joint and is attached to bones by tendons (**4**) ____________ both ends. One of the bones remains relatively fixed or stable; the (**5**) ____________ of the other bone moves as a result of muscle contraction.

—Adapted from "Structure of Skeletal Muscle." U.S. National Cancer Institute's Surveillance, Epidemiology and End Results (SEER) Program, 18 July 2004.

**Structure of a Skeletal Muscle**

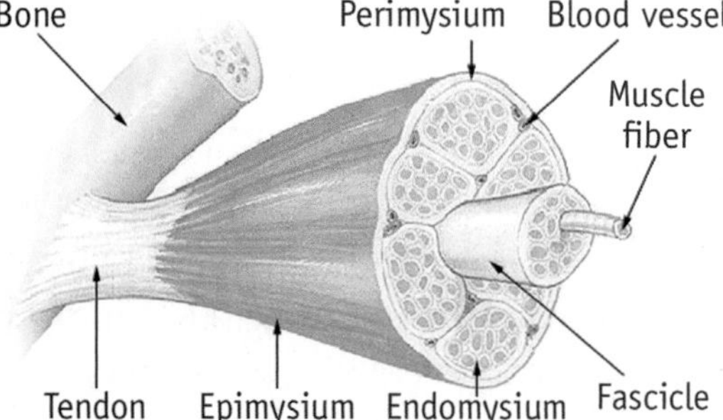


From U.S. National Cancer Institute's Surveillance, Epidemiology and End Results (SEER) Program, via contract number N01-CN-67006, with Emory University, Atlanta SEER Cancer Registry, Atlanta, Georgia, U.S.A.

## PRACTICE 10

The following paragraph uses space order to discuss satellites in space. Complete the paragraph by inserting transitions. Fill in each blank with a word from the box. Use each word once.

| above | from | high | into | over |
|---|---|---|---|---|

Engineers design satellites to support instruments flown in space. Satellites must be light enough to be carried (**1**) _______________ space on rockets, yet strong enough to withstand the forces of launching. Earth-observing satellites observe our planet (**2**) _______________ paths called orbits, many of which are greater than 400 miles (**3**) _______________ the ground. That distance is at least as far as Washington, D.C. to Boston, Massachusetts. Satellites are so (**4**) _______________ above Earth and travel so quickly that, in the right orbit, a satellite can pass (**5**) _______________ every part of Earth once every few days. Such orbits allow satellites to study and take pictures of all of Earth's features: land, plant life, oceans, clouds, and polar ice. Some satellites, such as those used for weather forecasting, are placed in fixed orbits to look at Earth continuously.

—Adapted from United States. *Our Mission to Planet Earth: A Guide to Teaching Earth System Science*. NASA. March 1994. 18 March 2007. <http://kids.earth.nasa.gov/guide/earth_system.pdf>.

## The Listing Pattern

Often authors want to list a series or set of reasons, details, or points. These details are listed in an order that the author has chosen. Changing the order of the details does not change their meaning. Transitions of addition, such as *and*, *also*, and *furthermore*, are generally used to indicate a *listing pattern*.

| **Listing pattern** |
|---|
| Idea 1<br>Idea 2<br>Idea 3 |

Weightlifting builds *and* tones muscles; it *also* builds bone density.

Notice that in this statement, two words signal the addition of ideas: *and* and *also*. Transitions of addition signal that the writer is using a second idea along with the first one. The writer presents an idea and then adds other ideas to deepen or clarify the first idea.

**Addition Transitions Used in the Listing Pattern**

| | | | | |
|---|---|---|---|---|
| also | final | for one thing | last of all | second |
| and | finally | furthermore | moreover | third |
| another | first | in addition | next | |
| besides | first of all | last | one | |

**EXAMPLE** Refer to the box of addition transitions used in the listing pattern. Complete the following paragraph with transitions that show the appropriate relationship between sentences.

### Horse Care Checklist

An animal as large and beautiful as a horse needs to be cared for carefully and diligently. (**1**) ______________, cleaning a stall, or mucking it out on a regular basis, is absolutely necessary for the horse's health and comfort. (**2**) ______________, a horse needs to be groomed three to five times a week; grooming includes controlling insects, caring for hooves, bathing, brushing, and possibly braiding the tail and mane. (**3**) ______________, a horse needs to be fed and exercised on a daily basis.

**EXPLANATION** Compare your answers to the following:

### Horse Care Checklist

[1]An animal as large and beautiful as a horse needs to be cared for carefully and diligently. [2]**First**, cleaning a stall, or mucking it out on a regular basis, is absolutely necessary for the horse's health and comfort. [3]**In addition**, a horse needs to be groomed three to five times a week; grooming includes controlling insects, caring for hooves, bathing, brushing, and possibly braiding the tail and mane. [4]**Finally**, a horse needs to be fed and exercised on a daily basis.

The paragraph on horse care begins with a general idea that is then followed by three major supporting details. Each detail requires a transition to show addition.

## PRACTICE 11

The following paragraph uses the listing thought pattern. Finish the outline that follows it by listing the major supporting details in their proper order. (Hint: Circle the addition transition words.)

### The Value of Artifacts

[1]Artifacts reveal much about the people who made them and the time period in which they were made. [2]Studying artifacts is important for several reasons. [3]First, artifacts tell a story. [4]By thinking about the purpose and need of the particular object, we can learn about the nature of the humans who created the object. [5]Studying the great pyramids teaches us to appreciate the human drive and sacrifice that went into building such mammoth structures. [6]Second, artifacts connect us to the people who used them. [7]By thinking about the ways in which the object was used, we begin to understand more about the people who used them. [8]Consider children's lunchboxes popular from 1950 to 1980. [9]These lunchboxes, decorated with images from popular children's television shows, reflect the profound influence television has had on young children. [10]Finally, artifacts reflect and cause change. [11]Think of a typewriter and a computer. [12]Both are used for many of the same purposes; both reflect the change of their times, and both caused great change as well.

—Adapted from Lubar & Kendrick, "Looking at Artifacts, Thinking About History."

### The Value of Artifacts

Studying artifacts is important for several reasons.

1. ______________________________

2. ______________________________

3. ______________________________

## PRACTICE 12

Determine the logical order of the following sentences. Write 1 by the sentence that should come first, 2 by the sentence that should come second, 3 by the sentence that should come third, and so on. (Circle the classification listing words.)

Textbook Skills

### Avoiding Ageism

______ Third, avoid implying that relationships are no longer important. Older people continue to be interested in relationships.

_____ To avoid ageism, be on guard against the following:

_____ Ageism signifies discrimination against the old.

_____ Next, don't assume you have to finish an older person's memory each time you see the person.

_____ Finally, don't speak in abnormally high volume; don't maintain an overly close physical distance.

_____ First, avoid talking down to a person because he or she is older. Older people are not slow; most people remain mentally alert well into old age.

—Adapted from DeVito, Joseph A. (2005) *Essentials of Human Communication*, 5th ed. New York: Longman. pp. 93–94.

## The Classification Pattern

Authors use the **classification pattern** to sort ideas into smaller groups and describe the traits of each group. Each smaller group, called a *subgroup*, is based on shared traits or characteristics. The author lists each subgroup and describes its traits.

Because groups and subgroups are listed, transitions of addition are used in this thought pattern. These transitions are coupled with words that indicate classes or groups. Examples of classification signal words are *first type, second kind,* and *another group.*

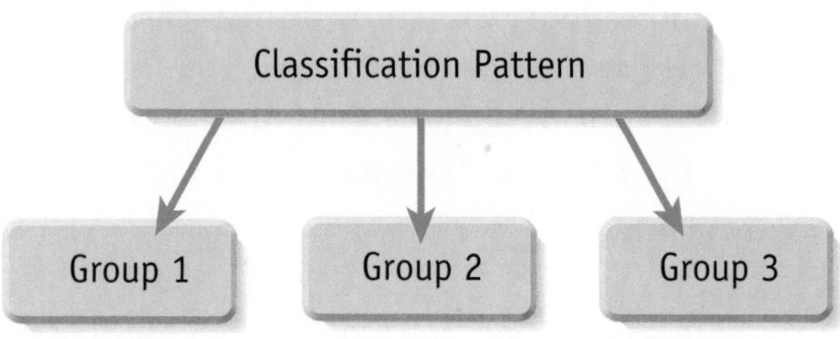


| Transitions Used in the Classification Pattern | | |
|---|---|---|
| another (group, kind, type) | first (group, categories, kind, type) | order |
| characteristics | second (group, class, kind, type) | traits |

**EXAMPLE** Determine the logical order for the following sentences. Write **1** by the sentence that should come first, **2** by the sentence that should come second, **3** by the sentence that should come third, and **4** by the sentence that should come last. (Hint: Circle the classification transition words.)

**Types of Wetlands**

______ Another type of wetland is the marsh, which is frequently or continually swamped with water; it is characterized by soft-stemmed vegetation adapted to saturated soil conditions.

______ One type of wetland is a bog, one of North America's most distinctive wetlands; it is characterized by spongy peat deposits, acidic waters, and a floor covered by a thick carpet of sphagnum moss.

______ Finally, a swamp is a type of wetland dominated by woody plants.

______ *Wetlands* is a general term that includes several types of vital links between water and land.

—Adapted from U.S. Environmental Protection Agency, "America's Wetlands."

**EXPLANATION** Compare your answers to the sentences arranged in the proper order in the following paragraph. The transition words are in **bold** print.

**Types of Wetlands**

[1]*Wetlands* is a general term that includes several types of vital links between water and land. [2]**One type** of wetland is a bog, one of North America's most distinctive wetlands; it is characterized by spongy peat deposits, acidic waters, and a floor covered by a thick carpet of sphagnum moss. [3]**Another type** of wetland is the marsh, which is frequently or continually swamped with water; it is characterized by soft-stemmed vegetation adapted to saturated soil conditions. [4]**Finally**, a swamp is a **type** of wetland dominated by woody plants.

In this paragraph, transitions of addition work with the classification signal words. In this case, *another* and *finally* convey the order of the types listed.

## PRACTICE 13

The following paragraph uses the classification thought pattern. Fill in the outline that follows by giving the missing details in their proper order. (Hint: Circle the classification transition words.)

## Types of Volcanic Eruptions

[1]During an episode of activity, a volcano commonly displays a distinctive pattern or type of behavior. [2]One type of eruption is a Vesuvian eruption; during this type of eruption, great quantities of ash-laden gas are violently discharged. [3]These gases form a cauliflower-shaped cloud high above the volcano. [4]A second kind of eruption is the Strombolian. [5]In a Strombolian-type eruption, huge clots of molten lava burst from the summit crater to form luminous arcs through the sky. [6]The lava collects on the flanks of the cone, and then lava clots combine to stream down the slopes in fiery rivulets. [7]Another kind of eruption is the Vulcanian type. [8]In this eruption, a dense cloud of ash-laden gas explodes from the crater and rises high above the peak. [9]Steaming ash forms a whitish cloud near the upper level of the cone. [10]A fourth kind of eruption is a Peléan or Nuée Ardente (glowing cloud) eruption. [11]A large amount of gas, dust, ash, and incandescent lava fragments are blown out of a central crater, fall back, and form tongue-like glowing avalanches. [12]These avalanches move down slope at speeds as great as 100 miles per hour.

—Adapted from U.S. Geological Survey, "Types of Volcanic Eruptions."

## Types of Volcanic Eruptions

1. ______________________________
2. ______________________________
3. ______________________________
4. ______________________________

### VISUAL VOCABULARY

______ The best meaning of the word **plume** is

a. feather.
b. column.
c. rope.

▲ On May 18, 1980, Mount St. Helens exploded in one of the most powerful types of volcanic eruptions, called "plinian." For more than nine hours, a vigorous plume of ash erupted, eventually reaching 12 to 15 miles above sea level. The plume moved eastward at an average speed of 60 miles per hour.

## PRACTICE 14

The following paragraph uses the classification thought pattern. Complete the concept map by giving the missing details in their proper order. (Hint: Circle the classification transition words.)

Textbook Skills

### Types of Societies

[1]Several types of societies emerged in Latin America and the Caribbean prior to the European Conquest of the sixteenth century. [2]The first group, bands, are small-scale and highly mobile societies, typically numbering several dozen households related through kinship ties. [3]Bands gather edible wild plants, as well as occasionally hunt game. [4]Members have an equal right to the resources in their territories. [5]And there is an absence of political and coercive power, and of institutionalized political offices and leadership. [6]For the greater part of history, most human societies were organized into bands. [7]At the moment of the European Conquest, some bands or foraging societies were present in northern Mexico, but more were in Amazonia, southern Chile, and southern Argentina. [8]The second type, tribes, are larger and are often less mobile. [9]Tribes are typically comprised of distinct groups, whose members claim a kinship to each other. [10]Tribes tend to cultivate plants and raise livestock. [11]Tribes display formal political positions and clearly recognizable political leaders, whose major role is to mediate disputes. [12]Many tribal groups still exist in Latin America, especially in Amazonia. [13]Another type of society is the chiefdoms. [14]Chiefdoms are much larger societies. [15]Sometimes chiefdoms number in the hundreds or thousands of households. [16]This society has control over wider, larger landscapes. [17]Higher population densities mean that the chiefdom develops more sophisticated fishing, farming, and ranching skills. [18]There is political and economic inequality. [19]Typically, there are formal, clearly named political positions and hereditary leadership or political offices ("chiefs"). [20]And, for the first time, coercive power surfaces. [21]Chiefdoms were widespread in Latin America and the Caribbean at the moment of the European Conquest. [22]Finally, states often have huge populations divided into many culturally distinct groups, and they exercise rule over much larger, far-flung territories. [23]States almost always have emerged through conflict and warfare; they display an extreme concentration of political and coercive power; they are highly structured and have standing armies. [24]Another key trait of states is mon-

umental architecture. [25]These building programs showed the state's ability to wrench labor from large segments of the population.

—Adapted from Sanabria, Harry. (2007) *The Anthropology of Latin America and the Caribbean,* pp. 50–52.

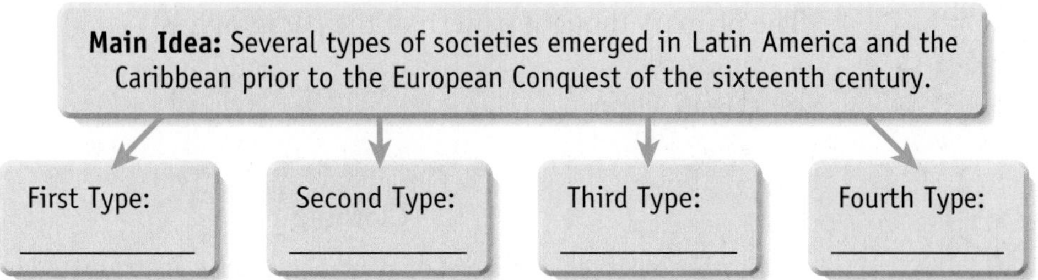


## Thought Patterns in Textbooks

Textbook authors often use transitions to make relationships between ideas clear and easy to understand. However, often an author will use more than one type of transition. For example, classification combines words that indicate addition and types. Sometimes addition and time words are used in the same paragraph or passage for a specific purpose. Furthermore, authors may mix thought patterns in the same paragraph or passage. Finally, be aware that relationships between ideas still exist even when transition words are not explicitly stated. The effective reader looks for the author's primary thought pattern.

**EXAMPLE** Read the following paragraphs from college textbooks. Circle the transitions or signal words used in each paragraph. Then identify the primary thought pattern used in the paragraph.

**A.**

**A Dangerous Diet**

Depriving the body of food for prolonged periods forces it to make adjustments to prevent the shutdown of organs. The body depletes its energy reserves to obtain the necessary fuels. The body first turns to protein tissue in order to maintain its supply of glucose. As this occurs, weight is lost rapidly because protein contains only half as many calories per pound as fat. At the same time, significant water stores are lost. Over time, the body begins to run out of liver tissue, heart muscle, blood, and so on, as these readily available substances are burned to supply energy.

—Adapted from Donatelle, *Health: the Basics,* 5th ed., p. 271.

_____ The primary thought pattern of the paragraph is
a. time order.
b. classification.

B.

**Clothing**

Clothing serves a variety of purposes. First, it protects you from the weather and, in sports like football, from injury. In addition, it helps you conceal parts of your body and so serves a modesty function. Clothing also serves as a cultural display. It communicates your cultural and subcultural affiliations. In the United States, where there are so many different ethnic groups, you can see examples of dress that indicate what country the wearers are from.

—Adapted from DeVito, *The Interpersonal Communication Book,* 10th ed., p. 204.

_____ The primary thought pattern of the paragraph is
a. time order.
b. listing.

C.

**Types of Interest Groups**

Whether they are lobbying politicians or appealing to the public, interest groups are everywhere in the American political system. As with other aspects of American politics and policymaking, political scientists loosely categorize interest groups into clusters. Among the most important clusters are those that deal with economic issues, environmental concerns, equality issues, and the interests of consumers. A study of these four distinct types of interest groups will give you a good picture of the American interest group system.

—Adapted from Edwards, Wattenberg, & Lineberry, *Government in America: People, Politics, and Policy,* 5th ed., p. 253.

_____ The primary thought pattern of the paragraph is
a. time order.
b. classification.

## PRACTICE 15

Read the following paragraph from a college communications textbook. Circle the transitions or signal words used in the paragraph. Then identify the primary thought pattern used.

Textbook Skills

**Culture Shock**

Culture shock refers to the psychological reaction you experience when you're in a culture very different from your own. Anthropologist Kalervo Oberg, who first used the term, notes that it occurs in stages. Stage one is the honeymoon. At first you experience fascination with the new culture and its people. This stage is characterized by cordiality and friendship in these early and superficial relationships. Stage two is the crisis. Here the differences between your own culture and the new one create problems. This is the stage at which you experience the actual shock of a new culture. Stage three is the recovery. During this period, you gain the skills necessary to function. You learn the language and ways of the new culture. Stage four is the adjustment. At this final stage, you adjust to and come to enjoy the new culture and experiences. You may still experience periodic difficulties and strains, but on the whole, the experience is pleasant.

—Adapted from DeVito, *The Interpersonal Communication Book,* 10th ed., p. 59.

_____ The primary thought pattern of the paragraph is
a. time order.
b. classification.

## Chapter Review

Test your understanding of what you have read in this chapter by filling in the blank with a word or phrase from the box.

| adjacent | first type | space order | thought pattern | transitions |
|---|---|---|---|---|
| classification | listing | steps | time order | when |

1. ______________________ are words and phrases that signal thought patterns by showing the logical relationship within a sentence and between sentences.

2. A ______________________ is established by using transitions to show the logical relationship between ideas in a paragraph or passage.

3. Narration and process are two uses of the ______________________ thought pattern.

4. Transitions of time signal that the writer is describing ____________ something occurred.

5. In addition to showing a chain of events, the time order pattern is used to show ______________________, stages, or directions that can be repeated at any time with similar results.

6. Transitions of addition, such as *and*, *also*, and *furthermore*, are generally used to indicate a ______________________ pattern.

7. Authors use the ______________________ pattern to sort ideas into smaller groups and describe the traits for each group.

8. Examples of classification signal words are ______________________, *second kind*, or *another group*.

9. The ______________________ pattern allows authors to describe a person, place, or thing based on its location or the way it is arranged in space.

10. Some of the words used to establish the space order pattern include ______________________, *below*, and *underneath*.

## Applications

### Application 1: Identifying Transitions

Fill in each blank with one of the words from the box. Use each word once.

| another | finally | furthermore | next |
|---|---|---|---|

1. Research has shown that cancers of the lip, tongue, mouth, throat, larynx, lung, and esophagus are connected to cigar smoking. ______________, facts strongly suggest a link between cigar smoking and cancer of the pancreas.

—National Cancer Institute, "Questions and Answers About Cigar Smoking and Cancer."

2. Some of the television shows that become classic favorites focus on relationships. One such show was *I Love Lucy*, which was based on the marriage of Lucy and Ricky and their friendship with Ethel and Fred; ______________ more recent example is *Friends*, which is based on the friendships among six friends.

3. Arturo's morning routine rarely varies: immediately after he wakes up, he makes his coffee. ______________, he fetches the newspaper, feeds the animals, and wakes up the children. ______________, he reads the paper while he drinks his coffee.

### Application 2: Identifying Transitions

Fill in each blank with one of the words from the box. Use each word once.

| afterward | currently | eventually | previously |
|---|---|---|---|

1. Rebecca and Sean drove 120 miles round trip to see John Mayer in concert. ______________, they agreed that the trip had been well worth the time, cost, and effort.

2. Juan came to the United States without money, family, or friends. He found a job, worked hard, and saved his money. ______________, he bought a home and brought his family from Mexico to live with him.

3. In the United States, more than 550,000 people have died as a result of AIDS since the epidemic began in 1981. Experts believe that nationwide over one million people ______________ live with HIV, the virus that causes AIDS.

4. George finally bought a new car off a dealer's lot that had never been owned before—a red convertible Mustang. ______________, he had bought only used cars.

## Application 3: Identifying Thought Patterns

Identify the thought pattern suggested by each of the following topic sentences.

_____ **1.** Alcoholics Anonymous recommends the following 12-step recovery process to overcome addiction.
a. time order b. classification

_____ **2.** Psychologists often discuss personality by types.
a. time order b. classification

_____ **3.** Breaking a bad habit is a multistep process.
a. time order b. listing

_____ **4.** Health care costs are soaring for several reasons.
a. space order b. listing

_____ **5.** A health spa offers several types of services aimed at rejuvenating the body and the spirit.
a. space order b. classification

_____ **6.** Five points need to be made about the Marshall Plan.
a. classification b. listing

_____ **7.** Hearing involves three stages.
a. time order b. classification

_____ **8.** Columbus set sail toward the West in search of new trade routes.
a. time order b. space order

_____ **9.** The United States has three branches of government.
a. time order b. classification

_____ **10.** Several forms of psychological stress affect a person's well-being.
a. space order b. classification

# REVIEW Test 1

## Transition Words and Thought Patterns

Match each of the thought patterns to the appropriate group of transition words. Thought patterns will be used more than once.

a. time order
b. space order
c. listing
d. classification

_____ 1. one type, several kinds, another group

_____ 2. first, second, third, fourth

_____ 3. before, after, while, during

_____ 4. behind, below, above, over

_____ 5. currently, eventually, previously

_____ 6. furthermore, moreover, besides

_____ 7. characteristics, traits, order

_____ 8. beneath, nearby, within

_____ 9. here, there

_____ 10. and, also, for one thing

## REVIEW Test 2

### Transition Words

Select a transition word for each of the blanks. Then identify the type of transition you chose.

**A.** Pilates develops a strong and supple spine by extending the space __________ each vertebra.

_____ **1.** The best transition word for the sentence is
a. between.
b. after.
c. before.

_____ **2.** The relationship between the ideas is one of
a. classification.
b. space order.

**B.** Proper posture is a matter of correctly positioning your body; place the joints between your big and second toes under your knees; pull your abdominals _______________ your spine, relax your shoulders down, and lengthen your body through the crown of your head.

_____ **3.** The best transition word for the sentence is
a. toward.
b. eventually.
c. one.

_____ **4.** The relationship between the ideas is one of
a. space order. b. addition.

**C.** The best course of action to take _______________ one has made a mistake is to admit it, learn from it, and avoid making it again.

_____ **5.** The best transition word for the sentence is
a. when.
b. before.
c. since.

_____ **6.** The relationship between the ideas is one of
a. listing. b. time order.

**D.** A character in a work of fiction is often studied on the basis of two groups of traits. The first group identifies whether the character is dynamic and changes or is static and stays the same. The _______________ identifies whether the character is round and fully developed or remains flat with only one main personality feature.

_____ **7.** The best transition word or phrase for the sentence above is
a. additional part.
b. second group.
c. later time.

_____ **8.** The relationship between the ideas is one of
a. classification. b. time order.

**E.** A monarch butterfly has four stages in its life cycle. The first stage begins _______________ a female monarch mates and lays eggs on leaves. The second stage occurs when a tiny larva hatches and begins to eat its eggshell and the leaves of the plant. The larva changes into the pupa or chrysalis, the third major stage of the monarch's life cycle. The final stage involves the adult monarch emerging from its chrysalis to dry its wings.

_____ **9.** The best transition word for the sentence is
a. before.
b. and.
c. as.

_____ **10.** The relationship between the ideas is one of
a. time order. b. addition.

## VISUAL VOCABULARY

_____ This insect is in what stage of its life cycle?

a. egg.
b. larva.
c. chrysalis.

# REVIEW Test 3

## Transition Words

Fill in each blank with a transition from the box. Use each transition once. Then complete the concept map with information from the paragraph.

| at the same time | next | then |
|---|---|---|
| first | subsequently | |

Textbook Skills

### Stimulus-Response Communication

One common model of communication is circular and sequential between a sender and listener. (**1**) _______________, the sender creates and sends a message, which acts as a stimulus. (**2**) _______________, listeners process the information. (**3**) _______________, based on their understandings, listeners send a response or feedback to the sender. Senders (**4**) _______________ use this feedback to adjust the message. In this process, senders become listeners as they respond to the feedback listeners send. (**5**) _______________, listeners become senders.

—Adapted from Brownell, *Listening: Attitudes, Principles, and Skills,* 2nd ed., p. 39.

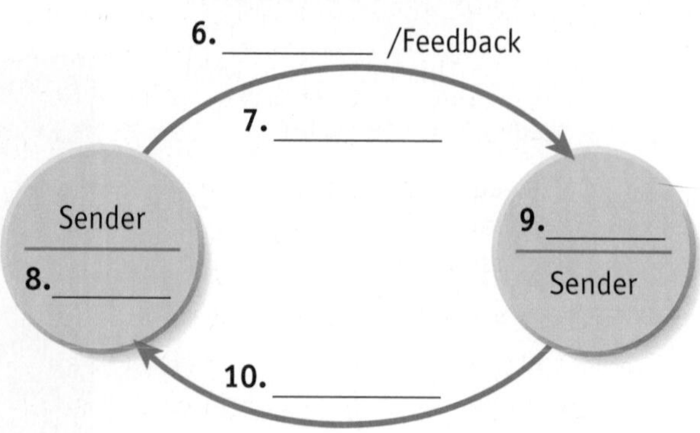


▲ A Stimulus Response Model of Communication

—From Judi Brownell, *Listening: Attitudes, Principles, and Skills*, 2/e. Published by Allyn and Bacon, Boston, MA. 

## REVIEW Test 4

### Transition Words and Thought Patterns

The following essay is from a college social science textbook. Before you read, skim the passage and answer the **Before Reading** questions. Read the essay. Then answer the **After Reading** questions.

#### The Early History of Human Motivation

[1]In your imagination, **transport** yourself back 100,000 years to the banks of the local river in your area. [2]Your tribe spent most of the day traveling up and down the river's banks hunting and fishing and gathering grubs, fruits, and other edibles. [3]However, not everyone worked equally hard. [4]Some individuals produced a lot of food for the tribe, while others produced none at all. [5]You may have **reflected** to yourself, "Some people in our tribe are not motivated," or "I wish everybody in our tribe were as motivated as I am." [6]In other words, you invented the concept of motivation to account for these differences in behavior. [7]The point of this imaginary scene is that humans have probably been thinking about their own and others' motivation for a long time, certainly before the beginning of psychology in 1879.

[8]Two bumper stickers from a much later time read: "If it feels good, do it" ______________ "If it's no fun, why do it?" [9]Are these **edicts** accurate descriptions of human conduct? [10]If so, are we merely pursuers of pleasure

and avoiders of pain? [11]Some early philosophers believe that we are. [12]The study of human motivation has a long history.

[13]Nearly 2,400 years ago, Greek philosophers were already discussing motivation under a principle known as hedonism. [14]Hedonism is the pursuit of pleasure and the avoidance of pain. [15]Although today the term often refers to sensory pleasures derived from food, drink, and sex, for philosophers this term meant striving for the greater good. [16]The phrase "the pursuit of happiness" from the Declaration of Independence most likely means a striving for the greater good. [17]It is doubtful that the signers of the Declaration meant for people to stop working and party all the time. [18]While it is true that sensory pleasure might be attained from spending your tuition money to pay for nightly partying, a hedonically greater benefit would result if that money were used to pay for your tuition and subsequent education.

[19]One of the first proponents of hedonism was the famous Greek philosopher Socrates (470–399 B.C.), who claimed a person should follow a course of action for which pleasure exceeds pain. [20]Further, Socrates claimed that the only reason a person would not do so is because he lacks complete knowledge of the pleasure or pain that can result. [21]For Democritus (460–370 B.C), it was both natural and good for people to follow this course. [22]However, he could not identify what was pleasurable or painful apart from a person's behavior. [23]Something was pleasurable if an individual strived for it, and something was painful if an individual avoided it. [24]But what was pleasurable or painful could differ for each individual. [25]No matter what these things were, pleasure was to be pursued, and pain was to be avoided.

[26]One might get the idea that Socrates and Democritus meant that we should "eat, drink, and be merry as if there is no tomorrow." [27]On the contrary, they felt that our pursuits should be followed in moderation. [28]They believed that moderation would lead to greater pleasure in the long run. [29]This idea was developed further a century later by Epicurus (341–271 B.C.). [30]He believed that pleasure and pain average out. [31]Thus, we might give up certain intense pleasures if subsequent pain of greater degree is a result. [32]For instance, an individual might drink alcohol in moderation to avoid the painful aftereffects of drinking too much. [33]Likewise, moderation may require experiencing pain prior to pleasure. [34]A person may endure immediate pain because longer-lasting pleasure may result. [35]For example, a student may give up the short-term benefit of earning money at an unskilled job to earn a college degree; her hope is that the college degree will lead to more meaningful and fruitful employment later.

—Adapted from Deckers, *Motivation: Biological, Psychological, and Environmental*, pp. 22–23.

## BEFORE READING

### Vocabulary in Context

______ **1.** The word **transport** in sentence 1 means
a. delight.
b. convey.
c. carry.
d. pass.

______ **2.** The word **reflected** in sentence 5 means
a. thought.
b. counted.
c. fumed.
d. planned.

______ **3.** The word **edicts** in sentence 9 means
a. actions.
b. steps.
c. stickers.
d. statements.

## AFTER READING

### Concept Maps

**4.** Finish the concept map by filling in the missing idea with information from the passage.

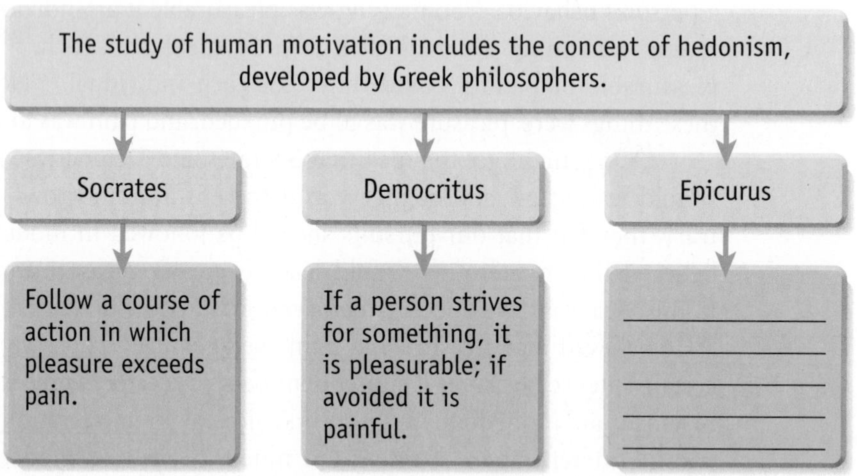


### Central Idea and Main Idea

______ **5.** Which sentence states the central idea of the essay?
a. sentence 1
b. sentence 6
c. sentence 12
d. sentence 13

## Supporting Details

______ **6.** What type of supporting detail is sentence 35?
a. major supporting detail b. minor supporting detail

## Transitions and Thought Patterns

______ **7.** The word **while** in sentence 4 is a transition that shows
a. time order. b. comparison and contrast.

______ **8.** What thought pattern is suggested by sentence 12?
a. time order b. space order

______ **9.** What is the relationship between sentence 19 and sentence 20?
a. time order b. addition

______ **10.** Which is the best transition for the blank in sentence 8?
a. and c. first
b. a type of d. finally

## Discussion Questions

**1.** What is hedonism, and how is it a source of motivation?

**2.** What is moderation, and how is it a source of motivation?

**3.** In what actions do you see hedonism and moderation in daily life?

## Writing Topics

**1.** In a paragraph, define hedonism in your own words and give an example.

**2.** In one or two paragraphs, discuss the differences between today's meaning of hedonism (as defined in sentence 15) and the way philosophers define the term. Use examples.

**3.** Discuss a situation in which you or someone you know gave up immediate reward for the greater good.

**4.** In one or two paragraphs, using the concepts of hedonism and moderation, give advice to a first-year college student.

## EFFECTIVE READER Scorecard

**Transitions and Thought Patterns**

| Test | Number Correct | | Points | | Score |
|---|---|---|---|---|---|
| Review Test 1 | ______ | × | 10 | = | ______ |
| Review Test 2 | ______ | × | 10 | = | ______ |
| Review Test 3 | ______ | × | 10 | = | ______ |
| Review Test 4 | ______ | × | 10 | = | ______ |
| Review Test 5 (website) | ______ | × | 10 | = | ______ |
| Review Test 6 (website) | ______ | × | 10 | = | ______ |

Enter your scores on the Effective Reader Scorecard: Chapter 6 Review Tests inside the back cover.

## After Reading About Transitions and Thought Patterns

Before you move on to the mastery tests on transitions and thought patterns, take time to reflect on your learning and performance by answering the following questions. Write your answers in your notebook.

What did I learn about the following: transitions and thought patterns; time order, space order, listing pattern, and classification pattern?

What do I need to remember about the following: transitions and thought patterns; time order, space order, listing pattern, and classification pattern?

How has my knowledge base or prior knowledge about transitions and thought patterns changed?

### More Review and Mastery Tests

For more practice, go to the book's website at http://ablongman.com/henry/ and click on *The Effective Reader.* Then select "More Review and Mastery Tests." The tests are organized by chapter.

MASTERY **Test 1**

Name ______________________ Section __________

Date __________ **Score** (number correct) ______ × 10 = ______%

**A.** The following items are from a college math textbook. Fill in the blanks with the correct transition word from the box. Use each word once.

| before | during | in | then | when |
|---|---|---|---|---|

Textbook Skills

**1–2.** Reading and highlighting a section of your textbook ______________ your instructor lectures on it allows you to maximize your learning and understanding ______________ the lecture.

**3–4.** Try to keep one section ahead of your syllabus. ______________ you study ahead of your lectures, you can ______________ concentrate on what is being explained in them instead of trying to write everything down.

**5.** Highlight key points ______________ your textbook as you study.

—Adapted from Bittinger & Beecher, *Introductory and Intermediate Algebra*, 2nd ed., p. 43.

**B.** Read the following paragraph from a college communications textbook. Fill in each blank with the correct transition word from the box. Use each word once.

| frequently | immediate | past | then | when |
|---|---|---|---|---|

Textbook Skills

**Gunnysacking**

A gunnysack is a large bag, usually made of burlap. As a conflict strategy, gunnysacking refers to the practice of storing up grievances to unload them at another time. The (**6**) ______________ occasion may be relatively simple (or so it may seem at first), such as someone's coming home late without calling. Instead of arguing about this, the gunnysacker unloads all

(**7**) ______________ grievances: the birthday you forgot two years ago, the time you arrived late for dinner last month, and the hotel reservations you forgot to make. As you probably know from experience, gunnysacking leads to more gunnysacking. (**8**) ______________ one person gunnysacks, the other person often does so as well. (**9**) ______________ two people end up dumping their stored up grievances on one another. (**10**) ______________, the original problem never gets addressed. Instead, resentment and hostility build up.

—Adapted from DeVito, *Essentials of Human Communication,* 4th ed., p. 177.

Name ______________________ Section ____________

MASTERY **Test 2**

Date ____________ **Score** (number correct) ______ × 10 = ______%

A. Fill in each blank with the correct transition word from the box. Use each word once.

| another | during | in | occasionally | often |
|---|---|---|---|---|

1. Although it doesn't happen frequently, American society has ____________ been gripped by fear, and its responses have not done credit to the nature of freedom.
2. The Red Scare, the hunt for communist traitors living in America, is one example of a fear that occurred following World War I. ____________ this time, hundreds of innocent immigrants were rounded up, imprisoned, and deported, for no reason other than fear of their allegedly radical ideas.
3. Even though the great fears of the first Red Scare were unfounded, the conflict between the United States and its allies and the Soviet Union and its allies, known as the Cold War, unleashed ____________ Red Scare in the late 1940s and early 1950s.
4. The hunt for alleged traitors started during World War II and was furthered by congressional committees. These committees ____________ abused their powers and harassed people who did not share their political views.
5. In February 1950, Senator Joseph McCarthy of Wisconsin began a witch hunt for so-called traitors; he claimed that communists were working ____________ the State Department. For four years, he used his power improperly as he led a senate investigation. He and his aides made wild accusations, browbeat witnesses, ruined reputations, and threw mud at harmless people. Moreover, even the president of the United States was afraid to stand up to him.

—Adapted from U.S. Department of State, "Censure of Senator Joseph McCarthy."

B. Read the following paragraph from a college social science textbook. Then answer the question that follows it. (Hint: Circle the transition words.)

xtbook
Skills

**Relax and Listen**

[1]Learning to relax is among the best ways to improve concentration during listening. [2]A variety of physical and mental exercises will help you sustain attention as you listen. [3]One activity is relaxing your muscles. [4]Tighten a single muscle group such as your neck, your lower

arm, or your foot for five or six seconds, and then completely relax it. [5]Begin at the extremities of your body and work inward. [6]You will realize that you were experiencing muscle stress as normal. [7]A second exercise is imagery. [8]To relax before the listening session, vividly recall a positive experience; relive all of the sights, smells, and sounds. [9]Your mind will relax as it focuses on these memories. [10]This effect can also be reached through fantasy by calling up imaginary events or images. [11]A third exercise is mental rehearsal, trying out in your mind various solutions to a stressful problem; when athletes have rehearsed mentally and see themselves winning, they have gone on to be highly successful. [12]Finally, deep breathing clears your mind and enables you to relax; this technique is helpful for any stressful listening event.

—Adapted from Brownell, *Listening: Attitudes, Principles, and Skills,* 2nd ed., p. 88.

______ **6.** The thought pattern of the paragraph is
a. time order. b. listing.

**C.** Read the following paragraph from a writing textbook. Fill in each blank with the correct transition from the box. Use each transition once.

| first | in addition | third |
|---|---|---|

Textbook Skills

### Composing Web Pages

In general, Web sites contain three basic elements. The (**7**) ______________ element is the text written by you. A Web page contains real writing: millions of people may see your page. Don't waste their time. The rule is "value-added." If you are not adding anything of value, do not add anything at all. The second element is any link to pages within your Web site or links to other appropriate Web pages on the Internet. Moving around in your Web site must be easy. Make sure your viewers know how to find something on your site and how to get back to where they started. (**8**) ______________, avoid dead-end pages. The (**9**) ______________ element is the choice of appropriate graphics; keep graphics simple; in most cases, images that move, flash, beep, or buzz simply annoy your viewers. And most viewers, research shows, will not wait more than ten or fifteen seconds for huge graphics to show up on their screens, no matter how wonderful they are.

—Adapted from DiYanni & Hoy, *The Scribner Handbook for Writers,* 3rd ed., pp. 825–26.

______ **10.** The thought pattern for the paragraph is
a. time order. b. listing.

MASTERY **Test 3**

Name ______________________ Section ____________

Date ____________ **Score** (number correct) ______ × 10 = ______%

**A.** The following information is from a college health textbook. Determine a logical order for the ideas to create a paragraph that makes sense. Write **1, 2, 3, 4,** and **5** in the spaces provided to indicate the proper order of ideas.

Textbook Skills

______ The first goal should be to help people establish enjoyable and stable patterns of eating and exercise.

______ Modern weight control programs should focus on several goals.

______ Finally, the program should set realistic goals.

______ An additional goal should be to focus on small gains to health and well-being at first and later focus on long-term effects such as higher energy levels and reduced risk of disease.

______ A third goal should be to teach one how to become a wise food consumer.

—Adapted from Donatelle, *Access to Health*, 7th ed., p. 275.

______ **6.** What thought pattern is used in the paragraph?
a. time order b. listing

**B.** Read the following paragraph from a business textbook. Fill in each blank with the correct transition from the box. Use each transition once.

| from | off | within |
|---|---|---|

**Garden Banks**

Located 110 miles (**7**) ______________ the coasts of Texas and Louisiana, Flower Garden Banks National Marine Sanctuary hosts the northernmost coral reefs in the United States. Rising to (**8**) ______________ 66 feet of the surface, the Banks are an attractive home for shallow water

Caribbean reef fishes and invertebrates. Today it has become a premier diving destination and attracts scientists (**9**) _______________ around the world.

—National Marine Sanctuaries. 18 July 2004.

_____ **10.** What thought pattern is used in the paragraph?
a. space order b. classification

MASTERY **Test 4**

Name ______________________ Section ____________

Date ____________ **Score** (number correct) ______ × 10 = ______%

**A.** The following information is from a college science textbook. Determine a logical order for the ideas to create a paragraph that makes sense. Write **1, 2, 3, 4,** and **5** in the spaces provided to indicate the proper order of ideas.

Textbook Skills

______ The transfer of heat between organisms and the environment takes place through several means.

______ A final important method of heat transfer is thermal radiation, such as the heat a fire gives off.

______ One important transfer is evaporation, the loss of moisture from a surface; evaporation releases heat, the energy needed to change water to vapor.

______ Another method of heat transfer is conduction, the movement of heat from a warmer solid object to a cooler one.

______ A third method is convection, the movement of fluid air or water over an object; a rotating fan cools by this method.

—Adapted from Smith & Smith, *Elements of Ecology,* 4th ed., p. 56.

______ **6.** What thought pattern is used in the paragraph?

a. time order b. listing

**VISUAL VOCABULARY**

______ The best meaning of the word **vapor** is

a. fog.
b. breath.
c. pollution.

**B.** Read the following paragraph from a college communications textbook. Fill in each blank with the correct transition from the box. Use each transition once.

| and | another type | types |
|---|---|---|

Textbook Skills

Among the (**7**) major _______________ of informative speeches are those of description, demonstration, (**8**) _______________ definition. (**9**) _______________ of informative speech is the "speech of introduction," in which you introduce someone to an audience. You may combine all four types into one speech, or you may devote your entire speech to just one kind. Keep in mind that each type has its own strategies.

—Adapted from DeVito, *Essentials of Human Communication,* 4th ed., pp. 360–61.

______ **10.** What thought pattern is used in the paragraph?
a. classification b. time order

MASTERY **Test 5**

Name ______________________ Section ____________

Date ____________ Score (number correct) ______ × 10 = ______%

**A.** Read the following paragraph from a college social science textbook.

Textbook Skills

### The Secret

[1]Harry McCharin is a very successful businessman. [2]Twenty years ago, he opened his first record store and has since developed the business. [3]He now owns a chain of twenty-seven music stores in Michigan, Ohio, and Indiana. [4]Harry is currently a happily married man with a family of three children. [5]Harry McCharin is a drug addict. [6]Every day, Harry gives himself an injection of heroin.

—Adapted from Fishbein & Pease, *The Dynamics of Drug Abuse*, p. 336.

**1.** What is the transition word used in sentence 4? ______________

______ **2.** What thought pattern is used in the paragraph?

a. listing b. time order

**B.** Read the following paragraph from a college English textbook.

Textbook Skills

### Learning the Stories Behind Words

[1]Learning the roots of words will surely help you build your vocabulary. [2]Another way is to learn the stories associated with some words. [3]Many words have interesting stories connected with people, places, and myths, and most dictionaries include at least some information about words that came from mythology as well as those connected with people and places. [4]______________, knowing the stories related to the words will help you remember their meanings and develop your vocabulary. [5]One good example is the phrase *Achilles' heel.* [6]If you know that the Greek hero Achilles was invulnerable except for one weak spot, his heel, you will know that *Achilles' heel* is a phrase meaning a small but important weakness.

—Adapted from DiYanni & Hoy, *The Scribner Handbook for Writers*, 3rd ed., p. 496.

______ **3.** In this paragraph, the author

a. lists a reason and example for learning the stories about words.

b. explains step by step how to add words to your vocabulary.

_____ **4.** The transition word that best fits the blank in sentence 4 is
a. First
b. Another
c. Furthermore

**C.** Read the following paragraph from a college social science textbook.

### Small Group Formats

[1]Small groups serve their functions in a variety of formats. [2]The following four basic types of small group formats are among the most popular. [3]The first format is the roundtable. [4]Group members arrange themselves in a circle or semicircle pattern. [5]Their discussions are informal as they share information or solve problems without any set pattern of who speaks when. [6]The second format is the panel. [7]Panel participants are "experts," and the panel is observed by an audience. [8]Panel discussions are informal, and there is no set pattern for who speaks when. [9]The third format is the symposium, which is made up of a series of prepared presentations or public speeches. [10]All speeches address different aspects of a single topic. [11]The leader of the symposium introduces each speaker. [12]The fourth popular format is the symposium-forum. [13]This small group consists of two parts: a symposium of prepared speeches and a forum. [14]A forum is made up of questions and comments from the audience and responses from the symposium. [15]The symposium leader introduces the speakers and moderates the forum.

—Adapted from DeVito, *Essentials of Human Communication,* 4th ed., pp. 244–45.

_____ **5.** What thought pattern is used in the paragraph?
a. time order
b. classification

**6–10.** Fill in the concept map with the topic sentence and major details from the paragraph.

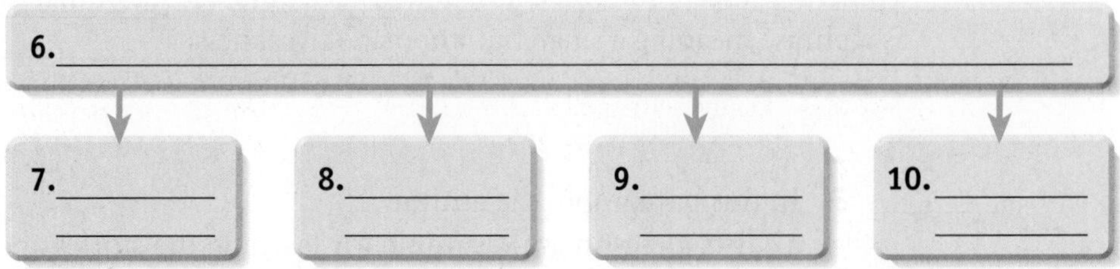

MASTERY **Test 6**

Name ______________________ Section ____________

Date ____________ **Score** (number correct) ______ × 10 = ______%

**A.** Read the following paragraph from a college accounting textbook.

Textbook Skills

[1]When Lisa arrived on campus for her first year of college, she did not open a checking account locally because she already had one in her hometown. [2]She knew that she could always use an Automated Teller Machine (ATM) to obtain cash. [3]For the first few months, she frequently visited an ATM; nearly every other day she needed a few dollars for some item or another. [4]It was only on a weekend trip back home, where she reviewed her latest bank statement that Lisa became aware of a problem. [5]Her statement showed 34 separate charges for ATM fees. [6]She had been charged $1.00 for each trip to an "out of network" ATM not owned by her bank. [7]She was also charged another $1.50 by the bank who owned the ATM, so each ATM visit created two charges. [8]Altogether, for her 17 visits to the ATM, Lisa had been charged $42.50 in ATM fees. [9]Lisa was shocked.

—Adapted from Madura, *Personal Finance,* 2nd ed., p. 125.

______ **1.** The relationship between sentence 6 and sentence 7 is one of
a. time. b. addition.

______ **2.** The overall thought pattern used in the paragraph is
a. classification. b. time order.

**B.** Read the following paragraph from a college mathematics textbook.

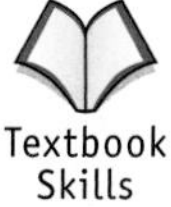
Textbook Skills

### A Five-Step Strategy for Solving Problems

[1]Many students fear solving mathematical problems so much that their thinking freezes with anxiety. [2]A five-step strategy can be very helpful in solving problems. [3]First, familiarize yourself with the problem situation; read it out loud or make and label a drawing, and assign a letter or variable to the unknown. [4]Second, translate the problem into an equation; use mathematical expressions and symbols and the letter or variable. [5]Third, solve the equation. [6]_______________, check the answer in the original wording of the problem. [7]Finally, clearly state the answer to the problem with the appropriate units, such as dollars and cents or inches.

—Adapted from Bittinger & Beecher, *Introductory and Intermediate Algebra,* 2nd ed., p. 387.

_____ **3.** The transition word that best fits the blank in sentence 6 is

a. First

b. Third

c. Next

_____ **4.** The thought pattern used in the paragraph is

a. classification.    b. time order.

**5–10.** Fill in the concept map with the topic sentence and major supporting details from the passage.

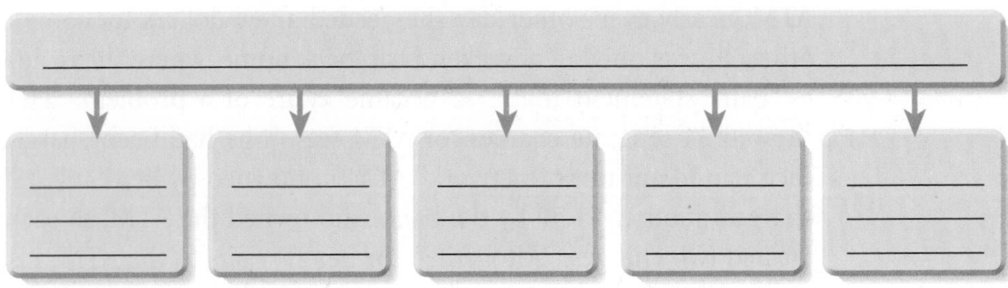

CHAPTER

7

# More Thought Patterns

## CHAPTER PREVIEW

## Before Reading About More Thought Patterns

In Chapter 6, you learned several important ideas that will help you as you work through this chapter. Use the following questions to call up your prior knowledge about transitions and thought patterns.

What are transitions? (Refer to page 242.) ______________________

______________________________________________

______________________________________________

What are thought patterns? (Refer to page 242.) ______________________

______________________________________________

______________________________________________

What is important to know about mixed thought patterns? Give an example from Chapter 6. (Refer to page 269.) ______________________

______________________________________________

______________________________________________

______________________________________________

______________________________________________

______________________________________________

You have learned that transitions and thought patterns show the relationships of ideas within sentences as well as between sentences and paragraphs, and you studied four common types: time order, space order, listing, and classification. In this chapter, we will explore some other common thought patterns:

- The comparison-and-contrast pattern
- The cause-and-effect pattern
- The generalization-and-example pattern
- The definition-and-example pattern

## The Comparison-and-Contrast Pattern

Many ideas become clearer when they are thought of in relation to one another. For example, comparing the prices different grocery stores charge makes us smarter shoppers. Likewise, noting the difference between loving and selfish behavior helps us choose partners in life. The comparison-and-contrast patterns enable us to see these relationships. This section discusses both comparison and contrast, starting with comparison. The discussion then turns to the important and effective comparison-and-contrast pattern, in which these two basic ways of organizing ideas are combined when writing an explanation, a description, or an analysis.

### Comparison

**Comparison** points out the ways in which two or more ideas are alike. Sample signal words are *similar, like*, and *just as.*

**Words and Phrases of Comparison**

| | | | | |
|---|---|---|---|---|
| alike | in a similar fashion | just as | resemble | similarly |
| as | in a similar manner | just like | same | |
| as well as | in like manner | like | similar | |
| equally | in the same way | likewise | similarity | |

Here are some examples:

**Just as** we relate to others based on their personality traits, we tend to interact with our personal computers based on their performance.

Writing, **like** farming, follows a cycle of planting, growing, and reaping.

African and European artists use many of the **same** subjects in their art.

Each of these sentences has two topics that are similar in some way. The similarity is the author's main point. For example, the first sentence compares human personality traits to the way a personal computer performs. The comparison is introduced by the phrase *just as.* The second sentence compares the writing process to the farming process using the signal word *like.* And the third sentence compares the subjects African artists choose to the subjects European artists choose for their art.

## PRACTICE 1

Complete the following ideas with a transition that shows comparison. Use each expression only once.

1. Physical fatigue affects the body; ________________, mental stress affects the mind.
2. Jealousy destroys a relationship ________________ thoroughly as a wildfire consumes a forest.
3. Compulsive gambling is an addiction ________________ in some ways to drug addiction.
4. The toddler and the teenager often behave ________________.
5. In her poem "Because I Could Not Stop for Death," Emily Dickinson writes that death ________________ a gentleman.

When comparison is used to organize an entire paragraph, the pattern looks like this.

| Comparison Pattern | | |
|---|---|---|
| **Idea 1** | | **Idea 2** |
| Idea 1 | *like* | Idea 2 |
| Idea 1 | *like* | Idea 2 |
| Idea 1 | *like* | Idea 2 |

**EXAMPLE** Determine a logical order for the following three sentences. Write **1** by the sentence that should come first, **2** by the sentence that should come second, and **3** by the sentence that should come last. Then use the information to fill in the chart.

_____ Another important similarity is the use of the opposing thumb to grasp objects.

_____ Humans and apes share similar characteristics.

_____ The defining trait of a human is the ability to walk upright on two feet; likewise, apes have the bone structure to allow for the same ability.

| Similarities between Humans and Apes | |
|---|---|
| **Humans** | **Apes** |
| 1. ______________________ | 1. ______________________ |
| ______________________ | ______________________ |
| 2. ______________________ | 2. ______________________ |

**EXPLANATION** Here are the sentences arranged in the proper order. The organization and transition words are in **bold** type.

> Humans and apes share **similar** characteristics. The defining trait of a human is the ability to walk upright on two feet; **likewise**, apes have the bone structure to allow for the same ability. **Another** important **similarity** is the use of the opposing thumb to grasp objects.

The addition signal word *another* provided an important context clue for understanding the proper order of the ideas. You should have filled in the chart with the following information.

| Humans | Apes |
|---|---|
| 1. bone structure to walk upright on two feet | 1. bone structure to walk upright on two feet |
| 2. opposing digits grasp objects | 2. opposing digits grasp objects |

## PRACTICE 2

Read the following paragraph. Complete the ideas with transitions from the box that show comparisons. Use each word once.

| | | |
|---|---|---|
| both | likewise | similarities |
| in the same way | similar | |

### The Similarities between Christianity and Islam

Two of the most influential religions, Christianity and Islam, actually share many (**1**) ______________. Both religions are monotheistic, worshipping one God, and the God of both religions is an all-powerful and all-knowing being. (**2**) ______________ Islam and Christianity believe God has a special relationship with humans. Muslims and Christians have a (**3**) ______________ view of God as the creator to whom they submit in obedience. Islam and Christianity share a moral code based on a Covenant, or agreement, established by God. Both religions view Satan (**4**) ______________, as an enemy of God and humanity. (**5**) ______________, Muslims and Christians agree that humans have free will and will face a final judgment based on their actions in light of God's moral code. In a similar fashion, both believe in the return of Jesus Christ at the end of this age to defeat Satan and judge humanity.

## Contrast

**Contrast** points out the ways in which two or more ideas are different. Sample signal words are *different*, *but*, and *yet*.

| Words and Phrases of Contrast | | | | |
|---|---|---|---|---|
| although | conversely | different from | in spite of | on the other hand |
| as opposed to | despite | differently | instead | still |
| at the same time | differ | even though | nevertheless | to the contrary |
| but | difference | however | on the contrary | unlike |
| by contrast | different | in contrast | on the one hand | yet |

Here are some examples:

Capitalism and socialism are two very **different** worldviews.

Women **differ** from men in their styles of communication.

Weather refers to the current atmospheric conditions, such as rain or sunshine. Climate, **on the other hand**, describes the general weather conditions in a particular place during a particular season or all year round.

Each of these sentences has two topics that differ from each other in some way. The difference is the author's main point. For example, the first sentence sets up a contrast between two points of view: capitalism and socialism. The contrast is introduced by the word *different*. The second sentence states that the communication styles of women *differ* from the communication styles of men. And the third sentence contrasts the definitions of *weather* and *climate*; the author connects the definitions with the signal phrase *on the other hand*.

### PRACTICE 3

Complete the following sentences with a transition that shows contrast. Use each expression only once.

1. ______________ his family is originally from Mexico, Juan does not speak Spanish.
2. Some people such as Oprah Winfrey choose to work ______________ the fact that they no longer need the money.
3. Marie knows that she needs to take her allergy medicine every day; ______________, she forgets unless she is reminded.

**4.** ______________ of cramming for the test the night before, Jordan and his study group started studying two weeks before the scheduled exam date.

**5.** Every member of the study group performed well on the exam, __________ the students who waited and crammed.

When contrast is used to organize an entire paragraph, the pattern looks like this.

**Contrast Pattern**

| **Idea 1** | | **Idea 2** |
|---|---|---|
| Idea 1 | *differs from* | Idea 2 |
| Idea 1 | *differs from* | Idea 2 |
| Idea 1 | *differs from* | Idea 2 |

**EXAMPLE** Determine a logical order for the following five sentences. Write **1** by the sentence that should come first, **2** by the sentence that should come second, **3** by the sentence that should come third, and so on. Then use the information to fill in the chart.

_____ Even though Alec had rarely spoken to others in the hallways, he had often interrupted coworkers who were speaking during meetings.

_____ In contrast, after counseling, he listened politely to others as they spoke during meetings.

_____ Quiet and withdrawn before counseling, Alec rarely spoke, smiled, or made eye contact with his coworkers as he passed them in the hallways or at their desks.

_____ However, after counseling, he became more friendly and outgoing, taking time to make eye contact and speak with colleagues.

_____ Alec behaved very differently after attending a series of counseling sessions aimed at improving his communication skills.

**Changes in Alec's Communication Skills**

| **Alec Before Counseling** | **Alec After Counseling** |
|---|---|
| 1. quiet and withdrawn in hallways | 1. ______________________ |
| 2. interrupted others during meetings | 2. ______________________ |
| | ______________________ |

**EXPLANATION** Here are the sentences arranged in the proper order. The transition and signal words are in **bold** type.

> [1]Alec behaved very **differently after** attending a series of counseling sessions aimed at improving his communication skills. [2]Quiet and withdrawn **before** counseling, Alec rarely spoke, smiled, or made eye contact with his coworkers as he passed them in the hallways or at their desks. [3]**However, after** counseling, he became more friendly and outgoing, taking time to make eye contact and speak with colleagues. [4]**Even though** Alec had rarely spoken to others in the hallways, he had often interrupted coworkers who were speaking during meetings. [5]**In contrast, after** counseling, he listened politely to others as they spoke during meetings.

The time signal words *before* and *after* provided important context clues for understanding the proper order of the ideas. You should have filled in the chart with the following information.

| Alec Before Counseling | Alec After Counseling |
|---|---|
| 1. quiet and withdrawn in hallways | 1. friendly and outgoing |
| 2. interrupted others during meetings | 2. listened politely to others during meetings |

## PRACTICE 4

Read the following paragraph. Complete the ideas with transitions from the box that show contrasts. Use each word once.

| difference | differs | instead |
|---|---|---|
| differences | in contrast | |

In anticipation of your move from the Miami-Dade area in Florida to Austin, Texas, I have prepared an analysis of the (**1**) _______________ in the cost of living between the two areas. The first (**2**) _______________ is the price range of homes. The average home sells for $433,000 in Miami-Dade (**3**) _______________ to the average selling price of $222,000 for a home in Austin. However, you may choose to rent an apartment (**4**) _______________ of buying a home. The average rent rate for a decent apartment in Miami-Dade is around $1100 per month as opposed to $954 for an apartment in Austin. The cost of utilities also (**5**) _______________ between the two regions. Total energy costs for a typical Miami-Dade residence average $170 a month, but the energy costs in Austin average at $157. Even in the service sector, the cost of living in Austin is much less than in the Miami-Dade area.

## Comparison and Contrast

The **comparison-and-contrast pattern** shows how two things are similar and also how they are different.

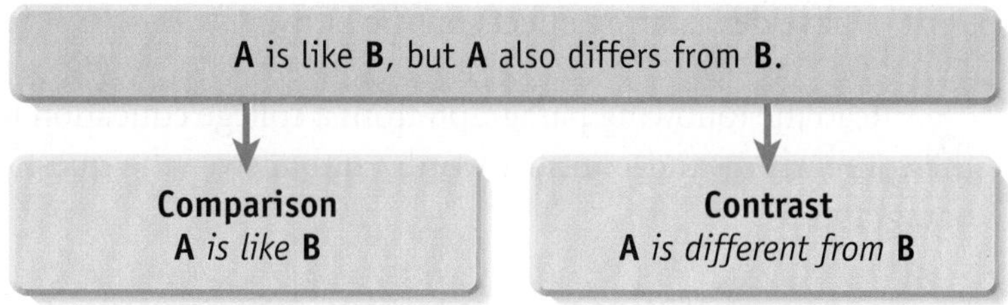


**Yoga and Pilates: The Similarities and Differences**

[1]Although yoga and Pilates share *similar* characteristics, an important *difference* exists. [2]*Both* yoga and Pilates are low-impact forms of exercise that improve posture, flexibility, and concentration. [3]In addition, *both* emphasize that a balance between body and mind is important. [4]*However*, the primary goal of Pilates is to strengthen the midsection and buttocks. [5]Pilates calls this area of the body the "powerhouse." [6]*On the other hand*, yoga does not focus on any one part of the body. [7]*Rather*, yoga works the opposing muscles of the entire body.

In the paragraph, two kinds of exercise are being compared and contrasted: yoga and Pilates. Remember, a topic sentence contains the topic and the author's controlling point about the topic. In this topic sentence, the author uses the words *similar* and *difference* to set up the points of comparison and contrast. The author's supporting details are a list of similarities introduced by the word *both.* The second similarity is introduced with the addition transition phrase *in addition*. The shift in the paragraph from similarities to differences is introduced in sentence 4 with the word *however*. The supporting details that explain these differences are introduced with the expressions *on the other hand* and *rather.*

**EXAMPLES** Determine a logical order for the following four sentences. Write **1** by the sentence that should come first, **2** by the sentence that should come second, **3** by the sentence that should come third, and **4** by the sentence that should come fourth.

______ Yet anorexia and bulimia are two different eating disorders.

______ Although anorexia and bulimia share certain similarities, they are very different.

______ Bulimia occurs when a person binges on large amounts of food and then induces vomiting; in contrast, anorexia occurs when a person refuses to eat much of anything.

______ Both arise out of a perceived need to be thin and lose weight, and both have devastating effects on the body.

Read the following paragraph from a college education textbook. Underline the comparison-and-contrast words, and answer the questions that follow the paragraph.

Textbook Skills

**What's the Difference?**

[1]Those with a disability and those with a handicap often face similar reactions from others. [2]They are often misunderstood. [3]And both are often given the same labels. [4]However, the two conditions have a distinct difference. [5]The distinction between the two is important. [6]A disability is an inability to do something specific, such as see or walk. [7]On the contrary, a handicap is a disadvantage only in certain situations. [8]Sometimes a disability leads to a handicap, but not always. [9]For example, being blind (a visual disability) is a handicap if you want to drive. [10]But blindness is not a handicap when you are creating music or talking on the telephone.

—Adapted from Woolfolk, *Educational Psychology*, 8th ed., pp. 107–08.

**1.** What two ideas are being compared and contrasted? ________________

____________________________________________

**2.** List four different comparison-and-contrast words or phrases in the paragraph. ________________________________

**EXPLANATIONS** Here are the four sentences about eating disorders arranged in the proper order. The transition words are in **bold** type.

[1]**Although** anorexia and bulimia share certain **similarities**, they are very **different**. [2]**Both** arise out of a perceived need to be thin and lose weight, and **both** have devastating effects on the body. [3]Yet anorexia and bulimia are two **different** eating disorders. [4]Bulimia occurs when a person binges on large amounts of food and then induces vomiting; **in contrast**, anorexia occurs when a person refuses to eat much of anything.

Here are the answers to the questions about the paragraph from an education textbook: The paragraph compares and contrasts a disability and a handicap. You were correct to choose any four of the following comparison-and-contrast words: *similar, same, however, both, distinction, on the contrary, but, difference.*

## PRACTICE 5

The following paragraph from a college psychology textbook uses comparison and contrast. Read the paragraph, and underline the comparison-and-contrast signal words. Then answer the questions that follow the paragraph.

Textbook Skills

[1]Parents have two distinctly different choices of punishment that can bring similar results. [2]On the one hand, positive punishment responds to the child's misbehavior with an action that improves the behavior. [3]For example, if Mom's frown in response to Pete's rude remark causes Pete to be less rude, then Mom's frown is a positive punishment. [4]On the other hand, negative punishment removes a freedom or privilege. [5]After grabbing and pulling his sister's hair, Raymond is punished by having to leave the table and go without dinner. [6]Just as Pete changed his behavior, Raymond no longer mistreats his sister.

—Adapted from Jaffe, *Understanding Parenting*, 2nd ed., p. 194.

_____ **1.** What pattern is used in this passage?
a. comparison
b. contrast
c. comparison and contrast

**2.** What two ideas are being discussed? ____________________ and ____________________

## PRACTICE 6

Read the following paragraph. Complete the ideas with transitions from the box. Use each word once.

| | | | | |
|---|---|---|---|---|
| conversely | different | even though | in contrast | same |
| despite | differs | however | just as | similar |

The similarities between high school and college are numerous and even obvious. Both levels teach many of the (**1**) ________________ subject areas: English, history, algebra, physics, and so on. Often the physical environment is (**2**) ________________ with the same kinds of classroom configurations, desks, chalkboards, and technology. (**3**) ________________ high school students can participate in various extra-curricular activities such as student government, sports, and clubs, so too can college students. However, (**4**) ________________ these apparent similarities, the college experience (**5**) ________________ significantly from the high school experience. First, high school is required and free; (**6**) ________________, college is voluntary and expensive. Second, high school students must obtain parental permission to participate in extracurricular activities; (**7**) ________________, college students only have to volunteer to participate. Finally, high school students often expect to be reminded about deadlines or guided through assignments. (**8**) ________________, college students are expected to take full responsibility and to think independently. Overall, (**9**) ________________ high school and college seem to be similar experiences, they are very (**10**) ________________ indeed.

## The Cause-and-Effect Pattern

Sometimes an author talks about *why* something happened or *what* results came from an event. A **cause** states why something happens. An **effect** states a result or outcome. Sample signal words include *because* and *consequently.*

| Cause-and-Effect Words | | | |
|---|---|---|---|
| accordingly | consequently | leads to | therefore |
| affect | due to | outcome | thus |
| as a result | if . . . then | results in | |
| because | impact | since | |
| because of | influence | so | |

Here are some examples:

**Because** Selena memorized the algebra formulas and practiced using them, she did well on the chapter test.

Lance seeks out personal and sensitive details in a conversation; he often repeats this information to others. **As a result,** those who know Lance have come to distrust him.

**Due to** the amount of snow on the streets and highways, schools and businesses have shut down.

Each of these sentences has two topics: one topic causes or has an effect on the second topic. The cause or effect is the author's controlling point. For example, the two topics in the first sentence are memorizing formulas and doing well on the test. This main idea states that memorizing is the cause of doing well. The cause is introduced by the word *because.* The two topics of the second sentence are Lance's behavior and the effect of that behavior. The effect is introduced by the signal phrase *as a result.* And the two topics in the third sentence are the amount of snow and the closing of schools and businesses; the author focuses on the cause by using the signal phrase *due to.* Note that cause and effect has a strong connection to time, and many of the transitions for this thought pattern therefore have a time element. Although many of these transition words have similar meanings and may be interchangeable, authors carefully choose the transition that best fits the context.

## PRACTICE 7

Complete each sentence with a cause-and-effect word or phrase from the box. Use each word only once.

| accordingly | consequently | if . . . then | leads to | results in |
|---|---|---|---|---|

1. Reading magazines, newspapers, and books _______________ a large vocabulary.
2. Over the summer, Molly grows to be several inches taller than all her peers.

   Her additional height _______________ better performance and more playing time on the basketball court.
3. Maurice surfed the Internet and bought an essay for his history class. His teacher, who suspected that Maurice didn't write the essay he submitted, surfed the Internet and found the essay Maurice had bought.

   _______________, Maurice received a failing grade for the assignment.

4. The American dream is based on the premise that _______________ you work hard, _______________ you will succeed.

5. Hurricane Katrina was a category 5 hurricane by the time it hit the Gulf Coast in August 2005. _______________, the hurricane destroyed many communities.

**VISUAL VOCABULARY**

_____ The best meaning for **catastrophic** is

a. unexpected.

b. disastrous.

c. minimal.

▲ The intensity of Hurricane Katrina caused catastrophic damage, destroying businesses and homes, leaving hundreds homeless, and costing $150 billion.

The writer using cause and effect introduces an idea or event and then provides supporting details to show how that idea *results in* or *leads to* another idea. Many times, the second idea comes about because of the first idea. Thus the first idea is the cause, and the following ideas are the effects.

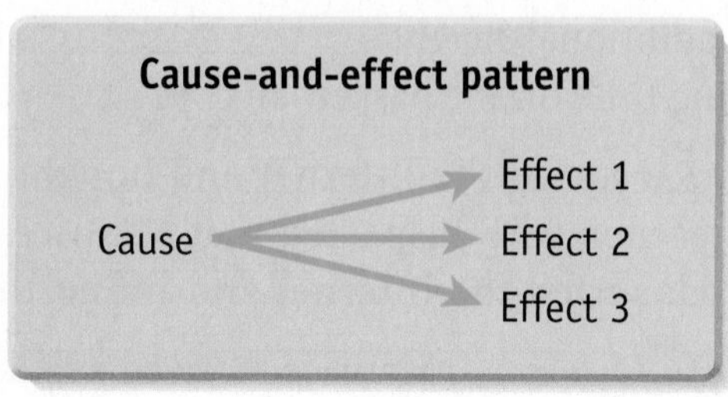

For example, read the following topic sentence:

> Over time, the eating disorder bulimia may damage the digestive system and the heart.

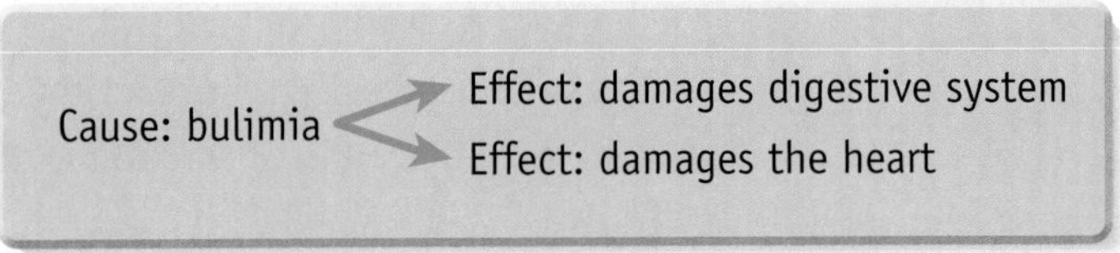


Often an author will begin with an effect and then give the causes.

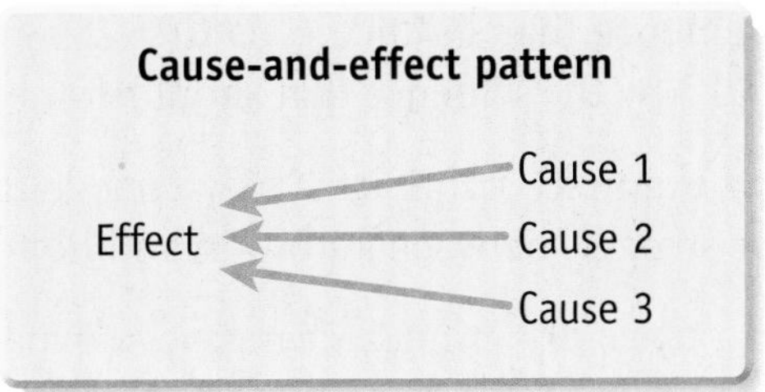


For example, read the following topic sentence:

> The eating disorder bulimia may be the result of poor self-esteem and cultural values.

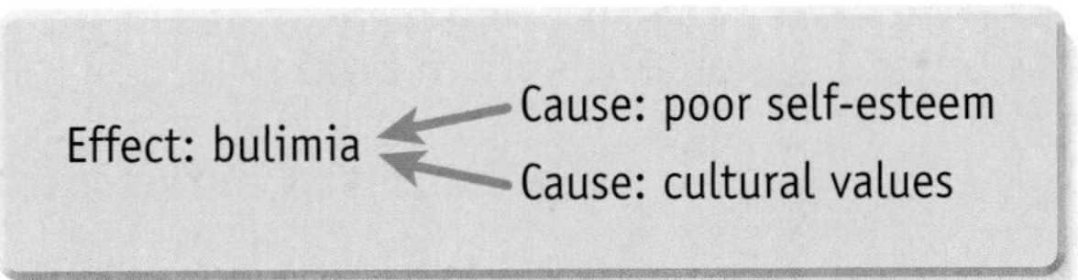


Sometimes the author may wish to emphasize a chain reaction.

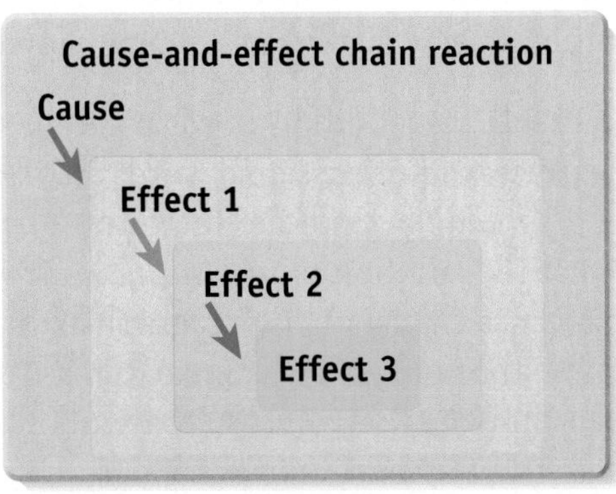

For example, read the following topic sentence.

> Low self-esteem leads to dissatisfaction with one's appearance, which leads to control issues and can ultimately result in bulimia.

**Cause-and-effect chain reaction**

Cause: low self-esteem → Effect: dissatisfaction with appearance → Effect: control issues → Effect: bulimia

**EXAMPLES** Determine a logical order for the following three sentences. Write **1** by the sentence that should come first, **2** by the sentence that should come second, and **3** by the sentence that should come last.

_____ For example, a character may change due to an inner conflict such as the struggle between ambition and honor.

_____ In a piece of fiction, a change in a dynamic character is usually the result of conflict.

_____ In addition, a character may change because of a conflict with another person or group of people, such as a struggle between a father and son or between a citizen and the government.

**EXPLANATION** Here are the sentences arranged in the proper order. The transition and signal words are in **bold** type.

### What Causes a Character to Change?

[1]In a piece of fiction, a change in a dynamic character is usually the **result of** conflict. [2]**For example**, a character may change **due to** an inner conflict **such as** the struggle between ambition and honor. [3]**In addition**, a character may change **because of** a conflict with another person or group of people, **such as** a struggle between a father and son or between a citizen and the government.

In this paragraph, two addition words combine with the cause-and-effect signal words. The cause-and-effect signal words are *result of*, *due to*, and *because of*. *For example* and *in addition* indicate the order of the cause-and-effect discussion. Also note that the addition phrase *such as* introduces examples of the kinds of conflict that cause change. This paragraph actually uses two patterns of organization to make the point—the listing pattern is used to add the cause-and-effect details. Even though two patterns are used, the cause-and-effect pattern is the primary pattern of organization.

## PRACTICE 8

The following paragraph from a college science textbook uses the cause-and-effect pattern of organization. Read the paragraph, underline the cause-and-effect signal words in it, and complete the concept map that follows it.

Textbook Skills

### An Evolutionary Arms Race

[1]Predators have a negative effect on the animals they consume, obviously. [2]As a result, in response, prey animals have evolved defenses against being consumed. [3]This change in the prey leads to the predator's developing more effective strategies. [4]There is an evolutionary arms race: predators change strategies, going one step farther, which causes prey to change strategies in the same general way. [5]As a result, both groups evolve at a fast pace. [6]As the predator becomes more successful, the pressure builds on the prey to improve defenses. [7]Conversely, the better the defense, the greater the need for the predator to develop its skills.

—Adapted from Maier, *Comparative Animal Behavior: An Evolutionary and Ecological Approach,* pp. 129–30.

**Cause-and-effect chain reaction**

Cause: ________ catches prey → Effect: _____ develops new defenses → Effect: ________ adjusts and becomes more effective → Effect: evolutionary ________

## PRACTICE 9

Read the following paragraph. Complete the ideas with transitions from the box. Use each word once.

| | | | | |
|---|---|---|---|---|
| affects | effects | influences | outcomes | results in |
| consequence | impact | leads to | result | therefore |

### The Effect of Violence in the Media

More than 1,000 studies on the (**1**) ______________ of television and film violence have been done during the past 40 years. Each study has reached the same (**2**) ______________: television violence (**3**) ______________ real-world violence. The majority of these studies, taken together, agree that the following are likely (**4**) __________ of media violence. Overall, constant viewing of televised violence has a negative (**5**) __________ on human character and attitudes. In addition, television violence encourages violent forms of behavior and (**6**) __________ moral and social values about violence in daily life. Watching significant amounts of television violence (**7**) __________ a greater likelihood of aggressive behavior in children. Television violence (**8**) __________ viewers of all ages, intellect, socioeconomic levels, and both genders. One sad (**9**) __________ of media violence is a warped view of the world. Viewers who watch significant amounts of television violence see a meaner world and, (**10**) __________, overestimate the risk of being a victim of violence.

—Adapted from United States. "Children, Violence, and the Media." Senate Committee on the Judiciary. 14 September 1999. 19 March 2007 <http://judiciary.senate.gov/oldsite/mediavio.htm.>.

## The Generalization-and-Example Pattern

> As technology evolves, it saves time; broadband Internet access cuts down on the time needed to access information on the World Wide Web.

Some people may read this sentence and think that the author's focus is on the topic of broadband Internet access. But evolving technology saves time in many other areas of our lives, such as in traveling, cooking, or cleaning. Adding an **example word** makes it clear that broadband Internet access is only one instance in which technology saves time.

Read the sentence about technology and the Internet again. Note how the use of the example word makes the relationship between ideas clear.

> As technology evolves, it saves time; *for example*, broadband Internet access cuts down on the time needed to access information on the World Wide Web.

In the generalization-and-example thought pattern, the author makes a general statement and then offers an example or a series of examples to clarify the generalization.

**The Generalization-and-Example Pattern**

Statement of a general idea
  Example
  Example

Example words signal that a writer is giving an instance of a general idea.

**Words and Phrases That Introduce Examples**

| | | | |
|---|---|---|---|
| an illustration | for instance | once | to illustrate |
| for example | including | such as | typically |

**EXAMPLE** Read each of the following items and fill in the blanks with an appropriate example word or phrase.

1. Food labels provide important information. _______________, the label on Rich Harvest Sweet Dark Whole Grain bread states that one slice has 120 calories.
2. Fatigue can interfere with performance. _______________, Carla was so tired after working straight through two shifts at the restaurant that she made careless mistakes on her math exam.
3. Tyler's intelligence and energy allows him to excel in a variety of areas _______________ sports, academics, and community service.

**EXPLANATION** Many words and phrases that introduce examples are easily interchanged. Notice that in the first two examples, the phrases *for example* and *for instance* are similar in meaning. In the third example, the use of the transition phrase *such as* signals a list. Even though transition words or phrases have similar meanings, authors carefully choose transitions based on style and meaning.

## PRACTICE 10

Complete each selection with an example word. Fill in the blanks with words from the box.

1. Luis is a gracious host ready for an instant party; he always keeps his pantry stocked with items _______________ soft drinks, bottled water, wine, and a variety of crackers, chips, and nuts.

2. Although Gene and Paula love each other deeply, they face significant problems in their relationship. ______________, Paula wants to continue her education, yet Gene wants to have children right away.
3. Leigh seems to have a number of allergy symptoms, ______________ extreme itching, scaly patches on her skin, watery eyes, and headaches.
4. Hunter will go to great lengths to have fun; ______________ he drove for 22 hours round trip to attend a Saturday afternoon beach party with a group of friends.
5. Watching television can have a soothing effect. ______________, when Jean has trouble falling asleep after a long, difficult day at the office, she turns the television volume down low, turns off all the lights, and lies down; the rhythm of the flickering images and low tones puts her right to sleep.

## PRACTICE 11

Read the following passage. Complete the ideas with transitions from the box. Use each word once.

| | | |
|---|---|---|
| exemplifies | for instance | such as |
| for example | illustrated | |

Groups use different decision-making methods when deciding, (**1**) ______________, which solution to accept. The method to be used should, naturally, be stated at the outset of the group discussion. The three main decision-making methods are as follows:

*Decision by authority:* Group members voice their feelings and opinions, but the leader, boss, or chief executive, (**2**) ______________ the president of the company, makes the final decision. This method has the advantages of being efficient and of giving greater importance to the suggestions of more experienced members. The big disadvantage is that members may feel that their contributions have too little influence and therefore may not participate with real enthusiasm.

*Majority rule:* The group agrees to abide by the majority decision and may vote on various issues as the group searches to solve its problem. The United States Senate often (**3**) ______________ majority rule. Like decision by authority, this method is efficient. A disadvantage is that it may lead the group to limit discussion by calling for a vote once a majority has agreed. Also, members not voting with the majority may feel disenfranchised and left out.

*Consensus:* In some situations, consensus means unanimous agreement; (**4**) ______________, a criminal jury must reach a unanimous decision to convict or acquit a defendant. In most business groups, consensus means that members agree that they can live with the solution; they agree that they can do whatever the solution requires. Consensus is especially helpful when the group wants each member to be satisfied and committed to the decision and to the decision-making process as a whole. Consensus obviously takes the most time of any of the decision-making methods and can lead to a great deal of inefficiency, especially if members wish to prolong the discussion process needlessly or selfishly. Two groups that have historically (**5**) ______________ decisions by consensus include the Iroquois Grand Council and the Quakers, a religious sect.

—Adapted from DeVito, Joseph A. (2005). *Essentials of Human Communication*, 5th ed., pp. 199.

## The Definition Pattern

Textbooks are full of new words and special terms. Even if the word is common, it can take on a special meaning in a specific course. To help students understand the ideas, authors often include a definition of the new or special term. Then, to make sure the meaning of the word or concept is clear, the author also gives examples.

**Emblems** are body gestures that directly translate into words or phrases—for example, the OK sign, the thumbs-up for "good job," and the V for victory.

—Adapted from DeVito, *Messages: Building Interpersonal Communication Skills,* 4th ed., p. 141.

In this sentence, the term *emblem* is defined first. Then the author gives three examples to make the term clear to the reader.

**The Definition Pattern**

Term and definition
  Example
  Example

- The **definition** explains the meaning of new, difficult, or special terms. Definitions include words like *is, are,* and *means*: "Emblems *are* body gestures that directly translate into words or phrases . . ."
- The **examples** follow a definition to show how the word is used or applied in the content course. Examples are signaled by words like *for example* and *such as:* "for example, the OK sign, the thumbs-up for 'good job,' and the V for victory."

**EXAMPLES**

**A.** Determine a logical order for the following three sentences. Write **1** by the sentence that should come first, **2** by the sentence that should come second, and **3** by the sentence that should come last. Then read the explanation.

_____ For example, a person may give up a high-paying job in the city to take a lower-paying job in a small town.

_____ Downshifting is a deliberate effort to reduce stress by choosing to live more simply.

_____ Some people who choose to downshift may also avoid the use of televisions, computers, and cell phones.

**B.** Read the following paragraph from a college communications textbook. Annotate the paragraph: circle the term being defined, and underline the key words in the definition. Then answer the questions that follow it.

**Paralanguage**

[1]**Paralanguage** is the meaning that is perceived along with the actual words used to deliver a message. [2]It is how we say something. [3]This is a broad

category that includes a number of traits such as dialects, accents, pitch, rate, vocal qualities, pauses, and silence. [4]A pleasing voice, for example, will make people more likely to listen to us. [5]And a modulated voice indicates higher social status and educational levels.

—Adapted from Harris & Sherblom, *Small Group and Team Communication,* 2nd ed., p. 112.

**1.** What are the two examples that illustrate the term being defined?

____________________ and ____________________.

**2.** Which words signal each example? ____________ and ____________.

**EXPLANATIONS**

**A.** The sentences have been arranged in the proper order in the following paragraph. The definition, example, and transition words are in **bold** type.

### Downshifting

Downshifting **is** a deliberate effort to reduce stress by choosing to live more simply. **For example**, a person may give up a high-paying job in the city to take a lower-paying job in a small town. Some people who choose to downshift may **also** avoid the use of televisions, computers, and cell phones.

This sequence of ideas begins by introducing the term *downshifting.* The term is linked to its definition with the verb *is.* The author provides two examples of behaviors common to people who downshift. The sentence that contains *for example* would logically follow the definition. The example that contains the addition transition *also* would come last.

**B.** By circling and underlining only key terms, you highlight the most important information for easy review. Compare your annotations to the following:

Textbook Skills

### Paralanguage

[1]**Paralanguage** is the meaning that is perceived along with the actual words used to deliver a message. [2]It is how we say something. [3]This is a broad category that includes a number of traits such as dialects, accents, pitch, rate, vocal qualities, pauses, and silence. [4]A pleasing voice, for example, will make people more likely to listen to us. [5]And a modulated voice indicates higher social status and educational levels.

—Adapted from Harris & Sherblom, *Small Group and Team Communication,* 2nd ed., p. 112.

**1.** The two examples are *a pleasing voice* and *a modulated voice.*

**2.** The signal words that introduce the examples are for *example* and *and.*

## PRACTICE 12

Read the paragraph. Finish the definition concept map that follows it by adding the missing details in the proper order.

### Sexual Cannibalism

[1]**Sexual cannibalism** occurs when one mate eats the other before, during, or after mating. [2]For example, the male redback spider is made in such a way that it can mate while it is being eaten. [3]Some half-eaten redback males actually survive to mate again. [4]And the female black widow occasionally eats the male immediately after mating. [5]However, if the female black widow is already well fed, the male usually escapes to mate again another day. [6]Praying mantises and scorpions are also known to engage in this violent mating behavior.

**Term:** ______________________________

**Definition:** ______________________________

**Example:** ______________________________

**Example:** ______________________________

**Example:** ______________________________

### VISUAL VOCABULARY

______ The best meaning of **spherical** is

a. round.
b. large.
c. oblong.

▶ The female black widow, with her spherical abdomen, is about 1.5 inches in length, nearly twice the size of the male.

## PRACTICE 13

Read the following passage. Finish the definition concept map that follows it by adding the missing details in proper order.

### What is Child Abuse and Neglect?

[1]Each State provides its own definitions of child abuse and neglect based on minimum standards set by Federal law. [2]The Federal Child Abuse Prevention and Treatment Act (CAPTA) defines child abuse and neglect as the following:

- [3]Any recent act or failure to act on the part of a parent or caretaker which results in death, serious physical or emotional harm, sexual abuse or exploitation.
- [4]An act or failure to act which presents an imminent risk of serious harm.

[5]Four major types of **maltreatment** are recognized in most States: neglect, physical abuse, sexual abuse, and emotional abuse. [6]Although any of the forms of child maltreatment may be found separately, they often occur in combination. [7]The following examples are for general informational purposes only. [8]Not all States' definitions will include all of the examples listed below, and individual States' definitions may cover additional situations not mentioned here.

[9]**Neglect** is failure to provide for a child's basic needs. [10]Neglect may be:

- [11]Physical (failure to provide necessary food or shelter, or lack of appropriate supervision)
- [12]Medical (failure to provide necessary medical or mental health treatment)
- [13]Educational (failure to educate a child or attend to special education needs)
- [14]Emotional (inattention to a child's emotional needs, failure to provide psychological care, or permitting the child to use alcohol or other drugs)

—Adapted from Child Welfare Information Gateway. "What is Child Abuse and Neglect?" U.S. Department of Health and Human Services April 2006 1 August 2007 <http://www.childwelfare.gov/pubs/factsheets/whatiscan.pdf>.

**Terms:** ______________________________

**Definition:** Any recent act or failure to act on the part of a parent or caretaker which results in death, serious physical or emotional harm, sexual abuse or exploitation. An act or failure to act which presents an imminent risk of serious harm.

**Term:** ______________________________

**Definition:** Neglect, physical abuse, sexual abuse, and emotional abuse.

**Term:** Neglect

**Definition:** ______________________________

**Examples:** Failure to provide ________ ________ medical treatment, an education, emotional support. Permitting the child to use drugs.

Textbook Skills

## Thought Patterns and Textbooks

Textbook authors rely heavily on the use of transitions and thought patterns to make information clear and easier to understand.

**EXAMPLES** The following topic sentences have been taken from college textbooks. Identify the *primary* thought pattern that each sentence suggests.

______ **1.** Issuing orders or making it clear that we have the power to control the behavior of others results in others' defensiveness.
a. cause and effect
b. comparison and contrast
c. definition

______ **2.** Distress is stress that brings about negative mental or physical responses such as having trouble relaxing.
a. cause and effect
b. comparison and contrast
c. definition

______ **3.** When stock prices fully reflect information that is available to investors, the stock market is efficient; in contrast, when stock prices do not reflect all information, the stock market is inefficient.
a. cause and effect
b. comparison and contrast
c. definition

**EXPLANATIONS** Topic sentence 1, from a psychology textbook, uses (a) cause and effect, signaled by the phrase *results in*. Topic sentence 2, from a health textbook, is organized according to (c) definition, using the verb *is* and the phrase *such as* to signal examples. Note that the sentence includes the phrase *brings about*, which suggests cause and effect; however, the sentence is set up in the form of a definition. Therefore, definition is the *primary* thought pattern. Topic sentence 3, from an economics textbook, uses (b) comparison and contrast as the primary thought pattern. Some readers may pick up on the author's use of time order, signaled by the word *when*. The use of time order can suggest cause and effect. However, in this sentence, *when* is used to describe two instances or events. The signal phrase *in contrast* joins these two events to point out the differences between them.

## PRACTICE 14

The following sentences are from college textbooks. Identify the thought pattern that each topic sentence suggests. (The type of textbook is identified after each topic sentence.)

_____ **1.** Creativity is the result of looking at things in a new way. (social science)
a. cause and effect
b. comparison and contrast
c. generalization and example

_____ **2.** The occasional drinker differs slightly from the social drinker. (health)
a. cause and effect
b. comparison and contrast
c. generalization and example

_____ **3.** Some pressed for war because they were suffering an agricultural depression. (history)
a. cause and effect
b. comparison and contrast
c. definition

_____ **4.** Several factors influence the way we relate to and use space in communicating. (communication)
a. cause and effect
b. comparison and contrast
c. generalization and example

_____ **5.** Analgesics, such as aspirin and ibuprofen, are pain relievers. (health)
a. cause and effect
b. comparison and contrast
c. definition

## Chapter Review

Test your understanding of what you have read in this chapter by filling in the blank with a word or phrase from the box. One answer is used twice.

| alike | comparison | effect | examples |
|---|---|---|---|
| cause | contrast | effects | |
| cause-and-effect | definition | example | |

**1.** Comparison points out the ways in which two or more ideas are _______________.

**2.** _______________ points out the ways in which two or more ideas are different.

**3.** The words *like*, *similarly*, and *likewise* signal the _______________ pattern.

4. A ______________ states why something happens.

5. An ______________ states a result or outcome.

6. An author will often begin with a ____________ and then give the ____________.

7. The expressions *as a result, leads to,* and *therefore* show the ______________ pattern.

8. ______________ words signal that a writer is giving an instance of a general idea to clarify a point.

9. A ______________ explains the meaning of a new, difficult, or special term.

10. ______________ follow a definition to show how the word is used or applied.

## Applications

### Application 1: Using Example and Definition Patterns

**A.** The following paragraph lists a series of supporting details using the generalization-and-example thought pattern. Complete the outline that follows with the missing details of example.

> Maxine excels at whatever she attempts. First, Maxine is a talented hostess. For example, she is able to create gourmet meals on short notice. She is also an avid competitor, excelling in sports such as tennis, golf, and swimming. In addition, Maxine is an award-winning student. For instance, she was awarded a full two-year scholarship at her local community college.

Main idea stated as a topic sentence: Maxine excels at whatever she attempts.

First major supporting detail: a talented hostess

Minor supporting detail of example: creates gourmet meals on short notice

1. Second major supporting detail: ______________________________

   Minor supporting detail of example: excels in tennis, golf, and swimming

2. Third major supporting detail: an award-winning student

   Minor supporting detail of example: ______________________________

   ______________________________________________

**B.** The following paragraph from a college science textbook contains a definition and three examples. In the spaces provided, write the term, the definition, and the missing example.

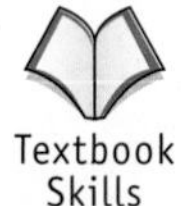
Textbook Skills

**Noise Pollution**

[1]Noise pollution is the mix of sounds connected to working with machines. [2]This mix could include the following: car engines, radios, lawn mowers, gardener blowers, factory machinery, office equipment, home appliances, televisions, and overhead jets. [3]Noise pollution is linked to urban cities such as New York City. [4]And noise pollution is more intense in some work settings. [5]For example, an automobile repair shop would have a high level of noise pollution.

—Adapted from McGuigan, *Encyclopedia of Stress*, p. 148.

**3.** Term: ________________________________

**4.** Definition: ________________________________

**5.** Example: car engines, radios, lawn mowers, gardener blowers, factory machinery, office equipment, home appliances, televisions, and overhead jets

Example: ________________________________

Example: an automobile repair shop

## Application 2: Using the Contrast Pattern

The following paragraph uses the contrast thought pattern. Underline the main idea. Then complete the concept map that follows.

Textbook Skills

**Listening and Gender**

[1]Deborah Tannen's bestselling book *You Just Don't Understand: Women and Men in Conversation* explores some of the differences in how men and women listen to one another. [2]Tannen shows that when men and women talk, men lecture while women listen. [3]The lecturer is set up as the superior, as the teacher, the expert; on the other hand, the listener is the inferior, the student, the nonexpert. [4]In addition, women use listening skills to build rapport and close relationships. [5]In contrast, men interrupt more and often change the topic to one they know more about or that is more factual, for example, sports or finance. [6]Finally, men, research shows, play up their expertise, using it to dominate the conversation. [7]However, women play down their expertise.

—Adapted from DeVito, *Messages: Building Interpersonal Communication Skills*, 4th ed., p. 98.

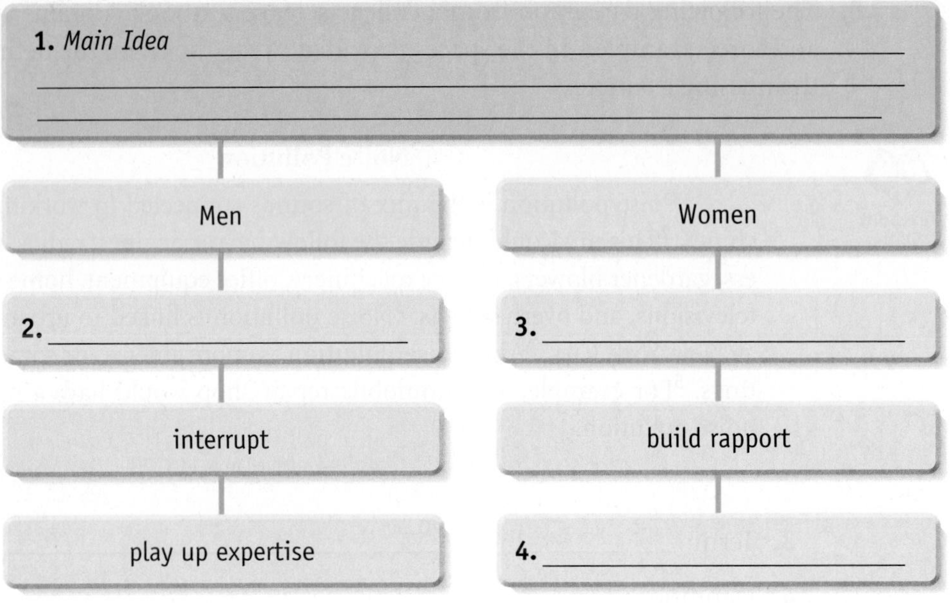


## Application 3: Using the Cause-and-Effect Pattern

The following series of sentences from a college psychology textbook uses the cause-and-effect thought pattern. Fill in each missing cause or effect.

1. Classical conditioning has an effect on deaths caused by drug overdose.

   Cause: ______

   Effect: deaths caused by drug overdose

2. A user who generally takes a drug in a particular place—the bathroom, say—develops a conditioned response to that place.

   Cause: generally taking a drug in a specific place

   Effect: ______

3. Because of classical conditioning, as soon as the user walks into the bathroom, his or her body begins to get ready for the influx of drugs that is about to come.

   Cause: classical conditioning

   Effect: ______

4. The conditioned response causes the body to counteract or dampen the effects of the drug.

Cause: ______________________________

Effect: counteracts or dampens effects of drug

Textbook Skills

**Classically Conditioned Animal Training**

◂ Dogs learn not to go beyond the boundary of an "invisible fence" because the fence delivers a mild shock through their collars.

—Adapted from Kosslyn & Rosenberg, *Psychology: The Brain, The Person, The World*, p. 173.

_____ 5. The primary thought pattern used in this figure is
- a. cause and effect.
- b. comparison and contrast.

# REVIEW Test 1

## Transition Words and Thought Patterns

A. Based on the thought pattern used to state each idea, fill in the blanks with the transition words from the box. Use each choice only once.

| because | even though | for example | on the other hand | so |
|---|---|---|---|---|

1. _______________ Chloe is afraid of heights, she went bungee jumping to celebrate her birthday.

2. Distance education is learning that takes place when the student is in a location apart from the classroom, building, or site; _______________, online courses and telecourses are distance learning courses.

3. As a student, Armando likes distance education _______________ he works a full-time job, and online courses offer a more flexible schedule.

4. Isabella wanted to become a professional stage actress, ______________ she moved to New York City.

5. A person who takes too much of a group's time may be poorly perceived; ______________, a person in an influential position may be granted more leeway in bending expectations regarding the use of time.

**B.** Underline the signal words. Then identify the thought pattern used in each short passage, as follows:

a. cause and effect
b. comparison and contrast
c. generalization and example

_____ **6.** The purpose of a documentary is to give depth and context for important public issues. One memorable example is *Harvest of Shame*, which exposed the mistreatment of migrant workers.

_____ **7.** Assertive communicators speak calmly, directly, and clearly to those around them; in contrast, nonassertive communicators may speak too rapidly, use a tone too low to be heard easily, or fail to say directly what is on their minds.

_____ **8.** Research shows that low doses of aspirin are beneficial to heart patients due to the blood-thinning properties of the drug.

_____ **9.** Rebekah overeats when she is under stress. Rebekah is overeating; therefore, she must be experiencing stress.

_____ **10.** The eureka experience is a sudden rush of understanding. I can recall one early instance of a eureka experience when the meaning of the word *frown* suddenly dawned on me. In that moment, by understanding one simple word, I became aware of the value of words.

# REVIEW Test 2

## Thought Patterns

**A.** Arrange the following sentences from a college health textbook in their proper order. Write **1** by the sentence that should come first, write **2** by the sentence that should come second, and so on. Use the transitions to figure out the proper order.

Textbook Skills

_____ In contrast, Gilligan believes that men have an ethic based on justice.

_____ According to Harvard Professor Carol Gilligan, men and women make very different decisions when facing moral choices.

_____ Gilligan believes that women have an ethic based on care.

_____ For example, men are more interested in fair play and individual rights.

_____ For example, women value loyalty, self-sacrifice, and peacemaking.

—Adapted from Donatelle, *Access to Health,* 7th ed., p. 135.

_____ **6.** What is the primary thought pattern used here?

a. generalization and example
b. cause and effect
c. comparison and contrast

**B.** Identify the thought pattern used in the following paragraphs, as follows:

a. cause and effect
b. comparison and contrast
c. definition

Textbook Skills

_____ **7.** Parenting style is the blend of attitudes and behaviors toward a child that creates an emotional climate. For example, a parent's style includes the parent's tone, a parent's body language, and signs of affection or hostility toward the child.

—Adapted from Jaffe, *Understanding Parenting,* 2nd ed., pp. 163–64.

_____ **8.** Marijuana has several short-term effects. First, physically, it speeds up the heart and reddens the eyes. In addition, psychologically, it may cause feelings of giddiness and increased hunger or sexual desire.

_____ **9.** Even though Gary and Tony are identical twins, their personalities differ greatly. On the one hand, Gary is outspoken, outgoing, and overcommitted. He serves on several service clubs, volunteers, and leads study sessions. On the other hand, Tony is shy and withdrawn and has few commitments. He enjoys reading, creating music, and drawing and prefers to study alone.

_____ **10.** Cassie suffered several long-term effects from the constant teasing she endured during her childhood. Because her peers ridiculed her for being too heavy, Cassie felt embarrassed about her body even as an adult and became unrealistic about what her ideal weight should be. In addition, the teasing caused Cassie to fear rejection; as a result, she often gave in to her children's demands in order to win their affection. Another impact of the teasing showed in Cassie's inability to trust people; she always had a vague feeling that others were judging her or saying negative things about her behind her back.

## REVIEW Test 3

### Transitions and Thought Patterns

Read each group of transition words and phrases, and identify the thought pattern they suggest.

_____ **1.** Consequently, because, if . . . then, accordingly
a. comparison and contrast
b. cause and effect
c. time

_____ **2.** On the one hand, on the other hand, likewise, in contrast, in comparison
a. comparison and contrast
b. definition
c. cause and effect

_____ **3.** Is, means, for example, such as, that is
a. comparison and contrast
b. definition
c. cause and effect

_____ **4.** Instead, differences, similarities, similarly
a. summary
b. comparison and contrast
c. cause and effect

_____ **5.** Results in, leads to, thus, therefore
a. time
b. cause and effect
c. generalization and example

## REVIEW Test 4

### Transitions and Thought Patterns

Before you read the following essay from the college textbook *Encyclopedia of Stress,* skim the passage and answer the **Before Reading** questions. Read the essay. Then answer the **After Reading** questions.

Textbook Skills

**Vocabulary Preview**

*provokes* (4): causes, stirs up
*phobia* (5): deep, irrational fear

*interacting with* (13): relating to, working with
*inflammation* (21): swelling

**Technostress**

[1]The computer revolution has created a new form of stress that is threatening the physical and mental health of many workers. [2]"Technostress" is a modern disorder caused by an inability to cope in a healthy manner with the new computer technology.

[3]Technostress reveals itself in several distinct ways. [4]It can surface as a person struggles to learn how to use computers in the workplace, which often **provokes** anxiety. [5]Some people develop a **phobia** about modern technology and need professional help to deal with their fears.

[6]Technostress can also surface as overidentification with computers. [7]Some people develop a machinelike **mind-set** that reflects the traits of the computer itself. [8]Some who were once warm and sensitive people become cold, lose their friends, and have no patience for the easy give-and-take of conversation. [9]In addition, they watch television as their major or only leisure activity.

[10]Further, *technostress* is the term used for such physical stress reactions as computer-related eyestrain, headaches, neck and shoulder tension, and backache. [11]Also, many people who use computer keyboards often develop carpal tunnel syndrome.

[12]These various reactions to technostress arise from long-term use of computers. [13]If someone spends most of their working hours **interacting with** only a computer screen and a keyboard, then that person may develop a number of the following symptoms.

[14]Eyestrain is caused by focusing continuously on a screen at close range. [15]The person who focuses for a long time on one specific colored screen may see the **complementary** color when looking up at a blank wall or ceiling. [16]This color reversal is normal and quickly lessens. [17]Headaches, though sometimes caused by eyestrain, are most often due to tension involving muscles of the brow, temples, jaw, upper neck, and base of the skull. [18]These headaches can be affected by improper height of the chair and screen. [19]Even the lack of an armrest can contribute. [20]Lack of an armrest causes the arms to pull down on the shoulders, creating, in turn, tension at the shoulder tip and base of the skull and spasms radiating up into the head. [21]Carpal tunnel syndrome, a numbness, tingling, or burning sensation in the fingers or wrists, may be induced by **inflammation** of the ligaments and tendons in fingers and wrists.

—Adapted from McGuigan, *Encyclopedia of Stress,* pp. 237–38.

VISUAL VOCABULARY

______ The best meaning of ergonomic is

a. poorly designed.
b. well designed.
c. cheaply produced.

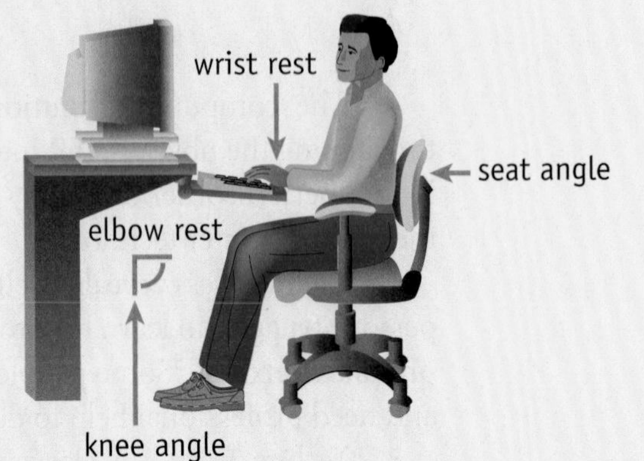


▲ An ergonomic chair will provide appropriate support to the back, legs, buttocks, and arms. This support can reduce contact stress, overexertion, and fatigue. It will also promote proper circulation to the extremities.

"Ergonomic Solutions: Workstation Chair." Occupational Safety and Health Administration U. S. Department of Labor. Online 16 June 2003. http://www.osha.gov/SLTC/computerworkstations_ecat/chair.html

## BEFORE READING

### Vocabulary in Context

______ **1.** The term **mind-set** in sentence 7 means

a. stubbornness.
b. decision.
c. attitude.
d. opinion.

______ **2.** The best synonym for **complementary** in sentence 15 is

a. beautiful.
b. opposite.
c. praise.
d. similar.

## AFTER READING

### Concept Map

**3–4.** Finish the concept map by filling in the missing idea with information from the passage.

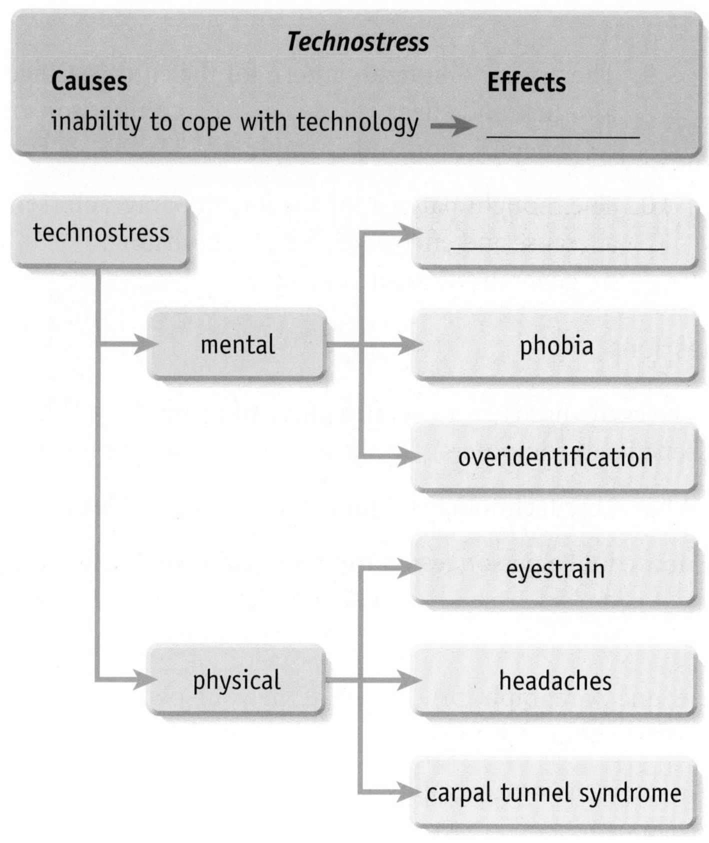


## Central Idea and Main Idea

______ **5.** Which sentence states the central idea of the passage?

a. sentence 1
b. sentence 2
c. sentence 12
d. sentence 13

## Supporting Details

______ **6.** Sentence 19 is a

a. major supporting detail.
b. minor supporting detail.

## Transitions

______ **7.** The word **further** in sentence 10 is a signal word that shows

a. comparison.
b. cause.
c. addition.

______ **8.** The word **though** in sentence 17 signals

a. cause and effect.
b. contrast.
c. addition.

## Thought Patterns

_____ **9.** The primary thought pattern for the entire passage is
a. cause and effect.
b. generalization and example.
c. comparison and contrast.

_____ **10.** The thought pattern for the fourth paragraph (sentences 10–11) is
a. cause and effect.
b. generalization and example.
c. listing.

## Discussion Questions

1. The essay discusses a negative effect of technology. What are some of the benefits of computers? Do the advantages balance the disadvantages?
2. What other technology besides computers could lead to "technostress"?
3. How could a person lessen the stress associated with technostress?

## Writing Topics

1. In one paragraph, briefly restate in your own words the author's main points about technostress.
2. In one or two paragraphs, give advice to someone who is suffering from technostress.

## EFFECTIVE READER Scorecard

### More Thought Patterns

| Test | Number Correct | | Points | | Score |
|---|---|---|---|---|---|
| Review Test 1 | _____ | × | 10 | = | _____ |
| Review Test 2 | _____ | × | 10 | = | _____ |
| Review Test 3 | _____ | × | 20 | = | _____ |
| Review Test 4 | _____ | × | 10 | = | _____ |
| Review Test 5 (website) | _____ | × | 10 | = | _____ |
| Review Test 6 (website) | _____ | × | 10 | = | _____ |

Enter your scores on the Effective Reader Scorecard: Chapter 7 Review Tests inside the back cover.

## After Reading About More Thought Patterns

Before you move on to the mastery tests on more thought patterns, take time to reflect on your learning and performance by answering the following questions. Write your answers in your notebook.

What did I learn about the following: transitions and thought patterns, compare and contrast pattern, the cause-and-effect pattern, the generalization-and-example pattern, the definition-and-example pattern?

What do I need to remember?

How has my knowledge base or prior knowledge about transitions and thought patterns changed?

## More Review and Mastery Tests

For more practice, go to the book's website at **http://ablongman.com/henry/** and click on *The Effective Reader.* Then select "More Review and Mastery Tests." The tests are organized by chapter.

# MASTERY Test 1

Name ______________________ Section ______________

Date ____________ **Score** (number correct) ______ × 10 = ______%

**A.** Fill in the blanks with the correct transition word or phrase from the box. Use each transition once.

| for example | in contrast | leads to | result in | subsequently |
|---|---|---|---|---|

**Rest Well**

Adequate rest (**1**) ______________________ improved performance. (**2**) ______________, sleep deprivation causes a host of problems. (**3**) ______________, lack of rest may (**4**) ______________________ loss of concentration and loss of energy. (**5**) ______________, poor concentration and lack of energy could lead to slow and flawed work.

**B.** Write the letter of the appropriate thought pattern before each item, as follows:

a. generalization and example
b. comparison and contrast
c. cause and effect

______ **6.** Marcel began to practice yoga because of a shoulder injury.

______ **7.** Marcel compared several types of yoga to determine which method was best for him.

______ **8.** For example, he considered Iyengar yoga, a style of yoga emphasizing body placement and alignment.

______ **9.** In addition, he thought about Ashtanga yoga, also known as power yoga, which focuses on high-energy, free-flowing movement.

______ **10.** Marcel chose Ashtanga because he enjoys an intense workout.

MASTERY **Test 2**

Name ______________________ Section ____________

Date ____________ **Score** (number correct) ______ × 10 = ______%

Read the paragraph. Fill in each blank with a suitable transition word from the box. Use each transition once. Then answer the questions that follow the paragraph.

| cause | caused | led | reasons | similar | therefore |
|---|---|---|---|---|---|

### Mindbender

[1]An expression from the past recently drifted into my mind as I thought about how to get along with my difficult, unrealistic, and controlling boss. [2]Among my crowd, during the early 1970s, the term *mindbender* usually referred to an intense drug trip that (**1**) ______________ one to see the world differently. [3]At least, that's what I heard. [4]I stayed clean of drugs for two main (**2**) ______________. [5]A strong desire to be in control of my own senses was the first (**3**) ______________ of my abstinence. [6]Second, a strong sense of rebellion (**4**) ______________ me to resist peer pressure. (**5**) [7]______________, a "mindbending" experience seemed to me a hassle much better avoided. [8]I wondered what made that term pop into my head. [9]Suddenly, it occurred to me that my boss's desire to force his distorted views upon others was (**6**) ______________ to a mindbender. That's why I felt so uncomfortable. [10]The rebel in me still wants control.

______ **7.** The phrase "the term *mindbender* usually referred to" in sentence 2 signals

a. definition.

b. comparison and contrast.

c. cause and effect.

______ **8.** The transition used to fill blank 1 in sentence 2 signals
a. definition.
b. comparison and contrast.
c. cause and effect.

______ **9.** The transition used to fill blank 5 in sentence 7 signals
a. generalization and example.
b. comparison and contrast.
c. cause and effect.

______ **10.** The transition used to fill blank 6 in sentence 9 signals
a. generalization and example.
b. comparison and contrast.
c. cause and effect.

MASTERY **Test 3**

Name ______________ Section ______________

Date ______________ **Score** (number correct) ______ × 10 = ______%

Write the numbers **1** to **9** in the spaces provided to show the correct order of the ideas. Then answer the question that follows the list.

Textbook Skills

**Expected Effects of Cocaine**

_____ The first effect the user can expect is a powerful burst of energy.

_____ However, if snorted through the nose, the effect begins in about three to five minutes; it peaks after fifteen to twenty minutes and wears off in sixty to ninety minutes.

_____ If the cocaine is injected through the veins, the effect is immediate and intense; it peaks in three to five minutes and wears off in thirty to forty minutes.

_____ Cocaine users can expect certain effects.

_____ The time it takes to feel the effects vary, based on whether the cocaine is injected or snorted.

_____ Users can also expect to experience a general sense of well-being.

_____ However, in some instances, cocaine may cause a panic attack.

_____ Finally, these uncomfortable aftereffects create a powerful craving for another dose.

_____ Once the cocaine wears off, the user becomes irritable and depressed.

—Adapted from Levinthal, *Drugs, Behavior, and Modern Society*, 3rd ed., p. 81.

_____ **10.** The primary thought pattern is

a. generalization and example.

b. comparison and contrast.

c. cause and effect.

MASTERY **Test 4**

Name ______________________ Section __________

Date __________ **Score** (number correct) ______ × 10 = ______%

Read the following paragraphs from college textbooks. Then answer the questions and complete the outlines.

### Systemic Violence

[1]A key source of social violence and criminal behavior comes from within the drug world. [2]Researchers use the term *systemic violence* to refer to the violence that is linked to drug dealing. [3]For example, this kind of violence can result from fights about boundaries and territory. [4]In addition, selling poor-quality drugs leads to unhappy and even violent customers. [5]Systemic violence can also erupt because of "messing up the money," that is, misusing the funds. [6]Research shows that youth who are involved in selling and buying cocaine are also more likely than their peers to be involved in other criminal acts, including felonies.

—Adapted from Levinthal, *Drugs, Behavior, and Modern Society,* 3rd ed., p. 43.

______ **1.** The primary thought pattern suggested by sentence 2 is
- a. definition.
- b. comparison and contrast.
- c. cause and effect.

______ **2.** The paragraph
- a. discusses the similarities between social violence and criminal behavior.
- b. lists some of the causes of violence in general.
- c. defines systemic violence.

### Systemic Violence

Main idea: A key source of social violence and criminal behavior comes from within the drug world.

I. Systemic violence

(**3**) A. ______________________________________

(**4**) B. ______________________________________

______________________________________

(5) C. ______________________________

II. Criminal behavior

A. Youth who sell and buy cocaine involved in criminal acts

B. Youth who sell and buy cocaine involved in felonies

Textbook Skills

### Creative and Logical Thought

[1]Creative thinking is an alternative to logical thinking. [2]Since the two kinds of thinking differ in important ways, you should know the special qualities of each. [3]For example, creative thinking puts things together; it synthesizes. [4]On the other hand, logical thinking analyzes things; it takes them apart. [5]A second difference is that creative thinking generates new ideas while logical thinking builds on and assesses existing ideas. [6]Creative thinking is inclusive, yet logical thinking is selective, screening out doubtful ideas. [7]The difference between creative and logical thinking makes them equally important. [8]We need to use both to effectively read, write, and think.

—Adapted from DiYanni & Hoy, *The Scribner Handbook for Writers,* 3rd ed., pp. 54–55.

_____ **6.** The primary thought pattern is
a. definition.
b. cause and effect.
c. comparison and contrast.

### Creative and Logical Thought

Main idea: Creative thinking is an alternative to logical thinking.

| | **Creative Thinking** | **Logical Thinking** |
|---|---|---|
| **First difference** | (7) ______________________ | analyzes things, takes them apart |
| **Second difference** | generates new ideas | (8) ______________________ |
| **Third difference** | (9) ______________________ | (10) ______________________ |

MASTERY **Test 5**

Name _______________ Section _______________

Date _______________ **Score** (number correct) _____ × 10 = _____%

Read the paragraphs from college textbooks. Then answer the questions and complete the concept maps.

## Public Speaking Anxiety

[1]Fear of public speaking causes major anxiety for a number of Americans. [2]Understanding some of its causes and effects often helps relieve public speaking anxiety. [3]This anxiety is triggered by the anticipation of performing in front of an audience. [4]Many fear public speaking because they fear they will make a mistake and look foolish. [5]In some instances, lack of preparation contributes to the problem. [6]A few obvious physical effects are a quavering voice, stuttering, vomiting, cold and sweaty hands, dry mouth, and even fainting. [7]This fear can also have mental effects, such as blocked ideas or short-term memory loss.

—Adapted from McGuigan, *Encyclopedia of Stress*, p. 210.

_____ **1.** The relationship between sentence 4 and sentence 5 is
a. cause and effect.
b. addition.
c. comparison.

### Causes and Effects of Public Speaking Anxiety

Main idea: Understanding some of its causes and effects often helps lessen the fear of speaking in public.

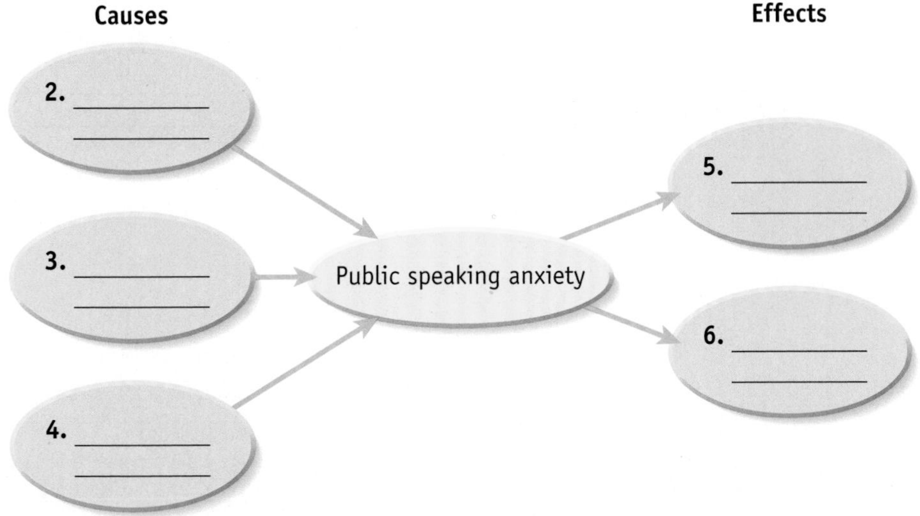

Textbook Skills

### Different Perspectives

[1]The same event in a family has a different meaning for each of its family members, based on age and cognitive ability. [2]This difference in perspectives can be clearly seen in studies on the effects of parents' divorce on their children. [3]Children who are 5 years old when parents divorce respond in predictable ways that are different from the predictable ways that 11-year-olds respond. [4]Five-year-olds assume the divorce is a result of something they did, whereas 11-year-olds can reason and understand that the divorce may be caused by other factors.

—Adapted from Kosslyn & Rosenberg, *Psychology: The Brain, The Person, and The World,* p. 378.

_____ **7.** The relationship between sentence 1 and sentence 2 is
- a. definition.
- b. comparison and contrast.
- c. cause and effect.

_____ **8.** The thought patterns used in the paragraph are comparison and contrast and
- a. generalization and example.
- b. time order.
- c. cause and effect.

The same event in a family has a different meaning for each of its family members, based on age and cognitive ability.

**9.** 5-year-olds ______________________
______________________
______________________

**10.** 11-year-olds ______________________
______________________
______________________

MASTERY **Test 6**

Name ______________________ Section ____________

Date ____________ **Score** (number correct) ______ × 10 = ______%

**A.** Read the following paragraph from a college finance textbook. Then answer the question and complete the concept map.

Textbook Skills

### Buying a Car Online Versus Buying a Car on a Lot

[1]Buying a new car online is still not as efficient as buying a car off a dealer's lot. [2]The personal options of a car make online buying difficult. [3]First, at a dealership, a customer can actually see the difference in the design of the two models of a particular car. [4]It is not as easy to detect the differences on a Web site. [5]Second, unlike a Web site, a dealer can also anticipate your questions and arrange for a test drive. [6]It is also more difficult to communicate with an online service. [7]For example, it is difficult to force an online service to meet its delivery promise to you because you have limited access to them through email and phone messages. [8]However, you can place pressure on a local dealership to meet its promise by showing up at the dealership to express your concerns in person.

—Adapted from Madura, *Personal Finance*, 2nd ed., p. 235.

______ **1.** The thought patterns used in the paragraph are listing and
a. definition.
b. comparison and contrast.
c. cause and effect.

### Buying a Car Online Versus Buying a Car on a Lot

Main idea: Buying a new car online is still not as efficient as buying a car off a dealer's lot.

| | **Online** | **Dealership** |
|---|---|---|
| **First difference** | Customer can't see differences in cars. | Customer can see differences in cars. |
| **Second difference** | (2) ______________________ | (3) ______________________ |
| **Third difference** | (4) ______________________ | (5) ______________________ |

**B.** Read the following paragraph from a college psychology textbook. Then answer the question and complete the outline with the major supporting details.

### Effects of Sleep Deprivation

[1]If you have ever stayed up late, say, studying or partying, and then awakened early the next morning, you have probably experienced sleep deprivation. [2]In fact, you may be sleep-deprived right now. [3]What happens as a result of sleep deprivation? [4]Young adults who volunteered for a sleep deprivation study were allowed to sleep for only five hours each night, for a total of seven nights. [5]After three nights of restricted sleep, volunteers complained of mental, emotional, and physical difficulties. [6]Moreover, their abilities to perform visual motor tasks declined after only two nights. [7]Hormones are also affected by sleep deprivation. [8]For example, the loss of even one night's sleep can lead to increases in the next day's level of cortisol. [9]Cortisol helps the body meet the demands imposed by stress. [10]Finally, going without sleep for long stretches of time, such as 4 to 11 days, causes profound psychological effects. [11]Long-term sleep deprivation can lead to feelings of losing control and anxiety.

—Adapted from Kosslyn & Rosenberg, *Psychology: The Brain, The Person, and The World*, p. 138.

______ **6.** The thought patterns used in the paragraph are listing and
a. generalization and example.
b. comparison and contrast.
c. cause and effect.

### Effects of Sleep Deprivation

(**7**) ______________________________

(**8**) ______________________________

(**9**) ______________________________

(**10**) ______________________________

CHAPTER

8

# Implied Main Ideas and Implied Central Ideas

## CHAPTER PREVIEW

## Before Reading About Implied Main Ideas and Implied Central Ideas

Take a moment to study the chapter preview. Underline key words that refer to ideas you have already studied in previous chapters. Each of these key words represents a great deal of knowledge upon which you will build as you learn about implied main ideas and implied central ideas. These key terms have been listed below. In the given spaces, write what you already know about each one.

- Main ideas: ______________________________

______________________________

- Supporting details: ______________________________________________

______________________________________________

______________________________________________

______________________________________________

- Thought patterns: ______________________________________________

______________________________________________

______________________________________________

- A summary: ______________________________________________
- Central ideas: ______________________________________________

______________________________________________

Compare what you wrote to the following paragraph, which summarizes this vital prior knowledge:

> Main ideas are stated in a topic sentence. A topic sentence includes a topic and the author's controlling point. Supporting details explain the main idea. There are two types of supporting details. Major supporting details directly explain the topic sentence (or thesis statement), and minor supporting details explain the major supporting details. Authors use transition words to create thought patterns. Thought patterns organize details. Some examples are time order, cause and effect, and comparison and contrast. A summary condenses a paragraph or passage to its main idea. Central ideas are the main ideas of longer passages. Stated central ideas are called thesis statements.

Recopy the list of key words in your notebook; leave several blank lines between each idea. As you work through this chapter, record how you apply each idea in the list to the new information you learn about implied main ideas and implied central ideas.

## What Is an Implied Main Idea?

As you learned in Chapter 3, sometimes authors state the main idea of a paragraph in a topic sentence. However, other paragraphs do not include a stated main idea. Even though the main idea is not stated in a single sentence, the paragraph still has a main idea. In these cases, the details clearly suggest or imply the author's main idea.

An **implied main idea** is a main idea that is not stated directly but is strongly suggested by the supporting details in the passage.

When the main idea is not stated, you must figure out the author's controlling point about a topic. One approach is to study the facts, examples, descriptions, and explanations given—the supporting details. Another approach is to identify the author's thought pattern. An effective reader often uses both approaches. Learning how to develop a main idea based on the supporting details and thought patterns will help you develop several skills. You will learn how to study information, value the meaning of supporting details, value the relationship between ideas, and use your own words to express an implied main idea.

Many different types of reading material use implied main ideas. For example, many paragraphs in college textbooks do not provide a topic sentence. In these passages, the author uses supporting details to imply the main idea. In addition, you will often need to formulate the implied main idea when you read literature. Short stories, novels, poems, and plays rely heavily on vivid details to suggest the author's point. The following short story is taken from a college literature textbook. Read the story, asking yourself, "What is the main idea?"

**Independence**

*Written by Chuang Tzu and Translated by Herbert Giles*

[1]Chuang Tzu was one day fishing, when the Prince of Ch'u sent two high officials to interview him, saying that his highness would be glad of Chuang Tzu's assistance in the administration of his government. [2]The latter quietly fished on, and without looking round, replied, "I have heard that in the State of Ch'u there is a sacred tortoise, which has been dead for three thousand years, and which the prince keeps packed up in a box on the altar in his ancestral shrine. [3]Now do you think that tortoise would rather be dead and have its remains thus honored, or be alive and wagging its tail in the mud?" [4]The two officials answered that no doubt it would rather be alive and wagging its tail in the mud; whereupon Chuang Tzu cried out, "Begone! I too elect to remain wagging my tail in the mud."

—Tzu, Chuang. "Independence." Translated by Herbert Giles. Reprinted in Kennedy, X. J. & Dana Gioia. *Literature: An Introduction to Fiction, Poetry, and Drama,* 8th ed., pp. 6–7.

Did you notice that every sentence in this paragraph is a supporting detail? No single sentence covers all the other ideas. To figure out the implied main idea, ask the following questions.

**Questions for finding the implied main idea:**

1. What is the topic, or subject, of the paragraph?
2. What are the major supporting details?
3. Based on the details about the topic, what point or main idea is the author trying to get across?

Apply these three questions to the passage above by writing your responses to each question in the following blanks.

**1.** What is the topic of the story? ______________________________

The title of the story gives us a strong clue that the topic is about independence. But each detail in the story also supports this topic.

**2.** What are the major supporting details?

a. ______________________________

b. ______________________________

c ______________________________

d. ______________________________

**3.** What is the main idea the author is trying to get across? ______________

______________________________

In order to formulate this main idea statement, you had to consider each of the details. For example, the author uses a vivid contrast between a dead tortoise which has an "honored" place on the Prince's "ancestral shrine" and a live tortoise "wagging its tail." In addition, the author has the two officials agree that the tortoise would have been better off alive and living freely. The tortoise serves as an example of independence, and helps the reader understand the significance of Chuang Tzu's choice. Tzu did not value power or public honor as much as he valued his own freedom to live simply.

Asking and answering these questions allows you to think about the impact of each detail and how the details fit together to support the author's controlling point. Searching for an implied main idea is like a treasure hunt. You must carefully read the clues provided by the author. This kind of careful reading is a skill that improves dramatically with practice. The following examples and practices are designed to strengthen this important skill.

## Using Supporting Details and Thought Patterns to Find Implied Main Ideas

Remember that the main idea of a paragraph is like a frame of a house. Just as a frame includes all the rooms, a main idea must cover all the details in a paragraph. Therefore, the implied main idea will be general enough to cover all the details, but it will not be so broad that it becomes an overgeneralization or a sweeping statement that suggests details not given; nor can it be so narrow that some of the given details are not covered. Instead, the implied main idea must cover *all* the details given.

The skill of identifying a stated main idea will also help you grasp the implied main idea. You learned in Chapter 3 that the stated main idea (the topic sentence) has two parts. A main idea is made up of the topic and the author's controlling point about the topic. One trait of the controlling point is the author's opinion or bias. A second trait is the author's thought pattern. Consider, for example, the topic sentence "Older people benefit from volunteer work for several reasons." "Older people" and "volunteer work" make up the topic. "Benefit" states the opinion, and "several reasons" states the thought pattern. When you read material that implies the main idea, you should mentally create a topic sentence based on the details in the material.

**EXAMPLE** Read the following list of supporting details. Circle the topic as it recurs throughout the list of details. Underline transition words and biased (opinion) words. Then choose the statement that best expresses the author's controlling point about the topic.

- Fear drains color from our faces; it makes our teeth chatter, our hearts pound, our breath quicken, and our knees knock.
- Fear churns our stomachs, raises goose bumps, and causes the jitters.
- Fear also raises feelings of anxiety and distrust and may even cause us to change our behaviors.
- Finally, fear can become a phobia that keeps us from enjoying life.

______ Which statement best expresses the implied main idea?

a. Phobias keep us from enjoying life.
b. Fear affects us in several ways.
c. Fear is the result of distrust and anxiety.
d. Fear affects many people.

**EXPLANATION** The topic that recurs throughout the list is *fear.* The transition words include *and*, *also*, and *finally*. These transitions of addition suggest the listing thought pattern. A study of the listed details reveals the effects of fear. The sentence that best combines the topic, thought pattern, and details is (b) "Fear affects us in several ways." The word *affects* signals cause and effect. The phrase *several ways* suggests listing, and the details are a list of the effects of fear. Options (a) and (c) are both too narrow to cover all the supporting details mentioned in the paragraph, and option (d) is too broad to be the main idea. Remember, the main idea must be neither too broad nor too narrow.

## PRACTICE 1

Read the following groups of supporting details. Circle the topic as it recurs throughout the list of details. Underline transition words to help you locate the major details. Also underline biased words to determine the author's opinion. Then select the sentence that best expresses the implied main idea.

### Group 1

- Liposuction is the surgical removal of fat deposits between the skin and muscle.
- Liposuction does not help people who are unable to lose weight by dieting and exercise.
- Without making healthy lifestyle choices, obese patients usually regain weight after liposuction.
- Serious health problems are more likely to occur when large amounts of fat are removed by liposuction.
- Removing more than 8 to 10 pounds of fat by liposuction in a single day is dangerous.

_____ **1.** Which statement best expresses the implied main idea?
a. Liposuction is not a good treatment for obesity.
b. Liposuction is the removal of fat deposits.
c. Liposuction is risky for some people.
d. Removing too much fat in one day is dangerous.

Textbook Skills

### Group 2

- Egypt's pyramids are the oldest existing buildings in the world.
- These ancient tombs are also among the world's largest structures.
- The largest pyramid stands taller than a 40-story building and covers an area greater than that of ten football fields.
- More than 80 pyramids still exist, and their once-smooth limestone surfaces hide secret passageways and rooms.

- The pyramids of ancient Egypt served a vital purpose: to protect the pharaohs' bodies after death.
- Each pyramid held not only the pharaoh's preserved body but also all the goods he would need in his life after death.

—Adapted from Sporre, *The Creative Impulse,* 6th ed., p. 45.

_____ **2.** Which sentence best states the implied main idea?

a. Pyramids are large, ancient buildings.
b. Pyramids are massive structures with several distinctive traits.
c. Pyramids are tombs that were built for the pharaohs.
d. Pyramids are remarkable.

## Group 3

- In 1986, a small number of British cattle came down with a new illness called mad cow disease.
- Within a few years, the disease had become an epidemic among British herds.
- Over 3 million cattle in Great Britain were destroyed, crippling the country's cattle industry.
- This fatal brain disease probably infected cows when they ate a food supplement made with the remains of sheep infected with a similar form of the illness.
- People who have eaten infected beef have come down with a new form of the disease.

_____ **3.** Which sentence best states the implied main idea?

a. Mad cow disease probably began when cows were fed tainted food.
b. Mad cow disease poses a health hazard for people.
c. Mad cow disease has crippled Great Britain's cattle industry and threatens the health of people who eat infected beef.
d. Mad cow disease is a horrible illness.

## Group 4

- Cognitive therapy helps a person deal with negative or painful thoughts and behaviors.
- This therapy, a psychological treatment, was developed by a medical doctor, Aaron T. Beck, in the 1970s.
- First, a person seeks to change thinking patterns such as assumptions and core beliefs.
- Changes in feelings and actions will follow.

- To aid change, a person learns how to replace harmful thoughts and behaviors with positive coping tactics.
- Some of these tactics may include anger management and relaxation training.

______ **4.** Which sentence best states the implied main idea?

a. Cognitive therapy is a psychological treatment.

b. Cognitive therapy is a psychological treatment that helps a person replace negative or painful thoughts and behaviors with positive coping skills.

c. Cognitive therapy was developed by Aaron T. Beck, M.D., in the 1970s.

d. Cognitive therapy focuses on negative or painful thoughts and behaviors.

## Finding the Implied Main Ideas of Paragraphs

So far, you have learned to recognize the implied main idea by studying the specific details in a group of sentences. In this next step, the sentences will form a paragraph, but the skill of recognizing the implied main idea is exactly the same. The implied main idea of paragraphs must not be too broad or too narrow, so study the supporting details and look for thought patterns that suggest the main idea.

**EXAMPLE** Read the following paragraph. Circle the topic as it recurs throughout the paragraph. Underline transition words to help you locate the major details. Also underline biased words to determine the author's opinion. Then select the sentence that best expresses the implied main idea.

**The Effects of Piracy**

[1]The Motion Picture Association of America estimates that as many as one million movies are pirated or downloaded illegally from the Internet each day. [2]Pirated DVD copies of *Harry Potter and the Sorcerer's Stone* were available in parts of China even before the film had hit theaters anywhere in the world, let alone been released for home viewing. [3]Imagine the number of people who choose not to go to the movie theater or rent a film because they are able to retain a pirated copy. [4]And imagine the amount of money sapped from our economy. [5]Finally, imagine the number of jobs lost as a result.

—Adapted from Biden, "Theft of American Intellectual Property."

_____ The best statement of the implied main idea is

a. Piracy robs the movie industry of profits and workers of jobs, and it hurts the nation's economy.
b. Illegally downloading movies is a serious problem.
c. Copies of *Harry Potter and the Sorcerer's Stone* were available worldwide before the film was shown in theaters.

**EXPLANATION** This paragraph requires the reader to interact with the information to fully understand the author's point. The title provides part of the topic "the effects of piracy," but you had to skim every sentence to see that all the details relate piracy to the movie industry. Thus the topic is "piracy in the movie industry." In sentence 2, details, biased words, and transition words work together (*even before*, *anywhere*, and *let alone*) to reveal the scope of the problem; it is worldwide. In sentences 3 to 5, transition words of addition and cause and effect (*and*, *finally*, *or*, *because*, and *result*) create a list of three ideas about which you are to think or "imagine." You are to imagine the amount of money lost to the movie industry *because* of piracy.

The author implies facts about lost jobs; for example, without the profits made from selling tickets or renting movies, fewer dollars are available for jobs such as staffing a video store or the ticket counter at the theater complex or operating a camera during the shooting of a film. The author is relying on you to think about the wide range of jobs and large amounts of money that are lost because of the volume of illegally downloaded movies.

Implied main ideas require that the reader be actively involved in the meaning-making process. You must use information you already have to make the connections between ideas that the author is suggesting. Item (a) is the best statement of the implied main idea of this paragraph. Note that this sentence uses the title and words from several sentences in the paragraph. Item (b) is too broad, and item (c) is too narrow.

## PRACTICE 2

Read the following paragraphs. In each paragraph, circle the topic as it recurs throughout the paragraph. Underline transition words to help you locate the major details. Also underline the biased words to determine the author's opinion. Then select the sentence that best expresses the implied main idea for each.

### Overcoming Writer's Block

[1]Countless numbers of college students in first-year composition classes face writer's block. [2]One way to overcome writer's block is to read. [3]Beginning writers may not have enough information or prior knowledge

about a topic to generate a paper. [4]Therefore, reading about a topic gives the writer information and ideas on which to draw. [5]Another way to overcome this problem is through discussion. [6]Talking to peers, teachers, and others about ideas and beliefs helps novice writers clarify their own understandings so that they can more easily share them on paper. [7]A third way to overcome writer's block is to brainstorm. [8]Brainstorming is just a way to focus thoughts through listing, freewriting, or making concept maps. [9]Brainstorming also allows a writer to discover what to say without worrying about how to say it. [10]Finally, writer's block can be reduced by the wise use of time management skills. [11]Beginning writers need to understand that writing is an outgrowth of thinking, and thinking takes time. [12]Often writer's block is the result of too much stress and too little time; therefore, to avoid this problem, writers should begin the assignment days before it is due.

_____ **1.** Which sentence best states the implied main idea?

a. Writer's block is a problem for many first-year college students.
b. Reading is an excellent way to overcome writer's block.
c. Beginning writers can overcome writer's block in several ways.
d. The writing process should be broken into three phases: prewriting, writing, and revising.

### Green Tea: The Miracle Drink

[1]Green tea has been used for thousands of years in Asia as both a beverage and an herbal medicine. [2]This herbal tea contains catechin, which is a type of tannin that acts as an astringent. [3]Research suggests that men and women in Japan who drink five to six cups of green tea each day have much lower rates of cancer than people who do not. [4]Green tea is also thought to lower cholesterol and blood sugar, control high blood pressure, stop tooth decay, and fight viruses. [5]Green tea has even been credited with the power to slow down the aging process.

_____ **2.** Which sentence best states the implied main idea?

a. Green tea is an ancient herbal drink.
b. Green tea has caught the attention of medical researchers.
c. Green tea lowers cholesterol and blood sugar and controls high blood pressure.
d. Green tea, an ancient Asian herbal drink, is thought to have many health benefits.

**One Handsome Young Man**

[1]At 6-foot-4, Van stood taller than most young men. [2]The Florida sun tanned his skin to a deep bronze and bleached his dark brown hair to varying shades of sandy blond. [3]Endowed with the high cheekbones of his Indian ancestors, sapphire eyes, and a luminous smile, he drew attention. [4]He moved like an athlete at ease in his own skin. [5]In neighborhood orange wars, Van could throw an orange farther and more accurately than any of us. [6]In fact, he could outrun, outswim, outhunt, outfish, outdo all of us, and still we loved him. [7]Guys felt proud to be his friend; girls clamored to be his sweetheart. [8]Even now, 30 years later, at our high school reunion, Van looms larger than life to those of us he left behind: an unaging memory, a tragic loss.

_____ **3.** Which sentence best states the implied main idea?

a. Van was a handsome, talented, well-liked young man who died young and is still missed.
b. Van was a tall, good-looking young man.
c. Van is a tragic figure.
d. Van is still missed by his high school friends.

## Creating a Summary from the Supporting Details

You have developed the skill of figuring out main ideas that are not directly stated. This ability to reason from specific details to main ideas will serve you well throughout college. One further step will also prove helpful in your reading and studying: the ability to state the implied main idea in your own words. You must learn to summarize the most important details in a one-sentence statement; in other words, you must create a topic sentence. To formulate this one-sentence summary, find the topic, determine the author's opinion by examining the biased words, and use the thought pattern to locate the major details. Then combine these ideas in a single sentence. The summary sentence includes the topic and the author's controlling point, just like a topic sentence. The statement you come up with must not be too narrow, for it must cover all the details given. On the other hand, it must not be too broad or go beyond the supporting details.

Remember that a main idea is always written as a complete sentence.

**EXAMPLE** Read the list of specific ideas that follows. Circle the topic as it recurs throughout each group of details. Underline words that reveal thought patterns and bias to discover the controlling point. Then write a sentence that best states the implied main idea.

- Ranked number one on the Forbes list for most powerful and best paid celebrities, Oprah Winfrey earns around $1.5 billion a year.
- At number two, Tiger Woods is the first athlete in history to bank $100 million.
- Number three on the list, Madonna traveled the globe for her tour, "Confessions," which drew over 1 million fans and grossed $194 million.
- By 2007, the Rolling Stones ranked fourth on the list by earning $437 million with their "Bigger Bang Tour."
- Rounding out the top five on the Forbes list is Brad Pitt with $35 million in annual earnings.

**1.** Implied main idea: ______________________________________________

______________________________________________________________

**EXPLANATION** To formulate an implied main idea statement, you must learn to summarize the important details into a one-sentence summary. The topic is the "Forbes list of most influential celebrities." The transition phrases include *ranked number one, at number two, number three, by 2007… ranked fourth, rounding out the top five.* To properly formulate a one-sentence summary, you should have noted that the details were organized as a list of celebrities from all walks of life. The details of their earnings provided the basis of their ranking on the list. The implied main idea could be expressed as follows: "The 2007 Forbes list of most influential celebrities is a diverse group ranked by their earnings."

**EXAMPLE** Read the following paragraph. Circle the topic as it recurs throughout the paragraph. Underline words that reveal thought patterns and bias to discover the controlling point. Then write a sentence that best states the implied main idea. Remember: not too narrow, not too broad—find that perfect fit!

**Beep Baseball**

[1]Each year as the baseball season gears up, "beep baseball" players take to diamonds across the country. [2]A beep baseball team is made up of six blind or visually impaired defensive players. [3]Sighted players include a pitcher and a catcher, neither of whom bats. [4]Each game has one sighted umpire and two sighted spotters on the field. [5]When a batter hits a ball, a spotter calls out to alert the player in the field nearest the ball. [6]The pitcher throws a 16-inch baseball that is equipped with a beeping device. [7]This specially designed baseball is activated by the pitcher, who pulls a pin in the ball; the pitcher says "ready" before the ball is thrown and "pitch" or "ball" as the ball is thrown. [8]The pitcher tries to

put the ball on the batter's bat, rather than strike the batter out. [9]A batter gets four swings before a strikeout. [10]Beep baseball has just two bases, which are 4 feet tall, are padded, and emit a buzzing sound. [11]If the ball is hit at least 40 feet, one of the two bases is activated. [12]A run is scored when the batter reaches a base before a fielder has full control of the ball. [13]An out occurs when the fielder has full control of the ball before the batter reaches a base. [14]Full control means that the ball is off the ground and held away from the fielder's body.

**2.** Implied main idea: ______________________________________________

______________________________________________________________

**VISUAL VOCABULARY**

_____ The best meaning of the word **audible** is

a. able to be seen.
b. able to be touched.
c. able to be heard.

▸ This beep baseball player relies on audible cues to make the play.

**EXPLANATION** To formulate an implied main idea statement, you must learn to summarize the most important details of the paragraph into a one-sentence summary. Keep in mind that using your own words to formulate an implied main idea means that everyone's answer will be slightly different. The following sentence is one way to state the main idea of the paragraph: "Beep baseball is a competitive baseball game adapted for blind and visually impaired players." The word *competitive* is a good summary word for all the rules that are discussed in the paragraph. Note that the transition words signaled time and space to describe the rules. The biased word *specially* in sentence 7 clearly suggests that the game had to be adapted.

## PRACTICE 3

**A.** Read each group of supporting details. Circle the topic as it recurs throughout each group of details. Underline words that reveal thought patterns and bias to discover the controlling point. Then write a sentence that best states the implied main idea. After writing, check the sentence by asking if all the major details support it.

### Group 1

- Recent DNA testing has proved several people on death row innocent of the crimes for which they were sentenced to death.
- The cost to taxpayers for death penalty appeals is staggeringly high.
- Many people believe that the death penalty is morally wrong and a form of legalized homicide.
- Many also believe that the death penalty does not deter crime.
- Finally, many believe that the death penalty unfairly targets the poor and the African American population.

**1.** Implied main idea: ____________________________________________

______________________________________________________________

### Group 2

- Narcotics used to control postsurgery pain cause side effects and don't always provide relief.
- A new technique is to drip a local anesthetic directly into the wound for two to five days while healing begins.
- One version, the ON-Q system, slowly drips the drug from a balloonlike ball into a tiny catheter inserted near the stitches, where it oozes out.
- The direct dose of pain medicine avoids the grogginess and other body-wide effects of narcotics.

—Neergaard, "Doctors Go to Source to Treat Pain from Surgery." 27 May 2003. *The Daytona Beach News-Journal.* 2A.

**2.** Implied main idea: ____________________________________________

______________________________________________________________

______________________________________________________________

**VISUAL VOCABULARY**

______ The best meaning of the word **catheter** is

a. the top layer of skin.
b. an incision.
c. pain medicine.
d. a medical tube.

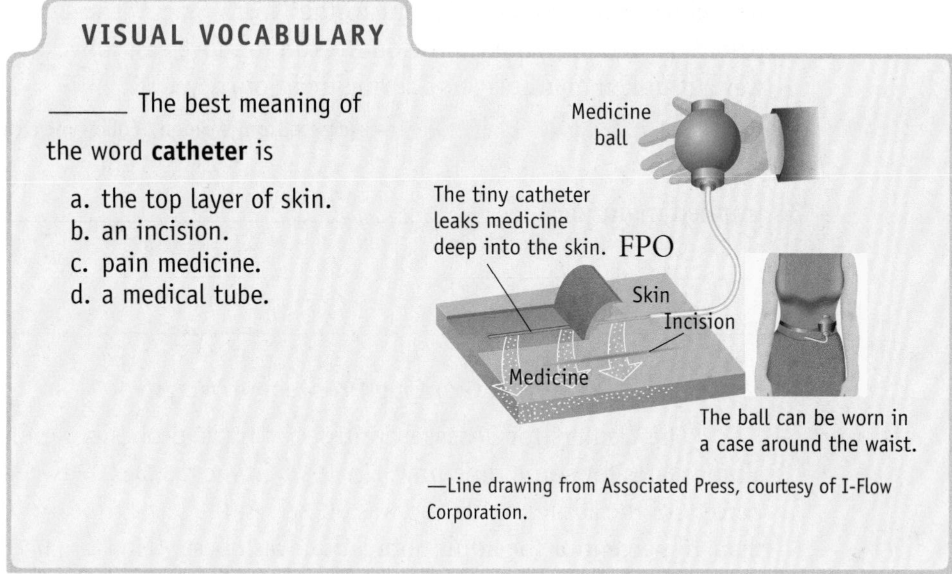


—Line drawing from Associated Press, courtesy of I-Flow Corporation.

**B.** Read the following paragraphs. Circle the topic as it recurs throughout each paragraph. Underline words that reveal thought patterns and bias to discover the controlling point. Then write a sentence that states the implied main idea.

### Slave Quilts: The Maps to Freedom

[1]Some historians believe that a number of African Americans escaped slavery through a network of supporters called the Underground Railroad. [2]In order for the Underground Railroad to work effectively, it was necessary to relay information to those attempting to make the trip to freedom. [3]Direct communication, however, was not an option. [4]Any overt signal would be quickly discovered. [5]In order to overcome this problem, the principals involved created a system based on designs sewn into quilts that could be conspicuously displayed in appropriate places. [6]Like any good system of subterfuge, the quilts appeared as commonplace items to the adversaries of fugitive slaves. [7]However, to those in flight, the quilts were an encouraging symbol that advised them of the who, what, when, and how of their journey to freedom. [8]Many of the symbols sewn into the patterns are obvious in their meanings, such as the monkey wrench, which denoted that it was time to gather the tools required to make the journey, or sailboats, which indicated the availability of boats for the crossing of crucial bodies of water. [9]Other symbols were more cryptic, such as the star pattern, which had several variations

but whose purpose was to point to the North Star. [10]The Drunkard's Path pattern served to remind those on the run to move east to west (in much the way a drunken man staggers) during their journey.

—Adapted from Weadon, "Follow the Drinking Gourd."

**3.** Implied main idea: ________________________________________

__________________________________________________________

__________________________________________________________

**A Growing Problem of Weight**

[1]The Centers for Disease Control has tracked obesity among adults in all the states for some time now. [2]In 1990, in most states, between 10 and 15 percent of the adult population was obese. [3]At the same time, in 10 states, less than 10 percent of the adult population was obese. [4]No state had more than 15 percent of its population obese. [5]By 1995, the situation had changed dramatically: more than half of the states had more than 15 percent of their populations obese, and none had less than 10 percent obese any longer. [6]In 2000, all the states except Colorado were over 15 percent, and almost half of the states were over 20 percent. [7]The prevalence of obesity among Maryland adults went from 11.2 percent in 1991 to 19.5 percent in 2000. [8]Across the nation, 61 percent of adults are either obese or overweight.

—Wechsler, "Trends in Dietary Behaviors and Overweight Among Young People."

**4.** Implied main idea: ________________________________________

__________________________________________________________

## The Implied Central Idea

Just as a single paragraph can have an implied main idea, longer passages made up of two or more paragraphs can also have an implied main idea. You encounter these longer passages in articles, essays, and textbooks. As you learned in Chapter 3, the stated main idea or central idea of these longer passages is called the *thesis statement*. When the main idea of several paragraphs is implied, it is called the **implied central idea**. You use the same skills to formulate the implied central idea of a longer passage that you use to formulate the implied main idea of a paragraph.

**The implied central idea** is the main idea suggested by the details of a passage made up of two or more paragraphs.

Annotating the text is a helpful tool in determining the implied central idea. Just as you did to grasp the implied main idea for paragraphs, circle the topic. Underline the signal words for thought patterns. Remember, transition words introduce supporting details. An author often pairs a transition word with a major supporting detail. Consider the following examples: *the first reason*, *a second cause*, *the final effect*, *another similarity*, an *additional difference*, and so on. When you see phrases such as these, your one-sentence summary may include the following kinds of phrases: *several effects, a few differences,* and so on.

A longer passage often contains paragraphs with stated main ideas. The stated main idea of a paragraph is a one-sentence summary of that paragraph and can be used as part of your summary of the implied central idea.

**EXAMPLE** Read the following passage from a college psychology textbook. Annotate the text. Then select the sentence that summarizes its central idea.

Textbook Skills

**Chunking**

[1]A chunk is a meaningful unit of information. [2]A chunk can be a single letter or number, a group of letters or other items, or even a group of words or an entire sentence. [3]For example, the sequence 1-9-8-4 consists of four digits, each of which is a chunk when they are remembered separately. [4]However, if you see the digits as a year or the title of George Orwell's novel *1984*, they constitute only one chunk, leaving you much more capacity for other chunks of information.

[5]See how many chunks you can find in this sequence of 20 numbers: 19411917186518211776. [6]You can answer "20" if you see the sequence as a list of unrelated digits or "5" if you break down the sequence into the dates of major wars in U.S. history. [7]If you do the latter, it's easy for you to recall all the digits in the proper sequence after one quick glance. [8]It would be impossible for you to remember them from a short exposure if you saw them as 20 unrelated items.

—Gerrig & Zimbardo, *Psychology and Life*, 16th ed., p. 225.

_____ The sentence that best summarizes the central idea is:

a. A chunk is a small part of a larger set of information.

b. Chunking is a strategy that increases memory by organizing large pieces of information into smaller units of thought.

c. Chunking is an excellent method of memorizing important dates in history.
d. Chunking is helpful.

**EXPLANATION** This passage demonstrates the challenge of grasping the implied central idea. The thought pattern used in the first three sentences is definition. Sentences 1 and 2 introduce and define the term "chunk," and the transition *or* is used to add details to the definition. Sentence 3 introduces an example by using the signal phrase *for example.* Interestingly, the transition *however* adds a minor supporting detail to the example in sentence 4. Sentences 5 through 8 explain the process of chunking using an example. The author has mixed patterns (definition and process) to describe a memory strategy called "chunking." The sentence that best summarizes these details and thought patterns is (b) *Chunking is a strategy that increases memory by organizing large pieces of information into smaller units of thought.* This sentence presents a definition of the term and indicates that a process is going to be discussed. Sentences *a* and *c* are too narrow; sentence *d* is too broad.

## PRACTICE 4

Read the following passage. Annotate the text. Then select the sentence that summarizes its central idea.

### The Three Phases of Lyme Disease

[1]The first stage of Lyme disease shows up three to 30 days after a person is bitten by an infected tick. [2]During this phase, a red-rimmed circular spot or spots emerge, often described as a "bull's-eye" rash. [3]The centers of these expanding spots become pale, and the infected person experiences exhaustion, headaches, a fever, and joint and muscle pains.

[4]The second stage of Lyme disease can develop within weeks or take months to appear. [5]One symptom is Bell's palsy which causes one side of the face to droop and the eye on that side to stay opened. [6]In addition, nerve problems can occur, the heart can become inflamed, and the rash seen in stage one can return.

[7]The third stage of Lyme disease, which can occur within weeks or take years to develop, is arthritis, the painful swelling of joints.

[8]Of course, not all cases of Lyme disease exhibit all these symptoms. [9]Some cases may have only one or two of these signs.

_____ The sentence that best summarizes the central idea is
a. Lyme disease can have long-term consequences.
b. Lyme disease affects different people in different ways.
c. Lyme disease can attack the nerves and heart.
d. Lyme disease, a serious illness caused by a tick bite, occurs in three stages.

**EXAMPLE** Read the following passage from a college history textbook. Annotate the text. Write a sentence that summarizes the central idea of the passage.

Textbook Skills

### *Why It's Called Brown* v. *Board of Education of Topeka, Kansas*

[1]Seven-year-old Linda Brown of Topeka, Kansas, lived close to a good public school, but it was reserved for whites. [2]So every day she had to cross railroad tracks in a nearby switching yard on her way to catch a run-down school bus that would take her across town to a school reserved for African American students. [3]Her father, Oliver Brown, concerned for her safety and the quality of her education, became increasingly frustrated with his youngster's having to travel far from home to get an education.

[4]"The issue came up, and it was decided that Reverend Brown's daughter would be the goat, so to speak," recalled a member of the Topeka NAACP. [5]"He put forth his daughter to test the validity of the law, and we had to raise the money."

[6]The NAACP continued to gather cases from around the nation. [7]The Supreme Court first agreed to hear *Brown and Briggs* v. *Elliot* (South Carolina) in 1952. [8]Two days before they were to be heard, the Court issued a postponement and added *Davis* v. *Prince Edward County* (Virginia) to its docket. [9]Just a few weeks later, the Court added *Bolling* v. *Sharpe* from the District of Columbia and *Gebhart* v. *Belton* (Delaware). [10]According to U.S. Supreme Court Justice Tom Clark of Texas, the Court "consolidated them and made Brown the first so that the whole question would not smack of being purely a Southern one." [11]Thus the case came to be known as *Brown* v. *Board of Education of Topeka, Kansas.*

—O'Connor & Sabato, *American Government: Continuity and Change,* 2000 ed., p. 190.

Implied central idea: ______________________________________________

______________________________________________

______________________________________________

______________________________________________

**EXPLANATION** This passage shows the importance of a title or heading. Turn the heading into the question: *Why is it called "Brown v. Board of Education of Topeka, Kansas"?* Reading to find the answer to this question helps you decide what to annotate as you read. The opening two paragraphs use a narrative to give the history of this landmark court case. It is safe to infer that the events in this case are similar to the events in other cases. The problem of racial discrimination was widespread. Instead of underlining the time order transition words, an effective reader might write in the margin the phrase "racial discrimination." This label summarizes the point of the narrative. The third paragraph begins with a topic sentence about bringing in other cases to join *Brown*. The supporting details (the additional cases) that follow are joined by time and addition words. All these details lead up to the final sentence, which restates the title. The transition word *thus* reinforces that this court case was the result of a widespread fight against racial discrimination.

The wording of answers will vary. One possible answer is "The Supreme Court Case *Brown v. Board of Education of Topeka, Kansas* was actually four cases brought from different areas of the nation to challenge discrimination against African Americans in public education." This sentence covers all the supporting details but does not go beyond the information given in the passage. For example, this was a landmark case that could be considered the most important civil rights case of the twentieth century. The effect of the ruling dramatically changed our society. However, these details are not included in the passage; thus the thesis statement does not mention them.

## PRACTICE 5

**A.** Read the following passage from a college communications textbook. Annotate the text. Write a sentence that summarizes the central idea.

Textbook Skills

### Unspoken Messages

[1]Bob leaves his apartment at 8:15 A.M. and stops at the corner drugstore for breakfast. [2]Before he can speak, the counterman says, "The usual?" [3]Bob nods yes. [4]While he savors his Danish, a fat man pushes onto the adjoining stool and overflows into his space. [5]Bob scowls and the man pulls himself in as much as he can. [6]Bob has sent two messages without speaking a syllable.

[7]George is talking to Charley's wife at a party. [8]Their conversation is entirely trivial, yet Charley glares at them suspiciously. [9]Their physical proximity and the movements of their eyes reveal that they are powerfully attracted to each other.

[10]Jose Ybarra and Sir Edmund Jones are at the same party, and it is important for them to establish a cordial relationship for business reasons.

[11]Each is trying to be warm and friendly, yet they will part with mutual distrust, and their business transaction will probably fall through.

[12]Jose, in Latin fashion, moved closer and closer to Sir Edmund as they spoke, and this movement was miscommunicated as pushiness to Sir Edmund, who kept backing away from this intimacy, which was miscommunicated to Jose as coldness. [13]The silent languages of Latin and English cultures are more difficult to learn than their spoken languages.

—DeVito, *Messages: Building Interpersonal Communication Skills,* 4th ed., p. 139.

Implied central idea: ________________________________________

________________________________________

Textbook Skills

## Graphics as Details That Imply a Main Idea

Textbook authors often use pictures, drawings, or graphs to make the relationship between the main idea and supporting details clear.

**EXAMPLE** Study the following figure from a health textbook. State the main idea suggested by the details in a sentence.

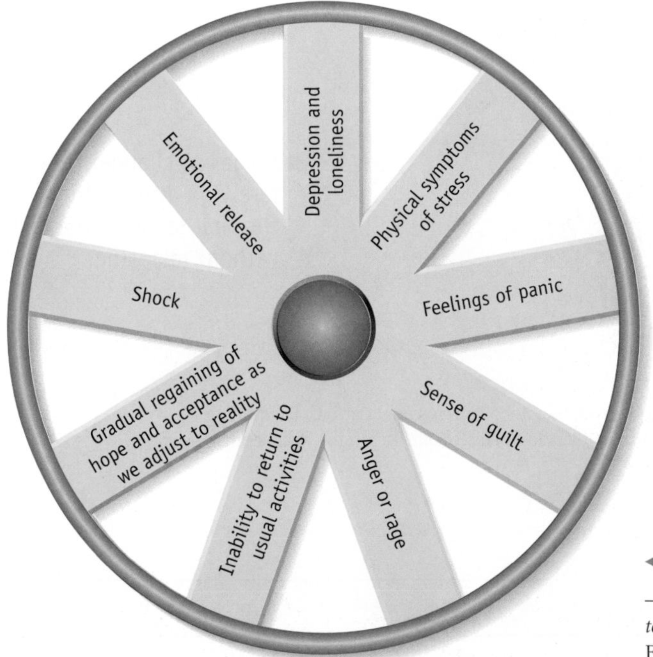


◄ Stages of Grief

—Image reprinted from Donatelle, Rebecca J., *Access to Health,* 7th ed., p. 545. Copyright © 2002 Pearson Education, publishing as Benjamin Cummings.

Implied main idea: ______________________________________________

______________________________________________

**EXPLANATION** This diagram is a circle graph. Circles often suggest a cycle or process. The caption tells us that each spoke is labeled with a different stage of grief. Each of the nine spokes that radiate from the center of the circle represents a stage of grief. The labels identify each stage. Therefore, by counting the number of spokes and using the caption, we can formulate a possible statement for the main idea: "Grief has nine stages." Since the main idea statement is a summary of the author's main point, it is not necessary to name each stage. Simply stating the number of stages indicates that a list of supporting details is given.

## PRACTICE 6

Study the following figure from a health textbook. Put the main idea suggested by the details into a sentence.

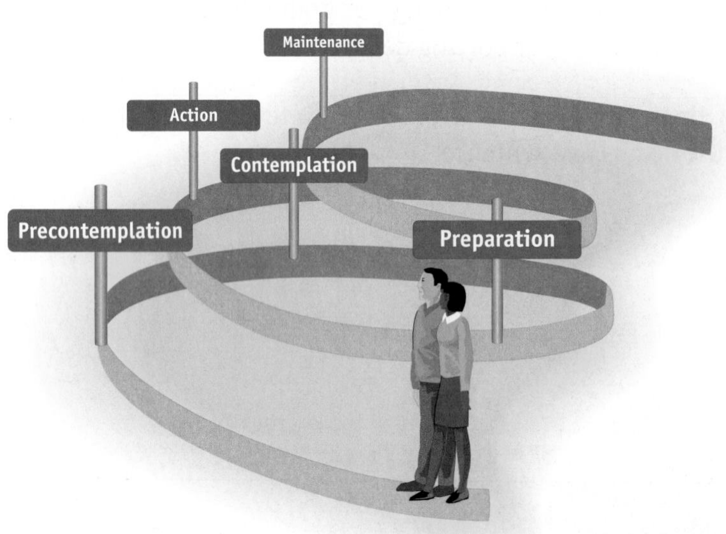


◂ Stages of change: People rarely go directly from the first stage to the last without relapsing.

—Figure reprinted from *Changing for Good* by James O. Prochaska, John Norcross and Carlo C. Diclemente. 

Implied main idea: ______________________________________________

______________________________________________

______________________________________________

## A Final Note About Experience and Perspective

As you have worked through this chapter, hopefully you have had some lively discussions about the possible answers for activities that asked for implied main ideas to be stated. Often a set of details will suggest many things to many people. Determining main ideas requires that the reader bring personal understandings and experience to the task. Thus people with different perspectives may disagree about what the details suggest. Another complex aspect of determining main ideas is that authors may choose to give a collection of details because the idea suggested is difficult to sum up in one sentence. The author intends several meanings to co-exist. The important point to remember is that the main idea you formulate should be strongly supported by the details in the paragraph or longer passage.

## Chapter Review

Test your understanding of what you have read in this chapter by filling in the blank with a word from the box.

| | | | |
|---|---|---|---|
| actively | implied main idea | point | topic |
| central idea | narrow | summarize | |
| connections | overgeneralization | supporting details | |

1. A main idea that is not stated directly but is strongly suggested by the supporting details in the paragraph is a(n) _______________.
2. Questions for finding the implied main idea:
   a. What is the _______________ or subject of the paragraph?
   b. What are the major _______________?
   c. Based on the details about the topic, what _______________ or main idea is the author trying to get across?
3. The implied main idea will be general enough to cover all the details, but it will not be so broad that it becomes a(n) _______________ or sweeping statement that suggests details not given.
4. Implied main ideas must be neither too broad nor too _______________.
5. To formulate an implied main idea, you must learn to _______________ the most important details into one sentence.

6. Formulating implied main ideas requires that the reader be _________ involved in the reading process.

7. You must use information you already have to make the _____________ between ideas that the author is suggesting.

8. The _______________ is the main idea of a passage made up of two or more paragraphs.

## Applications

### Application 1: Using Supporting Details to Determine Implied Main Ideas

A. Read each group of supporting details. Annotate the text by circling the topic and underlining key words of support and transition. In the spaces provided, write the letter of the best implied main idea for each group.

1. Supporting details:

- A category 1 hurricane has winds of 74 to 95 miles per hour and causes some damage to trees, shrubbery, and unanchored mobile homes.
- A category 5 hurricane has winds up to 155 miles per hour and causes extreme damage to homes and buildings and can blow away small structures.
- During a major hurricane, storm surges can cause the sea to flow inland for several miles.
- A category 1 hurricane brings surges of 4 to 5 feet; a category 5 hurricane causes surges of 18 feet or more.
- Heavy rainfall also causes dangerous flooding.
- Floodwaters cause most of the deaths associated with hurricanes.

______ Implied main idea:

a. Hurricanes are powerful storms.
b. People should evacuate when threatened by a hurricane.
c. Hurricanes pose several threats.
d. Hurricanes are driven by powerful winds.

2. Supporting details:

- Some experts believe that compulsive gambling is often linked to divorce.
- This type of gambling has also been tied to cases of neglected or abused children.

- Compulsive gambling also often leads to the gambler's loss of employment and income.
- Finally, gambling disorders may be a factor in some cases of homelessness.

______ Implied main idea:

a. Compulsive gambling is a disease.
b. Compulsive gambling leads to economic problems for the gambler.
c. Compulsive gambling is linked to child abuse.
d. Compulsive gambling may have several devastating consequences.

**B.** Read the following paragraph. Annotate the text by circling the topic and underlining key words of support and transition. In the spaces provided, write the letter of the best implied main idea for the paragraph.

**Genetically Modified Foods to Fight Malnutrition**

[1]Malnutrition is an urgent concern in Third World countries. [2]In these countries, many poor people rely on a single crop such as rice as the main staple of their diet. [3]However, rice does not have all the necessary nutrients to prevent malnutrition. [4]Thus scientists wanted to find a way to alter the genetic makeup of rice to improve its nutritional value. [5]For example, blindness due to a lack of vitamin A is a common problem in Third World countries. [6]Swiss researchers have created a strain of "golden" rice. [7]Golden rice contains an unusually high content of beta-carotene (vitamin A).

______ **3.** Which sentence best states the implied main idea?

a. Beta-carotene prevents blindness.
b. Genetically modified foods such as golden rice may help fight malnutrition in Third World countries.
c. Scientists are developing genetically modified foods.
d. Golden rice is a genetically modified food that has added vitamin A.

## Application 2: Creating a Summary from Supporting Details

**A.** Read each group of supporting details. Annotate the text by circling the topic and underlining key words of support and transition. In the spaces provided, use your own words to write the implied main idea for each group.

Textbook Skills

**1.** Supporting details from a college algebra textbook:

- The first step for solving problems is to *familiarize* yourself with the problem situation.
- You can try several approaches to become familiar with a problem.

- For example, read the problem out loud as if you were explaining it to someone else.
- Make and label a drawing with the information in the problem.
- Also, find needed information by looking up formulas or definitions.
- Once you have familiarized yourself with the problem, the second step for solving problems is to *translate* the problem to an equation.
- The third step is to *solve* the equation.
- The fourth step is to *check* the answer in the original problem.
- And, finally, the fifth step is to *state* the answer to the problem clearly.
- In summary, familiarize, translate, solve, check, and state.

—Adapted from Bittinger & Beecher, *Introductory and Intermediate Algebra,* 2nd ed., p. 127.

Implied main idea: ______________________________________________

____________________________________________________________

Textbook Skills

**2.** Supporting details from a college history textbook:

- During the Revolutionary War, women had to take over the management of countless farms, shops, and businesses.
- Women also became involved in other day-to-day matters that men had normally managed.
- Their experiences made the women and their families more aware of their abilities.
- At the same time, women made significant contributions to the war effort.
- And their efforts made them aware of their importance.

—Adapted from Garraty & Carnes, *The American Nation,* 10th ed., p. 130.

Implied main idea: ______________________________________________

____________________________________________________________

**B.** Read the following paragraph from a college history textbook. Annotate the text. In the space provided, write a sentence that states the implied main idea for the paragraph.

Textbook Skills

### Thomas Jefferson

[1]Thomas Jefferson was in some ways a typical, pleasure-loving southern planter. [2]However, he had in him something of the Spartan. [3]He grew tobacco

but did not smoke, and he rarely ate meat or drank alcohol. [4]Unlike most planters, he never hunted or gambled. [5]Yet he was a fine horseman and enjoyed dancing, music, and other social interests. [6]His practical interests ranged enormously: from architecture and geology to natural history and scientific farming. [7]Yet he displayed little interest in managing men. [8]Controversy dismayed him, and he tended to avoid it by assigning to some thicker-skinned associate the task of attacking his enemies. [9]Nevertheless, he wanted to have a say in shaping the future of the country. [10]And once engaged, he fought stubbornly and at times deviously to get and hold power. [11]He became the fourth President of the United States and held the office for two terms.

—Adapted from Garraty & Carnes, *The American Nation*, 10th ed., p. 170.

**3.** Implied main idea: ______________________________

______________________________

## Application 3: Implied Central Idea

Read the following passages from a college science textbook. Annotate the text. Answer the questions that follow each passage.

Textbook Skills

### Crying: A Stress Management Method?

[1]Researchers have asked why people cry and how crying might help with stress. [2]Although the eyes of all mammals are moisturized and soothed by tears, only human beings shed tears in response to emotional stress. [3]Yet we know little about this uniquely human behavior. [4]One theory suggests that tears help relieve stress by ridding the body of potentially harmful stress-induced chemicals. [5]One finding is that emotionally induced tears have a higher protein content than tears produced in response to eye irritation, such as those caused by an onion.

[6]Other interesting evidence includes a report that people with stress-related illnesses cry less than their healthy peers. [7]Reports based on experience are that people feel better "after a good cry." [8]It has been documented that men cry less often than women. [9]In America, two triggers of crying episodes are most common. [10]One involves personal relationships, such as arguments, and the second trigger is movie or television scenes. [11]Thus a primary crying time in this country is between seven and ten in the evening, when people are likely to be with others and/or watching television. [12]So when one is feeling stressed, crying is thought by some to be beneficial.

—Adapted from McGuigan, *Encyclopedia of Stress*, p. 61.

_____ **1.** Which is the best statement of the implied central idea?
a. Crying may be used primarily as a method of stress management.
b. Crying most frequently occurs in the evening.
c. Crying has physical benefits.
d. The human act of crying has prompted research into its causes and its role as a stress management method.

Textbook Skills

**Humor: A Stress Management Method?**

[1]Stress has been cited as a contributing cause of depression, anxiety, and other psychological problems. [2]Several studies indicate that a sense of humor helps in dealing with the stresses of life. [3]It mitigates depression, and laughter can overcome the fear of death itself.

[4]Laughter has been likened to "stationary jogging." [5]It relieves tension while exercising heart, lungs, and muscles. [6]Laughter increases heart rate and blood pressure. [7]Circulation of blood is thus improved. [8]Better circulation increases the amount of oxygen and other metabolic and nutritional components that are carried to various parts of the body. [9]It can help relieve pain through the release of endorphins into the bloodstream. [10]Laughter's most profound effects may occur on the immune system. [11]Natural killer cells that destroy viruses and tumors apparently increase during a state of mirth.

[12]The science of laughter is thought of as a legitimate field of study. [13]Studies indicate that humor can be helpful in treating various problems due to stress. [14]It can be incorporated into groups as a learned interaction.

—Adapted from McGuigan, *Encyclopedia of Stress,* pp. 107–108.

**2.** Implied central idea: ______________________________

______________________________

______________________________

# REVIEW Test 1

## Implied Main Ideas

**A.** Read each group of supporting details. Annotate the list. Then choose the sentence that best expresses the implied main idea for each group.

**1.** Supporting details:

- Birthrates fell for teens overall throughout the 1990s and for unmarried teens starting in the mid-1990s.
- However, the ratio of births to teenagers that are unmarried continued to rise.
- The number of unmarried teenage mothers rose from 14 percent in 1940 to 67 percent in 1990 and to 79 percent in 2000.
- This is because very few teens are marrying today, and the birthrate for married teens has dropped substantially.

—Adapted from National Center for Health Statistics, "New CDC Report Tracks Trends in Teen Births."

______ Implied main idea:

a. Although birthrates fell for teenagers during the 1990s, the proportional number of births to unmarried teens continued to rise.
b. The birthrate for married teenagers has dropped significantly.
c. Teenage marriage and parenthood are on the rise.
d. Birthrates for teenagers have fallen in recent years.

**2.** Supporting details:

- Maria focused all her attention on the television set even when she was flipping through the channels.
- By the time her husband Jesse entered the room, one of the shows had caught her attention.
- Jesse tried to talk to Maria about an issue that had come up at work.
- Jesse felt anxious and needed to talk.
- Although Maria nodded at everything Jesse said, her eyes never left the television set.
- In addition, she offered no comments, nor did she ask any questions.
- Jesse finally fell silent, then sighed deeply, and quietly left the room.

______ Implied main idea:

a. Jesse and Maria are not happily married.
b. Maria's lack of attention discouraged her husband at a time when he needed her support.
c. Maria and Jesse do not listen to each other.
d. Jesse's rude behavior of interrupting Maria's television show led to the couple's lack of communication.

**B.** Read the following chart, and study the details given. In the space provided, write the letter of the sentence that best states the implied main idea of the chart.

**3.** Supporting details:

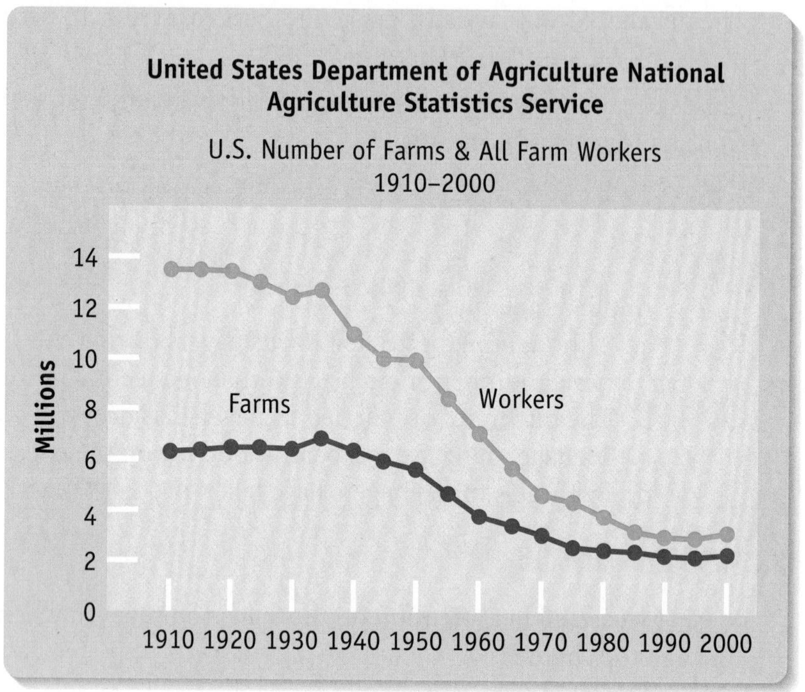


______ Implied main idea:

a. Fewer people were farmworkers in 2000 than in 1910.
b. The numbers of farms declined from a little over 6 million farms in 1910 to only 2 million in 2000.
c. The numbers of farms and farmworkers steadily declined from 1910 to 2000.
d. Millions of people have fled farm life for jobs in towns and cities.

Textbook Skills

**C.** Read the following paragraph. Annotate the text. In the space provided, write the letter of the best statement of the implied main idea.

Most people think "Anything worth doing is worth doing well." In contrast, perfectionists think, "Anything worth doing is worth doing perfectly."

Nothing less than perfection will do. "Procrastinating perfectionists" find the task so daunting that they wait until too late to prepare. They excuse themselves by thinking they could have done wonderfully, if only they had not procrastinated. "Tedious perfectionists" hone each step of preparation in great detail, but run out of time. For example, while preparing to deliver a speech, this perfectionist will gather volumes of material, write detailed outlines, but never practice delivering the speech.

—Adapted from Kelly, Marylin S. (2006). *Communication @ Work,* p. 70.

_____ **4.** The best statement of the implied main idea is

a. Don't aim for perfection; aim to do a very good job.
b. Perfection is an excuse.
c. Two types of perfectionists have unrealistic expectations.
d. Perfectionists are failures.

## REVIEW Test 2

### Implied Main Ideas

**A.** Read each group of supporting details. Annotate the lists. Then use your own words to state the main idea for each group.

#### Group 1

- The U.S. Board of Geographic Names does not recognize the Bermuda Triangle as an official name.
- The Bermuda Triangle is the unofficial name for a part of the ocean that extends from Bermuda to Miami, Florida, to San Juan, Puerto Rico.
- According to the U.S. Coast Guard, "The 'Bermuda or Devil's Triangle' is an imaginary area located off the southeastern Atlantic coast of the United States."
- However, the Bermuda Triangle is noted as a place where a high number of ships, small boats, and aircraft have been lost.
- Once, an entire squadron of American fighter planes disappeared in the Bermuda Triangle shortly after take-off from Fort Lauderdale, Florida.

- Some people believe that the Bermuda Triangle has mysterious, supernatural qualities.

**1.** Implied main idea: ______________________________

______________________________

## Group 2

- *Echolocation* is the use of sound and its echoes to establish direction and location.
- In addition, echolocation can determine the size, structure, material composition, and shape of objects.
- Dolphins make sounds similar to clicks, trills, moans, grunts, squeaks, and creaking doors.
- These sounds bounce off objects in the water and return to the dolphin in the form of an echo.
- In this way, dolphins can swim and hunt in murky water.

**2.** Implied main idea: ______________________________

______________________________

## Group 3

Textbook Skills

- Mary Pipher is the author of *Reviving Ophelia: Saving the Selves of Adolescent Girls.*
- According to Pipher, only one-seventh of all illustrations in children's textbooks are girls.
- In addition, girls are exposed to three times as many boy-centered stories as girl-centered stories.
- Boys tend to be portrayed as clever, brave, creative, and resourceful.
- In contrast, girls are depicted as kind, dependent, and docile.
- Girls read six times as many biographies of males as females.
- Even in animal stories, the animals are twice as likely to be males.

—Adapted from Teri Kwai Gamble and Michael W. Gamble. (2003).
*The Gender Communication Connection*, p. 248.

**3.** Implied main idea: Answers will vary in wording: ______________________________

______________________________

**VISUAL VOCABULARY**

The best meaning of docile is

_______

a. dangerous.
b. admirable.
c. passive.

▲ Domesticated animals are more docile than wild animals.

**B.** Read the following paragraph. Annotate the text. In the spaces provided, use your own words to write a sentence that states the implied main idea.

### Seth's Secret

[1]Every cell of Seth's body screamed for a fix. [2]He tried to ignore the urge but found that he was unable to concentrate on anything else long enough to distract himself from his desire. [3]He paced through rooms, setting out to fetch a particular object only to forget what he was looking for. [4]He called himself names for being so weak. [5]How could he let himself get in this condition? [6]If only he could hold on until the urge passed. [7]One more time he settled in to work at his computer. [8]Once more the urge surged up to overwhelm him. [9]He bolted from his chair and walked with quick determination to his secret stash—the little bottle he held back for times just like this. [10]Instead of working to meet his deadline, Seth took several deep chugs and felt the whiskey's familiar warmth rush through him. [11]He would stop tomorrow. [12]This would be the last time, for sure, just this once more.

**4.** Implied main idea: _______________________________________________

_______________________________________________________________

# REVIEW Test 3

## Implied Main Ideas and Implied Central Ideas

**A.** Read each group of supporting ideas. Annotate the lists. Then use your own words to write the best statement of the implied main idea for each group.

### Group 1

**Oil Pollution**

- Used engine oil can end up in waterways.
- Coral reefs and mangroves are more likely to be damaged by oil pollution than are sandy beaches or sea-grass beds.
- Oil-covered fur or feathers do not provide the needed insulation for marine mammals and diving birds in cold water.
- When an animal cleans itself, it also swallows oil.
- Fish exposed to oil pollution such as tanker spills may develop liver disease and reproductive and growth problems.
- Oil pollution occurs through major oil spills, runoff from city and industrial wastes, and exhaust particles from automobiles.

**1.** Implied main idea: ______________________________________________

______________________________________________

### Group 2

**A Few Duties for June for Florida Gardeners**

- In June, Florida gardeners fertilize blackberries and blueberries.
- They also plant the herbs that thrive in heat, such as basil, chives, and lemongrass.
- Florida gardeners know that June is a good month to spread thick layers of mulch in flowerbeds to smother quickly growing weeds.
- With June come the early days of the hurricane season, so Florida gardeners also take notice of weak or rotting trees or limbs that need pruning.

**2.** Implied main idea: ______________________________________________

______________________________________________

## Group 3

**"Do Not Call" Registry to Block Telemarketing Calls.**

- In July 2003, the Federal Trade Commission (FTC) began registering consumers for the free online "do not call" registry.
- In September, telemarketers and other sellers will have access to the registry.
- They will be required to check their call lists against the national "do not call" registry at least once every 90 days.
- In October, the FTC and the states will start to enforce the national "do not call" registry provisions of the Amended Telemarketing Sales Rule.
- Violators are subject to a fine of up to $11,000 per violation.

—Federal Trade Commission, "The 'Do Not Call' Registry."

**3.** Implied main idea: ______________________________________________

______________________________________________

______________________________________________

**B.** Read the following poem, and then write a sentence that states the implied central idea.

**Batteries and Bottled Water**

*by Dustin Weeks*

I'm making a list of the things I need
To ride out the storm:
Candles and cans of tuna,
A deck of cards,
Tape for the windows,
Or better yet sheets of plywood
Securely screwed.

I'm still making my list
As the wind begins to rise.
How long will half a jar of peanut butter last
In desperate hours?
I decide to drink the milk
Before it's too late and
A white frown trickles down my chin.

I decide I am good at making lists
While watching the water rising from under the door.

Right here I listed the wet/dry vac,
Just after the chain saw
And before the first aid kit.
The TV says it pays to be prepared
And they will let me know in the event of an actual emergency.

I have almost completed my list
When the roof lifts off
Like a giant Japanese kite
And the list is torn from my hands.
I watch it whipped higher and higher
Into the raging sky
A bottleless message urging evacuation.

**4.** Implied central idea: ________________________________________

________________________________________________________________

________________________________________________________________

## REVIEW Test 4

### Implied Main Ideas and Implied Central Ideas

Before you read, skim the following passage from a college social science textbook. Answer the **Before Reading** questions. Read the passage and annotate the text. Then answer the **After Reading** questions.

Textbook Skills

### Two Types of Language: Denotation and Connotation

[1]Consider a word such as *death.* [2]To a doctor, this word might mean the point at which the heart stops beating. [3]This is a denotative meaning, a rather **objective** description of an event. [4]To a mother whose son has just died, however, the word means much more. [5]It recalls the son's youth, his ambitions, his family, his illness, and so on. [6]To her, the word is emotional, subjective, and highly personal. [7]These emotional, subjective, and personal associations are the word's connotative meaning. [8]The **denotation** of a word is its objective definition; the **connotation** is its subjective or emotional meaning.

[9]Now consider a simple nod of the head in answer to the question, "Do you agree?" [10]This gesture is largely denotative and simply says yes. [11]What about a wink, a smile, or an overly rapid speech rate? [12]These nonverbal

expressions are more connotative; they express your feelings rather than objective information.

[13]The denotative meaning of a message is general or **universal;** most people would agree with the denotative meanings and would give similar definitions. [14]Connotative meanings, however, are extremely personal, and few people would agree on the precise connotative meaning of a word or nonverbal behavior.

[15]"Snarl words" and "purr words" may further clarify the distinction between denotative and connotative meaning. [16]Snarl words are highly negative ("She's an idiot," "He's a pig," "They're a bunch of losers"). [17]Sexist, racist, and heterosexist language and hate speech provide lots of other examples. [18]Purr words are highly positive ("She's a real sweetheart," "He's a dream," "They're the greatest"). [19]Although they may sometimes seem to have denotative meaning and refer to the "real world," snarl and purr words are actually connotative in meaning. [20]They don't describe people or events, but rather, they reveal the speaker's feelings about these people or events.

—Adapted from DeVito, *The Interpersonal Communication Book,* 10th ed., p. 162.

## BEFORE READING

### Vocabulary in Context

_____ **1.** The best definition of the word **objective** in sentence 3 is

a. personal.
b. factual.
c. honest.
d. biased.

_____ **2.** The best meaning of the word **universal** in sentence 13 is

a. lofty.
b. narrow.
c. common to many people.
d. exact.

### Thought Patterns

_____ **3.** What is the thought pattern suggested by the title of the passage?

a. cause and effect
b. classification
c. spatial order
d. comparison

## AFTER READING

### Main Ideas

_____ **4.** Which sentence is the topic sentence for the last paragraph (sentences 15–20)?

a. sentence 15
b. sentence 16
c. sentence 18
d. sentence 19

## Supporting Details

______ **5.** Based on the passage, a simple nod of the head
- a. is the only way to communicate agreement with an idea or person.
- b. can have many different meanings.
- c. is largely denotative and simply says yes.
- d. carries connotative meanings.

______ **6.** Based on the passage, "snarl words" and "purr words"
- a. describe people or events.
- b. communicate denotative meanings.
- c. reveal the speaker's feelings about people or events.
- d. are highly positive.

## Concept Maps and Charts

**7.** Complete the concept map with information from the passage.

**Two Types of Language**

| Denotation | Connotation |
|---|---|
| Objective descriptions | ______________ associations |
| Nod of the head | Wink, smile, rapid rate of speech |
| Universal meanings | Extremely personal meanings |
| | Snarl and purr words |

## Implied Main Ideas and Implied Central Ideas

______ **8.** Which sentence best states the implied main idea of the second paragraph (sentences 9–12)?
- a. Nonverbal language can also have denotative or connotative meanings.
- b. A nod of the head is an example of denotative language.
- c. A wink is an example of connotative language.
- d. Nonverbal language is powerful.

______ **9.** Which sentence best states the implied main idea of the third paragraph (sentences 13–14)?
a. Most people agree with the denotative meanings.
b. Most people disagree over connotative meanings.
c. Denotative meanings are more widely agreed on than connotative meanings.
d. Denotative and connotative meanings are very similar.

______ **10.** Which sentence best states the implied central idea of the passage?
a. Language has the ability to communicate many meanings.
b. Verbal and nonverbal language express both denotation and connotation.
c. Gestures are part of nonverbal language that can express both denotation and connotation.
d. Racist language is an example of connotative meaning.

## Discussion Questions

1. Which type of meaning is more powerful: denotative or connotative? Why?
2. Choose a few words, and as a group, discuss their denotations and connotations. Consider such terms as *pride*, *excellence*, or *envy*.
3. What kind of process do people go through to come to agreement about a universal denotative meaning of a word? Of a gesture?

## Writing Topics

1. In one or two paragraphs, describe an event during which connotative "snarl" and "purr" words were used powerfully.
2. In one or two paragraphs, describe an event during which gestures conveyed both connotative and denotative messages.
3. Write a letter that advises someone how to use connotative and denotative meanings to improve the person's ability to get along with others. For example, explain to a teenager how to talk to a teacher about a grade or how to talk a police officer out of giving a speeding ticket.

## EFFECTIVE READER Scorecard

**Implied Main Ideas and Implied Central Ideas**

| Test | Number Correct | | Points | | Score |
|---|---|---|---|---|---|
| Review Test 1 | ______ | × | 25 | = | ______ |
| Review Test 2 | ______ | × | 25 | = | ______ |
| Review Test 3 | ______ | × | 25 | = | ______ |
| Review Test 4 | ______ | × | 10 | = | ______ |
| Review Test 5 (website) | ______ | × | 25 | = | ______ |
| Review Test 6 (website) | ______ | × | 20 | = | ______ |

Enter your scores on the Effective Reader Scorecard: Chapter 8 Review Tests inside the back cover.

## After Reading About Implied Main Ideas and Implied Central Ideas

Before you move on to the mastery tests on implied main ideas and implied central ideas, take time to reflect on your learning and performance by answering the following questions. Write your answers in your notebook.

What did I learn about implied main ideas and implied central ideas?

What do I need to remember about implied main ideas and implied central ideas?

How has my knowledge base or prior knowledge about implied ideas changed?

## More Review and Mastery Tests

For more practice, go to the book's website at **http://ablongman.com/henry/** and click on *The Effective Reader.* Then select "More Review and Mastery Tests." The tests are organized by chapter.

**MASTERY Test 1**

Name ____________________ Section __________

Date __________ **Score** (number correct) ______ × 25 = ______%

**A.** Read and annotate the following paragraphs; then choose the letter of the best statement of the implied main idea for each paragraph.

### Differences between Males and Females

Textbook Skills

[1]Males produce 10 to 20 times more testosterone than women do. [2]Testosterone profoundly affects physique, behavior, moods, and self understanding. [3]In contrast, females produce estrogen. [4]Estrogen aids in the production of the good cholesterol, increases the flexibility of blood vessels, and helps to ward off infections and viruses. [5]Males and females also differ in the use of their brains. [6]Males are more skilled using the left lobe of the brain; the left lobe controls linear and analytical thinking. [7]Females excel at using the right lobe of the brain; the right lobe controls creativity and insight. [8]Finally, females mature physically more quickly than males.

—Teri Kwai Gamble and Michael W. Gamble. (2003). *The Gender Communication Connection*. New York: Longman, p. 35.

______ **1.** Which sentence best states the implied main idea?

a. Males and females differ emotionally and physically.
b. Males and females differ biologically.
c. Males are inferior to females.
d. Females are stronger and healthier than males.

### Turn Taking: With Respect to the Japanese

Textbook Skills

[1]A common American conversational habit is to try to help complete sentences or phrases begun by the other person. [2]Some people do this more than others; research conducted in America shows that higher status people will "help" complete sentences of lower status people rather than the other way around. [3]American men finish sentences for women far more than do women for men, and Americans end sentences for Japanese more than Japanese for Americans. [4]It may be meant primarily to show that one is listening and following along, but the Japanese may interpret it as impatience, aggressiveness, failure to show respect, or a simple exercise of power.

—Adapted from Condon, John C. (1984). *With Respect to the Japanese: A Guide for Americans*, p. 42.

______ **2.** Which sentence best states the paragraph's main idea?
   a. American men are rude and domineering.
   b. The American conversational habit of turn taking can be misunderstood by the Japanese.
   c. Americans finish the thoughts of other people.
   d. Japanese are polite in their conversational habits.

### Pollen Allergy

[1]Each spring, summer, and fall, tiny particles are released from trees, weeds, and grasses. [2]These particles, known as pollen, hitch rides on currents of air. [3]Although their mission is to fertilize parts of other plants, many never reach their targets. [4]Instead, they enter human noses and throats, triggering a type of seasonal allergic rhinitis called pollen allergy, which many people know as hay fever or rose fever (depending on the season in which the symptoms occur). [5]Of all the things that can cause an allergy, pollen is one of the most widespread. [6]Many of the foods, drugs, or animals that cause allergies can be avoided to a great extent; even insects and household dust are escapable. [7]Short of staying indoors when the pollen count is high—and even that may not help—there is no easy way to evade windborne pollen.

—National Institute of Allergy and Infectious Diseases, "Something in the Air: Airborne Allergens."

______ **3.** Which sentence best states the implied main idea?
   a. Pollen allergies occur in summer, spring, and fall.
   b. The symptoms caused by pollen allergies are uncomfortable.
   c. Pollen is one of the most widespread and difficult-to-avoid causes of allergies.
   d. Pollen irritates some people's noses and throats.

**B.** Read and annotate the following passage from a college history textbook. Write the central idea in the space provided.

Textbook Skills

### Native Americans Face Change

[1]Native American cultures had dominated North America until the arrival of large numbers of white men and women. [2]Indians found that conquest strained their time-honored ways of life. [3]As daily life changed almost beyond recognition, native peoples had to find new ways to survive both physically and socially. [4]Historian James Merrell reminded us that the Indians also

faced a world that from their view was just as "new" as the one which greeted European invaders.

[5]Europeans tried to "civilize" the Indians. [6]They wanted natives to dress like the colonists, attend white schools, and live in permanent buildings. [7]However, their deepest desire was to convert natives to Christianity. [8]In addition, English planters cleared the forests and fenced the fields. [9]In doing so, they changed the ecological system on which the Indians depended. [10]These actions reduced the supply of deer and other animals vital to native cultures.

[11]It was disease, however, that created the greatest threat to native cultures. [12]The new arrivals brought with them bacteria and viruses. [13]The immune systems of the native people had no ability to fight these types of germs. [14]As a result, smallpox, measles, and the flu nearly wiped out the Native American people. [15]Other diseases such as alcoholism also took a terrible toll.

—Adapted from Divine, Breen, Fredrickson, & Williams, *The American Story,* pp. 9–13.

**4.** Implied central idea: ________________________________________

________________________________________________________________

# MASTERY Test 2

Name ______________________ Section ______________

Date ______________ **Score** (number correct) ______ × 25 = ______%

**A.** Read and annotate the following paragraphs. In the spaces provided, use your own words to write the best statement of the main idea for each.

[1]Kickboxing as an aerobic exercise uses a bouncing base move. [2]Added to the base move are a variety of self-defense moves such as punches, kicks, and knee strikes. [3]Some cardio-kickboxing classes may also include sparring routines. [4]In addition, some kickboxing classes may incorporate traditional exercises, such as jumping jacks, leg lifts, push-ups, and abdominal crunches.

**1.** Implied main idea: ______________________________________________

______________________________________________

______________________________________________

[1]Lassie, one of the most famous animals ever on television, became a beloved symbol of loyalty and courage. [2]The popular sitcom *Friends* featured Marcel the monkey, who came to be regarded by the character Ross as a friend as much as a pet. [3]Another successful sitcom, *Married with Children*, had a dog named Buck—the sole trapping of normality in that dysfunctional family. [4]And who can forget the Taco Bell Chihuahua, who helped sell countless tacos?

**2.** Implied main idea: ______________________________________________

______________________________________________

[1]Mohandas Gandhi was a 20th-century leader of the Indian Nationalist movement. [2]Mahatma, or "great soul," was the name by which he became known later in his life. [3]His use of nonviolent confrontation, or civil disobedience, won freedom for his own people and influenced leaders around the world. [4]Gandhi believed in hard work and humility; he spun his own thread and wove the material for his clothes. [5]Gandhi fought for the rights of the imprisoned and impoverished.

**3.** Implied main idea: ______________________________________________

______________________________________________

**B.** Read and annotate the following passage from a college health textbook. Write the central idea in the space provided.

Textbook Skills

### Water: The Essential Nutrient

[1]Without water, you could live only about one week. [2]About 65 to 70 percent of your body weight is made up of water in the form of blood, saliva, urine, cellular fluids, and digestive enzymes. [3]In all these various forms, water helps transport nutrients, remove wastes, and control body temperature.

[4]Water carries nutrients along the digestive path and to the cells. [5]First, it does this by liquefying food and moving it through the stomach, small intestine, and large intestine. [6]When the food is absorbed into the blood, water plays an important role by regulating the amount of nutrients on both sides of the cell wall.

[7]Water needs vary, depending on the climate and a person's activity level. [8]In a cold climate, the demand by the body for water is less than in a warm climate. [9]An active person's demand for water is much greater than an inactive person's demand. [10]Also, more water is needed at higher altitudes than at lower altitudes.

[11]There are many ways to get liquid from your diet. [12]The most obvious source is a glass of water. [13]Most experts agree that six to eight glasses of water per day provide an adequate supply to an average adult. [14]Other healthy beverages are skim or low-fat milk and fruit juices. [15]In addition, many fruits and vegetables are excellent sources of water.

—Adapted from Pruitt & Stein, *Health Styles: Decisions for Living Well*, 2nd ed., p. 107.

**4.** Implied central idea: ______________________________________________

______________________________________________________________

## MASTERY Test 3

Name ______________________ Section ____________

Date ____________ Score (number correct) ______ × 25 = ______%

Read and annotate the following paragraphs. In the spaces provided, write the letter of the sentence that best states the implied main idea for each paragraph.

### Paragraph from a college history textbook

#### Growth of National Feelings

[1]Most modern revolutions have been prompted by strong national feelings, and most have resulted in independence. [2]In the case of the American Revolution, the desire to be free came before any national feeling. [3]The colonies did not enter into a political union because they felt an overwhelming desire to bring all Americans under one rule. [4]Instead they united as the only hope of winning a war against Great Britain. [5]The fact that the colonies chose to stay together after the war shows how much national feeling had developed during the war.

—Adapted from Garraty & Carnes, *The American Nation,* 10th ed., p. 130.

______ **1.** Which sentence best states the implied main idea?

a. One result of the American Revolution was the growth of national feelings.
b. Most wars are caused by national feelings.
c. The American Revolution was caused by a need for independence.
d. The fact that the colonies stayed united after the Revolution was a miracle.

### Paragraph from a college mass media textbook

#### The Vital Role of Magazines

[1]Magazines began in colonial America as a forum for the essay. [2]Since then, magazines have helped develop the nation's social awareness. [3]By 1900, an educated middle class used magazines as the tool for social protest. [4]Today, consumer magazines and literary journals make up the bulk of magazine publishing. [5]In the future, magazines will continue to change to provide vital voices to national discussions about political and social issues.

—Adapted from Folkerts & Lacy, *The Media in Your Life: An Introduction to Mass Communication,* 2nd ed., p. 141.

______ **2.** Which sentence best states the implied main idea?

a. Magazines are a unique American product.
b. Magazines were an important part of colonial America.
c. Magazines have provided many important services.
d. Magazines have been and will remain an important forum for American voices.

## Paragraph from a college algebra textbook

Textbook Skills

### Three Ways to Study

[1]During systematic study, you begin studying on November 1 for an exam scheduled on November 15, and you continue to study every day until the day of the test. [2]During intense study, you wait until November 14 to begin studying, and you cram all day and through the night. [3]Which of these methods would produce a better result on an exam? [4]Research shows that students who are successful use a third system that combines the first two. [5]They study systematically well ahead of the test, but they also do intense study the day before the test. [6]This works so long as they don't stay up all night.

—Adapted from Bittinger & Beecher, *Introductory and Intermediate Algebra,* 2nd ed., p. 805.

_____ **3.** Which sentence best states the implied main idea?

a. Systematic study requires that a student begin studying weeks before a test.

b. Intense study drives a student to "cram" the day before the test.

c. The most effective study system combines systematic and intense study sessions.

d. There are two basic ways to study for an exam: systematic and intense.

## Paragraph from a college science textbook

Textbook Skills

### Biology's Connection to Life

[1]Endangered species, genetically modified crops, global warming, air and water pollution, the cloning of embryos, nutrition controversies, emerging diseases, medical advances—is there ever a day that we don't see several of these issues featured in the news? [2]These topics and many more have biological underpinnings. [3]Most of these issues of science and society also involve technology. [4]Science and technology are interdependent, but their basic goals differ. [5]The goal of science is to understand natural phenomena. [6]In contrast, the goal of technology is generally to apply scientific knowledge for some specific purpose. [7]For example, discovery of the structure of DNA has created new technologies in many fields including medicine, agriculture, and forensics (DNA fingerprinting, for example).

—Adapted from Campbell, Reece, Taylor, and Simon. *Biology: Concepts and Connections,* 5th ed., Benjamin Cummings 2005. p. 12.

_____ **4.** Which sentence best states the implied main idea?

a. DNA fingerprinting is the result of applying biology to real-life issues.

b. Biology has a vital connection to everyday life issues.

c. Biology and technology go hand in hand.

d. Advances in technology affect the study of biology.

Name ______________________ Section ____________

# MASTERY Test 4

Date ____________ **Score** (number correct) ______ × 25 = ______%

Read and annotate the following paragraphs. In the spaces provided, use your own words to state the implied main idea.

## Paragraph from a college science textbook

### What Causes Motion Sickness?

[1]Boating, flying, or even riding in a car can make us dizzy and nauseated, a condition called motion sickness. [2]Some people start feeling ill just from thinking about getting on a boat or plane. [3]Many others get sick only during storms at sea or during turbulence in flight. [4]Motion sickness is thought to result from the brain's receiving signals from equilibrium receptors in the inner ear that conflict with visual signals from the eyes. [5]When a susceptible person is inside a moving ship, for instance, signals from the equilibrium receptors in the inner ear indicate, correctly, that the body is moving (in relation to the environment outside the ship). [6]In conflict with these signals, the eyes may tell the brain that the body is in a stationary environment, the cabin. [7]Somehow the conflicting signals make the person feel ill. [8]Symptoms may be relieved by closing the eyes, limiting head movements, or focusing on a stable horizon. [9]Many sufferers of motion sickness take a sedative such as Dramamine or Bonine to relieve their symptoms.

—Adapted from Campbell, Reece, Taylor, and Simon. *Biology: Concepts and Connections,* 5th ed., Benjamin Cummings 2005. p. 600.

**1.** Implied main idea: ______________________________________________

______________________________________________

______________________________________________

## Paragraph from a college social science textbook

### Audience Demand in Movie Markets

[1]In the early days, movies catered to the family audience. [2]From the era of the nickelodeon to the age of Panavision, mothers, fathers, and children flocked to neighborhood movie houses and to the theater palaces in the cities. [3]After the advent of television, as couples settled down to raise children in the suburbs, the movies became less attractive. [4]For parents, going to a movie meant paying for a babysitter, tickets, and transportation. [5]So many chose to stay home and watch television. [6]Slowly, the audience changed. [7]From the late 1960s until the late 1990s, the 17-year-old was the most reliable moviegoer. [8]Now, aging baby boomers far outnumber teenagers in the United States and present a viable group for studios to target.

—Adapted from Folkerts & Lacy, *The Media in Your Life: An Introduction to Mass Communication,* 2nd ed., p 166.

**2.** Implied main idea: ______________________________________________

______________________________________________

## Paragraph from a college history textbook

Textbook Skills

### America Isolated

[1]America was isolated from Europe by 3,000 miles of ocean or, as a poet put it, "nine hundred leagues of roaring seas." [2]The crossing took anywhere from a few weeks to several months, depending on wind and weather. [3]No one undertook an ocean voyage lightly, and few who made the westward crossing ever thought seriously of returning. [4]The modern mind can scarcely grasp the awful isolation that enveloped settlers. [5]One had to build a new life or perish—if not of hunger, then of loneliness.

—Adapted from Garraty & Carnes, *The American Nation*, 10th ed., p. 38.

**3.** Implied main idea: ______________________________________________

______________________________________________

## Visual graphic or concept map from a college communications textbook

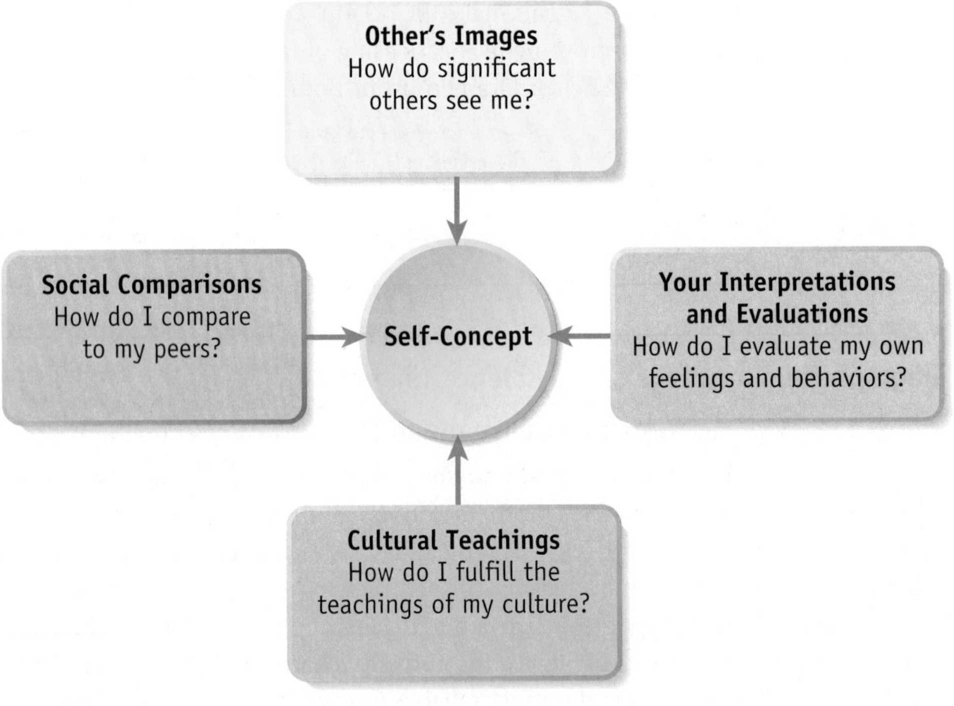


**4.** Implied main idea: ______________________________________________

______________________________________________

______________________________________________

—Adapted from DeVito, Joseph A. (2005). *The Interpersonal Communication Book, 11th ed.* New York: Longman, p. 57.

Name ______________________ Section ____________

# MASTERY Test 5

Date ____________ **Score** (number correct) ______ × 25 = ______%

---

**A.** Read and annotate the following selections. In the spaces provided, use your own words to state the implied main idea of each.

### Poem reprinted in a college literature textbook

**To See a World in a Grain of Sand**

*by William Blake (1803)*

To see a world in a grain of sand
And a heaven in a wild flower,
Hold infinity in the palm of your hand
And eternity in an hour.

**1.** Implied main idea: ______________________________________________

______________________________________________

### Paragraph from a college social science textbook

**One Way to Fight Fair**

[1]When you air your conflicts in front of others, you create a wide variety of other problems. [2]You may not be willing to be totally honest when third parties are present. [3]You may feel you have to save face and therefore must win the fight at all costs. [4]This may lead you to use strategies to win the argument rather than to resolve the conflict. [5]Also, you run the risk of embarrassing your partner in front of others. [6]This in turn could lead to resentment and hostility.

—DeVito, *Messages: Building Interpersonal Communication Skills,* 4th ed., p. 297.

**2.** Implied main idea: ______________________________________________

______________________________________________

**Paragraph from a college English textbook**

Textbook Skills

### Formal Outlines

[1]A formal outline requires you to use a set of rules that dictate how to display relationships among ideas. [2]You need to adhere strictly to the numbering and lettering requirements. [3]A formal outline can be either a topic outline or a sentence outline. [4]In a topic outline, each entry is a word or phrase. [5]In a sentence outline, each entry is a complete sentence. [6]Never mix the two types. [7]Creating a topic outline of textbook sections may help some readers comprehend the information. [8]Creating a sentence outline of original ideas seems to help writers create a first draft. [9]It is important to choose the outline that works best for your study needs.

—Adapted from Troyka, *Simon & Schuster Handbook for Writers,* 6th ed., p. 42.

**3.** Implied main idea: ______________________________________________

______________________________________________

**B.** Read and annotate the following passage from a college communications textbook. In the space provided, use your own words to state the implied central idea.

Textbook Skills

### The Power of Video

[1]On August 1, 1981, MTV began broadcasting. [2]Within ten years, MTV reached more than 204 million homes in forty-one countries around the world. [3]MTV and other music channels offer another source of income for musicians and recording companies. [4]Videos are promotion tools as well. [5]A well-thought out and well-made music video can boost recording sales greatly.

[6]Video promotion is a creative art. [7]Some videos are built with story lines that enhance the music. [8]Other music videos contain appealing images that may be unrelated to the specific lyrics. [9]Either way, videos have become so important that some top stars can spend more than $1 million on a video.

—Adapted from Folkerts & Lacy, *The Media in Your Life: An Introduction to Mass Communication,* 2nd ed., p. 269.

**4.** Implied central idea: ______________________________________________

______________________________________________

MASTERY **Test 6**

Name ____________________ Section __________

Date __________ **Score** (number correct) ______ × 25 = ______%

**A.** Read and annotate the following paragraphs from an educational psychology textbook. In the spaces provided, use your own words to state the implied main idea of each.

Textbook Skills

### Trust Versus Mistrust

[1]In the first months of life, babies begin to find out whether they can depend on the world around them. [2]According to psychologist Erik Erikson, the infant will develop a sense of trust if its needs for food and care are met with comforting regularity. [3]In this first year, infants are in Piaget's sensorimotor stage. [4]They are just beginning to learn that they are separate from the world around them. [5]This realization is part of what makes trust so important. [6]The infant must form a first loving, trusting relationship with the caregiver or develop a sense of mistrust.

—Adapted from Woolfolk, *Educational Psychology,* 8th ed., p. 65.

**1.** Implied main idea: ______________________________________________

______________________________________________

______________________________________________

Textbook Skills

### Defining the Problem

[1]Tenants were angry about the slow elevators in their building. [2]Consultants hired "to fix the problem" reported that the elevators were no slower than average and that improvements would be very expensive. [3]Then one day, as the building supervisor watched people waiting impatiently for an elevator, he realized that the problem was not slow elevators but the fact that people were bored. [4]They had nothing to do while they waited. [5]When the boredom problem was identified and seen as an opportunity to improve the "waiting experience," the simple solution of installing a mirror by the elevator on each floor eliminated the complaints. [6]Research indicates that many people skip the important first step of finding the problem and "leap" to naming the first problem that comes to mind.

—Adapted from Woolfolk, *Educational Psychology,* 8th ed., p. 291.

**2.** Implied main idea: ______________________________________________

______________________________________________

**B.** Read and annotate the following passage from a college composition textbook. In the spaces provided, use your own words to state the implied main idea and the implied central idea.

Textbook Skills

### Writing as a Process of Discovery

[1]Think of a task or an activity that you understand and do well: playing a card or board game, solving a mathematical equation, riding a bicycle, or playing a song on a musical instrument. [2]The task is now so simple that you no longer even think about it. [3]You just do it.

[4]Now think back to a time before you understood that activity. [5]It seemed anything but simple then. [6]It probably seemed mystifying, confusing, or overpowering. [7]"There's no way I'll ever be able to do this," you may have told yourself then. [8]But you did learn, and now the task or activity seems natural to you. [9]In fact, you probably wonder how you ever could *not* have understood it.

[10]There is a simple explanation for this change in attitude and ability: experience. [11]The more you worked at the activity, the better you became. [12]Practice made you confident and competent.

[13]That's exactly how it is with writing. [14]At first, writing can seem mystifying, confusing, or overpowering. [15]This is especially true if you haven't had much experience with it. [16]But regular practice with writing will change all that. [17]You'll discover that writing a paper involves the writing process—a series of stages called prewriting, composing, and revising. [18]You'll discover that a successful piece of writing is not a onetime effort but the result of several versions. [19]And you'll discover that when you write effectively, you communicate ideas clearly and directly to a reader, and you fulfill an identifiable purpose.

—Adapted from Kelly & Lawton, *Discovery: An Introduction to Writing*, 2nd ed., p. 2.

**3.** Implied main idea of paragraph 1 (sentences 1–3): ______________________

______________________________________________

**4.** Implied central idea of passage: ______________________________________

______________________________________________

CHAPTER

9

# Fact and Opinion

## CHAPTER PREVIEW

## Before Reading About Fact and Opinion

You are most likely already familiar with the commonly used words *fact* and *opinion*, and you probably already have an idea about what each one means. Take a moment to clarify your current understanding about fact and opinion by writing a definition for each one in the spaces below:

Fact: ______________________________________________

______________________________________________

Opinion: ______________________________________________

______________________________________________

______________________________________________

As you work through this chapter, compare what you already know about fact and opinion to new information that you learn about each one using the following method:

On a blank page in your notebook draw a line down the middle of the page to form two columns. Label one side "Fact" and the other side "Opinion." Just below each heading, copy the definition you wrote for each one. As you work through the chapter, record new information you learn about facts and opinions in their corresponding column.

## What Is the Difference Between Fact and Opinion?

Fact: Jennifer Lynn Lopez is an award-winning actress, singer, songwriter, dancer, and fashion designer.

Opinion: Jennifer Lopez is one of the most influential Hispanics in Hollywood.

Effective readers must sort fact from opinion to properly understand and evaluate the information they are reading.

A **fact** is a specific detail that is true based on objective proof. A fact is discovered.
An **opinion** is an interpretation, value judgment, or belief that cannot be proved or disproved. An opinion is created.
**Objective proof** can be physical evidence, an eyewitness account, or the result of an accepted scientific method.

Most people's points of view and beliefs are based on a blend of fact and opinion. Striving to remain objective, many authors rely mainly on facts. The main purpose of these authors is to inform. For example, textbooks, news articles, and medical research rely on facts. In contrast, editorials, advertisements, and fiction often mix fact and opinion. The main purpose of these types of writing is to persuade or entertain.

Separating fact from opinion requires you to think critically because opinion is often presented as fact. The following clues will help you separate fact from opinion.

| Fact | Opinion |
|---|---|
| Is objective | Is subjective |
| Is discovered | Is created |
| States reality | Interprets reality |
| Can be verified | Cannot be verified |
| Is presented with unbiased words | Is presented with biased words |
| *Example of a fact* | *Example of an opinion* |
| Spinach is a source of iron. | Spinach tastes awful. |

A fact is a specific, objective, and verifiable detail; in contrast, an opinion is a biased, personal view created from feelings and beliefs.

**EXAMPLE** Read the following statements, and mark each one **F** if it states a fact or **O** if it expresses an opinion.

_____ **1.** Two films by Michael Moore, *Bowling for Columbine* and *Fahrenheit 9/11*, are based on actual events.

_____ **2.** Filmmaker Michael Moore is a radical thinker whose two main goals are to stir up trouble and profit from the tragedy of others.

_____ **3.** Michael Moore won an Oscar for *Bowling for Columbine*, and he was awarded the Palme d'Or at the Cannes Film Festival for *Fahrenheit 9/11*.

_____ **4.** Michael Moore is a true patriot whose main goal is to unmask evil and apathy.

**EXPLANATION** Sentences 1 and 3 state facts that can be verified through research. *Bowling for Columbine* is the filmmaker's treatment of gun ownership in America based on the events of the shootings at Columbine High School. *Fahrenheit 9/11* is an anti-Bush documentary about President Bush that aims to expose his alliances with oil-producing nations, among other things. Sentences 2 and 4 express opinions, personal reactions to Michael Moore's work as a filmmaker. Sentence 2 expresses a negative personal opinion; sentence 4 expresses a positive personal opinion.

## PRACTICE 1

Read the following statements and mark each one **F** if it states a fact or **O** if it expresses an opinion.

_____ **1.** Michelangelo is the greatest painter of all time.

_____ **2.** The Sistine Chapel is the private chapel of the popes in Rome.

_____ **3.** Between 1508 and 1512, Michelangelo produced frescos for the chapel's ceiling; the murals depict scenes from the Book of Genesis, from the Creation to the Flood.

_____ **4.** One cannot really understand what a human is capable of producing until one sees Michelangelo's work in the Sistine Chapel.

## Ask Questions to Identify Facts

To test whether a statement is a fact, ask these three questions:

- Can the statement be proved or demonstrated to be true?
- Can the statement be observed in practice or operation?
- Can the statement be verified by witnesses, manuscripts, or documents?

If the answer to any of these questions is no, the statement is not a fact. Instead, it is an opinion. Keep in mind, however, that many statements blend both fact and opinion.

**EXAMPLE** Read the following statements, and mark each one

**F** if it states a fact or **O** if it expresses an opinion.

_____ **1.** Mel Gibson produced *The Passion of Christ* and *Apocalypto*.

_____ **2.** Both movies are too violent.

_____ **3.** Both movies earned millions of dollars.

_____ **4.** A spinning class is a group exercise program of about 45 minutes of riding on a stationary bike.

_____ **5.** Spinning classes are indoor group bike rides led by instructors who set the pace and degree of difficulty of the rides.

_____ **6.** A spinning class is a form of torture.

**EXPLANATION**

**1. F:** This statement can be easily verified in newspapers.

**2. O:** This is a statement of personal opinion. Some movie viewers may think the violence in the films is realistic and necessary.

3. **F:** How much money the movies made is easy to prove.
4. **F:** This statement can be easily verified by attending a spinning class or doing research.
5. **F:** It is a fact that spinning classes are held indoors and led by an instructor who sets the pace and degree of difficulty. Again, this statement can be proved by attending a class or doing research.
6. **O:** This is a statement with which others may disagree. Some people who spin probably enjoy the experience.

## PRACTICE 2

Read the following statements, and mark each one **F** if it states a fact or **O** if it expresses an opinion.

_____ 1. In 2008, reality shows like *American Idol*, *Survivor*, and *America's Next Top Model* still appealed to the American television market.

_____ 2. The poet Emily Dickinson composed over 1,000 poems.

_____ 3. The chemicals in marijuana smoke can cause cancer.

_____ 4. Florida, with its mild winters, is the ideal place to retire.

_____ 5. Small dogs make the best house pets.

_____ 6. Spanking of any kind is a form of child abuse.

_____ 7. Television reduces the intelligence of viewers.

_____ 8. The Harry Potter books and films have stimulated many children's interest in reading.

_____ 9. Within the next decade, as the "baby boom" generation retires, a shortage of teachers is likely to occur.

_____ 10. The mass production of the automobile changed the way people and goods moved from one place to another.

## Note Biased Words to Identify Opinions

Be on the lookout for biased words. **Biased words** express opinions, value judgments, and interpretations. They are often loaded with emotion. The box contains a small sample of these kinds of words.

**Biased Words**

| | | | | | |
|---|---|---|---|---|---|
| awful | best | favorite | great | miserable | stupid |
| amazing | better | frightful | greatest | more | unbelievable |
| bad | disgusting | fun | handsome | most | ugly |
| beautiful | exciting | good | horrible | smart | very |

Realize that a sentence can include both facts and opinions. The part of the sentence that includes a biased word may be an opinion about another part of the sentence that is a fact.

**EXAMPLE** Read the following sentences. Underline the biased words.

1. Even though actor Bruce Willis has a receding hairline, he is still very handsome.
2. The grasslands of the American West were tragically plowed under for crops.

**EXPLANATION**

In the first sentence, "Bruce Willis has a receding hairline" is a fact that can be proved by research or an eyewitness account. However, the second part of the sentence, "he is still very handsome," is an opinion about his appearance. In the second sentence, the grasslands of the American West *were* plowed under to make way for crops, but whether that fact is tragic is a matter of opinion.

## PRACTICE 3

Read the following sentences. Underline the biased words.

1. Even though spinach is low in calories and rich in fiber, iron, folate and vitamin A, its bitter taste makes it a less desirable food.
2. A Labrador retriever is a medium-sized dog with a distinctive double coat that requires brushing; loyal and friendly, this breed makes an excellent pet for a family.

## Note Qualifiers to Identify Opinions

Be on the lookout for words that qualify an idea. A qualifier may express an absolute, unwavering opinion using words like *always* or *never*. Other times a qualifier expresses an opinion in the form of a command as in *must*, or the desirability of an action with a word like *should*. Qualifiers may indicate different degrees of doubt with words such as *seems* or *might*. The box below contains a few examples of these kinds of words.

**Words That Qualify Ideas**

| | | | | | |
|---|---|---|---|---|---|
| all | could | likely | never | possibly, possible | sometimes |
| always | every | may | often | probably, probable | think |
| appear | has/have to | might | only | seem | usually |
| believe | it is believed | must | ought to | should | |

Remember that a sentence can include both fact and opinion. Authors use qualifiers to express opinions about facts.

**EXAMPLE** Read the following sentences. Underline the qualifiers.

1. Every citizen who wants to be informed about current events should subscribe to at least two newspapers and never miss the nightly news.
2. Amber, fossilized tree resin, was one of the first substances used for decoration; it is believed to exert a healthful influence on the endocrine system, spleen, and heart.

**EXPLANATION**

1. The qualifiers in this sentence are *every*, *should*, and *never*. The fact is that newspapers and the nightly news do cover current events, but these qualifiers express a personal opinion about this fact.
2. The qualifier in this sentence is the phrase *it is believed*. The author has signaled that what follows is not a proven fact, only a belief.

## PRACTICE 4

Read the following sentences. Underline the qualifiers.

1. While swimming, the woman suddenly disappeared from sight, possibly pulled underwater by an alligator.
2. You have to let me go to the annual New Year's Eve celebration in Times Square; everybody is going. I will be the only one who can't go.

## Think Carefully About Supposed "Facts"

Beware of **false facts,** or statements presented as facts that are actually untrue. At times, an author may mislead the reader with a false impression of the facts. Political and commercial advertisements often present facts out of context, exaggerate the facts, or give only some of the facts. For example, a retailer publishes the following claim in a local newspaper: "Batteries for $.10 each." However, the batteries are sold in packets of one hundred; they are not sold individually. Even though the advertisement told a partial truth, it misled consumers by leaving out an important fact. A truthful advertisement of the same situation states, "Batteries for $.10 each, sold only in packages of 100 for $10.00 per package."

Sometimes an author deliberately presents false information. Janet Cooke, a reporter for the *Washington Post,* concocted a false story about a boy named Jimmy, whom she described as "8 years old and a third-generation heroin addict," and whose ambition was to be a heroin dealer when he grew up. After she won a Pulitzer Prize for this story, it was learned that she had never met Jimmy and most of the details were simply not true. The *Washington Post* also learned that she had falsified facts on her résumé. She was fired, and the *Washington Post* returned the Pulitzer Prize. Cooke's use of false facts ruined her career and embarrassed the prestigious newspaper.

Read the following two examples of false facts:

1. The earliest humans lived at the same time as the dinosaurs.
2. The virus that causes mononucleosis, also known as the kissing disease, can be spread through the air.

Fossil records and scientific research have proved that the first statement is a false fact. The second statement is a false fact because the virus that causes mononucleosis can be spread only through contact with saliva. Often some prior knowledge of the topic is needed to identify false facts. The more you read, the more effective you will become at evaluating facts as true or false.

False facts can be used to mislead, persuade, or entertain. For example, read the following headline and four sentences published in the *National Enquirer* on March 2, 1976:

**Carol Burnett and Henry K. in Row**

> In a Washington restaurant, a boisterous Carol Burnett had a loud argument with another diner, Henry Kissinger. Then she traipsed around the place offering everyone a bite of her dessert. But Carol really raised eyebrows when she accidentally knocked a glass of wine over one diner and started giggling instead of apologizing. The guy wasn't amused and "accidentally" spilled a glass of water over Carol's dress.
>
> —*Carol Burnett* v. *National Enquirer, Inc.*

As a result of this article, Carol Burnett sued and won a settlement against the tabloid for making false statements. Note the value words the author used to describe Burnett's behavior: *boisterous, loud, traipsed, giggling,* and *raised eyebrows.*

### VISUAL VOCABULARY

What does the word **row** in the title of the paragraph about Carol Burnett and Henry K. mean?

Look up the different definitions of ***row*** in your dictionary.

1. Check two of the following words that mean roughly the same thing as the word *row* used in this sense.

   ___ propel ___ quarrel

   ___ brawl ___ convey

2. What pronunciation is given for *row* used in this sense? Select the word that *row* rhymes with.

   ___ cow ___ go

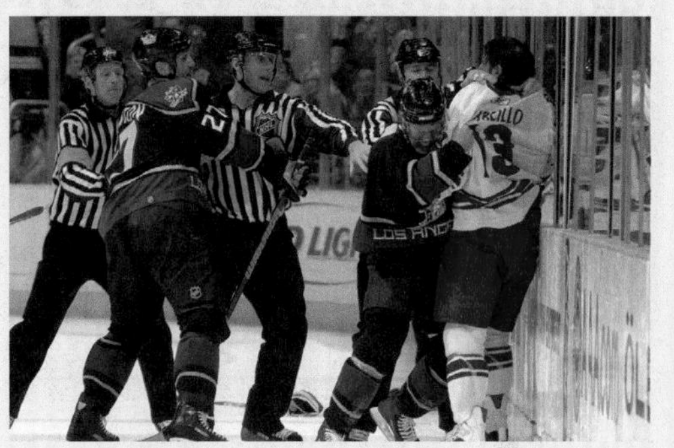

▲ The people in this photo are having a ***row***.

In addition to thinking carefully about false facts, beware of opinions stated to sound like facts. Remember that facts are specific details that can be researched and verified as true. However, opinions may be introduced as facts with phrases like "in truth," "the truth of the matter," or "in fact." Read the following two statements:

1. In point of fact, computers make life miserable.
2. Computers make life miserable; in point of fact, on November 2, 1988, Robert Morris sent out a computer "worm" that caused many computers around the country to crash. Damages to each computer ranged from $200 to $53,000.

—*United States* v. *Robert Morris*

The first statement is a general opinion that uses the value word *miserable*. The second statement is a blend of fact and opinion. It begins with a biased statement but then uses the phrase "in point of fact" to introduce factual details.

**EXAMPLES** Read the following statements, and mark each one as follows:

**F** if it states a fact

**O** if it expresses an opinion

**F/O** if it combines fact and opinion

_____ **1.** The syndicated television comedy *Friends* won numerous awards.

_____ **2.** The comedy *Friends* is still the funniest show on television.

_____ **3.** *Friends* has remained popular only because most television viewers have no taste.

_____ **4.** Nearly 700 Americans die of hypothermia each year.

_____ **5.** Because the alligator has been listed as an endangered species since 1976, killing alligators for their skins should be against the law.

**EXPLANATIONS**

1. **F:** This is a statement of fact that can be researched through news articles.
2. **O:** This is a statement of opinion that includes the biased word *funniest.*
3. **F/O:** This is a blend of fact and opinion. It is a fact that *Friends* is successful, but the statement also includes the biased words *only* and *no taste.*
4. **F:** This is a statement of fact that can be verified through research.
5. **F/O:** This statement blends fact and opinion. The biased word is *should.*

**EXAMPLE** Look at the cartoon. Then write one fact and one opinion about the cartoon.

Fact: ____________________________________________

____________________________________________

____________________________________________

Opinion: ____________________________________________

____________________________________________

____________________________________________

**EXPLANATION** Answers will vary; these are samples.

Fact: Tiger Woods has nothing to do with the General's duties.

Opinion: One of the female office workers is prettier than the other one.

## PRACTICE 5

**A.** Read the following statements, and mark each one as follows:

**F** if it states a fact

**O** if it expresses an opinion

**F/O** if it combines fact and opinion

_____ **1.** Unhealthy diets and lack of exercise are serious national problems; in fact, 300,000 deaths each year are linked to these two problems.

_____ **2.** Tobacco use kills more Americans than motor vehicle crashes, AIDS, cocaine use, heroin use, homicide, and suicide combined.

_____ **3.** Tobacco products should be outlawed.

_____ **4.** Diets high in fruits, vegetables, and fiber lower the risk for some types of cancer.

_____ **5.** Public schools ought to serve fruits and vegetables instead of pizza and hamburgers.

_____ **6.** Exercise is the only sure way to lose weight.

_____ **7.** Executives of tobacco companies murder millions of people with their products.

_____ **8.** All cancers caused by cigarette smoking could be prevented.

_____ **9.** The sugar glider, which is a small opossum, is smaller than a gerbil, larger than a mouse, and more adorable than a teddy bear.

_____ **10.** Pot-bellied pigs make great pets.

**B.** Read the following short reviews of destinations, restaurants, movies, and plays. Mark each one as follows:

**F** if it states a fact

**O** if it expresses an opinion

**F/O** if it combines fact and opinion

_____ **11.** The Palms Casino Resort in Las Vegas offers the absolute best in entertainment, restaurants, clubs, and spas.

_____ **12.** *The Lion King* is the story of a young lion cub named Simba who struggles to accept the responsibilities of adulthood and his destiny as king.

_____ **13.** The Nine Steakhouse, which serves prime aged steaks and imported spirits, is Chicago's most popular night spot.

_____ **14.** Set at the edge of Texas Hill Country on the Colorado River, Austin, the capital of Texas, offers many unexpected pleasures to the visitor.

_____ **15.** After pirates, hurricanes, and wars, Key West, Florida, survives as a great tourist town, with superb sunsets, informal living, wonderful festivals, relaxing beaches, top fishing possibilities, and all the services that a visitor could want.

_____ **16.** Wake up and break out of your old routine with breakfast at Sonic. Our one-of-a-kind breakfast menu offers a variety of tempting items like Toaster Sandwiches, breakfast burritos, smoothies and other morning favorites—all with the same, friendly Carhop service!

—Sonic, "Breakfast."

_____ **17.** Peter Jackson's Oscar-winning film of the *Lord of the Rings* epic by J. R. R. Tolkien remains one of the greatest achievements in cinema history.

_____ **18.** *Phantom of the Opera* is the longest-running production in Broadway history.

_____ **19.** Half of the land on Sanibel Island, Florida, is designated as natural areas, with two preserves protecting the island ecosystem and wildlife.

_____ **20.** The *Internet Movie Database* remains the ultimate source for movie and movie star information.

## Read Critically: Evaluate Details as Fact or Opinion in Context

Because the printed word seems to give authority to an idea, many of us accept what we read as fact. Yet much of what is published is actually opinion. Effective readers question what they read. Reading critically is noting the use of fact and opinion in the context of a paragraph or passage, the author, and the type of source in which the passage is printed.

### Evaluate the Context of the Passage

**EXAMPLE** Read the passage, and identify each sentence as follows:

**F** if it states a fact

**O** if it expresses an opinion

**F/O** if it combines fact and opinion

**Alexander the Great**

[1]Alexander III, more commonly known as Alexander the Great, was one of the greatest military leaders in world history. [2]He was born in Pella, Macedonia. [3]The exact date of his birth was probably July 20 or 26, 356 B.C. [4]Shortly before his 33rd birthday, Alexander the Great died. [5]The cause of his death remains unknown.

**1.** _____ **2.** _____ **3.** _____ **4.** _____ **5.** _____

**EXPLANATION**

1. **F/O:** His name and title are factual, but the value word *greatest* is an opinion with which some people may disagree.
2. **F:** This statement can be verified in historical records.

3. **O:** The word *probably* makes this a statement of opinion.

4. **F:** This statement can be checked and verified as true.

5. **F:** This is a factual statement that something isn't known.

## PRACTICE 6

**A.** Read the passage, and identify each sentence as follows:

**F** if it states a fact
**O** if it expresses an opinion
**F/O** if it combines fact and opinion

### Segway: An Invention That Moves People

[1]Dean Kamen's invention of the Segway may change modern life. [2]"This is the world's first self-balancing human transporter," Kamen said. [3]"You stand on this Segway Human Transporter and you think forward and then you go forward; if you think backward, you go backward." [4]The transporter, which can go up to 12 miles an hour, looks more like a lawn mower than a scooter and has no brakes; it is designed to mimic the human body's ability to maintain its balance. [5]Riders control the speed and direction of the device simply by shifting their weight and using a manual turning mechanism on one of the handlebars. [6]Bob Metcalf, a computer engineer who helped create the building blocks for the Internet, endorses the Segway. [7]"I've seen it," Metcalf said, "and it is more important than pantyhose, and it's more important than the Internet." [8]The Segway can take its rider up to 15 miles on a six-hour charge from a regular wall socket. [9]The machine is an environmentally friendly alternative to cars. [10]In the future the devices will replace cars in urban centers.

—Adapted from ABC News, "'IT' Gets Around."

1. _____ 2. _____ 3. _____ 4. _____ 5. _____

6. _____ 7. _____ 8. _____ 9. _____ 10. _____

**B.** Now that you have read the article about the Segway, study the picture of one on the next page. Provide a caption that combines fact and opinion.

______________________________

______________________________

______________________________

## Evaluate the Context of the Author

Even though opinions can't be proved true like facts can, many opinions are still sound and valuable. To judge the accuracy of the opinion, you must consider the source, the author of the opinion. Authors offer two types of valid opinions: informed opinions and expert opinions.

> An author develops an **informed opinion** by gathering and analyzing evidence.
> An author develops an **expert opinion** through much training and extensive knowledge in a given field.

**EXAMPLE** Read the topic and study the list of authors who have written their opinions about the topic. Identify each person as **IO** if he or she is more likely to offer an informed opinion and **EO** if he or she is more likely to offer an expert opinion.

**How to Discipline a Toddler**

_____ **1.** Dr. James Dobson, psychologist and best selling author of *Dare to Discipline,* giving advice on his daily radio show *Focus on the Family*

_____ **2.** An advice columnist such as Ann Landers or Dear Abby responding to a reader's question

_____ **3.** A pediatrician giving advice to the parents of one of his patients

_____ **4.** A high school science teacher who writes a lesson plan about disciplining children for a unit on human development in a health class

**EXPLANATION**

1. Dr. Dobson is considered to be an expert opinion in the field of childrearing. One way to identify an expert opinion is to note if the person giving the opinion holds an advanced degree or title or has published articles or books about the topic being discussed. Dobson has both the education and the achievement of being a successful author about this topic.
2. Advice columnists offer informed opinions on a wide range of topics. They often cite experts in their advice.
3. A pediatrician is a medical doctor for children. A pediatrician has had extensive training in childhood development.
4. A health teacher offers an informed opinion based on research to prepare the lesson. The teacher's main field is not childhood development, but science.

## Evaluate the Context of the Source

Often people turn to factual sources to find the factual details needed to form informed opinions and expert opinions. A medical dictionary, an English handbook, and a world atlas are a few excellent examples of factual sources.

**EXAMPLE** Read the passage, and then answer the questions that follow it.

### Statement by the Secretary of the Norwegian Nobel Committee

[1]There are more than 300 peace prizes in the world. [2]None is in any way as well known and as highly respected as the Nobel Peace Prize. [3]The *Oxford Dictionary of Twentieth-Century World History*, to cite just one example, states that the Nobel Peace Prize is "the world's most prestigious prize awarded for the 'preservation of peace.'" [4]Personally, I think there are many reasons for this prestige: the long history of the Peace Prize; the fact that it belongs to a family of prizes, the Nobel family, where all the family members benefit from the relationship; the growing political independence of the Norwegian Nobel Committee; and the monetary value of the prize, particularly in the early years and in the most recent years of its history. [5]One important element of the history of the prize has been the committee's broad definition of peace.

—Adapted from Lundestad, "The Nobel Peace Prize, 1901–2000," p. 163.

______ **1.** Sentence 1 is a
a. fact. b. opinion.

______ **2.** The *Oxford Dictionary of Twentieth-Century World History* in sentence 3 serves as
a. an informed opinion. b. factual resource.

______ **3.** Sentence 4 states
a. a fact. b. an expert opinion.

**EXPLANATION**

1. Sentence 1 is a statement of fact.
2. In sentence 3, the *Oxford Dictionary of Twentieth-Century World History* serves as a factual resource on which expert and informed opinions are based.
3. Sentence 4 is the author's expert opinion backed up by facts. As the secretary of the Norwegian Nobel Committee, Lundestad offers a list of fact-based reasons to back up his personal, expert opinion.

## PRACTICE 7

Read the passage, and then answer the questions that follow it.

> [1]Dreams, those mysterious worlds we enter once we fall asleep, have fascinated humankind for generations. [2]According to the *Grolier Encyclopedia of Knowledge*, dream interpretation dates back to 2000 B.C. [3]People in ancient Greece, Rome, Egypt, and China recorded and studied their dreams. [4]Views on dreams have been as varied and as vivid as the cultures of the people who have studied them. [5]Some believed dreams to be messages from God. [6]Others thought them to be signs of indigestion. [7]Neil Carlson and William Buskist, authors of the textbook *Psychology: The Science of Behavior,* state that people have long used dreams to wage war, predict the future, or detect the guilt or innocence of people accused of a crime. [8]Sigmund Freud, noted psychiatrist, believed that dreams are connected to our subconscious; he believed that our dreams are the result of emotions and desires we cannot express while awake. [9]Carl Jung, a widely published psychologist who studied under Freud, thought dreams were a way to work out problems we face in our waking lives. [10]No matter what the truth is, one-third of our life is spent dreaming, which adds up to a total of 27 years of our lifetime. [11]And everybody dreams!

_____ **1.** Sentence 1 is
a. a fact. b. an opinion.

_____ **2.** In sentence 2, the *Grolier Encyclopedia of Knowledge* offers
a. a factual source. b. an opinion.

_____ **3.** Sentence 2 is
a. a fact. b. an opinion.

_____ **4.** In sentence 8, Sigmund Freud's ideas are
a. fact. b. expert opinion.

_____ **5.** In sentence 9, Carl Jung's ideas are
a. fact. b. expert opinion.

_____ **6.** Overall, this paragraph serves as
a. a factual resource.
b. an informed opinion.
c. an expert opinion.

**VISUAL VOCABULARY**

The names of Freud's and Jung's professions share a prefix and a suffix. What are they?

What does each mean? Use your dictionary if necessary to fill in the blanks.

Prefix: ______________________

Meaning: ______________________

Suffix : ______________________

Meaning: ______________________

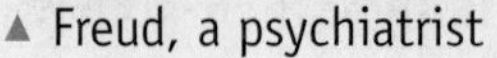
▲ Freud, a psychiatrist

▲ Jung, a psychologist

Textbook Skills

## Fact and Opinion in Textbook Passages

Most textbook authors are careful to present only ideas based on observation, research, and expert opinion. Read the following passage from a college health textbook, and identify each sentence as follows:

**F** if it states a fact

**O** if it expresses an opinion

**F/O** if it combines fact and opinion

**EXAMPLE** **Safety Guidelines During Weight Training**

[1]During a weight training program, the following guidelines should be followed. [2]First, when you use free weights (like barbells), spotters or helpers should assist you as you perform an exercise. [3]They can help if you are unable to complete a lift. [4]Second, tightening the collars on the end of the bars of free weights prevents the weights from falling off. [5]Dropping weight plates on toes and feet can result in serious injuries. [6]Third, warming up before weightlifting protects muscles from injuries. [7]Finally, using slow movements during weightlifting is a wise approach. [8]Debate among experts continues as to whether high-speed weightlifting is superior to slow-speed lifting in terms of strength gains. [9]However, slow movements may reduce the risk of injury. [10]And slow movement during weightlifting does increase muscle size and strength.

—Adapted from Powers & Dodd, *Total Fitness and Wellness*, 3rd ed., p. 111.

**1.** _____ **2.** _____ **3.** _____ **4.** _____ **5.** _____

**6.** _____ **7.** _____ **8.** _____ **9.** _____ **10.** _____

**EXPLANATION** Compare your answers to the ones below.

1. **O:** The word *should* indicates that this is an opinion or a suggestion. However, keep in mind that textbook authors offer information based on a great deal of research. This particular textbook lists the resources the authors used to form their opinions. This statement is therefore an expert opinion.
2. **O:** The word *should* indicates an opinion.
3. **F:** This is a statement of fact about what spotters can do.
4. **F:** This is a statement of fact that is supported by observation.
5. **F:** This is a statement of fact that can be verified by research and observation.
6. **F:** This is a statement of fact that can be verified through research. In fact, this textbook offers a list of expert and factual sources at the end of the chapter so that students can research the ideas for themselves.
7. **O:** This is an expert opinion based on research. The following sentences state facts to support this opinion.

**8.** **F:** This is a statement of fact. Experts do debate which method is best. This sentence does not favor one method over the other; it notes there is a debate and states both sides.

**9.** **F/O:** This is a statement that qualifies the facts. The facts can be verified through research and observation; however, the verb "may" indicates that results can vary.

**10.** **F:** This is a statement of fact that can be verified through research and observation.

## PRACTICE 8

**A.** Read the following passage from a college history textbook. Then identify each sentence as follows:

**F** if it states a fact

**O** if it expresses an opinion

**F/O** if it combines fact and opinion

Textbook Skills

### The TV President

[1]John Fitzgerald Kennedy was made for television. [2]His tall, lean body gave him the strong vertical line that cameras love, and his weather-beaten good looks appealed to women without intimidating men. [3]He had a full head of hair, and even in the winter he maintained a tan. [4]Complementing his appearance was his attitude. [5]He was always "cool" in public. [6]This too was tailor-made for the "cool medium," television. [7]Wit, irony, and understatement, all delivered with a studied ease, translate well on television. [8]Table-thumping, impassioned speech, and even earnest sincerity often just do not work on television.

[9]The first presidential debate was held in Chicago on September 26, 1960, only a little more than a month before the election. [10]Richard Nixon arrived looking ill and weak. [11]During the previous six weeks, he had banged his kneecap, which became infected, and he had spent several weeks in the hospital. [12]Then he caught a bad cold that left him hoarse and weak. [13]By the day of the debate, he looked like a nervous corpse. [14]He was pale, 20 pounds underweight, and haggard. [15]Makeup experts offered to hide his heavy beard and soften his jaw line, but Nixon accepted only a thin coat of Max Factor's "Lazy Shave," a pancake makeup base.

[16]Kennedy looked better, very much better. [17]He didn't need any makeup to appear healthy, nor did he need special lighting to hide a weak

profile. [18]He did, however, change suits. [19]He believed that a dark blue suit rather than a gray suit would look better under the bright lights. [20]Kennedy was right, of course, as anyone who watches a nightly news program realizes.

[21]When the debate started, Kennedy spoke first. [22]Although he was nervous, he slowed down his delivery. [23]His face was controlled and smooth. [24]He smiled with his eyes and perhaps the corners of his mouth, and his laugh was a mere suggestion of a laugh. [25]His body language was perfect.

[26]Nixon fought back. [27]He perspired, scored debating points, gave memorized facts, and struggled to win. [28]But his efforts were "hot"—bad for television. [29]Viewers saw a nervous, uncertain man, one whose clothes did not fit and whose face looked pasty and white.

[30]After the debate, Kennedy inched ahead of Nixon in a Gallup poll. [31]Most of the people who were undecided before watching the debate ended up voting for Kennedy.

—Adapted from Martin et al., *America and Its Peoples: A Mosaic in the Making*, 3rd ed., pp. 1001–02.

_____ **1.** His tall, lean body gave him the strong vertical line that cameras love, and his weather-beaten good looks appealed to women without intimidating men.

_____ **2.** The first presidential debate was held in Chicago on September 26, 1960, only a little more than a month before the election.

_____ **3.** During the previous six weeks, he had banged his kneecap, which became infected, and he had spent several weeks in the hospital.

_____ **4.** By the day of the debate, he looked like a nervous corpse.

_____ **5.** He was pale, 20 pounds underweight, and haggard.

_____ **6.** Kennedy looked better, very much better.

_____ **7.** He did, however, change suits.

**B.** Study the two pictures, and read the caption below them. Then identify each sentence based on the pictures as follows:

**F** if it states a fact

**O** if it expresses an opinion

**F/O** if it combines fact and opinion

▲ Tom Torlino, a Navajo Indian, photographed before and after his "assimilation." Torlino attended the Carlisle Indian School in Pennsylvania.

_____ **8.** Some Native Americans gave up their traditional dress to fit into white society.

_____ **9.** Native American men adorned themselves with long hair and jewelry.

_____ **10.** Tom Torlino was more handsome dressed in his native attire than in white attire.

## Chapter Review

Test your understanding of what you have read in this chapter by filling in each blank with a word or phrase from the box. Use each choice once.

| | | |
|---|---|---|
| biased words | informed opinion | scientific method |
| expert opinion | interprets | states |
| fact | opinion | unbiased words |

1. A _______________ is a specific detail that is true based on objective proof.
2. An _______________ is an interpretation, value judgment, or belief that cannot be proved or disproved.
3. Objective proof can be physical evidence, an eyewitness account, or the result of an accepted _______________.
4. An _______________ is developed by gathering and analyzing evidence.

**5.** An _______________ is developed through much training and extensive knowledge in a given field.

**6.** A fact _______________ reality.

**7.** An opinion _______________ reality.

**8.** A fact uses _______________.

**9.** An opinion uses _______________.

_____ **10.** Which of the following is a qualifier?

a. percent
b. probably
c. measurement

## Applications

### Application 1: Fact and Opinion

The accompanying graph comes from a health textbook. Study the graph, and label each statement based on the graph as follows:

**F** if it states a fact

**O** if it expresses an opinion

**F/O** if it combines fact and opinion

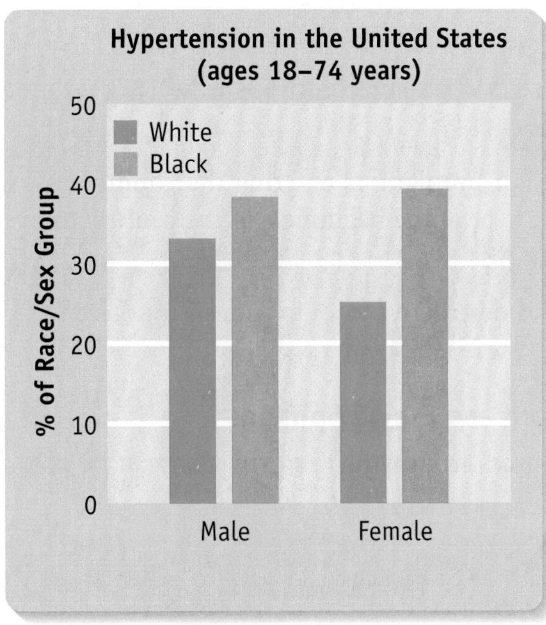


◄ The occurrence of hypertension (high blood pressure) in selected groups in the United States.

—Reprinted from Scott K. Powers and Stephen L. Dodd, *Total Fitness and Wellness,* 3rd ed. Figure 9.6. © Benjamin Cummings, 2003.

______ **1.** The occurrence of hypertension in the United States is remarkably high.

______ **2.** More men suffer from hypertension than women do.

______ **3.** More blacks suffer from hypertension than whites do.

______ **4.** Because hypertension affects so many adults between the ages of 18 and 74, the federal government should fund research for prevention and treatment.

### Application 2: **Opinions, Biased Words, and Qualifiers**

Read the following statements. Underline any biased words or qualifiers that are used. Then mark each statement as follows:

**F** if it states a fact

**O** if it expresses an opinion

**F/O** if it combines fact and opinion

______ **1.** Created in 1977, the perfume Opium has a sickening scent.

______ **2.** You are probably most attracted to the people who live or work close to you.

______ **3.** Violence linked to organized crime in the 1830s can be traced to several causes.

______ **4.** The number of immigrants entering the country rose alarmingly from 5,000 a year at the beginning of the century to over 50,000 a year in the 1830s.

______ **5.** Television is a destructive force in American society.

### Application 3: **Informed and Expert Opinions**

Following is a list of sources from which information can be obtained. Label each source as follows:

**IO** if it offers an informed opinion

**EO** if it offers an expert opinion

**FS** if it is a factual source

______ **1.** *World Book Encyclopedia*

______ **2.** A carefully researched and documented student essay about global warming

______ **3.** *Webster's Dictionary*

______ **4.** A statement about current fashion trends by a newly trained salesperson in the men's department at a major department store.

______ **5.** A family physician's recommendation for treatment of cancer

______ **6.** An English teacher's advice about the best way to write an essay

______ **7.** A college course catalog

______ **8.** A newspaper medical advice column written by a physician

______ **9.** A statement about football by Super Bowl–winning coach Jon Gruden

______ **10.** Botany.com, the Encyclopedia of Flowers and Plants, an online resource about gardening

# REVIEW Test 1

## Fact and Opinion

**A.** Read the following statements, and mark each one as follows:

**F** if it states a fact

**O** if it expresses an opinion

**F/O** if it combines fact and opinion

______ **1.** Government should do more to help the poor and needy.

______ **2.** Affirmative action programs give preference to qualified African Americans, women, and other minorities.

______ **3.** Denying welfare benefits to unwed mothers is not likely to affect the number of children born out of wedlock.

______ **4.** In 1998, one-third of all births were to unmarried women.

______ **5.** By 2020, more than one in five children in the United States will be of Hispanic origin; Spanish should therefore be a required subject for all school children.

**B.** Study the graph and its accompanying text. Then read the statements that follow it, based on the given information. Mark each statement as follows:

**F** if it states a fact

**O** if it expresses an opinion

**F/O** if it combines fact and opinion

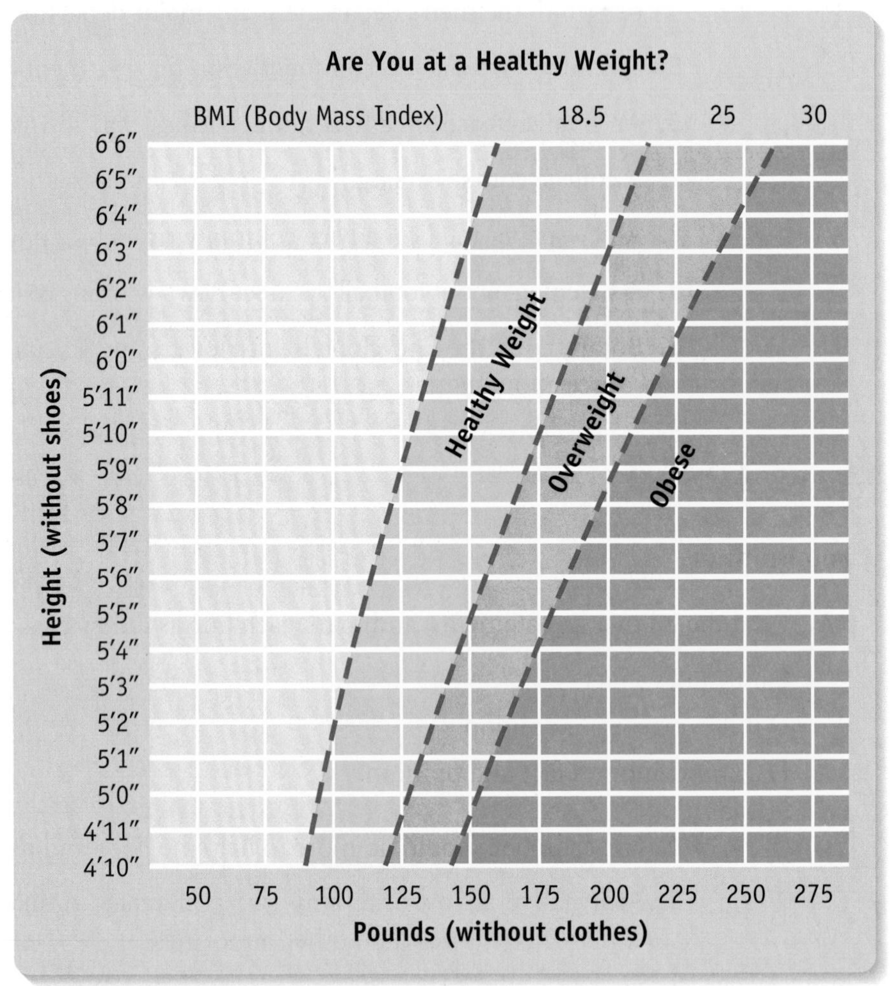


—Bren, Linda. "Losing Weight: Start By Counting Calories." *FDA Consumer* April 2004. 3 April 2007. U.S. Food and Drug Administration. <http://www.cfsan.fda.gov/~dms/fdweigh3.html>.

_____ **6.** The higher a person's BMI, the greater the risks for health problems.

_____ **7.** A 5′ 7″ person who weighs 175 lbs. is overweight.

_____ **8.** A 5′ 10″ person who weighs 225 lbs is obese due to bad eating habits.

_____ **9.** Obesity is the result of moral choices.

_____ **10.** A BMI of 30 or above indicates obesity.

**C.** Read the passage. Then identify each sentence as follows:

**F** if it states a fact

**O** if it expresses an opinion

**F/O** if it combines fact and opinion

**The Senior Market: A New Image of Aging**

[11]A few years ago a young market researcher sat down with three senior executives: one from a cosmetics firm, one from an egg producing plant, and one from a panty hose company. [12]She explained that she wanted to study the spending patterns of older people. [13]The executives laughed at her idea.

[14]Executives from companies like these might respond differently today. [15]Business has discovered the older market. [16]Economists tell us that older people today make up the richest generation of older people in history. [17]As a group they sit on a pile of wealth that includes their homes, pensions, savings, investments, and in some cases income from work. [18]Most likely, the older market will grow in the future. [19]But few companies have an idea of how to attract this older consumer. [20]Attempts to target this market have done poorly.

—Adapted from Novak, *Issues in Aging: An Introduction to Gerontology*, 1997.

**11.** _____ **12.** _____ **13.** _____ **14.** _____ **15.** _____

**16.** _____ **17.** _____ **18.** _____ **19.** _____ **20.** _____

# REVIEW Test 2

## Fact and Opinion

**A.** Read the following statements, and mark each one as follows:

**F** if it states a fact

**O** if it expresses an opinion

**F/O** if it combines fact and opinion

_____ **1.** The Super Bowl is the most watched show on television.

_____ **2.** The Super Bowl is America's favorite sporting event.

_____ **3.** In an open society such as the United States, secrecy in government is difficult to maintain, or should be.

_____ **4.** Hollywood exports movies to all parts of the world.

_____ **5.** Hollywood is to blame for the worldwide view that Americans are immoral and selfish.

_____ **6.** *Letter to My Mother* by Edith Bruck is an extraordinary incisive retelling of her life in wartime Auschwitz. It is one of the most important and impressive works of its kind. This book is a necessary and urgent read.

_____ **7.** In 1837, Michigan became the 26th state.

_____ **8.** The Hispanic population is one of the fastest-growing groups in America.

_____ **9.** Doctors fear that they will not be able to offer quality services due to the looming crisis caused by the rising costs of malpractice insurance.

_____ **10.** Doctors should not strike because of insurance malpractice issues.

**B.** Following is a list of sources from which information can be obtained. Label each source as follows:

**IO** if it offers an informed opinion

**EO** if it offers an expert opinion

**FS** if it is a factual source

_____ **11.** Sheehy, Gail. (1992). *The Silent Passage: Menopause.* New York: Morrow.

_____ **12.** A college mathematics textbook

_____ **13.** A friend who has recently researched the best bargain for a flat-screen television

_____ **14.** Internal Revenue Service. (1994). *Your Federal Income Tax* (Publication 17). Washington, D.C.: U.S. Government Printing Office.

_____ **15.** A college history teacher with 25 years of experience

_____ **16.** The Modern Language Association's *Handbook for Writers of Research Papers*, 6th ed., 2003.

______ **17.** A student research essay on the collapse of communism

______ **18.** Randolph, J. (1992). "Recycling of Materials." In *The New Grolier Multimedia Encyclopedia.* [CD-ROM]. Danbury, Conn.: Grolier Electronic.

______ **19.** A syllabus for a college course

______ **20.** Roger Ebert, film critic for the *Chicago Sun-Times* and host of his own television show that reviews movies called *Ebert and Roeper at the Movies*

# REVIEW Test 3

## Fact and Opinion

**A.** Read the following statements, and mark each one as follows:

**F** if it states a fact

**O** if it expresses an opinion

**F/O** if it combines fact and opinion

______ **1.** Florida offers its residents a mild year-round climate.

______ **2.** Florida is a paradise for senior citizens.

______ **3.** California is the birthplace of many radical ideas.

______ **4.** California struggles with immigration because it shares a border with Mexico.

______ **5.** The borders of the United States should not be as open as they are.

**B.** Read the following short reviews. Mark each one as follows:

**F** if it states only facts

**O** if it expresses opinions

**F/O** if it combines fact and opinion

______ **6.** *Catch Me If You Can* by Frank W. Abagnale with Stan Redding (Broadway, $14.95). Paperback.

______ **7.** *Wrapped in Rainbows* by Valerie Boyd (Scribner, $30.00; 527 pages). A splendid biography of Zora Neal Hurston. Boyd unravels many of the secrets in the life of the famed African American author.

_____ **8.** *"P" is for Peril* by Sue Grafton (Putnam, $26.95). Like all Grafton's alphabet mysteries featuring female sleuth Kinsey Malone, "*P*" will leave you panting for more!

_____ **9.** *Almanac of the 50 States* (Burlington, VT: Information Publications, 1985–). Annual. (Arizona State University owns 1985–. Latest year in Reference; earlier years in Journals.) This handy one-volume source is a collection of many different statistics collected by the U.S. government agencies and various business sources.

_____ **10.** *Gallup Poll Monthly*. Princeton, N.J.: Gallup Organization; http://www.gallup.com. A Web-based version of the Gallup poll, which has been in existence for over 70 years. An excellent source for important social issues and attitudes in the United States. The surveys come with large tables and helpful graphs and analyses.

**C.** Read the movie review. Then identify each sentence as follows:

**F** if it states a fact

**O** if it expresses an opinion

**F/O** if it combines fact and opinion

[11]The film **300** is based on the graphic novel by Frank Miller. [12]The film is a ferocious retelling of the ancient Battle of Thermopylae. [13]In this battle, King Leonidas (played by Gerard Butler) and 300 Spartans fight to their death against Xerxes and his massive Persian army. [14]Facing insurmountable odds, their valor and sacrifice inspire all of Greece to unite against their Persian enemy. [15]The film is an epic and awesome experience. [16]The film brings Miller's acclaimed graphic novel to life by combining live action with virtual backgrounds. [17]The film captures the author's distinct version of this ancient historical tale. [18]Fierce and formidable, the Spartans are one of the most mysterious cultures in history. [19]The Spartan warriors represent a type of hero that the world has never seen before. [20]**300** isn't just a movie; it's the next step in filmmaking.

**11.** _____ **12.** _____ **13.** _____ **14.** _____ **15.** _____

**16.** _____ **17.** _____ **18.** _____ **19.** _____ **20.** _____

# REVIEW Test 4

## Fact and Opinion

Textbook Skills

Before you read the following passage from a psychology textbook, skim the passage and answer the **Before Reading** questions. Read the passage. Then answer the **After Reading** questions.

### Vocabulary Preview

*ritual* (4): formal process or procedure
*charismatic* (6): appealing, fascinating
*dictates* (8): orders, commands
*celibate* (11): refraining from sex
*omnipotence* (19): state of being all-powerful
*omniscience* (19): state of being all-knowing
*coercive* (21): using force
*litany* (28): long list

### Why Do People Join Cults?

[1]Cults have no doubt forced themselves into your awareness in recent years. [2]Their extreme, often bizarre behaviors are widely covered in the media. [3]In the United States, 39 members of Heaven's Gate committed suicide in March 1997. [4]They did so in an orderly **ritual** that was planned by their leader. [5]Nearly 20 years earlier, more than 900 American citizens committed mass suicide-murder in a jungle compound in Guyana. [6]They did so at the urging of their **charismatic** leader, Reverend Jim Jones. [7]In France, Canada, and Switzerland, members of The Order of the Solar Temple also took their lives in **ritualized** cult deaths. [8]Meanwhile, in Japan, members of Aum Shin Rikyo gased subway riders, and they had planned mass destruction to fulfill the **dictates** of their cult leader. [9]Beyond these clearly dramatic examples, there are members of literally thousands of groups that qualify as cults. [10]They give total loyalty to their groups and leaders. [11]Members obey every command: they marry a partner they have never met in mass ceremonies; beg, recruit, work long hours for no pay; give all their money and possessions to the group; or become **celibate.**

[12]Can you imagine doing such things? [13]Are there any circumstances under which you would join a cult and become subject to the pressures that cults bring to bear on their members? [14]Obviously, most of you would say, "No way!" [15]But as psychologists, our task is to understand how such groups

and leaders develop their coercive power and to recognize the conditions that make many people at risk to their persuasive message.

[16]So what exactly are cults? [17]Cults vary widely in their activities, but they typically are nontraditional religious groups led by a strict, controlling leader who is the sole source of the group's thoughts, beliefs, and actions. [18]This leader is often charismatic, filled with energy and intense dedication. [19]And sometimes he or she claims special godlike powers of **omnipotence, omniscience,** and immortality. [20]Despite differences in the traits of particular cult groups, what is common are the recruiting promises. [21]The group's **coercive** power undercuts the personal exercise of free will and critical thinking of its members.

[22]Why, then, would people want to join a cult? [23]First of all, no one ever joins a *cult*, as such. [24]People join interesting groups to fulfill their pressing needs. [25]The groups are known as cults later on when they are seen as deceptive, dangerous, or opposing society's basic values. [26]Cults become appealing when they promise to fulfill an individual's personal needs. [27]The need may be for instant friendship, an identity, or an organized daily agenda. [28]Cults also promise to make up for a **litany** of societal failures. [29]By eliminating people's feelings of isolation and alienation, cults make their slice of the world safe, healthy, caring, predictable, and controllable. [30]Cult leaders offer simple solutions to a complex world by offering a path to happiness, success, and salvation.

[31]Although the mass suicides of cult members make media headlines, most cults operate quietly to achieve their goals. [32]When they deliver on their promises, they can serve a valuable function for some people by helping fill voids in their lives. [33]But when they are deceptive, coercive, and distort basic values of freedom, independence, and critical thinking, they become dangerous to members and to society. [34]One question worth raising is, Can society provide what most cults promise so they need not become an alternate lifestyle for so many people throughout the world?

—Adapted from Gerrig & Zimbardo, *Psychology and Life,* 16th ed., p. 588.

## BEFORE READING

### Vocabulary in Context

_____ **1.** What does the word **ritualized** mean in sentence 7?

a. violent
b. senseless
c. organized
d. dramatic

### Topic

______ **2.** The topic of this passage is
a. the benefits of joining a cult.
b. reasons to legally ban cults.
c. cults, what they are and why people join.
d. cults, freedom of religious expression.

## AFTER READING

### Central Idea

______ **3.** The central idea of the article is stated in paragraph
a. 1 (sentences 1–11).
b. 2 (sentences 12–15).
c. 4 (sentences 22–30).
d. 5 (sentences 31–34).

### Supporting Details

______ **4.** According to the authors, people join cults when
a. they want to commit suicide.
b. they are in need.
c. they are deceptive.
d. they need to control others.

### Transitions

______ **5.** The relationship of ideas between sentence 27 and sentence 28 is one of
a. cause and effect.
b. time order.
c. contrast.
d. addition.

### Thought Patterns

______ **6.** The thought pattern for the first paragraph of the passage (sentences 1–11) is one of
a. cause and effect.
b. time order.
c. examples.
d. contrast.

### Implied Main Ideas

______ **7.** Which of the following best states the implied main idea of paragraph 4 (sentences 22–30)?
a. Cults offer security.
b. People join cults for a variety of reasons.
c. Loneliness is the major reason people join cults.
d. People who fail at life join cults.

## Fact and Opinion

_____ **8.** Sentence 1 of the article is
a. fact.
b. opinion.
c. a mixture of fact and opinion.

_____ **9.** Sentence 5 is
a. fact.
b. opinion.
c. a mixture of fact and opinion.

_____ **10.** Sentence 23 is
a. fact.
b. opinion.
c. a mixture of fact and opinion.

## EFFECTIVE READER Scorecard

### Fact and Opinion

| Test | Number Correct | | Points | | Score |
|---|---|---|---|---|---|
| Review Test 1 | _____ | × | 5 | = | _____ |
| Review Test 2 | _____ | × | 5 | = | _____ |
| Review Test 3 | _____ | × | 5 | = | _____ |
| Review Test 4 | _____ | × | 10 | = | _____ |
| Review Test 5 (website) | _____ | × | 5 | = | _____ |
| Review Test 6 (website) | _____ | × | 5 | = | _____ |

Enter your scores on the Effective Reader Scorecard: Chapter 9 Review Tests inside the back cover.

## After Reading About Fact and Opinion

Before you move on to the mastery tests on fact and opinion, take time to reflect on your learning and performance by answering the following questions. Write your answers in your notebook.

### Your Reading Skills

What did I learn about fact and opinion?

What do I need to remember about fact and opinion?

How has my knowledge base or prior knowledge about fact and opinion changed?

## More Review and Mastery Tests

For more practice, go to the book's website at **http://ablongman.com/henry/** and click on *The Effective Reader.* Then select "More Review and Mastery Tests." The tests are organized by chapter.

## MASTERY Test 1

Name ______________________ Section __________

Date __________ **Score** (number correct) ______ × 5 = ______%

**A.** Read the following statements, and mark each one as follows:

**F** if it states a fact

**O** if it expresses an opinion

**F/O** if it combines fact and opinion

_____ **1.** Hydrogen is a perfect fuel and is undoubtedly the best that will be available for future use.

_____ **2.** In the United States, 39 states run lotteries to raise funds; this practice is immoral and should be stopped.

_____ **3.** Over 50 percent of Americans participate in state lotteries.

_____ **4.** State lotteries lure people who are poor and uneducated into playing by promising a quick way to get rich.

_____ **5.** Lotteries, which raise billions of dollars, are the only way for state governments to raise money for education and other services.

_____ **6.** Many of the people who play state lotteries have average to above-average levels of income and education.

_____ **7.** Road traffic is a growing source of pollution in Europe.

_____ **8.** Gas-guzzling cars account for half the oil consumed in the United States.

_____ **9.** Sport utility vehicles (SUVs) should be heavily taxed by the government because they require so much gasoline.

_____ **10.** The drawbacks of automobiles far outweigh their benefits.

**B.** Read the following short reviews. Mark each one as follows:

**F** if it states only facts

**O** if it expresses opinions

**F/O** if it combines fact and opinion

______ **11.** Three times the danger! Three times the drama! Three times the enjoyment! Fast-paced and action-packed, *Driving Dangerous* will air for the first time on television Thursday night at 9 P.M. and run for three nights in a row, same time, same channel.

______ **12.** Outrageously fun and funny, don't miss *Blades of Glory* with Will Farrell and Jon Heder as two disgraced Olympic ice skaters who were banned from the sport but agree to perform together in the pairs figure skating category to get back into the competition.

______ **13.** *Meet the Press* is the longest running United States television series.

______ **14.** *American Idol* exploits people who have no talent for the sake of high ratings.

______ **15.** Jennifer Hudson is the most talented and successful singer to have appeared on *American Idol.*

**C.** Study the advertisement for a lost dog prepared to run in a local newspaper and fliers. Then identify each item from the ad as follows:

**F** if it states a fact

**O** if it expresses an opinion

**F/O** if it combines fact and opinion

**Our Dog, Brutus, is missing!**

[16]Our dog, Brutus is missing! [17]Brutus weighs four pounds and is a tan-colored Chihuahua. [18]Although he is a swift-moving little dog with a saucy personality, he has been well-trained. [19]Therefore, he should obey the command "come." [20]We are offering a $100 reward for his safe return.

______ **16.** Our dog, Brutus, is missing!

______ **17.** Brutus weighs four pounds and is a tan-colored Chihuahua.

______ **18.** Although he is a swift-moving little dog with a saucy personality, he has been well-trained.

______ **19.** Therefore, he should obey the command "come."

______ **20.** We are offering a $100 reward for his safe return.

MASTERY **Test 2**

Name ______________________ Section __________

Date __________ **Score** (number correct) ______ × 5 = ______%

**A.** Read the following statements, and mark each one as follows:

**F** if it states a fact

**O** if it expresses an opinion

**F/O** if it combines fact and opinion

______ **1.** Don't take Math 101 from Dr. Harvey; he gives too much homework.

______ **2.** The college catalog states that two semesters of English and math are required.

______ **3.** Small dogs such as toy poodles make annoying pets.

______ **4.** Animals have a positive effect on shut-ins such as the elderly in nursing homes and children with serious illnesses who face long hospital stays.

______ **5.** Hip-hop music is the authentic voice of people oppressed by social injustice.

______ **6.** Maya Angelou, Toni Morrison, and Oprah Winfrey are the three most influential African American women of their generation.

______ **7.** African American scientists have made significant contributions through inventions and discoveries.

______ **8.** It is not wise to get medical advice from online sources.

______ **9.** Several types of cancer have been linked to diet.

______ **10.** Airlines should weigh everyone who travels by air to ensure everyone's safety.

**B.** Read the following advertisements for used cars. Mark each one as follows:

**F** if it states only facts

**O** if it expresses opinions

**F/O** if it combines fact and opinion

______ **11.** 2006 Nissan Maxima GLE. Black, V6 3.0 liter, automatic, black leather interior, A/C, power windows, power locks, dual heated seats, cruise control, Bose sound system with CD, sliding sun roof, alloy wheels. Excellent condition. 38,000 miles. $19,900.

_____ **12.** Well kept SUV, Aztec Red. Mostly highway miles. Still has plastic under floor mats—A MUST SEE! 29,300 miles. $21,500.

_____ **13.** 2006 1500 Silverado. Truck is in excellent condition. Contains LS Decor package, 5300V8 engine with reclining bucket seats & armrest, all power locks, alarm system, includes towing special equip. package, CD player, aluminum alloy wheels, etc. Has sprayed bed liner with fiberglass tonneau cover. Black and pewter color—very nice appearance with smooth ride. 21,000 miles. $20,995.

_____ **14.** 1994 Corvette. White with tan leather seats, automatic, A/C, 80,500 miles. $18,500.

_____ **15.** Lexus LS 430. Someone once said that perfection is a road, not a destination. If this is true, then the engineers and designers at Lexus probably have the route memorized. With no apparent fear of losing their way, the Lexus team has allowed their flagship sedan, the LS 430, to momentarily detour from its journey. For the time being, it is parked comfortably at the crossroads where science and art converge to create an extraordinary driving experience.

—*Kelley Blue Book.*

C. Following is a list of sources from which information can be obtained. Label each source as follows:

**IO** if it offers an informed opinion

**EO** if it offers an expert opinion

**FS** if it is a factual source

_____ **16.** The National Aeronautics and Space Administration (NASA) at http://www.nasa.gov

_____ **17.** Nicholas D. Kristof, award-winning column writer for the *New York Times*

_____ **18.** A news article on the front page of the *New York Times*

_____ **19.** *The Encyclopedia of Indians of the Americas*, published by Scholarly Publications in 1974

_____ **20.** A letter to the editor of a local paper from a concerned citizen who has researched the topic that is the subject of the letter

## MASTERY Test 3

Name ______________________ Section ____________

Date ____________ **Score** (number correct) _____ × 5 = _____%

**A.** Read the following statements, and mark each one as follows:

**F** if it states a fact

**O** if it expresses an opinion

**F/O** if it combines fact and opinion

_____ **1.** People over the age of 70 should not be allowed to drive.

_____ **2.** Insurance statistics show that teenagers have a high rate of automobile accidents; this proves that teenagers are the most reckless drivers.

_____ **3.** With their mindless content and showcasing of shocking behavior, most reality television shows are harmful to society.

_____ **4.** All politicians are crooks.

_____ **5.** Since the United States was founded, a number of senators have been charged with and convicted of corruption.

_____ **6.** Men are not as concerned with feelings and relationships as women are.

_____ **7.** In 2003, prime-time television began airing programs that showed a level of violence never before allowed on TV.

_____ **8.** Parents should be screening what their children are watching instead of trying to limit what Hollywood produces.

_____ **9.** Reality television shows take unfair advantage of the everyday person's desire to be famous.

_____ **10.** Education may not be the only way to get ahead, but statistics show that it is a key factor in achieving economic security.

**B.** Read the following passage. Then mark each sentence as follows:

**F** if it states a fact

**O** if it expresses an opinion

**F/O** if it combines fact and opinion

### Ecstasy and Raves

[11]"Ecstasy" is a synthetic drug with both psychedelic and stimulant effects. [12]The drug was created by a German company in 1912. [13]It was to be used as a possible appetite suppressant. [14]Currently, Ecstasy is mainly a "club drug" and is commonly used at all-night dance parties known as "raves." [15]However, the use of this drug is moving to settings other than nightclubs, such as private homes, high schools, college dorms, and shopping malls.

[16]Raves often are promoted as alcohol-free events, which gives parents a false sense of security that their children will be safe attending these parties. [17]In reality, raves may actually be havens for the illicit sale and abuse of club drugs. [18]Raves first appeared in the United States in the late 1980s in cities such as San Francisco and Los Angeles. [19]By the early 1990s, rave parties and clubs were present in most American metropolitan areas. [20]Raves are characterized by high entrance fees, extensive drug use, and overcrowded dance floors.

—Office of National Drug Control Policy, "MDMA."

11. _____ 12. _____ 13. _____ 14. _____ 15. _____

16. _____ 17. _____ 18. _____ 19. _____ 20. _____

MASTERY **Test 4**

Name ______________________ Section ____________

Date ____________ **Score** (number correct) ______ × 10 = ______%

**A.** The following information and illustration were published together in a health textbook. First read the information, and identify each numbered sentence as follows:

**F** if it states a fact

**O** if it expresses an opinion

**F/O** if it combines fact and opinion

**Tobacco-induced Illnesses**

_____ **1.** Tobacco is the single most preventable cause of death in the United States.

_____ **2.** Currently, about 48 million Americans smoke.

_____ **3.** Smoking is an impossible habit to break.

_____ **4.** Young children are the most vulnerable to passive smoke.

_____ **5.** The government should ban smoking in all public places.

—Pruitt & Stein, *Health Styles: Decisions for Living*, 2nd ed., p. 201.

**B.** Now study the graph on page 444. Read the statements based on the figure. Identify each one as follows:

**F** if it states a fact

**O** if it expresses an opinion

**F/O** if it combines fact and opinion

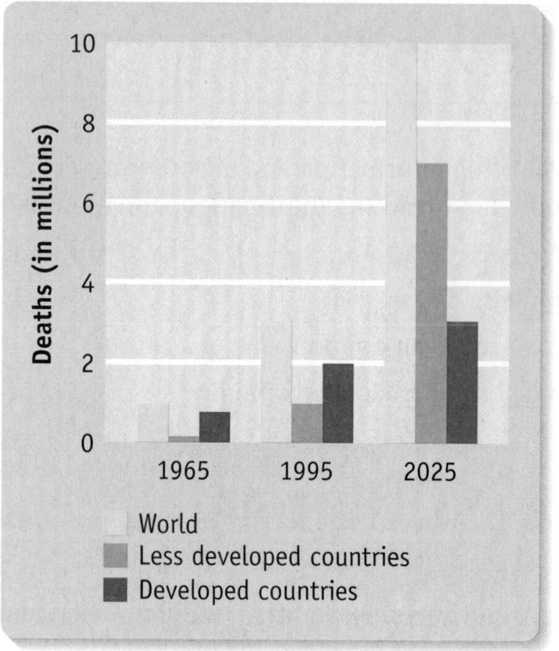


_____ **6.** Without doubt, by 2005, 10 million people worldwide will die of tobacco-induced illnesses.

_____ **7.** In 1965, more people in developed countries died of tobacco-induced illnesses than those in less developed countries.

_____ **8.** In 1965, people in less developed countries probably could not afford to buy tobacco products.

_____ **9.** In 1995, around 2 million people in developed countries died of tobacco-induced illnesses.

_____ **10.** Every one of these deaths is preventable.

MASTERY **Test 5**

Name ______________________ Section ____________

Date ____________ **Score** (number correct) ______ × 10 = ______%

**A.** Read the following passage from a history textbook. Then identify each excerpt from the passage as follows:

**F** if it states a fact

**O** if it expresses an opinion

**F/O** if it combines fact and opinion

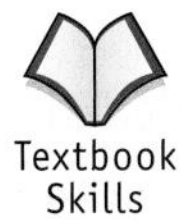


### A Nation Divided

[1]To the delight of the media, the race for the White House in 2000 proved to be close and exciting. [2]George Bush led in the polls until Al Gore moved ahead after the Democratic Convention in August. [3]Gore's running mate, Joe Lieberman, proved popular. [4]In contrast, Bush's choice of running mate, former defense secretary Dick Cheney, failed to excite the public. [5]But Gore's surprisingly uneven performance in three televised debates allowed Bush to regain a narrow lead in the polls in October. [6]Then, in the final week of the campaign, Gore began to draw even with Bush.

[7]The early returns on election night proved that the polls were right in stressing the closeness of the presidential race. [8]Gore seemed the likely winner when the networks mistakenly predicted a Democratic victory in Florida. [9]When the TV analysts put Florida back in the undecided column, Bush began to forge ahead, sweeping the rest of the South. [10]After midnight, when the networks again mistakenly called Florida, this time for Bush, Gore telephoned Bush to concede. [11]An hour later, however, he recanted when it became clear that the Bush margin in Florida was paper thin.

______ **1.** To the delight of the media, the race for the White House in 2000 proved to be close and exciting.

______ **2.** But Gore's surprisingly uneven performance in three televised debates allowed Bush to regain a narrow lead in the polls in October.

______ **3.** In the final week of the campaign, Gore began to draw even with Bush.

______ **4.** After midnight, when the networks again mistakenly called Florida, this time for Bush, Gore telephoned Bush to concede.

______ **5.** An hour later, however, he recanted when it became clear that the Bush margin in Florida was paper thin.

[12]For the next five weeks, all eyes were on the outcome in Florida. [13]Gore had a lead of more than 200,000 nationwide in the popular vote and 267 electoral votes. [14]Yet Bush, with 246 votes in the electoral college, could win the presidency with Florida's 25 electoral votes. [15]Both sides sent phalanxes of lawyers to Florida. [16]Bush's team sought to certify the results that showed him with a lead of 930 votes out of nearly six million cast. [17]Citing many voting problems disclosed by the media, Gore asked for a recount in three heavily Democratic counties in south Florida. [18]All three used old-fashioned punch card machines that resulted in some ballots not being clearly marked for any presidential candidate.

[19]The decision finally came in the courts. [20]Democrats appealed the first attempt to certify Bush as the victor to the Florida Supreme Court, where most of the judges had been appointed by Democrats. [21]The Florida court ordered recounts two times, but the Bush team appealed to the United States Supreme Court. [22]On December 12, five weeks after the election, the Supreme Court overturned the state's call for recounts. [23]The Supreme Court ruling was a 5–4 decision that reflected a long-standing divide in thought among the nine judges. [24]The next day, Gore gracefully conceded, and Bush finally became the president-elect. [25]Although the rule of law prevailed, neither the winner nor the loser could take much pride in his party's behavior.

—Adapted from Divine, Breen, Frederickson, & Williams, *The American Story,* pp. 1116–17.

______ **6.** For the next five weeks, all eyes were on the outcome in Florida.

______ **7.** Gore had a lead of more than 200,000 nationwide in the popular vote and 267 electoral votes.

______ **8.** Bush's team sought to certify the results that showed him with a lead of 930 votes out of nearly six million cast.

______ **9.** The next day, Gore gracefully conceded, and Bush finally became the president-elect.

______ **10.** Although the rule of law prevailed, neither the winner nor the loser could take much pride in his party's behavior.

MASTERY **Test 6**

Name ______________ Section ______________
Date ______________ **Score** (number correct) ______ × 10 = ______%

**A.** Read the following statements, and mark each one as follows:

**F** if it states a fact

**O** if it expresses an opinion

**F/O** if it combines fact and opinion

______ **1.** The reentry of the space shuttle *Columbia* into the earth's atmosphere on February 1, 2003, ended in disaster.

______ **2.** Ilan Roman, the first Israeli astronaut, was one of the seven crew members who lost their lives on the *Columbia.*

______ **3.** The witch's brew of rocket fuel on a space shuttle makes it very dangerous.

______ **4.** Michael Jordan, named NBA world champion six times, is the best player in the history of basketball.

______ **5.** Some people believe that crime rates increase during the full moon.

______ **6.** A reliable way to gain information about people is by studying their handwriting style.

**B.** Read the following passage from a college textbook. Then identify each excerpt from the passage as follows:

**F** if it states a fact

**O** if it expresses an opinion

**F/O** if it combines fact and opinion

Textbook Skills

**Love**

[1]Violins and valentines, roses and romance—this is the stuff relationships are made of. [2]Or is it? [3]Love itself completely defies definition. [4]It is not a product of the logical, analytical left side of the brain. [5]Instead, love stems from the right side of the brain, which feels rather than thinks. [6]Although the two sides of the brain do communicate well with each other, feelings cannot

be described; only the expression or outward behavior caused by the feeling can be explained. [7]One of humanity's greatest frustrations throughout history has been the inability to define and explain feelings, especially love. [8]That, of course, has been a boon to poets, Valentine's Day card manufacturers, florists, and others who make a living from our inability to express the feelings we have for that special person in our life.

[9]Love is like a stimulant drug. [10]It lifts our spirits and makes us giddy, and the crash from a lost love is comparable to the depression that follows the withdrawal from a powerful drug. [11]In between are the highs and lows that make our emotions feel like a roller-coaster ride. [12]Actually, there are degrees and stages of love. [13]Being in love occurs at the beginning of a relationship. [14]After a period of time, the "in love" stage fades, and a couple either breaks up or develops what is referred to as second-stage or mature love. [15]This is the kind of love that sustains a relationship or a marriage. [16]Although everyone is capable of this type of love, some people never do accomplish or experience it.

—Adapted from Girdano, Everly, & Dusek, *Controlling Stress and Tension,* 6th ed., pp. 159–60.

_____ **7.** Violins and valentines, roses and romance—this is the stuff relationships are made of.

_____ **8.** One of humanity's greatest frustrations throughout history has been the inability to define and explain feelings, especially love.

_____ **9.** Love is like a stimulant drug.

_____ **10.** Actually, there are degrees and stages of love.

CHAPTER

10

# Tone and Purpose

## CHAPTER PREVIEW

## Before Reading About Tone and Purpose

Study the chapter preview and underline words that relate to ideas you have already studied. Did you underline the following terms: subjective, objective, and main idea? What you already know about these topics will help you learn about tone and purpose. Use the blanks that follow to write a short one- or two-sentence summary about each topic.

Subjective words ______________________________________________

______________________________________________________________.

Objective words ______________________________________________

______________________________________________________________.

Main idea ____________________________________________________

______________________________________________________________.

Refer to the chapter preview and draw upon your prior knowledge to create at least five questions that you can answer as you study about tone and purpose:

________________________________________________?

________________________________________________?

________________________________________________?

________________________________________________?

________________________________________________?

Compare the questions you created with the following questions. Then write the ones that seem the most helpful in your notebook, leaving enough space between each question to record the answers as you read and study the chapter.

What are tone and purpose? How is tone established? How will objective facts and subjective opinions help me identify tone? Will fact and opinion help me identify purpose? How will the main idea help me discover the general purpose? What is the primary purpose, and how do I figure it out? How is irony used for special effects?

## What Are Tone and Purpose?

Read the following two paragraphs. As you read, think about the difference in the tone and purpose of each one:

> Tobacco is one of the strongest cancer-causing agents. It has been estimated to account for about 30% of cancer deaths in the United States. Smoking increases the risk of many types of cancer. For example, smoking raises the risk of cancers of the lung, throat, mouth, pancreas, kidney, bladder, cervix, and others. Smoking is also linked to other diseases besides cancer. These include heart disease, stroke, and lung diseases such as emphysema and bronchitis. In addition, tobacco also has a negative effect on the outcomes of pregnancy. Well over 400,000 premature deaths in the United States each year are caused by cigarette smoking.
>
> —Adapted from "Prevention and Cessation of Cigarette Smoking." 10 June 2003. National Cancer Institute.

> When I was your age, I started smoking. Yeah, I was 13 years old, trying to be cool, fit in, and look grown up, and I had no idea what a stupid

decision I was making. Today, I battle small-cell lung cancer. This cancer grows quickly, and by the time it was discovered, it had spread beyond my lungs. So now I endure chemotherapy and radiation treatments. I have lost my hair. I have problems thinking clearly and remembering things. I am plagued by nausea, vomiting, headaches, and mouth sores. My doctors tell me that this could have been avoided—if only I hadn't smoked. Chances are that I may not make it. Don't get me wrong. I am a fighter, and as long as I have breath, I have hope of beating this thing. Still, I live with that "If only." If only I hadn't started smoking. I just never dreamed this could happen to me. Listen! If you smoke—stop now before it's too late. If you don't smoke—don't start.

The differences in the tone and purpose of these two paragraphs are obvious. The first paragraph was written and published by the government to inform the public about the dangerous health effects of tobacco. The paragraph uses unbiased words and an objective, formal tone. The second paragraph approaches the same subject with a different purpose—to persuade young people to avoid smoking. The second paragraph conveys a painful personal experience using biased words and a subjective, informal tone.

As the two paragraphs demonstrate, tone and purpose work together to convey the author's meaning.

Every piece of information is created by an author who has a specific attitude toward the chosen topic and a specific reason for writing and sharing that attitude. The author's attitude is conveyed by the tone. **Tone** is the emotion or mood of the author's written voice. Understanding tone is closely related to understanding the author's reason for writing about the topic. This reason for writing is known as the author's **purpose.**

Tone and purpose are greatly influenced by the audience the author is trying to reach. The audience for the first paragraph is members of the general public who need factual information; the objective presentation of facts best serves such a wide-ranging audience. The audience for the second example is teenagers who need to be persuaded; the informal, personal approach is much more likely to reach this audience. Tone and purpose are established with word choice. Effective readers read to understand the author's tone and purpose. To identify tone and purpose, you need to build on several skills you have already studied: vocabulary, fact and opinion, and main ideas.

**Tone** is the author's attitude toward the topic.
**Purpose** is the reason the author writes about a topic.

## Understand How Tone Is Established

The author's attitude is expressed by the tone of voice he or she assumes in the passage. An author chooses carefully the words that will make an impact on the reader. Sometimes an author wants to appeal to reason and just gives facts and factual explanations. At other times, an author wants to appeal to emotions and stir the reader to feel deeply.

For example, in an effort to share reliable information, textbooks strive for an objective tone. An objective tone includes facts and reasonable explanations. It is matter-of-fact and neutral. The details given in an objective tone are likely to be facts. In contrast, sharing an author's personal worldview through fiction and personal essays often calls for a subjective tone. A subjective tone uses words that describe feelings, judgments, or opinions. The details given in a subjective tone are likely to include experiences, senses, feelings, and thoughts. Study the following list of words that describe the characteristics of tone.

**Characteristics of Tone Words**

| **Objective Tone** | **Subjective Tone** |
|---|---|
| **impartial** | **personal** |
| unbiased | biased |
| neutral | emotional |
| formal | informal |

An *unbiased* or *neutral* tone does not show any feelings for or against a topic. Instead, it focuses on facts. A *formal* tone chooses higher-level words and avoids using the pronouns *I* and *you,* thereby creating a sense of distance between the writer and the reader. An *objective* tone is thus impartial, unbiased, neutral, and most often formal. In contrast, a *biased* tone does show favor for or against a particular topic. A biased tone uses *emotional* words that focus on feelings. Finally, an *informal* tone uses the pronouns *I* and *you* to create a connection between the writer and the reader. A *subjective* tone is thus personal, biased, emotional, and often informal. In summary, to grasp the author's tone, you need to carefully note the author's choice of vocabulary and details.

**EXAMPLES** Look at the following list of expressions. Based on word choice, choose the tone word that best describes each statement.

_____ **1.** "Mom, please," she said as she rolled her eyes, "I would rather do it myself."

a. emotional b. neutral

_____ **2.** "Mother, I would like to introduce you to my professor, Dr. Rigolosi."
a. formal b. informal

_____ **3.** "Mom, I'm having a terrible time; could you please, please come over?"
a. details of facts b. details of experience

_____ **4.** "Mom, quick! Get over here, now!"
a. informal b. formal

_____ **5.** "My mother's name is Gerta Powell, and she was born in 1933."
a. objective b. subjective

**EXPLANATIONS**

**1.** (a) The speaker's desire for independence and the eye-rolling gesture appeal to and express emotions.

**2.** (a) The tone here is polite. Formal titles are used, such as "Mother" and "Dr. Rigolosi."

**3.** (b) The author does not give any factual details about the nature of the speaker's need. However, the speaker comments on her experience by saying it is "terrible."

**4.** (a) The use of "Mom" and short commands imply a familiar tone.

**5.** (a) Just the facts are given. None of the details are about feelings.

## PRACTICE 1

Read the following list of expressions. Based on word choice, choose a basic tone word that best describes each statement.

_____ **1.** "Diet Pepsi is light, crisp, and refreshing."
a. objective c. neutral
b. subjective

_____ **2.** No one should have the right to burn the American flag.
a. neutral c. biased
b. objective

_____ **3.** "Four score and seven years ago, our forefathers brought forth on this continent a new nation . . ."
a. biased c. informal
b. formal

_____ **4.** The gangs known as the Crips and the Bloods formed during the late 1960s in California; they still exist today.
a. emotional
b. biased
c. neutral

_____ **5.** "Give me liberty or give me death."
a. objective
b. unbiased
c. emotional

## Identify Subjective and Objective Tone Words

Recognizing tone and describing an author's attitude deepens your comprehension and helps you become a more effective reader. A small sample of words used to describe tone are listed here. Look up the meanings of any words you do not know. Developing your vocabulary helps you better understand an author's word choice to establish tone.

| Subjective | | | Objective |
|---|---|---|---|
| admiring | disbelieving | persuasive | accurate |
| angry | discouraged | pleading | factual |
| annoyed | disdainful | poetic | impartial |
| anxious | dramatic | reverent | matter-of-fact |
| approving | earnest | rude | straightforward |
| arrogant | elated | sad | truthful |
| argumentative | entertaining | sarcastic | |
| assured | fearful | self-pitying | |
| belligerent | friendly | serious | |
| biting | funny | sincere | |
| bitter | gloomy | supportive | |
| bored | happy | suspenseful | |
| bubbly | hostile | sympathetic | |
| calm | humorous | tender | |
| candid | idealistic | tense | |
| cold | informal | thoughtful | |
| comic | informative | threatening | |
| complaining | irritated | timid | |
| confident | joking | urgent | |
| cynical | jovial | warning | |
| demanding | joyful | wistful | |
| direct | lively | wry | |
| disappointed | loving | | |

**EXAMPLES** Read the following items. Choose a word that best describes the tone of each statement. Use each word once.

| | | |
|---|---|---|
| anxious | encouraging | persuasive |
| elated | gloomy | tender |

1. "If you care about saving lives, you should vote for gun control."

   Tone: ______________________

2. "You can do anything if you put your mind to it. Come on! You can do it!"

   Tone: ______________________

3. "I hope I do all right on this test. Even though I studied all night, I might forget important information."

   Tone: ______________________

4. "I won! I won!" Snively shouted as he realized he held the winning lottery ticket.

   Tone: ______________________

5. Thick, heavy clouds hung low in the sky, like a soggy gray blanket. The trees were winter bare, and the ground was brown and wet. Though it was only 2 o'clock in the afternoon, a dusky shroud covered the neighborhood.

   Tone: ______________________

6. Study the picture. Use a word to label the attitude of the grandfather toward his grandchild.

   Tone: ______________________

**EXPLANATIONS** Compare your answers to these:

1. persuasive. As you learned when you studied fact and opinion, the words "should," "ought," and "must" are opinion words. They suggest a persuasive tone.
2. encouraging
3. anxious
4. elated
5. gloomy
6. tender

## PRACTICE 2

Read the following items. Based on word choice, choose a word from the box that best describes the tone of each statement. Use each word once.

| admiring | arrogant | factual | informative | warm |
|---|---|---|---|---|
| angry | bitter | happy | sad | wistful |

1. "It is with sorrow that I must submit my resignation."

   Tone: ______________________________

2. "The best days were growing up on the farm before life became so fast-paced."

   Tone: ______________________________

3. "It is so good to see you again after such a long time. How is your wonderful family?"

   Tone: ______________________________

4. Manny shoots for the basket at an awkward angle. He hesitates. The ball is knocked out of his hands. The lost points may have just cost his team the win.

   Tone: ______________________________

5. "Animals can be divided into three groups based on the way they maintain body temperature."

   Tone: ______________________________

6. A quiet yet thrilling feeling of peace swept over her. Her children were healthy, she was successful in her job, and she was in love with her husband. It seemed she had all a person could want.

   Tone: ______________________________

7. "It isn't enough to say you are sorry after years of doing wrong. You just can't say you are sorry! How dare you think you can! Don't expect forgiveness, either!"

   Tone: ______________________________

8. "It is with pleasure and pride that I offer this recommendation on behalf of Kareem Smith. He is hardworking, intelligent, and honest."

   Tone: ______________________________

9. "Who broke the vase in the foyer? When I find out who did it, that person is going to be so sorry. Do you know how much that vase cost?"

   Tone: ______________________________

10. "I am the best there is, and don't you forget it. There is no one who beats me."

    Tone: ______________________________

## Discover the General Purpose in the Main Idea

Many reasons can motivate a writer. These can range from the need to take a stand on a hotly debated issue to the desire to entertain an audience with an amusing story. Basically, an author writes to share a main idea about a topic. An author's main idea, whether stated or implied, and the author's purpose are directly related. One of the following three general purposes will drive a main idea: to inform, to entertain, and to persuade.

In Chapter 3, you learned that a main idea is made up of a topic and the author's controlling point. You identified the controlling point by looking for thought patterns and biased (tone) words. The next two sections will build on what you have learned. First, you will study the relationship between the three general purposes and the author's main idea. You will practice using the main idea to discover the general purpose. Then you will apply what you have learned to figure out an author's primary purpose.

- **To inform.** When a writer sets out to inform, he or she shares knowledge and information or offers instruction about a particular topic. A few of the tone words usually used to describe this purpose include *objective, matter-of-fact,* and *straightforward.* Authors use facts to explain or describe the main idea to readers. Most textbook passages are written to inform. The following topic sentences reflect the writer's desire to inform.

  1. The main causes of road rage are stress and anxiety.
  2. A healthful diet includes several daily servings from each of the major food groups.

In sentence 1, the topic is *road rage*, and the words that reveal the controlling point are *main causes, stress,* and *anxiety*. The author uses a tone that is unbiased and objective, so the focus is on the information. In sentence 2, the topic is *diet*, and the words that reveal the controlling point are *healthful, several daily servings,* and *major food groups*. Again, the author chooses words that are matter-of-fact and that suggest factual details will follow. Both topic sentences indicate that the author's purpose is to provide helpful information.

- **To persuade.** A writer who sets out to persuade tries to bring the reader into agreement with his or her view on the topic. A few of the tone words often used to describe this purpose include *argumentative, persuasive, forceful, controversial, positive, supportive, negative,* and *critical.* Authors combine facts with emotional appeals to sway the reader to their point of view. Politicians and advertisers often write and speak to persuade. The following topic sentences reflect the writer's desire to persuade.

  3. Violence that arises from road rage must be harshly and swiftly punished.
  4. How to achieve should be a part of public school education from elementary through high school.

In sentence 3, the topic is *violence*. The words that reveal the author's controlling point include *arises from, must be, harshly,* and *swiftly punished*. This sentence deals with the same general topic as sentence 1. Notice the difference in the treatments of this topic. Sentence 3 refocuses the topic from the causes of road rage to the effect of road rage: the *violence* that *arises from* road rage. The author then introduces a forceful, biased viewpoint.

In sentence 4, the topic is *public school education*. The author uses the process thought pattern to limit the topic with the phrase *how to achieve*. Additional words that reveal the controlling point are *should be,* which are followed by a recommendation for action. The author is offering a controversial personal opinion about how children should be educated. In both of these sentences, the authors want to convince others to agree with them about taking a specific course of action.

- **To entertain.** A writer whose purpose is to entertain sets out to captivate or interest the audience. A few of the tone words often used to describe this purpose include *amusing, entertaining, lively, humorous,* and *suspenseful.* To entertain, authors frequently use expressive language and creative thinking. Most readers are entertained by material that stirs an emotional reaction such as laughter, sympathy, or fear. Thus, authors engage readers creatively through vivid images, strong feelings, or sensory details (such as sights, sounds, tastes, textures, and smells). Both fiction and nonfiction writers seek to entertain. The following topic sentences reflect the writer's desire to entertain.

    5. Think of our highways as a place to study how operating a powerful machine can turn normal people into four types of maniacs: the bully, the loudmouth, the speed-demon, and the exterminator.
    6. I am zealously committed to eating a balanced diet from the four basic food groups: low-calorie, low-carbohydrate, low-fat, and low-taste.

You may have found identifying the topic and controlling point a little more challenging in these two sentences. Often, when writers entertain, they imply the main idea. And when they use an implied main idea, they rely much more heavily on tone words. Sentence 5, like sentences 1 and 3, deals with the topic of the stresses of driving. In this sentence, the author focuses the topic on the drivers with the phrase *four types of maniacs*. The use of *maniacs* (a biased word) offers a strong clue that the author's purpose is to entertain. Other words that reveal tone include *powerful*, *normal*, *bully*, *loudmouth*, *speed-demon*, and *exterminator*. The author seeks to amuse the reader with the contrast between "normal people" and what they become behind the wheel of a vehicle.

Sentence 6, like sentence 2, deals with the topic of a *diet*. In this case, the words that reveal the author's controlling point are *balanced* (which suggests healthful) and *four basic food groups* (which indicates the classification thought pattern). However, the main idea is not really about a balanced diet. The point seems to be about dieting. Clearly, the author is trying to make us smile by setting up an unexpected contrast. In most cases, the words *four food groups* are followed by a very different list of details. Surprising contrasts often set up an ironic tone. And irony often amuses the reader. You will learn more about irony later in this chapter. Authors also use other methods to entertain such as exaggerations, vivid details, and dramatic descriptions.

These six sentences show that a topic can be approached in a variety of ways. The author chooses a topic and a purpose. The purpose shapes the focus of the main idea. The author carefully chooses tone words to express the main idea in light of the purpose. Each of these choices then controls the choices of supporting details and the thought pattern used to organize them.

**EXAMPLES** Read each of the following paragraphs. Annotate them for main idea and tone.

**I** = to inform **P** = to persuade **E** = to entertain

_____ **1.** So there we were, in the standing yoga pose known as the warrior. My right leg stretched out to its max behind me, my left leg bent at the knee to bring my thigh parallel to the floor, and my torso twisted toward the left knee. My arms stretched out at shoulder height, the left one in front and the right one in back of me. The fingertips on both hands were "stretching for those unseen objects just beyond reach." *Hey,* I thought, *I can do this.* Then the seconds stretched into eternity, and my fifty-something, never-exercised-much body began to tremble and sweat. My mind focused on my struggling body: *Hold on just a little longer.* Finally, the pencil-thin, thirty-something, human-pretzel teacher said, "Slowly straighten your left leg." *See,* I thought, *no problemo.* Then she said, "As you straighten your left leg, bend your torso forward and bring your right leg up off the ground for a balanced pose. And don't forget: Breathe." *Oh, yeah! Breathe, breathe!* I thought as my body fought for balance.

**VISUAL VOCABULARY**

Write a one-sentence description of what parts of the body the torso includes and excludes.

______________________________

______________________________

______________________________

______________________________

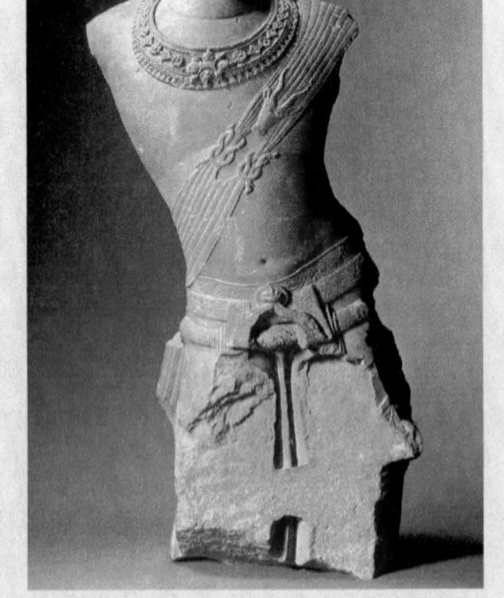

▸ This statue is the torso of a human body.

_____ **2.** Yoga exercises benefit a person in three ways. Yoga leads to physical balance, mental alertness, and fewer injuries. The practice of yoga uses slow, steady motions to enter and hold poses that stretch and strengthen the body's muscles. Because each pose is held for at least 10 seconds, the body learns to adjust and find its natural balance. To find this balance, the mind must be actively involved. And as the muscles are stretched and strengthened, injuries are less likely to occur.

______ **3.** Yoga is a much healthier practice than simple stretching. Stretching relies on a jerky movement that forces the body into a certain position. Often stretching is dynamic, using a bouncing motion, and the stretch is only held for a moment or two. Such stretching can lead to injuries. In contrast, yoga uses a static stretch that relies on inner balance to hold the pose for at least 10 to 15 seconds. To successfully enter and hold a yoga pose, the mind must focus on what the body needs to stay balanced. By holding a stretch, the body becomes strong and flexible, and the connection between the mind and body is strengthened more so than with simple stretching.

**4.** Study each of the three photos of people in public speaking situations. Label the purpose of each speaker as follows:

**I** = to inform **P** = to persuade **E** = to entertain

______ a.

______ b.

______ c.

## EXPLANATIONS

**1.** The topic of this paragraph is presented in the first sentence—yoga. However, the main idea is implied: yoga is a strenuous exercise for a beginner. The author uses the narrative thought pattern to share a personal experience. Throughout the narrative, the author uses vivid details, descriptions, and exaggerations (E) *to entertain* the reader.

2. This paragraph opens with the main idea stated in a topic sentence. The topic is yoga exercises, and the words that reveal the author's controlling points are *benefit* and *three ways.* The details consist of a list and explanations of these benefits. The author's purpose here is simply (I) *to inform* the reader about three benefits of yoga.

3. This paragraph also opens with the main idea stated in a topic sentence. Again, the topic is yoga, and the words that reveal the controlling point are *much healthier* (which is an opinion) and *than simple stretching* (which indicates the contrast thought pattern). The author clearly believes that yoga is better than simple stretching and gives details (P) *to persuade* the reader that this view is correct.

4. a. E, b. P, c. I.

## PRACTICE 3

Read the following topic sentences. Label each according to its purpose:

**I** = to inform **P** = to persuade **E** = to entertain

_____ 1. Cloning human beings should be banned.

_____ 2. The National Hurricane Center predicts a record number of hurricanes in the upcoming months.

_____ 3. Friends don't let friends drive drunk.

_____ 4. Bulimia and anorexia are two serious eating disorders.

_____ 5. A celebrity is a person who works hard all his life to become well known, then wears dark glasses to avoid being recognized.

—James B. Simpson

_____ 6. Spanking as a way to discipline a child has a long history in many cultures.

_____ 7. Age is strictly a case of mind over matter. If you don't mind, it doesn't matter. —Jack Benny

_____ 8. Kwanzaa is an African American tradition that is based on the African celebration of the "first fruits" of the harvest.

_____ 9. When I was a boy of fourteen, my father was so ignorant I could hardly stand to have the old man around. But when I got to be twenty-one, I was astonished at how much he had learned in seven years. —Mark Twain

_____ **10.** Rely on Denta-Fresh toothpaste to stop bad breath just as millions of others have.

## Figure Out the Primary Purpose

In addition to the three general purposes, authors often write to fulfill a more specific purpose. The following table offers several examples of specific purposes.

**General and Specific Purposes**

| **To inform** | **To entertain** | **To persuade** |
|---|---|---|
| to analyze | to amuse | to argue against |
| to clarify | to delight | to argue for |
| to discuss | to frighten | to convince |
| to establish | | to criticize |
| to explain | | to inspire (motivate a change) |

Often a writer has two or more purposes in one piece of writing. Blending purposes adds interest and power to a piece of writing. Take, for example, the award-winning documentary *Fahrenheit 9/11.* This film attempts to inform and entertain, but its primary purpose is to argue. The film uses facts, personal bias, and humor to take a strong stand against President Bush. Comics like Jon Stewart and Conan O'Brien use facts from daily events to entertain their audiences. In these cases, when an author has more than one purpose, only one purpose is in control overall. This controlling purpose is called the **primary purpose.**

You have studied several reading skills that will help you grasp the author's primary purpose. For example, the author's primary purpose is often suggested by the main idea, the thought pattern, and the tone of the passage. Read the following topic sentence. Identify the author's primary purpose by considering the main idea, thought pattern, and tone.

_____ Spanking must be avoided as a way to discipline due to its long-term negative effects on the child.

a. to discuss the disadvantages of spanking
b. to argue against spanking as a means of discipline
c. to make fun of those who use spanking as a means of discipline

This topic sentence clearly states a main idea "against spanking" using the tone words "must" and "negative." The details will be organized using the thought pattern "long-term effects." Based on the topic sentence, the author's primary purpose is (b) to argue against spanking as a means of discipline. Even when the main idea is implied, tone and thought patterns point to the author's primary purpose.

You should also take into account titles, headings, and prior knowledge about the author. For example, it's easy to see that Jay Leno's primary purpose is to entertain us with his book *If Roast Beef Could Fly*. The title is funny, and we know Jay Leno is a comedian. An effective reader studies the general context of the passage to find out the author's primary purpose.

> **Primary purpose** is the author's main reason for writing the passage.

**EXAMPLES** Read each of the following paragraphs. Identify the primary purpose of each.

**1.** **The American Dream: Ideal Bodies**
***by Dave Barry***

If there's one ideal that unites all Americans, it's the belief that every single one of us, regardless of ethnic background, is fat. It was not always this way. There was a time, not so long ago, when Americans did not obsess about fat. In those days, a man could be portly and still be considered attractive. The standards were also more lenient for women: Marilyn Monroe, whom nobody ever called skinny, was a major sex goddess.

—Barry, "Build Yourself a Killer Bod with Killer Bees," p. 168.

_____ The main purpose of this paragraph is
a. to explain how to lose weight.
b. to amuse the reader with humorous details about weight.
c. to convince readers about the danger of being overweight.

**2.** **Letter from Birmingham Jail**
***by Martin Luther King Jr.***

We know through painful experience that freedom is never voluntarily given by the oppressor; it must be demanded by the oppressed. Frankly, I have yet to engage in a direct-action campaign that was "well timed" in the view of those who have not suffered unduly from the disease of segregation. For years now I have heard the word "Wait!" It rings in the ear of every Negro with piercing familiarity. This "Wait" has almost always meant "Never." We must come to see, with one of our distinguished jurists, that "justice too long delayed is justice denied."

—DiYanni, *One Hundred Great Essays*, p. 406.

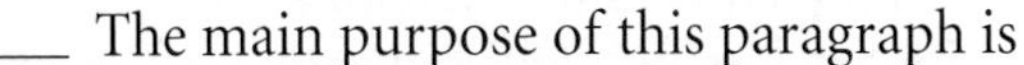

______ The main purpose of this paragraph is
a. to entertain the reader with details from the civil rights movement.
b. to convince the reader that the Negro deserves justice now.
c. to explain why the Negro has been treated unfairly.

Textbook Skills

**3.** **Long-Term Memory**

Think of long-term memory as a "data bank" or warehouse for all of your feelings and ideas. Information you heard hours, days, weeks, even years ago is stored in long-term memory. Long-term memory differs from short-term memory in several ways. Long-term memory can handle large amounts of information; short-term memory has less space for storage. Putting information in and getting it out again is a slow process in long-term memory. On the other hand, short-term memory is a rapid process.

—Adapted from Brownell, *Listening: Attitudes, Principles, and Skills,* 2nd ed., p. 150.

______ The main purpose of this paragraph is
a. to argue against poor memory skills.
b. to amuse the reader with humorous details about long-term memory.
c. to inform the reader about the differences between long-term and short-term memory.

**EXPLANATIONS**

1. Dave Barry is a well-known comic. Thus, a reader can expect his primary purpose to be (b) to amuse the reader with humorous details about weight. His use of tone words hints that this is an amusing piece. For example, the title suggests a lighthearted play on words. The phrase "The American Dream" makes most people think of freedom or wealth, not "ideal bodies." This unexpected contrast is amusing. Likewise, the phrase "one ideal that unites all Americans" usually suggests patriotism, civil rights, or some other grand idea. Thus, it is ironic and funny that Barry uses this phrase to introduce "fat." He also uses understatement to describe Marilyn Monroe as one "whom nobody ever called skinny" to amuse the reader. Overall, the tone is lighthearted.
2. It is common knowledge that Dr. Martin Luther King, Jr. is a beloved martyr of the civil rights movement. He is famous for his stand against injustice.

The title tells us that this piece was written from the Birmingham jail. He was jailed for his stand against segregation. His main purpose is (b) to convince the reader that the Negro deserves justice now.

3. Based on the source note, you know that this paragraph comes from a textbook, and the primary purpose of a textbook is to inform. In addition, the tone of the title and details is factual and objective. Its main purpose is (c) to inform the reader about the differences between long-term and short-term memory.

## PRACTICE 4

Read each of the following paragraphs. Identify the primary purpose of each.

1. **Different Words, Different Worlds**
***by Deborah Tannen***

Many years ago, I was married to a man who shouted at me, "I do not give you the right to raise your voice to me, because you are a woman and I am a man." This was frustrating because I knew it was unfair. But I also knew just what was going on. I ascribed his unfairness to his having grown up in a country where few people thought women and men have equal rights. Now I am married to a man who is a partner and friend. We come from similar backgrounds and share values and interests. It is a continual source of pleasure to talk to him. It is wonderful to have someone I can tell everything to, someone who understands. But he doesn't always see things as I do, doesn't always react to things as I expect him to. And I often don't understand why he says what he does.

—DiYanni, *One Hundred Great Essays*, p. 678.

_____ The main purpose of this paragraph is
a. to entertain with amusing details about marriage.
b. to explain that men and women often perceive things differently.
c. to argue against the idea that men are superior to women.

Textbook Skills

2. **Human Impact on Lakes**

Wakes created by motorboating disturb vegetation and the birds that nest in it. Motorboats discharge an oily mixture with gas exhausts beneath the surface of the water. This mixture escapes notice. One gallon of oil per million gallons of water imparts an odor to lake water. Eight gallons per million taints fish. These oily discharges can lower oxygen levels and hurt the growth and life span of fish.

—Adapted from Smith & Smith, *Elements of Ecology*, 4th ed., p. 462.

_____ The main purpose of this paragraph is

a. to inform the reader about the impact of human motorboating activity on lakes.
b. to argue against the use of boats in lakes.
c. to entertain the reader with interesting details about boating.

Textbook Skills

**3.** **The Metamorphosis**
***by Franz Kafka***

As Gregor Samsa awoke one morning from uneasy dreams he found himself transformed in his bed into a gigantic insect. He was lying on his hard, as it were armor-plated, back and when he lifted his head a little he could see his dome-like brown belly divided into stiff arched segments on top of which the bed quilt could hardly keep in position and was about to slide off completely. His numerous legs, which were pitifully thin compared to the rest of his bulk, waved helplessly before his eyes.

—Kennedy & Gioia, *Literature,* 8th ed., pp. 345–346.

_____ The main purpose of this paragraph is

a. to explain to the reader that a human has turned into a bug.
b. to convince the reader that a human has turned into a bug.
c. to engage the reader with an absurd story.

**4.** Study the mock advertisement. Using your own words, identify its primary purpose in the space provided.

◄ "Build your dream home on one of Horseshoe Bend's many beautiful wooded building lots."

The main purpose of this mock advertisement is to _______________

_______________________________________________

## Recognize Irony Used for Special Effects

Irony is a tone often used in both conversation and written text. An author uses **irony** when he or she says one thing but means something else. Irony is the contrast between what is stated and what is implied, or between actual events and expectations.

Irony is often used to entertain and enlighten. For example, in the novel *Huckleberry Finn* by Mark Twain, the boy Huckleberry Finn believes he has done something wrong when he helps his older friend Jim escape slavery. The ironic contrast lies between what Huckleberry Finn thinks is wrong and what really is wrong: slavery itself. Twain set up this ironic situation to reveal the shortcomings of society.

Irony is also used to persuade. In her essay "I Want a Wife," Judy Brady seems to be saying she wants a wife to take care of the children, do the household chores, and perform all the other countless duties expected of a wife in the mid-twentieth century. However, she doesn't really want a wife; she wants equality with men. As she describes the role of a wife as a submissive servant, she argues against the limitations that society placed on women.

Due to its powerful special effects, authors use irony in many types of writings. For example, you will come across irony in fiction, essays, poetry, comedy routines, and cartoons. When authors use irony, they imply their main ideas and rely heavily on tone. Thus you need to understand two common types of irony so that you can see and enjoy their effects: verbal irony and situational irony.

**Verbal irony** occurs when the author's words state one thing but imply the opposite.

During a violent storm, your friend says, "Nice weather, eh?"

At the finish line of a marathon, a tired runner says, "Why, I'm ready to run another 24 miles."

A father reviews his son's straight A report card and says, "Well, you have certainly made a mess of things!"

**Situational irony** occurs when the events of a situation differ from what is expected.

A high school dropout eventually becomes a medical doctor.

An Olympic swimmer drowns.

A multimillionaire clips grocery coupons.

**EXAMPLES** Read the items, and identify the type of irony used in each.

_____ **1.** Martha and Charlotte, who can't stand each other, show up at the prom wearing the exact same dress.
a. verbal irony
b. situational irony
c. no irony

_____ **2.** The burglar who had robbed the neighborhood garages of golf clubs and bicycles turned out to be a grandmother of six.
a. verbal irony
b. situational irony
c. no irony

_____ **3.** After getting stuck babysitting for her younger brothers and sisters, Kerry said, "This must be my lucky day."
a. verbal irony
b. situational irony
c. no irony

_____ **4.** Dark- or bright-colored foods are the healthiest because of their nutrients.
a. verbal irony
b. situational irony
c. no irony

**EXPLANATIONS**

**1.** (b) situational irony: The fact that people who can't stand each other have similar taste in fashion is unexpected.

**2.** (b) situational irony: Most would not suspect a grandmother to be a thief.

**3.** (a) verbal irony: The author provides a clue to the tone by using the phrase "getting stuck babysitting." These words let us know that Kerry is not pleased and doesn't mean what she is saying.

**4.** (c) no irony: The author provides facts without emotion.

## PRACTICE 5

Read the items, and identify the type of irony used in each.

_____ **1.** Looking out the window at the gray skies and wind-blown trees, Robert said, "Great day for a picnic."
a. verbal irony
b. situational irony
c. no irony

_____ **2.** On opening night, the beautiful, talented, and famous actress stood frozen with stage fright as the curtain rose.
a. verbal irony
b. situational irony
c. no irony

_____ **3.** "Driving while under the influence of drugs or alcohol is really smart."

a. verbal irony
b. situational irony
c. no irony

_____ **4.** Kim stayed up all night typing the paper that was due the next day. Just as she was ready to print, her computer crashed, and she lost all her information. She had failed to save her work as she wrote. It was the best paper she had ever written.

a. verbal irony
b. situational irony
c. no irony

_____ **5.** Algebra is a challenging course for many college students.

a. verbal irony
b. situational irony
c. no irony

Textbook Skills

## Author's Tone and Purpose

Read the excerpt from the textbook *Messages: Building Interpersonal Communication Skills.* Then answer these questions about the author's purpose and tone.

_____ **1.** The author's primary purpose for this section of the text is

a. to inform.
b. to entertain.
c. to persuade.

_____ **2.** The tone of the main text is

a. biased.
b. objective.

_____ **3.** The purpose of the cartoon "Accountants in Love" is

a. to inform.
b. to entertain.
c. to persuade.

_____ **4.** The tone of the quote by Erich Segal is

a. earnest.
b. loving.
c. irritated.
d. sarcastic.

_____ **5.** The tone of the quote by Erich Fromm is

a. biting.
b. cheerful.
c. poetic.
d. insulting.

**264** PART 3: Messages in Context

How would you explain the cartoon to the right in terms of social exchange theory?

### Intimacy

At the intimacy stage you commit yourself still further to the other person and, in fact, establish a kind of relationship in which this individual becomes your best or closest friend, lover, or companion. Usually the intimacy stage divides itself quite neatly into two phases: an *interpersonal commitment* phase in which you commit yourselves to each other in a kind of private way and a *social bonding* phase in which the commitment is made public—perhaps to family and friends, perhaps to the public at large through formal marriage. Here the two of you become a unit, a pair.

True love comes quietly, without banners or flashing lights. If you hear bells, get your ears checked.
—*Erich Segal*

Commitment may take many forms; it may be an engagement or a marriage; it may be a commitment to help the person or to be with the person, or a commitment to reveal your deepest secrets. It may consist of living together or an agreement to become lovers. The type of commitment varies with the relationship and with the individuals. The important characteristic is that the commitment made is a special one; it's a commitment that you do not make lightly or to everyone. This intimacy stage is reserved for very few people at any given time—sometimes just one, sometimes two, three, or perhaps four. Rarely do people have more than four intimates, except in a family situation.

Immature love says: "I love you because I need you."
Mature love says: "I need you because I love you."
—*Erich Fromm*



## Chapter Review

Test your understanding of what you have read in this chapter by filling in the blank with a word or phrase from the box.

| | | | | |
|---|---|---|---|---|
| to entertain | to persuade | primary purpose | situational | tone |
| to inform | objective | purpose | subjective | verbal |

**1.** The ________________ is the author's attitude toward the topic.

**2.** The ________________ tone words usually present facts and reasonable explanations.

3. The _______________ tone words describe feelings, judgments, or opinions.

4. The _______________ is the author's reason for writing about a topic.

5. An author's purpose in using facts to teach or explain a main idea is _______________.

6. Authors combine facts with emotional appeals to sway readers to their point of view when their purpose is _______________.

7. A writer whose purpose is _______________ sets out to amuse or interest the audience.

8. The main reason the author writes the passage is his or her _______________.

9. _______________ irony occurs when the author's words state one thing but imply the opposite.

10. _______________ irony occurs when the events of a situation differ from what is expected.

## Applications

### Application 1: Tone

Read each of the following items. Choose the tone word from the box that best describes each item.

| | | | |
|---|---|---|---|
| doubtful | sad | self-pitying | sympathetic |
| irritated | sarcastic | straightforward | threatening |

_______________ 1. "Please note in your checkbook how much money you spent using your ATM card today."

_______________ 2. "Hey, lay off, you don't have to nag me. I was going to do it anyway!"

_______________ 3. "When are you going to take the garbage out? Sometime this year, maybe?"

_______________ **4.** "You know how hard it's been. I have been working two jobs and going to school nights just to make ends meet and get ahead. I hardly have time to do any of the things I need to do, much less have any fun. No one else works as hard as I do."

_______________ **5.** "I know it's been hard. And I appreciate all you are going through right now. If you will just put the receipts on the counter, I will take care of the paperwork for you."

## Application 2: Author's Purpose

Read each item, and identify the author's purpose: to inform, to entertain, or to persuade.

**1.** Pain is a normal part of a physical process that lets us know something is wrong.

_______________________________________________

**2.** The death penalty is deeply flawed and should be abolished.

_______________________________________________

**3.** "Yes, I have gained weight. I weighed only 8 pounds when I was born."

_______________________________________________

**4.** Each of our cozy, long-sleeved knit shirts is available in an array of colors. They're the perfect additions to your wardrobe for any season. Hurry! The marked-down sale price is good only through Saturday.

_______________________________________________

**5.** The sound of glass shattering downstairs startled Kalein out of her sleep. She held her breath as she listened to the sound of footsteps coming closer to her bedroom. Frantically, she dialed 911. "Hurry," she whispered into the phone, "someone is in the house." She knew as soon as the words were out that help was too far away. Her eyes cast about the room in search of a weapon to use to defend herself.

_______________________________________________

## Application 3: Author's Primary Purpose

Identify the primary purpose of each passage.

1. **Sequoya and the Cherokee Alphabet**

Sequoya was a brilliant and proud Cherokee. He was born in Tennessee around 1770 and lived in Georgia until 1843. He is best known for his amazing feat of creating the Cherokee alphabet. This remarkable man is thought to be the son of Nathaniel Gist, an English trader, and a part-Cherokee woman. He was also known by his English name, George Guess. In a heroic effort to save Cherokee culture, Sequoya created a system of writing for the Cherokees. He began this work around 1809, and by 1821, he had created an alphabet made up of over 80 symbols. With the alphabet, the Cherokees published newspapers and books in their own language. Thousands of Cherokees learned to read and write in the new written language. The giant sequoia trees and Sequoia National Park in California are named after him.

Purpose: _____
a. to inform
b. to entertain
c. to persuade

2. **Justice Fulfilled or Justice Denied?**

On January 12, 2003, the governor of Illinois, George Ryan, commuted death penalties into life sentences for 167 inmates on death row. The debate about the death penalty usually focuses on the fear that an innocent person sits on death row. However, Governor Ryan spared the lives of many vicious killers. In his effort to combat the unfairness of the death penalty, he abused his power. And he hurt the chances of true and lasting reform of the death penalty.

Purpose: _____
a. to inform
b. to entertain
c. to persuade

3. **The Reconstruction Period**
***by Booker T. Washington***

The years from 1867 to 1878 I think may be called the period of Reconstruction. This included the time that I spent as a student at Hampton and as a teacher in West Virginia. During the whole of the Reconstruction period two ideas were constantly agitating the minds of the coloured people, or, at least, the minds of a large part of the race. One of these was the craze for Greek and Latin learning, and the other was a desire to hold office.

It could not have been expected that a people who had spent generations in slavery, and before that generations in the darkest heathenism, could at first form any proper conception of what an education meant. In every part of the

South, during the Reconstruction period, schools, both day and night, were filled to overflowing with people of all ages and conditions, some being as far along in age as sixty and seventy years. The ambition to secure an education was most praiseworthy and encouraging. The idea, however, was too prevalent that, as soon as one secured a little education, in some unexplainable way he would be free from most of the hardships of the world, and, at any rate, could live without manual labour. There was a further feeling that a knowledge, however little, of the Greek and Latin languages would make one a very superior human being, something bordering almost on the supernatural. I remember that the first coloured man whom I saw who knew something about foreign languages impressed me at that time as being a man of all others to be envied.

—Washington, Booker T. *Up from Slavery: An Autobiography.* New York: Doubleday, Page, 1901; Bartleby.com, 2000. www.bartleby.com/1004/. 6 April 2007.

Purpose: ______

a. to inform b. to entertain c. to persuade

## Application 4: Irony

Read each item, and identify the type of irony used, if any.

______ **1.** A student says, "I really love a teacher who gives meaningless busywork."

a. verbal irony
b. situational irony
c. no irony

______ **2.** In O. Henry's short story "The Gift of the Magi," a wife named Della cut off and sold her long, beautiful hair to buy her husband, Jim, a gold chain for his prized pocket watch as a Christmas present. Meanwhile, Jim sold his watch to buy a beautiful comb for his wife's lovely, long hair.

a. verbal irony
b. situational irony
c. no irony

_____ **3.** What is the tone of the cartoon?
a. verbal irony
b. situational irony
c. no irony

_____ **4.** "No, no, don't bother to get up. I can manage to bring all the groceries in by myself. After all, I bought them by myself and I put them in the car by myself, so why should I mind hauling them in the house all by myself?"
a. verbal irony
b. situational irony
c. no irony

# REVIEW Test 1

## Tone

Read the following items, and choose a tone word from the box that best describes each.

| | | | |
|---|---|---|---|
| angry | encouraging | pessimistic | sympathetic |
| confident | joking | pleading | timid |
| disbelieving | joyful | sarcastic | warning |

_______________ **1.** "Quitting smoking is easy; I quit two or three times a day."

_______________ **2.** "Very funny, Joe, I can hardly stop laughing. I mean, risking cancer is just so funny."

_______________ **3.** "I am not going to get cancer because I can kick the smoking habit any time I choose to."

_______________ **4.** "You'd better think again, Joe. That's what my uncle thought, too."

_______________ **5.** "Oh, yeah, I'm sorry, how is he doing? I know you must be worried."

_______________ **6.** "Not so good. The chemotherapy is making him really sick. I'm afraid he might not make it."

______________ 7. "Don't worry, Sue, the treatment is going to work. The doctors said he had an 80 percent chance of beating the cancer."

______________ 8. "Well, those odds don't mean anything when you act as stupidly as my uncle. He still smokes at least a pack a day!"

______________ 9. "You have to be kidding! Still smoking? That's hard to believe!"

______________ 10. "Please, Joe, don't end up like my uncle. Please, stop smoking now before it becomes impossible for you to quit, too."

# REVIEW Test 2

## Tone

Read the following items. Choose a tone word from the box below that best describes each.

| admiring | factual | humble | ironic | pleading |
|---|---|---|---|---|
| cautionary | hopeful | humorous | persuasive | prayerful |

______________ 1. When you become senile, you won't know it.—Bill Cosby

—Simpson, James B., comp. *Simpson's Contemporary Quotations.* Boston: Houghton Mifflin, 1988. www.bartleby.com/63/. 6 April 2007].

______________ 2. I believe that unarmed truth and unconditional love will have the final word in reality. This is why right, temporarily defeated, is stronger than evil triumphant.—Martin Luther King, Jr., accepting Nobel Peace Prize 10 Dec 64

—Simpson, James B., comp. *Simpson's Contemporary Quotations.* Boston: Houghton Mifflin, 1988. www.bartleby.com/63/. [6 April 07].

______________ 3. Tennis is a perfect combination of violent action taking place in an atmosphere of total tranquillity.—Billie Jean King, tennis player

—Simpson, James B., comp. *Simpson's Contemporary Quotations.* Boston: Houghton Mifflin, 1988. www.bartleby.com/63/. [6 April 07].

_______________ **4.** Let every nation know, whether it wishes us well or ill, that we shall pay any price, bear any burden, meet any hardship, support any friend, oppose any foe to assure the survival and the success of liberty.—John F Kennedy, 35th US President

—Simpson, James B., comp. *Simpson's Contemporary Quotations.* Boston: Houghton Mifflin, 1988. www.bartleby.com/63/. [6 April 07].

_______________ **5.** Tell him, if he doesn't mind, we'll shake hands.—John F Kennedy, 35th US President, On meeting Soviet Premier Nikita S Khrushchev

—Simpson, James B., comp. *Simpson's Contemporary Quotations.* Boston: Houghton Mifflin, 1988. www.bartleby.com/63/. [6 April 07].

_______________ **6.** Mama and Daddy King represent the best in manhood and womanhood, the best in a marriage, the kind of people we are trying to become.—Coretta Scott King

—Simpson, James B., comp. *Simpson's Contemporary Quotations.* Boston: Houghton Mifflin, 1988. www.bartleby.com/63/. [6 April 07].

_______________ **7.** God give me the serenity to accept things which cannot be changed; Give me courage to change things which must be changed; And the wisdom to distinguish one from the other.

—Respectfully Quoted: A Dictionary of Quotations Requested from the Congressional Research Service. Washington D.C.: Library of Congress, 1989; Bartleby.com, 2003. www.bartleby.com/73/. [6 April 2007].

_______________ **8.** The term embryology, in its widest sense, is applied to the various changes which take place during the growth of an animal from the egg to the adult condition.

—Gray, Henry. *Anatomy of the Human Body.* Philadelphia: Lea & Febiger, 1918; Bartleby.com, 2000. www.bartleby.com/107/. [6 April 2007].

_______________ **9.** A novel everyone should read is H. G. Well's *Invisible Man*, a tale of psychological terror. Wells created a gripping masterpiece on the destructive effects the invisibility has on the scientist and the insane and murderous chaos left in his malicious wake.

—Bartleby.com, 2000. www.bartleby.com/1003/. [6 April 2007].

______________ **10.** "Yet, I implore you, pause! Yield to my advice, do not do this deed."—Jocaste, *Oedipus the King*.

## REVIEW Test 3

### Author's Purpose

**A.** Read the following topic sentences. Label each according to its purpose:

**I** = to inform

**P** = to persuade

**E** = to entertain

_____ **1.** The best way to survive babysitting a set of triplets is to come armed with plenty of energy, lots of patience, and a first-aid kit.

_____ **2.** The Trail of Tears is the name of the journey that more than 70,000 Indians took when they were forced to give up their homes and move to Oklahoma.

_____ **3.** According to fitness specialist Jack Tremagne, a long-term weightlifting program is the only effective method for losing and keeping off unhealthy body fat.

_____ **4.** The northbound lane of State Road 17 will be shut down for several days this week due to road construction.

_____ **5.** The death penalty is unfair and cruel and should be abolished.

_____ **6.** The sound of a thousand motorcycles fills the night air as leather-clad, tough-looking, party-minded bikers roar into the sleepy coastal town for one wild, crazy, unforgettable week.

**B.** Read the following items, and identify the primary purpose of each.

#### Historical Passage Published on an Internet Site

**President Johnson's Views in 1965 on America's Role in the Vietnam War**

Why are we in South Vietnam? We are there because we have a promise to keep. Since 1954, every American president has offered support to the people of South Vietnam. We have made a national pledge to help South Vietnam defend its independence. And I intend to keep our promise.

We are also there to strengthen world order. Around the globe, from Berlin to Thailand, are people whose well-being rests, in part, on the belief that they can count on us if they are attacked. To leave Vietnam to its fate would shake the confidence of all these people in the value of American commitment, the value of America's word. The result would be increased unrest and instability and even wider war.

We are also there because there are great stakes in the balance. Let no one think for a moment that retreat from Vietnam would bring an end to conflict. The battle would be renewed in one country and then another. The central lesson of our time is that the appetite of aggression is never satisfied.

—President Lyndon B. Johnson's Address at Johns Hopkins University: "Peace Without Conquest" April 7, 1965. *Public Papers of the Presidents of the United States: Lyndon B. Johnson, 1965.* Volume I, entry 172, pp. 394–399. Washington, D. C.: Government Printing Office, 1966.

_____ **7.** The primary purpose of this passage is
- a. to inform the reader about the causes of the Vietnam War.
- b. to entertain the reader with President Johnson's opinions about the Vietnam War.
- c. to convince the reader of America's need to be involved in the Vietnam War.

**Editorial Cartoon Published in a Newspaper**

_____ **8.** The primary purpose of this cartoon is
a. to inform the reader about the need to ban smoking.
b. to entertain the reader with a funny situation about smoking bans.
c. to persuade the reader to ban smoking outside.

## Literary Passage Published in a Book

**Fog**

***by Carl Sandburg***

The fog comes
on little cat feet.
It sits looking
over harbor and city
on silent haunches
and then moves on.

—Sandburg, *Chicago Poems* (1916).

_____ **9.** The primary purpose of this passage is
a. to inform the reader about the traits of fog.
b. to entertain the reader with its poetic language and the similarities between the fog and a cat.
c. to persuade the reader to see the fog as a threat to the city.

## Paragraph from a Health Textbook

Textbook Skills

**Smokeless Tobacco**

Smokeless tobacco is used by approximately 5 million U.S. adults. Most users are teenage (20 percent of male high school students) and young adult males, who are often emulating a professional sports figure or family member. There are two types of smokeless tobacco—chewing tobacco and snuff. Chewing tobacco contains tobacco leaves treated with molasses and other flavorings. The user places a "quid" of tobacco in the mouth between the teeth and gums and then sucks or chews the quid to release the nicotine. Once the quid becomes ineffective, the user spits it out and inserts another. Dipping is another method of using chewing tobacco. The dipper takes a small amount of tobacco and places it between the lower lip and teeth to stimulate the flow of saliva and release the nicotine. Dipping rapidly releases the nicotine into the bloodstream.

Snuff can come in either dry or moist powdered form or sachets (teabaglike pouches) of tobacco. The most common placement of snuff is inside the cheek. In European countries, inhaling dry snuff is more common than in the United States.

—Donatelle, *Access to Health,* 7th ed., p. 365.

_____ **10.** The primary purpose of this passage is
a. to inform the reader about smokeless tobacco.
b. to entertain the reader with graphic details about smokeless tobacco.
c. to persuade the reader to avoid using smokeless tobacco.

# REVIEW Test 4

## Combined Skills Test

The following selection was published in newspapers around the country. Before you read, skim the passage and answer the **Before Reading** questions. Read the passage, and answer the **After Reading** questions that follow.

### Vocabulary Preview

*officiated* (4): performed official duties
*wavering* (6): hesitant, unsure
*salvation* (6): eternal life
*honorary* (9): given as a mark of honor
*brim* (13): rim, lip
*grist* (14): grain for grinding
*surname* (15): last name
*sparked* (21): courted

**Last Recognized Widow of a Union Veteran in Civil War Dies at 93**

***by Duncan Mansfield***

Jan. 19, 2003

[1]Gertrude Janeway, the last widow of a Union veteran from the Civil War, has died in the three-room log cabin where she lived most of her life. [2]She was 93.

[3]Bedridden for years, she died Friday, more than six decades after the passing of the man she called the love of her life, John Janeway, who married her when he was 81 and she was barely 18.

[4]"She was a special person," said the Rev. Leonard Goins, who **officiated** at her funeral Sunday.

[5]"Gertie, as she was called, had a vision beyond that [cabin] that kept her going. [6]She never had any **wavering** or doubt in her **salvation.** [7]She was strong in that," he said.

[8]She was to be buried Monday near her husband's slender military tombstone at tiny New Corinth Church cemetery.

[9]An **honorary** member of the Daughters of Union Veterans of the Civil War, Mrs. Janeway was the last recognized Union widow. [10]She received a $70 check each month from the Veterans Administration.

[11]Mrs. Janeway, who lived her whole life in Blaine [Tennessee], about 30 miles north of Knoxville, was born 44 years after the Civil War ended.

[12]In a 1998 interview, she said her husband rarely spoke about the war.

[13]"He says the **nighest** he ever got to gettin' killed was when they shot a hole through his hat **brim,**" she said, but he never told her where that happened.

[14]Her husband was a 19-year-old Grainger County farm boy who ran away to enlist in 1864 after being encouraged by a group of Union horse soldiers that he met on his way to a Blount County **grist** mill.

[15]He sent his horse home and signed up under the **surname** January because "he was afraid his people would come and claim him," Mrs. Janeway said.

[16]Two months later, he was captured by Confederates near Athens, Georgia. [17]He was later released and rejoined his unit, the 14th Illinois Cavalry. [18]After the war, he spent many years in California before returning home to Tennessee and meeting then 16-year-old Gertrude.

[19]Mrs. Janeway said her mother refused to sign papers to let her marry him before she turned 18. [20]"So my man says, 'Well, I will wait for her until you won't have to,'" she recalled. [21]"We **sparked** for three years."

[22]She remembered getting married in the middle of a dirt road in 1927 with family and friends gathered around. [23]He bought her the cabin in 1932, and it was there that he died in 1937, at 91, from pneumonia.

[24]"After he died, why it just seemed like a part of me went down under the ground with him," she said in the 1998 interview. [25]"He is the only one I ever had. [26]There wasn't anybody else."

—Associated Press. "Last Widow of Union Veteran Dies at Age 93." *Los Angeles Times*. 20 Jan. 2003, p. A-16.

## BEFORE READING

### Vocabulary in Context

_____ **1.** What does the word **nighest** mean in sentence 13?

a. highest
b. straightest
c. nearest
d. shortest

### Purpose

_____ **2.** The primary purpose of this passage is
a. to entertain the reader with vivid details about Gertrude and John Janeway's lives.
b. to persuade the reader to agree with the opinion that Gertrude Janeway was an extraordinary woman.
c. to inform the reader about the death of a woman and the end of the era she represented.

## AFTER READING

### Central Idea and Main Idea

_____ **3.** Which sentence best states the central idea of the passage?
a. sentence 1
b. sentence 5
c. sentence 4
d. sentence 6

### Supporting Details

_____ **4.** Which detail about John Janeway is correct?
a. He died from complications of a wound he received during the Civil War.
b. He was 63 years older than his wife Gertrude.
c. He was well liked by Gertrude's family.
d. He built the log cabin in which Gertrude spent most of her life.

_____ **5.** Sentence 15 is a
a. main idea.
b. major supporting detail.
c. minor supporting detail.

### Transitions

_____ **6.** The relationship between the ideas in sentence 13 is one of
a. cause and effect.
b. time order.
c. classification.
d. contrast.

### Thought Patterns

_____ **7.** The overall thought pattern for the passage is
a. cause and effect.
b. time order.
c. classification.
d. contrast.

## Fact and Opinion

_____ **8.** Which of the following is a statement of opinion?

a. Mrs. Janeway, who lived her whole life in Blaine, about 30 miles north of Knoxville, was born 44 years after the Civil War ended.
b. "She was a special person."
c. Her husband was a 19-year-old Grainger County farm boy who ran away to enlist in 1864 after being encouraged by a group of Union horse soldiers that he met on his way to a Blount County grist mill.
d. Mrs. Janeway said her mother refused to sign papers to let her marry him before she turned 18.

_____ **9.** "Gertrude Janeway, the last widow of a Union veteran from the Civil War, has died in the three-room log cabin where she lived most of her life." The tone of this statement is

a. matter-of-fact.
b. sorrowful.
c. harsh.
d. insensitive.

_____ **10.** "After he died, why it just seemed like a part of me went down under the ground with him."

The tone of this statement is

a. respectful.
b. bitter.
c. mournful.
d. peaceful.

## Discussion Topics

1. What kinds of changes in society did Gertrude Janeway witness during her lifetime?
2. What kinds of changes in society do you think you will witness during your lifetime?
3. Why do you think Gertrude's parents opposed her marriage to John?
4. In what ways do differences between people (such as gender, age, race, or religion) place strains on relationships?

## Writing Topics

1. Write a tribute to or an obituary for a person of interest.
2. Discuss one way society has changed due to technology.
3. Give advice to an engaged couple who are significantly different from each other in age, race, or religion.

## EFFECTIVE READER Scorecard

**Tone and Purpose**

| Test | Number Correct | | Points | | Score |
|---|---|---|---|---|---|
| Review Test 1 | ______ | × | 10 | = | ______ |
| Review Test 2 | ______ | × | 10 | = | ______ |
| Review Test 3 | ______ | × | 10 | = | ______ |
| Review Test 4 | ______ | × | 10 | = | ______ |
| Review Test 5 (website) | ______ | × | 10 | = | ______ |
| Review Test 6 (website) | ______ | × | 10 | = | ______ |

Enter your scores on the Effective Reader Scorecard: Chapter 10 Review Tests inside the back cover.

## After Reading About Tone and Purpose

Before you move on to the mastery tests on tone and purpose, take time to reflect on your learning and performance by answering the following questions. Write your answers in your notebook.

What did I learn about tone and purpose?

What do I need to remember about tone and purpose?

How has my knowledge base or prior knowledge about tone and purpose changed?

### More Review and Mastery Tests

For more practice, go to the book's website at **http://www.ablongman.com/henry** and click on *The Effective Reader.* Then select "More Review and Mastery Tests." The tests are organized by chapter.

MASTERY **Test 1**

Name ______________________ Section ____________
Date ____________ **Score** (number correct) ______ × 10 = ______%

**A.** Read the following items. Choose a tone word from the box that best describes each item.

| amazed | argumentative | factual | logical | reflective |
|---|---|---|---|---|

______________ **1.** Just imagine for a moment what life in this country might have been if women had been properly represented in Congress. Would a Congress where women in all their diversity were represented tolerate the countless laws now on the books that discriminate against women in all phases of their lives? Would a Congress with adequate representation of women have allowed this country to reach the 1970s without a national health care system? Would it have permitted this country to rank fourteenth in infant mortality among the developed nations of the world? Would it have allowed the situation we now have in which thousands of kids grow up without decent care because their working mothers have no place to leave them? Would it allow fraudulent packaging and cheating of consumers in supermarkets, department stores and other retail outlets? Would it consent to the perverted sense of priorities that has dominated our government for decades, where billions have been appropriated for war while our human needs as a people have been neglected?—Bella Abzug

—*Bella*! "February 7" section (1972). *The Columbia World of Quotations*. New York: Columbia University Press, 1996. www.bartleby.com/66/. [6 April 2007].

______________ **2.** The sky was as full of motion and change as the desert beneath it was monotonous and still,—and there was so much sky, more than at sea, more than anywhere else in the world. The plain was there, under one's feet, but what one saw when one looked about was that brilliant blue world of stinging air and moving cloud. Even the mountains were mere ant-hills under it. Elsewhere the sky is the roof of the world; but here the earth was the floor of the sky. The landscape one longed for when one was away, the thing all about one, the world one actually lived in, was the sky, the sky!—Willa Cather, *Death Comes for the Archbishop*.

—*The Columbia World of Quotations*. New York: Columbia University Press, 1996. www.bartleby.com/66/. [6 April 2007].

_______________ **3.** When things are investigated, then true knowledge is achieved; when true knowledge is achieved, then the will becomes sincere; when the will is sincere, then the heart is set right (or then the mind sees right); when the heart is set right, then the personal life is cultivated; when the personal life is cultivated, then the family life is regulated; when the family life is regulated, then the national life is orderly; and when the national life is orderly, then there is peace in this world.—Confucius

—*Liki* (*Record of Rites*), chapter 42.—*The Wisdom of Confucius*, ed. and trans. Lin Yutang, chapter 4, pp. 139–40 (1938). Respectfully Quoted: A Dictionary of Quotations Requested from the Congressional Research Service. Washington D.C.: Library of Congress, 1989; Bartleby.com, 2003. www.bartleby.com/73/. [6 April 2007].

_______________ **4.** We are all citizens of one world; we are all of one blood. To hate a man because he was born in another country, because he speaks a different language, or because he takes a different view on this subject or that, is a great folly. Desist, I implore you, for we are all equally human. . . . Let us have but one end in view, the welfare of humanity.—John Amos Comenius

—Respectfully Quoted: A Dictionary of Quotations Requested from the Congressional Research Service. Washington D.C.: Library of Congress, 1989; Bartleby.com, 2003. www.bartleby.com/73/. [6 April 2007].

_______________ **5.** The United Arab Emirates is a federation of sheikhdoms (1995 est. pop. 2,925,000), c.30,000 sq mi (77,700 sq km), SE Arabia, on the Persian Gulf and the Gulf of Oman. The federation, commonly known as the UAE, consists of seven sheikhdoms: Abu Dhabi (territorially the largest of the sheikhdoms), Ajman, Dubai, Fujairah, Ras al-Khaimah, Sharjah, and Umm al-Qaiwain. The city of Abu Dhabi (1991 est. pop. 798,000) in Abu Dhabi is the capital.—World Fact Book, 2003.

—*The World Factbook.* Washington, D.C.: Central Intelligence Agency, 2003; Bartleby.com, 2003. www.bartleby.com/151/. [7 April 2007].

**B.** Read the following topic sentences. Label each one according to its purpose:

**I** = to inform
**P** = to persuade
**E** = to entertain

_____ **6.** Florida offers a wide variety of fun vacation activities, from traditional tourist attractions to pristine natural retreats.

_____ **7.** Paris never sleeps; at night, the River Seine glistens as the City of Light comes alive.

_____ **8.** Explore the nature of Armada—with our all natural hair care products, offering the purest of ingredients designed to bring out the shine and body of healthy hair.

_____ **9.** The number of teenagers who are choosing to not have sex is growing for a variety of reasons.

_____ **10.** Congress must act quickly to head off the looming health care crisis.

MASTERY **Test 2**

Name ______________________ Section __________

Date __________ **Score** (number correct) ______ × 10 = ______%

Read the following items. Choose a tone word from the box that best describes each.

| | | | |
|---|---|---|---|
| annoyed | bitter | curious | humorous |
| apologetic | comforting | excited | sarcastic |
| appreciative | confused | friendly | scared |

______________ **1.** "Hey, sweetie, how is your work going?"

______________ **2.** "Please, can't you see that I am trying to concentrate? You made me forget what I was thinking."

______________ **3.** "Well, forgive me for trying to be nice."

______________ **4.** "I'm sorry. I don't mean to be rude. I just have so much work to do."

______________ **5.** "I thought you were caught up. What happened?"

______________ **6.** "Mr. Wilkerson took a two-week vacation and left me with all his unfinished work. He gets a vacation, and I get twice the workload."

______________ **7.** "Hmm, what a bummer! Can I get you anything? A snack or a drink?"

______________ **8.** "Well, how about a new boss?"

______________ **9.** "Hey, I know what will cheer you up. How about this weekend we take off for a romantic two days in San Antonio! Just the two of us, and no work. What do you say? It will be fun! It will give you something to look forward to."

______________ **10.** "You are so wonderful. You always seem to make things better."

MASTERY **Test 3**

Name ______________ Section ______________
Date ______________ **Score** (number correct) ______ × 25 = ______%

Read each item; then answer the questions that follow it.

**Poem**

**Richard Cory**

***by Edwin Arlington Robinson***

Whenever Richard Cory went down town,
We people on the pavement looked at him:
He was a gentleman from sole to crown,
Clean favored, and imperially slim.

And he was always quietly arrayed,
And he was always human when he talked;
But still he fluttered pulses when he said,
"Good-morning," and he glittered when he walked.

And he was rich—yes, richer than a king—
And admirably schooled in every grace:
In fine, we thought he was everything
To make us wish that we were in his place.

So on we worked, and waited for the light,
And went without the meat, and cursed the bread;
And Richard Cory, one calm summer night,
Went home and put a bullet through his head.

______ **1.** The primary purpose of this poem is to
a. inform.
b. persuade.
c. entertain.

______ **2.** The overall tone of this poem can be described as
a. ironic.
b. humorous.
c. disbelieving.
d. excited.

**Paragraph from an Ecology Textbook**

**The Ecosystem**

Consider a natural ecosystem, a forest. The physical part of the forest consists of the atmosphere, climate, soil, and water. The many different plants and animals that live in the forest make up the biotic component. Each organism not only responds to the physical environment but also changes it. Each organism becomes a part of the environment. The trees in the canopy of a forest intercept the sunlight and use this energy for food. In doing so, they change the environment for the plants below them. The canopy reduces the sunlight and lowers air temperature. Birds foraging on insects in the litter layer of the forest reduce insect numbers. This changes the environment for other organisms that depend on this shared food resource. Thus in ecosystems, the living and the physical environment interact in ways that are complex.

—Adapted from Smith & Smith, *Elements of Ecology*, 4th ed., p. 3.

_____ **3.** The primary purpose of this paragraph is to
a. argue in favor of protecting ecosystems.
b. offer amusing details about the organisms in ecosystems.
c. give information about the complexity of ecosystems.

_____ **4.** The tone of this paragraph can be described as
a. academic.
b. informal.
c. bored.
d. lively.

MASTERY **Test 4**

Name ______________ Section ______________
Date ______________ **Score** (number correct) ______ × 25 = ______%

Read each item, and answer the questions that follow it.

**Paragraph from a Short Story**

## An Occurrence at Owl Creek Bridge
***by Ambrose Bierce***

A man stood upon a railroad bridge in northern Alabama, looking down into the swift water twenty feet below. The man's hands were behind his back, the wrists bound with a cord. A rope closely encircled his neck. It was attached to a stout cross-timber above his head and the slack fell to the level of his knees. Some loose boards laid upon the sleepers supporting the metals of the railway supplied a footing for him and his executioners—two private soldiers of the Federal army, directed by a sergeant who in civil life may have been a deputy sheriff. At a short remove upon the same temporary platform was an officer in the uniform of his rank, armed. He was a captain. A sentinel at each end of the bridge stood with his rifle in the position known as "support," that is to say, vertical in front of the left shoulder, the hammer resting on the forearm thrown straight across the chest—a formal and unnatural position, enforcing an erect carriage of the body. It did not appear to be the duty of these two men to know what was occurring at the center of the bridge; they merely blockaded the two ends of the foot planking that traversed it.

—Bierce, "An Occurrence at Owl Creek Bridge," 1891.

______ **1.** The primary purpose of this paragraph is to
a. persuade.
b. entertain.
c. inform.

______ **2.** The tone of this paragraph can be described as
a. horrified.
b. bitter.
c. matter-of-fact.
d. panicked.

**Passage from a Health Textbook**

Textbook Skills

## Eating for Health

Americans consume more calories per person than any other group of people in the world. A *calorie* is a unit of measure that indicates the amount of energy we get from a particular food. Calories are eaten in the form of protein, fats, and carbohydrates. These are three basic nutrients needed for life. Three other nutrients—vitamins, minerals, and water—are necessary for bodily function but do not add any calories to our diets.

Taking in too many calories is a major factor in our tendency to be overweight. However, it is not the amount of food we eat that is likely to cause weight problems and related diseases. It is the relative amount of nutrients in our diets and lack of exercise. Most Americans get about 38 percent of their calories from fat, 15 percent from proteins, 22 percent from complex carbohydrates, and 24 percent from simple sugars. Experts recommend that complex carbohydrates be increased to make up 48 percent of our total calories. They also suggest that we reduce proteins to 12 percent, simple sugars to 10 percent, and fats to no more than 30 percent of our total diets.

—Adapted from Donatelle, *Access to Health,* 7th ed., p. 217.

_____ **3.** The primary purpose of this passage is to
- a. convince students to lose weight.
- b. condemn the typical American diet.
- c. share useful information that will lead to a healthy lifestyle.

_____ **4.** The overall tone of this passage can be described as
- a. critical.
- b. bossy.
- c. cynical.
- d. neutral.

MASTERY **Test 5**

Name ______________________ Section ____________

Date __________ **Score** (number correct) ______ × 25 = ______%

Read each passage; then answer the questions that follow it.

**Paragraph from a Health Textbook**

### Alcohol

Since the beginning of recorded history, there has always been a part of the world population that has problems with alcohol. The Old Testament of the Bible includes stories of the Jewish people dealing with problems related to drinking alcohol. Plato, the great Greek philosopher, noted problems linked to public drunkenness. Some of his recommendations for dealing with the problem serve as models for current laws in the United States. (Plato recommended no alcohol for those under eighteen years of age.) The Institute of Medicine in 1990 estimated that 25 percent of U.S. citizens consume large amounts of alcohol. According to their data, nearly 5 percent of the population are dependent on alcohol, and 5 to 15 percent are problem drinkers. Problem drinkers include those who struggle to control or limit their alcohol intake, those who drink despite growing health problems, and those who lose control over their behavior or mood while drinking.

—Adapted from Fishbein & Pease, *The Dynamics of Drug Abuse,* p. 103.

______ **1.** The primary purpose of this paragraph is to
- a. encourage the reader to avoid alcohol.
- b. inform the reader about widespread alcohol use.
- c. delight the reader with interesting information about alcohol's history.

______ **2.** The tone of this paragraph can be described as
- a. accusing.
- b. helpful.
- c. objective.
- d. depressing.

**Passage from an American History Textbook**

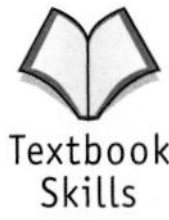


### The Question of Slavery

Early on the evening of January 21, 1850, Senator Henry Clay of Kentucky trudged through knee-deep snowdrifts to visit Senator Daniel

Webster of Massachusetts. Clay, 73 years old, was a sick man, wracked by a severe cough. But he braved the snowstorm. He feared for the Union's future.

For four years, Congress had bitterly debated the issue of the expansion of slavery in new territories. Ever since Daniel Wilmot had proposed that slavery be banned from any territory acquired from Mexico, those against slavery had argued that Congress had the right to ban slavery in all of the territories. Southerners who were for slavery strongly disagreed.

Politicians had been unable to work out a compromise. One simple proposal had been to extend the Missouri Compromise line to the Pacific Ocean. Thus slavery would have been outlawed north of 36'30" north latitude, but it would have been allowed south of that line. Moderate southerners supported this proposal, but few others agreed. Another proposal was known as "squatter sovereignty." It stated that the people who lived in a territory should decide whether or not to allow slavery.

Neither idea offered a solution to the whole range of issues dividing the North and the South. It was up to Henry Clay, who had just returned to Congress after a seven-year absence, to work out a solution. For an hour on the evening of January 21, Clay outlined the following plan to save the Union:

- California be admitted as a free state.
- Mexico and Utah have no restrictions on slavery.
- Texas give up land in exchange for unpaid debts.
- Congress enact a strict Fugitive Slave Law.
- Slave trade, but not slavery, be banned in the District of Columbia.

Clay's proposal set off an eight-month debate in Congress and led to threats of southern succession. Eventually parts of Clay's compromise were accepted. The compromise gave the false sense that the issue had been resolved. Hostility was defused, and calm returned. But as one southern editor correctly noted, it was "the calm of preparation, and not of peace."

—Adapted from Martin et al., *America and Its Peoples: A Mosaic in the Making,* 3rd ed., pp. 455–57.

_____ **3.** The primary purpose of this passage is to
a. inform.
b. entertain.
c. persuade.

_____ **4.** The overall tone of this passage can be described as
a. argumentative.
b. factual.
c. bitter.
d. stern.

**MASTERY Test 6**

Name ______________________ Section ____________

Date ____________ **Score** (number correct) ______ × 25 = ______%

Study the following photographs and caption taken from the textbook *The American Nation: A History of the United States Since 1865, Volume 2*, by John A. Garraty and Mark C. Carnes. Answer the questions that follow.

Textbook Skills

Many immigrant women worked in garment industry sweatshops. In 1911, a fire at the Triangle Shirtwaist Company caused workers to leap to their deaths (*top*) when blocked exit doors and the lack of fire escapes trapped them. The tragic fire, which claimed 146 victims, gave impetus to labor organizations such as the Women's Trade Union League and the International Ladies' Garment Workers Union (ILGWU). The Women's League sponsored demonstrations (note the sign on the right of the lower photo: "Do You Want Fire Protection? ORGANIZE") and pushed for better pay and conditions for women workers.

720

_____ **1.** The authors' primary purpose for this entire page is
a. to inform the reader about workplace conditions for women in the early 1900s.
b. to entertain the reader with graphic historical details about women in the early 1900s.
c. to persuade the reader that women have been treated unfairly throughout history.

_____ **2.** What is the tone suggested by the photograph at the top?
a. comic
b. gruesome
c. mocking
d. urgent

_____ **3.** What is the tone of the text between the two photographs?
a. objective
b. biased

_____ **4.** What was the primary purpose of the women in the second photograph as expressed by their signs?
a. to inform the public about their poor working conditions
b. to persuade employers to improve working conditions
c. to amuse the public with a parade

CHAPTER

11

# Inferences

## CHAPTER PREVIEW

## Before Reading About Inferences

Study the chapter preview and underline words that relate to ideas you have already studied. Did you underline the following terms: facts, prior knowledge, and bias? What you already know about these topics will help you learn about inferences. Use the blanks that follow to write a short one- or two-sentence summary about each topic:

Facts ______________________________________________

______________________________________________.

Prior knowledge ______________________________________________

______________________________________________.

Bias ______________________________________________

______________________________________________.

Now, skim the chapter to find three additional topics that you have already studied. List those topics:

___

___

Copy the following study outline in your notebook. Leave ample blank spaces between each topic. Use your own words to fill in the outline with information about each topic as you study about inferences:

**Reading Skills Needed to Make VALID Inferences:**

I. Verify facts.

II. Assess prior knowledge.

III. Learn from text.

  a. Context clues

  b. Thought patterns

  c. Implied main ideas

IV. Investigate bias.

V. Detect contradictions.

## Inferences: Educated Guesses

Read the following passage.

> The air in the darkened movie theater felt chilly on Crystal's bare shoulders and arms. Her best friend, Julie, who had seen the movie three times already, had been smart to wear layered shirts, even if they were short-sleeved. Crystal placed the icy soft drink she had been holding in her chair's cup holder. Her right hand was freezing cold. She shivered as she watched the shark's fin, larger than life on the big screen, approaching the pretty young woman swimming in the ocean. As the music became faster and louder and the shark moved closer, a tingle ran up her spine. The shark struck. The victim screamed. At the same time, Crystal's right hand suddenly grabbed Julie's arm. Julie screamed too.

Which of the following statements might be true, based on the ideas in the passage?

_____ Crystal shivered because she was cold.

_____ Crystal shivered because she felt fear.

______ Julie screamed because Crystal's cold hand surprised her.

______ Julie screamed because she was afraid.

Did you choose the first three statements? Congratulations! You just made a set of educated guesses or **inferences**. An author suggests or **implies** an idea, and the reader comes to a conclusion and makes an inference about what the author means.

In the paragraph about Crystal and Julie, the first three statements are all firmly based on the information in the passage. However, the last statement is not backed by the supporting details. The facts point to Crystal's being cold and afraid, yet there is no hint of any fear on Julie's part. The only evidence given that could explain Julie's scream is Crystal's cold hand suddenly grabbing her.

## What Is a Valid Inference?

People constantly draw conclusions about what they notice. We observe, gather information, and make inferences all the time.

> An **inference** or **conclusion** is an idea that is suggested by the facts or details in a passage.

For example, study the photo, and then answer the accompanying question.

**VISUAL VOCABULARY**

What are the emotions shown in this photo? ______________

______________

______________

If you wrote *happiness, joy, tenderness,* or *pride,* you made a valid inference based on the clues given in the man's facial expression, his gestures, and the details of the situation.

A **valid inference** is a rational judgment based on details and evidence. The ability to make a valid inference is a vital life skill. Making valid inferences aids us in our efforts to care for our families, succeed in our jobs, and even guard our health.

For example, doctors strive to make inferences about our health based on our symptoms. A red throat and swollen glands may lead a doctor to conclude that a patient has a strep infection. The doctor then orders a strep test to find out if her educated guess (a guess based on evidence) is correct. If it is correct, she prescribes an antibiotic to treat the infection.

A **valid inference** is a logical conclusion based on evidence.

**EXAMPLE** Read the following passage. Write **V** beside the three valid inferences. (Hint: valid inferences are firmly supported by the details in the passage.)

[1]At 15 years old, José is the oldest child in a family of five brothers and one sister. [2]His family came to the United States from Mexico when José was 6 years old. [3]His parents are still unable to speak much English. [4]The only work his father and mother have been able to find is picking crops. [5]They are migrant workers. [6]To earn a living, the family constantly moves to find new crops to help harvest. [7]Because their pay is based on how much they pick, often the older children join their parents in the fields and work from dawn to dusk. [8]Over the years, José and his siblings have attended more than a dozen different schools. [9]All of the children receive low scores and are several grade levels behind other children their age. [10]José has learned to speak English fairly well, and he reads whenever he can find discarded newspapers, magazines, or books. [11]His mother and father always take José with them when they buy food or clothes.

______ **1.** José and his family work hard and sacrifice to make a living.

______ **2.** José's parents don't care about their children's education.

______ **3.** Migrant work does not provide a stable lifestyle.

______ **4.** José is not very smart.

______ **5.** José's ability to speak English is a help to his parents.

**EXPLANATION** Statements 1, 3, and 5 are valid inferences firmly based on the information in the passage. It is valid to infer that picking crops is hard work. It is also valid to infer that the family's need to move around to follow the work demands sacrificing friends and stability. Finally, it is valid to infer that José's parents take him shopping because he speaks English better than they do, so he is a help to them.

Statements 2 and 4 are not based on the information in the passage. It is invalid to assume that José's parents don't care about education. The facts only support the idea that the family's need to move interferes with the children's education. It is also wrong to infer that José is not smart. In fact, his desire to read is a sign of intelligence.

## PRACTICE 1

Each of the following items contains a short passage and three inferences. In each item, only one inference is valid. In the space provided, write the letter of the inference that is clearly supported by each passage.

_____ **1.** Randall took great notes in class and from his textbooks. He studied every night for a week before the test. Of all the students in his class, Randall earned the highest grade on the test.

a. Randall is smarter than his classmates.
b. Randall is the teacher's favorite student.
c. Randall worked hard for his grade.

_____ **2.** Sandra was 20 pounds overweight, so she decided to cut out all carbohydrates (such as cereal, rice, potatoes, and bread) from her diet. Instead, she ate a bowl of fruit every morning and extra helpings of meat, colorful vegetables, and salads for lunch and dinner. Sandra lost the 20 pounds in four months.

a. Sandra did not look good before she changed her diet.
b. Eating too many carbohydrates may cause weight gain.
c. Sandra enjoyed her new diet.

_____ **3.** Mark takes charge of the TV's remote control every night. He watches three or four different sports events at the same time. During the commercials or when the sportscasters are talking, he switches to the other games. By doing this, Mark is able to follow racing, basketball, tennis, and golf.

a. There is nothing else good on television, so Mark watches only sports.
b. Mark is rude to his family.
c. Mark is a dedicated sports fan.

## Making VALID Inferences and Avoiding Invalid Conclusions

Two of the most common pitfalls of making inferences are ignoring the facts and relying too much on personal opinions and bias. Often we are tempted to read too much into a passage because of our own prior experiences or beliefs. Of course, to make a valid inference, we must use clues based on logic and our experience. However, the most important resource must be the written text. As effective readers, our main goal is to find out what the author is saying, stating, or implying. Sound inferences come from orderly thinking. Effective readers learn to use the VALID thinking process to make valid inferences. The VALID approach avoids drawing false inferences or coming to invalid conclusions.

> An **invalid conclusion** is a false inference that is not based on the details, or facts in the text or on reasonable thinking.

The VALID approach is made up of 5 steps:

Step 1: **V**erify and value the facts.

Step 2: **A**ssess prior knowledge.

Step 3: **L**earn from the text.

Step 4: **I**nvestigate for bias.

Step 5: **D**etect contradictions.

### Step 1: Verify and Value the Facts

Develop a devotion to finding the facts. In Chapter 9, you learned to identify facts and to beware of false facts. You learned that authors may mix fact with opinion or use false information for their own purposes. Just as authors may make this kind of mistake, readers may, too. Readers may draw false inferences by mixing the author's facts with their own opinions or by misreading the facts. So it is important to find, verify, and stick to factual details. Once you have all the facts, only then can you begin to interpret the facts by making inferences.

**EXAMPLE 1** Read the following short passage. Then write **V** next to the two valid inferences firmly supported by the facts.

[1]Korea has long been known as the "Eastern Land of Courtesy." [2]When happy, a Korean simply smiles or gently touches the one who brings the

happiness. [3]When angry, a Korean simply stares directly at the person, and that person's humble smile is a powerful apology.

_____ **1.** Koreans are quiet and reserved people.

_____ **2.** Koreans show their emotions.

_____ **3.** Koreans are afraid of hurting the feelings of other people.

**EXPLANATION** The first two statements are correct inferences based on the facts. However, there is no hint or clue that Koreans are afraid of hurting anyone's feelings. In fact, directly staring at someone when angry is a bold act in this Asian culture. The third statement goes beyond the facts without any reason to do so. Effective readers draw conclusions that are supported by the facts.

**EXAMPLE 2** Study the photo. Then write **V** next to the inference firmly supported by the details in the picture.

_____ **1.** The tennis player feels angry.

_____ **2.** The tennis player feels triumphant.

_____ **3.** The tennis player feels defeated.

**EXPLANATION** Based on the details in the photo, the correct inference is number 2.

## Step 2: Assess Prior Knowledge

Once you are sure of the facts, the next step is to draw on your prior knowledge. What you have already learned and experienced can help you make accurate inferences.

**EXAMPLE 1** Read the following passage from a college science textbook. Identify the facts. Check those facts against your own experience and understanding. Write **V** next to the five inferences firmly supported by the facts in the passage.

Textbook Skills

**Animals Use Foraging Strategies**

[1]A robin flies into the yard, lands, hops for a short distance as if sizing up the situation, and stops. [2]Then it moves deliberately in a series of irregular paths across the grass. [3]The bird pauses every few feet, staring ahead as if in deep concentration or cocking its head toward the ground. [4]It then either moves on or crouches low as if to brace itself. [5]It pecks quickly in the ground and pulls out an earthworm. [6]On occasion, the earthworm pulls back, and in the tug-of-war, the worm wins. [7]The robin does not push the action. [8]It lets go and hops to another spot to repeat the food-seeking activity. [9]This activity is the robin's foraging strategy.

—Smith & Smith,
*Elements of Ecology*, 4th ed., p. 200.

______ **1.** Robins hunt for food.

______ **2.** Earthworms are a part of a robin's diet.

______ **3.** Robins are easily frightened.

______ **4.** Robins are able to sense their prey beneath the ground.

______ **5.** Robins fight for their food.

______ **6.** A foraging strategy is the way in which an animal gets food.

______ **7.** Robins are one example of animals that have a foraging strategy.

**EXPLANATION** Items 1, 2, 4, 6, and 7 are valid inferences based on information in the passage. However, we have no evidence that robins are easily frightened (item 3) or that they fight for their food. In fact, sentence 7 gives a detail showing that the opposite is true: if an earthworm fights back, robins give up and try somewhere else. Item 5 is therefore not a valid inference.

**EXAMPLE 2** Study the cartoon on page 509. Then choose the inference most firmly supported by the details.

______ In this cartoon, the boy's memory is being compared to
a. a computer.
b. his friend.
c. what he had learned before.

**"I forgot to make a back-up copy of my brain, so everything I learned last semester was lost."**

**EXPLANATION** The expression "back-up copy" is a computer term for saving your work into the computer's memory so that it won't be lost. Some understanding of computers is needed to be able to make this inference. The more you know about a wide range of topics, the easier making the right inference becomes.

## Step 3: Learn from the Text

When you value and verify facts, you are learning from the text. A valid inference is always based on what is stated or implied by the details in the text; in contrast, an invalid inference goes beyond the evidence. Thus, to make a valid inference, you must learn to rely on the information in the text. Many of the skills you have studied from previous chapters work together to enable you to learn from the text. For example, context clues unlock the meaning of an author's use of vocabulary. Becoming aware of thought patterns teaches you to look for the logical relationship between ideas. Learning about stated and implied main ideas trains you to examine supporting details. (In fact, you use inference skills to find the implied main idea.) In addition, tone and purpose reveal the author's bias and intent. (Again, you often use inference skills to grasp the author's tone and purpose.) As you apply these skills to your reading process, you are carefully listening to what the author has to say. You are learning from the text. Once you learn from the text, only then can you make a valid inference. The following examples show you how you learn from the text.

**EXAMPLE 1** Read the following set of ideas. Answer the questions that follow.

Nikki is not her usual **docile** self when she is playing basketball. She has more fouls called on her for unnecessary roughness than any of her teammates.

_____ **1.** The best *synonym* of the word **docile** is
a. meek.
b. aggressive.
c. brave.

_____ **2.** The best *antonym* of the word **docile** is
a. meek.
b. aggressive.
c. brave.

_____ **3.** What is the primary relationship of ideas within the first sentence?
a. time order
b. generalization and example
c. cause and effect

_____ **4.** What is the primary relationship of ideas within the second sentence?
a. time order
b. generalization and example
c. contrast

_____ **5.** What is the relationship of ideas between sentence 1 and sentence 2?
a. time order
b. generalization and example
c. contrast

_____ **6.** The author's tone is
a. admiring.
b. critical.
c. balanced.

_____ **7.** The author's purpose is
a. to inform the reader about the difference between Nikki's personality on the court and off the court.
b. to persuade Nikki to change her behavior.
c. to entertain the reader with vivid details of Nikki's behavior.

_____ **8.** Which of the following is a valid inference?
a. Nikki is an aggressive bully.
b. Nikki is an entertaining basketball player.
c. Nikki is not usually aggressive.

**EXPLANATION**

1. The synonym of *docile* is implied by the details in the sentences. Based on the context clues "not her usual self" and "unnecessary roughness," you can infer the meaning of the word is (a) *meek*.
2. Now that you have figured out the meaning of the word *docile,* it is important to recognize its antonym because the sentence says she is "*not* her

usual docile self." Again, context clues strongly suggest the best antonym for docile is (b) *aggressive.*

3. The relationship of ideas within the first sentence is time order based on the transition *when. When* she is playing basketball, Nikki is *not docile* or meek. You may at this point infer that when she is not playing basketball, she is docile or meek. Test this early inference as you continue reading.

4. The relationship of ideas in the second sentence is (c) *contrast* based on the transition words *more than.* She is *more* aggressive *than* other players.

5. The relationship of ideas between sentence 1 and sentence 2 is (b) *generalization and example.* Nikki is *not* her usual *meek* self while playing basketball; for example, she is *more aggressive than* other players.

6. The author's tone is (c) balanced. The author gives the reader two different views of Nikki. Nikki's docile nature off court is balanced against her aggressive nature on court.

7. The author's purpose is (a) to inform the reader about the difference between Nikki's personality on the court and off the court.

8. Based on what we have learned from analyzing the text, the valid inference is (c) *Nikki is not usually aggressive,* and your earlier inference is verified. Choices (a) and (b) are invalid conclusions because they are not supported by the details in the text.

**EXAMPLE 2** Read the following passage from the college textbook *Changing American Families.* Answer the questions.

Textbook Skills

### Women and Work

[1]A survey taken in 1987 gathered information about women who **elect** to stay at home or go to work. [2]First, women were influenced by their families. [3]A stable relationship with a male partner made marriage a safe, secure place that allowed women to stay at home. [4]A stable marriage also often resulted in family decisions that made the husband's job a top priority. [5]A second factor was the women's experience in the work force. [6]A rewarding job with chances of moving up made most working women less likely to quit work. [7]Third was the ability of the husband to provide a good income. [8]Low wages for husbands pushed wives into the paid labor force. [9]Fourth, women thought about the social rewards. [10]Those who had friends and neighbors that devalued being full-time housewives and mothers were more likely to seek paid work outside the home.

—Adapted from Aulette, *Changing American Families*, p. 145.

_____ **1.** The best meaning of the word **elect** in sentence 1 is
a. choose.
b. be unwilling to.
c. cause.

_____ **2.** What is the relationship of ideas within sentence 2?
a. listing
b. time order
c. cause and effect

_____ **3.** What is the primary thought pattern based on the following transitions: *first, second, third*, and *fourth*?
a. listing
b. time order
c. cause and effect

_____ **4.** Which of the following best describes the author's tone and purpose?
a. to criticize women who choose to work
b. to objectively inform the reader about why women choose to stay home or to work outside the home
c. to amuse the reader with the ironic details about women

_____ **5.** Which of the following states a valid inference?
a. Women don't want to work outside the home.
b. Four factors influence women to stay at home or go to work.
c. Women don't like being full-time housewives and mothers.

**EXPLANATION**

1. Based on the general context, the best meaning of the word **elect** is (a) *choose.*
2. The relationship of ideas within sentence 2 is (c) cause and effect based on the phrase "influenced by their families."
3. The primary thought pattern based on the transitions *first, second, third,* and *fourth* is (a) listing. The paragraph is made up of a list of the reasons that influence women's choices.
4. The author's tone and purpose is to (b) objectively inform the reader about why women choose to stay home or to work outside the home.
5. Based on what is learned from the text, the valid inference is (b) Four factors influence women to stay at home or go to work. Note that this inference states the implied main idea of the paragraph. The topic is women's choices to work or stay home. The controlling point is a list of factors that cause or influence their choices. Items (a) and (c) are invalid conclusions that are not based on the text.

## Step 4: Investigate for Bias

One of the most important steps in making a valid inference is confronting your biases. Each of us possesses strong personal views that influence the way we process information. Often our personal views are based on prior experiences. For example, if we have had a negative prior experience with a used car salesperson, we may become suspicious and stereotype all used car salespeople as dishonest. Sometimes, our biases are based on the way in which we were raised. Some people register as Democrats or Republicans and vote for only Democratic or Republican candidates simply because their parents were members of either the Democratic or Republican party. To make a valid inference, we must investigate our response to information for bias. Our bias can shape our reading of the author's meaning. To investigate for bias, note biased words and replace them with factual details as you form your conclusions.

**EXAMPLE 1** Read the following paragraph. Investigate the list of inferences that follow for bias. Underline biased words. Fill in each space with the following: write **V** if the inference is valid or **I** if the inference is invalid due to bias.

**Americans with Diabetes**

[1]Who would *choose* the peril or risk of blindness, a coma, or even death? [2]By 2002, some 17 million Americans suffered from diabetes. [3]This number raised great alarm, for it showed that over a million more people were affected than had been affected just two years before. [4]Most of these new cases were a kind of diabetes known as Type 2. [5]This type occurs because of high sugar levels in the blood, and it is usually found in people over 40. [6]However, many of the newer cases of Type 2 diabetes are occurring in younger people. [7]This form of diabetes is linked to obesity and lack of exercise, and in the long term, it can lead to kidney failure, heart disease, blindness, a coma, and even death. [8]However, research has shown that people can raise their chances of avoiding this disease. [9]They just need to *choose* a better lifestyle by eating healthy foods and exercising.

_____ **1.** Lifestyle choices in America have led to an increase in diabetes.

_____ **2.** The overindulgent and lazy habits of Americans have increased their health risks.

_____ **3.** Some types of diabetes may be preventable.

_____ **4.** Americans are deliberately choosing to put their lives in peril.

**EXPLANATION** Items 1 and 3 are (**V**) valid inferences that can be drawn based on information from the paragraph. These two sentences avoid the use of biased language. Item 2 is an (**I**) invalid inference. The biased words *overindulgent* and *lazy* are not supported by the paragraph's details. Item 4 is an (**I**) invalid inference. The word *deliberately* is a biased word that goes beyond the information in the paragraph. It is possible that many Americans are not aware of the connection between diet, exercising, and diabetes.

**EXAMPLE 2** Read the following paragraph. Investigate the list of inferences that follow for bias. Underline biased words. Mark each item as follows: **V** if the inference is valid or **I** if the inference is invalid due to bias.

### The Five Pillars of Islam

[1]The guiding principles of the Islamic faith are known as the Five Pillars of Islam. [2]Muslims, the believers of Islam, devote their lives to these principles. [3]The first principle is called *shahadah* (shah-HAH-dah). [4]*Shahadah* is the prayer of faith that says, "There is no God but Allah, and Muhammad is his messenger." [5]The second rule is known as *salat* (sah-LAHT); *salat* is the act of praying five times a day to Allah. [6]Prayer occurs at dawn, noon, afternoon, dusk, and night. [7]The third principle is *saum* (sah-OHM); *saum* is a fast from food or drink that lasts 30 days during the holy month of Ramadan. [8]The fourth pillar is called *zakat* (zeh-KAHT); this is the act of giving money to the poor and needy. [9]The final principle of Islam is *haj* (HAHDJ); this is the journey of pilgrimage that Muslims all over the world must make to the holy city of Mecca in Saudi Arabia at least once in their lifetime.

_____ **1.** The word *shahadah* is a word for a very specific prayer that is always worded the same way.

_____ **2.** Islam teaches one to seek God and to help others.

_____ **3.** Islam takes discipline to practice.

_____ **4.** Islam is a radical belief that teaches people to think selfishly of themselves first.

**EXPLANATION** Items 1, 2 and 3 are (**V**) valid inferences based on the details in the paragraph. Item 1 includes the qualifier *always* which usually indicates a bias. However, based on the fact that the paragraph gives the name and exact wording of the prayer, it is reasonable to infer that the exact wording is the unique trait of the prayer and always used. Item 4 is an (**I**) invalid inference. This sentence includes two biased words *radical* and *selfishly*. This biased statement is not grounded in the details.

## Step 5: Detect Contradictions

Have you ever misjudged a situation or had a wrong first impression? For example, have you ever assumed a person was conceited or rude, only to find out later that he or she was acutely shy? Many times, there may be a better explanation for a set of facts than the first one that comes to mind. The effective reader hunts for the most reasonable explanation. The best way to do this is to consider other explanations that could logically contradict your first impression.

**EXAMPLE 1** Read the following list of behaviors. Then, in the blank, write as many explanations for the behaviors as you can think of.

- Slurred words
- Poor balance
- Slow movement
- Uncontrolled shaking in limbs
- Rigid muscles and stooped posture
- Fatigue or tiredness
- Depression

________________________________________________

________________________________________________

**EXPLANATION** Some people may think the behaviors in this list describe an alcoholic or a drug addict. But the list is actually a list of symptoms for Parkinson's disease, a brain disease that affects body movement. Often, people with this disease, like actor Michael J. Fox, also suffer from depression. Alcoholics and drug addicts do share most of the listed symptoms, except for rigid muscles and stooped posture. Those who suffer from Parkinson's disease struggle with muscles that become stiff and even freeze into place.

A reader who does not think about other possible views can easily jump to a wrong conclusion. Effective readers consider all the facts and all the possible explanations for those facts. Effective readers look for contradictions.

**EXAMPLE 2** Study the photo. Then, using inference skills, answer the question.

_____ Identify the season shown in the picture.

a. summer
b. winter
c. spring
d. autumn

**EXPLANATION** Two clues in the photo point to (d) autumn: the leaves have begun to turn and some students are wearing long-sleeved flannel shirts and sweaters.

Use the 5 VALID steps to think your way through to logical conclusions based on sound inferences: (1) verify and value the facts, (2) assess prior knowledge, (3) learn from the text, (4) investigate for bias, and (5) detect contradictions.

## PRACTICE 2

Read the following passage. Investigate the list of inferences that follow for bias. Underline biased words. Mark each inference as follows: **V** for a valid inference firmly supported by the facts, **I** for an invalid inference.

### Obesity

[1]Nearly 54 million Americans weigh at least 30 pounds too much. [2]That means that one in six Americans is **obese**. [3]Being too heavy contributes to many other health problems, including heart disease, diabetes, and arthritis. [4]In addition, close to 300,000 people die each year from weight-related problems. [5]In 2002, the IRS ruled that obesity is a disease and is a real threat to life and well-being. [6]Therefore, the IRS started giving tax credits for weight-loss programs. [7]These tax credits apply to programs like Weight Watchers and Jenny Craig. [8]Many experts don't think that the tax break has had a very big effect and that further steps are needed. [9]For example, some also want to get rid of junk food at schools and build more running and biking paths.

_____ **1.** The word **obese** in sentence 2 means "at least 30 pounds overweight."

_____ **2.** Being overweight is a trait a person is born with; it is genetic.

_____ **3.** Obesity, or being overweight, is the only result of lifestyle choices.

_____ **4.** Weight Watchers and Jenny Craig can now be thought of as health care for people who are at risk.

_____ **5.** Being overweight is not a serious health problem because people can lose weight if they really want to.

## Inferences in Creative Expression

As you have learned, nonfiction writing, such as in textbooks and news articles, directly states the author's point. Everything is done to make sure that the meanings are clear and unambiguous (not open to different interpretations). However, in many other types of writing, both fiction and nonfiction, authors use creative expression to suggest layers of meaning. Creative expressions are also known as literary devices. The following chart is made up of a few common literary devices, their meanings, and an example of each:

| Creative Expression: Literary Devices | | |
|---|---|---|
| Connotations of words | The emotional meaning of words | Mother was never stingy with her advice. |
| Metaphor | A direct comparison | Lies are sinkholes. |
| Personification | Giving human traits to things that are not human | The sun woke slowly. |
| Simile | An indirect comparison | Lies are like sticky webs. |
| Symbol | Something that stands for or suggests something else | A skull and crossbones is a symbol for poison and death. |

By using these devices, a writer creates a vivid mental picture in the reader's mind. When a creative expression is used, a reader must infer the point the writer is making from the effects of the images. The following paragraph is the introduction to an essay about alcoholism. Notice its use of literary devices. After you read, write a one-sentence statement of the author's main idea for this paragraph.

### Trapped in the Darkness

[1]Jean squeezed her eyes tight against the painful light that poured into the room with daybreak. [2]She groaned, rolled over, and buried her head in her pillow. [3]Hiding was useless; her misery followed her. [4]As she lay there, fighting the jumping nausea, she tried to recall the night before, but the events seemed shrouded in a dense fog. [5]She lifted her fingers to press on her temples; she had her usual tequila headache. [6]Her stomach twisted with familiar shame. [7]I *am* going to quit, she promised herself—again. [8]She groaned and curled into the darkness of her blanket.

_______________________________________________

_______________________________________________

This paragraph uses several creative expressions. Darkness is often used as a symbol of death, pain and suffering, or denial. All of these meanings could apply to Jean's situation. Light is often used as a symbol for wisdom and truth. The use of contrast between dark and light suggests many meanings. The painful light (sentence 1) could represent Jean's inability to face the truth or act wisely. The phrase "jumping nausea" (sentence 4) is the use of personification. Live beings jump, so to give such an action to nausea is to give it lifelike qualities. The phrase "events seemed shrouded in a dense fog" (sentence 4) is a simile. Perhaps the author is comparing Jean's memory to a fog. Or maybe the author is referring to Jean being drunk the night before. The phrase "tequila headache" (sentence 5) is a metaphor for a hangover. Based on all the details, it is valid to infer that Jean has a drinking problem. The author could have simply stated "Jean suffers because of a serious drinking problem." But the creative expressions intensify the meaning. And they suggest many levels of meaning. Therefore, as an effective reader, carefully consider the shades and levels of meaning while reading examples of creative writing.

**EXAMPLE** A fable is a short story that makes a pointed statement. Read the following short fable written by Aesop in the sixth century B.C.E. Then answer the questions that follow it.

**The North Wind and the Sun**

[1]A dispute arose between the North Wind and the Sun, each claiming that he was stronger than the other. [2]At last they agreed to try their powers on a traveler, to see which could strip him of his cloak the fastest. [3]The North Wind had the first try; gathering up all his force for the attack, he came whirling furiously down upon the man and caught up the man's cloak as though he would **wrest** it from the man in a single effort. [4]But the harder he blew, the more closely the man wrapped the cloak around himself. [5]Then came the turn of the Sun. [6]At first, he beamed gently upon the traveler, who soon unclasped his cloak and walked on with it hanging loosely about his shoulders. [7]Then the Sun shone forth in full strength, and the man, before he had gone many steps, was glad to throw his cloak right off and complete his journey lightly clad.

**1.** Choose the three valid inferences that are firmly based on the information in the passage by writing a **V** next to each one.

_____ a. The North Wind and the Sun are given human traits.

_____ b. The traveler is not very smart.

_____ c. The North Wind uses force to try to make the man take off his cloak.

_____ d. The Sun uses heat to influence the man to take off his cloak.

_____ **2.** Based on context clues, we can infer that the meaning of the word **wrest** in sentence 3 is
a. wrap. b. rip. c. give.

_____ **3.** Based on the details in the passage, we can conclude that the implied main idea of the passage is
a. persuasion is better than force.
b. the Sun is harsher than the North Wind.
c. humans are easily controlled by nature.

**EXPLANATION**

1. The correct inferences are (a), (c), and (d). Often creative writers give human traits to things that are not human. In this fable, the wind and the sun, like some humans, are in competition with one another, each wanting to be the stronger one. The text clearly implies the North Wind's use of force in words such as *force, attack, whirling,* and *wrest.* However, the Sun's efforts are described with words such as *gently* and *shone forth.* There is nothing to suggest that the traveler is not smart. Instead, he acts very logically.
2. The words *force* and *attack* indicate that the best meaning of the word *wrest* is (b) "rip."
3. The main idea suggested by the details is (a) persuasion is better than force. To make logical inferences, we must use our common sense and life experiences. Based on our own experiences, we know that the wind and the sun are both strong, but they are harsh in different ways. Though humans are influenced by nature, that point is a supporting detail and not the main idea.

## PRACTICE 3

Read the following poem written by Robert Herrick in 1648. Choose the inferences that are most logical, based on the details in the poem.

**To the Virgins, to Make Much of Time**

Gather ye rose-buds while ye may,
    Old Time is still a-flying;
And this same flower that smiles today,
    Tomorrow will be dying.

The glorious lamp of heaven, the sun,
    The higher he's a-getting,
The sooner will his race be run,
    And nearer he's to setting.

That age is best which is the first,
    When youth and blood are warmer;
But being spent, the worse, and worst
    Times still succeed the former.

Then be not coy, but use your time,
    And while ye may, go marry;
For having lost but once your prime,
    You may forever tarry.

**Vocabulary Preview**

*coy* (13): shy

*tarry* (16): delay

_____ **1.** The poet is speaking to
a. unmarried women.
b. married men.
c. married young people.

_____ **2.** In the first verse, the rosebuds represent
a. time.
b. death.
c. love.

_____ **3.** In the second stanza (group of lines), the sun measures
a. a person's life span.
b. a footrace.
c. the time span of one day.

_____ **4.** In the third stanza, the poet implies that
a. the wisdom of old age is best.
b. it is better to be young than to be old.
c. the young are foolish.

_____ **5.** The main idea of the poem is to
a. enjoy life now.
b. wait for wisdom.
c. get married.

Textbook Skills

# Inferences and Visual Aids

Textbook authors often use pictures, photos, and graphs to imply an idea. These visuals are used to reinforce the information in that section of the textbook.

**EXAMPLE** This "Dilbert"cartoon was reprinted in a textbook. Based on the cartoon, what was the topic of the textbook chapter?

Dilbert © 1997 Reprinted by permission of United Features Syndicate, Inc.

______ marriage and communication in intimate relationships

______ women and low self-esteem

______ effects of nonverbal communication

**EXPLANATION** The woman in the cartoon is obviously self-confident and outspoken about what she wants, so the chapter is not about women and low self-esteem. In addition, the artist did not include any gestures in the cartoon, so the chapter is not about the effect of nonverbal communication. Indeed, the humor is based on the kind of communication the woman expects. The cartoon was in a chapter about marriage and communication in intimate relationships.

## PRACTICE 4

Study the figure on page 522, taken from the textbook *Access to Health*. Then answer the questions.

______ **1.** What is the topic of the chapter?
a. benefits of exercise
b. overall health of a man
c. causes of cancer

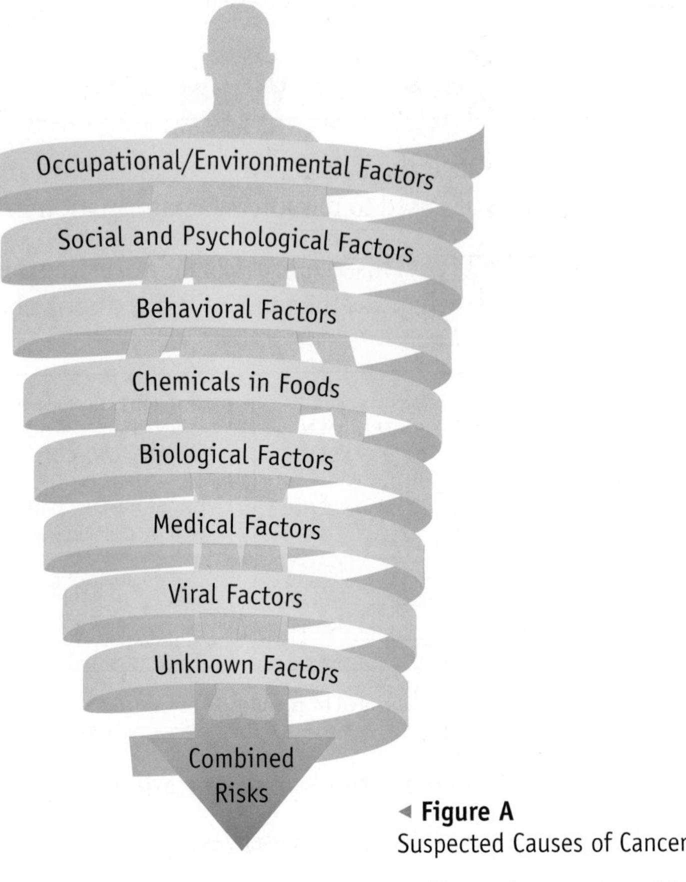


◄ **Figure A**
Suspected Causes of Cancer

—Donatelle, Rebecca J., *Access to Health,* 7th ed., p. 432. 

**2.** Write a caption in a complete sentence that best states the implied main idea of the figure.

___________________________________________

## Chapter Review

Test your understanding of what you have read in this chapter by filling in the blanks with words from the box. Use each expression once.

| | | |
|---|---|---|
| assess prior knowledge | implies | learn from the text |
| false inference | inference | |

1. An ______________ or conclusion is an idea that is suggested by the facts or details in a passage.

2. An author suggests or ______________ an idea.

3. A ______________ is a wrong conclusion that is not based on the details or facts.

4–5. The five steps for making sound inferences are

   a. Verify and value the facts.

   b. ______________________________

   c. ______________________________

   d. Investigate for bias.

   e. Detect contradictions.

## Applications

Textbook Skills

### Application 1: Making Inferences from a List

Read the following list of details. Write **V** for valid by the three inferences that are firmly based on the information.

**Traits of a Successful Team Member**

- Commits to the team's goals
- Has high standards for self and others
- States disagreements
- Accepts differing views as sources of information
- Listens carefully
- Shares information
- Attends all meetings
- Completes assignments
- Looks for solutions

—Adapted from Barker & Gaut, *Communication*, 8th ed., p. 151.

______ Successful team members should always agree with one another.

______ Successful team members challenge one another to do their best.

______ Successful team members are responsible and dependable.

______ Successful team members are problem solvers.

______ Successful team members set personal goals as a top priority.

______ Successful team members rarely offer differing views.

### Application 2: Making Inferences from a Visual

Read the following comic strip in the series known as "Blondie," by Dean Young and Denis Lebrun. Write **V** for valid by the two inferences that are firmly based on the details.

Reprinted with Special Permission of King Features Syndicate.

______ Dagwood, the man walking the dog, is very interested in the book he is reading.

______ Life is usually full of danger.

______ Dagwood's dog remains calm during the walk.

______ Dagwood does not notice what is going on around him.

______ Blondie, the woman in the final panel, is worried about Dagwood.

### Application 3: Making Inferences from a Poem

Read the following poem, which was written by James Stephens in 1915. Write **V** for valid by the three inferences that are firmly based on the details.

**The Wind**

The wind stood up and gave a shout.
He whistled on his fingers and
Kicked the withered branches about

And thumped the branches with his hand
And said he'd kill and kill and kill,
And so he will and so he will.

_____ The poet is referring to a gentle breeze.

_____ The poet is referring to a gale or hurricane-force wind.

_____ The wind is given human traits.

_____ The wind acts like a gentleman.

_____ The wind is like a strong, wild man.

_____ The wind is not dangerous.

# REVIEW Test 1

## Making Inferences

**A.** Write **V** for valid by the three inferences that are firmly based on the information in each passage.

**1–3.** [1]Damon knew he had to pass this test to get a decent final grade. [2]He had always struggled during tests. [3]Even when he knew the answers, he froze up on tests so much that he couldn't think or recall clearly. [4]All semester he had studied and learned the information, only to freeze up during the test. [5]As a result, he was barely passing the course. [6]So he carefully wrote the answers to the test's study guide on several small strips of paper. [7]He folded these and tucked them into the inside band of his cap. [8]Later, during the test, Damon took off his cap, slipped the papers out of their hiding place, and used them to complete the test.

_____ The study guide covered the same information that was on the test.

_____ Damon did not study for the test.

_____ Damon suffers from test anxiety.

_____ Damon is not very smart.

_____ Damon cheated on the test.

**4–6.** [1]Before AIDS, Botswana was known as an African success story. [2]Rich diamond mines were discovered within its borders after it gained independence from Britain in 1966. [3]But it avoided the warfare and corruption that followed the discovery of gemstones elsewhere in the region. [4]It evolved into a well-run democracy with a fast-growing economy. [5]It had the continent's strongest credit rating and lowest infant mortality rate.

[6]Now the nation spends its weekends at funerals. [7]More than one-third of Botswana's adults are HIV-positive. [8]Life expectancy has plunged from over 65 to under 40. [9]More than 65,000 children have lost their parents to AIDS, and that number is projected to double or triple by 2010. [10]If the United States had Botswana's rate of AIDS deaths, it would lose 15,000 citizens per day.

—Adapted from Grunwald, "A Small Nation's Big Effort Against AIDS," *Washington Post*, 2 Dec. 2002.

_____ AIDS has devastated the country of Botswana.

_____ The growing number of orphans in Botswana is a social crisis.

_____ Botswana loses 15,000 people a day to AIDS.

_____ Botswana is a poor country.

_____ Botswana's government has a history of making good decisions for the nation.

**VISUAL VOCABULARY**

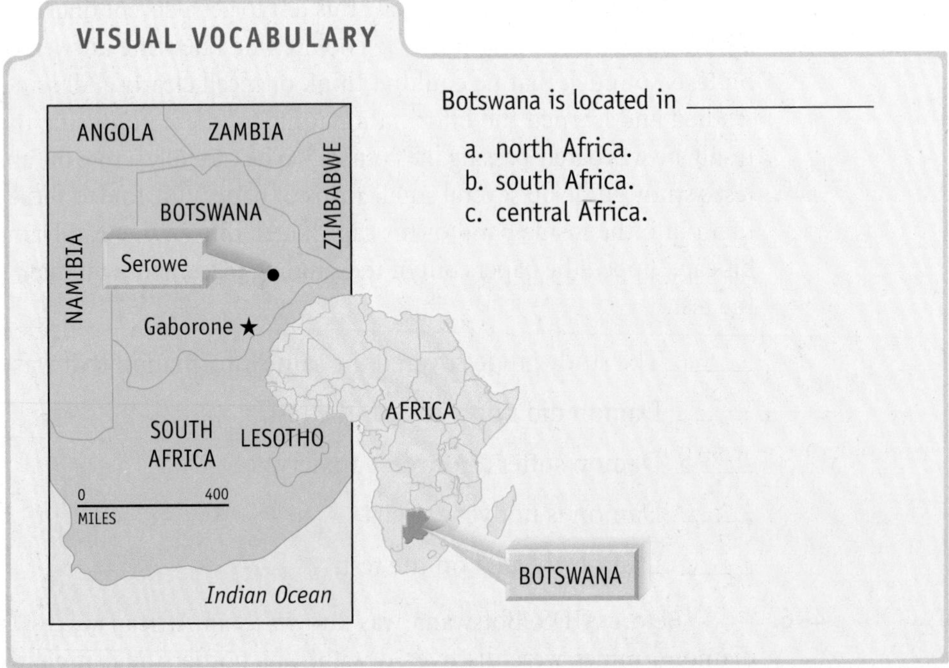


Botswana is located in ___________

a. north Africa.
b. south Africa.
c. central Africa.

**B. (7–10).** Write **V** for valid by the four inferences that are firmly based on the information in the label that follows the paragraph.

**Reading Nutritional Labels**

[1]The first place to start when you look at the Nutrition Facts panel is the serving size and the number of servings in the package. [2]Serving sizes are given in familiar units, such as cups or pieces, followed by the metric amount, such as the number of grams. [3]Serving sizes are based on the amount of food people typically eat, which makes them realistic and easy to compare to similar foods. [4]Calories are a measure of how much energy you get from a serving of this food. [5]The nutrients listed first are the ones Americans generally eat in adequate amounts, or even too much. [6]Eating too much fat or too much sodium may increase your risk of certain chronic diseases, like heart disease, some cancers, or high blood pressure. [7]Eating too many calories is linked to being overweight and obesity. [8]Americans often don't get enough dietary fiber, vitamin A, vitamin C, calcium, and iron in their diets. [9]Eating enough of these nutrients can improve your health, and they help reduce the risk of some diseases. [10]For example, getting enough calcium can reduce the risk of osteoporosis. [11]This disease causes bones to become brittle and break as one ages. [12]The Percent Daily Value section of the Nutrition Facts panel tells you whether the nutrient (fat, sodium, fiber, etc.) in a serving of food adds a lot or a little to your total daily diet.

—"Guidance on How to Understand and Use the Nutrition Facts Panel on Food Labels," U.S. Food and Drug Administration: Center for Food Safety and Applied Nutrition, June 2000.

**▼ Sample Label for Macaroni and Cheese**

**Nutrition Facts**

Serving Size 1 cup (228g)
Serving Per Container 2

| Amount Per Serving | |
|---|---|
| **Calories** 250 | Calories from Fat 110 |
| | **% Daily Value*** |
| **Total Fat** 12g | **18%** |
| Saturated Fat 3g | **15%** |
| **Cholesterol** 30mg | **10%** |
| **Sodium** 470mg | **20%** |
| **Total Carbohydrate** 31g | **10%** |
| Dietary Fiber 0g | **0%** |
| Sugars 5g | |
| **Protein** 5g | |
| Vitamin A | 4% |
| Vitamin C | 2% |
| Calcium | 20% |
| Iron | 4% |

*Percent Daily Values are based on a 2000 calorie diet. Your Daily Values may be higher or lower depending on your calorie needs:

| | Calories: | 2,000 | 2,500 |
|---|---|---|---|
| Total Fat | Less than | 85g | 80g |
| Sat Fat | Less than | 20g | 25g |
| Cholesterol | Less than | 300mg | 300mg |
| Sodium | Less than | 2,400mg | 2,400mg |
| Total Carbohydrate | | 300g | 375g |
| Dietary Fiber | | 25g | 30g |

_____ Food labels are designed to make it easier for you to use nutrition labels to make quick, informed food choices that contribute to a healthy diet.

_____ Macaroni & cheese is not a healthy food.

_____ An entire package of macaroni & cheese has a total fat of 24g.

_____ Macaroni & cheese does not contain enough iron to be of value in a healthy diet.

_____ Macaroni & cheese has 20% of the recommended daily amount of calcium for a healthy diet.

_____ Macaroni & cheese is a good food to eat to reduce the risk of osteoporosis.

_____ A person who eats macaroni & cheese runs the risk of becoming obese.

# REVIEW Test 2

## Making Inferences

Read the poem by Gary Soto. Then, answer the questions that follow it.

**How Things Work**

Today it's going to cost us twenty dollars
To live. Five for a softball. Four for a book,
A handful of ones for coffee and two sweet rolls,
Bus fare, rosin for your mother's violin.

We're completing our task. The tip I left
For the waitress filters down
Like rain, wetting the new roots of a child
Perhaps, a belligerent cat that won't let go

Of a balled sock until there's chicken to eat.
As far as I can tell, daughter, it works like this:
You buy bread from a grocery, a bag of apples
From a fruit stand, and what coins

Are passed on helps others buy pencils, glue,
Tickets to a movie in which laughter
Is thrown into their faces.
If we buy a goldfish, someone tries on a hat.

If we buy crayons, someone walks home with a broom.
A tip, a small purchase here and there,
And things just keep going. I guess.

_____ **1.** The poem suggests that the narrator
a. does not have much money.
b. is a father talking to his daughter.
c. owns a cat.

_____ **2.** The narrator's tone is
a. depressed.
b. worried.
c. matter of fact.

_____ **3.** The narrator and his daughter are
a. going to a movie.
b. eating a meal.
c. shopping for various items.

_____ **4.** The lines "Tickets to a movie in which laughter/Is thrown into their faces" implies that

a. those who watch the movie are being laughed at or poked fun at by the movie makers.
b. those who watch the movie are laughing because the movie is funny.
c. going to the movies is a rare treat.

_____ **5.** The topic of the poem is

a. how the economy works.
b. how to save money.
c. how a family works together.

# REVIEW Test 3

## Making Inferences

A. **(1–2).** Write **V** for valid by the two inferences that are firmly supported by the ideas in the passage.

### Scalded

[1]Stella Liebeck, 79, ordered breakfast in a McDonald's drive-through lane, and her grandson parked the car so she could add some cream and sugar to her coffee. [2]She tugged at the cup to try to get the top off. [3]Her dashboard was slanted and had no cup holder. [4]So she put the cup between her knees and tried to pull the top off. [5]She tugged, and scalding coffee gushed into her lap.

[6]Desperately, she pulled at her sweatsuit as she squirmed in the bucket seat. [7]The coffee seared her skin. [8]By the time she reached an emergency room, second- and third-degree burns had spread across her buttocks and her lap.

[9]Mrs. Liebeck spent seven days in the hospital and three weeks recuperating at home with her daughter. [10]She was later hospitalized again to receive skin grafts. [11]She lost 20 percent of her body weight—down to 83 pounds—and was unable to care for herself. [12]The grafts were almost as painful as the burn.

[13]Mrs. Liebeck wrote to McDonald's and asked the company to reduce the temperature of its coffee. [14]She asked to be paid for her out-of-pocket expenses of $2,000. [15]She also wanted her daughter to be paid the wages she lost when she stayed home to care for her mother. [16]McDonald's offered Mrs. Liebeck $800. [17]She sued, asking for at least $100,000 in damages, including pain and suffering. [18]Just before trial, she offered to settle for $300,000, but McDonald's refused the offer.

[19]Coffee at 170 degrees causes second-degree burns within 3.5 seconds of hitting the skin. [20]McDonald's had gotten more than 700 burn complaints over ten years, yet had not lowered the heat. [21]A jury awarded Liebeck $2.9 million. [22]Later a judge knocked the amount down to $640,000.

______ Liebeck spilled her coffee because the car she was in was moving.

______ The sweatsuit Liebeck wore sucked the hot coffee in next to her skin.

______ Liebeck wanted to get rich through her lawsuit against McDonald's.

______ McDonald's could not have prevented Liebeck's injuries.

______ McDonald's could have saved money by settling the lawsuit before the trial.

______ The judge who awarded Liebeck $640,000 thought the jury was too easy on McDonald's.

**B.** Study the map, and read the passage. Then answer the questions.

**▼ World Seismic Activity on May 7, 2003**

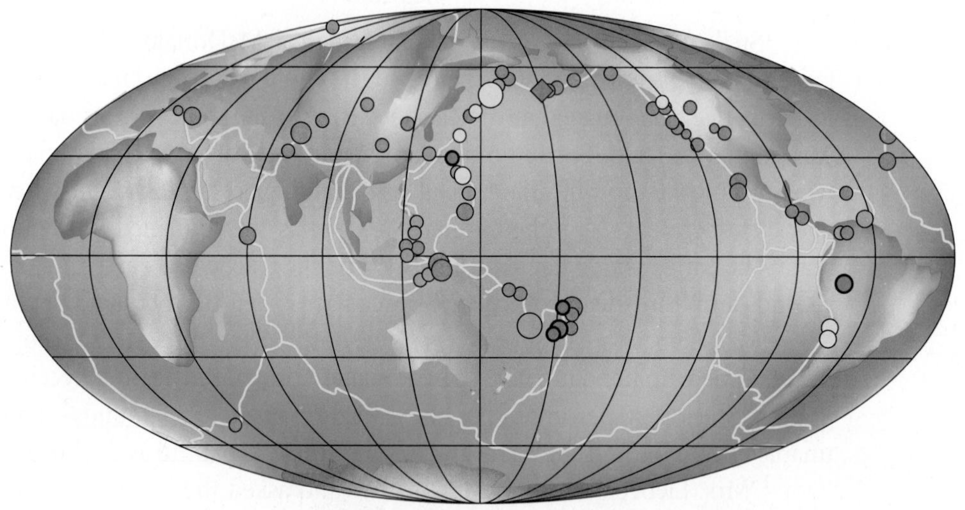

**Plate boundaries in yellow.**

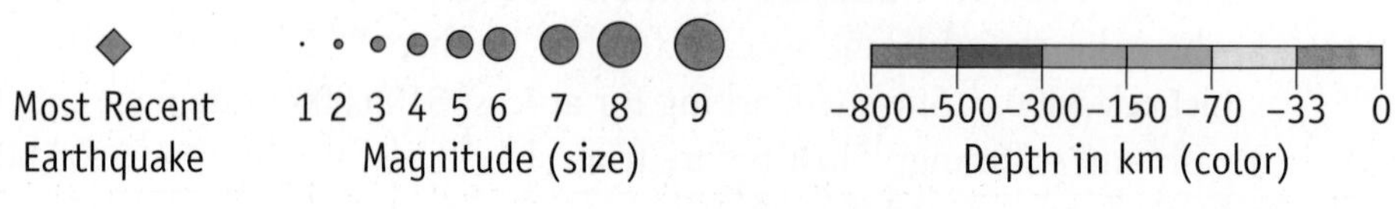


—From U.S. Geological Survey <http://neic.usgs.gov/neis/current/world.html>, Dec. 9, 2002.

### Facts About Earthquakes

[1]Most earthquakes and volcanic eruptions occur along plate boundaries, such as the boundary between the Pacific Plate and the North American Plate. [2]One of the most active plate boundaries where earthquakes and eruptions are frequent is around the massive Pacific Plate. [3]This area is commonly referred to as the Pacific Ring of Fire. [4]In 1760, British engineer John Michell, one of the pioneers of **seismology,** correctly stated the cause of earthquakes. [5]He wrote that earthquakes and the waves of energy that they make are caused by "shifting masses of rock miles below the surface."

—U.S. Geological Survey

_____ **3.** The word **seismology** in sentence 4 means
- a. the study of earthquakes.
- b. the study of landmasses.
- c. the study of the Pacific Ring of Fire.

_____ **4.** The passage and map suggest that "plates" are
- a. large masses of rock miles below the earth's surface.
- b. small areas of land.
- c. large areas of ocean.

_____ **5.** The map suggests that most earthquakes
- a. occur on large landmasses.
- b. occur under the sea or on smaller islands.

## REVIEW Test 4

### Making Inferences

Textbook Skills

Before you read the following passage from a college history textbook skim the passage. Answer the **Before Reading** questions. Then read the passage and answer the **After Reading** questions.

**Vocabulary Preview**

*prosperity* (1): wealth
*mania* (3): craze
*deprivation* (15): lack
*optimistic* (20): hopeful
*vagrants* (32): homeless persons

### The Great Depression

[1]The **prosperity** of the 1920s came to an abrupt halt in October 1929. [2]The stock market, which had boomed during the decade, suddenly faltered. [3]Investors who had borrowed heavily to take part in the buying **mania** that had swept Wall Street were suddenly forced to sell their securities to cover their loans. [4]The wave of selling triggered an avalanche of trading.

[5]On October 24, later known as Black Thursday, nearly 13 million shares were traded as **highfliers** such as RCA and Westinghouse lost nearly half their value. [6]The stock market rallied for the next two days, but on Tuesday, October 29, the downslide resumed. [7]Frightened sellers dumped more than 16 million shares, and the industrial stock price average fell by 43 points. [8]The panic ended in November, with stocks at 1927 levels. [9]For the next four years, there was a steady drift downward. [10]By 1932, prices were at only 20 percent of their 1920 highs.

[11]The Great Depression that followed the crash of 1929 was the most devastating economic blow ever suffered by the nation. [12]It lasted for more than ten years, and it dominated every aspect of American life during the 1930s. [13]Unemployment rose to 12 million by 1932. [14]Though it dipped midway through the decade, it still stood at 10 million by 1939. [15]Children grew up thinking that economic **deprivation** was the norm rather than the exception in America. [16]Year after year, people kept looking for a return to wealth. [17]But the outlook remained dismal. [18]The Depression loosened its grip on the nation only after the outbreak of World War II in 1939. [19]Even then, it left lasting mental and emotional scars. [20]The Americans who lived through it would never again be so **optimistic** about their economic future.

[21]It is difficult to measure the human cost of the Great Depression. [22]The material hardships were bad enough. [23]Men and women lived in lean-tos made of scrap wood and metal. [24]Families went without meat and fresh vegetables for months. [25]They existed on a diet of soup and beans. [26]The emotional burden was even greater: Americans suffered through year after year of grinding poverty with no relief in sight. [27]The unemployed stood in lines for hours waiting for relief checks. [28]Veterans sold apples or pencils on street corners.

[29]Many Americans sought escape in movement. [30]Men, boys, and some women rode the rails in search of jobs. [31]They hopped freight trains to move south in the winter or west in the summer. [32]One town in the Southwest hired special police to keep **vagrants** from leaving the boxcars. [33]Those who became tramps had to keep on the move, but they did find a sense of community in the hobo jungles that sprang up along the major railroad routes. [34]Here the unfortunate could find a place to eat and sleep and people with whom to share their misery. [35]Louis Banks told interviewer Studs Terkel what the informal camps were like:

> [36]Black and white, it didn't make any difference who you were, 'cause everybody was poor. [37]All friendly, sleep in a jungle. [38]We used to take a big pot and cook food, cabbage, meat, and beans all together. [39]We all set together, we made a tent. [40]Twenty-five or thirty would be

out on the side of the rail, white and colored. [41]They didn't have no mothers or sisters, they didn't have no home, they were dirty, they had overalls on, they didn't have no food, they didn't have anything.

—Adapted from Divine, Breen, Fredrickson, & Williams, *The American Story*, pp. 834–839.

## BEFORE READING

### Vocabulary in Context

_____ **1.** The word **highflier** in sentence 5 means
a. stocks usually sold at a higher price than other stocks.
b. stocks usually sold at a lower price than other stocks.
c. stocks usually sold at the same price as most stocks.

### Tone and Purpose

_____ **2.** Which of the following best describes the author's tone and purpose?
a. to delight the reader with entertaining details
b. to inform the reader with factual details
c. to persuade the reader with emotional details

## AFTER READING

### Concept Maps

Finish the timeline with information from the passage.

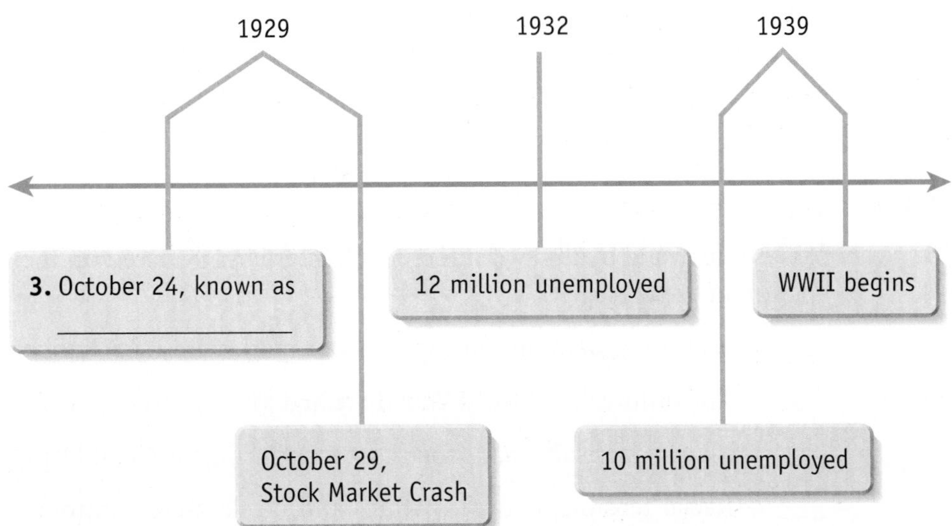

## Central Idea and Main Idea

_____ **4.** Choose the best statement of the central idea of the passage.
a. The Great Depression was a devastating economic and emotional blow to the United States.
b. The Great Depression put millions of people out of work.
c. The Great Depression lasted for more than ten years.

## Supporting Details

_____ **5.** Sentence 6, "The stock market rallied for the next two days, but on Tuesday, October 29, the downslide resumed," is a
a. major supporting detail. b. minor supporting detail.

## Transitions

_____ **6.** "Year after year, people kept looking for a return to wealth. But the outlook remained dismal."

The relationship between the ideas in these two sentences is one of
a. cause and effect. c. contrast.
b. time order.

## Thought Patterns

_____ **7.** The thought pattern used in the second paragraph (sentences 5–10) is
a. cause and effect. c. classification.
b. time order. d. definition.

## Fact and Opinion

_____ **8.** Sentence 11 is a statement that expresses
a. a fact. c. a mixture of fact and opinion.
b. an opinion.

## Inferences

**9–10.** Write **V** for valid by the two inferences that are firmly based on the information in the passage.

_____ Fear was a factor in causing the stock market crash in October 1929.

_____ The outbreak of World War II created jobs for Americans.

_____ Many Americans made their fortunes during the Great Depression.

_____ Racial tensions between whites and blacks were common in the "hobo jungles."

### Discussion Questions

1. Why did October 24, 1929, become known as "Black Thursday"?
2. What was the link between the crash of the stock market and the Great Depression?
3. Why would World War II trigger the end of the Great Depression?
4. What are the chances of another Great Depression occurring?

### Writing Topics

1. Summarize the causes of the Great Depression.
2. Discuss the effects of the Great Depression on families.
3. Explain why the time period from 1929 to 1939 is called the Great Depression.

## EFFECTIVE READER Scorecard

**Inferences**

| Test | Number Correct | | Points | | Score |
|---|---|---|---|---|---|
| Review Test 1 | ______ | × | 10 | = | ______ |
| Review Test 2 | ______ | × | 20 | = | ______ |
| Review Test 3 | ______ | × | 20 | = | ______ |
| Review Test 4 | ______ | × | 10 | = | ______ |
| Review Test 5 (website) | ______ | × | 10 | = | ______ |
| Review Test 6 (website) | ______ | × | 10 | = | ______ |

Enter your scores on the Effective Reader Scorecard: Chapter 11 Review Tests inside the back cover.

## After Reading About Inferences

Before you move on to the mastery tests on inferences, take time to reflect on your learning and performance by answering the following questions. Write your answers in your notebook.

What did I learn about inferences?

What do I need to remember about inferences?

How has my knowledge base or prior knowledge about inferences changed?

## More Review and Mastery Tests

For more practice, go to the book's website at **http://www.ablongman.com/henry** and click on *The Effective Reader.* Then select "More Review and Mastery Tests." The tests are organized by chapter.

Name ______________________ Section ____________

# MASTERY Test 1

Date ____________ **Score** (number correct) ______ × 20 = ______%

**A.** Read the passage. Then answer the questions that follow it.

Textbook Skills

## Diagnosing Alcoholism

[1]Alcoholism involves the development of certain harmful behaviors associated with long-term use of great amounts of alcohol. [2]It is a **chronic** illness with medical and social effects. [3]Alcoholism advances slowly as tolerance and dependence develop. [4]Although there is some disagreement about what alcoholism is, the following eight symptoms usually aid in its diagnosis:

1. Being drunk frequently in ways that are obvious and destructive
2. Failing in marriage and increasing absences from work
3. Being fired
4. Seeking medical treatment for drinking
5. Suffering physical injury
6. Being arrested for driving under the influence
7. Being arrested for drunkenness
8. Being hospitalized for cirrhosis of the liver or DTs [delirium tremens, or mental confusion that may include hallucinations]

—Adapted from Fishbein & Pease, *The Dynamics of Drug Abuse*, p. 116.

**1.** Write **V** for valid by the inference that is firmly supported by the passage.

______ Alcoholism can be difficult to diagnose.

______ Most people who drink become alcoholics.

______ Alcoholism is not a life-threatening disease.

______ **2.** The word **chronic** in sentence 2 implies

a. short-term.
b. curable.
c. constant.

**B.** Read the following excerpt from a 2000 report based on research by Stanford University. Then answer the questions that follow it.

### What Do Users Do on the Internet?

[1]We asked each of our 4,000 respondents to select among a list of 17 common Internet activities and tell us which they did or did not do. [2]This is what we found:

- [3]E-mail is by far the most common Internet activity. [4]Ninety percent of all Internet users claim to be e-mailers.
- [5]For the most part, the Internet today is a giant public library with a definite commercial tilt. [6]A widespread use of the Internet today is as a search tool for products (62 percent of users), travel (54 percent), hobbies (63 percent), and general information (77 percent). [7]Almost all users who were interviewed stated that they engaged in one or more of these activities.
- [8]A little over a third of all Internet users report using the Web to engage in entertainment such as computer games (online chess, role games, and the like). [9]Thus the Internet is also emerging as an entertainment utility.
- [10]Chat rooms are for the young and the anonymous. [11]While a quarter of Internet users claim to have used chat rooms, this activity largely decreases after age 25. [12]And the chatters report that the vast portion of their chat room time is spent with others whose identities remain unknown.
- [13]Consumer activity, such as buying, stock trading, online auctions, and e-banking, are engaged in by much smaller fractions of Internet users. [14]Only a quarter of those surveyed reported making purchases online, and less than 15 percent do any of the other activities. [15]Despite all the sound and fury, consumer commercial online transactions are in their earliest stages.

—Adapted from O'Toole, "What Do Users Do on the Internet?"
*The Internet Study*, Institute for the Quantitative
Study of Society, Stanford University.

**3–5.** Write **V** for valid by the three inferences that are firmly supported by details in the passage.

______ More Internet users use the Internet to find travel information than to e-mail others.

______ The Internet offers a wide variety of activities.

______ Use of the Internet cuts down on time spent with family and friends.

______ All information located on the Internet is reliable.

______ People rarely use chat rooms to talk with friends and loved ones.

______ Most Internet users do not use online banking services.

MASTERY **Test 2**

Name ______________________ Section ____________

Date ____________ **Score** (number correct) ______ × 20 = ______%

Read the passage. Then answer the questions that follow it.

### Criticism

[1]Kay has been married less than a month. [2]But she's ready to give up on Don for his habit of dumping his clothes and belongings wherever he happens to be. [3]"When he left his muddy running shoes on top of my new microwave, I screamed at him like a fishwife," she says, "and asked him why his mother had brought up such a slob. [4]He immediately defended his mother and started to criticize mine. [5]Then we both got on the defensive and had a knock-down fight."

[6]Dr. Harriet Lefkowith, a Tenafly, N.J., human resource development specialist who leads workshops on communication throughout the country says, "Because criticism has such a negative **connotation,** we get into situations where the people we criticize invariably react defensively.

[7]"Before you know it, the act of criticism turns into an armed camp with two sides. [8]Nobody's thinking. [9]There's no problem solving. [10]Everyone's defending himself or herself."

[11]Since each of us has our own systems and standards, it's human to criticize. [12]But in order to do it in a manner that keeps personal and working relationships from landing on the rocks, it's important to understand how we can give it in a way that won't make temperatures rise.

[13]Depending on how you criticize, you can look for a variety of responses. [14]Jean, for instance, got a good response when she appeared to be taking responsibility for the situation. [15]In another case, Susan got the hoped-for results by getting to the point instead of beating around the bush. [16]Initially, she was critical of her husband Steve, in a general way. [17]But Steve never got the message—especially about visiting her mother.

[18]"In a situation such as this, it's not useful to say 'You hate my relatives and you never visit my mother,'" states Dr. Clifford Swenson, clinical psychologist of Purdue University. [19]"A **concrete** suggestion such as 'I think my mom would really like it if you could come along with me when I go down to visit her this Saturday' will always get a better reaction than 'You never want to come with me.'"

—Adapted from Roesch, "How to Take a Bite Out of Criticism," as appeared in *Relationships Today*, August 1988.

_____ **1.** The word **connotation** in sentence 6 means
a. meaning.
b. action.
c. reaction.

_____ **2.** Kay's mistake in criticizing Don was
a. expecting Don to be neat.
b. telling him what she thought.
c. attacking his mother.

_____ **3.** The word **concrete** in sentence 19 means
a. helpful.
b. specific.
c. polite.

_____ **4.** Most people criticize others because of
a. the desire to control.
b. low self-esteem.
c. a desire to hurt others.

_____ **5.** The best statement of the implied central idea of the passage is
a. Criticism builds strong relationships.
b. Criticism is unavoidable.
c. Criticism can be harmful if not handled properly.

MASTERY **Test 3**

Name ______________________ Section ____________

Date ____________ **Score** (number correct) ______ × 20 = ______%

Read the following short article by Richard Willing, originally published in *USA Today.* Then choose five inferences that are firmly supported by the ideas in the passage. Write V for valid by your choices.

### Latchkey Children

[1]Today, over 65 million American women and over 70 percent of mothers work outside of the home. [2]One of the major problems faced by the large number of working mothers is finding adequate child care for their children. [3]The problem is so widespread that the phrase "latchkey children" has been coined to describe the numerous children who return home after school to an empty house.

[4]Brandon and Mica are latchkey kids. [5]They step off the school bus at approximately 4 P.M. every day. [6]They wave good-bye to their bus driver and all their friends on the bus. [7]Then they walk the two blocks to their home. [8]When they reach their house, Brandon, who is the older of the two at age 12, reaches into his shoe to retrieve his house key and unlocks the door for his 8-year-old sister; they go inside. [9]Once inside, they relock the door. [10]Brandon pours each of them their usual glass of milk while Mica unwraps the cookies, brownies, or other snack that is always waiting for them. [11]Then they retire to the family room, where Mica watches her favorite cartoon show and Brandon begins his homework.

[12]Brandon and Mica have been carefully schooled in their role of latchkey children. [13]Their mother and father have established some basic house rules. [14]The children are not allowed to play outside or have houseguests. [15]They are strictly forbidden to do any cooking, and they do not answer the door under any circumstances. [16]If the phone rings, they take a message, informing the caller that their mother "is in the shower and cannot come to the phone at the moment." [17]Their mother's and father's work numbers are posted near each of the telephones right below the emergency number.

—Adapted from Bynum & Thompson, *Juvenile Delinquency: A Sociological Approach*, 5th ed., pp. 238–239.

______ Finding child care is still considered the responsibility of the mother.

______ There needs to be more organized and safe child care available to help working parents.

_____ Brandon seems to be a mature and responsible 12-year-old.

_____ Latchkey children are neglected or abused.

_____ Brandon and Mica's parents worry about the children being home alone.

_____ Brandon and Mica's parents are unfit parents.

_____ Brandon and Mica's parents are more concerned about the children's interactions with other people than about trouble the children might cause by themselves.

**VISUAL VOCABULARY**

Children who return home from school each day to an empty house to await the arrival of their parents are known as _______________ children.

MASTERY **Test 4**

Name ______________________ Section ____________

Date ____________ **Score** (number correct) ______ × 20 = ______%

Read the following information. Then use inference skills to label each movie review with a movie rating of G, PG, PG-13, R, or NC-17.

### The Movie Rating System

The movie rating system is a voluntary system sponsored by the Motion Picture Association of America and the National Association of Theater Owners. The purpose of the rating system is to provide parents with information about films, so that they can make judgments about what they want or do not want their children to see. The rating board uses the following six criteria to determine a movie rating: theme, language, violence, nudity, sex, and drug use. Here are descriptions used by the rating board for each rating.

*General Audiences.* All ages admitted. This signifies that the film rated contains nothing most parents will consider offensive for even their youngest children to see or hear. Nudity, sex scenes, and scenes of drug use are absent; violence is minimal; snippets of dialogue may go beyond polite conversation but do not go beyond common everyday expressions.

*Parental Guidance Suggested.* Some material may not be suitable for children. This signifies that the film rated may contain some material that parents might not like to expose to their young children—material that will clearly need to be examined or inquired about before children are allowed to attend the film. Explicit sex scenes and scenes of drug use are absent; nudity, if present, is seen only briefly, horror and violence do not exceed moderate levels.

**PG-13** | **PARENTS STRONGLY CAUTIONED**

Some Material May Be Inappropriate for Children Under 13 ®

*Parents Strongly Cautioned.* Some material may be inappropriate for children under 13. This signifies that the film rated may be inappropriate for pre-teens. Parents should be especially careful about letting their younger children attend. Rough or persistent violence is absent; sexually oriented nudity is generally absent; some scenes of drug use may be seen; one use of the harsher sexually derived words may be heard.

*Restricted-Under 17 requires accompanying parent or adult guardian* (age varies in some locations). This signifies that the rating board has concluded that the film rated contains some adult material. Parents are urged to learn more about the film before taking their children to see it. An R may be assigned due to, among other things, a film's use of language, theme, violence, sex or its portrayal of drug use.

*No One 17 and Under Admitted.* This signifies that the rating board believes that most American parents would feel that the film is patently adult and that children age 17 and under should not be admitted to it. The film may contain explicit sex scenes, an accumulation of sexually-oriented language, or scenes of excessive violence. The NC-17 designation does not, however, signify that the rated film is obscene or pornographic.

—*Movie Ratings.* Motion Picture Association of America. 24 July 2007.
http://www.mpaa.org/movieratings/index.htm

_____ **1.** *Hairspray,* released in July 2007 by New Line Cinema, is a feature film adaptation of the Tony award-winning Broadway production *Hairspray* about star-struck teenagers on a local Baltimore dance show. The film has suggestive content, teen smoking, and crude language.

_____ **2.** *Arctic Tale,* a documentary narrated by Queen Latifah about the life cycle of a mother walrus and her calf, and the life of a polar bear and her cubs illustrates the harsh realities of existence in the Arctic. This family movie is a real adventure in the coolest place on earth.

_____ **3.** *Crash,* released in 1997, is about a group of people who get sexually aroused by car crashes. The film, starring Holly Hunter, has numerous explicit sex scenes.

_____ **4.** *Dream Catcher,* released in 2003 by Castle Rock, is a Stephen King novel adapted to the screen about how four friends who share telepathic gifts must fight against an alien invasion. The film includes extreme profanity and much intense, disturbing violence.

_____ **5.** *The Simpson's Movie,* released in 2007, brings Homer, Marge, Bart, Lisa, Maggie and the rest of the cast to the big screen with this feature-length version of the animated TV show. Irreverent humor runs throughout the movie.

MASTERY **Test 5**

Name ________________ Section ________
Date ________ **Score** (number correct) ______ × 10 = ______%

**A.** Read the following passage. Then answer the questions that follow it.

Textbook Skills

### Japanese Hiring Practices

[1]Japanese employees are hired as a group or "class," once a year, much like students entering a school. [2]Though their activities may differ, they work together, eat together, and many will live together in a company dormitory. [3]The ability to get along with others is therefore a very important criterion for being hired. [4]Character, along with family background and school attended, usually count for much more than specialized training or outstanding personal abilities. [5]Individual achievement could work against one's ability to fit in comfortably. [6]A Japanese-American was being interviewed for a position with a major Japanese corporation known throughout the world. [7]The student had lived in Japan many years and was fluent in both English and Japanese. [8]Each of the persons who interviewed the candidate was apparently most concerned about his American background. [9]Each stressed "there is no room for individualism in this company."

[10]Another young employee of a prestigious trading company became disillusioned with company policies after about one year. [11]He was an idealist and some of what went on did not meet his ideals. [12]Few Japanese fortunate enough to work for the company would have thought about leaving his job, yet he considered leaving the company and perhaps returning to graduate school and then going into teaching. [13]He sought advice from many persons, and finally decided to remain. [14]What most persuaded him to stay? [15]"I realized," he said, "that if I left the company, it would make it much more difficult for others from this college to be hired by the company in the future."

—Condon, John. *With Respect to the Japanese: A Guide for Americans*. Intercultural Press. 1984. p. 10.

______ **1.** Three traits valued by the Japanese workforce are
a. character, family background, and getting along with others.
b. character, individual achievement, and getting along with others.
c. school attended, character, and outstanding personal achievement.

______ **2.** In the Japanese workforce, individual achievement is
a. rewarded and admired.
b. expected.
c. viewed with suspicion.

______ **3.** For a Japanese worker, having an "American background" offers a __________ impression.
a. positive
b. negative

______ **4.** The disillusioned worker remained with his company because
a. he couldn't find another job as good as the one he had.
b. he wanted to save up his money to further his college education to become a teacher.
c. he didn't want to hurt the reputation of his college.

______ **5.** The best statement of the implied central idea of this passage is:
a. In the Japanese workforce, the group is more important than the individual.
b. Japanese hiring practices are unfair.
c. American workers stress individual achievement.
d. Most Japanese would feel fortunate to work for a large company.

**B.** Read the following opening paragraphs to Flannery O'Connor's short story about a woman who finds herself in conflict with others. Then write **V** for valid by the five inferences that are firmly supported by the details in the passage.

### From "Revelation"

[1]The doctor's waiting room, which was very small, was almost full when the Turpins entered and Mrs. Turpin, who was very large, made it look even smaller by her presence. [2]She stood looming at the head of the magazine table set in the center of it, a living demonstration that the room was inadequate and ridiculous. [3]Her little bright black eyes took in all the patients as she sized up the seating situation. [4]There was one vacant chair and a place on a sofa occupied by a blond child in a dirty blue romper who should have been told to move over and make room for the lady. [5]He was five or six, but Mrs. Turpin saw at once that no one was going to tell him to move over. [6]He was slumped down in the seat, his arms idle at his sides and his eyes idle in his head; his nose ran unchecked.

[7]Mrs. Turpin put a firm hand on Claud's shoulder and said in a voice that included anyone in the room who wanted to listen, "Claud, you sit in

that chair there," and gave him a push down into the vacant one. [8]Claud was florid and bald and sturdy, somewhat shorter than Mrs. Turpin, but he sat down as if he were accustomed to doing what she told him to.

[9]Mrs. Turpin remained standing. [10]The only man in the room besides Claud was a lean stringy old fellow with a rusty hand spread out on each knee, whose eyes were closed as if he were asleep or dead or pretending to be so as not to get up and offer her his seat. [11]Her gaze settled agreeably on a well-dressed gray-haired lady whose eyes met hers and whose expression said: if that child belonged to me, he would have some manners and move over—there's plenty of room there for you and him too.

**6–10.**

_____ Mrs. Turpin likes to be in control of a situation.

_____ Mrs. Turpin likes children.

_____ Mrs. Turpin thinks the little boy with the runny nose is rude.

_____ Mr. Turpin is a strong male figure.

_____ Mrs. Turpin is at the doctor's office because she is sick.

_____ Mrs. Turpin is annoyed.

_____ The narrator suggests that Mrs. Turpin thinks her comfort is more important than that of a child.

_____ The well-dressed gray-haired lady and Mrs. Turpin share the same values.

# MASTERY Test 6

Name ____________________ Section ____________

Date ____________ **Score** (number correct) ______ × 10 = ______%

**A.** Study the cartoon. Then answer the questions.

*"Because my genetic programming prevents me from stopping to ask directions—that's why!"*



______ **1.** The cartoon is about

a. communication.

b. cars.

c. differences between men and women.

**2–4.** Write **V** for valid by the three inferences that are firmly supported by the details in the cartoon.

______ The couple is getting along well.

______ The couple is lost in the country.

______ The woman has asked the man why he doesn't ask for directions.

______ The woman knows where they are.

______ The cartoon suggests that most men do not ask for directions when they are lost.

**B.** Read the following textbook passage; then answer the questions that follow it.

Textbook Skills

## Questions for Effective Listening

[1]Often a communicator wrongly assumes what you already know, or she leaves out important information. [2]Since she is familiar with her topic and purpose, it is often hard for her to make wise choices about what to tell you. [3]Consequently, you end up with gaps in your information.

[4]By asking questions, you can obtain clarification on points that seem vague. [5]Don't be discouraged by speakers who seem annoyed or impatient with your questions. [6]Your goal is effective listening. [7]There are many types of questions; each has its own purpose. [8]For example, closed questions ask for very specific information in a short response. [9]On the other hand, probing questions are meant to increase understanding. [10]The chart below defines four basic types of questions.

*Types of Questions*

[11]**Closed:** Ask closed questions when you want a short, direct response.

[12]"What grade did you get on the exam?"

[13]**Open:** Open questions allow your partner alternatives in how he or she responds: there is more than one way of answering.

[14]"What did you think of the lecture in class today?"

[15]**Leading:** Your partner can tell from the way you ask the question what you expect as his or her response. [16]These questions bias the information you receive.

[17]"Wasn't that a boring lecture today?"

[18]**Probes:** There are many kinds of probes, questions that encourage your partner to expand on a specific topic. [19]Probes are often useful after your partner has made an initial incomplete response.

[20]"Why did you think the lecture was boring?"

—Brownell, *Listening: Attitudes, Principles, and Skills,* pp. 117–118.

______ **5.** What is the best statement of the implied central idea of the passage?
a. Probing is an important part of the listening process.
b. Effective questions are used both for clarification and to obtain information.
c. Different questions serve different impatient listeners.

**6–10.** Write **V** for valid by the five inferences that are firmly supported by the details in the passage.

______ Some speakers resent being questioned.

______ Asking questions is a sign that the listener has not been paying attention.

______ Gaps in information may occur because speakers do not know their audience very well.

______ Leading questions should be avoided.

______ "For whom did you vote in the election?" is an example of a closed question.

______ "Wasn't that a stupid-looking Web page Marisa put together for her campaign?" is an example of a leading question.

______ Probing questions are used to get a short, direct response.

CHAPTER

12

# The Basics of Argument

## CHAPTER PREVIEW

Before Reading About the Basics of Argument
What Is an Argument?
Step 1: Identify the Author's Claim and Supports
Step 2: Decide Whether the Supports Are Relevant
Step 3: Decide Whether the Supports Are Adequate
Step 4: Check the Argument for Bias
Textbook Skills: The Logic of Argument

## Before Reading About the Basics of Argument

Many of the same skills you learned to make valid inferences will help you master the basics of argument. Take a moment to review the five steps in the VALID approach to making sound inferences. Fill in the following blanks with each of the steps.

Step 1: ______________________________

Step 2: ______________________________

Step 3: ______________________________

Step 4: ______________________________

Step 5: ______________________________

Skim the chapter and list any other reading skills you have studied from prior chapters that seem to apply to the basics of argument: ______________________________

______________________________

Use your prior knowledge about valid inferences, other reading skills, and the chapter preview to create at least three questions that you can answer as you study:

1. ________________________________________________________________

________________________________________________________________?

2. ________________________________________________________________

________________________________________________________________?

3. ________________________________________________________________

________________________________________________________________?

Reading skills that you have studied in prior chapters that will help you master the basics of arguments are main ideas, supporting details, fact and opinion, and tone and purpose (to persuade). Compare the questions you created based on your prior knowledge and the chapter preview with the following questions. Then write the ones that seem the most helpful in your notebook, leaving enough space between questions to record your answers as you read and study the chapter.

How will verifying and valuing the facts help me decide if supports in an argument are relevant? How will learning from the text help me decide if supports in an argument are adequate? How does an argument use bias? What is the relationship between main ideas and the author's claim? How does opinion affect an argument? What is the connection between tone, purpose, and the basics of argument?

## What Is an Argument?

Have you noticed how many of us enjoy debating ideas and winning arguments? You can see this on television, where many shows thrive on conflict and debate. For example, the *Jerry Springer* show uses the conflicts between guests to amuse the audience. Programs such as *Meet the Press,* hosted by Tim Russert, or *The O'Reilly Factor* with Bill O'Reilly debate political and social issues. Likewise, talk radio fills hours of air time with debate about issues related to culture and politics. Two examples are *The Drudge Report* with Matt Drudge and *The Larry Elder Show.*

Some people are so committed to their ideas that they become emotional, even angry. However, effective **argument** is reasoned: It is a process during which a claim is made and logical details are offered to support that claim.

An **argument** is made up of two types of statements:
1. The author's claim—the main point of the argument
2. The supports—the evidence or reasons that support the author's claim

The purpose of an argument is to persuade the reader that the claim is valid. To decide if a claim is valid, you must analyze the argument in four basic steps.

1. Identify the author's claim and supports.
2. Decide whether the supports are relevant.
3. Decide whether the supports are adequate.
4. Check the argument for bias.

## Step 1: Identify the Author's Claim and Supports

Read the following claim:

*Dream Girls* is a movie worth seeing.

The claim certainly states the speaker's point clearly. But it probably wouldn't inspire most of us to go see the movie. Instead, our first response to the claim is likely to be "why?" We need reasons before we can decide if we think a claim is valid. Notice that a claim, like any main idea, is made up of a topic and a controlling point. Here, *Dream Girls* is the topic, and the controlling point is "worth seeing." Notice that the details that follow answer a question about the controlling point: "Why is *Dream Girls* a movie worth seeing?"

1. *Dream Girls* won 5 Oscars.
2. *Dream Girls* is about love, ambition, and success.
3. *Dream Girls* is full of great music.

These three sentences offer the supports for the author's claim. We are now able to understand the basis of the argument, and we now have details about which we can agree or disagree.

Writers frequently make claims that they want us to accept as valid. To assess whether the claim is valid, an effective reader first identifies the claim and the supports. Identifying the author's claim and supports for that claim is the first step in analyzing an argument.

**EXAMPLES**

**A.** Read the following groups of ideas. Identify the claim and supports in each group. Write C if the sentence states the author's claim or S if the sentence offers support for the claim.

**Group 1**

[1]Dog bites pose a serious national problem. [2]Dogs bite an estimated 4.7 million people each year, with 800,000 individuals needing medical treatment.

_____ **1.** Sentence 1

_____ **2.** Sentence 2

**Group 2**

[1]They never wave or say hello. [2]Our neighbors are unfriendly people.

_____ **3.** Sentence 1

_____ **4.** Sentence 2

**Group 3**

[1]Popcorn contains only 15 calories per cup when it is air-popped. [2]Popcorn is a good snack. [3]Popcorn is a good source of fiber.

_____ **5.** Sentence 1

_____ **6.** Sentence 2

_____ **7.** Sentence 3

**Group 4**

[1]Mrs. Overby takes time to explain difficult ideas in class. [2]Mrs. Overby is always available for student conferences. [3]Mrs. Overby's students have a high passing rate. [4]Mrs. Overby is a good teacher.

_____ **8.** Sentence 1

_____ **9.** Sentence 2

_____ **10.** Sentence 3

_____ **11.** Sentence 4

**B.** Editorial cartoons offer arguments through the use of humor. The cartoonist has a claim to make and uses the situation, actions, and words in the cartoon as supporting details. Study the cartoon reprinted here. Then write a claim based on the supports in the cartoon.

—*The Detroit News,* Larry Wright © 2002

________________________________________

________________________________________

________________________________________

## EXPLANATIONS

**A.**

### Group 1

1. Sentence 1 states the author's claim (C); 2. Sentence 2 offers support for the claim (S).

### Group 2

3. Sentence 1 offers support for the claim (S); 4. Sentence 2 states the author's claim (C).

### Group 3

5. Sentence 1 offers support for the claim (S); 6. Sentence 2 states the author's claim (C); 7. Sentence 3 offers support for the claim(s).

### Group 4

8. Sentences 1, 2, and 3 offer support for the claim (S). Sentence 4 states the author's claim (C).

**B.** The note from school came from the school's administration. The horrible spelling is a sign that the people running the school do not have basic writing or thinking skills. Several claims can be suggested by the details in the cartoon. The following are a few possibilities.

Students must not be receiving a good education.

School administrators should not allow teachers to teach outside their fields.

School administrators are the main problem in education.

School administrators are not smart.

School administrators must not care about education.

## PRACTICE 1

Read the following groups of ideas. Identify the claim and supports in each group. Write C if the sentence states the author's claim or S if the sentence offers support for the claim.

### Group 1

[1]Jennifer Hudson has earned respect from the movie industry for her role in *Dream Girls.* [2]Hudson won an Academy Award, a Golden Globe, and the Screen Actors Guild award in 2007.

_____ **1.** Sentence 1

_____ **2.** Sentence 2

### Group 2

[1]Drinking plenty of water helps to keep your breath sweet, flush out toxins, and reduce infection. [2]You should drink at least eight glasses of water every day.

_____ **3.** Sentence 1

_____ **4.** Sentence 2

### Group 3

[1]Public schools will need to hire about 200,000 new teachers each year to meet classroom needs. [2]The need for teachers will become a crisis in the

next few years. [3]Currently, 100,000 new teachers are entering the workforce each year.

_____ **5.** Sentence 1

_____ **6.** Sentence 2

_____ **7.** Sentence 3

### Group 4

[1]A window on the back of Jermaine's house is broken, and the screen is torn. [2]Jermaine must have been robbed. [3]Jermaine's microwave, DVD/CD player, and three small televisions are missing.

_____ **8.** Sentence 1

_____ **9.** Sentence 2

_____ **10.** Sentence 3

### Group 5

[1]Dr. Martin announced that all students who had a B average on their unit tests did not have to take the final exam. [2]Shantel has a B average on her unit tests. [3]Shantel should not have to take the final exam.

_____ **11.** Sentence 1

_____ **12.** Sentence 2

_____ **13.** Sentence 3

### Group 6

[1]Working long hours on the computer should be avoided. [2]While working on the computer our eyes don't blink as often, and they dry out, causing eyestrain. [3]Extended computer sessions may cause blurred vision and sensitivity to light.

_____ **14.** Sentence 1

_____ **15.** Sentence 2

_____ **16.** Sentence 3

### Group 7

[1]Cars, planes, and trains have freed people from living and doing business in the same place they were born. [2]Technology brings more choices and has improved life. [3]Washing machines, vacuum cleaners, dryers, stoves, ovens, refrigerators, and microwaves have cut down on the time and labor needed to do household chores.

______ **17.** Sentence 1

______ **18.** Sentence 2

______ **19.** Sentence 3

### Group 8

[1]Caffeine has benefits. [2]Caffeine produces a feeling of well-being. [3]Caffeine gives some people the ability to memorize simple numbers, concepts, and thought sequences more easily.

______ **20.** Sentence 1

______ **21.** Sentence 2

______ **22.** Sentence 3

### Group 9

[1]A 30-second commercial during the Super Bowl costs advertisers $1.2 million. [2]The Super Bowl audience is the largest television audience during the year. [3]Many Americans say they watch the Super Bowl for the commercials as much as for the football. [4]Super Bowl commercials are as big an event as the football game.

______ **23.** Sentence 1

______ **24.** Sentence 2

______ **25.** Sentence 3

______ **26.** Sentence 4

### Group 10

[1]Pete Rose, famous baseball player, was banned from the sport for gambling. [2]Bobby Knight, a university basketball coach, was fired for losing his temper on the court. [3]A California father of a little leaguer was jailed for 45 days for attacking his son's team manager for benching the boy. [4]Unsportsmanlike behavior is a problem in organized sports.

_____ **27.** Sentence 1

_____ **28.** Sentence 2

_____ **29.** Sentence 3

_____ **30.** Sentence 4

## Step 2: Decide Whether the Supports Are Relevant

In Step 1, you learned to identify the author's claim and supports. The next step is to decide whether the supports are relevant to the claim. Remember, a claim, like any main idea, is made up of a topic and a controlling point. Irrelevant supports change the topic or ignore the controlling point. Relevant supports will answer the reporter's questions (*Who? What? When? Where? Why?* and *How?*). Use these questions to decide whether the supports for a claim are relevant.

For example, read the following argument a teenager makes about her curfew. Identify the support that is irrelevant to her claim.

> [1]"I am mature enough to make my own decisions about my curfew. [2]When I work the closing shift at McDonald's, I am out until 2 A.M., and no matter where I am, I always make sure to stick with a group of people. [3]And I am not just out roaming the streets; I only want to stay out late for specific events like a concert or a late movie. [4]None of my friends even have curfews. [5]Just like always, I will tell you ahead of time where I will be and when I will be home, and I do have my cell phone in case you get worried and want to call me. [6]Or I can call you if I need help."

By turning this teenager's claim into a question, she and her parents can test her ability to offer valid reasons: "How have I shown I am mature enough to make my own decisions about my curfew?" Sentences 2, 3, 5, and 6 offer relevant examples of her maturity. However, sentence 4 states an irrelevant support that changes the topic. The argument is about *her* curfew based on *her* maturity, not her friends' curfews.

When evaluating an argument, it is important to test each piece of supporting evidence to determine whether it is relevant.

**EXAMPLES**

**A.** Read the following lists of claims and supports. Mark each support **R** if it is relevant to the claim or **N** if it is not relevant to the claim.

1. Claim: Online shopping offers a lot of benefits.

   Supports

   ______ a. You can shop at any time of the day or night.

   ______ b. You don't have to leave your house.

   ______ c. You can't try on clothes to see if they fit.

   ______ d. You may have to pay postage to return items.

   ______ e. You can save money because comparison shopping takes less time.

2. Claim: Water supplies should have fluoride added to prevent tooth decay.

   Supports

   ______ a. Research shows that drinking fluoride from birth reduces tooth decay by as much as 65 percent.

   ______ b. Fluoride is a safe, natural mineral that makes bones and teeth stronger.

   ______ c. Drinking eight glasses of water every day promotes good health.

   ______ d. Although fluoride is present in plants, animals, and water, the amount is too low to offer protection against tooth decay.

   ______ e. Fluoride is tasteless and odorless.

3. Claim: Sports utility vehicles (SUVs) are unsafe and should be banned.

   Supports

   ______ a. SUVs can average as little as 12 miles per gallon of gasoline.

   ______ b. SUVs emit more harmful chemicals, such as carbon monoxide and nitrogen oxides, into the air than cars do.

   ______ c. SUVs are expensive.

   ______ d. The size of SUVs makes them more likely to roll over and cause greater damage to other vehicles during accidents.

   ______ e. Smaller cars are safer and more fuel-efficient.

**B.** Argument is also used in advertisements. It is important for you to be able to understand the claims and supports of ads. Many times advertisers appeal to emotions, make false claims, or give supports that are not relevant because their

main aim is to persuade you to buy their product. Study the advertisement for milk put out by America's Dairy Farmers and Milk Processors. Mark each support **R** if it is relevant to the claim or **N** if it is not relevant to the claim.

**4.** Claim: Drinking milk is good for your health.

Supports

______ a. Marvin Harrison drinks milk.

______ b. Marvin Harrison is a successful athlete.

______ c. The protein in milk helps build muscle.

______ d. Marvin Harrison is good looking.

______ e. Sugary drinks aren't healthful choices.

**EXPLANATIONS**

1. Items (a), (b), and (e) are relevant to the claim. Items (c) and (d) are not relevant because they point out drawbacks to online shopping instead of supporting the claim that online shopping offers a lot of benefits.
2. Items (a), (b), and (d) are relevant to the claim. Items (c) and (e) are not relevant. The benefits of drinking water are not the issue. The taste and odor of fluoride are not directly tied to its ability to prevent tooth decay.
3. Items (b) and (d) are relevant to the claim; the others are not relevant. The amount of gasoline an SUV uses does not affect its safety. Neither does its cost. The author's claim is about SUVs, not smaller cars, so the safety of smaller cars is also beside the point.
4. Only (c) is relevant to the claim that drinking milk is good for your health. Advertisers often use celebrities as spokespeople, but personal remarks about Marvin Harrison are not relevant to the healthfulness of milk. The detail about sugary drinks is a true statement, but has nothing to do with the claim about milk.

## PRACTICE 2

**A.** Read the following lists of claims and supports. Mark each support **R** if it is relevant to the claim or **N** if it is not relevant to the claim.

1. Claim: Use of steroids is harmful and should be avoided.

   Supports

   ______ a. Excessive use of steroids can cause rage.

   ______ b. One short-term effect of steroid use is acne.

   ______ c. One long-term effect of steroid use is stunted growth in teenagers.

   ______ d. Other long-term effects of steroid use may be liver damage, prostate cancer, and a higher risk of heart disease.

   ______ e. Drinking alcohol poses greater risks than using steroids.

2. Claim: Left-handed people face obstacles in the classroom and in school activities.

   Supports

   ______ a. In school sports, standard equipment (for example, hockey sticks and baseball gloves) is designed for right-handed players.

_____ b. Musician Kurt Cobain, who dropped out of high school, was left-handed.

_____ c. The word *left* comes from an old Anglo-Saxon word that means "weak."

_____ d. In schools, colleges, and universities, the standard desk has a small top attached to the right side of the desk, which makes it difficult for left-handed students to write.

_____ e. School supplies such as scissors, three-ring binders, and keyboards are mostly made for right-handed writers.

**3.** Claim: Migrant farmworkers boost the economy.

Supports

_____ a. Most migrant farmworkers are legal residents or U.S. citizens.

_____ b. The efforts of migrant workers support the multibillion-dollar farming business.

_____ c. Most of the vegetables and fruits in this country are grown and picked with the aid of migrant workers.

_____ d. Without migrant workers, farmers would not be able to produce and harvest their crops.

_____ e. Farming is ranked as one of the three most dangerous jobs in the nation.

**4.** Claim: Easter Seals is a nonprofit organization worthy of support in terms of time and money.

Supports

_____ a. Easter Seals provides adult and senior service programs across the country.

_____ b. Easter Seals runs hundreds of camping and recreation programs nationwide for children and adults with disabilities.

_____ c. Easter Seals offers job training and employment programs.

_____ d. Dr Pepper/Seven Up is a corporate sponsor of Easter Seals.

_____ e. Easter Seals uses the lily as its official logo.

**B.** Study the mock advertisement that encourages viewers to consume a soy product. Read the claim, and then mark each support **R** if it is relevant to the claim or **N** if it is not relevant to the claim.

**5.** Claim: Soy-Sublime is a healthful food that you should buy.

Supports

______ a. Soy reduces the risks of certain types of cancer.

______ b. Soy alleviates symptoms of menopause.

______ c. Soybeans grow abundantly and actually replenish the soil they grow in.

______ d. Consuming 25 grams of soy protein per day, as part of a diet that is low in saturated fat and cholesterol, may reduce the risk of heart disease.

______ e. Good cooks use soy.

Now that you have practiced identifying relevant supports in a list format, you are ready to isolate relevant supports in reading passages. In a paragraph, the topic sentence states the author's claim. Each of the supporting details must be evaluated as relevant or irrelevant supports for the topic sentence.

**EXAMPLE** Read the following paragraph.

**Children of Substance-Abusing Parents**

[1]Substance abuse and addiction are leaving a path of wreckage in the form of abused and neglected children. [2]From 1986 to 1997, the number of abused and neglected children in America jumped from 1.4 million to some 3 million.

[3]This stunning rise was more than eight times faster than the increase in the children's population. [4]The *reported* number of abused and neglected children killed by substance-abusing parents climbed from 98 in 1985 to 1,185 in 1996. [5]But the U.S. Advisory Board on Child Abuse and Neglect set the actual number higher, at 2,000. [6]This means that five abused and neglected children die each day. [7]The use of drugs such as alcohol, crack cocaine, and heroin are fueling this explosion of abuse. [8]Heroin and marijuana should not be legalized.

—Adapted from Califano, "Foreword."

**1.** Underline the topic sentence (the sentence that states the author's claim).

_____ **2.** Which sentence is *not* relevant to the author's point?

a. sentence 2
c. sentence 3
b. sentence 7
d. sentence 8

**EXPLANATION**

**1.** Sentence 1 is the topic sentence that states the author's claim.

**2.** The sentence that is *not* relevant to the author's point is (d), sentence 8. The author's claim is that substance abuse is a cause of the abuse of children. Based on the information in the passage, parents are abusing both legal and illegal drugs. Legalizing drugs is a separate issue.

## PRACTICE 3

Read the following paragraphs.

### "At Risk" with AD/HD

[1]Occasionally, we may all have difficulty sitting still, paying attention, or controlling impulsive behavior. [2]For some people, the problems are so severe that they interfere with their lives. [3]AD/HD is the common label for Attention-deficit/hyperactivity disorder. [4]This disorder is marked by developmentally inappropriate levels of behavior in three areas: inattention, impulsivity, and hyperactivity. [5]Until recently, experts believed that children outgrew AD/HD because hyperactivity diminishes during the teen years. [6]However, many symptoms continue into adulthood. [7]Individuals with AD/HD can be very successful. [8]Nevertheless, without proper treatment AD/HD may have serious long-term consequences. [9]Some consequences may include school failure, problems with relationships, substance abuse, risk for accidental injures, and job failure.

—Adapted from CHADD, "The Disorder Named AD/HD."

1. Underline the topic sentence (the sentence that states the author's claim).

_____ 2. Which sentence is *not* relevant to the author's point?

a. sentence 3
b. sentence 4
c. sentence 7
d. sentence 9

**Acquaintance Rape**

[1]Violent behavior during dating or courtship is not rare. [2]In a national study of college students, 27.5 percent of the women surveyed said that they had suffered rape or attempted rape at least once since age 14. [3]The term "hidden rape" has come about because sexual assaults are rarely reported. [4]Over half of more than 1,000 female students surveyed at a large urban university had faced some form of unwanted sex. [5]Twelve percent of these acts were committed by casual dates, and 43 percent were committed by steady dating partners. [6]From 1992 to 1993, nearly half of the 500,000 rapes and sexual assaults reported to the police by women of all ages were carried out by friends or acquaintances. [7]Of the rapes that occur on college campuses, 80 to 95 percent are perpetrated by someone the victim knows.

—Adapted from National Center for Injury Prevention and Control, "Dating Violence."

3. Underline the topic sentence (the sentence that states the author's claim).

_____ 4. Which sentence is *not* relevant to the author's point?

a. sentence 3
b. sentence 4
c. sentence 6
d. sentence 7

## Step 3: Decide Whether the Supports Are Adequate

In Step 1 you learned to identify the author's claim and supports. In Step 2 you learned to make sure the supports are relevant. In Step 3 you must decide whether the supports are adequate. A valid argument is based not only on a claim and relevant support but also on the amount and quality of the support given. That is, supports must give enough evidence for the author's claim to be convincing. Just as you used the reporter's questions to decide whether supports are relevant, you can use them to test whether supports are adequate. Supporting details fully explain the author's controlling point about a topic. Remember, those questions are *Who? What? When? Where? Why?* and *How?*

For example, you may argue, "A vegetarian diet is a more healthful diet. I feel much better since I became a vegetarian." However, the reporter's question

"Why?" reveals that the support is inadequate. The answer to "Why is a vegetarian diet a more healthful diet?" should include expert opinions and facts, not just personal opinion. Often in the quest to support a claim, people oversimplify their reasons. Thus, they do not offer enough information to prove the claim. Instead of logical details, they may offer false causes, false comparisons, forced choices, or leave out facts that hurt the claim. You will learn more about inadequate argument in Chapter 13.

In Chapter 11, you studied how to avoid invalid conclusions and make valid inferences (see pages 506–516). The same thinking steps you use to make valid inferences help you identify valid claims: consider the facts, don't infer anything that is not there, and make sure nothing contradicts your conclusion.

**EXAMPLE** Read the list of supports.

Supports

- One pound of muscle burns 50 calories a day.
- One pound of fat burns 2 calories a day.
- Two pounds of muscle can burn up 10 pounds of fat in one year.
- Lean muscle mass weighs more than fat.

Write V for valid by the claim that is adequately supported by the evidence in the list.

______ a. Building muscles will help one lose weight.

______ b. Muscles burn more calories than fat.

______ c. It is hard to lose weight.

______ d. Weight training is the best way to lose weight.

**EXPLANATION** Choices (a), (c), and (d) use the evidence to jump to false conclusions about losing weight. However, none of the evidence mentions weight loss. In fact, since muscle weighs more than fat, adding muscle can cause a weight gain. The only logical conclusion based on the evidence is (b), *muscles burn more calories than fat.*

## PRACTICE 4

**A.** Read the list of supports.

**1.** Supports

- When a couple fights, name-calling creates distrust, anger, and a sense of helplessness.

- Assigning blame makes others defensive during a fight.
- When two people fight, words like *never* or *always* are usually not true and create more anger.
- Exaggerating or making up a complaint can keep the couple's real issues hidden during a fight.
- A couple bringing up gripes and hurt feelings stockpiled over time can lead to explosive anger in a fight.

Write **V** for valid by the claim that is adequately supported by the evidence.

______ a. Fighting leads to violence.

______ b. Using unfair methods during a fight makes the situation worse.

______ c. Everyone uses unfair fighting methods.

______ d. Fighting cannot be avoided.

**B.** Study the graph.

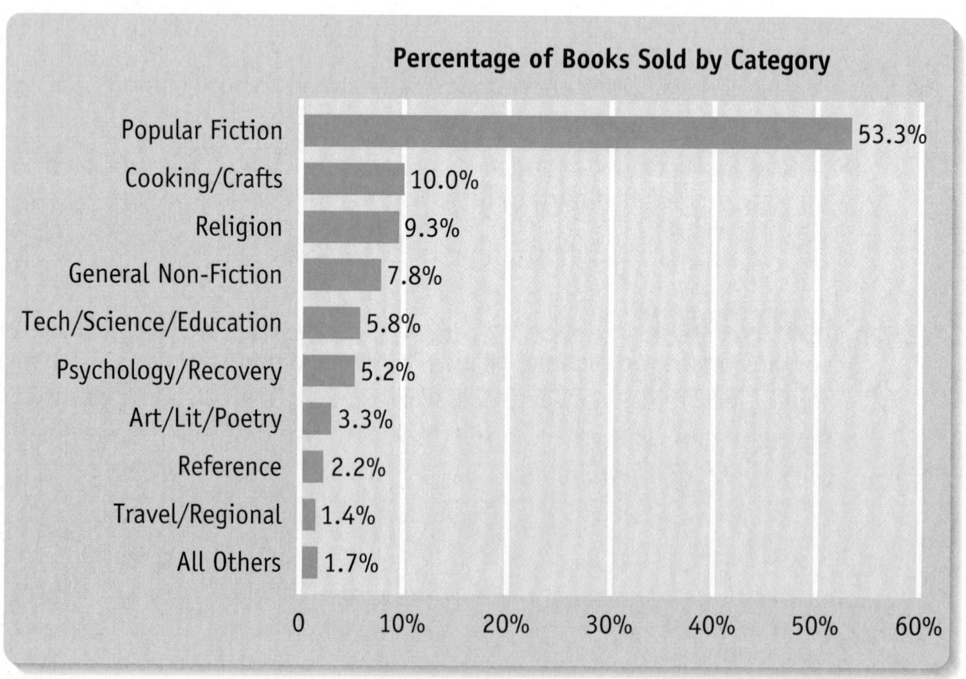


—1999 Consumer Research Study on Book Purchasing. *American Booksellers Association, Book Industry Study Group, 2000. CQ Researcher* Jan.–Dec. (2000); 549.

**2.** Write V for valid by the claim that is adequately supported by the evidence.

_____ a. Not very many people are reading books.

_____ b. The majority of adults in the United States are reading books.

_____ c. Popular fiction leads the sales charts.

_____ d. The number of people buying books about travel has increased.

## Step 4: Check the Argument for Bias

In Step 1, you learned to identify the author's claim and supports. In Step 2, you learned to make sure the supports are relevant to the claim. In Step 3, you learned to avoid false inferences and identify valid claims based on adequate supports. Again, the skills you use to make sound inferences help you determine whether an argument is valid. In Step 4, you must also check for the author's bias for or against the topic. Authors may use emotionally slanted language or biased words to present either a favorable or a negative view of the topic under debate. In addition, authors may include only the details that favor the stances they have taken. A valid argument relies on objective, factual details. As you evaluate the argument for the author's bias, ask the following questions:

- Does the author provide mostly positive or negative supports?
- Does the author provide mostly factual details or rely on biased language?
- Does the writer include or omit opposing views?

**EXAMPLE** Read the following paragraphs from the August 7, 2004 radio address of President George W. Bush to the nation. Then answer the questions.

**President Bush's Radio Address of the President to the Nation**

[1]Good morning. [2]My most solemn duty as President is to protect our country, and in the three years since our country was attacked, we have taken important steps to overcome terrorist threats to this nation.

[3]We have pursued terrorists across the world, destroying their leadership and denying them sanctuaries. [4]We are working with other governments to break up terror cells and stop planned attacks, on virtually every continent. [5]We've created a new Department of Homeland Security to win the battle against terror on the home front. [6]We are working to secure our borders,

air and sea ports and critical infrastructure. [7]We are bringing the best technologies to bear against the threat of chemical and biological warfare.

[8]We're using the tools of the Patriot Act to track terrorists within our borders, and stop them before they kill our people. [9]We have transformed the FBI to focus on the prevention of terrorist attacks. [10]We've established a Terrorist Threat Integration Center, to merge and analyze foreign and domestic intelligence on global terror in a single place. [11]And we are sharing that intelligence in unprecedented ways with local officials and first responders who need it to protect our communities.

[12]I agree with the conclusion of the 9/11 Commission. [13]Because of these steps at home and abroad, our country is safer than it was on September the 11th, 2001. [14]Yet, we're still not safe.

—"Radio Address of the President to the Nation, August 7, 2004." White House. Homepage. 10 August 2004.

______ **1.** Overall, the passage relies on
- a. factual details.
- b. emotionally slanted language.

______ **2.** Which of the following statements is true?
- a. Sentence 1 offers an opposing view.
- b. Sentence 2 offers an opposing view.
- c. Sentence 14 offers an opposing view.
- d. No opposing view is offered in the passage.

______ **3.** In this passage, President Bush expressed a biased attitude
- a. in favor of the findings of the 9/11 Commission.
- b. in favor of chemical and biological warfare.
- c. against the FBI.
- d. against local officials and first responders.

**EXPLANATION**

**1.** Although he uses emotionally slanted words, President Bush mostly relies on (a) factual details that can be verified through research. He provides a list of actions that his administration has taken against terrorism since September 11, 2001. Even though the reader may not agree with these actions or agree that the actions have been effective, the list is based on facts. A few examples of biased language include *most solemn duty, destroying, sanctuaries, virtually, critical, best, transformed,* and *safer.*

2. (c) Sentence 14 refers to findings of the Commission that by 2004, the United States was still not safe from terror attacks. Sentences 12 and 14 offer a counter view to the list of accomplishments that the President has mentioned in his speech.

3. In the passage, President Bush expresses a bias (a) in favor of the 9/11 Commission by expressing agreement with its report.

## PRACTICE 5

Read the following paragraphs taken from a speech given by Senator Edward Kennedy at the 2004 Democratic National Convention. Then answer the questions.

### Senator Edward Kennedy's Address to the Democratic National Convention

[1]The eyes of the world were on us and the hearts of the world were with us after September 11th—until this administration broke that trust. [2]We should have honored, not ignored, the pledges we made. [3]We should have strengthened, not scorned, the alliances that won two World Wars and the Cold War.

[4]Most of all, we should have honored the principle so fundamental that our nation's founders placed it in the very first sentence of the Declaration of Independence—that America must give "a decent Respect to the Opinions of Mankind."

[5]We failed to do that in Iraq. [6]More than 900 of our servicemen and women have already paid the ultimate price. [7]Nearly 6,000 have been wounded in this misguided war. [8]The administration has alienated long-time allies. [9]Instead of making America more secure, they have made us less so. [10]They have made it harder to win the real war on terrorism, the war against Al Qaeda. [11]None of this had to happen.

[12]How could any President have possibly squandered the enormous goodwill that flowed to America from across the world after September 11th?

[13]Most of the world still knows what we can be—what only we can be—and they want us to be that nation again.

[14]America must be a light to the world, and under John Kerry and John Edwards, that's what America will be.

[15]We need a President who will bind up the nation's wounds. [16]We need a President who will be a symbol of respect in a world yearning to be at peace again. [17]We need John Kerry as our President.

—Senator Edward M. Kennedy Address to the Democratic National Convention. 27 July 2004. 10 August 2004.

______ **1.** Overall, the passage offers supports that are
a. mainly positive.
b. mainly negative.

______ **2.** Which of the following statements is true?
a. Sentence 1 offers an opposing view.
b. Sentence 5 offers an opposing view.
c. Sentence 12 offers an opposing view.
d. No opposing view is offered in the passage.

______ **3.** In this passage, the author expresses a biased attitude
a. in favor of President Bush's administration.
b. in favor of John Kerry for President of the United States.
c. against the war in Iraq.
d. against America providing global leadership.

Textbook Skills

## The Logic of Argument

Most of the subjects you will study in college rely on research by experts, and these experts may have differing views on the same topic. Often textbooks spell out these arguments. Sometimes textbook authors will give several experts' views. But sometimes only one view will be presented. In this case, be aware that there may be other sides to the story.

Textbook arguments are usually well developed with supports that are relevant and adequate. These supports may be studies, surveys, expert opinions, experiments, theories, examples, or reasons. Textbooks may also offer graphs, charts, and photos as supports. An effective reader tests passages in textbooks for the logic of the arguments they present. The exercises that follow are designed to give you practice evaluating the logic of arguments in textbooks.

### PRACTICE 6

**A.** Read the following paragraph from a college psychology textbook, and study the figure that accompanies it. Mark each statement in the passage and the figure **C** if it is an author's claim or **S** if it provides support for the claim.

Textbook Skills

**Locus of Control**

[1]Locus of control is the most important trait of a person's personality. [2]**Locus of control** is a person's belief about who or what controls the consequences of actions. [3]A person who expects to control his or her own fate has an *internal* locus of control. [4]This person thinks that rewards come through

effort. [5]A person who sees his or her life as being controlled by forces outside himself or herself has an *external* locus of control. [6]This person thinks that his or her own behavior has no effect on outcomes.

—Carlson & Buskist, *Psychology: The Science of Behavior,* 5th ed., pp. 460–461.

**Internal Locus of Control**

| Poor performance on test | Good performance on test |
|---|---|
| It's my own fault. I should have spent more time studying. | Great! I knew all that studying would pay off. |

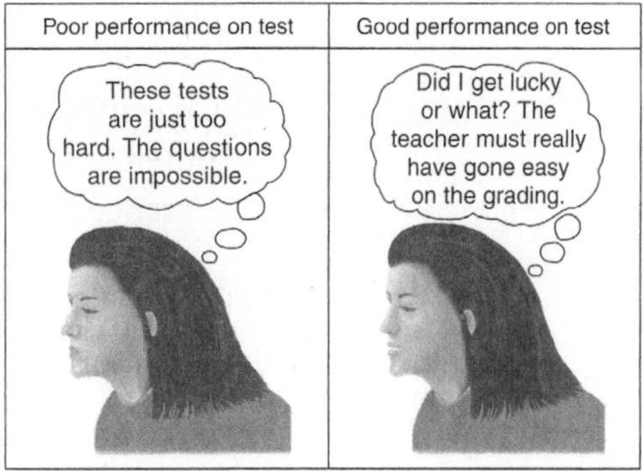


—From Carlson, N. & Buskist, W. *Psychology: The Science of Behavior,* 5/e © 1994. Published by Allyn & Bacon, Boston, MA. Copyright © 2004 by Pearson Education. Reprinted by permission of the publisher.

_____ **1.** sentence 1

_____ **2.** sentence 2

_____ **3.** sentence 3

_____ **4.** sentence 4

_____ **5.** sentence 5

_____ **6.** sentence 6

_____ **7.** The person's will is the most powerful driving force in a person who has an internal locus of control.

_____ **8.** "It's my own fault. I should have spent more time studying."

_____ **9.** The environment is the most powerful driving force in a person who has an external locus of control.

_____ **10.** "Did I get lucky or what? The teacher must really have gone easy on the grading."

**B.** Read the following paragraph from a textbook on parenting.

Textbook Skills

### Chinese Children

[1]Some American experts believe that the good behavior of Chinese children is the result of the way Chinese parents and teachers treat their children and students. [2]Chinese children are quiet, quick to follow instructions, and rarely act selfishly. [3]Chinese children do not cry, whine, throw tantrums, or suck their

thumbs. [4]American children are taught to be independent. [5]Chinese parents and the teachers in nurseries and kindergarten tend to be warm, kind, and attentive. [6]Chinese parents strive to promote intense closeness between themselves and their children. [7]They do not use physical punishment or harsh verbal rebukes.

—Adapted from Jaffe, *Understanding Parenting*, 2nd ed., p. 150.

**11.** Underline the topic sentence that states the claim of the author's argument.

______ **12.** Which sentence is *not* relevant to the author's point?

a. sentence 1
b. sentence 5
c. sentence 4
d. sentence 7

**C.** The following information comes from a college health textbook. Read each list of supports. Choose the claim that is adequately supported by the evidence in the list.

Textbook Skills

**13.** Supports

- People who chronically skip breakfast burn an average of 150 fewer calories per day than regular breakfast eaters.
- Breakfast eaters awake with a souped-up metabolism.
- Breakfast skippers greet each day cold and tired with the "metabolic furnace" set on low until lunch.

Write **V** for valid by the claim that is adequately supported by the evidence.

______ a. People who skip breakfast lose more weight than people who eat breakfast.

______ b. People who skip breakfast use less energy.

______ c. Breakfast is the most important meal of the day.

______ d. People who skip breakfast are more hungry than people who eat breakfast.

**14.** Supports

- Eat a juicy apple or a cup of soup instead of a dry granola bar or a bag of popcorn.
- Dehydration stimulates the appetite.
- Foods with high water content will make you feel even more full than drinking water to wash down dry foods with the same calorie count.

Write **V** for valid by the claim that is adequately supported by the evidence.

_____ a. Wet foods are healthier than dry foods.

_____ b. Dry foods are not appropriate diet foods.

_____ c. The water content of foods plays an important role in weight control.

_____ d. Water intake is the most important part of a diet aimed at weight control.

**VISUAL VOCABULARY**

The context given in the three supports, along with this photo, suggests that dehydrated means _____________. The word **dehydrated** is composed of three word parts: a prefix, root, and a suffix. What is the root, and what does it mean?

Root: _____________

Meaning: _____________

▲ Dehydrated food

**15.** Supports

- A Tufts University study of women who took up moderate weightlifting found that they increased their strength by 35 to 75 percent.
- The women increased their balance by 14 percent.
- And they increased their bone density by 1 percent.
- The greater your muscle mass, the greater your metabolic rate and hence the more calories you burn.

Write V for valid by the claim that is adequately supported by the evidence.

_____ a. Women who lift moderate weights develop large muscle mass.

_____ b. Beginning a moderate weightlifting program demands time and dedication.

_____ c. Weightlifting is the best way to lose weight.

_____ d. A moderate weightlifting program has several health benefits in addition to burning calories.

—Adapted from Donatelle, *Health Basics*, 5th ed., p. 271.

## Chapter Review

Test your understanding of what you have read in this chapter by filling in each blank with a word from the box. Use each choice once.

| | | |
|---|---|---|
| adequate | claim | personal |
| amount | evidence | relevant |
| argument | making an invalid conclusion | topic sentence |
| bias | | |

**1.** Effective _______________ is a reasonable process during which a claim is made and logical details are offered to support that claim.

**2–3.** An argument is made up of two types of statements:

a. The author's _______________

b. The _______________ or reasons that support the author's claim

**4–5.** List the two missing steps that will help you analyze an argument:

Step 1: Identify the author's claim and supports.

Step 2: Decide whether the supports are relevant.

Step 3: Decide whether the supports are _______________.

Step 4: Check the argument for _______________.

**6.** When evaluating an argument, it is important to test each piece of supporting evidence with the question, "Is this support _______________ to the author's claim?"

**7.** In a paragraph, the _______________ states the author's claim.

**8.** A valid argument is based not only on a claim and relevant support but also on the _______________ and quality of the support given.

**9.** The _______________ opinion and experience of one person do not carry enough weight to make an adequate claim.

**10.** Making a claim without providing adequate support for the claim is an error known as ________________________.

## Applications

### Application 1: Argument: Author's Claim and Supports

**A.** Read the following groups of ideas. Mark each statement **C** if it is an author's claim or **S** if it provides support for the claim.

**1.** ______ a. The television show *America's Most Wanted* has helped capture more than 700 criminals.

______ b. *Sesame Street* has taught millions of preschoolers about the alphabet, arithmetic, and social values.

______ c. Television can be a force for good.

______ d. The Discovery Channel supports education by offering high-interest programs about history, science, and various cultures.

______ e. News channels like CNN, MSNBC, and Fox News bring up-to-the-minute information to the audience.

**B.** Study the photograph of people protesting for legal reforms in the medical field. Then mark each statement that follows **C** if it is an author's claim or **S** if it provides support for the claim.

▲ Physicians, nurses and support staff of Flagler Hospital in St. Augustine gather in front of the hospital for a noon protest Wednesday to urge Florida lawmakers to pass medical malpractice law reform. Doctors are calling for a $250,000 cap on noneconomic malpractice awards, saying out-of-control jury awards are behind insurance increases.

**2.** ______ a. Protesters are calling for a cap on malpractice suits.

______ b. Doctors, nurses, and support staff of Flagler Hospital in St. Augustine, Florida, are gathered in front of the hospital.

______ c. Without a cap on malpractice suits, doctors may "pull up roots" by leaving Florida.

______ d. Florida lawmakers should put a cap on malpractice insurance costs.

______ e. Out-of-control jury awards are behind insurance increases.

### Application 2: Argument: Relevant Supports

**A.** Read the following outline of a claim and its supports. Mark each support **R** if it is relevant to the claim or **N** if it is not relevant to the claim.

Claim: For senior citizens who live alone, owning a pet increases physical and mental well-being.

Supports

______ **1.** Seniors who own a pet must be physically active in order to take care of the pet.

______ **2.** Pets offer companionship and lessen loneliness.

______ **3.** Pets cost money.

______ **4.** Senior citizens may have to give their pets up when they move into assisted living homes.

______ **5.** Caring for a pet can give a senior citizen a sense of purpose, a reason to get up each day.

**B.** Read the following paragraph.

**Shark Attacks Decline Overall but Not in the Shark-Bite Capital**

[1]Shark attacks declined globally for the third straight year, but the figures show that Volusia County remains the unofficial shark-bite capital of the world. [2]Sharks bit 22 people in Volusia waters—tying a record set in 2001, according to Capt. Scott Petersohn, who keeps such statistics for Volusia's Beach Patrol. [3]For the third year in a row, more than half the attacks in the United States occurred in Florida. [4]However, the 29 bites reported in Florida were down from 37 in 2001 and 38 in 2000, according to the Shark File Web site.

[5]Three people were killed by sharks out of 60 attacks across the globe last year—down from five deaths in 72 attacks in 2001 and 13 deaths in 85 attacks in 2000. [6]Florida had a slow tourist season in 2002.

—Adapted from Johnson, "Shark Attacks Decline Globally, Stay Same in Area," *The Daytona Beach News-Journal*, 7 Feb. 2003, p. 8A.

**6.** Underline the topic sentence (the sentence that states the claim).

_____ **7.** Which sentence is *not* relevant to the author's point?

a. sentence 2
b. sentence 4
c. sentence 5
d. sentence 6

## Application 3: Argument: Adequate Supports and Author's Bias

**1.** The following paragraph consists only of supports. Choose the claim (topic sentence) that the evidence adequately supports.

### They Can Get Away With It

[1]A person who uses your Social Security number, credit card numbers, checking account information, and birth date has committed identity theft. [2]As many as 1 in 20 Americans say that they have been the victim of identity theft during their lives. [3]The total loss so far due to identity theft may reach as high as $23 billion. [4]But in the year 2000, the FBI reported making only 922 arrests for identity theft. [5]"This is the fastest-growing crime today because the thieves know they can get away with it," said Linda Foley, director of the Identity Theft Resource Center. [6]"If you talk to law enforcement and ask them why they aren't prosecuting, they will say they have limited resources," said Barbara Span, vice president of Star Systems (the largest network of bank ATM machines). [7]"And they prosecute crimes that are easier to prove. [8]Also, violent crimes tend to take priority."

—Adapted from Sullivan, "ID Theft Victims Get Little Help."

_____ a. Identity theft happens every day and costs billions of dollars.

_____ b. Police don't care about identity theft crimes.

_____ c. Identity theft, a costly crime, is easy to get away with due to a lack of response from law enforcement.

_____ **2.** The details in the paragraph are mostly

a. negative.
b. positive.

**3.** Study the graph; then indicate which conclusion is *not* adequately supported by evidence.

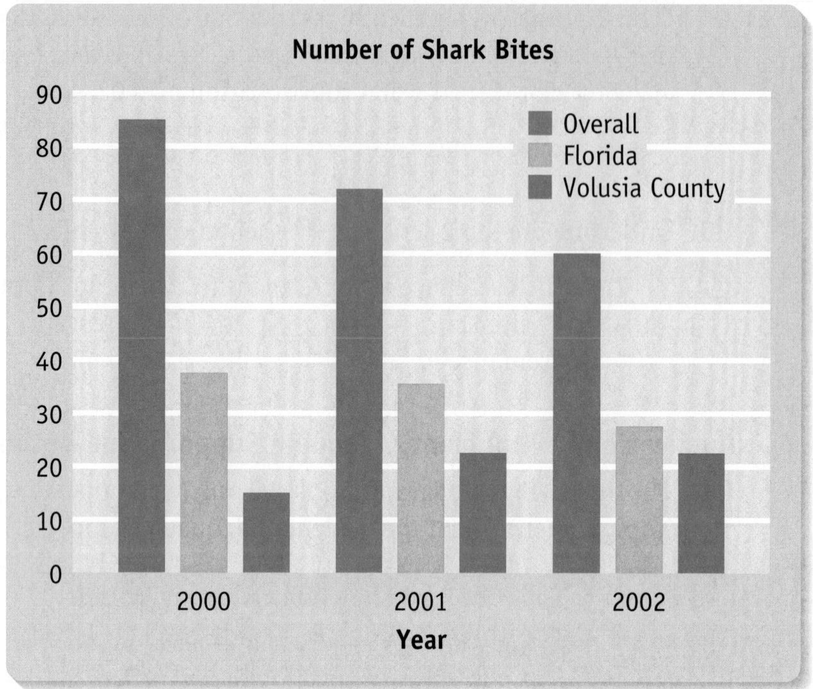


*Source:* Graph reprinted from *Daytona Beach News-Journal,* "Shark Bites," 7 Feb. 2003.

______ a. The number of shark bites per year is declining globally.

______ b. The number of shark bites per year is declining in Florida.

______ c. The number of shark bites per year is declining because there are fewer sharks.

______ d. The number of shark bites per year has remained the same in Volusia County for two years.

## REVIEW Test 1

### Argument

**A.** Read the following groups of ideas. Mark each statement **C** if it is an author's claim or **S** if it provides support for the claim.

#### Group 1

______ **1.** Julie has a high fever.

______ **2.** Julie has the flu, not just a common cold.

______ **3.** Julie's symptoms came on suddenly.

______ **4.** Julie also has a cough, chills, and muscle aches.

### Group 2

______ **5.** Veterinary pet insurance is a good investment for a pet owner.

______ **6.** A good insurance policy can cost as little as \$15 a month for cats and \$18 a month for dogs.

______ **7.** Benefits cover the cost of tests, treatments, and medicine.

______ **8.** After a \$50 deductible, all the pet's medical bills are covered.

**B.** Read the following lists of claims and supports. Mark each support **R** if it is relevant to the claim or **N** if it is not relevant to the claim.

Claim: A negative outlook on life is a key barrier to success.

Supports

______ **9.** Many people play a "tape" of negative messages in their heads, and these negative messages control their thoughts.

______ **10.** Messages like "I can't do this" or "No one cares what I do" are often untrue statements that block positive action.

______ **11.** Most actions begin as thoughts or beliefs.

______ **12.** Success begins with the belief or thought that the goal is attainable.

______ **13.** Everybody fails sometimes.

______ **14.** Success leads to more success.

Claim: The study of mathematics is essential to becoming a well-educated person with a large number of career options.

Supports

______ **15.** Knowledge of mathematics makes one a smarter, better-informed consumer.

______ **16.** The study of mathematics is difficult for many people.

______ **17.** Solving mathematical problems helps develop critical thinking skills.

______ **18.** Mathematics has always been a part of a good education.

______ **19.** Understanding mathematical concepts helps one understand and use technology better.

______ **20.** Mathematical skills are the basis of hundreds of good-paying jobs in accounting, engineering, and computer programming.

# REVIEW Test 2

## Argument

**A.** Read the following groups of ideas. Mark each statement **C** if it is an author's claim or **S** if it provides support for the claim.

_____ **1.** In California, Senator Deborah Ortiz proposed a law that would ban soft drinks from all public schools in the state.

_____ **2.** In Maine, State Representative Sean Faircloth sponsored the "Maine Obesity Package"; this law would force fast-food chains to place nutritional information on menus.

_____ **3.** The obesity bill would also set aside dollars for walking trails, bike lanes, and cross-country ski trails in Maine.

_____ **4.** Lawmakers in several states believe that Americans should become more active and eat healthier fare.

—Adapted from Hellmich, "Legislators Try to Outlaw Soft Drinks, Sugary Snacks at Schools."

**B.** Study the following mock advertisement for gun locks. Read the claim and the list of supports. Mark each support **R** if it is relevant to the claim or **N** if it is not relevant to the claim.

***An Unlocked Gun is an Open Door to Disaster***

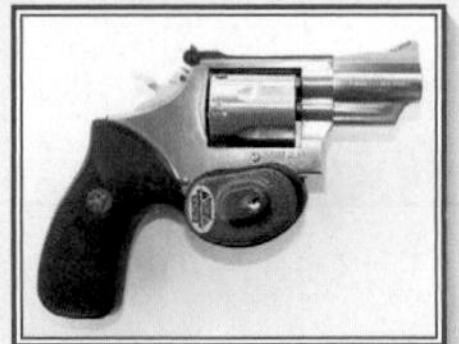

Most often, you do not leave home without locking your front door in order to ensure your personal safety. Locking the door just makes sense. Use common sense also when you own and use firearms. A gun lock ensures personal safety. When not in use, a gun should be kept unloaded, in a gun safe, and equipped with a gun lock.

*Shut the door on disaster. Lock your firearms.*

Claim: Gun owners should use gun locks on their firearms to ensure safety.

Supports

_____ **5.** Most often, you do not leave home without locking your front door in order to ensure your personal safety.

_____ **6.** Locking the door just makes sense.

_____ **7.** Use common sense also when you own and use firearms.

_____ **8.** A gun lock ensures personal safety.

_____ **9.** When not in use, a gun should be kept unloaded, in a gun safe, and equipped with a gun lock.

_____ **10.** Responsible gun ownership is just common sense.

**C.** Read the following lists of claims and supports. Mark each support **R** if it is relevant to the claim or **N** if it is not relevant to the claim.

Claim: Anger can be controlled.

Supports

_____ **11.** Relaxation skills such as deep breathing and slowly repeating words like *relax* can ease angry feelings.

_____ **12.** Avoiding situations that cause anger can help prevent anger; for example, a person who is angered by traffic should take less traveled roads when possible.

_____ **13.** Anger is healthy and normal.

_____ **14.** Some people are hotheads and just can't help themselves.

Claim: Ephedra, an herb used to lose weight, is unsafe and should be banned.

Supports

_____ **15.** Ephedra increases the heart rate and narrows blood vessels.

_____ **16.** Some experts say the drug is safe compared to other drugs used to lose weight.

_____ **17.** The Food and Drug Administration has recorded nearly 100 deaths due to ephedra.

_____ **18.** The Bush administration has ordered a study on ephedra and its dangers.

—Caruso, "Study Urges Ephedra Restrictions," p. A11.

**D.** Read the following paragraph.

### A Serious Sadness: SAD

[1]Seasonal affective disorder (SAD) is a type of depression also known as the "winter blues." [2]SAD is a real illness, and people with SAD can have severe symptoms. [3]Young people and women are at the highest risk for the disorder. [4]But it can affect anyone. [5]In fact, an estimated 25 percent of the population suffers from mild winter SAD. [6]About 5 percent suffer from a more severe form of the disorder. [7]The symptoms of SAD occur regularly during the fall or winter months. [8]Those who suffer from SAD experience changes in their sleeping and eating habits; they feel sad, anxious, or "empty"; and they feel a loss of pleasure in activities they once enjoyed. [9]They also crave sugary or starchy foods. [10]All of these symptoms lead to exhaustion, irritability, poor concentration, and weight gain. [11]A brisk walk in the morning sunlight can be helpful.

—National Health Association, "Depression: Seasonal Affective Disorder."

**19.** Underline the sentence that states the author's claim.

______ **20.** Which sentence is *not* relevant to the author's claim?

a. sentence 1
b. sentence 3
c. sentence 10
d. sentence 11

## REVIEW Test 3

### Argument

**A.** Read the following claim and its supports. Mark each support **R** if it is relevant to the claim or **N** if it is not relevant to the claim.

Claim: Young people use their style of dress to express a sense of belonging.

Supports

______ **1.** One group of teenagers might choose to wear the "'60s retro look."

______ **2.** Another group may prefer loose-fitting clothes such as oversized shirts and baggy pants.

______ **3.** Some groups use accessories like earrings, necklaces, or sunglasses to set themselves apart.

______ **4.** A permanent way to identify with a group is through body art, such as tattooing.

______ **5.** Parents, teachers, and other adults do not approve of many of these group dress codes.

**B.** Read the following paragraph.

**Working Benefits Teenagers**

[1]Teenagers should enter the workforce as soon as possible due to the personal and financial benefits of working. [2]The first benefit is the opportunity to build lasting relationships. [3]Coworkers who share common interests and career goals offer an extra source of support and friendship. [4]In addition, young workers learn how to build positive relationships with supervisors. [5]These relationships may be a priceless source of references and future job connections. [6]Second, when young people work, they learn the value of earning their own money. [7]Working teens are more likely to budget and save. [8]They are more likely to have checking and savings accounts and even credit cards in their own names, thus building up a record of good credit for themselves. [9]Teenagers who work are also more likely to value the goods they buy with their own money.

**6.** Underline the sentence that states the author's claim.

______ **7.** In this paragraph, the author expresses a biased attitude
a. against teenagers going to college immediately after graduating from high school.
b. in favor of teenagers learning financial responsibility.
c. against teenagers working full time.
d. in favor of teenagers working full time to earn their own living.

**C.** Read the following paragraph.

[1]In the United States, HIV infection is increasing most rapidly among young people; one in every four new infections occurs in people younger than 22. [2]The United States has more than double the teenage pregnancy rate of any other Western industrialized country; more than a million teenagers become pregnant each year. [3]In addition, teenagers have the highest rates of sexually transmitted diseases (STDs) of any age group. [4]In fact, one in four young people contracts an STD by the age of 21.

—Adapted from De Carlo, "Educating for Sexual Responsibility."

______ **8.** Which of the following claims is adequately supported by the evidence in the paragraph?
a. Sex education should be taught in high school.
b. Young people need help protecting themselves from disease and unwanted pregnancy.
c. Sex education programs encourage young people to engage in dangerous activities.
d. The United States has the highest teen pregnancy rate in the world.

**D.** Study the following table.

**College Students' Top Ten Reasons for Cheating**

1. The instructor gave too much material.
2. The instructor left the room.
2.* A friend asked me to cheat, and I couldn't say no.
4. The instructor doesn't seem to care if I learn the material.
5. The course information is useless.
6. The course material is too hard.
6.* Everyone else seems to be cheating.
8. I'm in danger of losing a scholarship due to low grades.
9. I don't have time to study because I'm working to pay for school.
10. People sitting around me made no effort to protect their work.

* = tied

—"College Cheating," Research in Higher Education, p. 52.

**9–10.** Choose the *two* claims that are *not* adequately supported by the evidence.

______ a. Instructors are unfair in their expectations.

______ b. Students blame their actions on teachers and other students.

______ c. Students may cheat because of grades and time concerns.

______ d. Most students take responsibility for their own cheating.

## REVIEW Test 4

### Argument

Before you read, skim the following article, which addresses the debate about our rights as citizens to privacy. Answer the **Before Reading** questions. Then read the passage, and answer the **After Reading** questions.

### Vocabulary Preview

*furor* (2): uproar, fit of anger
*surveillance* (2): close watch, observation
*sphere* (9): area
*permanent* (10): long-term, lasting

## No, You're Not Paranoid . . .

[1]You don't have to be a sports fan to remember the 2001 Super Bowl. [2]The name of the winner may have faded from memory, but who can forget the **furor** over the **surveillance** system used to scan the 100,000 fans as they entered Tampa Stadium?

[3]Although signs advised fans that they were being videotaped, most probably never realized the extent of the surveillance. [4]The Facefinder biometric system picked out 19 petty criminals whose faces matched mug shots in a police database. [5]Since it was just an experiment, no one was arrested. [6]But the surveillance sparked a flood of media attention and a call for public hearings by the American Civil Liberties Union (ACLU).

[7]The experiment was **dubbed** "Snooper Bowl" by the ACLU. [8]And it renewed the debate about the use of technology. [9]It is feared that new technologies may be shrinking the **sphere** of privacy that Americans once considered a birthright. [10]Some also say the test was just another step toward broad and **permanent** surveillance of American society.

[11] "We need a modern-day Paul Revere riding from city to city warning people: 'The cameras are coming; the cameras are coming!'" said Norman Seigel. [12](Seigel is the former executive director of the New York chapter of the ACLU.) [13]The chapter carried out a block-by-block search of Manhattan, and almost 2,500 cameras were found aimed at New Yorkers in public places.

[14]In Illinois, state officials have used face-recognition tools to put all photos taken for drivers' licenses into an electronic "mug book" of nearly every adult in the state.

[15]Actually, the Super Bowl was not the first use of the technology. [16]Casinos have been matching faces of gamblers captured on video cameras to a database of known cheaters. [17]This system was first installed at Trump Marina in Atlantic City, N.J.

[18]Of course, banks, hospitals, jewelry stores, and other places of business have been using video cameras since the 1960s. [19]Then, in the 1990s, the price and size of video equipment shrank, and the quality of the images improved. [20]Thus videotaping people in public (and sometimes in private) became widespread.

[21]Now video cameras record activity on freeways, subways, and buses and in elevators, public parks, parking garages, schools, stores, restaurants, and post offices. [22]Moreover, the growing popularity of the Internet has given the practice worldwide coverage. [23]In cities across the country, bars are installing Webcams, which are video cameras that broadcast live over the World Wide Web. [24]Web surfers can check out the action at their local pubs before they go out on the town.

[25]Legal experts say surveillance devices are lawful in public places. [26]But in several recent cases, landlords and managers of buildings have been caught watching their tenants' bathrooms or bedrooms. [27]Video cameras have also been found in public restrooms and tanning salons.

[28]And the United States is not alone. [29]For example, in recent decades in Britain, terrorist bombings have become common; thus authorities have been using video cameras in public places for more than two decades. [30]With more than 1.5 million closed-circuit television cameras watching streets, parks, and public buildings, Britain is perhaps the most watched country on earth.

—"No, You're Not Paranoid," *CQ Researcher,* p. 512.

## BEFORE READING

### Vocabulary in Context

_____ **1.** What does the word **dubbed** mean in sentence 7?
a. repeated
b. recorded
c. named
d. admired

### Tone and Purpose

_____ **2.** The overall tone of the passage is
a. objective.
b. biased.

_____ **3.** The primary purpose of the passage is
a. to inform.
b. to entertain.
c. to persuade.

## AFTER READING

### Central Idea and Main Idea

_____ **4.** Which sentence best states the central idea of the passage?
a. The government is trying to take away everyone's right to privacy.
b. The growing use of surveillance systems stirs up controversy.

c. Controversial surveillance systems are used in public places to catch criminals.
d. The government must do whatever it must to protect law-abiding citizens.

**Supporting Details**

_____ **5.** Sentence 13 is a
a. main idea.
b. major supporting detail.
c. minor supporting detail.

**Transitions**

_____ **6.** The relationship between the ideas in sentences 25 and 26 is
a. time order.
b. comparison and contrast.
c. cause and effect.
d. definition.

**Thought Patterns**

_____ **7.** The overall thought pattern for the passage is
a. generalization and example.
b. time order.
c. classification.
d. contrast.

**Fact and Opinion**

_____ **8.** Sentence 11 is a statement of
a. fact.
b. opinion.

**Inferences**

_____ **9.** Sentences 11–13 imply that
a. people need to be warned that government may be taking away some of their freedoms.
b. cameras have become our enemies.
c. people are paranoid or afraid of government.
d. the government is doing what is necessary to protect its citizens.

**Argument**

_____ **10.** Reread sentences 25–27. Then choose the claim that is adequately supported by the evidence.
a. Surveillance of private acts is lawful.
b. Surveillance of private acts is illegal.
c. Some people are using surveillance devices to watch the private behaviors of others.

## Discussion Topics

1. In what ways are surveillance devices used in your school? The local mall? Other public places near you?
2. What are some of the arguments people make against the use of surveillance devices in public places?
3. What are the dangers of the government's putting driver's licenses into a photo bank? What are the benefits?

## Writing Topics

1. Should police cars have surveillance devices? Write a paragraph arguing one side of this issue.
2. Why do places of business that stay open 24 hours a day, such as Wal-Mart or convenience stores, use surveillance devices? Is this use justified? Write a paragraph to discuss the topic.
3. Do you think surveillance devices should be used in public places? Why or why not? Write a paragraph with a claim and reasons.

## EFFECTIVE READER Scorecard

### The Basics of Argument

| Test | Number Correct | | Points | | Score |
|---|---|---|---|---|---|
| Review Test 1 | ______ | × | 5 | = | ______ |
| Review Test 2 | ______ | × | 5 | = | ______ |
| Review Test 3 | ______ | × | 10 | = | ______ |
| Review Test 4 | ______ | × | 10 | = | ______ |
| Review Test 5 (website) | ______ | × | 5 | = | ______ |
| Review Test 6 (website) | ______ | × | 5 | = | ______ |

Enter your scores on the Effective Reader Scorecard: Chapter 12 Review Tests inside the back cover.

## After Reading About the Basics of Argument

Before you move on to the mastery tests on the basics of argument, take time to reflect on your learning and performance by answering the following questions. Write your answers in your notebook.

What did I learn about the basics of argument?

What do I need to remember about the basics of argument?

How has my knowledge base or prior knowledge about argument changed?

### More Review and Mastery Tests

For more practice, go to the book's website at **http://www.ablongman.com/henry** and click on *The Effective Reader.* Then select "More Review and Mastery Tests." The tests are organized by chapter.

# MASTERY Test 1

Name ______________________ Section ____________

Date ____________ **Score** (number correct) ______ × 10 = ______%

**A.** Read the following group of ideas. Mark each statement **C** if it is an author's claim or **S** if it provides support for the claim.

_____ **1.** On a Pennsylvania road on November 2, 1999, a driver using a cell phone ran a stop sign and broadsided Patricia N. Pena's family car, killing 1-year-old Morgan Lee.

_____ **2.** The harshest penalty the driver of the car could receive was a $50 fine and two traffic tickets.

_____ **3.** "My husband and I were outraged," Pena wrote later.

_____ **4.** Pena also believes the driver "would have gotten into more trouble if he had just threatened to kill my daughter; since he did kill her and blamed it on his cell phone, he walks away."

_____ **5.** Cell phones should be banned from use while driving.

—"Should Cell Phones Be Banned in Cars?" *CQ Researcher,* p. 210.

**B.** Read the author's claim and the list of supports. Then mark each support **R** if it is relevant to the claim or **N** if it is not relevant to the claim.

Claim: Parents and teachers disagree about whether state testing has a negative effect on students' learning.

Supports

_____ **6.** A poll taken of parents in 2000 showed that over 50 percent of the parents did not think testing was a problem.

_____ **7.** In the same poll, 18 percent of parents thought that teachers focused too much on "teaching to the test."

_____ **8.** In the same year, a poll taken of teachers showed that nearly 70 percent of teachers thought that state testing forced them to focus too much on teaching the information on the test.

_____ **9.** Many students may know the information but do not test well.

_____ **10.** Only 4 percent of teachers said they didn't know if state testing had negative effects, whereas 33 percent of the parents polled said they didn't know.

—"Is There Too Much Testing?" *CQ Researcher,* p. 327.

# MASTERY Test 2

Name ______________________ Section ____________

Date ____________ **Score** (number correct) ______ × 10 = ______%

**A.** Read the following group of ideas. Mark each statement **C** if it is an author's claim or **S** if it provides support for the claim.

______ **1.** You should accept the feelings of other people.

______ **2.** Accepting feelings is not the same thing as agreeing with them.

______ **3.** One of the only things that really belongs to anyone is his or her feelings.

______ **4.** And though we might want to stop or change the feelings of another, it is impossible to do so.

______ **5.** Thus it is not helpful or wise to tell another person that he or she should not feel a certain way.

**B.** Read the author's claim and the supports. Then mark each support **R** if it is relevant to the claim or **N** if it is not relevant to the claim.

Claim: A current law that violates a student's right to privacy should be changed.

Supports

______ **6.** The law gives universities the option of telling a student's parents about underage drinking and illicit drug use.

______ **7.** The law favors the belief that parents have the right to know about the personal lives of their grown children over the students' right to control who has access to the details of their personal lives.

______ **8.** Many parents don't even pay for their children's education.

**C.** Read the following paragraph, which consists of supports.

Textbook Skills

### The Forces That Rule Our Lives

[1]The first force in our lives is the voice of our social environment. [2]The social environment is made up of friends, family, school, and church. [3]As we become socialized by these people, we adopt their systems of beliefs. [4]Changes in society's beliefs occur slowly, over decades or even centuries. [5]The second force in our lives is the individual voice, the voice of the human

spirit. [6]This inner voice may come to recognize that all is not well, and it may begin to question the social voice. [7]The individual mind can change much more quickly than society's mind. [8]The third force in our lives is the voice of divine guidance. [9]We are so thoroughly trained to obey the laws of people and then urged by inner desires to take command of our own lives that it becomes difficult to release the self to the divine. [10]Lama Surya Das calls these the *outer*, *inner*, and *innate* powers or forces.

—Adapted from Girdano, Eeverly, & Dusek, *Controlling Stress and Tension,* 6th ed., p. 75.

______ **9.** Which claim is adequately supported by the evidence?

a. A person is not whole or complete until he or she listens to the outer, inner, and innate voices.
b. Everyone believes in God.
c. Several basic forces or voices exist within us.
d. Few people can change society or themselves.

**D.** Study the graph.

Textbook Skills

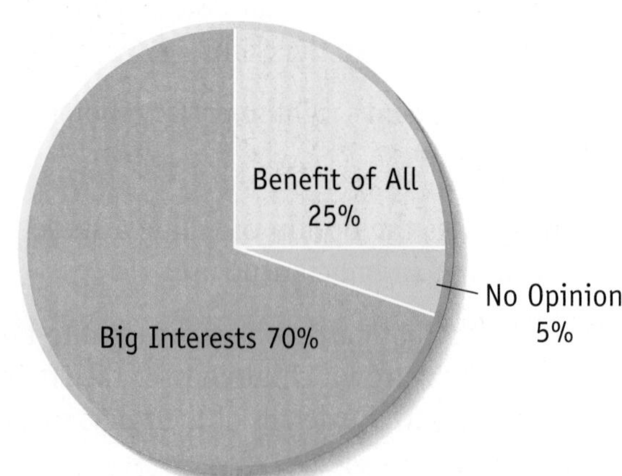


**Public Opinion about Who Runs the Country.** Would you say the government is pretty much run by a few big interests looking out for themselves or that it is run for the benefit of all the people?

*Source:* Copyright © 2000 The Gallup Organization. All rights reserved. Reprinted with permission from www.gallup.com and the poll conducted July 6–9, 2000.

______ **10.** Which claim is adequately supported by the evidence?

a. Most people believe that government is run for the benefit of all the people.
b. Most people believe that government is run by "big interest" groups looking out for themselves.
c. Most people don't know or care who is running government.
d. Most people are frustrated with government.

MASTERY **Test 3**

Name ______________________ Section ____________

Date ____________ **Score** (number correct) ______ × 10 = ______%

**A.** Read the following groups of ideas. Each group contains the author's claim and supports for that claim. Identify the author's claim in each group.

______ **1.** a. Reading short stories allows us to experience times and places other than our own.
b. Reading short stories stimulates our imagination.
c. Short stories should be read for a number of reasons.
d. Reading short stories helps us connect with the experiences and feelings of others.

______ **2.** a. Space tourism will someday be a money-making business.
b. Businessman Dennis Tito was the first space tourist.
c. Tito flew aboard a Russian rocket to the international space station on April 30, 2001.
d. In a survey of over 1,000 households, 60 percent of those surveyed said they were interested in traveling to space for a vacation.

______ **3.** a. Daytona Beach plays host to hundreds of thousands of race fans during the world-famous Daytona 500 NASCAR race every February.
b. Year-round mild climate and beautiful beaches make Daytona a perfect family vacation spot.
c. Every October and March, thousands of motorcycles thunder into Daytona Beach for Oktoberfest and Bike Week, respectively.
d. Daytona Beach appeals to a wide array of tourists.

______ **4.** a. Some computer users complain about the amount of time their service provider is down and inaccessible.
b. Computers have some disadvantages.
c. Many computer users are discouraged by the amount of e-mail they must deal with on a daily basis.
d. A growing concern among parents is the access children have to unsuitable material on the Internet.

**B.** Read the following claim and its supports. Mark each support **R** if it is relevant to the claim or **N** if it is not relevant to the claim.

Claim: Animals become extinct mainly as a result of human action.

Supports

_____ **5.** Humans destroy the natural environment of a species by damming rivers, filling in swamps and marshes, and cutting down trees to build homes, roads, and other developments.

_____ **6.** Many species of fish and birds have been damaged by oil spills, acid rain, and water pollution created by industry.

_____ **7.** Many animals are hunted to extinction for their meat, furs, or other valuable parts.

_____ **8.** Some people have taken positive steps to protect endangered species.

_____ **9.** New species introduced into a habitat by humans can bring diseases that destroy the native species.

**C.** Read the following paragraph, which consists of supports.

[1]American poet Emily Dickinson lived from 1830 to 1886 in Amherst, Massachusetts, the small town in which she was born. [2]She was an unusual and gifted woman who in her later years dressed in white, rarely left her house, and composed over 1,000 poems. [3]Common themes that run throughout her works are death, immortality, love, and nature. [4]Her verses, known for their strong images and nontraditional form, won her wide acclaim after her death. [5]Only five poems were published during her lifetime. [6]The poems published after her death were marred by unskillful editing to make them conform to standard forms of rhyme and punctuation. [7]Both the life and poetry of Emily Dickinson defied traditional expectations. [8]But her reputation and influence have grown steadily over the years, and she is now considered one of America's greatest poets.

_____ **10.** In this paragraph, the author expresses a bias

a. in favor of Emily Dickinson for achieving widespread fame during her lifetime.
b. against Emily Dickinson as a woman writer.
c. in favor of Emily Dickinson because she defied tradition to become one of America's greatest poets.
d. against Emily Dickinson because she did not want to publish her work during her lifetime.

MASTERY **Test 4**

Name ______________________ Section ____________

Date __________ **Score** (number correct) ______ × 10 = ______%

The following article was published in a daily newspaper. Read the article, and then answer the questions that follow it.

### Tough Talk, Very Little Action

[1]For all the tough talk out of Washington on immigration, illegal immigrants caught along the Mexican border have almost no reason to fear they will be prosecuted.

[2]Ninety-eight percent of those arrested between Oct. 1, 2000, and Sept. 30, 2005, were never prosecuted for illegally entering the country, according to an Associated Press analysis of federal data. [3]Those 5.3 million immigrants were simply escorted back across the Rio Grande and turned loose. [4]Many presumably tried to slip into the U.S. again.

[5]The number of immigrants prosecuted annually tripled during that five-year period, to 30,848 in the fiscal year 2005, the most recent figures available. [6]But that still represented less than 3 percent of the 1.17 million people arrested that year. [7]The prosecution rate was just under 1 percent in 2001.

[8]The likelihood of an illegal immigrant being prosecuted is "to me, practically zero," said Kathleen Walker, president-elect of the American Immigration Lawyers Association.

[9]Federal prosecutors along the nation's southern border have come under pressure from politicians and from top officials in the Justice Department to pursue more cases against illegal immigrants.

[10]But few politicians are seriously suggesting the government prosecute everyone caught slipping across the border. [11]With about 1 million immigrants stopped each year, that would overwhelm the nation's prisons, break the Justice Department's budget, and paralyze the courts, immigration experts say.

[12]The Justice Department itself says it has higher priorities.

—Caldwell, Alicia A. "Tough Talk, Very Little Action." *The Daytona Beach News-Journal*, 8 April 2007, 2B.

Read the author's claim and the supports. Mark each support **R** if it is relevant to the claim or **N** if it is not relevant to the claim.

Claim: For all the tough talk out of Washington on immigration, illegal immigrants caught along the Mexican border have almost no reason to fear they will be prosecuted. (sentence 1)

Supports

_____ **1.** Ninety-eight percent of those arrested between Oct. 1, 2000, and Sept. 30, 2005, were never prosecuted for illegally entering the country, according to an Associated Press analysis of federal data. (sentence 2)

_____ **2.** Those 5.3 million immigrants were simply escorted back across the Rio Grande and turned loose. (sentence 3)

_____ **3.** Many presumably tried to slip into the U.S. again. (sentence 4)

_____ **4.** The number of immigrants prosecuted annually tripled during that five-year period, to 30,848 in the fiscal year 2005, the most recent figures available. (sentence 5)

_____ **5.** But that still represented less than 3 percent of the 1.17 million people arrested that year. The prosecution rate was just under 1 percent in 2001. (sentences 6–7)

_____ **6.** The likelihood of an illegal immigrant being prosecuted is "to me, practically zero," said Kathleen Walker, president-elect of the American Immigration Lawyers Association. (sentence 8)

_____ **7.** Federal prosecutors along the nation's southern border have come under pressure from politicians and from top officials in the Justice Department to pursue more cases against illegal immigrants. (sentence 9)

_____ **8.** But few politicians are seriously suggesting the government prosecute everyone caught slipping across the border. (sentence 10)

_____ **9.** With about 1 million immigrants stopped each year, that would overwhelm the nation's prisons, break the Justice Department's budget, and paralyze the courts, immigration experts say. (sentence 11)

_____ **10.** The Justice Department itself says it has higher priorities. (sentence 12)

MASTERY **Test 5**

Name ____________________ Section ____________

Date ____________ **Score** (number correct) ______ × 20 = ______%

**A.** Read each list of supports. Choose the claim that is adequately supported by the evidence in each list.

Supports

- The push to create public schools began in earnest in the 1820s.
- Many people saw public education as the answer to poverty.
- Others saw public education as a way to fight crime and help immigrants fit into society.
- At first, many thought Sunday schools were the way "to reclaim the vicious, to instruct the ignorant, and to raise the standard of morals among the lower classes of society."
- But soon these religious reformers called for public schools, too.

—Adapted from Martin et al., *America and Its Peoples: A Mosaic in the Making*, 3rd ed., p. 340.

______ **1.** Which claim is adequately supported by the evidence?

a. Public schools were created for the good of both the individual and the country.

b. Public schools were created so that everyone in the country could have free education.

c. Education is the only way a person can become successful.

d. Education is a basic right owed to everyone.

Supports

- Whole grains are packed with vitamins, minerals, and fiber that you just don't find in plain white bread, processed cereals, white rice, or even many healthful-looking enriched "multigrain" breads.
- Researchers have found disease-fighting properties in the nutrients in whole grains.
- In addition to being nutritious, whole grains are loaded with flavor and texture, adding interest to meals.

—Donatelle, *Health*, 5th ed., p. 231.

______ **2.** Which claim is adequately supported by the evidence?

a. Whole grains are the most healthful food available.

b. Multigrain breads are not good for you.

c. Whole-grain foods are hard to beat for nutrition, taste, and texture.

d. The easiest way to get whole grain in the diet is by eating whole-wheat bread.

Textbook Skills

Supports

- Infant mortality rates are higher for boys, and women live an average of seven years longer than men.
- Females have a more acute sense of smell and taste than males, and women's hearing is better and lasts longer than men's.
- While alcoholism is twice as common in men as in women, alcoholic women are at much greater risk for death from drinking.
- Women have a higher risk than men of developing diabetes, and a heart attack is more likely to be fatal for a woman than for a man.

—Adapted from Benokraitis, *Marriages and Families*, 4th ed., p. 75.

______ **3.** Which claim is adequately supported by the evidence?
a. Women are stronger than men.
b. Men are stronger than women.
c. Women live longer than men.
d. Men and women are different from each other.

**B.** Read the following paragraph. Then answer the questions that follow it.

Textbook Skills

**Power Goes to the Less Interested**

[1]If you can walk away from the rewards that your partner controls or can suffer the punishment your partner gives, then you control the relationship. [2]If, on the other hand, you need the rewards that your partner controls or are unable or unwilling to suffer the punishments that your partner can give, then your partner has the power and controls the relationship. [3]Power corrupts people. [4]In a love relationship, for example, the person who maintains the greater power is the one who would find it easier to break up the relationship. [5]The person who is unwilling or unable to break up has little power. [6]This lack of power is due to the fact that he or she is dependent on the relationship and the rewards provided by the other person.

—Adapted from DeVito, *Messages: Building Interpersonal Communication Skills*, 4th ed., p. 328.

______ **4.** Which sentence states the author's claim?
a. In any interpersonal relationship, the person who holds the power is the one who is less interested in and less dependent on the other person.
b. Some people like to be controlled by others.
c. Some people like to control others.
d. Powerful people do not make lasting commitments to others.

______ **5.** Which sentence is *not* relevant to the argument?
a. sentence 1
b. sentence 2
c. sentence 3
d. sentence 6

MASTERY **Test 6**

Name ______________ Section ______________

Date ______________ Score (number correct) ______ × 20 = ______%

**A.** Read the following paragraphs. Identify the sentence that is *not* a logical support for the claim in each.

### Retrospective Voting

[1]Voters can influence the direction of future policies through retrospective voting. [2]Retrospective voting is the act of casting votes based on the performance of those who are already in office by either reelecting them or throwing them out of office. [3]Personal ambition is the reason most people run for office. [4]Voters may not know what politicians will do in the future, but they can judge how well politicians performed in the past. [5]When officeholders are defeated, it is reasonable to assume that voters did not like their performance. [6]And newly elected officials should change the course of policy if they do not want to meet a similar fate in the next election.

—Adapted from Dye, *Politics in America,* 5th ed., p. 250.

______ **1.** Which sentence is *not* a relevant support for the claim that retrospective voting can influence future policy?

a. sentence 3
b. sentence 4
c. sentence 5
d. sentence 6

### The Elitist Perspective

[1]"Government is always government by the few whether in the name of the few, the one, or the many." [2]This quotation expresses the basic idea of *elitism*. [3]All societies, including democracies, divide themselves into the few who have power and the many who do not. [4]In every society, there is a division of labor. [5]Most people are content to let others undertake the tasks of government. [6]The elite are the few who have power. [7]The masses are the many who do not. [8]The theory of elitism holds that an elite is inevitable in any social organization. [9]Leaders may take advantage of their power. [10]We cannot form a club, a church, a business, or a government without selecting some people to provide leadership.

—Adapted from Dye, *Politics in America,* 5th ed., p. 22.

______ **2.** Which sentence is *not* a relevant support for the claim that the elite rule government?

a. sentence 2
b. sentence 8
c. sentence 9
d. sentence 10

**B.** Read the list of supports. Choose the claim that is adequately supported by the evidence in the list.

Supports

- Women's bones can become weak and brittle as they age.
- Calcium, ingested through diet or supplements, can keep bones healthy as they age.
- Exercise also builds bones.
- Many women do not get enough calcium or exercise enough to keep bones healthy and strong as they age.

_____ **3.** Which claim is adequately supported by the evidence?
a. Women need to exercise and eat properly to protect their bones as they age.
b. Most women are malnourished and will suffer bone loss as they age.
c. Most women are too busy to find the time to get the exercise they need.
d. Women are not aware of the danger posed by lack of exercise and calcium deficiencies.

**C.** Read the following paragraph. Then answer the questions that follow it.

Textbook Skills

### The Human Eye

[1]A camera views the world through a lens that gathers and focuses light. [2]The eye also gathers and focuses light. [3]Light enters the **cornea,** a transparent bulge on the front of the eye, and passes through the **pupil,** an opening in the iris. [4]To focus a camera, you move its lens closer to or farther from the object viewed; to focus light in the eye, a bean-shaped lens changes its shape. [5]It thins to focus on faraway objects and thickens to focus on near ones. [6]To control the amount of light coming into a camera, you change the opening of the lens; in the eye, the muscular disk of the iris changes the size of the pupil. [7]At the back of the camera body is photosensitive film that records the changes in light that have come through the lens. [8]This film can be very expensive. [9]Likewise, in the eye, light strikes the **retina,** a thin sheet that lines the rear wall of the eyeball.

—Adapted from Gerrig & Zimbardo, *Psychology and Life,* 16th ed., pp. 89–90.

_____ **4.** Which sentence states the author's claim?
a. The human eye is similar to a camera.
b. The human eye is a marvelous invention.
c. The human eye is far superior to a camera.
d. The human eye sees differently than a camera.

_____ **5.** Which sentence is *not* relevant to the argument?
a. sentence 5
b. sentence 6
c. sentence 7
d. sentence 8

CHAPTER

13

# Advanced Argument: Persuasive Techniques

## CHAPTER PREVIEW

## Before Reading About Advanced Argument: Persuasive Techniques

In this chapter, you will build on the concepts you studied about the basics of argument. Take a moment to review the four steps in analyzing an argument. Fill in the following blanks with each of the steps.

Step 1: ______________________________

Step 2: ______________________________

Step 3: ______________________________

Step 4: ______________________________

Based on the chapter preview and what you learned about the basics of argument, complete the following idea:

A valid argument is made up of relevant and adequate supports.

Biased arguments that use logical fallacies and propaganda techniques are composed of ____________ and ____________ supports.

To help you master the material in the chapter, create a three-column chart in your notebook. In the left column write the headings from the chapter preview, as in the example that follows. Leave enough room between each heading to fill in definitions and examples as you work through the chapter.

**General definition: A fallacy is**

| **Fallacy** | **Definition** | **Example** |
|---|---|---|
| Personal attack | | |
| Straw man | | |

**General definition: Propaganda is**

| **Propaganda technique** | **Definition** | **Example** |
|---|---|---|
| Name calling | | |
| Testimonials | | |

## Biased Arguments

Much of the information that we come in contact with on a daily basis is designed to influence our thoughts and behaviors. Advertisements, editorials, and political campaigns constantly offer one-sided, biased information to sway public opinion.

This biased information is based on two types of reasoning: the use of **fallacies** in logical thought and the use of **propaganda**. An effective reader identifies and understands the use of these persuasion techniques in biased arguments.

## What Is a Fallacy in Logical Thought?

You have already studied logical thought in Chapter 12, "The Basics of Argument." Logical thought or argument is a process that includes an author's claim, relevant support, and a valid conclusion. A **fallacy** is an error in the process of logical thought. A fallacy leads to an invalid conclusion. You have also studied two general types of fallacies: irrelevant details and inadequate details. By its nature, a fallacy is not persuasive because it weakens an argument. However, fallacies are often used to convince readers to accept an author's claim. In fact, the word *fallacy* comes from a Latin word that means "to deceive" or "trick." You will learn more about irrelevant and inadequate arguments in the next two sections of this chapter.

Fallacies are not to be confused with false facts. A fact, true or false, is stated without bias, and facts can be proven true or false by objective evidence. In contrast, a fallacy is an invalid inference or biased opinion about a fact or set of facts. Sometimes the word *fallacy* is used to refer to a false belief or the reasons for a false belief.

A **fallacy** is an error in logical thought.

**EXAMPLE** Read the following sets of ideas. Mark each statement as follows:

**UB** for unbiased statements
**B** for biased arguments

_____ **1.** Thomas Edison invented the light bulb.

_____ **2.** Every time Ralph has worn his New York Mets t-shirt, he has passed his math exams; therefore, to pass the next exam he will wear it again.

_____ **3.** Lashonda trusts the news story because it's printed in the newspaper.

_____ **4.** Randall attended classes regularly, took detailed notes during classes and from his textbooks, reviewed his notes daily, asked questions during classes, and, as a result, earned a high grade point average.

_____ **5.** Even though sunlight travels approximately 93 million miles to reach earth, its ultraviolet rays cause premature aging of the skin, cataracts, and skin cancer.

**EXPLANATION**

1. This is an unbiased statement (UB); however, it is a false fact. Thomas Edison did not invent the light bulb. Research reveals that several men had produced various types of electrical lights before Edison. Edison improved upon a 50-year-old idea based on a patent he bought from inventors Henry Woodward and Matthew Evans. This idea is not a fallacy; it does not represent an error in thinking. The detail is simply incorrect information. Logical thinking begins with verifying the facts.
2. This is a biased argument (B) based on a fallacy in logical thought. Ralph has jumped to the wrong conclusion about why he did well on his math exams. By not considering other reasons for his success, he has identified a false cause and made an invalid inference. You will learn more about the fallacy of false cause later in this chapter.
3. This is also a biased argument (B) based on a fallacy in logical thought. Lashonda is arguing in a circle. She has a favorable bias toward words in print. She trusts the news because it is in the paper. Unfortunately, publication does not guarantee accuracy. You will learn more about the fallacy of circular reasoning later in this chapter.
4. This is an unbiased statement (UB). Every detail can be verified through testimony or eyewitness accounts of Randall's classmates, teachers, and transcripts.
5. This is an unbiased statement (UB). This statement is factual and can be proven with objective evidence, case histories, and expert opinions.

## PRACTICE 1

Read the following sets of ideas. Mark each statement as follows:

**UB** for unbiased statements
**B** for biased arguments

______ **1.** Birds evolved from dinosaurs.

______ **2.** Teenager to his friend, "You are jealous because I have my own car."

______ **3.** People under the age of 18 should not be allowed to vote because they are too young.

______ **4.** British soldiers fired in self-defense on American colonists in the Boston Massacre.

## What Is Propaganda?

Propaganda is a means by which an idea is widely spread. The word *propaganda*, first used by Pope Gregory XV, comes from a Latin term that means to "propagate" or "spread." In 1612, the Pope created a department within the church to spread the Christian faith throughout the world by missionary work. Centuries later, President Woodrow Wilson used propaganda to sway the American people to enter World War I. **Propaganda** is a biased argument that advances or damages a cause. Propaganda is often used in politics and advertising.

Read the following two descriptions of the same car. The first description includes facts known by the owner. The second description includes details advertised by the owner.

**Facts:** This 2001 300M made by Chrysler is fully loaded with power windows and locks, AM/FM radio and CD player, leather upholstery, and a 3.5-liter V6, 250-horsepower engine. Owner's price of $16,000 is non-negotiable. The car's mileage is unknown because the odometer was disconnected at 10,000 miles. The 3-year-old car also has a high level of road noise, even when the windows are closed.

**For Sale:** This is your chance to own a high-performance luxury sedan; the 300M has been the heavy-hitter in the Chrysler lineup for several years. This 2001 black 300M sedan is in superb condition with lush leather upholstery, a whisper-quiet ride, and a 3.5-liter V6, 250-horsepower engine that delivers heart-pumping power and speed. Hurry! This beauty is priced to sell quickly.

The first description offers objective, fact-based information about the car. However, the second description includes details that appeal to emotions and personal values by using tone words (for more information on tone, see Chapter 10, "Tone and Purpose") such as *luxury*, *superb*, *lush*, *whisper-quiet*, *heart-pumping*, and *beauty*. In addition, the owner did not include the discrepancy between the actual mileage and the mileage clocked on the odometer. Nor did the owner disclose the level of road noise. This description offers only a positive view of the vehicle, and thus, it is an example of **propaganda**. Propaganda uses fallacies to spread biased and misleading information.

> **Propaganda** is an act of persuasion that systematically spreads biased information that is designed to support or oppose a person, product, cause, or organization.

Propaganda uses a variety of techniques that are based on **emotional appeal**. If you are not aware of these techniques, you may be misled by the way information is presented and come to invalid conclusions. Understanding propaganda techniques will enable you to separate factual information from emotional appeals so that you can come to valid conclusions.

For example, the second description of the 300M uses emotional appeals. Its concluding statement, "Hurry! This beauty is priced to sell quickly," appeals to emotions linked to competition. The suggestion is to hurry and *beat* everyone else to this superb luxury car. It may also appeal to emotions linked to self-gratification and needs of acceptance. Hurry! Satisfy a desire for luxury and power. Many people will desire this popular, powerful luxury car. The first description of the car gives only facts; in contrast, the second description uses emotional language to make the car more appealing and the need for action urgent.

> **Emotional appeal** is the arousal of emotions to give a biased meaning or power to an idea.

**EXAMPLE** Read the following sets of ideas. Mark each statement as follows:

**UB** for unbiased statements
**B** for biased arguments

_____ **1.** A healthful diet includes a variety of foods including grain, fresh fruits and vegetables, fats, and protein.

_____ **2.** Use your vote to put Grace McKinney in the Senate because, like you and me, she comes from a hardworking, middle-class family and wants to give control of government back to the people.

_____ **3.** Spicy foods and stress cause stomach ulcers.

_____ **4.** Don't buy your insurance from DealState; that outfit is a bunch of crooks. Instead trust us, TruState, to meet your insurance needs.

_____ **5.** To avoid identity theft, do not give out personal information, periodically obtain a copy of your credit report, and keep detailed records of your banking and financial accounts.

**EXPLANATION**

1. This is an unbiased statement (UB). It is factual and can be proven with objective evidence, case histories, and expert opinions.
2. This is a biased argument (B) using the emotional appeal of propaganda. The statement uses the "plain folks" appeal. Grace McKinney is described as an everyday person with the same values of everyday people. You will learn more about this propaganda technique later in this chapter.
3. This is an unbiased statement (UB); however, it is a false fact. Research reveals that stomach ulcers are caused by an infection from a bacterium or by use of pain medications such as aspirin or ibuprofen. Cancer can also cause stomach ulcers. Stress and spicy food can aggravate an ulcer, but they do not cause one to occur.
4. This is a biased argument (B) using the emotional appeal of the propaganda technique of "name calling." You will learn more about this propaganda technique later in this chapter.
5. This is an unbiased statement (UB). This statement offers factual advice, based on research, about how to respond to the crime of identity theft.

## PRACTICE 2

Read the following sets of ideas. Mark each statement as follows:

**UB** for unbiased statements
**B** for biased arguments

_____ 1. Buy Gold Plus Jeans; they are made in America by Americans.

_____ 2. Advertisement: "This beautiful and famous actress wears Gold Plus Jeans."

_____ 3. Cortisol is a hormone triggered by stress that causes fat to collect in the abdomen.

_____ 4. Charles Darwin is respected by many in the scientific community for his theory of evolution.

Often the emotional appeal of propaganda is found in the supporting details, which are either irrelevant or inadequate (for more information on irrelevant and inadequate details, see Chapter 12, "The Basics of Argument"). The following sections of this chapter offer in-depth discussions and practices to help you identify irrelevant and inadequate arguments that use fallacies in logical thought and propaganda techniques.

## Irrelevant Arguments: Fallacies

Writing based in logical thought offers an author's claim and relevant supporting details, and it arrives at a valid conclusion. Fallacies and propaganda offer irrelevant arguments based on irrelevant details. Irrelevant details draw attention away from logical thought by ignoring the issue or changing the subject.

### Personal Attack

**Personal attack** is the use of abusive remarks in place of evidence for a point or argument. Also known as an *ad hominem* attack, a personal attack attempts to discredit the point by discrediting the person making the point.

For example, Sam, a convicted felon, takes a stand against smoking in public places and calls for a law to ban smoking in restaurants. Those who oppose the law focus attention on Sam's criminal record and ignore his reasons for being against smoking in restaurants with statements like "Now the lawbreakers want to make the laws" or "Don't listen to a loser who can't stay out of jail." However, Sam's criminal past has nothing to do with smoking laws; making it a part of the argument is a personal attack.

**EXAMPLE** Read the following paragraph. Underline two uses of the logical fallacy of *personal attack*.

> [1]Teenager Tyrone is trying to persuade his father that he, Tyrone, should have a motorcycle. [2]Tyrone points out that he has held a steady part-time job for three years and has saved enough money to pay for the motorcycle. [3]Tyrone's father asks, "What about the cost of insurance?" [4]Tyrone replies that he has checked with several insurance companies and found a reasonable rate. [5]He added that he has enough money in his budget to cover the costs. [6]When his father still hesitates, Tyrone says, "You don't like this because it wasn't your idea; you would rather be the one in control." [7]His father retorts, "Well, it's hard to trust your judgment when you have a dozen piercings in your face."

**EXPLANATION** The point Tyrone implies is that he is mature enough to handle the responsibility of owning a motorcycle. He begins with logical reasons to support this claim. He works, saves, and budgets his own money. In addition, he took the initiative to shop for the best price for insurance. These are impressive supports for his argument. However, when his father resists his logic, Tyrone falls into the use of personal attack in sentence 6. Tyrone accuses his father of selfishly trying to stay in control of his life. Tyrone's father responds in sentence 7 with his own personal attack on the way Tyrone looks. The issue of the motorcycle is no longer the focus of their discussion.

## Straw Man

A **straw man** is a weak argument substituted for a stronger one to make the argument easier to challenge. A straw man fallacy distorts, misrepresents, or falsifies an opponent's position. The name of the fallacy comes from the idea that it is easier to knock down a straw man than a real man who will fight back. The purpose of this kind of attack is to shift attention away from a strong argument to a weaker one that can be more easily overcome. Study the following example:

> Governor Goodfeeling opposes drilling for oil in Alaska. But the United States is too dependent on foreign oil supplies, and the American economy would benefit from having an American supply of oil. Governor Goodfeeling is opposed to American-based oil drilling and wants to keep us dependent on foreign oil cartels.

This passage doesn't mention Governor Goodfeeling's reasons for opposing drilling for oil in Alaska. Instead, the writer restates the governor's position in ways that are easy to attack: continued dependence on foreign supplies and the implied economic hardships this might bring.

**EXAMPLE** Read the following paragraph. Underline the *straw man* fallacy in it.

> *Candidate Manual Cortez:* [1]"We must protect our natural environment. [2]Unique and irreplaceable habitats are being devoured by uncontrolled growth. [3]I propose that we set the area known as the Loop aside as a natural reserve. [4]The Loop is a 30-mile stretch of road that cuts through a section of the vanishing Florida forests and marshes. [5]Let us work together to halt McRay's Building Corporation's plans for a new housing development in the Loop once and for all."
>
> *Candidate Rory Smith:* [6]"New construction is a sign of healthy economic development." [7]Candidate Cortez is against economic development.

**EXPLANATION** Candidate Rory Smith uses the straw man fallacy when he accuses his opponent of being against economic development in sentence 7. Candidate Manual Cortez has not said he is against economic development. He is against this particular development in this one specific area known as the Loop. He is for protecting the environment.

## Begging the Question

**Begging the question** restates the point of an argument as the support and conclusion. Also known as *circular reasoning*, begging the question assumes that an unproven or unsupported point is true. For example, the argument, "Spinach is an awful tasting food because it tastes bad" begs the question. The point "Spinach is an awful tasting food" is assumed to be true because it is restated in the phrase "tastes bad" without specific supports that give logical reasons or explanations. Compare the same idea stated without begging the question: "I never eat spinach because it has a bitter taste, and I don't like foods that taste bitter."

**EXAMPLE** Read the following paragraph. Underline the irrelevant argument of *begging the question.*

**Superman Returns**

[1]Christopher Reeve's portrayal of Superman seemed to be definitive. [2]He was ridiculously good-looking, and with the chisled face of a god, he made gallantry and innocence heroic. [3]Christopher Reeve was the best actor of all time for the role because he was the only actor who could convincingly play the role. [4]Then, *Superman Returns* flew into theatres in 2006. [5]And Brandon Routh proved that "he has what it takes to reinvent Superman for a new generation," as stated by Peter Travers in his review of the movie for *Rolling Stone.*

**EXPLANATION** Sentence 3 begs the question. To say that Christopher Reeve was the *only actor who could convincingly play the role* is simply restating the idea that he *was the best actor of all time for the role.* If he is the only one, then he is the best. As an effective reader, you want to know the reasons that explain why he is the best or the only one who could play this role.

## PRACTICE 3

Identify the fallacy in each of the following items. Write **A** if it begs the question, **B** if it constitutes a personal attack, or **C** if it is a straw man.

_____ **1.** Vote the knuckleheads out of office.

_____ **2.** Ice cream is my favorite dessert because I like it.

_____ **3.** Algebra is too hard because the concepts are difficult.

_____ **4.** Raina should not be class president because she is a cheerleader.

_____ **5.** We don't need Alfred Simons in Congress; he is a multimillionaire.

# Irrelevant Arguments: Propaganda Techniques

## Name-Calling

**Name-calling** uses negative labels for a product, idea, or cause. The labels are made up of emotionally loaded words and suggest false or irrelevant details that cannot be verified. Name-calling is an expression of personal opinion. For example, a bill for gun control may be labeled "anti-American" to stir up opposition to the bill. The "anti-American" label suggests that any restriction to the ownership of guns is against basic American values.

**EXAMPLE** Read the following paragraph. Underline the irrelevant details that use *name-calling.*

**From Good Girl to Diva**

[1]Christina Singer has veered a long way from the bubblegum pop music and teeny-bop image that made her famous. [2]In her newest album, *Taunt and Tease*, she has the air of a raunchy diva. [3]Even though her voice delivers a decent mix of pop, rock, soul, and R&B, her vampire-in-leather costume and wicked-witch makeup makes her act scary to watch.

**EXPLANATION** The first sentence uses two labels to name the kind of appeal of this fictitious singer: *bubblegum pop* is a kind of music aimed at the preteen market, and *teeny-bop image* is usually linked to this market. Sentence 2 calls Christina Singer a raunchy diva. The word *raunchy* means "crude" or "vulgar," and the word *diva* suggests the large ego of a star. So saying she has the air of a raunchy diva is calling her rude and full of herself. Sentence 3 includes three negative labels: *vampire-in-leather costume, wicked-witch*, and *scary*. These names evoke images of the singer's evil and dark side.

## Testimonials

**Testimonials** use irrelevant personal opinions to support a product, idea, or cause. Most often the testimonial is provided by a celebrity whose only qualification as a spokesperson is fame. For example, a famous actor promotes a certain brand of potato chips as his favorite, or a radio talk show host endorses a certain type of mattress.

**EXAMPLE** Read the following paragraph. Underline the irrelevant details that use a *testimonial.*

### The Benefits of Milk

[1]Milk and milk products are important dietary sources of calcium. [2]Milk and milk products are also good sources of other vital nutrients, including high-quality protein for building and repairing body tissues and vitamin A for better eyesight and healthy skin. [3]They are also rich in riboflavin, vitamin $B_{12}$, and phosphorus. [4]Famous athlete Jerome High-Jumper says, "Drinking milk every day makes me the athlete I am."

**EXPLANATION** Sentences 1 through 3 offer factual details about milk and milk products. However, sentence 4 uses the testimonial of a famous athlete. Being a famous athlete doesn't make the spokesperson an expert about the nutritional value of milk. A doctor, nurse, or nutritionist could offer a relevant expert opinion.

## PRACTICE 4

Identify the propaganda technique used in each of the following items. Write **A** if the sentence is an example of name-calling or **B** if it is a testimonial.

_____ **1.** Senator Hillary Clinton has a wishy-washy voting record on the war in Iraq. First, she voted for the war; but as soon as the war became unpopular, she said she would have voted differently.

_____ **2.** President Bush proved to be a war monger.

_____ **3.** "I have been to Darfur. I have seen the heartbreaking suffering of starvation. We cannot delay. The United Nations must intervene, now!"—Jean Powell, a relief volunteer

_____ **4.** To raise money for stem cell research, Nancy Reagan gave several speeches about her experiences with President Reagan's 10-year battle with Alzheimer's disease.

_____ **5.** "I have known Tamika Greer since she was a child. She is honest, hard working, and compassionate, with a large dose of common sense. She will be excellent as mayor of our city."

## Bandwagon

The **bandwagon** appeal uses or suggests the irrelevant detail that "everyone is doing it." This message plays on the natural desire of most individuals to conform to group norms for acceptance. The term *bandwagon* comes from the 19th-century use of a horse-drawn wagon that carried a musical band to lead circus parades and political rallies. To *jump on the bandwagon* meant to follow the crowd, usually out of excitement and emotion stirred up by the event rather than out of thoughtful reason or deep conviction.

**EXAMPLE** Read the following paragraph. Underline the irrelevant details that use the *bandwagon* appeal.

**Prom Curfew**

[1]Alissa, a sophomore, has been asked to the senior prom by a popular football player. [2]Her parents are protective and strict, so she has a curfew that will force her to come home long before the after-prom parties are over. [3]As she is talking over her plans with her parents, she offers to pay for her dress with her own money, and she reassures them that her date is trustworthy and comes from a family that her parents know and respect. [4]She also tells them that all her friends' parents are letting them stay out until 3 A.M. [5]She reminds them that she has a cell phone and can call if she needs to for any reason. [6]When her parents resist, she says, "I'm the only one who isn't allowed to stay out late on prom night."

**EXPLANATION** Alissa uses the bandwagon appeal in two sentences. In sentence 4, she implies that her parents should jump on the bandwagon and conform to what other parents are doing when she says all her friends' parents are letting them stay out until 3 A.M. She then follows this argument in sentence 6 with "I am the only one who isn't allowed," a statement that shows she has already jumped on the bandwagon and wants to do what everyone else is doing. Read the paragraph with the bandwagon details removed.

**Prom Curfew**

Alissa, a sophomore, has been asked to the senior prom by a popular football player. Her parents are protective and strict, so she has a curfew that will force her to come home long before the after-prom parties are over. As she is talking over her plans with her parents, she offers to pay for her dress with her own money, and she reassures them that her date is trustworthy and comes from a family that her parents know and respect. She reminds them that she has a cell phone and can call if she needs to for any reason.

## Plain Folks

The **plain folks** appeal uses irrelevant details to build trust based on commonly shared values. Many people distrust the wealthy and powerful, such as politicians and the heads of large corporations. Many assume that the wealthy and powerful cannot relate to the everyday concerns of plain people. Therefore, the person or organization of power puts forth an image to which everyday people can more easily relate. For example, a candidate may dress in simple clothes, pose for pictures doing everyday chores like shopping for groceries, or talk about his or her own humble beginnings to make a connection with "plain folks." These details strongly suggest that "you can trust me because I am just like you." The appeal is to the simple, everyday experience, and often the emphasis is on a practical or no-nonsense approach to life.

**EXAMPLE** Read the following paragraph. Underline the irrelevant details that appeal to *plain folks.*

### Cooking with Helen

[1]A woman dressed in everyday casual clothes, wearing a sleeveless blue-collared shirt and khaki slacks, is busy preparing food in a television studio that has been created to look like a cozy kitchen. [2]She says, "Hello, my name is Helen. [3]Welcome to my kitchen. [4]For the next hour, I will share with you a few of the family-secret, down-home cooking techniques that have put my book, *Helen's Favorite Southern Recipes,* on the national best-seller list for the past three years."

**EXPLANATION** The woman, Helen, is described as wearing clothes that many plain folks also wear: She is *dressed in everyday casual clothes, wearing a sleeveless blue-collared shirt and khaki slacks.* So plain folks can relate to the woman based on her style of clothing. The kitchen is described as *cozy,* which suggests basic or simple values common to many people. Helen sets a friendly tone with the use of her first name, and the word *my* in *my kitchen* suggests that she is inviting the audience into her home. She then taps into everyday family values with the phrases *family-secret* and *down-home.* All of these details suggest that this best-selling author and television spokesperson is just one of the "plain folks." Once you identify these irrelevant details, you can come to a conclusion based on the relevant details. Read the paragraph with the appeals to plain folks removed; the remaining details are facts that can be verified.

### Cooking with Helen

A woman is busy preparing food in a television studio that has been created to look like a kitchen. She says, "Hello, my name is Helen. Welcome to this kitchen. For the next hour, I will share with you a few of the cooking techniques that have put my book, *Helen's Favorite Southern Recipes,* on the national best-seller list for the past three years."

## PRACTICE 5

Label each of the following items according to the propaganda techniques they employ:

A. plain folks
B. bandwagon
C. testimonial
D. name calling

_____ **1.** A candidate running for the United States Senate dressed in blue jeans and plaid shirt is eating a hot dog at a community cookout.

_____ **2.** Join the millions of satisfied customers who use Grime-Be-Gone.

_____ **3.** People who burn the flag are traitors.

_____ **4.** A headline on the Web site of PETA (People for the Ethical Treatment of Animals) read, "Music legend B. B. King protests injustice and violence toward animals." It then presented the following excerpt from an interview with B. B. King that appeared in *Guitar World:* "I came home one morning and saw an English actress on TV who was talking about how a lot of fast-food companies fix chicken, for example. They showed how the chicken would be coming around like on an assembly line, and when they get to each place, this thing would cut the heads off and something else would do something else to them. And they showed some place in northern Canada where they were killin' the baby seals. They were white and pretty out on the snow, and then they'd kill them and there would be blood and stuff. They showed how we make mink coats in the U.S. We electrocute the minks through their testicles so it won't hurt the fur. I was sitting there and I just got angry. One of my sons who usually cooks for me came over the next morning to make me some bacon and eggs, and I couldn't eat it. And from that time on that's been my protest—I haven't eaten any meat since."

—Drozdowski, "B. B. King: Rambling, Gambling Man."

_____ 5. Which propaganda technique does this World War II poster use?
   a. plain folks
   b. bandwagon

## Inadequate Arguments: Fallacies

In addition to offering relevant supporting details, logical thought relies on adequate supporting details. A valid conclusion must be based on adequate support. Fallacies and propaganda offer inadequate arguments that lack details. Inadequate arguments oversimplify the issue and do not give a person enough information to draw a proper conclusion.

### Either-Or

**Either-or** assumes that only two sides of an issue exist. Also known as the *black-and-white fallacy*, either-or offers a false dilemma because more than two options are usually available. For example, the statement "If you don't give to the toy drive, you don't care about children" uses the either-or fallacy. The statement assumes there is only one reason for not giving to the toy drive—not caring about children. Yet it may be that a person doesn't have the money to buy a toy for the drive, or the person may help children in other ways. Either-or leaves no room for the middle ground or other options.

**EXAMPLE** Read the following paragraph. Underline the *either-or* fallacy in it.

**Peer Pressure**

[1]Clay, Chad, Diego, and Stefan are spending the night together at Chad's house. [2]Around 3 A.M., Chad suggests that they sneak out, take his father's car, and go for a ride around town.

[3]Diego says, "I don't know. [4]What if we get caught?"

[5]"We won't," Chad says. [6]"Don't be such a wuss. [7]It will be fun."

[8]"Yeah," Clay chimes in. [9]"Everyone sneaks out at least once in their life—no big deal."

[10]"Listen, Diego," Chad says in a low, serious voice, "either you're with us or you're not. [11]What's it going to be?"

[12]Diego is still not sure and says, "I don't know, guys, we will be grounded for life if we get caught. [13]Why can't we just stay here and watch movies like we planned?"

[14]"Fine," Stefan says, "you just stay home like a good little boy."

**EXPLANATION** Sentence 10 asserts the either-or fallacy "either you're with us or you're not." Chad makes it sound like Diego will be an enemy if he doesn't go along with the plans. Diego is actually looking out for their best interests. He reminds them of the punishment they will face if they are caught.

## False Comparison

**False comparison** assumes that two things are similar when they are not. This fallacy is also known as a *false analogy*. An analogy is a point-by-point comparison that is used to explain an unfamiliar concept by comparing it to a more familiar one.

For example, an author may draw an analogy between a computer and the human anatomy. The computer's motherboard is like the human nervous system; the computer's processor is like the part of the human brain that tells the other parts of the body what to do. Just like a human brain, a computer's brain also has memory. However, the analogy breaks down when one considers all the differences between a computer and the human anatomy. The human body can repair itself, and the human brain can think creatively and critically. A false comparison occurs when the differences outweigh the similarities.

**EXAMPLE** Read the following paragraph. Underline the logical fallacy of *false comparison*.

[1]A community college president is giving a speech at a local gathering of business professionals. [2]He says, "The community college is just like your

own business. [3]We charge fees for our services. [4]We worry about public relations. [5]We have to pay for buildings, water, and electricity. [6]We hire, train, and promote employees. [7]And we both have the same bottom line."

**EXPLANATION** Sentences 1 through 6 state traits that community colleges do have in common with businesses. However, sentence 7 draws a false analogy. Businesses do not receive public funding from tax dollars. And the primary purpose of a community college is to educate the public, not make large profits. So in significant ways, a community college's bottom line is very different from the bottom line of a business.

## False Cause

**False cause,** also known as **Post Hoc,** assumes that because events occurred around the same time, they have a cause-and-effect relationship. For example, Tyrell wears a blue baseball cap and hits a record number of homeruns. To continue hitting homeruns, he feels he must wear his blue baseball cap. Tyrell has made the mistake of believing that his blue baseball cap has something to do with his ability to hit a record number of homeruns. What are the other possible causes? The Post Hoc fallacy is the false assumption that because event B *follows* event A, event B *was caused by* event A. An effective reader does not assume a cause without thinking about other possible causes.

**EXAMPLE** Read the following paragraph. Underline the logical fallacy of *false cause.*

[1]Haley's family moved from the small town in which she was born and had lived her entire 16 years to a large city. [2]At first, the separation from her lifelong friends caused her to feel lonely and depressed. [3]Eventually she made new friends. [4]They were very different from any friends she had before. [5]They wore body art in the form of tattoos and piercings, and they loved heavy metal music. [6]Around the same time, her parents noticed that Haley was drinking alcohol frequently and heavily. [7]Her parents blamed her new bad habits on her new friends and forbade Haley to see them anymore.

**EXPLANATION** Haley's parents jumped to a false conclusion based on a false cause in sentence 7. Because Haley made new friends around the same time they noticed her drinking habits, her parents blamed her new friends. Instead, they should consider other explanations. Perhaps Haley is still depressed and is using alcohol as a means of self-medication. Or maybe Haley began drinking long before they moved, but her parents just now noticed the behavior.

## PRACTICE 6

Identify the fallacy in each of the following items. Write **A** if the sentence states a false cause, **B** if it makes a false comparison, or **C** if it employs the either-or fallacy.

_____ **1.** A true patriot serves in the military.

_____ **2.** Animals deserve the same legal rights as humans.

_____ **3.** I shouldn't have gone to bed with my hair wet; now I have a cold.

_____ **4.** If you don't vote, you have no right to complain.

_____ **5.** Corbin smoked marijuana before he became addicted to heroin. Marijuana use leads to addiction to hard drugs.

_____ **6.** Which logical fallacy does this World War II poster use?

a. false cause
b. false comparison
c. either-or

## Inadequate Arguments: Propaganda Techniques

### Card Stacking

**Card stacking** omits factual details in order to misrepresent a product, idea, or cause. Card stacking intentionally gives only part of the truth. For example, a commercial for a snack food labels the snack "low in fat," which suggests that it is healthier and lower in calories than a product that is not low in fat. However, the commercial does not mention that the snack is loaded with sugar and calories.

**EXAMPLE** Read the following paragraph and the list of details used to create the paragraph. Place a check beside the details that were omitted by *card stacking*.

**BriteTeeth**

[1]BriteTeeth will turn yellow teeth into a dazzling smile. [2]Recent research revealed that 9 out of 10 people who used BriteTeeth had noticeably whiter teeth. [3]Apply BriteTeeth to your teeth every night before you go to sleep. [4]Then in the morning, brush your teeth as you normally do. [5]Results should be apparent in two applications.

Omitted Details:

_____ BriteTeeth is made of a special mix of baking soda and carbamide peroxide.

_____ BriteTeeth has been used by more than 300,000 people.

_____ BriteTeeth has a temporary effect and must be used on a daily basis.

_____ BriteTeeth was linked in the research to softer teeth and higher rates of tooth decay.

**EXPLANATION** The detail that should not have been left out but was as a method of card stacking is the last detail in the list: *BriteTeeth was linked in the research to softer teeth and higher rates of tooth decay.* Consumers who are truly concerned about their teeth will not want a product that is likely to cause softening and tooth decay.

## Transfer

**Transfer** creates an association between a product, idea, or cause with a symbol or image that has positive or negative values. This technique carries the strong feelings we may have for something over to something else.

Symbols stir strong emotions, opinions, or loyalties. For example, a cross represents the Christian faith; a flag represents a nation; a white lab coat represents science and medicine; and a beautiful woman or a handsome man represents acceptance, success, or sex appeal. Politicians and advertisers use symbols like these to win our support. For example, a political candidate may end a speech with a prayer or the phrase "God bless America," to suggest that God approves of the speech. Another example of transfer is the television spokesperson who wears a white lab coat and quotes studies about the health product she is advertising.

Transfers can also be negative. For example, skull and crossbones together serve as a symbol for death. Therefore, placing a skull and crossbones on a bottle transfers the dangers of death to the contents of the bottle.

**EXAMPLE** Read the following paragraph. Underline the irrelevant details that use *transfer*.

**Governor Edith Public**

[1]Governor Edith Public, who is appearing at a campaign rally in her bid for reelection, says, "Let me begin by saying thank you to the president of the United States for being here today. [2]Your support is deeply appreciated, particularly now that your numbers in the public opinion polls are soaring again." [3]The president, the governor, and the audience laugh good-naturedly. [4]"Good people," the governor continues, "examine my record. [5]Like the president, I have vetoed every bill that attempted to raise your taxes. [6]At the same time, I have carried out new legislation designed to lower the rising cost of living and still provide good health care."

**EXPLANATION** Governor Public opens her remarks with a statement that creates a strong link between the president of the United States and her campaign. The weight, authority, and grandeur of the presidency are carried in the physical presence of the president. Thus his mere appearance transforms any occasion into a powerful event. However, Governor Public's thank-you to the president lays claim to his personal and official support. The phrase "particularly now that your numbers in the public opinion polls are soaring again" combines bandwagon appeal with transfer by suggesting that many people in a poll support the president. If many support the president, and the governor has the same values as the president, then many support the governor as well. Governor Public uses transfer again when she says, "Like the president," in sentence 5.

## Glittering Generalities

**Glittering generalities** offer general positive statements that cannot be verified. A glittering generality is the opposite of name-calling. Often words of virtue and high ideals are used, and the details are inadequate to support the claim.

For example, words like *truth, freedom, peace,* and *honor* suggest shining ideals and appeal to feelings of love, courage, and goodness.

**EXAMPLE** Read the following paragraph. Underline the irrelevant details that use *glittering generalities.*

**A Vote for Education**

[1]A candidate for political office has been asked about her views on education. [2]She responds, "Our democracy is based on the rights of all individuals to be educated. [3]The ability to read and write allows citizens to express their views to those who represent them in government. [4]A society that is uneducated is less likely to enjoy the right to pursue happiness and is less able to protect hard-won freedoms. [5]Research indicates that those with at least a two-year college education are better able to make a good living and pay taxes. [6]And I applaud those teachers who hold their students to standards of moral and academic excellence. [7]I propose that we raise the beginning salaries of teachers and limit class size."

**EXPLANATION** Most of the glittering generalities used by the candidate call to mind American virtues. Sentence 2 includes *democracy* and *rights.* Sentence 4 includes *right to pursue happiness,* which is a paraphrase from the U.S. Constitution, and *freedoms.* Sentence 6 includes *applaud* which is a glittering generality that expresses a feeling, not an action, and *standards of moral and academic excellence.* These are all noble ideals that few people would argue against; however, they do not add any substance to her ideas. Read the paragraph with the glittering generalities removed.

**A Vote for Education**

A candidate for political office has been asked about her views on education. She responds, "The ability to read and write allows citizens to express their views to those who represent them in government. Research indicates that those with at least a two-year college education are better able to make a living and pay taxes. I propose that we raise the beginning salaries of teachers and limit class size."

## PRACTICE 7

For **1–4**, label each of the following items according to the propaganda techniques they employ:

A. transfer
B. glittering generality
C. card stacking

_____ **1.** A vote for candidate Anthony Vacarro is a vote for honesty and integrity.

_____ **2.** Fans can own a dress just like the one Julia Roberts wore to the Oscars. The black velvet vintage dress made by Italian designer Valentino is now available in sizes 0 through 16 at an affordable price.

_____ **3.** The right to burn the flag is part of the right of freedom of speech.

_____ **4.** Be like Alicia Silverstone, Bill Maher, Woody Harrelson, and a host of other successful people. Go vegetarian; don't eat meat.

_____ **5.** Identify the detail from the list of details that was **omitted** from the paragraph for purposes of card stacking.

Truck for sale. This low-mileage 2006 Dodge Dakota offers four-wheel drive and heavy-duty towing power. The Dakota Quad Cab provides comfortable seating for six. In addition, Dodge Dakota Quad Cab trucks have received the highest, five-star government rating for side-crash safety.

a. The Dodge Dakota Quad Cab is the widest and largest truck in its category.
b. The Dodge Dakota Quad Cab truck was named *Four Wheeler* magazine's truck of the year on December 9, 2006.
c. The five-star government rating was awarded to the 2003 Dodge Dakota Quad Cab; no information was available on the 2006 model.

Textbook Skills

## Examining Biased Arguments

Textbooks strive to present information in a factual, objective manner with relevant and adequate support, in keeping with their purpose to inform. However, textbook authors may choose to present biased arguments for your examination. As an effective reader, you are expected to evaluate the nature of the biased argument and the author's purpose for including the biased argument.

**EXAMPLE** The following passage appears in a college mass communication textbook. It serves as an introduction for the chapter "Radio." As you read the passage, underline biased information. After you read, answer the questions.

Textbook Skills

### Limbaugh Speaks: His Listeners Act

[1]His program is unabashedly biased. [2]He sneers at liberals as "ditto-heads" and worse. [3]He calls other members of the media liars. [4]He brags about himself on the air.

[5]Millions of his fans love it. [6]They devour his liberal-bashing and accept his statements as political gospel.

[7]That is Rush Limbaugh, the glib commentator who has been called the "800 pound gorilla of talk radio." [8]He is heard on more than 600 radio stations.

[9]Limbaugh's influence on his listeners is enormous. [10]Claiming that the media were distorting the Republican plan in Congress to transfer the federal school lunch program to the states, he urged listeners to call their newspapers, the national networks, and the news magazines to protest.

[11]"All you say is, 'Stop lying about the school lunch program' and hang up," he told them.

[12]Thousands from coast to coast immediately did so, many using his exact words. [13]Typically, Cable News Network in Atlanta received more than 300 calls.

[14]Critics of Limbaugh's bombastic style recognize his power but contend that he is preaching to the converted. [15]William Rentschler observed in *Editor & Publisher:* "His program is largely a love feast of like-minded listeners massaging the giant ego of their hero."

—Agee, Ault, and Emery, *Introduction to Mass Communications,* 12th ed., p. 213.

______ **1.** Overall, the tone of the passage is
a. positive about Rush Limbaugh.
b. negative about Rush Limbaugh.
c. neutral toward Rush Limbaugh.

______ **2.** The primary purpose of the passage is
a. to encourage readers to condemn Rush Limbaugh.
b. to inform the reader about the power of radio, using Rush Limbaugh as an example.
c. to persuade readers to listen to Rush Limbaugh by giving entertaining details about his show.

______ **3.** In sentence 2, Rush Limbaugh uses the propaganda technique
a. name calling.
b. testimonial.
c. bandwagon.
d. false cause.

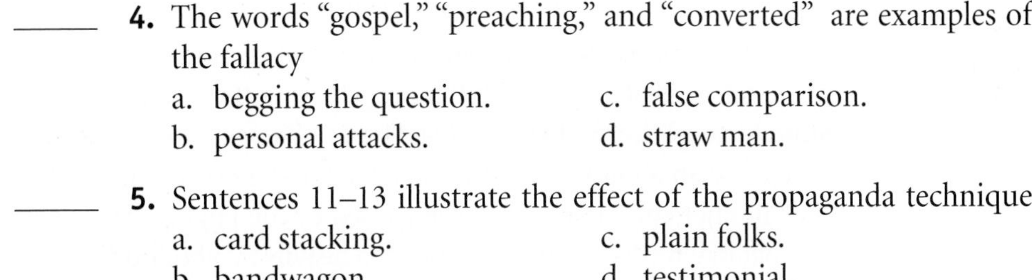

_____ **4.** The words "gospel," "preaching," and "converted" are examples of the fallacy

a. begging the question.
b. personal attacks.
c. false comparison.
d. straw man.

_____ **5.** Sentences 11–13 illustrate the effect of the propaganda technique

a. card stacking.
b. bandwagon.
c. plain folks.
d. testimonial.

**EXPLANATION** The biased information includes the following words: *Unabashedly, sneers, liberals, "dittoheads," liars, brags, devour, liberal-bashing, gospel, glib, 800 pound gorilla, enormous, distorting, bombastic, preaching, converted, love feast,* and *giant ego.*

1. This list of biased words indicates the negative tone (b) used in the discussion about Rush Limbaugh.
2. The primary purpose of the passage is (b) to inform the reader about the power of radio by using Rush Limbaugh as an example. As a well-known and controversial radio talk show host, Rush Limbaugh is an excellent example with which to open a chapter about radio and its influence on society. The authors' purpose was not to condemn or endorse Rush Limbaugh, but to make a point about the power of radio. Radio is a medium of mass communication, and Rush Limbaugh uses propaganda and fallacies in logical thought successfully in his daily broadcast. The authors of this mass communication textbook highlight the powerful relationship between radio and persuasion by using Rush Limbaugh as an example.
3. In sentence 2, Rush Limbaugh uses the propaganda technique (a) name calling.
4. The words "gospel," "preaching," and "converted" are examples of the fallacy (c) false comparison. These words compare Limbaugh and his listeners to a religious leader and followers.
5. Sentences 11-13 illustrate the effect of the propaganda technique (b) bandwagon. Rush Limbaugh has earned the loyalty of a large audience that he can get to jump on the bandwagon of his choice.

## PRACTICE 8

The following passage appears in a college history textbook. As you read the passage, underline biased words. After you read, answer the questions.

Textbook Skills

### "Uncle Tom's Cabin"

[1]Tremendously important in increasing sectional tensions and bringing home the evils of slavery to still more people in the North was Harriet Beecher Stowe's novel *Uncle Tom's Cabin* (1852). [2]Stowe was neither a professional writer nor an abolitionist, and she had almost no firsthand knowledge of slavery. [3]But her conscience had been roused by the Fugitive Slave Act. [4]In gathering material for the book, she depended heavily on abolitionist writers, many of whom she knew. [5]She dashed it off quickly; as she later recalled, it seemed to write itself. [6]Nevertheless, *Uncle Tom's Cabin* was an enormous success: 10,000 copies were sold in a week; 300,000 in a year. [7]It was translated into dozens of languages. [8]Dramatized versions were staged in countries throughout the world.

[9]Harriet Beecher Stowe was hardly a distinguished writer; it was her approach to the subject that explains the book's success. [10]Her tale of the pious, patient slave Uncle Tom, the saintly white child Eva, and the callous slave driver Simon Legree appealed to an audience far wider than that reached by the abolitionists. [11]She avoided the self-righteous, accusatory tone of most abolitionist tracts and did not seek to convert readers to belief in racial equality. [12]Many of her southern white characters were fine, sensitive people, while the cruel Simon Legree was a transplanted Connecticut Yankee. [13]There were many heart-rending scenes of pain, self-sacrifice, and heroism. [14]The story proved especially effective on the stage: The slave Eliza crossing the frozen Ohio River to freedom, the death of Little Eva, Eva and Tom ascending to Heaven—these scenes left audiences in tears.

[15]Southern critics pointed out, correctly enough, that Stowe's picture of plantation life was distorted, her slaves atypical. [16]They called her a "coarse, ugly, long-tongued woman" and accused her of trying to "awaken rancorous hatred and malignant jealousies" that would undermine national unity. [17]Most Northerners, having little basis on which to judge the accuracy of the book, tended to discount southern criticism as biased. [18]In any case, *Uncle Tom's Cabin* raised questions that transcended the issue of accuracy. [19]Did it matter if every slave was not as kindly as Uncle Tom, as determined as George Harris? [20]What if only one white master was as evil as Simon Legree? [21]No earlier white American writer had looked at slaves as people.

[22]*Uncle Tom's Cabin* touched the hearts of millions. [23]Some became abolitionists; others, still hesitating to step forward, asked themselves as they put the book down: Is slavery just?

—Garraty and Carnes. *The American Nation: Volume One, A History of the United States to 1877*, pp. 378–79.

_____ **1.** Overall the tone of the passage
a. is positive about *Uncle Tom's Cabin.*
b. is negative about *Uncle Tom's Cabin.*
c. remains neutral toward *Uncle Tom's Cabin.*

_____ **2.** The author's purpose is
a. to argue against the injustices of slavery.
b. to inform the reader about the importance of *Uncle Tom's Cabin.*
c. to delight the reader by sharing the success of a nineteenth-century woman writer.

_____ **3.** The "heart-rending scenes of pain, self-sacrifice, and heroism" included in *Uncle Tom's Cabin* were most likely examples of the propaganda technique
a. bandwagon.
b. testimonials.
c. transfer.
d. name calling.

_____ **4.** In sentence 16, Stowe's critics use the propaganda technique
a. bandwagon.
b. testimonials.
c. transfer.
d. name calling.

## Chapter Review

Complete these sentences by filling in each blank with a term from the box. Use each term once.

| | | |
|---|---|---|
| ad hominem | fallacy | post hoc |
| begging the question | false analogy | propaganda |
| black and white | ignoring | |
| emotional appeal | oversimplify | |

**1.** A _______________ is an error in logical thought.

**2.** Irrelevant details draw attention away from logical thought by _______________ the issue.

**3.** Inadequate details _______________ the issue and do not give a person enough information to draw a proper conclusion.

4. ______________ is an act of persuasion that systematically spreads biased information that is designed to support or oppose a person, product, cause, or organization.

5. ______________ is the arousal of emotions to give meaning or power to an idea.

6. ________________ is also known as circular reasoning.

7. Personal attack is also known as an ___________ attack.

8. False cause is also known as ______________.

9. False comparison is also known as ______________.

10. Either-or is also known as the ______________fallacy.

## Applications

### Application 1

Read the following mock advertisement for a weight loss system. Label each sentence using one of the following letters (some answers may be used more than once):

| | |
|---|---|
| a. unbiased statement | e. transfer |
| b. bandwagon | f. testimonial |
| c. plain folks | g. glittering generality |
| d. false cause | h. false comparison |

**The Beauty of LeanBody**

[1]Join the 3.1 million people who are already using LeanBody. [2]In just seven days you can lose from four to fourteen inches guaranteed with the LeanBody System. [3]You can have a body as beautiful as Jennifer Anniston, Halle Berry, or Jennifer Lopez. [4]LeanBody introduces a new technique known as power breathing. [5]LeanBody's specially designed power breathing supercharges your blood with fat-burning oxygen causing you to lose inches fast. [6]With power breathing, your body acts like a fat-burning furnace. [7]Whether you are a busy homemaker, on-the-go teenager, harried office worker, or retired senior citizen, LeanBody is for you. [8]The LeanBody workout takes only minutes a day and can be performed sitting down. [9]You can easily attain a

healthy, toned body with LeanBody and still enjoy your favorite foods. [10]Just listen to what superstar Charlene Lovely has to say about LeanBody: "With LeanBody I lost 45 pounds and 3 dress sizes; LeanBody saved my career."

______ **1.** Sentence 1

______ **2.** Sentence 2

______ **3.** Sentence 3

______ **4.** Sentence 4

______ **5.** Sentence 5

______ **6.** Sentence 6

______ **7.** Sentence 7

______ **8.** Sentence 8

______ **9.** Sentence 9

______ **10.** Sentence 10

## Application 2

Study the following tobacco advertisement from the nineteenth century.

______ **1.** Which of the following propaganda techniques is used in the advertisement?

a. testimonial
b. plain folks
c. transfer

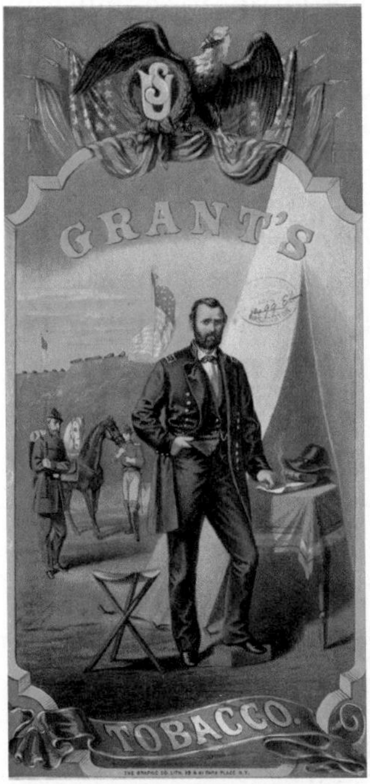

**2.** Write a caption for the advertisement that uses a propaganda technique.

______________________________________

______________________________________

______________________________________

# REVIEW Test 1

## Biased Arguments

Read the following sets of ideas. Write **UB** if the statement is unbiased, or **B** if the idea is a biased argument.

______ **1.** Joe E. Jones, nationally known film critic, writes, "*Troy*, starring Brad Pitt, is a must-see cinematic event. Clearly Brad Pitt's best performance of his career thus far."

______ **2.** Drink orange juice; it contains potassium and vitamins A and C, and it lowers blood pressure.

______ **3.** A study released by the National Academy on an Aging Society found that care for people with Alzheimer's Disease can be costly. The average cost for a person with Alzheimer's who is still living at home is $12,572 a year.

______ **4.** Obviously a politician cannot wear his heart on his sleeve when he is working for the success of his country. Only hypocrites and innocent dreamers would demand that he speak openly about his plans. Just as a businessman does not divulge his secrets to his rival, so also in politics, with even greater justification, much must remain a secret.

—Lehmann, Ernst Herbert. "How They Lie." ©1939 by Nibelungen-Verlag, GmbH., Berlin W9 Preliminary translation by Katherine Lynch. Final page copyright ©2000 by Randall L. Bytwerk. http://www.calvin.edu/academic/cas/gpa/lugen0.htm

______ **5.** A college sophomore says to her parents, "I can't believe you won't let me go to Cancun for spring break. Everyone I know is going. Not only do their parents let them go, but their parents pay for the trip, too. At least I am willing to pay my own expenses."

# REVIEW Test 2

## Biased Arguments: Fallacies in Logical Thought

**A.** Write the letter of the fallacy next to its definition.

a. begging the question
b. personal attack
c. straw man
d. false cause
e. false comparison
f. either-or

_____ **1.** In this fallacy, the original argument is replaced with a weaker version that is easier to challenge than the original argument.

_____ **2.** This fallacy assumes that two things are similar when they are not.

_____ **3.** This fallacy assumes that because events occurred around or near the same time, they have a cause-and-effect relationship.

_____ **4.** This fallacy assumes that only two sides of an issue exist.

_____ **5.** This fallacy restates the point of an argument as the support and conclusion.

_____ **6.** This fallacy uses abusive remarks in place of evidence for a point or argument.

**B.** Write the letter of the fallacy used in each of the following items.

_____ **7.** The truly patriotic citizen supports all elected officials.

a. straw man
b. begging the question
c. false comparison
d. either-or

_____ **8.** During the 2004 presidential campaign, Senator Tom Harkin said that Vice President Dick Cheney was a coward.

a. straw man
b. false comparison
c. personal attack
d. false cause

_____ **9.** I knew I was going to see you today because my horoscope said that I was going to meet with someone special today.

a. either-or
b. false cause
c. begging the question
d. straw man

_____ **10.** I love going to the movies because watching movies is my favorite leisure time activity.

a. straw man
b. false cause
c. either-or
d. begging the question

# REVIEW Test 3

## Biased Arguments: Propaganda

**A.** Write the letter of the propaganda technique next to its definition.

a. plain folks
b. bandwagon
c. testimonial
d. transfer
e. name-calling
f. glittering generality
g. card stacking

_____ **1.** This technique uses irrelevant personal opinions to support a product, idea, or cause.

_____ **2.** This technique uses or suggests the irrelevant detail that "everyone is doing it."

_____ **3.** This technique omits factual details in order to misrepresent a product, idea, or cause.

_____ **4.** This technique uses irrelevant details to build trust based on commonly shared values.

_____ **5.** This technique creates an association between a product, idea, or cause with a symbol or image that has positive or negative values.

_____ **6.** This technique uses negative labels for a product, idea, or cause.

_____ **7.** This technique offers general positive statements that cannot be verified.

**B.** Write the letter of the propaganda technique used in each of the following items.

_____ **8.** Want a meal that tastes like mom's? For downhome hospitality, eat at Mom's Diner.

a. bandwagon
b. glittering generalities
c. plain folks
d. transfer

_____ **9.** A devoted mother who knows the value of character, a war-tested veteran who knows the value of courage, and a hardworking business woman who knows the value of honesty, Li Ming wants to serve you as your next senator.

a. bandwagon
b. glittering generalities
c. plain folks
d. transfer

______ **10.** 16 million people can't be wrong: Buy your next computer online from CompuBuy.com.

a. bandwagon
b. glittering generalities
c. plain folks
d. transfer

# REVIEW Test 4

## Advanced Argument

Before you read, skim the following speech given by Mrs. Corinne Roosevelt Robinson. The sister of President Theodore Roosevelt, she supported the Republican ticket of Senator Harding and Governor Coolidge in the 1920 presidential election. Answer the **Before Reading** questions. Then read the passage and answer the **After Reading** questions.

### Vocabulary Preview

*efficiency* (sentence 2): skill, competence
*prestige* (sentence 11): status, reputation
*deplorable* (sentence 11): dreadful, shameful
*resolution* (sentence 17): motion, decision
*sentinel* (sentence 18): guard, lookout

**Safeguard America!**

[1]I am behind Senator Harding and Governor Coolidge for President and Vice-President of the United States for two reasons. [2]First, because they are the nominees of the Republican party, and secondly because I believe them to be 100% American, of true patriotism, who have not failed to show marked **efficiency** and ability in public office.

[3]I am one who believes that the Republican party and the Democratic party have different ideas. [4]And I believe that the issues of the two parties are not as blurred and as **indistinguishable** as is sometimes said to be the case. [5]The Republican party is the party of concrete nationalism, as opposed to the hazy internationalism of the Democratic party. [6]The Republican party preached preparedness. [7][And] the Democratic party, influenced by its President, mind you I say the President of the Democratic party and not of the whole United States, was keeping us out of war. [8]Keeping us out of war until he was re-elected President.

[9]We need the Republican party in office during the hard days to come, when there must be the [up-building] and rebuilding of our nation. [10]We need preparedness for days of peace and against the always possible dangers

of war. [11]Shall we choose again the party which blindly turns from the right, and in so doing, dragged down the **prestige** of America and brought on our nation unbearable criticism and **deplorable** confusion?

[12]Fellow citizens, we are at the turning of the ways. [13]Theodore Roosevelt said in October, 1916, "I demand at this election that each citizen shall think of America first." [14]Who now does not regret that the country did not respond to that demand? [15]Let us, the Republican party, again make this demand.

[16]Senator Harding stood for a League of Nations with strong, Americanizing reservations, as Theodore Roosevelt did. [17]He also stood with the Senate in passing the **resolution** which would have enabled Theodore Roosevelt to lead a division into France when the morale of France and of America was at a low ebb. [18]And Senator Harding, in making the memorial address on Theodore Roosevelt before the Ohio Joint Legislative Assembly in January, 1919, said, "Colonel Roosevelt was the great patriotic **sentinel**, pacing the parapets of the republic, alert to danger and every menace, and in love with duty and service, and always unafraid."

[19]Those words of our presidential nominee, in admiration of my great brother, are almost a promise of what his own attitude will be. [20]Let us stand behind him, looking forward and onward as Theodore Roosevelt would have done. [21]And let us try with might and main to put our beloved country in the safe keeping of Warren Harding and Calvin Coolidge.

—Robinson, Corinne Roosevelt. "Safeguard America." *American Leaders Speak: Recordings from World War I and the 1920 Election, 1918–1920.* American Memory. Library of Congress. 20 August 2004.

## BEFORE READING

### Vocabulary

_____ **1.** What is the best meaning of the word **indistinguishable** in sentence 4?

a. alike
b. vague
c. different
d. clear

### Tone and Purpose

_____ **2.** The author's tone and purpose is

a. to entertain with inspiring details.
b. to inform with objective evidence.
c. to persuade with praise and warnings.

## AFTER READING

### Central Idea

_____ **3.** Which sentence states the author's central idea?

a. sentence 1
b. sentence 8
c. sentence 3
d. sentence 20

### Supporting Details

_____ **4.** Who said "…at this election each citizen shall think of America first"?

a. Calvin Coolidge
b. Senator Harding
c. the President of the Democratic party
d. Theodore Roosevelt

### Thought Patterns

_____ **5.** The relationship of ideas within sentence 5 is

a. time order.
b. cause and effect.
c. contrast.
d. generalization and example.

### Fact and Opinion

_____ **6.** Overall this passage relies on

a. fact. b. opinion. c. fact and opinion.

### Inferences

_____ **7.** Based on the details in the passage, which of the following is a valid inference?

a. Theodore Roosevelt is President of the United States at the time this speech is given.
b. Theodore Roosevelt supported Senator Harding and Governor Coolidge for President and Vice President of the United States.
c. Theodore Roosevelt died before January 1919.
d. Theodore Roosevelt was a popular president within both the Republican and Democratic parties.

### Argument

_____ **8.** In sentences 6 and 7, the author uses the fallacy of

a. begging the question.
b. straw man.
c. personal attack.
d. false cause.

_____ **9.** Paragraph 5 (sentences 16–18) uses the propaganda technique of

a. bandwagon.
b. transfer.
c. testimonial.
d. glittering generalities.

_____ **10.** In his description of Theodore Roosevelt (sentence 18), Senator Harding uses

a. glittering generalities.
b. plain folks.
c. name calling.
d. bandwagon.

## Discussion Topics

1. What does the phrase "100% American, of true patriotism" mean to the author? What does it mean to you?
2. In sentences 9–11, the author speaks of war, peace, and the reputation of America in the world during the time between World War I and World War II. Discuss the current status of war, peace, and the reputation of America in the world.
3. How can citizens "think of America first"?
4. What role should America take in international events?

## Writing Topics

1. Describe the most important character traits a person should possess to be an effective President of the United States.
2. Write a paragraph or two about the importance of voting.
3. Describe an important issue that a politician should address.

## EFFECTIVE READER Scorecard

**Advanced Argument: Persuasive Techniques**

| Test | Number Correct | | Points | | Score |
|---|---|---|---|---|---|
| Review Test 1 | _____ | × | 20 | = | _____ |
| Review Test 2 | _____ | × | 10 | = | _____ |
| Review Test 3 | _____ | × | 10 | = | _____ |
| Review Test 4 | _____ | × | 10 | = | _____ |
| Review Test 5 (website) | _____ | × | 20 | = | _____ |
| Review Test 6 (website) | _____ | × | 10 | = | _____ |

Enter your scores on the Effective Reader Scorecard: Chapter 13 Review Tests inside the back cover.

## After Reading About Advanced Argument: Persuasive Techniques

Before you move on to the mastery tests on advanced argument, take time to reflect on your learning and performance by answering the following questions. Write your answers in your notebook.

What did I learn about persuasive techniques?

What do I need to remember about persuasive techniques?

How has my knowledge base or prior knowledge about persuasive techniques changed?

### More Review and Mastery Tests

For more practice, go to the book's website at **http://ablongman.com/henry/** and click on *The Effective Reader*. Then select "More Review and Mastery Tests." The tests are organized by chapter.

MASTERY **Test 1**

Name ______________________ Section ______________

Date ____________ **Score** (number correct) ______ × 10 = ______%

Write the letter of the fallacy used in each of the following items.

______ **1.** Love America or leave it.

a. begging the question
b. either-or
c. personal attack
d. straw man

______ **2.** The senator doesn't care about the environment because it doesn't win him any votes to care.

a. false cause
b. either-or
c. begging the question
d. personal attack

______ **3.** Being in school is like being in a concentration camp.

a. false comparison
b. straw man
c. begging the question
d. false cause

______ **4.** I have won the football lottery at work three times. Every time I won, my boyfriend and I had a fight the night before. I am going to pick a fight with him tonight because I want to win the lottery tomorrow.

a. straw man
b. either-or
c. false cause
d. personal attack

______ **5.** The government should continue research in the area of human cloning. Just as space research has brought us useful byproducts such as Teflon, research in human cloning will lead to unexpected discoveries that will benefit humanity.

a. false comparison
b. begging the question
c. straw man
d. false cause

______ **6.** The candidate for city commission says, "We need lower taxes because the current taxes are too high."

a. straw man
b. personal attack
c. begging the question
d. either-or

______ **7.** I touched a toad. Now I have a wart.

a. false cause
b. straw man
c. either-or
d. personal attack

_____ **8.** Speaker 1: Our prisons are overcrowded, and we don't have the money to build additional prisons. We need to find other solutions. Many of those in prison for lesser, nonviolent crimes could be placed on house arrest and equipped with technology that tracks their whereabouts.

Speaker 2: My opponent wants to set prisoners free to live in the comfort of their own homes.

a. begging the question
b. false comparison
c. personal attack
d. straw man

_____ **9.** The charges against the police for brutality are untrue because police are officers of the law.

a. straw man
b. begging the question
c. personal attack
d. either-or

_____ **10.** I could never date Samantha; she looks like a horse.

a. personal attack
b. false cause
c. straw man
d. either-or

MASTERY **Test 2**

Name ______________________ Section ____________

Date ____________ **Score** (number correct) ______ × 10 = ______%

Write the letter of the fallacy used in each of the following items.

______ **1.** When the local newspaper printed a story accusing Senator Smith of skimming money from his constituents, the Senator pointed out that the editorial board of the newspaper endorsed the Senator's opponent in the last election.

a. straw man
b. either-or
c. begging the question
d. false cause

______ **2.** How can you believe anything that woman says? She is a lawyer.

a. begging the question
b. either-or
c. personal attack
d. false comparison

______ **3.** Recreational use of marijuana is against the law, and its use is still widespread. To reduce the use of marijuana, get rid of the laws that ban its use.

a. straw man
b. false cause
c. begging the question
d. personal attack

______ **4.** Smoking cigarettes helps me control my weight. So either I can smoke, or I can get fat.

a. begging the question
b. personal attack
c. either-or
d. false comparison

______ **5.** This administration knows nothing about economics—why, as soon as the president took office, the economy plummeted!

a. begging the question
b. false cause
c. personal attack
d. false comparison

______ **6.** We must either use animals for medical research or give up finding a cure for diseases like AIDS and cancer.

a. false cause
b. begging the question
c. straw man
d. either-or

______ **7.** "Mother, how can you tell me not to do drugs after all those stories you told me about your doing drugs when you were my age?"

a. begging the question
b. either-or
c. personal attack
d. false comparison

_____ **8.** The law in Florida says that a 13-year-old girl can have an abortion without her parent's consent, yet she cannot legally have sex or even get a tattoo without her parent's consent. This law makes no sense, and a law that doesn't make sense is a stupid law.

a. false comparison
c. either-or
b. begging the question
d. straw man

_____ **9.** We must wage a war on poverty with the weapon of compassion.

a. false comparison
c. straw man
b. begging the question
d. false cause

_____ **10.** Everyone has the right to health care; therefore, health care should be made available to everyone.

a. straw man
c. begging the question
b. false comparison
d. either-or

MASTERY **Test 3**

Name ______________________ Section ____________

Date ____________ **Score** (number correct) ______ × 10 = ______%

**A.** Identify the propaganda technique used in each of the following items. Some techniques are used more than once.

| | |
|---|---|
| a. plain folks | d. transfer |
| b. bandwagon | e. name-calling |
| c. testimonial | f. glittering generality |

______ **1.** A candidate promises, "Elect me, and I will serve the land of the free and the home of the brave with courage and humility."

______ **2.** I would never listen to, much less buy, Fergie's music; she is an immoral person and a horrible role model.

______ **3.** A commercial advertising ice cream shows a series of preschool children in settings that look like their homes reading the list of natural ingredients on the ice cream carton as they happily eat the ice cream.

______ **4.** Michael Jordan, a famous basketball player, recommends Hanes T-shirts because they are comfortable.

______ **5.** In a television commercial for a breath mint, a young woman is dripping with sweat. She pops a breath mint in her mouth; immediately a breeze begins to blow, she stops sweating, and she breathes out an icy cloud of air that turns the whole scene a refreshing blue color.

______ **6.** Don't take classes with that professor; he's a tough grader and a boring lecturer.

______ **7.** I am going to vote for gun control because all my friends and family are voting for gun control.

______ **8.** If you want a good, old-fashioned home-cooked meal, come into Andy's. We make the meals mom used to make.

______ **9.** Identify the propaganda technique used in this poster.

a. plain folks
b. bandwagon
c. testimonial
d. transfer
e. name calling
f. glittering generality

**B.** Read the following fictitious advertisement. Identify the detail that was **omitted** from the advertisement for the purpose of card stacking.

______ **10.** House for sale: Built in 2003, this four-bedroom, three-bath pool home with a total living space of 1,800 square feet is located close to shopping and in an excellent school district. All appliances are included.

a. The house is underpriced for a quick move because the owner received a job transfer.
b. The appliances are still under warranty.
c. The house is sitting on a recently filled sinkhole.

MASTERY **Test 4**

Name ______________________ Section ______________

Date __________ **Score** (number correct) ______ × 10 = ______%

**A.** Identify the propaganda technique used in each of the following items. Some techniques are used more than once.

a. plain folks
b. bandwagon
c. testimonial
d. transfer
e. name-calling
f. glittering generality

______ **1.** In 1970, Lawton Chiles walked more than 1,000 miles across the state of Florida and won his bid for the U.S. Senate. One of his campaign buttons read, "I am walking with Lawton Chiles."

______ **2.** In a 1964 political television advertisement, a little girl is counting the petals she is picking off a daisy. When she reaches the number 10, the audience hears another voice counting down, "ten . . . nine . . . eight." At the number zero, a deafening explosion is heard. The mushroom cloud of an atomic bomb is reflected in the little girl's eyes. Then the voice of Lyndon B. Johnson says, "These are the stakes—to make a world in which all God's children can live, or to go into the darkness. We must either love each other, or we must die." After this, another voice says, "Vote for Lyndon B. Johnson. The stakes are too high for you to stay home."

______ **3.** My opponent is a weak-minded liberal.

______ **4.** Kirstie Alley advertises how she lost weight using the Jenny Craig program.

______ **5.** Everyone smokes marijuana, so it should be legalized.

______ **6.** An advertisement for State Farm Insurance says, "Like a good neighbor, State Farm is there."

______ **7.** The Internet is one of the greatest tools of democracy and should be cherished and protected as a basic American right to access information. Stop censorship of the Internet in public libraries.

_____ **8.** Identify the propaganda technique used in this advertisement.

a. plain folks
b. bandwagon
c. testimonial
d. transfer
e. name calling
f. glittering generality

**B.** Read the following fictitious advertisements. Identify the detail from each list that was **omitted** from each advertisement for the purpose of card stacking.

_____ **9.** For sale: A 2006 white Malibu with low mileage. Maintenance work has been done on a regular basis. All new tires. AM/FM radio with CD player. Power steering. Only $6,000.

a. The car has had only one owner, an elderly woman who didn't often drive.
b. The car was recently in a wreck and has had major repairs.
c. The car seats five people comfortably and has an adequate amount of trunk space.

_____ **10.** Be the gorgeous redhead you have always wanted to be. ColorLife Russet will turn your hair a luscious shade of auburn while leaving it soft and manageable. Turn heads your way with ColorLife Russet.

a. ColorLife Russet is a temporary color that must be reapplied every two to three weeks.
b. ColorLife Russet meets the Food and Drug Administration's recommended levels of lead acetate.
c. ColorLife Hair Color comes in 26 other shades as well.

MASTERY **Test 5**

Name ______________________ Section __________

Date __________ **Score** (number correct) ______ × 10 = ______%

A. Identify the propaganda technique used in each of the following items. Some techniques are used more than once.

a. plain folks
b. bandwagon
c. testimonial
d. transfer
e. name-calling
f. glittering generality

______ **1.** Reese Witherspoon is my favorite actress because she has an all-American look that is wholesome and trustworthy.

______ **2.** The scene is a beach on a sunny day. A crowd of attractive, athletic-looking young men seem captivated by a pretty young woman clad in a skimpy bikini who is spreading suntan lotion on her body. The young woman turns to the camera and says, "Before I used SafeTan, I couldn't get a date." She nods her head toward the crowd of young men. "Now look at me," she says with a wink.

______ **3.** Senator De Germaine said, "My opponent is a jerk if he thinks lowering taxes will help the economy."

______ **4.** Be like millions of others, join the National Rifle Association.

______ **5.** An advertisement for Wrigley's Doublemint chewing gum shows tennis champion Serena Williams dressed in casual clothes, listening to music. Her eyes are closed, and she is smiling as if she is enjoying herself. In the lower corner is a picture of a pack of Wrigley's Doublemint chewing gum.

______ **6.** A group of average-looking men are sitting in a typical-looking living room in front of a television, watching a football game, and joyfully eating a bag of chips and Hot Salsalita salsa. The camera focuses in on a scoopful of salsa as it is lifted to be eaten. A voice says, "Spice up your party with Hot Salsalita salsa."

______ **7.** A woman is flying on a commercial airline. She leaves her seat and goes into the bathroom, where she washes her hair. Doing so, she says, "Yes, yes, yes," in loud, sensual tones of pleasure. The camera catches the surprised looks on the faces of the other passengers,

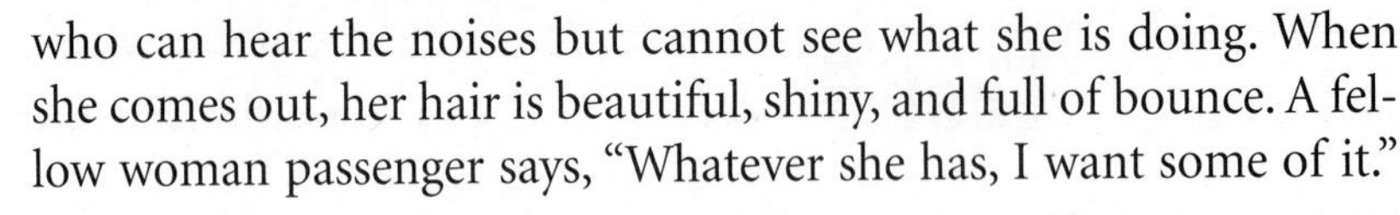
who can hear the noises but cannot see what she is doing. When she comes out, her hair is beautiful, shiny, and full of bounce. A fellow woman passenger says, "Whatever she has, I want some of it."

_____ **8.** Famed golfer Tiger Woods appears in a television commercial driving a Buick Rendezvous.

**B.** Read the following fictitious advertisements. Identify the detail from each list that was **omitted** from each advertisement for the purpose of card stacking.

_____ **9.** The BeCool Ice Shaver is designed to offer years of fun and save a lot of money. The BeCool Ice Shaver can turn your favorite fruits into frosty drinks, delicious frozen desserts, or cool sorbets. For only $19.99, you get the BeCool Ice Shaver, six ice cups, and a recipe booklet.

a. The BeCool Ice Shaver has a 90-day guarantee.
b. The BeCool Ice Shaver is a best-selling product.
c. The BeCool Ice Shaver was recalled because its stainless steel blade was reported to have caused injuries to fingers and hands.

_____ **10.** The YourChoice Adjustable Bed allows you and your sleep partner to choose the firmness each of you desires with a simple push of a button. The YourChoice Adjustable Bed can be ordered with a variety of mattresses. Choose a foam mattress that conforms to your body, a traditional innerspring mattress, or the unbelievably comfortable air mattress. The YourChoice Adjustable Bed offers ultimate comfort whether you are sleeping or watching television. Order online and receive a 10 percent discount.

a. Extreme cold or severe impact, such as those that can occur during shipping, can damage the power cord insulation and cause electric shock.
b. The YourChoice Adjustable Bed foam mattress reduces the soreness that comes from pressure points of the traditional mattress.
c. The YourChoice Adjustable Bed company offers low-interest financing.

MASTERY **Test 6**

Name ________________________ Section ____________

Date ____________ **Score** (number correct) ______ × 10 = ______%

**A.** Write the letter of the fallacy used in each of the following items.

______ **1.** Either you are a patriotic American or you are a member of the Council on Foreign Relations.

a. begging the question
b. either-or
c. personal attack
d. false comparison

______ **2.** The reporters for the *Report of the Daily News* are biased liberals who seek to radically change society.

a. false cause
b. either-or
c. personal attack
d. false comparison

______ **3.** Nightmares are the result of eating spicy foods.

a. false cause
b. straw man
c. false comparison
d. either-or

______ **4.** Callie Krandall is campaigning for the Democratic candidates in her district; however, her opinion is of little value since she is only a 13-year-old.

a. begging the question
b. either-or
c. personal attack
d. false comparison

______ **5.** Women should not be drafted to serve in the armed forces because women have never been drafted to serve in the armed forces.

a. begging the question
b. either-or
c. personal attack
d. false comparison

**B.** Write the letter of the propaganda technique used in each of the following items.

______ **6.** This season, everyone is buying genuine leather jackets, so you should, too.

a. transfer
b. bandwagon
c. plain folks
d. glittering generalities

_____ **7.** A college-aged actor dressed in blue jeans and a t-shirt is the spokesperson for a series of commercials selling personal computers.
a. transfer
b. bandwagon
c. plain folks
d. testimonial

_____ **8.** Former Speaker of the House Newt Gingrich told Republican politicians to use positive, governing words such as *choice, dream, hard work,* and *freedom* when discussing policies.
a. testimonial
b. bandwagon
c. plain folks
d. glittering generalities

_____ **9.** My opponent favors a unionized bureaucracy that will impose waste and failure upon the American people.
a. glittering generalities
b. bandwagon
c. name calling
d. transfer

_____ **10.** Read the following fictitious advertisement. Identify the detail that was omitted from the advertisement for the purpose of card stacking.

Enhance your children's education by giving them a library of classical literature. For just $10.00 a month, your child will receive a copy of a wide variety of classics such as *Alice in Wonderland*, *Romeo and Juliet*, *Pilgrim's Progress*, and *Huckleberry Finn*. Join the Classics for Your Child Book Club today.

a. The books contain color illustrations.
b. The books are abridged or shortened editions.
c. The book club membership can be cancelled at any time.

PART TWO

# Additional Readings

# The Connection Between Reading and Writing

The connection between reading and writing is a natural one. All of the tools that an effective reader uses to read are also used by an effective writer to write. Effective readers can become effective writers. The following discussion takes you through several steps that will show you how to become an effective writer. Each step is built on the same concepts you are studying to become an effective reader.

## Step 1: Prewrite

Just as you **preread** the ideas in a passage to get a general sense of what the author is saying (see Chapter 1, pages 11–14), you can explore what you want to say as a writer by surveying the ideas you have about a particular topic. **Prewriting** is thinking about what you want to say before you begin writing. Just as effective readers ask prereading questions to guide them as they seek to understand the author's main point, effective writers use prewriting techniques such as brainstorming. **Brainstorming** is thinking about a topic without stopping to criticize the ideas as they occur. Brainstorming is a thinking process; when you put the ideas you brainstorm on paper, you are prewriting. There are several ways to brainstorm for prewriting.

One way to brainstorm about a topic is to **ask and answer questions**. Answering the reporter's questions *who, what, when, where, why,* and *how* will get your ideas out of your head and onto paper. This kind of thinking may help you find your central idea, which will become your thesis statement or topic sentence.

A second way to brainstorm is to **list details** about a topic, *as many* as you can. The point of this activity is to get as many details as possible on paper, so don't stop to think about their proper order or logic. Just make the list.

A third way to brainstorm is to freewrite. **Freewriting** is writing down whatever comes into your head about a topic. Most writers set a time limit, such as five minutes, and during that time, they write down every thought. Freewriting is a good way to break writer's block. During a freewrite, you do not worry about grammar or spelling; your mission is to get ideas on paper. Later you can polish your style.

## Step 2: Organize Your Ideas

Once you have your ideas on paper, you need to organize them so that they are clear and easy to follow. Outlines or concept maps (Chapter 5) are very useful in this step. In general, writers use the following format: (1) tell the reader what you are going to say, (2) tell the reader your ideas, and (3) tell the reader what you said.

I. Write a Main Idea Statement (Chapter 3)
   A. The main idea statement tells the reader what you are going to say.
   B. The main idea statement for a paragraph is a topic sentence (page 112).
   C. The main idea statement for a longer piece that has several paragraphs is a thesis statement or central idea (page 128).

II. Give Supporting Details (Chapters 3–4)
   A. Most ideas need at least two or three supporting details.
   B. Major supporting details may need to be explained with minor supporting details (pages 163–164).
   C. Organize supporting details by using thought patterns (Chapters 6–7). Some ideas may need examples, while others may call for a discussion of cause or effects.

III. Offer a Conclusion. Remind your reader of the most important ideas you told them.

## Step 3: Write

Now that you have generated ideas, you are ready to write the first draft of your paper. Have a dictionary and a thesaurus nearby so that you can find the exact words to say what you mean. Link supporting details with transitions. Words like *first*, *second*, *for example*, and *in contrast* make ideas flow smoothly and show your readers the thought pattern. If your writing will respond or refer to another writer's text, annotating it to follow the writer's use of language and structure will increase your comprehension of that text.

## Step 4: Edit and Revise

After reading a selection, an effective reader reviews and reflects on the ideas in the written text. Again, the reading-writing connection is evident: an effective reader writes answers to questions formed before reading, records reactions to new information, or summarizes the passage. Likewise, after writing a draft, an effective writer takes time to revisit the written text. Often the writer tries to look at the piece of writing from a reader's perspective, checking to make sure ideas are clearly explained so that someone else could read and understand the main idea and flow of supporting details. Proofreading a paper ensures quality in the areas of unity (all ideas connect to the main idea), supporting details, clarity (thought patterns), and style (vocabulary and tone). Effective writers often produce several drafts of their work so they can focus on one of these areas at a time. (In similar fashion, effective readers reflect after they have read to focus on specific places or aspects of the passage.)

- Read your paper for **unity**. Make sure that the main idea statement and the details agree with each other. Edit out supporting details that go off topic. Details are off topic if they introduce or discuss ideas that you did not include or imply in your main idea.
- Read your paper for **support**. Make sure you have given enough major and minor supporting details to explain your main idea completely. Edit out any details that are not logical or relevant.
- Read your paper for **clarity**. Use a thought pattern. If you use more than one thought pattern, be sure you use transitions between patterns to signal your readers. Make sure you have included the proper transitions so your readers can follow the flow of ideas. Reading your work out loud is a good way to identify any areas that may need to be smoothed out.
- Read your paper for **style**. Edit carefully for grammar, spelling, and punctuation errors. Make effective use of vocabulary skills. Spend time with a thesaurus finding exactly the right vocabulary for impact. Mark Twain once noted that "the difference between the right word and the almost right word is the difference between lightning and a lightning bug." Word choice establishes your voice and sets a tone that helps you connect with your reader. Reading the work of other writers to see how they use words and tone for effect will help you develop this same skill.

Developing a strong connection between reading and writing will enable you to deepen your effectiveness with both. The more you read, the more you know; the more you know, the more you know about what and how to write. Take advantage of every opportunity to write throughout your college courses. Take notes, annotate the texts you read, and write journal entries, summaries, and critical responses. Read; then write about what you read.

## Annotating a Text

Using your writing skills throughout the reading process is an excellent way to ensure that you remain an active reader. Active reading requires that you respond to what you are reading while you read. You have been taught to ask questions before, during, and after reading. You should annotate your text as you find the answers to your questions. Annotating your textbook is an active reading and writing activity. The word *annotate* suggests that you "take notes" in your textbook. Writing notes in the margin of the textbook page as you read focuses your attention and improves your concentration. Annotating will also help you check and improve your comprehension. You can note questions quickly where they occur, move on in your reading, and later return to those questions for clarification. In addition to writing notes, you can underline, circle, or highlight important terms, definitions, examples, or other key ideas. After reading, your annotations will make reviewing the textbook material easier and more efficient.

The following techniques are often used to annotate a text:

- Circle important terms.
- Underline definitions and meanings.
- Place small question marks above unknown words.
- Point out important concepts with symbols such as a star or check.
- Signal steps in a process or lists by using numbers.
- Write recall questions in the margin where the answer is found. You can use these questions to test your comprehension and review the material. Cover up the text so that you only see the questions; then try to recall the answers.
- Write summaries at the end of long sections.

The following passage from a college health textbook has been annotated for you as an illustration.

Textbook Skills

## Adapting to Stress

HEALTH SKILLS

Although there will always be some stress in your life, that does not mean you cannot do anything about it. In fact, the best medicine for stress appears to be learning how to adapt to or cope with stress.

*Stress can be controlled!*

**Coping** is adaptation to stress. In primitive times, coping with stress meant little more than exercising the basic **fight-or-flight reaction** to threatening situations. For example, if a tiger threatened a primitive man, he would either stand and fight (and do so with added strength and cunning brought about by the stress reactions described by the general adaptation syndrome) or run from the threat (also with the added strength and cunning brought about by the stress reaction).

*What is "coping"? Describe "fight-or-flight." (F/F)*

Today, we are not threatened by tigers. Threats come instead from difficult working situations, unexpected bills, and disappointing news. Although survival is still at issue, it is not as much the survival of an individual or the species as maintaining self-esteem in stressful situations. The fight-or-flight response still works well in some cases, as do **defense mechanisms** such as avoidance and denial. These responses, however, are usually effective only for the short term. In our complex society, more adaptive methods of coping are necessary for a long-term adaptation to stress. Fleeing or denying a stress situation might be very useful in diminishing the acute pain of an unhappy event, but it does not help you deal with the source of the stress over the long run.

*What are two examples of defense mechanisms? (DM)*

*Summary: F/F and DM are 2 short-term ways to cope with stress.*

### Coping with Stress

There are several ways you can effectively minimize the negative effects of everyday stress, whether it is in school, on the job, or at home. One preventive action is to make sure that you take good care of your physical health. You do this by (1) eating nutritiously, (2) exercising, (3) not smoking or using drugs, and (4) getting an adequate amount of sleep. You will find tips on how to develop good health habits in the related chapters in this textbook. Being in good physical health can help your body fight the negative health effects that can accompany stress.

** Healthy, long-term coping technique*

*Be Good to MYSELF!*

—Reprinted from Pruitt, B.E. and Jane J. Stein. *Health Styles: Decisions for Living Well,* 2nd ed., Allyn & Bacon, 1999, p. 85.

## Writing a Summary

Writing a summary is an effective step in the reading and studying process.

A **summary** is a brief, clear restatement of a longer passage.

A summary includes only the passage's most important points. Often a summary is made up of the main idea and major supporting details. The length of a summary should reflect your study needs and the kind of passage you are trying to understand. For example, a paragraph might be summarized in a sentence or two, an article might be summarized in a paragraph, and a textbook chapter might be summarized in a page or two.

You can discover how well you understand a passage by writing a summary of it as an after reading activity. Use the annotations you make during reading to create your summary.

For example, read the following summary of "Adapting to Stress" from a college health textbook. Underline the words and phrases that were annotated in the earlier section:

> [1]By learning how to adapt to or cope with stress, stress can be controlled. [2]Two short-term ways to cope with stress are the fight-or-flight response and defense mechanisms. [3]During the primitive fight-or-flight response, a threat or stress creates a short-term burst of energy that allows a person to either stand and fight or turn and run with additional strength and skill. [4]Defense mechanisms include avoidance and denial. [5]However, healthy, long-term coping techniques for stress involve maintaining physical health. [6]To effectively cope with stress, eat a healthful diet, exercise, avoid use of tobacco and drugs, and get enough sleep.

This summary includes the author's main idea and the major supporting details. However, this summary also brings in a few minor supporting details. For example, sentence 3 explains the fight-or-flight reaction to stress. Including these details makes the summary longer than may be necessary. The following version includes only the main idea and the major supporting details.

> [1]Two short-term methods of adapting to stress include the fight-or-flight response and defense mechanisms such as avoidance and denial. [2]Healthy, long-term ways to cope with stress involve maintaining physical health by eating healthfully, exercising, avoiding use of tobacco and drugs, and getting enough sleep.

Remember, the length of the summary depends upon your study needs as well as the length of the passage you are summarizing.

READING 1

# One Person's Path to Literacy

*by Richard Wanderman*

Have you ever struggled in school? Or have you ever wanted to do something and faced overwhelming challenges? Did you find the challenges frustrating? Did you learn important lessons through the struggle to achieve? Richard Wanderman faced many challenges in his pursuit of literacy. He recounts the story of his struggle and his successes in this article that appears on his professional Web site, LD Resources, designed to offer resources for the learning disabled community.

### Vocabulary Preview

*consultant* (paragraph 1): adviser, mentor
*remediation* (paragraph 1): correction
*domain* (paragraph 3): area, field
*exposure* (paragraph 4): risk, experience

---

1 I'm 48 years old, married, live in a nice house, have a successful career as an educational **consultant,** and I have a learning disability, dyslexia. My life was not always so great. I was a premature breech birth, had meningitis, polio, and every childhood illness. I was tested for everything including language problems from an early age so I was labeled "dyslexic" early. I went to a special school until 6th grade where I had plenty of extra help and **remediation.** Still, I had to repeat 6th grade at that school. I suffered the rest of my school days in public schools where I did poorly.

2 When I went to college my life improved markedly because this is where I discovered art. The art world gave me a chance to express myself without words, so I took a lot of art courses. I got good at making things with clay and I learned my first important lesson about my language disability: I could be smart and articulate with clay and still have a language disability which made it hard to be smart and articulate with words.

My next big life lesson happened a few 3
years later. I drove Volkswagens because they were the only cars I could afford. I knew little about cars and had never even changed the oil in one. One day the engine in my VW bus seized up and I didn't have the money to have it fixed. I bought the book *How to Fix Your Volkswagen for the Complete Idiot.* I started reading, slowly. I bought a few metric tools, pulled the engine, and dragged it into the backyard where I took it apart. Two weeks later, when I got the engine into the car and it started I learned that when you feel good

about yourself and are willing to take risks you can transfer confidence from one **domain** to another. I knew nothing about engines but took the confidence I'd gotten with art into a totally new domain.

4 My next domain was rock climbing. Hey, I don't bungi jump; I'm not crazy. I got into climbing because it was a fun thing to do with friends. We all got into it at the same time and were all chicken from the start. However, we noticed that the more we did it the easier it was to take "**exposure.**" So we did it more. And the more I did it the better I got. It wasn't a talent thing; it was practice. After about five years of climbing I found myself in Yosemite Valley on a big wall. What had I learned? I'd learned that if you enjoy something and do it all the time, you get better at it. Practice makes better.

5 Later I took that idea into a very scary place. I decided to see if I could actually learn how to read and write by practicing. I read and wrote every day for two years. This may seem obvious to you, but it wasn't to me; I had no idea that most people read things every day. I had avoided reading things as much as possible and avoided writing completely. Nevertheless, for two years I took my prior experiences and mapped them into learning how to read and write, and at the end of two years I'd learned a lot. Most importantly, I was literate.

6 Then came the dawn of personal computers. Once I used one, and then bought one, my writing and then my reading improved at a rapid clip.

7 Here's the point: had I been given a computer as a child in school I doubt I'd have been mature enough to take full advantage of it and I doubt the school would have allowed me to use it in a way that would have been meaningful to me. I needed to go through the long, messy process that I went through with art, cars, climbing, and reading and writing to get to a place in my life where I knew I was smart enough to dive into an area that was totally unknown, hard, but interesting.

8 For me growing up was particularly painful and messy. My father used to tell me the bumps would build character and I would roll my eyes. Well, he was right. And even though I wouldn't want to go through it all again I have plenty of character because of it all. And I can read and write.

Choose the best meaning of each word in **bold**. Use context clues to make your choice.

Vocabulary in Context ______ **1.** "When I went to college my life improved **markedly** because this is where I discovered art." (paragraph 2)

a. somewhat
b. painfully
c. little
d. clearly

Vocabulary in Context ______ **2.** "I could be smart and **articulate** with clay and still have a language disability which made it hard to be smart and articulate with words." (paragraph 2)

a. hardworking
b. communicative
c. achievement-oriented
d. playful

Central Idea and Main Idea ______

**3.** Which sentence is the best statement of the central idea of the passage?

a. My struggles and triumphs as one who suffered with a learning disability taught me several important lessons.
b. My learning disability made my life difficult.
c. Bumps build character.
d. Reading is important.

Central Idea and Main Idea ______

**4.** Which sentence is the best statement of the main idea of the fourth paragraph?

a. My next domain was rock climbing.
b. I got into climbing because it was a fun thing to do with friends.
c. The more I did it, the better I got.
d. Practice makes better.

Supporting Details ______

**5.** The author learned how to fix his Volkswagen engine

a. by trial and error.
b. by reading and doing.
c. in an automotive repair class.
d. with a group of his friends.

Supporting Details ______

**6.** If the author had been given a computer as a child in school, he would have been

a. inspired to learn.
b. unable to benefit from it.
c. scared of using it.
d. grateful.

Thought Patterns ______

**7.** The main thought pattern for the overall passage is

a. comparison and contrast.
b. time order.
c. cause and effect.

Transitions ______

**8.** "I had avoided reading things as much as possible and avoided writing completely. Nevertheless, for two years I took my prior experiences and mapped them into learning how to read and write, and at the end of two years I'd learned a lot." (paragraph 5)

The relationship of ideas between these two sentences is

a. time order.
b. contrast.
c. addition.

Transitions ______ **9.** "My father used to tell me the bumps would build character and I would roll my eyes." (paragraph 8)

The relationship of ideas within this sentence is

a. time order.
b. contrast.
c. addition.

Fact and Opinion ______ **10.** Which of the following statements from paragraph 3 is a statement of opinion?

a. My next big life lesson happened a few years later.
b. I drove Volkswagens because they were the only cars I could afford.
c. One day the engine in my VW bus seized up, and I didn't have the money to have it fixed.
d. I bought the book *How to Fix Your Volkswagen for the Complete Idiot.*

Fact and Opinion ______ **11.** "We all got into it at the same time and were all chicken from the start." (paragraph 4)

This sentence is a statement of

a. fact.
b. opinion.
c. fact and opinion.

Tone and Purpose ______ **12.** The tone of paragraph 1 is

a. complaining.
b. matter-of-fact.
c. angry.
d. tender.

Tone and Purpose ______ **13.** The tone of paragraph 2 is

a. conceited.
b. hostile.
c. positive.
d. disappointed.

Tone and Purpose ______ **14.** The tone of paragraph 8 is

a. wry.
b. complaining.
c. discouraged.
d. bubbly.

Tone and Purpose ______ **15.** The main purpose of "One Person's Path to Literacy" is

a. to persuade educators to do more to help students with learning disabilities.
b. to entertain readers with a heartwarming story.
c. to inform others that a learning disability can be overcome.

Inferences ______ **16.** Based on the author's experiences with his learning disability, we can infer that other people with learning disabilities may

a. need to use nontraditional ways to learn.
b. have lower intellectual abilities.
c. need to be physically active.
d. create many of their own problems.

Inferences ______ **17.** The author implies that

a. early testing for learning disabilities helped him in his struggle to learn.
b. being labeled "dyslexic" did not help him in his struggle to learn.
c. the school system neglected his learning disability.
d. he didn't mind failing the sixth grade.

Inferences ______ **18.** When the author states in paragraph 4 "we noticed that the more we did it the easier it was to take 'exposure,'" he is implying that

a. rock climbing exposed him to the harsh elements of weather.
b. he and his friends learned rock climbing quickly and easily.
c. learning involves some kind of risk-taking.
d. rock climbing and learning requires courage.

Argument ______ **19.** "One day the engine in my VW bus seized up, and I didn't have the money to have it fixed. I bought the book *How to Fix Your Volkswagen for the Complete Idiot.*"

Which of the following points is supported by the evidence of this statement?

a. The author couldn't pay for repairs on his VW bus because he was out of work.
b. The VW bus was a constant source of worry.
c. The author seeks to solve his own problems.
d. The author thought that he was an idiot.

Argument ______ **20. Claim:** The author is very intelligent.

Which statement does *not* support this claim?

a. The author became good at expressing himself through art.
b. The author taught himself how to fix an engine in two weeks.
c. The author had to repeat the sixth grade.
d. The author transferred how to learn about art and engines to how to learn to read.

## Mapping

Complete the following time line with information for the passage.

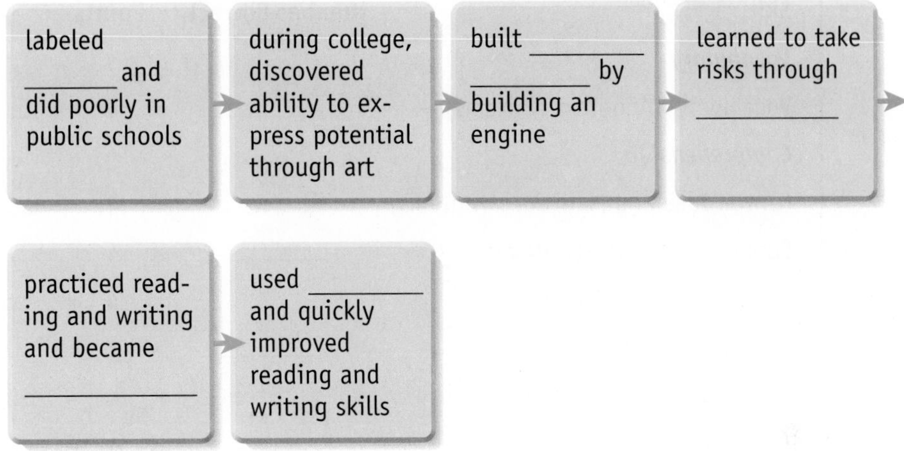


## Questions for Discussion and Writing

1. What are the author's central idea and major supporting details? Write your answers as a summary.
2. What are some of the difficulties that students who are learning disabled face?
3. Explain the cycle of success. How or why does success in one domain lead to success in another?
4. Recall an experience when you faced a stressful learning situation. How did you feel and respond?
5. How could teachers and schools help a student who has a learning disability?

## EFFECTIVE READER Scorecard

**"One Person's Path to Literacy"**

| Skill | Number Correct | | Points | | Total |
|---|---|---|---|---|---|
| ***Vocabulary*** | | | | | |
| Vocabulary in Context (2 items) | ______ | × | 4 | = | ______ |
| ***Comprehension*** | | | | | |
| Central Idea and Main Idea (2 items) | ______ | × | 4 | = | ______ |
| Supporting Details (2 items) | ______ | × | 4 | = | ______ |
| Thought Patterns (1 item) | ______ | × | 4 | = | ______ |
| Transitions (2 items) | ______ | × | 4 | = | ______ |
| Fact and Opinion (2 items) | ______ | × | 4 | = | ______ |
| Tone and Purpose (4 items) | ______ | × | 4 | = | ______ |
| Inferences (3 items) | ______ | × | 4 | = | ______ |
| Argument (2 items) | ______ | × | 4 | = | ______ |
| **Mapping** (5 items) | ______ | × | 4 | = | ______ |
| | | | Comprehension Score | | ______ |

READING 2

# Native American Sports Mascots

Have you noticed the different ways in which symbols are used in American culture? The fast-food restaurant McDonald's uses the clown Ronald McDonald to appeal to children. Advertisers seek someone like Tiger Woods to be a spokesperson for their product because he serves as a symbol of talent, hard work, and success. Sometimes the use of symbols can communicate a negative image of a particular group. The issue of the use of Native American names in sports has been debated since the early 1970s. Some people believe that the names honor Native Americans; others believe that the use of the names demeans Native Americans and their culture. The following article, from *Issues and Controversies,* offers a discussion of the controversy.

### Vocabulary Preview

*mascot* (paragraph 1): symbol of good luck
*gamut* (paragraph 1): range, scope
*conventional* (paragraph 1): usual, traditional
*engender* (paragraph 2): produce, cause
*denounced* (paragraph 4): condemned, criticized
*caricature* (paragraph 4): cartoon with exaggerated features
*degrade* (paragraph 9): humiliate, shame, demean

---

1 At all levels of sport—from professional down through college, high school and elementary school—teams adopt a name and **mascot** that is used to represent their organization. Sports team names run the **gamut** from the mundane, such as the Philadelphia Eagles of the National Football League (NFL), to the less **conventional,** like the Detroit Shock of the Women's National Basketball Association (WNBA).

2 For many athletes and fans, team names and mascots are rallying points. They provide a common image that everyone can identify with and support. But for some, team mascots are not sources of pride. Rather, some team names, like Indians and Braves, **engender** anger and charges of racial insensitivity toward Native Americans.

3 The Washington Redskins of the NFL have drawn some of the most intense criticism because the word *redskin* is considered offensive by Native Americans. Some say that it refers to the hue of Native American skin, but others say it dates to the days when traders and soldiers would bring Indian scalps, red with blood, back from battle in order to collect a bounty. Regardless of the etymology of the word, critics say, it is offensive.

4 Criticism of the Redskins has centered on their name, but other teams have been **denounced** because of their mascots. The Cleveland Indians, of Major League Baseball (MLB), have been targeted by activists because their mascot, Chief Wahoo, is a **caricature** of a Native American. The image shows the head of an Indian with an exaggerated smile revealing enormous teeth. A feather and headband complete the logo.

5 The University of Illinois has received its share of criticism for continuing to use Chief Illiniwek, its live-action mascot. A student, typically a white male, dresses up in buckskin and a turkey-feather headdress and dances before the crowd at football and basketball games in order to generate support for the home team.

6 Still other teams have been criticized for actions that their fans take during games. Perhaps the best known of these is the "tomahawk chop" employed by fans of the Atlanta Braves baseball team. Fans use either foam tomahawks or their arms to make a chopping motion while intoning a stereotypically Native American chant.

7 The issue has been simmering since the early 1970s, when colleges like Stanford University in California began to change their nicknames because of pressure from those who found it offensive. Stanford switched from the Indians to the Cardinals.

8 Recently, a group of students at the University of Northern Colorado propelled the issue into the spotlight when they renamed their intramural basketball team the Fightin' Whities. The group, made up of Native Americans, Hispanics, and whites, decided to change their team's name to protest the fact that a local high school refused to stop using the name Fightin' Reds for its sports teams. The story was carried by news organizations across the country, reigniting the debate over whether using Native American names is acceptable.

Supporters say that the team names and 9 mascots are meant to honor Native Americans, not **degrade** them. Sports teams especially like the names because many associate Native Americans with strength and courage, two attributes that athletes must exhibit on the field, supporters say.

Not only do the names honor the tra- 10 ditions of Native Americans, but they are also an important part of a team's or school's tradition, boosters say. Many schools chose their nicknames 70 or 80 years ago, and to change now is unfair to the students, they argue.

Critics, on the other hand, argue that al- 11 though teams and schools may not mean any harm when they adopt Native American names and mascots, harm is done anyway. First, they say, Indians are human beings, not symbols. Regardless of intent, using Native American imagery and names for sports teams is degrading, they argue. Also, to portray Native Americans simply as mascots is to ignore the complexities and hardships of their lives, opponents say.

**VISUAL VOCABULARY**

_______ The best meaning of **intramural** is

a. within the student body.
b. social.

▲ Many colleges and universities have strong intramural programs for their students.

Choose the best meaning of each word in **bold.** Use context clues to make your choice.

Vocabulary in Context _______ **1.** "Sports team names run the gamut from the **mundane,** such as the Philadelphia Eagles of the National Football League (NFL), to the less conventional, like the Detroit Shock of the Women's National Basketball Association (WNBA)." (paragraph 1)

a. offensive
b. ordinary
c. bizarre
d. playful

Vocabulary in Context _______ **2.** "Regardless of the **etymology** of the word, critics say, it is offensive." (paragraph 3)

a. history
b. emotions
c. future
d. meaning

Central Idea and Main Idea _______ **3.** Which sentence is the best statement of the implied central idea of the passage?

a. Teams adopt names and mascots to represent them.
b. For many athletes and fans, team names and mascots are rallying points.
c. The use of Native American icons to name sports teams is a hotly debated cultural issue.
d. Native Americans are deeply offended by the exploitation of their culture in the form of names for sports teams.

Central Idea and Main Idea ______ **4.** Which sentence is the best statement of the main idea of paragraph 3?

a. The Washington Redskins of the NFL have drawn some of the most intense criticism because the word *redskin* is considered offensive by Native Americans.
b. Some say that it refers to the hue of Native American skin, but others say it dates to the days when traders and soldiers would bring Indian scalps, red with blood, back from battle in order to collect a bounty.
c. Regardless of the etymology of the word, critics say, it is offensive.

Supporting Details ______ **5.** Team names provide

a. a rallying point for some teams and fans.
b. a common image for group identification and support.
c. sources of anger and charges of racial insensitivity toward Native Americans.
d. all of the above.

Supporting Details ______ **6.** The "Fightin' Whities" (paragraph 8) is the name of

a. a woman's professional basketball team.
b. a college football team.
c. a racist group.
d. an intramural basketball team made up of Native Americans, Hispanics, and whites.

Thought Patterns ______ **7.** The main thought pattern for the overall passage is

a. examples that contrast the two sides of the controversy about using Native American names to identify a sports team.
b. a discussion of the reasons against using Native American names to identify a sports team.
c. a narrative that tells of the Native Americans' struggle for dignity.
d. a step-by-step description of how a sports team name is chosen.

Thought Patterns ______ **8.** The thought pattern for paragraph 8 is

a. comparison and contrast.
b. definition.
c. time order.

Transitions ______ **9.** "Regardless of intent, using Native American imagery and names for sports teams is degrading, they argue. Also, to portray Native Americans simply as mascots is to ignore the complexities and hardships of their lives, opponents say." (paragraph 11)

The relationship of ideas between these two sentences is

a. time order.
b. contrast.
c. addition.

Transitions ______ **10.** "Fans use either foam tomahawks or their arms to make a chopping motion while intoning a stereotypically Native American chant." (paragraph 6)

The relationship of ideas within this sentence is

a. time order.
b. definition.
c. cause and effect.

Fact and Opinion ______ **11.** Overall, this passage

a. stresses the opinions of those who are against the use of Native American sports names and mascots.
b. stresses the opinions of those who are in favor of the use of Native American sports names and mascots.
c. uses graphically violent details.
d. lists and explains supporting details for the opinions on both sides of the issue.

Fact and Opinion ______ **12.** "Still other teams have been criticized for actions that their fans take during games."

This sentence from paragraph 6 is a statement of

a. fact.
b. opinion.
c. fact and opinion.

Tone and Purpose ______ **13.** The overall tone of the passage is

a. inflammatory.
b. soothing.
c. balanced.
d. outraged.

Tone and Purpose ______ **14.** The tone of paragraph 5 is

a. objective.
b. emotional.
c. positive.
d. negative.

Tone and Purpose ______ **15.** The tone of the name "Fightin' Whities" is

a. compromising.
b. humorous.
c. confrontational.
d. inspiring.

Tone and Purpose ______ **16.** The author's main purpose in "Native American Sports Mascots" is

a. to persuade sports teams and fans to stop using Native American names.
b. to entertain readers with interesting background information about the use of Native American names in sports.
c. to inform the reader about both sides of the issue concerning the use of Native American names in sports.

Inferences ______ **17.** The author implies that

a. sports teams choose names to deliberately offend Native Americans.
b. the names and mascots of sports teams reflect and influence how society views Native Americans.
c. Native Americans are overly sensitive to the issue.
d. sports teams will never give up the controversial names and mascots.

Inferences ______ **18.** The details in paragraph 8 imply that

a. the University of Northern Colorado students were racists.
b. the people most concerned about the ethical use of Native American names in sports are Native Americans.
c. a racially diverse group of college students hoped to pressure a high school team to change its team names.
d. a local high school decided to change the name of its sports team.

Inferences ______ **19.** Based on the description of the Cleveland Indians' mascot, we can infer that the mascot creates an image of the Native American as

a. aggressive and hostile.
b. silly and foolish.
c. a good sport.
d. intelligent and athletic.

Argument ______ **20. Claim:** Native American names should not be used to name teams or mascots.

Which statement does *not* support this claim?

a. The term *redskin* refers to the days when soldiers and traders brought back scalps red with blood for a bounty.
b. The mascot Chief Wahoo is a caricature of a Native American.
c. Although teams and schools may not mean any harm when they adopt Native American names and mascots, harm is done anyway.
d. Sports teams especially like the names because many associate Native Americans with strength and courage, two attributes athletes must exhibit on the field.

## Mapping

Complete the chart with information from the passage.

| Against the Use of Native American Names | In Favor of the Use of Native American Names |
|---|---|
| ______________________ ______________________ | provide a rally point for athletes and fans |
| are linked to violence against Native Americans | are an important part of a team's or school's traditions |
| encourage caricatures of Native Americans | ______________________ ______________________ ______________________ ______________________ |

## Questions for Discussion and Writing

1. What are the author's central idea and major supporting details? Write your answer as a summary.
2. Are Native American team names and mascots proper symbols for sports teams and schools to use?
3. Do you think it is dehumanizing for Native Americans to be reduced to symbols?
4. Why are Native Americans offended by the term *redskin*? How does knowing about the history of the term *redskin* affect the meaning of the term when it is applied to a football team? Are players on a *redskin* team similar to the soldiers and traders of days gone by?
5. How have other groups of people been used as symbols?

## EFFECTIVE READER Scorecard

"Native American Sports Mascots"

| Skill | Number Correct | | Points | | Total |
|---|---|---|---|---|---|
| ***Vocabulary*** | | | | | |
| Vocabulary in Context (2 items) | ______ | × | 4 | = | ______ |
| ***Comprehension*** | | | | | |
| Central Idea and Main Idea (2 items) | ______ | × | 4 | = | ______ |
| Supporting Details (2 items) | ______ | × | 4 | = | ______ |
| Thought Patterns (2 items) | ______ | × | 4 | = | ______ |
| Transitions (2 items) | ______ | × | 4 | = | ______ |
| Fact and Opinion (2 items) | ______ | × | 4 | = | ______ |
| Tone and Purpose (4 items) | ______ | × | 4 | = | ______ |
| Inferences (3 items) | ______ | × | 4 | = | ______ |
| Argument (1 item) | ______ | × | 4 | = | ______ |
| **Mapping** (2 items) | ______ | × | 10 | = | ______ |
| | | | Comprehension Score | | ______ |

READING 3

# Messages from a Welfare Mom: My Turn at 30

*by Ramona Parish*

To mark the 30th anniversary of "My Turn," the weekly column written by readers, *Newsweek* magazine republished some of the most memorable essays from the past three decades. The following essay first appeared May 23, 1988. In the essay, Ramona Parish, a struggling student and single mother at the time, offered a glimpse into the hardships of life on welfare.

## Vocabulary Preview

*penalizes* (paragraph 1): punishes
*extraction* (paragraph 6): pulling out, removal
*abundance* (paragraph 9): a great quantity

---

1 Like many other single mothers, I am on welfare. I have received Aid to Families with Dependent Children ever since I divorced my husband six years ago. Living on government aid does several things to people. It destroys their pride and dignity; it makes them dependent on a system that **penalizes** them for being willing to work. I am not lazy and I want to work. But at this time the best I can hope for is a minimum-wage job that would only undermine my attempts to get ahead. Instead of just being poor, I would become one of the nation's working poor. I cannot survive on $3.35 per hour with three children, without regular child-support payments or health insurance. So I live on AFDC and often feel guilty because I take advantage of this system and its services. But I'm also made to feel guilty because I cannot pay for things with my own hard-earned money.

**To the people behind me on the grocery store line:** You have helped me feel guilty. You chip away at what little pride I have left by snickering to others when I use my food stamps, at the time commenting loudly about the abuse of taxpayers' dollars. It is because of such comments that I shop in a town 15 minutes away, and even there my face reddens with shame. 2

**To all landlords:** Some of you believe that because I receive welfare I have no pride in my home or my surroundings. Many times I've called on the phone to ask about a rental and, sight unseen, been turned down when I mention I receive AFDC. I know you have heard that most welfare people will destroy your home and are completely unreliable in paying rent on time. It doesn't matter that I have excellent references from previous landlords or that I can have the rent payments 3 sent directly to you. On the other hand, there are some of you who will rent *only* to welfare. You like having the money sent to you from social services. You don't care what condition your apartment is in because when I complain about needed repairs (windows that won't open, doors with broken locks) you tell me: "So? Move out." Because there are only a few of you who will rent to AFDC, your apartment will not be empty long.

4 **To my ex-husband:** In the past six years I have asked very little from you. Although I appreciate the bags of "used clothing" you sent when I asked if you could help with school clothes, I would have preferred if you had sent child support. Why should I have been the one who was embarrassed when your father stopped by and gave our son a pair of tennis shoes and each of our daughters $10? You should be the one who is embarrassed—more help from you could make a difference in the way our children live. I make sure they have all their basic needs met, but I get tired of telling them, no, they can't have the things they want because I don't have the money.

5 **To my children:** I did not intend to raise you on welfare. Bear with me a few more years, for I am trying to make a bad situation better. All of you kids have complained about having to apply for the free-lunch program. I know how ashamed you must feel when you're singled out in the classroom as a free-luncher, and the hurt caused by whispers among your friends that you're poor and your mother is on welfare. I'm sorry for the things I can't afford. But my biggest apology is for the groceries and boxes of toys you saw delivered to the house four years ago by the Old Newsboys organization. Tears still come to my eyes when I think of the question that each of you asked so innocently, "Mom, I thought people collected these for the poor who can't afford food and toys for the holidays." Little did you know, we were one of the poor. Since that day my pride has not allowed me to accept any more gift baskets.

**To all doctors and dentists:** Would my hysterectomy, which was done three years ago when I was only 28 have been so urgent if I hadn't had Medicaid to pay for it? Could I have avoided having to take estrogen every day for the rest of my life? Although I had a choice of whether to have the surgery or not, I believe scare tactics were used. I wonder if some professionals take advantage of Medicaid recipients because women on AFDC are seen as uneducated and are expected to believe what they are told? And would that explain why so many AFDC women have lost all their teeth? After several **extractions**—six teeth lost in six years on AFDC with three more to go soon—I find it difficult to chew my food properly. It's a standard joke now that I'm always the last to leave the table; in reality, I'm too embarrassed to tell people that dentists suggest pulling teeth because Medicaid won't pay for root canals and crowns. 6

**To all pharmacists:** When there is a long line of customers waiting to have their prescriptions filled and I hand you mine, do not shout, "Do you have your current Medicaid card?" Because the shouting is an advertisement that I am on welfare, I will walk around the store until the line is gone. Welfare moms do have some dignity. 7

**To all social-service case workers:** When I am willing to help myself and work, why do you take everything away? Can't you at least let me keep the food stamps and the 8 medical insurance until I am above the poverty level? Without these benefits I cannot make it, so I stay on the soaring welfare rolls. I don't want a free ride, but I do need a lift.

9 **To whom it may concern:** Do not feel pity for me. I don't want it. I have been given an **abundance** of self-worth these past two years. Enrolling in college and getting an education is my key to a future without AFDC. Managing a full-time class load, 20 hours a week on a work-study program, and being a mother hasn't been easy, but I've survived. Every time I cash a work-study check, I get back a piece of my pride. I still use my food stamps in another town, but at the same time I use dollar bills that I have earned myself. With each passing semester my head lifts a little higher. What I could use is a smile of understanding and words of encouragement and support. With help, not hindrance, I will make it.

Choose the best meaning of each word in **bold**. Use context clues to make your choice.

Vocabulary in Context ______ **1.** "But at this time the best I can hope for is a minimum-wage job that would only **undermine** my attempts to get ahead." (paragraph 1)

a. cover
b. help
c. support
d. damage

Vocabulary in Context ______ **2.** "With help, not **hindrance**, I will make it." (paragraph 9)

a. an assist
b. an obstacle
c. understanding
d. malice

Central Idea and Main Idea ______ **3.** Which sentence is the best statement of the central idea of the passage?

a. Like many other single mothers, I am on welfare.
b. It [living on government aid] destroys their pride and dignity; it makes [aid recipients] dependent on a system that penalizes them for being willing to work.
c. What I could use is a smile of understanding and words of encouragement and support.
d. With help, not hindrance, I will make it.

Central Idea and Main Idea ______ **4.** Which sentence is the best statement of the implied main idea of paragraph 3?

a. Many landlords treat people who receive welfare unfairly.
b. Many landlords are patient and helpful toward people on welfare.
c. Many landlords will not rent to people who are on welfare.
d. Many landlords prefer to rent to people who are on welfare.

Supporting Details ______ **5.** The author shopped in a town 15 minutes away because
a. she wanted to compare prices and get the best buy for her money.
b. she was ashamed and embarrassed to shop in her own town.
c. she was abusing the taxpayers' money.
d. none of the above.

Supporting Details ______ **6.** When the author asked her ex-husband for help with the children's school clothes, he
a. sent extra child support money.
b. sent the money he owed her for child support.
c. sent a bag of used clothes.
d. ignored her request for help.

Thought Patterns ______ **7.** The main thought pattern for the overall passage is
a. a contrast between welfare mothers and working mothers.
b. a series of complaints and concerns, each addressed to a specific group of people or person in the author's life.
c. a narrative that tells of one woman's struggle for independence.
d. a step-by-step description of how to get off welfare.

Thought Patterns ______ **8.** The thought pattern for paragraph 2 is
a. cause and effect.
b. definition.
c. time order.

Transitions ______ **9.** "I am not lazy and I want to work. But at this time the best I can hope for is a minimum-wage job that would only undermine my attempts to get ahead." (paragraph 1)

The relationship of ideas between these two sentences is
a. time order.
b. contrast.
c. addition.

Transitions ______ **10.** "Since that day my pride has not allowed me to accept any more gift baskets." (paragraph 5)

The relationship of ideas within this sentence is
a. time order.
b. definition.
c. comparison.

Fact and Opinion ______ **11.** Overall, the ideas in this passage
a. are based on research and statistics.
b. are based on the personal experiences of the author.
c. objectively present the views of many other people.
d. bitterly describe the effects of divorce on women and children.

Fact and Opinion

______ **12.** "You chip away at what little pride I have left by snickering to others when I use my food stamps, at the time commenting loudly about the abuse of taxpayers' dollars."

This sentence from paragraph 2 is a statement of

a. fact.
b. opinion.
c. fact and opinion.

Tone and Purpose

______ **13.** The overall tone of the passage is

a. balanced.
b. bitter.
c. discouraged.
d. upbeat.

Tone and Purpose

______ **14.** The tone of paragraph 5 is

a. harsh.
b. hopeful.
c. regretful.
d. admiring.

Tone and Purpose

______ **15.** The tone of paragraph 9 is

a. depressed.
b. playful.
c. humble.
d. angry.

Tone and Purpose

______ **16.** The author's main purpose in "Messages from a Welfare Mom" is

a. to persuade others not to go on government assistance.
b. to entertain readers with an inspirational story of overcoming barriers.
c. to inform the reader about the shameful effects being on government assistance can have.

Inferences

______ **17.** From the article we may infer that

a. the author's divorce was a factor that led to her need for government assistance.
b. the author chose to be divorced and on welfare.
c. the author does not know how to get off welfare.
d. the author is doomed to remain on welfare indefinitely.

Inferences

______ **18.** In paragraph 5, the author implies that

a. accepting charity hurts self-esteem.
b. her children are difficult and whiny.
c. she and her family are not poor in spirit and courage.
d. she and her children deserve an apology from her ex-husband.

Inferences ______ **19.** The details in paragraph 6 imply that

a. the author had many medical problems.

b. government assistance was a big help with medical problems.

c. doctors exploit Medicaid patients for a profit by suggesting unnecessary and radical procedures.

d. doctors are a source of hope and encouragement.

Argument ______ **20.** The following list of ideas contains a claim and the supports for that claim. In the space, write the letter of the claim of the argument.

a. A person on welfare must often endure the loud, rude remarks of pharmacists, cashiers, and other customers who comment publicly on his or her use of government aid.

b. For a person who receives government aid, many aspects of life are demeaning.

c. Some doctors and dentists may see women on AFDC as uneducated and expect them to believe what they are told.

d. Often landlords either won't rent to welfare recipients or do not properly maintain the properties that they do rent to welfare families.

## Outlining

Complete the outline with information from the passage. ______________

Central idea: ______________________________

______________________________

I. ______________________________

A. People create feelings of shame by snickering and commenting loudly.

B. The author shops in a town 15 minutes away.

II. The landlords

A. ______________________________

B. Others rent only to welfare recipients but don't maintain property.

III. ______________________________

A. He is uninvolved and doesn't do his part to help support the family.

B. His lack of support causes hardship and embarrassment.

IV. The children

A. The author asks them to be patient.

B. The author tells them she is ashamed and sorry.

V. The doctors and dentists
   A. They use scare tactics and expect Medicaid patients to believe what they are told.
   B. Many AFDC women lose their teeth because Medicaid won't pay for root canals and crowns.

VI. The pharmacists
   A. Some pharmacists advertise with loud comments that a customer is on government aid.
   B. Welfare moms have some dignity.

VII. The social caseworkers
   A. Social caseworkers should help welfare recipients keep benefits instead of taking them away.
   B. People on welfare don't want a free ride but need a lift.

VIII. ________________________________________
   A. Don't offer pity.
   B. With help, not hindrance, I will make it.

## Questions for Discussion and Writing

1. What are the author's central idea and major supporting details? Write your answer as a summary.
2. What are the links between divorce and welfare?
3. How does living on government aid destroy people's pride and dignity?
4. What are some of the reasons people stay on welfare?
5. How does a person get off public assistance?
6. What are some of the benefits of government assistance?

## EFFECTIVE READER Scorecard

"Messages from a Welfare Mom"

| Skill | Number Correct | Points | Total |
|---|---|---|---|
| ***Vocabulary*** | | | |
| Vocabulary in Context (2 items) | ______ | × 4 = | ______ |
| ***Comprehension*** | | | |
| Central Idea and Main Idea (2 items) | ______ | × 4 = | ______ |
| Supporting Details (2 items) | ______ | × 4 = | ______ |
| Thought Patterns (2 items) | ______ | × 4 = | ______ |
| Transitions (2 items) | ______ | × 4 = | ______ |
| Fact and Opinion (2 items) | ______ | × 4 = | ______ |
| Tone and Purpose (4 items) | ______ | × 4 = | ______ |
| Inferences (3 items) | ______ | × 4 = | ______ |
| Argument (1 item) | ______ | × 4 = | ______ |
| **Outlining** (5 items) | ______ | × 4 = | ______ |
| | | Comprehension Score | ______ |

READING 4

# Darkness at Noon

*by Harold Krents*

How should we treat the handicapped? Blind author Harold Krents gives us a few lessons about judging people on their abilities rather than their disabilities.

### Vocabulary Preview

*narcissistic* (paragraph 1): vain, self-absorbed
*invariably* (paragraph 3): always
*intoned* (paragraph 12): chanted
*misconception* (paragraph 15): mistaken belief, false impression

---

1 Blind from birth, I have never had the opportunity to see myself and have been completely dependent on the image I create in the eye of the observer. To date it has not been **narcissistic**.

2 There are those who assume that since I can't see, I obviously also cannot hear. Very often people will converse with me at the top of their lungs, enunciating each word very carefully. Conversely, people will also often whisper, assuming that since my eyes don't work, my ears don't either.

3 For example, when I go to the airport and ask the ticket agent for assistance to the plane, he or she will **invariably** pick up the phone, call a ground hostess, and whisper: "Hi, Jane, we've got a 76 here." I have concluded that the word *blind* is not used for one of two reasons: Either they fear that if the dread word is spoken, the ticket agent's retina will immediately detach, or they are reluctant to inform me of my condition, of which I may not have been previously aware.

4 On the other hand, others know that of course I can hear, but believe that I can't talk. Often, therefore, when my wife and I go out to dinner, a waiter or waitress will ask Kit if "*he* would like a drink," to which I respond that "indeed *he* would."

5 This point was graphically driven home to me while we were in England. I had been given a year's leave of absence from my Washington law firm to study for a law degree at Oxford University. During the year I became ill and was hospitalized. Immediately after admission, I was wheeled down to the X-ray room. Just at the door sat an elderly woman—elderly I would judge from the sound of her voice. "What is his name?" the woman asked the orderly who had been wheeling me.

6 "What's your name?" the orderly repeated to me.

7 "Harold Krents," I replied.

8 "Harold Krents," he repeated.

9 "When was he born?"

10 "When were you born?"

11 "November 5, 1944," I responded.

12 "November 5, 1944," the orderly **intoned**.

13 This procedure continued for approximately five minutes, at which point even my saint-like disposition deserted me. "Look," I finally blurted out, "this is absolutely ridiculous. Okay, granted I can't see, but it's got to have become pretty clear to each of you that I don't need an interpreter."

14 "He says he doesn't need an interpreter," the orderly reported to the woman.

15 The toughest **misconception** of all is the view that because I can't see, I can't work. I was turned down by over forty law firms because of my blindness, even though my qualifications included a cum laude degree from Harvard College and a good ranking in my Harvard Law School class.

16 The attempt to find employment, the continuous frustration of being told that it was impossible for a blind person to practice law, the rejection letters, not based on my lack of ability but rather on my disability, will always remain one of the most disillusioning experiences of my life.

I therefore look forward to the day, with the expectation that it is certain to come, when employers will view their handicapped workers as a little child did me years ago when my family still lived in Scarsdale. 17

I was playing basketball with my father in our backyard according to procedures we had developed. My father would stand beneath the hoop, shout, and I would shoot over his head at the basket attached to our garage. Our next-door neighbor, aged five, wandered over into our yard with a playmate. "He's blind," our neighbor whispered to her friend in a voice that could be heard distinctly by Dad and me. Dad shot and missed; I did the same. Dad hit the rim; I missed entirely; Dad shot and missed the garage entirely. "Which one is blind?" whispered back the little friend. 18

I would hope that in the near future when a plant manager is touring the factory with the foreman and comes upon a handicapped and nonhandicapped person working together, his comment after watching them work will be, "Which one is disabled?" 19

Choose the best meaning of each word in **bold**. Use context clues to make your choice.

Vocabulary in Context

______ **1.** "This procedure continued for **approximately** five minutes, at which point even my saint-like disposition deserted me." (paragraph 13)

a. long
b. exactly
c. a mere
d. about

**VISUAL VOCABULARY**

_________ The best meaning of the word **disposition** is

a. nature.
b. livelihood.

▲ This teenager's expression is typical of her happy *disposition*.

Vocabulary in Context _______ **2.** "The attempt to find employment, the continuous frustration of being told that it was impossible for a blind person to practice law, the rejection letters, not based on my lack of ability but rather on my disability, will always remain one of the most **disillusioning** experiences of my life." (paragraph 16)

a. inspiring
b. disappointing
c. character-building
d. hardworking

Central Idea and Main Idea _______ **3.** Which sentence is the best statement of the implied central idea of the passage?

a. A disability poses many barriers.
b. Some day a person with a handicap will be treated the same as one who is not handicapped.
c. I have faced many instances of discrimination based on others' limited view of my abilities.
d. In spite of the discrimination I have faced, I have hope for the future.

Central Idea and Main Idea ______ **4.** Which sentence is the best statement of the implied main idea of paragraph 18?

a. In spite of my blindness, I was able to shoot a basketball as accurately as my father, a sighted man, could.
b. Children are not prejudiced.
c. My father was a patient and kind man.
d. My father had a disability as well.

Supporting Details ______ **5.** The name Kit in paragraph 4 refers to

a. the author.
b. the waiter.
c. the author's wife.
d. the author's child.

Supporting Details ______ **6.** During the author's hospital stay in England, he becomes frustrated because

a. he had to get an X-ray.
b. an elderly woman and an orderly treated him as if he needed an interpreter.
c. he didn't fell well.
d. he was unable to work due to his illness.

Thought Patterns ______ **7.** The main thought pattern for the overall passage is

a. examples of personal experiences and responses to discrimination based on misconceptions about blindness.
b. an argument against special treatment of the handicapped.
c. a discussion of the causes of prejudice.
d. a comparison and contrast between the life of a sighted person and that of a blind person.

Thought Patterns ______ **8.** The thought pattern for paragraph 2 is

a. cause and effect.
b. example.
c. time order.

Transitions ______ **9.** "Conversely, people will also often whisper, assuming that since my eyes don't work, my ears don't either. For example, when I go to the airport and ask the ticket agent for assistance to the plane, he or she will invariably pick up the phone, call a ground hostess, and whisper: 'Hi, Jane, we've got a 76 here.'" (paragraphs 2–3)

The relationship of ideas between these two sentences is

a. time order.
b. contrast.
c. example.

Transitions ______ **10.** "There are those who assume that since I can't see, I obviously also cannot hear." (paragraph 2)

The relationship of ideas within this sentence is

a. time order.
b. example.
c. cause and effect.

Fact and Opinion ______ **11.** Overall, the ideas in this passage

a. are based on research and statistics.
b. are based on the personal experiences of the author.
c. objectively present the views of many other people.
d. describe the reasons the author loves to practice law.

Fact and Opinion ______ **12.** "The toughest misconception of all is the view that because I can't see, I can't work."

This sentence from paragraph 15 is a statement of

a. fact.
b. opinion.
c. fact and opinion.

Tone and Purpose ______ **13.** The overall tone of the passage is

a. depressed.
b. humorous.
c. objective.
d. determined.

Tone and Purpose ______ **14.** The tone of paragraph 5 is

a. harsh.
b. hopeful.
c. matter of fact.
d. admiring.

Tone and Purpose ______ **15.** The tone of paragraph 18 is

a. depressed.
b. prideful.
c. humble.
d. humorous.

Tone and Purpose ______ **16.** The author's main purpose in "Darkness at Noon" is

a. to persuade others to be nice to people who have disabilities.
b. to entertain readers with an inspirational story of overcoming barriers.
c. to inform the reader through examples of personal experiences about the ways in which people with handicaps face discrimination.

Inferences ______ **17.** From the article, we can conclude that

a. the author is resentful about his disability.
b. the author is an activist who works on behalf of people with disabilities.
c. the author's experiences represent the experiences of many people who have disabilities.
d. the author is self-absorbed.

Inferences ______ **18.** From the passage, we can conclude

a. the author is unwilling to speak up for himself when he is discriminated against.
b. the author's blindness has limited his options.
c. the author depends very little on other people.
d. the author is shy by nature.

Inferences ______ **19.** The details in paragraphs 5–14 imply that

a. the author does not often lose his patience.
b. the author doesn't like the elderly lady.
c. the orderly is not very bright.
d. the author is terminally ill.

Argument ______ **20.** The following list of ideas contains a claim and the supports for that claim. In the given space, write the letter of the claim.

a. Some people think that being blind affects one's ability to hear.
b. Other people think that being blind affects one's ability to work.
c. Some people even believe that being blind affects one's ability to speak.
d. Some people judge others based on their disability rather than on their abilities.

## Mapping

Complete the concept map. Fill in the blanks with the central idea and the missing major supporting details from "Darkness at Noon."

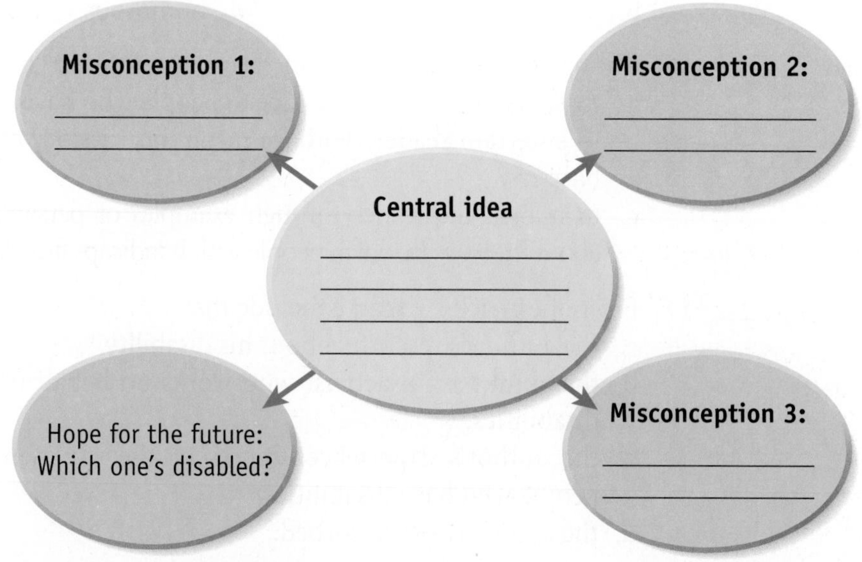

## Questions for Discussion and Writing

1. What are the author's central idea and major supporting details? Write your answer as a summary.
2. If you are a person with a disability, how do you respond to situations like those the author describes? If you do not have a disability, what would your attitude be if you did have one? How do you treat individuals who have a disability?
3. Why do people react to Krents's blindness as the ticket agents, hospital staff, and law firms did?
4. In what ways does society as a whole discriminate against people with disabilities?
5. Do you think the world Krents wishes for at the conclusion of his essay will come into being? What must happen in order to create such a world?

## EFFECTIVE READER Scorecard

"Darkness at Noon"

| Skill | Number Correct | Points | | Total |
|---|---|---|---|---|
| ***Vocabulary*** | | | | |
| Vocabulary in Context (2 items) | ______ | × 4 | = | ______ |
| **Comprehension** | | | | |
| Central Idea and Main Idea (2 items) | ______ | × 4 | = | ______ |
| Supporting Details (2 items) | ______ | × 4 | = | ______ |
| Thought Patterns (2 items) | ______ | × 4 | = | ______ |
| Transitions (2 items) | ______ | × 4 | = | ______ |
| Fact and Opinion (2 items) | ______ | × 4 | = | ______ |
| Tone and Purpose (4 items) | ______ | × 4 | = | ______ |
| Inferences (3 items) | ______ | × 4 | = | ______ |
| Argument (1 item) | ______ | × 4 | = | ______ |
| **Mapping** (4 items) | ______ | × 5 | = | ______ |
| | | Comprehension Score | | ______ |

## READING 5

# Curbing College Drinking Starts with a Change in Attitude

*by Sara Fritz*

College drinking is often seen as a harmless rite of passage into adulthood for American youth. Yet statistics reveal the seriousness of this behavior in the number of deaths, injuries, and assaults that occur each year in connection with college drinking. Sara Fritz, Washington Bureau Chief for the *St. Petersburg Times*, explores the problems of this long-standing dilemma and possible solutions for it.

### Vocabulary Preview

*trustee* (paragraph 4): board member
*intractable* (paragraph 8): stubborn

---

1 Drinking by college students has long been seen as a relatively harmless rite of passage for young people. But we now have solid statistics that demonstrate the seriousness of the problem.

2 Each year, about 1,400 college students between ages 18 and 24 die of alcohol-related injuries, including auto accidents, alcohol poisoning and suicide. Another 500,000 sustain injuries under the influence of alcohol. More than 600,000 students are assaulted by a student who has been drinking, and about 70,000 of those are sexual assaults.

3 Of course, these statistics do not begin to portray the incredible loss that is felt on a campus or within families when young people with promising lives are killed while partying. These students are dying or killing themselves at the very moment when their lives are beginning to flourish. These are people who might otherwise find cures for disease, become our next political leaders or, at minimum, get married and raise children of their own.

As a college **trustee,** I have spent many long hours in discussions with students about this problem. Even though they frequently see fellow students being carried out of the dorm by paramedics after long bouts of excessive drinking, many of them still think the problem is being exaggerated. 4

"Our parents drank, did drugs and partied in college," they say, "so why are they trying to prevent us from doing the same thing?" 5

There are a couple of answers to this very good question. First, many of their parents have come to regret the excesses of their youth. Some have struggled with drug and 6 alcohol problems ever since. Second, because we now talk more openly about date rape and sexual assault, the real consequences of college drinking binges are better understood than they were two or three decades ago.

7 Nearly every college and university tries to do something to curb the problem, especially after a student dies. They appoint a counselor for students who get in trouble while abusing alcohol or they post signs or distribute brochures outlining the dangers of alcohol. Some campuses even establish chapters of Alcoholics Anonymous.

8 When these measures fail to curb reckless drinking, college administrators conclude it is an insoluble problem. "With each failed effort," says a new NIH report, "the image of college drinking as an **intractable** problem is reinforced, administrators are demoralized, and the likelihood that schools will devote resources to prevent programs decreases."

9 Now we have a group of social scientists who think their discipline can help solve the problem of college drinking. The group issued a report last week outlining a number of approaches that promise to change the drinking culture on college campuses.

10 What a concept! You'd think the nation's academics might have thought of using the tools of their trade on a problem in their own back yard long before now.

"We need not accept high-risk drinking on our campuses as inevitable," says Mark Goldman, a researcher at the University of South Florida and co-chairman of the NIH task force working on this problem. "If colleges and communities work together, they can change these harmful drinking patterns." 11

The key to solving the problem, according to Goldman's task force, is to attack the problem from three different angles. The approach must try to change the entire student population, the environment in which they exist and the specific at-risk drinkers. This means there is probably no college or university in the country that is doing enough. Goldman and the task force deserve thanks for their work, even though their findings seem somewhat self-evident. But my guess is their report will be lost in the blizzard of paper that arrives on college campuses from the government. 12

Before any such program can succeed, students must be convinced that binge drinking is not normal behavior. Parents and college administrators have to be convinced that is it possible for them to influence students' behavior. 13

Choose the best meaning of each word in **bold**. Use context clues to make your choice.

Vocabulary in Context ______ **1.** "When these measures fail to curb reckless drinking, college administrators conclude it is an **insoluble** problem." (paragraph 8)

a. college
b. family
c. impossible to solve
d. easily solved

**VISUAL VOCABULARY**

The best definition of **proactively** is ________

a. after the fact.
b. in advance.

▸ SADD works *proactively* to stop college binge drinking.

Vocabulary in Context ______ **2.** " 'With each failed effort,' says a new NIH report, 'the image of college drinking as an intractable problem is reinforced, administrators are **demoralized,** and the likelihood that schools will devote resources to prevent programs decreases.' " (paragraph 8)

a. right
b. uninvolved
c. inspired
d. discouraged

Central Idea and Main Idea ______ **3.** Which sentence is the best statement of the implied central idea of the passage?

a. Drinking by college students is a serious problem.
b. A recent study suggests a program to address the serious and stubborn problems posed by college drinking.
c. College drinking is an insoluble problem.
d. Nearly every educational institution of higher learning is attempting to solve the problem of college drinking.

Central Idea and Main Idea ______ **4.** Which sentence is the best statement of the main idea of paragraph 12?

a. The key to solving the problem, according to Goldman's task force, is to attack the problem from three different angles.
b. The approach must try to change the entire student population, the environment in which they exist and the specific at-risk drinkers.

c. This means there is probably no college or university in the country that is doing enough.
d. Goldman and the task force deserve thanks for their work, even though their findings seem somewhat self-evident.

Supporting Details ______ **5.** The estimated number of students between the ages of 18 and 24 who die each year due to alcohol-related injuries is
a. 70,000.
b. 600,000.
c. 500.
d. 1,400.

Supporting Details ______ **6.** The author, as a college trustee,
a. participated in Goldman's NIH study about college drinking.
b. drank, did drugs, and partied in college.
c. spent many long hours in discussion with students about college drinking.
d. feels that she is doing her part to solve the problem of college drinking.

Thought Patterns ______ **7.** The main thought pattern for the overall passage is
a. comparing and contrasting drinking college students to non-drinking college students.
b. discussing the causes of college drinking.
c. listing and discussing the problems associated with college drinking and possible solutions.
d. a narrative account of college drinking.

Thought Patterns ______ **8.** The thought pattern for paragraph 6 is
a. comparison and contrast.
b. listing.
c. time order.

Transitions ______ **9.** "Each year, about 1,400 college students between ages 18 and 24 die of alcohol-related injuries, including auto accidents, alcohol poisoning and suicide. Another 500,000 sustain injuries under the influence of alcohol." (paragraph 2)

The relationship of ideas between these two sentences is
a. addition.
b. contrast.
c. effect.

Transitions ______ **10.** "Before any such program can succeed, students must be convinced that binge drinking is not normal behavior." (paragraph 13)

The relationship of ideas within this sentence is
a. time order.
b. example.
c. cause and effect.

Fact and Opinion

_____ **11.** Overall, the ideas in this passage
a. are based on research and statistics.
b. are based on the personal experiences of the author.
c. are based on a mix of statistics, research, and the personal experiences of the author.

Fact and Opinion

_____ **12.** "These are people who might otherwise find cures for disease, become our next political leaders or, at minimum, get married and raise children of their own."

This sentence from paragraph 3 is a statement of
a. fact.
b. opinion.
c. fact and opinion.

Tone and Purpose

_____ **13.** The overall tone of the passage is
a. pessimistic.
b. enthusiastic.
c. angry.
d. aloof.

Tone and Purpose

_____ **14.** The tone of paragraph 10 is
a. admiring.
b. sarcastic.
c. ungrateful.
d. pleased.

Tone and Purpose

_____ **15.** The tone of paragraph 13 is
a. forceful.
b. unsure.
c. bitter.
d. pleading.

Tone and Purpose

_____ **16.** The author's main purpose in this article is
a. to persuade students, parents, and educators to change the culture that leads to college binge drinking.
b. to entertain readers with a personal reflection about a current issue.
c. to inform the readers about the serious problem of college binge drinking.

Inferences

_____ **17.** From paragraphs 5 and 6, we can conclude that
a. some students who drink in college think that their parents' objections to college drinking is hypocritical.
b. most parents don't mind if their college-aged students drink alcohol.
c. all parents drank "drank, did drugs and partied in college."
d. college students are spoiled and selfish.

Inferences

_____ **18.** From the details in paragraph 2, we can conclude that
a. college drinking is on the rise.
b. college drinking is an isolated problem.

c. over a million students suffer serious problems as a result of college drinking each year.
d. the problem of college drinking cannot be solved.

Inferences ______ **19.** The article implies that
a. students are the only ones who can solve the problem of college drinking.
b. solving the problem of college drinking will require the efforts of students, parents, and educators.
c. the problem of college drinking cannot be solved.
d. the problem of college drinking is exaggerated.

Argument ______ **20.** **Claim:** Parents should share with their children their hard-won wisdom about college drinking.

Which statement does not support this claim?
a. Many parents have come to regret the excesses of their youth.
b. The real consequences of college drinking binges are better understood now than they were two or three decades ago.
c. No college or university in the country is doing enough to solve the problem of college binge drinking on their campuses.
d. Students who are at risk will not listen to their parents about college binge drinking.

## Outlining

Complete the following study outline with information from the passage.

I. The problem is very serious.

II. ______________ raise a question.

III. Colleges and universities respond to the problem.

IV. Social scientists study the problem.

A. ______________________________

B. Attack problem from three angles

1. Change the ______________________

2. ______________________________

3. ______________________________

V. Students, parents, and college administrators must change attitudes and work together to solve the problem.

## Questions for Discussion and Writing

1. What are the author's main idea and major supporting details? Write your answer as a summary.
2. Is binge drinking a problem at the college you attend? How does the college respond to student drinking? How do students respond? Is help available for students who want or need it?
3. What is the cause-and-effect relationship between alcohol use and injuries? Between alcohol use and assaults?
4. Just as Fritz challenges educators to change the climate of drinking, some writers have suggested that colleges should report a student's binge drinking to the student's parents. What do you think of this solution? What are some other steps colleges and universities can take to help solve this problem?
5. What would change students', parents', and colleges and universities' attitudes about college binge drinking? How can students be convinced that this behavior is not normal? What will convince parents and educators that they have influence over student behavior?

## EFFECTIVE READER Scorecard

"Curbing College Drinking Starts With a Change in Attitude"

| Skill | Number Correct | Points | Total |
|---|---|---|---|
| ***Vocabulary*** | | | |
| Vocabulary in Context (2 items) | ______ | × 4 = | ______ |
| ***Comprehension*** | | | |
| Central Idea and Main Idea (2 items) | ______ | × 4 = | ______ |
| Supporting Details (2 items) | ______ | × 4 = | ______ |
| Thought Patterns (2 items) | ______ | × 4 = | ______ |
| Transitions (2 items) | ______ | × 4 = | ______ |
| Fact and Opinion (2 items) | ______ | × 4 = | ______ |
| Tone and Purpose (4 items) | ______ | × 4 = | ______ |
| Inferences (3 items) | ______ | × 4 = | ______ |
| Argument (1 item) | ______ | × 4 = | ______ |
| **Outlining** (5 items) | ______ | × 4 = | ______ |
| | | Comprehension Score | ______ |

READING 6

# Time to Look and Listen

*by Magdoline Asfahani*

According to some experts, nearly 900,000 legal immigrants flow into the United States each year. These immigrants come from vastly different cultures and face tremendous challenges. In the following essay, published in *Newsweek* Magazine's "My Turn" column December 2, 1996, the author shares her love of America and the challenges of her multicultural upbringing.

### Vocabulary Preview

*conscious* (paragraph 1): mindful, aware
*incompatible* (paragraph 2): mismatched, unable to coexist
*heritage* (paragraph 3): tradition, custom, birthright
*monotheistic* (paragraph 5): the belief in one god
*nuances* (paragraph 8): subtle degrees of meaning
*collective* (paragraph 11): group

---

1 I love my country as many who have been here for generations cannot. Perhaps that's because I'm the child of immigrants, raised with a **conscious** respect for America that many people take for granted. My parents chose this country because it offered them a new life, freedom and possibilities. But I learned at a young age that the country we loved so much did not feel the same way about us.

2 Discrimination is not unique to America. It occurs in any country that allows immigration. Anyone who is unlike the majority is looked at a little suspiciously, dealt with a little differently. I knew that I was an Arab and a Muslim. This meant nothing to me. At school I stood up to say the Pledge of Allegiance every day. These things did not seem **incompatible** at all. Then everything changed for me, suddenly and permanently, in 1985. I was only in seventh grade, but that was the beginning of my political education.

That year a TWA plane originating in Athens was diverted to Beirut. Two years earlier the U.S. Marine barracks in Beirut had been bombed. That seemed to start a chain of events that would forever link Arabs with terrorism. After the hijacking, I faced classmates who taunted me with cruel names, attacking my **heritage** and my religion. I became an outcast and had to apologize for myself constantly. 3

After a while, I tried to forget my heritage. No matter what race, religion or ethnicity, a child who is attacked often retreats. I was the only Arab I knew of in my class, so I had 4 no one in my peer group as an ally. No matter what my parents tried to tell me about my proud cultural history, I would ignore it. My classmates told me I came from an uncivilized, brutal place, that Arabs were by nature anti-American, and I believed them. They did not know the hours my parents spent studying, working, trying to preserve part of their old lives while embracing, willingly, the new.

5 I tried to forget the Arabic I knew, because if I didn't I'd be forever linked to murderers. I stopped inviting friends over for dinner, because I thought the food we ate was "weird." I lied about where my parents had come from. Their accents (although they spoke English perfectly) humiliated me. Though Islam is a major **monotheistic** religion with many similarities to Judaism and Christianity, there were no holidays near Chanukah or Christmas, nothing to tie me to the "Judeo-Christian" tradition. I felt more excluded. I slowly began to turn into someone without a past.

6 Civil war was raging in Lebanon, and all that Americans saw of that country was destruction and violence. Every other movie seemed to feature Arab terrorists. The most common questions I was asked were if I had ever ridden a camel or if my family lived in tents. I felt burdened with responsibility. Why should an adolescent be asked questions like "Is it true you hate Jews and you want Israel destroyed?" I didn't hate anybody. My parents had never said anything even alluding to such sentiments. I was confused and hurt.

7 As I grew older and began to form my own opinions, my embarrassment lessened and my anger grew. The turning point came in high school. My grandmother had become very ill, and it was necessary for me to leave school a few days before Christmas vacation. My chemistry teacher was very sympathetic until I said I was going to the Middle East. "Don't come back in a body bag," he said cheerfully. The class laughed. Suddenly, those years of watching movies that mocked me and listening to others who knew nothing about Arabs and Muslims except what they saw on television seemed like a bad dream. I knew then that I would never be silent again.

I've tried to reclaim those lost years. I 8
realize now that I come from a culture that has a rich history. The Arab world is a medley of people of different religions; not every Arab is a Muslim, and vice versa. The Arabs brought tremendous advances in the sciences and mathematics, as well as creating a literary tradition that has never been surpassed. The language itself is flexible and beautiful, with **nuances** and shades of meaning unparalleled in any language. Though many find it hard to believe, Islam has made progress in women's rights. There is a specific provision in the Koran that permits women to own property and ensures that their inheritance is protected—although recent events have shown that interpretation of these laws can vary.

My youngest brother, who is 12, is now 9
at the crossroads I faced. When initial reports of the Oklahoma City bombing pointed to "Arab-looking individuals" as the culprits, he came home from school crying. "Mom, why do Muslims kill people? Why are the Arabs so bad?" She was angry and brokenhearted, but tried to handle the situation in the best way possible through education. She went to his class, armed with Arabic music, pictures, traditional dress and cookies. She brought a chapter of the social-studies book to life and the children asked intelligent, thoughtful

questions, even after the class was over. Some even asked if she was coming back. When my brother came home, he was excited and proud instead of ashamed.

10 I only recently told my mother about my past experience. Maybe if I had told her then, I would have been better equipped to deal with the thoughtless teasing. But, fortunately, the world is changing. Although discrimination and stereotyping still exist, many people are trying to lessen and end it. Teachers, schools and the media are showing greater sensitivity to cultural issues. However, there is still much that needs to be done, not for the sake of any particular ethnic or cultural groups but for the sake of our country.

11 The America that I love is one that values freedom and the differences of its people. Education is the key to understanding. As Americans we need to take a little time to look and listen carefully to what is around us and not rush to judgment without knowing the facts. And we must never be ashamed of our pasts. It is our **collective** differences that unite and make us unique as a nation. It's what determines our present and our future.

Choose the best meaning of each word in **bold.** Use context clues to make your choice.

Vocabulary in Context ______

**1.** "Their accents (although they spoke English perfectly) **humiliated** me." (paragraph 5)

a. provoked
b. harmed
c. embarrassed
d. inspired

Vocabulary in Context ______

**2.** "My parents had never said anything even alluding to such **sentiments**." (paragraph 6)

a. facts
b. details
c. ideals
d. feelings

Central Idea and Main Idea ______

**3.** Which sentence best states the central idea of the passage?

a. I love my country as many who have not been here for generations cannot.
b. After the hijacking, I faced classmates who taunted me with cruel names, attacking my heritage and my religion.
c. Although discrimination and stereotyping still exist, many people are trying to lessen and end it.
d. As Americans we need to take a little time to look and listen carefully to what is around us and not rush to judgment without knowing the facts.

Central Idea and Main Idea ______ **4.** Which sentence best states the main idea of paragraph 2?
a. Discrimination is not unique to America.
b. Anyone who is unlike the majority is looked at a little suspiciously, dealt with a little differently.
c. I knew that I was an Arab and a Muslim.
d. At school I stood up to say the Pledge of Allegiance every day.

Supporting Details ______ **5.** What significant event occurred in 1985?
a. The author's family immigrated into the United States.
b. The U.S. Marine barracks in Beirut was bombed.
c. A TWA plane originating in Athens was hijacked to Beirut.
d. The author's younger brother faced cruelty at school.

Supporting Details ______ **6.** What was the turning point in the author's acceptance of her heritage?
a. the hijacking of the TWA plane
b. the name calling by her peers
c. the chemistry teacher's response to her need to travel to the Middle East
d. her mother's visit to a classroom

Thought Patterns ______ **7.** The main thought pattern for the entire passage is
a. a series of events of the author's struggles as an Arab-Muslim immigrant in the United States.
b. a list of causes for discrimination against Arab-Muslims.
c. a discussion of the differences between American and Arab cultures.
d. a list of reasons in an argument for legal immigration.

Thought Patterns ______ **8.** The thought pattern for paragraph 6 is
a. listing.
b. comparison and contrast.
c. definition.

Transitions ______ **9.** "Civil War was raging in Lebanon, and all that Americans saw of that country was destruction and violence." (paragraph 6)

The relationship of ideas within this sentence is
a. cause and effect.
b. comparison and contrast.
c. addition.

Transitions ______ **10.** "Teachers, schools and the media are showing greater sensitivity to cultural issues. However, there is still much that needs to be done, not for the sake of any particular ethnic or cultural groups but for the sake of our country." (paragraph 10)

The relationship of ideas between these sentences is
a. cause and effect.
b. comparison and contrast.
c. addition.

Fact and Opinion ______ **11.** "I love my country as many who have been here for generations cannot."

This sentence from paragraph 1 is a statement of
a. fact.
b. opinion.
c. fact and opinion.

Fact and Opinion ______ **12.** "The Arabs brought tremendous advances in the sciences and mathematics, as well as creating a literary tradition that has never been surpassed."

This sentence from paragraph 8 is a statement of
a. fact.
b. opinion.
c. fact and opinion.

Tone and Purpose ______ **13.** The overall tone of the passage is
a. sincere.
b. sarcastic.
c. angry.
d. matter of fact.

Tone and Purpose ______ **14.** The tone of paragraph 8 is
a. embarrassed.
b. humble.
c. admiring.
d. neutral.

Tone and Purpose ______ **15.** The overall purpose of the passage is to
a. inform the reader about the strengths of the Arab-Muslim culture.
b. entertain the reader with a personal story.
c. persuade the reader to be more tolerant of different cultures.

Inferences ______ **16.** From the article, we can conclude that
a. discrimination can never be overcome.
b. all immigrants face prejudice and mistreatment.
c. prejudice can be overcome through education.
d. discrimination occurs more frequently in America than in other countries.

Inferences ______ **17.** From the details in paragraph 5, we can conclude that
a. the author was not well liked by her peers.
b. the author did not get along well with her family.
c. religious traditions can be a powerful force that unites or separates people.
d. separation of church and state is necessary.

Argument ______ **18. Claim:** Misconceptions about Arab-Muslim culture existed in America in the 1990s.

Which of the following statements does not support this claim?

a. Civil war was raging in Lebanon.
b. All that Americans saw of Lebanon was destruction and violence.
c. Every other movie seemed to feature Arab terrorists.
d. The author was often asked if she had ever ridden a camel or if her family lived in tents.

Argument ______ **19.** The following list of ideas contains a claim and supports for that claim. In the space, write the letter of the claim for the argument.

a. The Arab culture has a rich history.
b. Arabs brought tremendous advances in the sciences and mathematics, as well as creating a literary tradition that has never been surpassed.
c. The language itself is flexible and beautiful, with nuances and shades of meaning unparalleled in any language.
d. Islam has made progress in women's rights.

Argument ______ **20.** The following list of ideas contains a claim and supports for that claim. In the space, write the letter of the claim for the argument.

a. After a while, I tried to forget my heritage.
b. No matter what my parents tried to tell me about my proud cultural history, I would ignore it.
c. I tried to forget the Arabic I knew, because if I didn't I'd be forever linked to murderers.
d. I stopped inviting friends over for dinner, because I thought the food we ate was "weird."

## Outlining

Add the ideas needed to complete this outline of "Time to Look and Listen."

I. Immigration and discrimination
   A. Author expresses love for America.
   B. Author experiences discrimination in school.
   C. World events link Arabs with terrorism.
      1. TWA hijacking
      2. ______________________________

II. Rejection of Arab heritage
   A. ______________________________
   B. Author feels humiliated by her family's traditions.
   C. Author becomes confused and hurt.

III. The turning point
   A. ______________________________
   B. Teacher makes an insensitive remark.
   C. Classmates laugh.

IV. A rich history
   A. ______________________________
   B. The Arabic language is flexible and beautiful.
   C. Islam has made progress in women's rights.

V. Education: the key
   A. Author's brother faces prejudice of peers.
   B. ______________________________
   C. Author's brother feels pride in his heritage.

VI. America's need
   A. America is becoming somewhat more sensitive to cultural issues.
   B. Discrimination and stereotyping still exist.
   C. America's differences unite us and make us unique.

## Questions for Discussion and Writing

1. What are the author's central idea and major supporting details? Write your answer as a summary.
2. Have you experienced or witnessed someone else experience discrimination? What was its effect?
3. In paragraph 1, the author states, "I love my country as many who have been here for generations cannot." Do you think that immigrants have a deeper love for America than those who were born here? Why or why not?
4. The issue of immigration has long been debated. Should America limit the number of legal immigrants allowed into the country?
5. In what ways do our differences make us stronger as a country?

## EFFECTIVE READER Scorecard

**"Time to Look and Listen"**

| Skill | Number Correct | | Points | | Total |
|---|---|---|---|---|---|
| ***Vocabulary*** | | | | | |
| Vocabulary in Context (2 items) | ______ | × | 4 | = | ______ |
| ***Comprehension*** | | | | | |
| Central Idea and Main Idea (2 items) | ______ | × | 4 | = | ______ |
| Supporting Details (2 items) | ______ | × | 4 | = | ______ |
| Thought Patterns (2 items) | ______ | × | 4 | = | ______ |
| Transitions (2 items) | ______ | × | 4 | = | ______ |
| Fact and Opinion (2 items) | ______ | × | 4 | = | ______ |
| Tone and Purpose (3 items) | ______ | × | 4 | = | ______ |
| Inferences (2 items) | ______ | × | 4 | = | ______ |
| Argument (3 items) | ______ | × | 4 | = | ______ |
| **Outlining** (5 items) | ______ | × | 4 | = | ______ |
| | | | Comprehension Score | | ______ |

d whose bout with disease
hs. With the dedicated and
elen Keller overcame these
with honors from Radcliffe,
the Presidential Medal of
graphy, *The Story of My Life*
e following passage, an ex-
ugh the miraculous events

*succeeded* (paragraph 2): followed
*plummet* (paragraph 3): ball of lead
*sounding-line* (paragraph 3): a line or wire weighted, usually with a plummet, to measure the depth of water
*quiver* (paragraph 8): tremble, shiver

---

1 The most important day I remember in all my life is the one on which my teacher, Anne Mansfield Sullivan, came to me. I am filled with wonder when I consider the **immeasurable** contrast between the two lives which it connects. It was the third of March 1887, three months before I was seven years old.

2 On the afternoon of that eventful day, I stood on the porch, **dumb,** expectant. I guessed vaguely from my mother's signs and from the hurrying to and fro in the house that something unusual was about to happen, so I went to the door and waited on the steps. The afternoon sun penetrated the mass of honeysuckle that covered the porch and fell on my upturned face. My fingers lingered almost unconsciously on the familiar leaves and blossoms which had just come forth to greet the sweet southern spring. I did not know what the future held of marvel or surprise for me. Anger and bitterness had preyed upon me continually for weeks and a deep **languor** had **succeeded** this passionate struggle.

3 Have you ever been at sea in a dense fog, when it seemed as if a tangible white darkness shut you in, and the great ship, tense and

anxious, groped her way toward the shore with **plummet** and **sounding-line,** and you waited with beating heart for something to happen? I was like that ship before my education began, only I was without compass or sounding-line and had no way of knowing how near the harbor was. "Light! Give me light!" was the wordless cry of my soul, and the light of love shone on me in that very hour.

4 I felt approaching footsteps. I stretched out my hand as I supposed to my mother. Someone took it, and I was caught up and held close in the arms of her who had come to reveal all things to me, and, more than all things else, to love me.

5 The morning after my teacher came she led me into her room and gave me a doll. The little blind children at the Perkins Institution had sent it and Laura Bridgman had dressed it; but I did not know this until afterward. When I had played with it a little while, Miss Sullivan slowly spelled into my hand the word "d-o-l-l." I was at once interested in this finger play and tried to imitate it. When I finally succeeded in making the letters correctly I was flushed with childish pleasure and pride. Running downstairs to my mother I held up my hand and made the letters for doll. I did not know that I was spelling a word or even that words existed; I was simply making my fingers go in monkey-like imitation. In the days that followed I learned to spell in this uncomprehending way a great many words, among them *pin*, *hat*, *cup* and a few verbs like *sit*, *stand* and *walk*. But my teacher had been with me several weeks before I understood that everything has a name.

6 One day, while I was playing with my new doll, Miss Sullivan put my big rag doll into my lap also, spelled "d-o-l-l" and tried to make me understand that "d-o-l-l" applied to both. Earlier in the day we had had a tussle over the words "m-u-g" and "w-a-t-e-r." Miss Sullivan had tried to impress it upon me that "m-u-g" is mug and that "w-a-t-e-r" is water, but I persisted in confounding the two. In despair she had dropped the subject for the time, only to renew it at the first opportunity. I became impatient at her repeated attempts and, seizing the new doll, I dashed it upon the floor. I was keenly delighted when I felt the fragments of the broken doll at my feet. Neither sorrow nor regret followed my passionate outburst. I had not loved the doll. In the still, dark world in which I lived there was no strong sentiment or tenderness. I felt my teacher sweep the fragments to one side of the hearth, and I had a sense of satisfaction that the cause of my discomfort was removed. She brought me my hat, and I knew I was going out into the warm sunshine. This thought, if a wordless sensation may be called a thought, made me hop and skip with pleasure.

We walked down the path to the well- 7
house, attracted by the fragrance of the honeysuckle with which it was covered. Someone was drawing water and my teacher placed my hand under the spout. As the cool stream gushed over one hand she spelled into the other the word *water*, first slowly, then rapidly. I stood still, my whole attention fixed upon the motions of her fingers. Suddenly I felt a misty consciousness as of something forgotten—a thrill of returning thought; and somehow the mystery of language was revealed to me. I knew then that "w-a-t-e-r" meant the wonderful cool something that was flowing over my hand. The living word awakened my soul, gave it light, hope, joy, set it free! There were barriers still, it is true, but barriers that could in time be swept away.

I left the well-house eager to learn. 8
Everything had a name, and each name gave

birth to a new thought. As we returned to the house every object which I touched seemed to **quiver** with life. That was because I saw everything with the strange, new sight that had come to me. On entering the door I remembered the doll I had broken. I felt my way to the hearth and picked up the pieces. I tried vainly to put them together. Then my eyes filled with tears; for I realized what I had done, and for the first time I felt repentance and sorrow.

I learned a great many new words that 9
day. I do not remember what they all were; but I do know that *mother*, *father*, *sister*, *teacher* were among them—words that were to make the world blossom for me, "like Aaron's rod, with flowers."* It would have been difficult to find a happier child than I was as I lay in my crib at the close of that eventful day and lived over the joys it had brought me, and for the first time longed for a new day to come.

* Aaron's rod is an allusion to a miracle recorded in the Old Testament wherein God caused a dead stick to sprout with flowers.

Choose the best meaning of each word in **bold**. Use context clues to make your choice.

Vocabulary in Context ______

**1.** "Miss Sullivan had tried to impress it upon me that 'm-u-g' is mug and 'w-a-t-e-r' is water, but I persisted in **confounding** the two." (paragraph 6)
a. confusing
b. repeating
c. hating
d. remembering

Vocabulary in Context ______

**2.** "Then my eyes filled up with tears; for I realized what I had done and for the first time I felt **repentance** and sorrow." (paragraph 8)
a. hurt
b. resentment
c. remorse
d. relief

Central Idea and Main Idea ______

**3.** Which sentence best states the central idea of the passage?
a. The most important day I remember in all my life is the one on which my teacher, Anne Mansfield Sullivan, came to me.
b. I am filled with wonder when I consider the immeasurable contrast between the two lives which it connects.
c. I was like that ship before my education began, only I was without compass or sounding-line and had no way of knowing how near the harbor was.
d. It would have been difficult to find a happier child than I was as I lay in my crib at the close of that eventful day and lived over the joys it had brought me, and for the first time longed for a new day to come.

Central Idea and Main Idea ______ **4.** Which sentence is the best statement of the implied main idea of paragraph 3?

a. Helen Keller was afraid of the sea.
b. Helen Keller felt unloved.
c. Helen Keller couldn't wait to begin learning.
d. Helen Keller understood the sea.

Supporting Details ______ **5.** The morning after Miss Sullivan arrived, she gave Helen

a. a hug.
b. a cup of water.
c. a doll from the little blind children at the Perkins Institution.
d. a dose of discipline.

Supporting Details ______ **6.** Helen broke her doll because

a. she didn't care for it.
b. she was jealous of it.
c. she was angry at having to work with spelling words.
d. she was spoiled and mean.

Thought Patterns ______ **7.** The main thought pattern for the overall passage is

a. time order.
b. cause and effect.
c. definition.
d. classification.

Thought Patterns ______ **8.** The thought pattern for paragraph 3 is

a. cause and effect.
b. classification.
c. comparison and contrast.

Transitions ______ **9.** "I stood still, my whole attention fixed upon the motions of her fingers. Suddenly I felt a misty consciousness as of something forgotten—a thrill of returning thought; and somehow the mystery of language was revealed to me." (paragraph 7)

The relationship of ideas between these two sentences is

a. time order.
b. contrast.
c. example.

Transitions ______ **10.** "I felt my teacher sweep the fragments to one side of the hearth, and I had a sense of satisfaction that the cause of my discomfort was removed." (paragraph 6)

The relationship of ideas within this sentence is

a. time order.
b. example.
c. addition.

Fact and Opinion

______ **11.** "I learned a great many new words that day."

This sentence from paragraph 9 is a statement of

a. fact.
b. opinion.
c. fact and opinion.

Fact and Opinion

______ **12.** "I do not remember what they all were; but I do know that *mother*, *father*, *sister*, *teacher* were among them—words that were to make the world blossom for me, 'like Aaron's rod, with flowers.' "

This sentence from paragraph 9 is a statement of

a. fact.
b. opinion.
c. fact and opinion.

Tone and Purpose

______ **13.** The overall tone of the passage is

a. reflective and joyful.
b. angry and bitter.
c. matter of fact.
d. calm and soothing.

Tone and Purpose

______ **14.** "Then my eyes filled up with tears; for I realized what I had done, and for the first time felt repentance and sorrow."

The tone of this statement from paragraph 8 is

a. harsh.
b. hopeful.
c. regretful.
d. admiring.

Tone and Purpose

______ **15.** "As the cool stream gushed over one hand she spelled into the other the word *water*, first slowly, then rapidly. I stood still, my whole attention fixed upon the motions of her fingers. Suddenly I felt a misty consciousness as of something forgotten—a thrill of returning thought; and somehow the mystery of language was revealed to me."

The tone of these sentences from paragraph 7 is

a. excited.
b. confused.
c. pained.
d. humorous.

Tone and Purpose

______ **16.** The author's main purpose in "The Day Language Came into My Life" is

a. to persuade others about the joy of teaching the blind and deaf.
b. to entertain readers with a lighthearted story that has a happy ending.
c. to inform the reader about the significance of Anne Sullivan's impact on Helen Keller's life.

Inferences ______ **17.** From the passage, we can conclude that
a. the author was an intelligent and quick learner.
b. the author did not want to learn.
c. Helen Keller would never have learned to communicate without Anne Sullivan.
d. the author's family was ashamed of Helen's disabilities.

Inferences ______ **18.** Based on the details in paragraphs 5–7, we can conclude that
a. an important step in the learning of language is practicing skills.
b. Helen's stubbornness slowed down her learning process.
c. Anne Sullivan was a strict teacher.
d. Helen loved her doll.

Inferences ______ **19.** "On entering the door I remembered the doll I had broken. I felt my way to the hearth and picked up the pieces. I tried vainly to put them together. Then my eyes filled with tears; for I realized what I had done, and for the first time I felt repentance and sorrow."

These details from paragraph 8 imply that
a. the doll meant more to Helen once she understood it had a name.
b. the doll can be fixed.
c. the doll was cheaply made and easily broken.
d. Helen had never had a doll before.

Argument ______ **20.** The following list of ideas contains a claim and the supports for that claim. In the given space, write the letter of the claim.
a. Anne Sullivan was a loving and patient teacher to Helen Keller.
b. Helen says that Sullivan "had come to reveal all things to me, and, more than all things else, to love me."
c. When Helen did not make progress with the words *mug* and *water,* Sullivan dropped the subject for a time, only to renew it at the next opportunity.
d. When Helen broke the doll, Sullivan swept the fragments out of the way and continued the lesson at the well-house.

## Mapping

Complete the following time line with details for the passage.

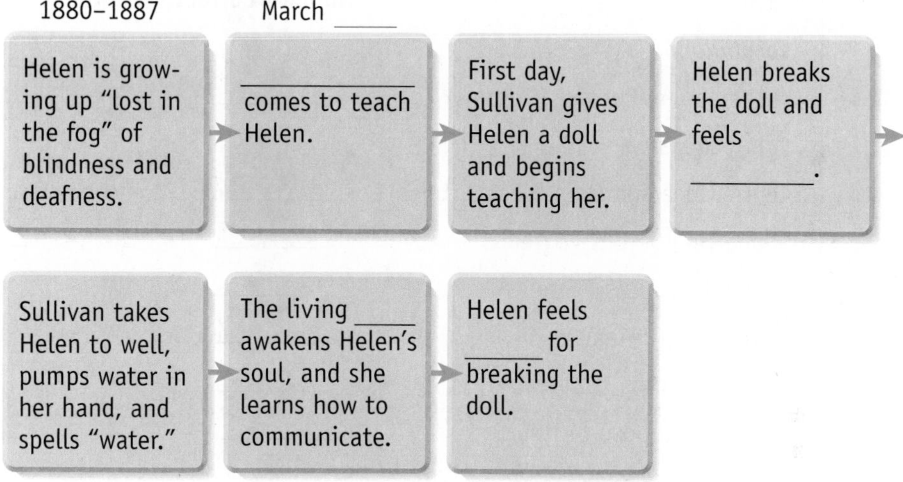


## Questions for Discussion and Writing

1. What are the author's central idea and major supporting details? Write your answer as a summary.
2. What difference did language make in Helen Keller's life? What was she feeling before and after she learned about words?
3. How would you contrast Helen's relationship to words when she spelled them by rote and when she learned the significance of their meanings?
4. How does Helen's changed attitude toward the doll reflect an inner change?
5. Have you ever experienced a sudden understanding? Did you struggle before understanding came? Describe your experience. If you have not experienced an exciting moment of learning, what has been missing? What causes a breakthrough in learning?

## EFFECTIVE READER Scorecard

"The Day Language Came into My Life"

| Skill | Number Correct | | Points | | Total |
|---|---|---|---|---|---|
| ***Vocabulary*** | | | | | |
| Vocabulary in Context (2 items) | ______ | × | 4 | = | ______ |
| ***Comprehension*** | | | | | |
| Central Idea and Main Idea (2 items) | ______ | × | 4 | = | ______ |
| Supporting Details (2 items) | ______ | × | 4 | = | ______ |
| Thought Patterns (2 items) | ______ | × | 4 | = | ______ |
| Transitions (2 items) | ______ | × | 4 | = | ______ |
| Fact and Opinion (2 items) | ______ | × | 4 | = | ______ |
| Tone and Purpose (4 items) | ______ | × | 4 | = | ______ |
| Inferences (3 items) | ______ | × | 4 | = | ______ |
| Argument (1 item) | ______ | × | 4 | = | ______ |
| **Mapping** (5 items) | ______ | × | 4 | = | ______ |
| | | | Comprehension Score | | ______ |

READING 8

# Neat People vs. Sloppy People

*by Suzanne Britt*

an was born in Winston-Salem, North Carolina, and at-
ge and Washington University. She is a journalist who has
ied in journals, newspapers, and news magazines. In this
two types of people to reveal some common human shortcomings.

### Vocabulary Preview

*rectitude* (paragraph 2): morally correct behavior or thinking
*métier* (paragraph 3): trade, art, job
*tentative* (paragraph 3): possible
*mementos* (paragraph 4): keepsakes
*accumulate* (paragraph 4): collect, gather
*excavation* (paragraph 5): dig, burrow
*meticulously* (paragraph 5): carefully
*scrupulously* (paragraph 5): thoroughly
*sentimental* (paragraph 9): emotional

---

1 I've finally figured out the difference between neat people and sloppy people. The distinction is, as always, moral. Neat people are lazier and meaner than sloppy people.

2 Sloppy people, you see, are not really sloppy. Their sloppiness is merely the unfortunate consequence of their extreme moral **rectitude**. Sloppy people carry in their mind's eye a heavenly vision, a precise plan, that is so stupendous, so perfect, it can't be achieved in this world or the next.

3 Sloppy people live in Never-Never Land. Someday is their **métier**. Someday they are planning to alphabetize all their books and set up home catalogues. Someday they will go through their wardrobes and mark certain items for **tentative** mending and certain items for passing on to relatives of similar shape and size. Someday sloppy people will make family scrapbooks into which they will put newspaper clippings, postcards, locks of hair, and the fried corsage from their senior prom. Someday they will file everything on the surface of their desks, including the cash receipts from coffee purchases at the snack shop. Someday they will sit down and read all the back issues of *The New Yorker.*

For all these noble reasons and more, 4
sloppy people never get neat. They aim too high and wide. They save everything, planning

someday to file, order, and straighten out the world. But while these ambitious plans take clearer and clearer shape in their heads, the books spill from the shelves onto the floor, the clothes pile up in the hamper and closet, the family **mementos accumulate** in every drawer, the surface of the desk is buried under mounds of paper and the unread magazines threaten to reach the ceiling.

5 Sloppy people can't bear to part with anything. They give loving attention to every detail. When sloppy people say they're going to tackle the surface of the desk, they really mean it. Not a paper will go unturned; not a rubber band will go unboxed. Four hours or two weeks into the **excavation,** the desk looks exactly the same, primarily because the sloppy person is **meticulously** creating new piles of papers with new headings and **scrupulously** stopping to read all the old book catalogs before he throws them away. A neat person would just bulldoze the desk.

6 Neat people are bums and clods at heart. They have cavalier attitudes toward possessions, including family heirlooms. Everything is just another dust-catcher to them. If anything collects dust, it's got to go and that's that. Neat people will toy with the idea of throwing the children out of the house just to cut down on the clutter.

7 Neat people don't care about process. They like results. What they want to do is get the whole thing over with so they can sit down and watch the rasslin' on TV. Neat people operate on two unvarying principles: Never handle any item twice, and throw everything away.

8 The only thing messy in a neat person's house is the trash can. The minute something comes to a neat person's hand, he will look at it, try to decide if it has immediate use and, finding none, throw it in the trash.

Neat people are especially vicious with 9
mail. They never go through their mail unless they are standing directly over a trash can. If the trash can is beside the mailbox, even better. All ads, catalogs, pleas for charitable contributions, church bulletins and money-saving coupons go straight into the trash can without being opened. All letters from home, postcards from Europe, bills and paychecks are opened, immediately responded to, then dropped in the trash can. Neat people keep their receipts only for tax purposes. That's it. No **sentimental** salvaging of birthday cards or the last letter a dying relative ever wrote. Into the trash it goes.

Neat people place neatness above every- 10
thing, even economics. They are incredibly wasteful. Neat people throw away several toys every time they walk through the den. I knew a neat person once who threw away a perfectly good dish drainer because it had mold on it. The drainer was too much trouble to wash. And neat people sell their furniture when they move. They will sell a La-Z-Boy recliner while you are reclining in it.

Neat people are no good to borrow from. 11
Neat people buy everything in expensive little single portions. They get their flour and sugar in two-pound bags. They wouldn't consider clipping a coupon, saving a leftover, reusing plastic non-dairy whipped cream containers or rinsing off tin foil and draping it over the unmoldy dish drainer. You can never borrow a neat person's newspaper to see what's playing at the movies. Neat people have the paper all wadded up and in the trash by 7:05 A.M.

Neat people cut a clean swath through 12
the organic as well as the inorganic world.

People, animals, and things are all one to them. They are so insensitive. After they've finished with the pantry, the medicine cabinet, and the attic, they will throw out the red geranium (too many leaves), sell the dog (too many fleas), and send the children off to boarding school (too many scuffmarks on the hardwood floors).

Choose the best meaning of each word in **bold**. Use context clues to make your choice.

Vocabulary in Context ______ **1.** Sloppy people carry in their mind's eye a heavenly vision, a precise plan, that is so **stupendous,** so perfect, it can't be achieved in this world or the next. (paragraph 2)

a. stupid
b. huge
c. predictable
d. complete

Vocabulary in Context ______ **2.** They have **cavalier** attitudes toward possessions, including family heirlooms. (paragraph 6)

a. worried
b. destructive
c. considerate
d. careless

Central Idea ______ **3.** Which sentence is the best statement of the central idea of the passage?

a. I've finally figured out the difference between neat people and sloppy people.
b. The distinction is, as always, moral.
c. Neat people are lazier and meaner than sloppy people.
d. Sloppy people, you see, are not really sloppy.

Main Idea ______ **4.** Which sentence is the best statement of the main idea of paragraph 3?

a. Sloppy people live in Never-Never Land.
b. Someday is their métier.
c. Someday they are planning to alphabetize all their books and set up home catalogues.
d. Someday they will go through their wardrobes and mark certain items for tentative mending and certain items for passing on to relatives of similar shape and size.

Supporting Details ______ **5.** Neat people are bums and clods at heart because

a. they can't bear to part with anything.
b. they save everything.
c. everything is a dust catcher to them.
d. they are vicious with the mail.

Supporting Details ______ **6.** The only messy thing in a neat person's house is
a. the trash can.
b. the La-Z-Boy recliner.
c. the moldy dish drainer.
d. the den.

Thought Patterns ______ **7.** The main thought pattern for the essay is
a. example.
b. time order.
c. definition.
d. comparison and contrast.

Thought Patterns ______ **8.** The thought pattern for paragraph 4 is
a. example.
b. time order.
c. definition.
d. comparison and contrast.

Transitions ______ **9.** "Four hours or two weeks into the excavation, the desk looks exactly the same, primarily because the sloppy person is meticulously creating new piles of papers with new headings and scrupulously stopping to read all the old book catalogs before he throws them away. A neat person would just bulldoze the desk." (paragraph 5)

The relationship of ideas between these sentences is
a. contrast.
b. cause and effect.
c. generalization and example.
d. time order

Transitions ______ **10.** "For all these noble reasons and more, sloppy people never get neat." (paragraph 4)

The relationship of ideas within this sentence is
a. time order.
b. example.
c. cause and effect.
d. comparison and contrast.

Fact and Opinion ______ **11.** Overall, the ideas in this passage
a. are based on research and statistics.
b. are based only on the personal experiences of the author.
c. objectively present the views of many people.
d. rely mostly on personal observations and opinions.

Fact and Opinion ______ **12.** "Sloppy people live in Never-Never Land." (paragraph 3)
This sentence from paragraph is a statement of
a. fact.
b. opinion.
c. fact and opinion.

Tone and Purpose ______ **13.** The overall tone of the passage is
a. frank.
b. humorous.
c. objective.
d. mean-spirited.

Tone and Purpose ______ **14.** The tone of paragraph 2 is
a. admiring.
b. ironic.
c. impatient.
d. prideful.

Tone and Purpose ______ **15.** The tone of paragraph 10 is
a. hateful.
b. objective.
c. sarcastic.
d. neutral.

Tone and Purpose ______ **16.** The author's main purpose in "Neat People vs. Sloppy People" is to
a. persuade her readers to avoid being neat people.
b. inform readers about the differences between neat and sloppy people.
c. entertain readers with a humorous observation about the differences between neat and sloppy people.

Inferences ______ **17.** From the article, we can conclude that
a. the author dislikes sloppy people.
b. the author is a sloppy person.
c. sloppy people are more noble than neat people.
d. all neat people are mean.

Inferences ______ **18.** From the details in paragraph 3, we can conclude that
a. sloppy people attach emotional significance to possessions.
b. all sloppy people read *The New Yorker*.
c. sloppy people like arts and crafts.
d. sloppy people are perfectionists.

Inferences ______ **19.** From the details in paragraphs 10 and 11, we can conclude that
a. neat people live in germ-free environments.
b. neat people are rich.
c. neat people are not sentimental.
d. neat people don't read the newspaper.

Argument ______ **20.** The following list contains a claim and supports for the claim. Identify the claim.
a. Neat people place neatness above everything, even economics.
b. Neat people throw away several toys every time they walk through the den.

c. I knew a neat person once who threw away a perfectly good dish drainer because it had mold on it.
d. And neat people sell their furniture when they move.

## Outlining

Complete the study outline with information from the passage.

Neat people are lazier and meaner than sloppy people.

I. Sloppiness is merely the unfortunate consequence of their

______________________.

A. They save everything, planning someday to file, order, and straighten out the world.

B. They give loving attention to __________.

II. Neat people are bums and clods at heart.

A. They never handle any item _____.

B. They ______ everything away.

## Questions for Discussion and Writing

1. What are the author's central idea and major supporting details? Write your answer as a summary.
2. A stereotype is a generalization that labels a person or a group of people. Do you think Suzanne Britt has stereotyped neat and sloppy people? Explain why or why not?
3. Suzanne Britt writes that the distinction between neat and sloppy people is "moral." What do you think she means by this statement? Do our behaviors reveal our morals or values? Support why or why not with example behaviors.
4. Do you agree with Suzanne Britt's claim "Neat people are lazier and meaner than sloppy people"? Why or Why not?
5. Write an essay in which you contrast two different groups of people: youth/elderly; shy/outgoing; ambitious/lazy; rich/poor.

## EFFECTIVE READER Scorecard

**"Neat People vs. Sloppy People"**

| Skill | Number Correct | | Points | | Total |
|---|---|---|---|---|---|
| ***Vocabulary*** | | | | | |
| Vocabulary in Context (2 items) | ______ | × | 4 | = | ______ |
| ***Comprehension*** | | | | | |
| Central Idea and Main Idea (2 items) | ______ | × | 4 | = | ______ |
| Supporting Details (2 items) | ______ | × | 4 | = | ______ |
| Thought Patterns (2 items) | ______ | × | 4 | = | ______ |
| Transitions (2 items) | ______ | × | 4 | = | ______ |
| Fact and Opinion (2 items) | ______ | × | 4 | = | ______ |
| Tone and Purpose (4 items) | ______ | × | 4 | = | ______ |
| Inferences (3 items) | ______ | × | 4 | = | ______ |
| Argument (1 item) | ______ | × | 4 | = | ______ |
| **Outlining** (4 items) | ______ | × | 5 | = | ______ |
| | | | Comprehension Score | | ______ |

READING 9

# How the Crab Apple Grew

*by Garrison Keillor*

Garrison Keillor is a storyteller, humorist, author, and creator and host of the award-winning weekly radio show *A Prairie Home Companion*, which has been on the air for over 30 years. Millions of listeners have been entertained by Keillor's yarns of the simple life in fictitious Lake Wobegon, where, according to Keillor, "the women are strong, the men are good-looking, and all the children are above average." His radio show inspired the 2006 movie, *A Prairie Home Companion*, for which he wrote the script and played the main character. In addition, he is the creator and host of the syndicated daily radio feature *A Writer's Almanac*, which has aired on NPR since 1993. A prolific writer, he has penned over a dozen books. The following essay, from *Leaving Home*, first published in 1986, stands as a classic example a well-crafted story of wit and wisdom.

**Vocabulary Preview**

*lanky* (paragraph 11): tall, thin, long-limbed
*en route* (paragraph 12): on the way
*aviator* (paragraph 12): pilot
*aerial* (paragraph 12): above ground, in flight, mid-air
*Vaya con Dios* (paragraph 12): Spanish expression for "Go with God"
*reckoned with* (paragraph 14): idiom for "taken seriously"
*aviation* (paragraph 17): flying
*address* (paragraph 18): speech

---

1 It has been a quiet week in Lake Wobegon. It was warm and sunny on Sunday, and on Monday the flowering crab in the Dieners' backyard burst into blossom. Suddenly, in the morning, when everyone turned their backs for a minute, the tree threw off its bathrobe and stood trembling, purple, naked, revealing all its innermost flowers. When you saw it standing where weeks before had been a bare stick stuck in the dirt, you had to stop; it made your head spin.

2 Becky Diener sat upstairs in her bedroom and looked at the tree. She was stuck on an assignment from Miss Melrose for English, a 750-word personal essay, "Describe your backyard as if you were seeing it for the first time." After an hour she had thirty-nine words, which she figured would mean she'd finish at 1:45 P.M. Tuesday, four hours late, and therefore would get an F even if the essay was great, which it certainly wasn't.

3 How can you describe your backyard as if you'd never seen it? If you'd never seen it, you'd have grown up someplace else, and wouldn't be yourself; you'd be someone else entirely, and how are you supposed to know what that person would think?

4 She imagined seeing the backyard in 1996, returning home from Hollywood. "Welcome Becky!" said the big white banner across McKinley Street as the pink convertible drove slowly along, everyone clapping and cheering as she cruised by, Becky Belafonte the movie star, and got off at her old house. "Here," she said to the reporters, "is where I sat as a child and dreamed my dreams, under this beautiful flowering crab. I dreamed I was a Chinese princess." Then a reporter asked, "Which of your teachers was the most important to you, encouraging you and inspiring you?" And just then she saw an old woman's face in the crowd, Miss Melrose pleading, whispering, "Say me, oh please, say me," and Becky looked straight at her as she said, "Oh, there were so many, I couldn't pick out one, they were all about the same, you know. But perhaps Miss-Miss—oh, I can't remember her name—she taught English, I think—Miss Milross? She was one of them. But there were so many."

5 She looked at her essay. "In my backyard is a tree that has always been extremely important to me since I was six years old when my dad came home one evening with this bag in the trunk and he said, 'Come here and help me plant this'—"

6 She crumpled the sheet of paper and started again.

7 "One evening when I was six years old, my father arrived home as he customarily did around 5:30 or 6:00 P.M. except this evening he had a wonderful surprise for me, he said, as he led me toward the car.

"My father is not the sort of person who does surprising things very often so naturally I was excited that evening when he said he had something for me in the car, having just come home from work where he had been. I was six years old at the time." 8

She took out a fresh sheet. "Six years old was a very special age for me and one thing that made it special was when my dad and I planted a tree together in our backyard. Now it is grown and every spring it gives off large purple blossoms . . ." 9

The tree was planted by her dad, Harold, in 1976, ten years after he married her mother, Marlys. They grew up on Taft Street, across from each other, a block from the ball field. They liked each other tremendously, and then they were in love, as much as you can be when you're so young. Thirteen and fourteen years old and sixteen and seventeen: they looked at each other a lot. She came and sat in his backyard to talk with his mother and help her shell peas but really to look at Harold as he mowed the lawn, and then he disappeared into the house and she sat waiting for him, and of course he was in the kitchen looking out at her. It's how we all began, when our parents looked at each other, as we say, "when you were just a gleam in your father's eye," or your mother's, depending on who saw who first. 10

Marlys was long-legged, **lanky**, had short black hair and sharp eyes that didn't miss anything. She came over to visit the Dieners every chance she got. Her father was a lost cause, like the Confederacy, like the search for the Northwest Passage. He'd been prayed for and suffered for and fought for 11 and spoken for, by people who loved him dearly, and when all was said and done, he just reached for the gin bottle and said, "I don't know what you're talking about," and he didn't. He was a sore embarrassment to Marlys, a clown, a joke, and she watched Harold for evidence that he wasn't similar. One night she dropped in at the Dieners' and came upon a party where Harold, now nineteen, and his friends were drinking beer by the pail. Harold flopped down on his back and put his legs in the air and a pal put a lit match up to Harold's rear end and blue flame came out like a blowtorch, and Marlys went home disgusted and didn't speak to him for two years.

12 Harold went crazy. She graduated from high school and started attending dances with a geography teacher named Stu Jasperson, who was tall and dark-haired, a subscriber to *Time* magazine, educated at Saint Cloud Normal School, and who flew a red Piper Cub airplane. Lake Wobegon had no airstrip except for Tollerud's pasture, so Stu kept his plane in Saint Cloud. When he was **en route** to and from the plane was almost the only time Harold got to see Marlys and try to talk sense into her. But she was crazy about Stu the **aviator**, not Harold the hardware clerk, and in an hour Stu came buzzing overhead doing loops and dives and dipping his wings. Harold prayed for him to crash. Marlys thought Stu was the sun and the moon; all Harold could do was sit and watch her, in the backyard, staring up, her hand shielding her eyes, saying, "Oh, isn't he marvelous?" as Stu performed **aerial** feats and then shut off the throttle and glided overhead singing "**Vaya con Dios**" to her. "Yes, he is marvelous," said Harold, thinking, "DIE DIE DIE."

That spring, Marlys was in charge of the Sweethearts Banquet at the Lutheran church. Irene Holm had put on a fancy winter Sweethearts Banquet with roast lamb, and Marlys wanted to top her and serve roast beef with morel mushrooms, a first for a church supper in Lake Wobegon. Once Irene had referred to Marlys's dad as a lush. 13

Morel mushrooms are a great delicacy. They are found in the wild by people who walk fifteen miles through the woods to get ten of them and then never tell the location to a soul, not even on their deathbeds to a priest. So Marlys's serving them at the banquet would be like putting out emeralds for party favors. It would blow Irene Holm out of the water and show people that even if Marlys's dad was a lush, she was still someone to be **reckoned with**. 14

Two men felt the call to go and search for morels: Harold put on his Red Wing boots and knapsack and headed out one evening with a flashlight. He was in the woods all night. Morels are found near the base of the trunk of a dead elm that's been dead three years, which you can see by the way moonlight doesn't shine on it, and he thought he knew where some were, but around midnight he spotted a bunch of flashlights behind him, a posse of **morelists** bobbing along on his trail, so he veered off and hiked five miles in the wrong direction to confuse them, and by then the sun was coming up so he went home to sleep. He woke at 2:00 P.M., hearing Stu flying overhead, and in an instant he knew. Dead elms! Of course! Stu could spot them from the air, send his ground crew to collect them for Marlys, and the Sweethearts Banquet would be their engagement dinner. 15

16 Stu might have done just that, but he wanted to put on a show and land the Cub in Lake Wobegon. He circled around and around, and came in low to the west of town, disappearing behind the trees. "He's going to crash!" cried Marlys, and they all jumped in their cars and tore out, expecting to find the young hero lying bloody and torn in the dewy grass, with a dying poem on his lips. But there he was standing tall beside the craft, having landed successfully in a field of spring wheat. They all mobbed around him, and he told how he was going up to find the morels and bring them back for Marlys.

17 There were about forty people there. They seemed to enjoy it, so he drew out his speech, talking about the lure of **aviation** and his boyhood and various things so serious that he didn't notice Harold behind him by the plane or notice the people who noticed what Harold was doing and laughed. Stu was too inspired to pay attention to the laughter. He talked about how he once wanted to fly to see the world but once you get up in the air you can see that Lake Wobegon is the most beautiful place of all, a lot of warm horse manure like that, and then he gave them a big manly smile and donned his flying cap and scarf and favored them with a second and third smile and a wave, and he turned and there was Harold to help him into the cockpit.

18 "Well, thanks," said Stu, "mighty kind, mighty kind." Harold jumped to the propeller and threw it once and twice, and the third time the engine fired, and Stu adjusted the throttle, checked the gauges, flapped the flaps, fit his goggles, and never noticed the ground was wet and his wheels were sunk in. He'd parked in a wet spot, and then during his **address** someone had gone around and made it wetter, so when Stu pulled back on the throttle the Cub just sat, and he gave it more juice and she creaked a little, and he gave it more and the plane stood on its head with its tail in the air and dug in.

It pitched forward like the *Titanic*, and 19
the propeller in the mud sounded like he'd eaten too many green apples. The door opened and Stu climbed out, trying to look dignified and studious as he tilted eastward and spun, and Harold said, "Stu, we didn't say we wanted those mushrooms sliced."

Harold went out that afternoon and col- 20
lected five hundred morel mushrooms around one dead elm tree. Marlys made her mark at the Sweethearts dinner, amazing Irene Holm, who had thought Marlys was common. Harold also brought out of the woods a bouquet of flowering crab apple and asked her to marry him, and eventually she decided to.

The tree in the backyard came about a 21
few years afterward. They'd been married awhile, had two kids, and some of the gloss had worn off their life, and one afternoon, Harold, trying to impress his kids and make his wife laugh, jumped off the garage roof, pretending he could fly, and landed wrong, twisting his ankle. He lay in pain, his eyes full of tears, and his kids said, "Oh poor Daddy, poor Daddy," and Marlys said, "You're not funny, you're ridiculous. "

He got up on his bum ankle and went 22
in the woods and got her a pint of morels and a branch from the flowering crab apple. He cut a root from another crab apple and planted the root in the ground. "Look, kids," he said. He sharpened the branch with his hatchet and split the root open and stuck the branch in and wrapped a cloth

around it and said, "Now, there, that will be a tree." They said, "Daddy, will that really be a tree?" He said, "Yes." Marlys said, "Don't be ridiculous."

23 He watered it and tended it and, more than that, he came out late at night and bent down and said, "GROW. GROW. GROW." The **graft** held, it grew, and one year it was interesting, and the next it was impressive and then wonderful, and finally it was magnificent. It's the most magnificent thing in the Dieners' backyard. Becky finished writing 750 words late that night and lay down to sleep. A backyard is a novel about us, and when we sit there on a summer day, we hear the dialogue and see the characters.

Choose the best meaning of each word in **bold**. Use context clues to make your choice.

Vocabulary in Context ______ **1.** ". . . but around midnight he spotted a bunch of flashlights behind him, a posse of **morelists** bobbing along on his trail . . ." (paragraph 15)

a. people who are moral
b. people hunting for morel mushrooms
c. Harold's friends
d. people who are immoral

Vocabulary in Context ______ **2.** "The **graft** held, it grew, and one year it was interesting, and the next it was impressive and then wonderful, and finally it was magnificent." (paragraph 23)

a. dishonest gain
b. split
c. new plant
d. idea

Central Idea and Main Idea ______ **3.** Which sentence is the best statement of the central idea of the passage?

a. She was stuck on an assignment from Miss Melrose for English, a 750-word personal essay, "Describe your backyard as if you were seeing it for the first time." (paragraph 2)
b. She imagined seeing the backyard in 1996, returning home from Hollywood. (paragraph 4)
c. The tree was planted by her dad, Harold, in 1976, ten years after he married her mother, Marlys. (paragraph 10)
d. A backyard is a novel about us, and when we sit there on a summer day, we hear the dialogue and see the characters. (paragraph 23)

Central Idea and Main Idea ______

**4.** Which sentence is the best statement of the main idea of paragraph 11?

a. Marlys was long-legged, lanky, and had short black hair and sharp eyes that didn't miss anything.
b. She came over to visit the Dieners every chance she got.
c. He was a sore embarrassment to Marlys, a clown, a joke, and she watched Harold for evidence that he wasn't similar.
d. Harold flopped down on his back and put his legs in the air and a pal put a lit match up to Harold's rear end and blue flame came out like a blowtorch, and Marlys went home disgusted and didn't speak to him for two years.

Supporting Details ______

**5.** How many times does Becky begin a new draft of her essay?

a. once
b. twice
c. four times
d. six times

Supporting Details ______

**6.** When was the crab apple tree planted?

a. 1986
b. 1976
c. 1996
d. when Harold and Marlys married

Thought Patterns ______

**7.** The main thought pattern for the overall passage is

a. time order.
b. comparison and contrast.
c. cause and effect.
d. definition and example.

Thought Patterns ______

**8.** The thought pattern for paragraph 14 is

a. definition and example.
b. space order.
c. comparison and contrast.
d. cause and effect.

Transitions ______

**9.** "They are found in the wild by people who walk fifteen miles through the woods to get ten of them and then never tell the location to a soul, not even on their deathbeds to a priest. So Marlys's serving them at the banquet would be like putting out emeralds for party favors." (paragraph 14)

The relationship of ideas between these two sentences is

a. space order.
b. time order.
c. cause and effect.
d. generalization and example.

Transitions ______ **10.** Marlys was long-legged, lanky, had short black hair and sharp eyes that didn't miss anything. (paragraph 11)

The relationship of ideas within this sentence is
a. space order.
b. listing.
c. cause and effect.
d. time order.

Fact and Opinion ______ **11.** Overall, the ideas in this passage
a. are based on research and statistics.
b. are based on an eyewitness account.
c. objectively record an historical event.
d. are fictitious in nature.

Fact and Opinion ______ **12.** "It has been a quiet week in Lake Wobegon."
This statement from paragraph 1 is a statement of
a. fact.
b. opinion.
c. fact and opinion.

Tone and Purpose ______ **13.** The overall tone of the passage is
a. hopeful.
b. bitter.
c. bored.
d. humorous.

Tone and Purpose ______ **14.** The tone of paragraph 3 is
a. hopeful.
b. fearful.
c. puzzled.
d. angry.

Tone and Purpose ______ **15.** The tone of paragraph 20 is
a. matter of fact.
b. disinterested.
c. romantic.
d. gleeful.

Tone and Purpose ______ **16.** The author's main purpose in "How the Crab Apple Grew" is
a. to inform the reader about how to write an essay and grow a crab apple tree.
b. to persuade the reader to appreciate family.
c. to entertain the reader with an instructive story.

Inferences ______ **17.** Which of the following statements is a valid conclusion based on the ideas in paragraph 17?
a. Stu is self-absorbed.
b. Stu has a good sense of humor.
c. Stu is humble.
d. Stu is smarter than Harold.

Inferences ______ **18.** From the passage, we can conclude that
a. The crab apple tree symbolizes love.
b. The crab apple tree symbolizes Becky's dreams of success.
c. The crab apple tree represents Harold's insecurity.
d. The crab apple tree and the Morel mushrooms are status symbols.

Inferences ______ **19.** The details in paragraphs 2 through 9 imply that
a. Becky enjoys writing essays.
b. Becky hates her English teacher.
c. Becky will have to turn her assignment in late.
d. Becky is frustrated and having a hard time writing her essay.

Argument ______ **20.** The following list of ideas contains a central claim and the supports for that claim. In the given space, write the letter of the claim.
a. They had been married for a while and had two kids.
b. One afternoon, Harold, trying to impress his kids and make his wife laugh, jumped off the garage roof, pretending he could fly, and landed wrong, twisting his ankle.
c. He lay in pain, his eyes full of tears, and his kids said, "Oh poor Daddy, poor Daddy."
d. Marlys said, "You're not funny, you're ridiculous."

## Mapping

"How the Crab Apple Tree Grew" is very well organized in its telling of the events. Keillor divided the story into four distinct phases to make his point.

Complete the time line below. Fill in the blanks with the central point and the missing supporting details from the passage. Paragraph numbers are given in parentheses.

**Central Point:** ____________________________________________

____________________________________________

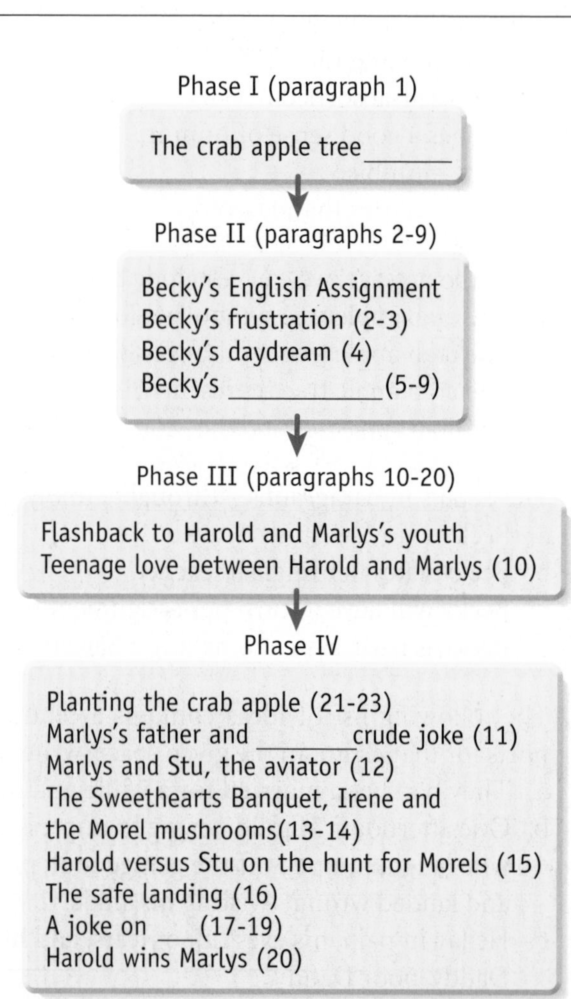


## Questions for Discussion and Writing

1. What are the author's central idea and major supporting details? Write your answer as a summary.
2. The first half of the essay describes Becky's struggle to write an essay for an English class. How does she feel about the assignment? Her teacher?

How do you know she feels these things? Describe Becky's writing process. Why was she stuck? How did she get started? How do your experiences as a writer compare to Becky's? Do you like to write? What is your writing process?

3. How would you describe Harold and Marlys's feelings for each other? Would you say this is a love story? Is Harold a loving father and husband? Support your answers with details from the passage.

4. The essay begins and ends with the image of the crab apple tree. What do you think the tree symbolizes? Support your answer with details from the passage.

5. Explain what the author means by the following statement: "A backyard is a novel about us, and when we sit there on a summer day, we hear the dialogue and see the characters."

## EFFECTIVE READER Scorecard

**How the Crab Apple Grew**

| Skill | Number Correct | | Points | | Total |
|---|---|---|---|---|---|
| ***Vocabulary*** | | | | | |
| Vocabulary in Context (2 items) | ______ | × | 4 | = | ______ |
| ***Comprehension*** | | | | | |
| Central Idea and Main Idea (2 items) | ______ | × | 4 | = | ______ |
| Supporting Details (2 items) | ______ | × | 4 | = | ______ |
| Thought Patterns (2 items) | ______ | × | 4 | = | ______ |
| Transitions (2 items) | ______ | × | 4 | = | ______ |
| Fact and Opinion (2 items) | ______ | × | 4 | = | ______ |
| Tone and Purpose (4 items) | ______ | × | 4 | = | ______ |
| Inferences (3 items) | ______ | × | 4 | = | ______ |
| Argument (1 item) | ______ | × | 4 | = | ______ |
| **Mapping** (5 items) | ______ | × | 4 | = | ______ |
| | | | Comprehension Score | | ______ |

READING 10

# Coming Out, the First Time

*by Betty DeGeneres*

Betty DeGeneres is the mother of comedian Ellen DeGeneres, who famously came out in 1997 as a lesbian on her hit television show, *Ellen*. Betty DeGeneres has served as the Human Rights Campaign's (HRC) National Coming Out spokesperson since 1978. She is the author of two books: *Love, Ellen* and *Just a Mom*. Betty also writes an advice column, "Ask Betty," for *PlanetOut* on issues of coming out and acceptance. The following essay is an excerpt from the prologue of *Love, Ellen*, in which she tells about her journey with her daughter.

**Vocabulary Preview**

*embarked* (paragraph 9): set out, started
*assumption* (paragraph 16): a guess, theory
*derogatory* (paragraph 16): insulting, belittling
*frivolous* (paragraph 17): thoughtless, silly
*retrospect* (paragraph 19): looking back

---

1 Three words, spoken two decades ago by my daughter Ellen at the age of twenty, changed my life forever. In an instant, her bombshell shattered many of my long-held beliefs about who she was, who I was, and about life itself.

2 Nothing in the months, days, hours, or minutes leading up to that moment could have prepared me for what she would tell me that day. Twenty minutes earlier, just before Ellen suggested we go for a walk on the beach, we had been enjoying a large, relatively uneventful family gathering in Pass Christian on the Mississippi Gulf Coast.

3 This small beach community is an hour's drive from New Orleans, Louisiana, where I grew up and raised my two kids, Vance and Ellen. It is where my oldest sister, Helen, lived for many years with her family in their lovely, comfortable home on West Beach Boulevard, facing the water. The house, set far back from the boulevard, has a wide screened porch and a large front yard full of shade trees. Inside, the spacious living room has a well-used fireplace and the large dining room opens onto a cozy sunroom.

4 From the time our kids were small, Helen's was an ideal place to gather for holidays and other happy occasions. At Thanksgiving, Christmas, summer picnic reunions, and other celebrations our number would swell, with grandparents, cousins, uncles, aunts, nieces, nephews, and a few neighbors and friends. Lots of us! Yet we never felt that

we were intruding or had overstayed our welcome.

5 For those winter holiday feasts, the dining room always managed to **accommodate** us all; afterward we'd share long, leisurely hours by the fire. In warm weather, we always ate outdoors, at picnic tables in the front yard. We have home movies of all the children swinging on a rope tied to a tall tree branch. They'd stand on a picnic table to catch it as it swung by.

6 To escape the heat we could sit on the screened porch or relax in a hammock. Of course, when it was really hot, everyone headed for the beach—to sit on the sand or swim or go sailing in the Sunfish.

7 The house on West Beach Boulevard has a wealth of cherished memories for me. Like old photographs, many of those happy moments have faded in my mind with the passage of time, the different years blurring one into the next. And yet, I can vividly recall this particular life-changing visit, which came at the end of the summer of 1978.

8 At the time, I was living eight hours away in Atlanta, Texas, with my then husband, whom I had married after divorcing Vance and Ellen's father several years earlier. Vance, the older of my two kids, couldn't be with us; he was in Yuma, Arizona, finishing up his two years of service in the Marines, after already having started to make a name for himself in comedy writing and rock music. Ellen, however, was able to make it. She was living just an hour away in New Orleans at her dad's house, so she rode over to Helen's with us.

9 That meant a chance to do some catching up. Living so far away from each other was hard on both of us. We were always extremely close and missed the luxury of being together on a daily basis. In those days, Ellen was still struggling to find a direction for herself. After graduating from high school, she had tried college for all of a month, only to conclude that wasn't for her. She then **embarked** on what would ultimately become one of the longest lists of jobs known to humankind—everything from vacuum cleaner salesperson to oyster shucker—before finding her true calling. But even then, Ellen had a knack for describing even the most mundane details of her struggles and making them sound hilarious or dramatic. That weekend was no exception. So I had no reason to suspect that anything was different or out of the ordinary about Ellen.

10 Nor did it seem unusual when, after we all finished dinner late that afternoon, El said to me, "Let's go out for one more walk on the beach."

11 When we crossed West Beach Boulevard and walked down the steps of the seawall, I began to sense that she had something on her mind. Probably, I imagined, it was her latest job, or maybe a new boyfriend. But we weren't really talking much as we walked across the broad, sandy beach down to the hard-packed sand by the water's edge. The cool salty breeze felt wonderful as we walked along and my daughter, at my side, was a pretty sight. With her straight blond hair and her sparkling blue eyes, she really was the essence of the girl next door. What a treat to be together, walking along quietly.

12 But suddenly Ellen stopped, and I turned back to see why. She had tears in her eyes, which alarmed me. As I walked toward her in concern, she began to cry, and it was then that she sobbed with a depth of emotion

I will never forget and spoke those three words: "Mom, I'm gay."

13 In my mind, everything stopped. This was the biggest shock of my life and the last thing I had ever expected to hear. Still reeling, I reached out to comfort her. She was upset and crying, so I did the most natural thing a mother would do—I took her into my arms and hugged her. No mother wants to see her child in pain.

14 Reassuring her that I loved her was my first priority. But it would take time for the words she had just spoken to sink in. There was no way I could comprehend or process or accept this news immediately. My shock was coupled with disbelief. As close as we were, this was not the Ellen I knew. On the other hand, if we had been living in the same city and had been in more constant touch, I probably would have had some clues.

15 It was my turn to talk, but I didn't know what to say. A hundred different thoughts and emotions were racing through me. In my mind I was frantically reaching, searching for any question, any argument, that would bring her back to her senses—back to being the lovely, young heterosexual daughter she always had been.

16 *Heterosexual daughter.* That thought gripped me. It is such a natural **assumption** that we don't even have to consider the word. It isn't even in our usual vocabulary. We just are. But now, I had to consider another word that wasn't in my usual vocabulary—homosexual. *My homosexual daughter—just* thinking those strange words brought on a new wave of emotion that I recognized as fear. I feared for Ellen's well-being, given society's prejudiced and negative attitudes. Though I had almost no exposure to gay people at all, I knew the **derogatory** names used for them, and I didn't want my daughter called those names.

And, then, of all things, as I was hugging 17
Ellen and waiting for her tears to subside, the most **frivolous** but upsetting thought came out of nowhere. Now, I sadly realized, El's engagement picture would never appear in the New Orleans newspaper.

In those days, whenever I was home for 18
a visit, I'd always look at the engagement announcements of young women in the *Times Picayune,* and I would often recognize the maiden name of the mother—a friend from high school or college. I had always fantasized about seeing Ellen's picture there and about her marrying some fine young man and about myself as the proud mother of the bride.

In **retrospect**, it's ironic that although 19
Ellen never had an engagement picture in my hometown paper, in years to come she would be a featured celebrity not only in the *Picayune* but on the covers of magazines and papers all over the world. At that time, however, such fame was far beyond my fantasies. I felt as if a dream had been shattered. Only later would I understand that my disappointment was not for Ellen. It was for me. I was the one whose marriages hadn't worked out according to expectations. Why on earth should she have to fulfill my dreams? Why not love her and support her as she fulfilled her own?

When I finally found my voice, I asked, 20
"Are you sure?" The question hung in the air. It sounded judgmental. I softened it, saying, "I mean, couldn't this just be a phase?"

Ellen almost smiled. "No, Mother," she 21
said. "It's not a phase. I'm sure."

22 More questions followed: "How do you know?" "How long have you known?"

23 Ellen tried to answer truthfully. "I think I've always known, but I didn't know what to call it. Now I do. I'm gay, Mom."

24 It was getting dark, and when we started back to the house, she reminded me of a movie we had seen together a couple of years earlier. As I recall, it was *Valley of the Dolls*, or something like that. Ellen said, "You know that scene when the two girls were touching and hugging, I thought that was gross. I'd never seen anything like that before. But then it happened to me, and it wasn't gross, Mom."

25 She told me more about her first experience. She also told me that a friendship formed after her return to New Orleans was more than that. Ellen felt that she was in love.

26 Even as I tried to understand, I was in a state of denial. "But, Ellen, boys have always liked you, and you're so popular. You just need to meet the right one."

27 She shook her head. "I've dated a lot of nice boys. That's not who I am." Ellen's expression was wistful and solemn, yet also relieved—as if a burden had been lifted off her. I was feeling many things at that point, but relief wasn't one of them.

We walked back into the house. We were 28
not the same mother and daughter who had left thirty minutes before. We looked the same, but we were not. Nobody else knew—not for a while. Now we had a secret.

Every family of a gay person has its own 29
story. This was ours, a story that would develop and unfold in many surprising ways.

Over the next years, we corresponded, 30
we wrote poems to each other, we talked on the phone, we laughed, and we cried. We never lost close contact. "Love, Ellen," or some form thereof, was how she signed off every time she ended a letter or said good-bye after a talk. That love was never taken for granted, on either side.

Ever so slowly, as I met her friends and 31
her partners, I relaxed, seeing how very happy she was—and is. Along the way, I learned many lessons about what it means to be human, lessons about love and courage and honesty.

Choose the best meaning of each word in **bold**. Use context clues to make your choice.

Vocabulary in Context ______ **1.** "For those winter holiday feasts, the dining room always managed to **accommodate** us all . . . " (paragraph 5)

a. accept
b. frustrate
c. contain
d. crowd

Vocabulary in Context ______ **2.** "But even then, Ellen had a knack for describing even the most **mundane** details of her struggles and making them sound hilarious or dramatic." (paragraph 9)

a. startling
b. ordinary
c. embarrassing
d. entertaining

Central Idea ______ **3.** Which sentence is the best statement of the central idea of the passage?

a. Three words, spoken two decades ago by my daughter Ellen at the age of twenty, changed my life forever. (paragraph 1)
b. Nothing in the months, days, hours, or minutes leading up to that moment could have prepared me for what she would tell me that day. (paragraph 2)
c. Twenty minutes earlier, just before Ellen suggested we go for a walk on the beach, we had been enjoying a large, relatively uneventful family gathering in Pass Christian on the Mississippi Gulf Coast. (paragraph 2)
d. Along the way, I learned many lessons about what it means to be human, lessons about love and courage and honesty. (paragraph 31)

Main Idea ______ **4.** Which sentence is the best statement of the main idea of paragraph 4?

a. From the time our kids were small, Helen's was an ideal place to gather for holidays and other happy occasions.
b. At Thanksgiving, Christmas, summer picnic reunions, and other celebrations our number would swell, with grandparents, cousins, uncles, aunts, nieces, nephews, and a few neighbors and friends.
c. Lots of us!
d. Yet we never felt that we were intruding or had overstayed our welcome.

Supporting Details ______ **5.** Pass Christian on the Mississippi Gulf Coast is

a. the town in which Betty DeGeneres currently lives.
b. where Betty DeGeneres's sister lived.
c. four hours from New Orleans, Louisiana.
d. the town in which Ellen's father lives.

Supporting Details ______ **6.** In 1978, Betty DeGeneres lived in

a. Pass Christian, Mississippi.
b. New Orleans, Louisiana.
c. Atlanta, Texas.

Thought Patterns ______ **7.** The main thought pattern for the overall passage is

a. a definition and example of tolerance and acceptance.
b. the causes and effects of being gay.
c. the series of events that occurred the day Betty DeGeneres learned that her daughter Ellen was gay.
d. an argument for tolerance and acceptance of others.

Thought Patterns ______ **8.** The thought pattern for paragraph 2 is

a. cause and effect.
b. time order.
c. definition and example.
d. listing.

Transitions ______ **9.** "What a treat to be together, walking along quietly. But suddenly Ellen stopped, and I turned back to see why." (paragraphs 11 and 12)

The relationship of ideas between these two sentences is

a. contrast.
b. cause and effect.
c. listing.
d. space order.

Transitions ______ **10.** "She was upset and crying, so I did the most natural thing a mother would do—I took her into my arms." (paragraph 13)

The relationship of ideas within this sentence is

a. contrast.
b. cause and effect.
c. listing.
d. space order.

Fact and Opinion ______ **11.** Overall, the ideas in this passage are based on

a. research.
b. the research, observations, and personal experience of the author.
c. a blend of factual details and the author's personal experience and observations.
d. an expert opinion.

Fact and Opinion ______ **12.** "This small beach community is an hour's drive from New Orleans, Louisiana, where I grew up and raised my kids."

This sentence from paragraph 3 is a

a. fact.
b. opinion.
c. fact and opinion.

Tone and Purpose ______ **13.** The overall tone of the passage is

a. forthright.
b. embarrassed.
c. preachy.
d. indignant.

Tone and Purpose ______ **14.** "The cool salty breeze felt wonderful as we walked along and my daughter, at my side, was a pretty sight. With her straight blond hair and her sparkling blue eyes, she really was the essence of the girl next door."

The tone of these sentences from paragraph 11 is

a. curious.
b. objective.
c. boastful.
d. satisfied.

Tone and Purpose ______ **15.** The tone of paragraph 16 is

a. neutral.
b. concerned.
c. condemning.
d. angry.

Tone and Purpose ______ **16.** The author's main purpose in "Coming Out, the First Time" is

a. to persuade readers to be more accepting of others.
b. to entertain readers with a personal glimpse into a celebrity's personal life.
c. to inform readers of the courage, honesty, and love necessary for acceptance.

Inferences ______ **17.** The reading suggests that

a. Ellen did not want to disclose her homosexuality to her mother.
b. a shocking event can have a positive outcome.
c. homosexuality is widely accepted in society.
d. Betty DeGeneres was angry at Ellen.

Inferences ______ **18.** The details in paragraph 4 imply that this family

a. is warm and loving.
b. gets together on a weekly basis.
c. rarely gets together.
d. doesn't keep secrets.

Inferences ______ **19.** The details in paragraph 12 imply that

a. Ellen is unhappy about being gay.
b. Betty is unhappy about Ellen being gay.
c. Ellen struggled with the task of telling her mother that she, Ellen, was gay.
d. Betty made it difficult for Ellen to confide in her.

Argument ______ **20.** The following list of ideas contains a central claim and the supports for that claim. In the given space, write the letter of the claim.

a. But even then, Ellen had a knack for describing even the most mundane details of her struggles and making them sound hilarious or dramatic.
b. That weekend was no exception.
c. So I had no reason to suspect that anything was different or out of the ordinary about Ellen.
d. Nor did it seem unusual when, after we all finished dinner late that afternoon, El said to me, "Let's go out for one more walk on the beach."

## Outlining

Complete the outline with ideas from the passage.

Central Idea: ______________________________________________

______________________________________________.

I. Where she spoke the three words
   A. The town, Pass Christian, Mississippi
   B. A family gathering at Helen's house

II. Living far away from each other
   A. Betty in ________, Texas
   B. Ellen in ___________, Louisiana

III. The disclosure
   A. A walk on the beach
   B. Ellen's tearful admission

IV. ________ reaction
   A. Shock
   B. Concern
   C. Acceptance

## Questions for Discussion and Writing

1. What is the author's central idea and major supporting points? Write your answers as a summary.
2. Have you or someone you know ever had to make a difficult confession that would disappoint or upset others? What makes such a confession so difficult? What advice would you give to someone who needed to disclose sensitive information?
3. Betty DeGeneres thought she knew her daughter. When she learned about Ellen's homosexuality, she was shocked. How do you think she handled the situation? What did she do that was admirable? Was there anything she said or did that she shouldn't have? Why or Why not?
4. Have you or someone you know suffered rejection or ridicule for being different? Why are people so quick to reject someone who is different?

What advice would you give to the person being rejected? The person who is intolerant?

5. Betty DeGeneres has devoted her life to promoting acceptance and tolerance. Her relationship with her daughter, and her daughter's struggle to fit into society inspired her commitment. Why is it that we often don't get involved unless an issue directly affects us? What is one cause you think is worthy of support? How can you become involved?

## EFFECTIVE READER Scorecard

**"Coming Out, the First Time"**

| Skill | Number Correct | | Points | | Total |
|---|---|---|---|---|---|
| ***Vocabulary*** | | | | | |
| Vocabulary in Context (2 items) | _____ | × | 4 | = | _____ |
| ***Comprehension*** | | | | | |
| Central Idea and Main Idea (2 items) | _____ | × | 4 | = | _____ |
| Supporting Details (2 items) | _____ | × | 4 | = | _____ |
| Thought Patterns (2 items) | _____ | × | 4 | = | _____ |
| Transitions (2 items) | _____ | × | 4 | = | _____ |
| Fact and Opinion (2 items) | _____ | × | 4 | = | _____ |
| Tone and Purpose (4 items) | _____ | × | 4 | = | _____ |
| Inferences (3 items) | _____ | × | 4 | = | _____ |
| Argument (1 item) | _____ | × | 4 | = | _____ |
| **Outlining** (4 items) | _____ | × | 5 | = | _____ |
| | | | Comprehension Score | | _____ |

PART THREE

# Combined-Skills Tests

Part Three contains 15 tests. The purpose of these tests is twofold: to track your growth as a reader and to prepare you for the formal tests you will face as you take college courses. Each test presents a reading passage and questions that cover some or all of the following skills: vocabulary in context, central ideas, supporting details, thought patterns, inferences, tone and purpose, fact and opinion, and argument.

# Test 1

Read the following passage, and then answer the questions.

**How Do You Rescue a Horse?**

[1]How do you rescue a horse? [2]That's a good question. [3]There are 7 million horses in the United States, and every year some of them will need to be rescued from overturned trailers, from collapsed barns, or after riding accidents in the woods or fields. [4]Rescue teams around the country train themselves to rescue people in all kinds of emergencies and disasters. [5]They train themselves to rescue animals, too.

[6]The Felton Volunteer Fire Department, in California, for example, is developing a training manual for how to rescue large animals. [7]They also do training using—listen to this—a horse mannequin!

[8]The horse mannequin is named Lucky. [9]He is life-sized—15 hands tall—so that firefighters and rescue workers get a taste of really what it would be like to work with such a large animal. [10]It can be used in all weather, even mud and water. [11]When emergency responders are trained to help large animals, they are much more likely to save the animal's life and keep themselves from being injured in the process.

—Federal Emergency Management Agency, "How Do You Rescue a Horse?"

**VISUAL VOCABULARY**

The best meaning of the word *cumbersome* is ________

a. awkward.
b. tedious.

► Rescuing a large animal like "Lucky" can be dangerous because of the animal's *cumbersome* size.

Vocabulary ______ **1.** The best meaning of the word *mannequin* as used in sentences 7 and 8 is
a. little man.
b. model.
c. volunteer.
d. little horse.

Vocabulary ______ **2.** The best meaning of the word *hand* as used in sentence 9 is
a. a person who helps with work.
b. a unit of measurement.
c. a nickname.
d. a training technique.

Implied Central Idea ______ **3.** Choose the sentence that best states the author's implied central idea.
a. Horses need the help of humans to stay safe and healthy.
b. Rescuing a large animal such as a horse requires training and practice.
c. Horses are prone to accidents.
d. Lucky is an effective training tool for responders to emergencies.

Main Idea, Details ______ **4.** Sentence 9 is a
a. main idea.
b. major supporting detail.
c. minor supporting detail.

Transitions ______ **5.** The relationship between sentences 6 and 7 is one of
a. cause and effect.
b. classification.
c. contrast.
d. addition.

Transitions ______ **6.** The relationship within sentence 11 is one of
a. cause and effect.
b. classification.
c. contrast.
d. example.

Inferences ______ **7.** Choose the inference most soundly based on sentences 8–10.
a. Lucky must be fed and groomed like any other horse.
b. Firefighters and rescue workers train in adverse weather conditions to be as prepared as possible.
c. Firefighters and rescue workers enjoy their work.
d. Lucky is used as a training tool across the country.

Argument ______ **8.** We can conclude that
a. rescuing large animals can be dangerous work.
b. the firefighters and rescue workers become attached to Lucky.
c. horses are the main types of animals that need to be rescued.
d. the Felton Volunteer Fire Department is ahead of the rest of the country in developing training procedures.

Tone ______ **9.** The tone of sentence 7 is
a. matter of fact.
b. bitter.
c. astonished.
d. reflective.

Fact and Opinion ______ **10.** Sentence 2 is a statement of
a. fact.
b. opinion.
c. fact and opinion.

# Test 2

Read the following passage, and then answer the questions.

### Green Power

[1]Green power is electricity generated through the use of renewable resources. [2]Renewable energy sources include the sun, wind, water, heat within the earth, and organic plant and waste material. [3]The terms most often used for these energy sources are solar, wind, hydro, geothermal and biomass energy. [4]These resources don't disappear forever when they are used to produce electricity because they are easily replenished by nature. [5]Some of the most common reasons why people buy green power are to

- Improve human health
- Preserve the earth for their children and grandchildren
- Reduce impact on the environment
- Conserve limited fossil resources

[6]Green power can also offer protection against rising electricity prices.

—American Wind Energy Association, "What Is Green Power?" and "Why Should I Buy Green Power?"

Vocabulary ______ **1.** The best meaning of the word *geothermal* as used in sentence 3 is
a. energy from the sun.
b. energy from wind.
c. energy from the heat within the earth.
d. energy from organic plant and waste material.

Vocabulary ______ **2.** The best meaning of the word *replenished* as used in sentence 4 is
a. depleted.
b. replaced.
c. substituted.
d. seen.

Implied Central Idea ______ **3.** Which is the best statement of the implied central idea of this passage?

a. Green power offers several benefits.
b. Green power is natural.
c. Green power is good for the environment.
d. Renewable resources will save fossil fuel sources.

Central Idea, Details ______ **4.** Sentence 6 is a

a. central idea.
b. major supporting detail.
c. minor supporting detail.

Thought Patterns ______ **5.** The thought pattern for sentences 1–4 is

a. definition.
b. comparison and contrast.
c. time order.
d. cause and effect.

Thought Patterns ______ **6.** The thought pattern for sentences 5–6 is

a. definition.
b. comparison and contrast.
c. time order.
d. cause and effect.

Purpose ______ **7.** The author's main purpose is to

a. inform.
b. entertain.
c. persuade.

**8–10.** Complete the study outline based on information from the passage.

I. Term: Green power

II. Definition: Green power is electricity generated through the use of renewable resources.

III. Examples: Sun (solar)

Wind (wind)

Water (hydro)

Heat within earth (______________)

______________________ (biomass)

IV. Effects: Improves human health

Preserves earth

______________________

Conserves fossil fuels

Protects against rising electricity prices

# Test 3

Read the following passage, and then answer the questions.

**Anorexia Nervosa**

[1]People who deliberately starve themselves or severely restrict their food intake suffer from an eating disorder called **anorexia nervosa.** [2]The disorder usually begins around the time of puberty and leads to extreme weight loss—at least 15 percent below normal body weight. [3]Those who struggle with this problem also have an intense fear of becoming fat, even though they are underweight. [4]Many people with the disorder look emaciated, yet they are convinced that they are overweight. [5]Sometimes they must be hospitalized to prevent death by starvation. [6]Still, they often continue to deny that they have a problem or face any health risk. [7]Food and weight become obsessions. [8]For some, the compulsiveness shows up in strange eating rituals or the refusal to eat in front of others. [9]It is not uncommon for people with anorexia to collect recipes and prepare lavish gourmet feasts for family and friends but not partake in the meals themselves. [10]They may adhere to strict exercise routines to keep off weight. [11]Ninety percent of all anorexics are women.

[12]The most important thing that family and friends can do to help individuals with anorexia is to love them unconditionally. [13]Talk to physicians or counselors for help in determining the best way to approach and deal with the situation. [14]People with anorexia will beg and lie to avoid eating and gaining weight; achieving a cure means giving up the illness and hence giving up the control. [15]Family and friends should not give in to the pleadings of an anorexic patient but should not nag the person incessantly either. [16]Anorexia is an illness that cannot be controlled by simple willpower; professional guidance is needed. [17]Most important is to support the individual without supporting the person's actions.

—Adapted from National Women's Health Information Center, "Anorexia Nervosa."

Vocabulary ______ **1.** The best meaning of the word *emaciated* as used in sentence 4 is

a. wasted.
b. heavy.
c. embarrassed.
d. willful.

Vocabulary ______ **2.** The best meaning of the word *incessantly* as used in sentence 15 is

a. endlessly, all the time.
b. in silence.
c. with violence.
d. with good intentions.

Main Idea ______ **3.** Which sentence best states the main idea of the second paragraph?

a. sentence 12
b. sentence 13
c. sentence 14
d. sentence 15

Implied Central Idea ______ **4.** What is the implied central idea of the passage?

a. Many people suffer with the condition known as anorexia nervosa.
b. Anorexia nervosa is an eating disorder that has horrible consequences.
c. The person suffering with anorexia nervosa faces mental and physical problems and requires the support of others.
d. Those who suffer with anorexia nervosa often deny that they have a life-threatening disorder.

Transitions ______ **5.** The relationship between sentences 5 and 6 is one of

a. time order.
b. example.
c. contrast.
d. cause.

Inferences ______ **6.** Choose the inference that is most soundly based on the information in the passage.

a. Anorexia nervosa is not a serious problem.
b. Anorexia nervosa is the result of childhood trauma.
c. People who suffer with anorexia nervosa are seeking some sort of control over their lives.
d. People who suffer with anorexia nervosa are selfish.

**7–10.** Complete the idea map based on the information in the passage.

7. ______________________________

8. ______________________________

Support of family and friends

Physical problems

9. ______________________________

Professional help

10. ______________________________

Extreme weight loss, possible death

Fear, denial, obsession

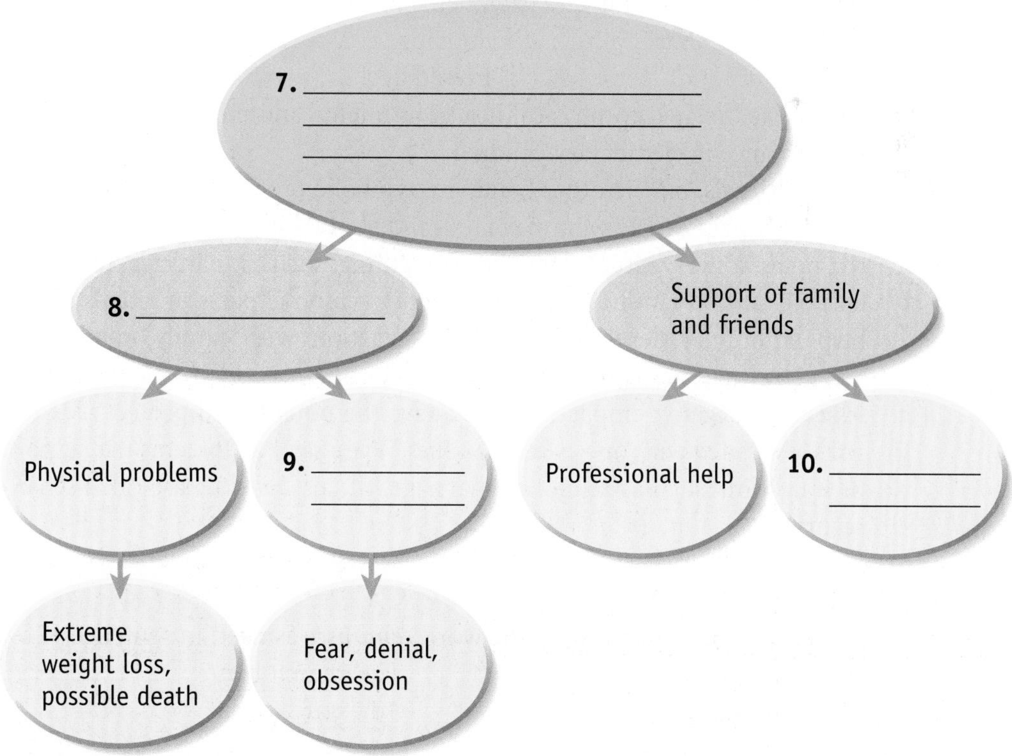

# Test 4

Read the following passage, and then answer the questions.

**The Health of Routines and Rituals**

[1]Routines and rituals are alive and well in the United States—and keeping people well in the process. [2]That's the claim of a review of 50 years of research that appears in the December 2002 issue of the *Journal of Family Psychology*. [3]Many Americans take part in routines and rituals, and these practices help to improve their mental and physical health and sense of belonging, according to the researchers who did the analysis of 32 studies. [4]Routine events, such as evening dinners eaten together as a family, provide comfort simply by being predictable events people can count on, says study author Barbara Fiese, a psychologist at Syracuse University in New York.

[5]Routines are acts done regularly that need to be done, such as eating or preparing for bed, and take time but are seldom thought about afterward, she says. [6]"Having some predictability in life around routines is positive," Fiese says. [7]Children flourish when they can predict things in their life, such as family dinners or regular bedtimes, the study found. [8]Regular family dinners, even if only for 20 minutes a day, are the most common routine. [9]"If you look at dinner time, for example, it's not happening seven days a week but usually four or five times," Fiese says. [10]"Even that short period of time has a positive effect. [11]It's related to physical health in infants and children and academic performance in elementary children."

[12]Rituals, on the other hand, are symbolic practices people do or celebrate that help define who they are—and about which they often reminisce, she notes. [13]Every ritual stands for something, such as marriage, which is an entrance into a family. [14]The meaningful, symbolic parts of rituals seem to help emotional development and satisfaction with family relationships. [15]When rituals are continued during times of stress, such as a divorce, they lessen the negative impact. [16]"They have the potential to protect kids from risks associated with one-parent families," Fiese says. [17]"It seems that at points of transition, such as school or marriage, rituals can increase one's sense of security."

—Adapted from Deutsch, "A Slave to Routine?"

Vocabulary ______ **1.** The best meaning of the word *reminisce* as used in sentence 12 is

a. guess.
b. harp.
c. remember.
d. stare.

Central Idea ______ **2.** The sentence that best states the central idea of the passage is
a. sentence 1.
b. sentence 2.
c. sentence 5.
d. sentence 12.

Transitions ______ **3.** The relationship between sentences 11 and 12 is one of
a. definition and example.
b. cause and effect.
c. time order.
d. comparison and contrast.

Transitions ______ **4.** The relationship of the ideas within sentence 5 is
a. definition and example.
b. cause and effect.
c. time order.
d. comparison and contrast.

Thought Patterns ______ **5.** Which thought pattern does the passage use in addition to definition?
a. comparison
b. effect
c. time order

Supporting Details ______ **6.** Sentence 16 is a
a. central idea.
b. major supporting detail.
c. minor supporting detail.

Purpose ______ **7.** The author's main purpose in the passage is to
a. inform.
b. entertain.
c. persuade.

Tone ______ **8.** The tone of the passage is
a. excited.
b. bossy.
c. objective.
d. pessimistic.

**9–10.** Complete the study outline with information from the passage.

Central idea: ____________________________________________

____________________________________________

I. Routines
   A. Definition: acts done regularly that need to be done and take time but are seldom thought about afterward
   B. Examples
      1. ____________________________________________
      2. Preparing for bed
   C. Effects
      1. Improve physical health in infants and children
      2. Improve academic performance in elementary children

II. Rituals
   A. Definition: symbolic practices people do or celebrate that help define who they are—and about which they often reminisce
   B. Example: Marriage
   C. Effects
      1. Protect children from risks linked to one-parent families
      2. Increase sense of security

# Test 5

Read the following passage, and then answer the questions.

**Wildfires**

[1]Wildfires leave problems behind them, even after the last ember has been extinguished. [2]In July 1994, a wildfire burned 2,000 acres of forest and scrub on the steep slopes of Storm King Mountain, near Glenwood Springs, Colorado. [3]In September 1994, torrential rains triggered debris flows, which poured from this burned area and inundated a 3-mile stretch of Interstate 70 with tons of mud, rock, and other debris. [4]The flows engulfed 30 cars, sweeping two of them into the Colorado River. [5]Some travelers were seriously injured, but fortunately there were no deaths.

[6]Scientists from the Landslides Hazards Program of the United States Geological Survey are studying the link between wildfires and debris flows at Storm King Mountain and sites in several other states. [7]During an intense wildfire, all vegetation may be destroyed; also, the organic material in the soil may be burned away or may decompose into water-repellent substances that prevent water from percolating into the soil. [8]As a result, even normal rainfall may result in unusual erosion or flooding from a burned area; heavy rain can produce destructive debris flows, as happened at Storm King Mountain.

—Adapted from U.S. Geological Survey, "USGS Wildland Fire Research."

Vocabulary ______ **1.** The best meaning of the word *ember* as used in sentence 1 is
a. person.
b. tree.
c. spark.
d. fire hose.

Vocabulary ______ **2.** The best meaning of the word *torrential* in sentence 3 is
a. light.
b. heavy.
c. dark.
d. frightening.

**VISUAL VOCABULARY**

The best meaning of the word *prescribed* is _______

a. set.
b. controlled.

▲ Fire, whether naturally occurring or *prescribed*, has a vital function; it can stimulate growth of native plants and suppress invasion of exotic species.

Central Idea ______ **3.** The central idea of the passage is stated in
a. sentence 1.
b. sentence 2.
c. sentence 6.
d. sentence 8.

Supporting Details ______ **4.** Sentence 4 is a
a. central idea.
b. minor supporting detail.
c. major supporting detail.

Transitions ______ **5.** The relationship between sentences 1 and 2 is one of
a. contrast.
b. effect.
c. example.
d. classification.

Thought Patterns ______ **6.** The overall thought pattern of the first paragraph is
a. time order.
b. comparison.
c. cause and effect.
d. contrast.

Argument ______ **7.** Which of these overall statements does not support the point that wildfires are destructive?
a. A wildfire can destroy thousands of acres of forests.
b. The ash from wildfire is rich with nutrients.
c. A wildfire leaves a water-repellent layer of substances on top of the soil.
d. Burned land is vulnerable to flooding.

Fact and Opinion ______ **8.** Sentence 1 is a statement of
a. fact.
b. opinion.
c. fact and opinion.

Inferences ______ **9.** Based on the information in the passage, we can conclude that
a. a link exists between wildfires and debris flows during flooding.
b. wildfires can be prevented.
c. the loss of human life during wildfires is avoidable.
d. wildfires are caused primarily by human carelessness.

**10.** Complete the study outline based on the information in the passage.

Central idea: Wildfires leave problems behind them, even after the last ember has been extinguished.

I. Example of Storm King Mountain
   A. July 1994 wildfire
   B. September 1994 torrential rains
   C. Combined effect: debris flow
      1. Tons of mud, rock, debris on a 3-mile stretch of Interstate 70
      2. 30 cars engulfed; 2 swept into Colorado River
      3. Human injuries, no deaths

II. ______________________________
   A. Vegetation and organic material burned away
   B. Water-repellent substances layer over soil
   C. Rainfall leads to erosion, flooding, and debris flows

# Test 6

Read the following passage, and then answer the questions.

**"Boyhood Days"**

**Taken from *Up from Slavery* by Booker T. Washington**

[1]From the time that I can remember having any thoughts about anything, I recall that I had an intense longing to learn to read. [2]I determined, when quite a small child, that, if I accomplished nothing else in life, I would in some way get enough education to enable me to read common books and newspapers. [3]Soon after we got settled in some manner in our new cabin in West Virginia, I induced my mother to get hold of a book for me. [4]How or where she got it I do not know, but in some way she procured an old copy of Webster's "blue-back" spelling-book, which contained the alphabet, followed by such meaningless words as "ab," "ba," "ca," "da." [5]I began at once to devour

this book, and I think that it was the first one I ever had in my hands. [6]I had learned from somebody that the way to begin to read was to learn the alphabet, so I tried in all the ways I could think of to learn it,—all of course without a teacher, for I could find no one to teach me. [7]At that time there was not a single member of my race anywhere near us who could read, and I was too timid to approach any of the white people. [8]In some way, within a few weeks, I mastered the greater portion of the alphabet. [9]In all my efforts to learn to read my mother shared full my ambition, and sympathized with me and aided me in every way that she could. [10]Though she was totally ignorant, so far as mere book knowledge was concerned, she had high ambitions for her children, and a large fund of good hard, common sense which seemed to enable her to meet and master every situation. [11]If I have done anything in life worth attention, I feel sure that I inherited the disposition from my mother.

[12]In the midst of my struggles and longing for an education, a young coloured boy who had learned to read in the state of Ohio came to Malden. [13]As soon as the coloured people found out that he could read, a newspaper was secured, and at the close of nearly every day's work this young man would be surrounded by a group of men and women who were anxious to hear him read the news contained in the papers. [14]How I used to envy this man! [15]He seemed to me to be the one young man in all the world who ought to be satisfied with his attainments.

[16]About this time the question of having some kind of a school opened for the coloured children in the village began to be discussed by members of the race. [17]As it would be the first school for Negro children that had ever been opened in that part of Virginia, it was, of course, to be a great event, and the discussion excited the widest interest.

* * *

[18]This experience of a whole race beginning to go to school for the first time, presents one of the most interesting studies that has ever occurred in connection with the development of any race. [19]Few people who were not right in the midst of the scenes can form any exact idea of the intense desire which the people of my race showed for an education. [20]As I have stated, it was a whole race trying to go to school. [21]Few were too young, and none too old, to make the attempt to learn. [22]As fast as any kind of teachers could be secured, not only were day-schools filled, but night-schools as well. [23]The great ambition of the older people was to try to learn to read the Bible before they died. [24]With this end in view, men and women who were fifty or seventy-five years old would often be found in the night-school. [25]Sunday-schools were formed soon after freedom, but the principal book studied in the Sunday-school was the spelling-

book. [26]Day-school, night-school, Sunday-school, were always crowded, and often many had to be turned away for want of room.

Washington, Booker T. *Up from Slavery: An Autobiography*. New York: Doubleday, Page, 1901; Bartleby.com, 2000. www.bartleby.com/1004/. 30 July 2007.

Vocabulary ______ **1.** The best meaning of the word *induced* in sentence 3 is
a. offered.
b. stopped.
c. persuaded.
d. allowed.

Vocabulary ______ **2.** The best meaning of the word *disposition* in sentence 11 is
a. situation.
b. character.
c. problem.
d. need.

Central Idea ______ **3.** Which sentence best states the central idea of this passage?
a. sentence 1
b. sentence 2
c. sentence 9
d. sentence 15

Transitions ______ **4.** The relationship between sentences 12 and 13 is one of
a. time order.
b. effect.
c. contrast.
d. example.

Main Ideas Details ______ **5.** Sentence 14 is
a. main idea.
b. major supporting detail.
c. minor supporting detail.

Fact and Opinion ______ **6.** Sentence 15 is
a. fact.
b. opinion.
c. fact and opinion.

Inferences ______ **7.** Based on the information in the passage, we can infer that Booker T. Washington

a. was a hardworking student.
b. neglected work and chores to learn to read.
c. was ashamed because he couldn't read.
d. was one of many of his race who could read.

**8–10.** Complete the following time line with information from the passage.

I. Washington determines to learn to read.

II. The influence of his (8) ______________

III. His envy of a man who can (9) ______________

IV. The opening of a (10) ______________

V. The whole race learns to read

# Test 7

Read the following passage, and then answer the questions.

**Lincoln's Gettysburg Address 1863**

[1]Fourscore and seven years ago our fathers brought forth on this continent a new nation, conceived in liberty, and dedicated to the proposition that all men are created equal.

[2]Now we are engaged in a great civil war, testing whether that nation, or any nation so conceived and so dedicated, can long endure. [3]We are met on a great battlefield of that war. [4]We have come to dedicate a portion of that field as a final resting-place for those who here gave their lives that the nation might live. [5]It is altogether fitting and proper that we should do this. [6]But, in a larger sense, we cannot dedicate, we cannot consecrate, we cannot hallow, this ground. [7]The brave men, living and dead, who struggled here have consecrated it, far above our poor power to add or detract. [8]The world will little note, nor long remember, what we say here, but it can never forget what they did here. [9]It is for us the living, rather, to be dedicated here to the unfinished work which they who fought here have thus far so nobly advanced. [10]It is rather for us to be here dedicated to the great task remaining before us—that from these honored dead we take increased devotion to that cause for which they gave the last full measure of devotion—that we here highly resolve that

these dead shall not have died in vain—that this nation, under God, shall have a new birth of freedom and that government of the people, by the people, for the people, shall not perish from the earth.

*American Historical Documents, 1000–1904.* Vol. XLIII. The Harvard Classics. New York: P.F. Collier & Son, 1909–14; Bartleby.com, 2001. www.bartleby.com/43/. 30 July 2007.

Vocabulary ______ **1.** A synonym of the word *proposition* in sentence 1 is
a. scheme.
b. idea.
c. conspiracy.
d. speech.

Vocabulary ______ **2.** The best meaning of the word *consecrate* in sentence 6 is
a. set apart.
b. see.
c. destroy.
d. own.

Thought Patterns ______ **3.** The main thought pattern used in the passage is
a. cause and effect.
b. time order.
c. comparison and contrast.
d. definition and example.

Main Idea, Details ______ **4.** Sentence 1 is a
a. main idea.
b. major supporting detail.
c. minor supporting detail.

Central Idea ______ **5.** The central idea of the passage is best stated in
a. sentence 1.
b. sentence 2.
c. sentence 3.
d. sentence 10.

Transitions ______ **6.** The relationship of ideas between sentence 5 and sentence 6 is
a. cause and effect.
b. addition.
c. time order.
d. comparison and contrast.

Purpose ______ **7.** The author's main purpose is to
a. inform the reader about the sacrifice of the soldiers.
b. to assert the ideal that all "are created equal."
c. to entertain the reader with a dramtic speech.

Tone ______ **8.** The overall tone of the passage is
a. unbiased.
b. cautious.
c. reverent.
d. sorrowful.

Fact and Opinion

______ **9.** Sentence 3 is a statement of
a. fact.
b. opinion.
c. fact and opinion.

**10.** Complete the following summary with information from the passage.

In his famous Gettysburg Address, President Abraham Lincoln calls upon the principles set forth by the Declaration of Independence and defines the Civil War as a struggle for "a new birth of freedom" that offers true ________ to all of its citizens.

# Test 8

Read the following passage, and then answer the questions.

**Unfasten Your Seat Belt**

[1]You may never cross the hot desert sands in an armored military vehicle. [2]But like NBC's David Bloom, the popular 39-year-old *Today Show* co-anchor who died while covering the war in Iraq, you could develop a fatal blood clot.

[3]Pulmonary embolism—a blocked artery in the lungs usually caused by a clot that first forms deep in a leg muscle—kills 60,000 Americans a year. [4]Lots of factors increase your odds: oral contraceptives, hormone therapy, some cancers, heart disease, pregnancy, paralysis, surgery, and overweight. [5]But in many cases, the clots are the result of simply sitting still for too, too long.

[6]Not drinking enough fluids makes it even worse, and age doesn't matter. [7]Nearly half of those who develop dangerous blood clots in their legs—deep-vein thrombosis, or DVT—are under 50. [8]Untreated, DVT can lead to pulmonary embolism.

[9]Here are five ways to cut your risk: [10]Wear "smart hose." [11]Stay hydrated. [12]On long trips, drink at least a liter of water every 5 hours. [13]At high risk? [14]Get this cheap, new therapy called warfarin. [15]If you've had DVT or pulmonary embolism once, the odds of a repeat event are higher. [16]Ask your doctor about long-term, low-dose warfarin. [17]Move! [18]On any long trip, do leg exercises in your seat. [19]Take these symptoms to the ER—fast! [20]Sudden breathlessness, chest pain when you inhale, coughing up blood-stained phlegm, and rapid pulse are signs of pulmonary embolism. [21]DVT symptoms include a red, swollen, or tender area over a leg vein.

—"Unfasten Your Seat Belt!" *Prevention,* July 2003, p. 30.

Vocabulary ______ **1.** The best meaning of the phrase *pulmonary embolism* as used in sentence 3 is

a. a heart attack.
b. a stroke.
c. a dangerous blood clot in the leg.
d. a blocked artery in the lung.

Vocabulary ______ **2.** The best meaning of the phrase *deep-vein thrombosis* as used in sentence 7 is

a. a heart attack.
b. a stroke.
c. a dangerous blood clot in the leg.
d. a blocked artery in the lung.

Main Idea, Details ______ **3.** Sentence 10 is a

a. a main idea.
b. a major supporting detail.
c. a minor supporting detail.

Transitions ______ **4.** The relationship between sentences 1 and 2 is one of

a. contrast.
b. addition.
c. cause.
d. effect.

Implied Central Idea ______ **5.** What is the best statement of the implied central idea of this passage?

a. Many factors cause pulmonary embolisms.
b. Not drinking enough fluids is a major cause of pulmonary embolisms.
c. Untreated blot clots in the legs can lead to a pulmonary embolism.
d. Although pulmonary embolisms are caused by many factors, steps can be taken to reduce the risk.

Transitions ______ **6.** The relationship of ideas within sentence 4 is one of

a. listing.
b. comparison.
c. cause.
d. time order.

Purpose ______ **7.** The author's main purpose is to

a. inform the reader about dangers of pulmonary embolisms.
b. entertain the reader with ways to overcome this problem.
c. persuade the reader to take precautions against pulmonary embolisms.

Tone ______ **8.** The tone of the passage is

a. alarming.
b. pessimistic.
c. fearful.
d. cautionary.

Fact and Opinion ______ **9.** Sentence 21 is a statement of

a. fact.
b. opinion.
c. fact and opinion.

**10.** Complete the following study outline with information from the passage.

Term: Pulmonary embolism

Definition: a blocked artery in the lungs, usually caused by a clot that first forms deep in a leg muscle.

Symptoms: ______________________________________________

______________________________________________

Contributing factors: oral contraceptives, some cancers, heart disease, pregnancy, surgery, overweight, dehydration, sitting still too long

Ways to cut risks: wear smart hose; drink plenty of water; consider taking low doses of warfarin; keep moving; get help if symptoms appear

# Test 9

Textbook Skills

Read the following passage from the college history textbook *The American Story*, and then answer the questions.

### The Enlightenment

[1]European historians often refer to the eighteenth century as the Age of Reason. [2]During this period, a body of new, often radical ideas swept the public meeting places and universities across Europe and America. [3]These ideas changed the way that educated Europeans thought about God, nature, and society. [4]This intellectual revolution was called the Enlightenment, and it involved the work of Europe's greatest minds, men such as Newton and Locke, Voltaire and Hume. [5]In time, the writings of these thinkers reached the American colonies, where they received a mixed reception. [6]On the one hand, the colonists welcomed new science; on the other hand, they defended the tenets of traditional Christianity.

[7]The thinkers in this new era replaced the idea of original sin with a much more positive view of human nature. [8]They believed that a loving God set the universe in motion and gave human beings the power of reason. [9]This ability to reason enabled them to understand the orderly workings of the created world. [10]Everything, even human society, was based on mechanical rules or natural laws. [11]The responsibility of right-thinking men and women, therefore, was to make certain that society followed these natural laws. [12]Some even believed that it was possible to achieve perfection in this world. [13]In fact, human suffering had come about only because people had lost touch with the basic insights of reason.

—Adapted from Divine, Breen, Fredrickson, & Williams, *The American Story*, pp. 117–118.

Vocabulary ______ **1.** The best meaning of the word *tenets* as used in sentence 6 is

a. people.
b. ideals.
c. tools.
d. ministers.

Vocabulary ______ **2.** The best meaning of the word *mechanical* as used in sentence 10 is

a. handmade.
b. obvious.
c. automatic.
d. flexible.

Central Idea ______ **3.** The sentence that best states the central idea of this passage is

a. sentence 1.
b. sentence 2.
c. sentence 3.
d. sentence 7.

Main Idea, Details ______ **4.** Sentence 7 serves what purpose in the second paragraph?

a. as a minor supporting detail
b. as a major supporting detail
c. as the main idea

Inferences ______ **5.** Sentence 7 implies that

a. original sin does not offer a positive view of human nature.
b. the thinkers of the Enlightenment agreed with the idea of original sin.
c. human nature is evil.
d. life after death exists.

Transitions ______ **6.** The relationship of ideas within sentence 6 is one of

a. listing.
b. contrast.
c. cause and effect.
d. time order.

Purpose ______ **7.** The author's main purpose is to

a. inform.
b. entertain.
c. persuade.

Tone ______ **8.** The tone of the passage is

a. objective.
b. emotional.

Fact and Opinion ______ **9.** Sentence 4 is a statement of

a. fact.
b. opinion.
c. fact and opinion.

Argument ______ **10.** Which sentence is not relevant to the claim that the ideas of the Enlightenment caused a worldwide revolution in thought?

a. sentence 2
b. sentence 3
c. sentence 4
d. sentence 5

# Test 10

Textbook Skills

Read the following paragraph from the college humanities textbook *The Creative Impulse,* and then answer the questions.

**The Human Journey**

[1]The human journey began long before the records of history. [2]Several million years may have passed as the human race evolved from a rudimentary rural society to city life, civilization, and history. [3]Humans grew culturally as they adapted to a changing environment. [4]The first stage of human culture was the Paleolithic period or Old Stone Age. [5]The Old Stone Age reaches back beyond 1 million years B.C.E., when humans were hunters and gatherers. [6]But in the Paleolithic period, humans discovered fire, clothing, basic techniques for hunting and gathering food, and simple social organization. [7]Toward the end of the period, our ancestors may have begun to think in artistic and religious terms. [8]The second stage of human culture was the Neolithic period or New Stone Age. [9]Between around 8000 and 3000 B.C.E., people began to settle down and to raise crops rather than to hunt animals and gather food. [10]This was the agricultural phase. [11]Stone tools improved dramatically, and humans learned to make pottery and textiles. [12]Social structure changed as well as humans learned how to live together in small villages.

—Adapted from Sporre, *The Creative Impulse: An Introduction to the Arts,* 6th ed., pp. 35–36.

Vocabulary ______ **1.** The best meaning of the word *rudimentary* as used in sentence 2 is

a. simple.
b. before the records of history.
c. before human life evolved.
d. before the Stone Age.

Vocabulary ______ **2.** The best meaning of the word *phase* as used in sentence 10 is

a. way.
b. crop.
c. answer.
d. era.

Implied Main Idea ______ **3.** What is the implied main idea of this paragraph?

a. Humankind began its journey long before records were kept.
b. Humans grow and change in response to their environment.
c. An early stage in human culture is the Paleolithic age.
d. Two early stages of human culture are the Paleolithic and Neolithic Stone Ages.

Thought Patterns ______ **4.** The main thought pattern used in this paragraph is
a. classification.
b. comparison and contrast.
c. definition.
d. time order.

Transitions ______ **5.** The relationship of ideas between sentences 5 and 6 is one of
a. listing.
b. contrast.
c. cause and effect.
d. time order.

Fact and Opinion ______ **6.** Sentence 2 is a statement of
a. fact.
b. opinion.
c. fact and opinion.

**7–10.** Complete the study outline with information from the passage.

Main idea: ______________________________

I. Paleolithic Period (Old Stone Age)
  A. Hunters and gatherers
  B. ______________________________
  C. ______________________________
II. Neolithic Period (New Stone Age)
  A. Raised crops
  B. Improved stone tools
  C. Made pottery and textiles
  D. ______________________________

# Test 11

Textbook Skills

Read the following paragraph from the college textbook *Essentials of Human Communication*. Then answer the questions.

### Territoriality

[1]One aspect of communication having to do with space is **territoriality**, a term that comes to us from ethology (the study of animals in their natural habitat). [2]Territoriality refers to an ownership-like reaction toward a particular space or object. [3]Many animals mark their territory. [4]Humans do too. [5]We make use of three types of markers: central, boundary, and ear markers.

[6]Central markers signify that the territory is reserved. [7]When you place a drink on a bar, books on your desk, or a sweater over your chair, you let others know that this territory belongs to you. [8]Boundary markers distinguish your territory from that belonging to others. [9]The divider in the supermarket checkout line, the armrests separating your theater seat from those on either side, the fence around your house, and the door to your apartment are examples. [10]Ear markers identify your possessions. [11]Trademarks, nameplates, and initials on a shirt or attaché case specify that this particular object belongs to you.

—Adapted from DeVito, *Essentials of Human Communication*, 4th ed., p. 135.

Vocabulary ______ **1.** The word *territoriality* in sentences 1 and 2 means
a. a study of animals.
b. a study of a natural habitat.
c. a study of animals in their natural habitat.
d. an ownership-like reaction.

Supporting Details ______ **2.** The divider in the supermarket checkout line is an example of a
a. central marker.
b. boundary marker.
c. ear marker.
d. none of the above.

Main Idea ______ **3.** The main idea of this paragraph is stated in
a. sentence 1.
b. sentence 2.
c. sentence 3.
d. sentence 5.

Inferences ______ **4.** Based on information in the paragraph, we can conclude that
a. humans can learn about themselves by studying other animals.
b. humans have evolved beyond the effects of territoriality.
c. animals use ear markers in their natural habitats.
d. other types of boundary markers exist.

Transitions ______ **5.** The relationship between sentences 10 and 11 is one of
a. cause and effect.
b. comparison and contrast.
c. time order.
d. definition and example.

Transitions ______ **6.** The relationship of ideas within sentence 5 is one of
a. listing.
b. comparison.
c. cause and effect.
d. time order.

Thought Patterns ______ **7.** The overall thought pattern used in the paragraph is
a. cause and effect.
b. classification.
c. comparison and contrast.
d. time order.

Purpose ______ **8.** The author's main purpose is to
a. inform.
b. entertain.
c. persuade.

Tone ______ **9.** The tone of the passage is
a. accusing.
b. objective.
c. comical.
d. controversial.

Fact and Opinion ______ **10.** The paragraph relies on details of
a. fact.
b. opinion.
c. fact and opinion.

# Test 12

Textbook Skills

Read the following passage from a college health textbook, and then answer the questions.

### The Anger Urge

[1]Although much has been said about how hotheaded, short-fused people are at risk for health problems, recent research provides even more compelling reasons for "chilling out." [2]A study of nearly 13,000 people found that anger, even in the absence of high blood pressure, can increase a person's risk of heart attack by more than 2.5 times. [3]Stress hormones released during anger may constrict blood vessels in the heart or actually promote clot formation, which can cause a heart attack.

[4]Anger results when our wants, desires, and dreams differ from what we actually get in life. [5]People who spend all their emotional energy in a quest for justice or grow frustrated over events that seem impossible to change can become driven by anger. [6]Because anger triggers the fight-or-flight reaction, these people operate with the stress response turned on long after it should have dissipated.

[7]Angry people usually display cynicism, which is a brooding, fault-finding view of their world. [8]Like anger, cynicism keeps the fight-or-flight reactions constantly flowing through their bodies. [9]Often thought of as "hostile," these constantly stressed folks may have weakened immune systems, and they may face an increased risk of disease.

—Adapted from Donatelle, *Health*, 5th ed., pp. 66–67.

Vocabulary ______ **1.** The best meaning of the word *compelling* as used in sentence 1 is
a. forceful.
b. obvious.
c. personal.
d. compiled.

Vocabulary ______ **2.** The best meaning of the word *quest* as used in sentence 5 is
a. question.
b. denial.
c. search.
d. thought.

Central Idea ______ **3.** The central idea of the passage is stated in
a. sentence 1.
b. sentence 2.
c. sentence 3.
d. sentence 4.

Transitions ______ **4.** The relationship between sentences 7 and 8 is
a. example.
b. contrast.
c. comparison.
d. time.

Transitions ______ **5.** The relationship of ideas within sentence 3 is one of
a. listing.
b. comparison.
c. cause and effect.
d. classification.

Purpose ______ **6.** The author's main purpose is to
a. inform the reader about dangers of anger.
b. entertain the reader with details about anger management.
c. persuade the reader to take specific steps against the anger urge.

Fact and Opinion ______ **7.** Sentence 6 is a statement of
a. fact.
b. opinion.
c. fact and opinion.

**8–10.** Complete the cause-and-effect flowchart with information from the passage.

**8.** Central idea: ______________________________________________

__________________________________________________________

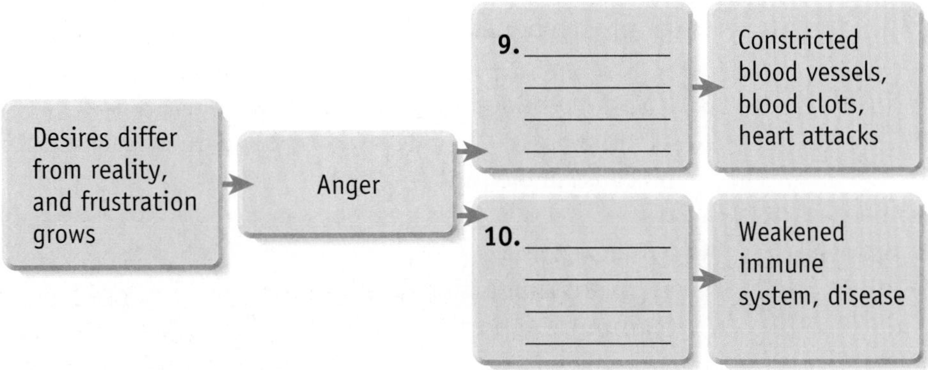

Desires differ from reality, and frustration grows → Anger → **9.** ______________ → Constricted blood vessels, blood clots, heart attacks

Anger → **10.** ______________ → Weakened immune system, disease

# Test 13

Textbook Skills

Read the following paragraph adapted from the college textbook *Educational Psychology,* and then answer the questions.

### Peer Relationships

[1]Peer relationships play a major role in healthy personal and social development. [2]Strong evidence exists to support the idea that adults who had close friends as children have higher self-esteem and are more able to maintain intimate relationships than adults who had lonely childhoods. [3]The types of friends and the quality of the friendships matter too. [4]Stable, caring relationships with friends who are socially skilled and mature aids in social development. [5]This is especially true during difficult times such as the divorce of parents or a move to a new school. [6]Adults who were rejected as children tend to have more problems, such as dropping out of school or committing crimes. [7]Friendships are central to students' lives. [8]When there has been a falling-out or an argument, when one child is not invited to a sleep-over, when rumors are started and pacts are made to ostracize someone, the results can be devastating to the children involved. [9]Even when students begin to mature and know intellectually that rifts will soon be healed, they may still be emotionally crushed by temporary trouble in friendships.

—Adapted from Woolfolk, *Educational Psychology,* 8th ed., p. 87.

Vocabulary ______ **1.** The best meaning of the word *ostracize* as used in sentence 8 is
a. brutalize.
b. exclude.
c. include.
d. help.

Vocabulary and Inference ______ **2.** The word *rifts* as used in sentence 9 suggests
a. broken feelings or relationships.
b. broken bones.
c. broken promises.
d. broken marriages.

Thought Patterns ______ **3.** The thought pattern suggested by sentences 8 and 9 is
a. time order.`
b. cause and effect.
c. comparison and contrast.

Supporting Details ______ **4.** Sentence 7 is a
a. major supporting detail.
b. minor supporting detail.

Central Idea ______ **5.** The central idea of the passage is best stated in
a. sentence 1.
b. sentence 2.
c. sentence 3.
d. sentence 9.

Transitions ______ **6.** The relationship of ideas within sentence 2 is one of
a. listing.
b. comparison and contrast.
c. time order.

Purpose ______ **7.** The author's main purpose is to
a. inform the reader about importance of peer relationships in personal and social development.
b. entertain the reader with details about self-esteem.
c. persuade the reader to be a good friend and make good friends.

Fact and Opinion ______ **8.** Sentence 9 is a statement of
a. fact.
b. opinion.
c. fact and opinion.

**9–10.** Complete the summary with ideas from the passage.

________________ play a major role in healthy personal and social development. Close, stable, and caring relationships with friends as children aid in social development. People who had these types of friendships have higher ________________ and are able to maintain intimate relationships and to cope with difficulties. In contrast, those who did not develop such relationships are more likely to drop out of school or commit crimes.

# Test 14

Read the following passage, and then answer the questions.

### Sweet Fifteen-La Quinceafiera

[1]The need to recognize the transition between childhood and adulthood is universal. [2]Civilizations over the centuries have established rites of passage for both boys and girls. [3]For young women in the United States, that event is often marked at age sixteen with Sweet Sixteen parties or debuts.

[4]This practice was promoted in the South in the nineteenth century with the debutante ball. [5]A similar event is the Jewish coming of age at thirteen with the bar mitzvah for boys and the bat mitzvah for girls.

[6]Coming-out parties were thought to have reached the New World during the French occupation of Mexico in the nineteenth century, but the *quinceañera's* roots go much deeper than that. [7]In her book *Quinceañera*, author Michele Salcedo explains, "The beginnings [of the *quinceañera*] go much further back, thousands of years back, to the indigenous people of our respective cultures. [8]The Tainos and Arawaks, the Quechua and Toltecs, the Aztecs and Mayas, to name but a few. [9]All had rites of passage to mark the point in a child's life when she was a child no longer, but ready to make her contribution to society as an adult."

[10]According to Mark Francis and Arturo J. Perez-Rodriguez in the book *Primero Dios: Hispanic Liturgical* Resource, both boys and girls initially participated in these rites of passage but only the celebration for girls has survived. [11]As part of the preparation, girls were separated at age fifteen from their playmates and instead instructed on their importance to the community and their future roles as wives and mothers. [12]"During the rite in its origins, the gods were thanked for the lives of these future mothers, and the young women pledged to fulfill their roles of service to the community," write the authors. [13]"The *quinceañera* was gradually Christianized by the missionaries to highlight a personal affirmation of faith by the young woman and her willingness to become a good Christian wife and mother. [14]It then became common to celebrate it in church, although apart from a Mass."

[15]Unlike many Latino traditions, however, the *quinceañera* tends to be cross denominational and not exclusively Catholic. [16]The social significance of the *quinceañera* may be what most attracts attention. [17]It bears a great similarity to many weddings, except in this case the "bride" wears pink. [18]The pink color symbolizes the girl's coming of age, but the preferred emphasis is on the girl's maturity rather than on her sexuality. [19]In many *quinceañeras*, the event begins with a Mass, but this is not always the case. [20]Because of the event's great cost to the parents—an average of $10,000—some churches discourage their members from adopting the tradition. [21]To offset the costs, families sometimes enlist the support of *padrinos* (sponsors) to cover particular items, from the dress to the cost of a band for the reception. [22]This practice is also carried over to weddings.

[23]The *quinceañera* chooses several of her friends to be her attendants, called the Court of Honor. [24]These girls—there are usually fourteen of them to represent the debutante's previous years—start the procession, accompa-

nied by their escorts. [25]The parents usually enter the procession next, before their daughter. [26]The *quinceañera* can have an escort, usually a brother, cousin, or friend, but some choose to have their parents as escorts instead.

[27]There are interesting twists to the celebration as well. [28]According to Salcedo, most Cuban families forgo the church service, while Mexican American, Dominican, and Colombian families will almost always include it. [29]The service can be a simple prayer or blessing from the priest, or a full Mass. [30]Puerto Ricans will also generally opt for the Mass, which culminates with the mother of the *quinceañera* placing a tiara on her daughter's head and her father replacing her flats with high heels.

[31]Despite the ceremony's high cost, many parents see *quinceañera* celebrations as a good investment. [32]It reinforces the fact that their daughter is expected to take on more responsibility, and that symbolism does not escape the *quinceañera*. [33]"Not to brag, but my daughter is unique in a lot of ways," says Mary Mendez, the mother of Brandy, who celebrated her *quinceañera* in 1994. [34]Brandy's *quinceañera* was featured in a June 15–21 article in the *New Times* of Phoenix, Arizona. [35]"I think it [the *quinceañera*] is good. [36]Half of what's wrong with kids nowadays is they don't think about their future."

—Menard, Valerie. (2004) *The Latino Holiday Book*, pp. 88–90.

**VISUAL VOCABULARY**

Based on the passage a debutante is also known as a

_______________.

▸ The debutante often dances her first dance of the ball with her father.

Vocabulary ______ **1.** The best meaning of the word *debutante* in sentence 4 is
- a. introduction.
- b. young person.
- c. young woman.
- d. finance.

Vocabulary ______ **2.** The best meaning of the word *affirmation* in sentence 13 is
a. statement.
b. denial.
c. ceremony.
d. marriage.

Implied Central Idea ______ **3.** Which sentence is the best statement of the implied central idea of the passage?
a. La Quinceafiera is a Hispanic debutante ball.
b. La Quinceafiera is a significant expense for the family.
c. La Quinceafiera reflects the religious beliefs of the Hispanic culture.
d. La Quinceafiera is a cultural event that recognizes the transition between childhood and adulthood for young Latino women.

Transitions ______ **4.** The relationship between sentences 15 and 16 is one of
a. time order.
b. contrast.
c. effect.
d. example.

Supporting Details ______ **5.** Sentence 27 is a
a. major supporting detail.
b. minor supporting detail.

Fact and Opinion ______ **6.** Sentence 4 is a statement of
a. fact.
b. opinion.
c. fact and opinion.

**7–10.** Complete the following summary with information from the passage.

A **(7)** ____________ is a social event, similar to a debutante ball, recognizing the transition between childhood and adulthood of a young woman. The *quinceafiera's* roots go back thousands of years. Historically, girls were separated at age fifteen from their playmates and instructed on their importance to the community and their future roles as **(8)** ______ and **(9)** ________. Eventually, missionaries used this ritual to highlight a personal affirmation of **(10)** _________ faith. The quinceafiera reinforces the fact that the daughter is expected to take on more responsibility.

# Test 15

Textbook Skills

Read the following passage from the college textbook *Politics in America.* Then answer the questions.

[1]Democracy means a person participates in the decisions that affect the person's life. [2]People should be free to choose for themselves how they want to live. [3]Personal participation in government is necessary for personal dignity. [4]People should not have decisions made *for* them but *by* them. [5]Even if they make mistakes, it is better that they be allowed to do so rather than take away their rights to make their own decisions. [6]The true democrat would reject even a wise and benevolent dictatorship because it would threaten the person's character, self-reliance, and dignity. [7]Perhaps in a democracy, the people will not always choose wise policies for themselves. [8]Yet people who cannot choose for themselves are not really free.

[9]Decisions in a democracy must be reached by majority rule. [10]Each person has one vote. [11]And each person's vote must be equal to every other person's vote. [12]Status, money, or fame must not be factors. [13]The government is not truly democratic when any person is denied political equality because of race, sex, or wealth. [14]Majorities are not always right. [15]But majority rule means that all persons have an equal say in decisions affecting them. [16]If people are truly equal, then their votes must count equally. [17]And a majority vote must decide the issue, even if the majority decides foolishly.

—Adapted from Dye, *Politics in America,* 5th ed., pp. 15–16.

Vocabulary ______ **1.** The best meaning of the word *benevolent* as used in sentence 6 is
a. cruel.
b. kind.
c. indifferent.
d. mature.

Vocabulary ______ **2.** The best meaning of the word *democrat* as used in sentence 6 is
a. one who rules by force.
b. one who believes in civil liberties.
c. one who is a member of the Democratic party.
d. one who believes in big government.

Thought Patterns ______ **3.** The thought pattern for the passage is
a. the effects of democracy.
b. the time order for the voting process.
c. the differences between a dictatorship and a democracy.
d. the traits of democracy.

Supporting Details ______ **4.** Sentence 10 is a supporting detail that gives information about
a. a reason for not voting.
b. an example of corruption in politics.
c. an effect of democracy.
d. a trait of a majority rule.

Central Idea ______ **5.** The best statement of the central idea of this passage is found in
a. sentence 1.
b. sentence 3.
c. sentence 7
d. sentence 17.

Transitions ______ **6.** The relationship of ideas within sentence 4 is one of
a. listing.
b. contrast.
c. cause and effect.
d. time order.

Purpose ______ **7.** The author's main purpose is to
a. inform the reader about the need to vote.
b. entertain the reader with the hope of democracy.
c. defend the ideal of democracy.

Tone ______ **8.** The tone of the passage is
a. quarrelsome.
b. jaded.
c. uncertain.
d. assertive.

Fact and Opinion ______ **9.** Sentence 7 is a statement of
a. fact.
b. opinion.
c. fact and opinion.

Inferences ______ **10.** The best title for the passage is
a. Democracy or Death.
b. Individual Dignity and Democracy.
c. The Risks of Majority Rule.
d. Democracy.

PART FOUR

# Reading Enrichment

APPENDIX A

# Reading Graphics in Textbooks

Reading comprehension involves more than just reading words. Authors also use visual images such as photographs, cartoons, and graphics to relay ideas. Graphics are helpful for several reasons. First, graphics can simplify difficult ideas and make relationships among ideas easier to see. Second, graphics can sum up ideas so that they can be more quickly digested. Third, graphics can sway a reader by pointing out trends or gaps in information. An effective reader should know how to read different types of graphics. This chapter will discuss three basic types: tables, graphs, and diagrams. Although a variety of graphics exist, a few basic guidelines can be applied as a reading process for any graphic.

## Basic Guidelines for Reading Graphics

Graphics give a great deal of information in a smaller space than it would take to write the ideas in the form of words. The following suggestions will help you understand the general format of a graphic. Apply the SQ3R strategies discussed in Chapter 1. Remember to survey, question, read, recite, and review the information.

1. **Read the Words Printed with the Graphic**
   A graphic has a main idea and supporting details, just as a paragraph does.

- ***Read the title or caption.*** The title or caption is usually at the top of the graphic.

  The title or caption states the main idea of the graphic.

  Ask: What is this graphic about? What is being described?

- ***Note the source.*** The source is usually at the bottom of the graphic. The source is the author or publisher of the ideas in the graphic.

*Note to Reader: Appendix B, Reading Textbooks, Appendix C, Figurative Language: Metaphors and Similes, and Appendix D, Reading the Dictionary appear online at http://www.ablongman.com/henry

Ask: Who collected the information? Is the source a trusted authority?

If the graphic reports the results of a survey, how many people took part? Who were they?

- ***Read any footnotes.*** The footnotes are also found at the bottom of a graphic. Footnotes can include important supporting details.

  Ask: Do the footnotes explain what any numbers or headings mean?

  How was the data collected?

- ***Read the labels.*** Many graphics use columns and rows. Other graphics use horizontal or vertical axes. Columns, rows, and axes are labeled. These labels give important supporting details for the graphic's main idea. Look up any words you do not know in a dictionary.

  Ask: Do the labels tell what the columns and rows represent?

  Are any symbols or abbreviations used? If so, what do they mean?

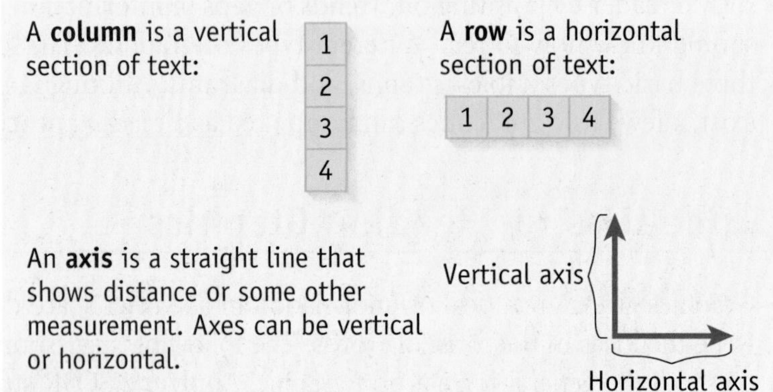


**2. Analyze the Graphic**

- ***Analyze the format.*** Each type of chart has its own organization. For example, a table uses columns and rows. A pie chart is a circle divided into parts.

  Ask: How is the graphic organized?

  Why did the author use this type of graphic?

- ***Analyze the unit of measurement.*** Study the legend. A legend will list and explain symbols used as labels. Study the labels of rows, columns, and axes.

  Ask: Do the numbers represent hundreds? Thousands? Millions? Inches? Feet? Miles? Pounds? Ounces? Or are metric units used?

- ***Analyze trends and patterns.*** Trends and patterns suggest or imply important ideas that support the graphic's main idea.

Ask: What are the extremes? How do the extremes compare to the total?

What are the averages?

What and how much are the increases? What and how much are the decreases?

Textbook Skills

**EXAMPLE** Study the accompanying graphic from the college textbook *Drugs, Behavior, and Modern Society*, 3rd ed. (Levinthal, p. 15). Answer the questions that follow with information from the graph.

**Drug Use in the United States Across the Life Span**

| | Percentage by Age Group for Use in Past Year/Past Month | | | | Estimated Total Number of Users |
|---|---|---|---|---|---|
| | 12–17 | 18–25 | 26 and Older | Total Sample | Past Year/ Past Month |
| Any illicit drug | 20/11 | 30/17 | 8/4 | 12/7 | 26,220,000/14,820,000 |
| Marijuana | 14/8 | 25/15 | 5/3 | 9/5 | 19,573,000/11,177,000 |
| Cocaine | 2/0.5 | 5/2 | 1/0.5 | 2/0.7 | 3,691,000/1,501,000 |
| Crack cocaine | 0.4/0.1 | 1/0.4 | 0.4/0.2 | 0.5/0.2 | 1,035,000/413,000 |
| Heroin | 0.3/0.02 | 0.5/0.2 | 0.1/0.1 | 0.2/0.1 | 403,000/208,000 |
| Hallucinogens | 4/1 | 7/2 | 0.2/0.1 | 1/0.4 | 3,169,000/907,000 |
| Alcohol | 35/19 | 75/58 | 64/49 | 63/47 | 138,346,000/104,603,000 |
| Nicotine (any tobacco use) | 27/17 | 54/45 | 34/30 | 36/30 | 79,778,000/66,766,000 |

Original source: Substance Abuse and Mental Health Services Administration (2000). *Summary of findings from the 1999 National Household Survey on drug abuse.* Rockville, MD: Office of Applied Studies, Substance Abuse and Mental Health Services Administration, Tables G.5–G.9, G.21–G.25.

**1.** What is the title of the table? ______________________________

______________________________

**2.** What is the source of the table? ______________________________

______________________________

______________________________

______________________________

______________________________

3. How many categories of drugs are listed in the table? ______________

4. What time spans of drug use are tracked in the table? ______________

______________________________________________

5. What are the three age groups the table uses? __________, __________, and __________

6. Which drug had the highest total number of users in the past year or past month? ______________

7. Which drug had the lowest total number of users in the past year or past month? ______________

8. Which age group had the highest level of marijuana use in the past year or past month? ______________

9. Which drug has the highest level of use by the 12- to 17-year-old age group?

______________________________________________

10. Based on the information in the table, which drug is most likely to have the greatest impact on the health of all age groups? ______________

**EXPLANATION**

1. What is the title of the table? Drug Use in the United States Across the Life Span

2. What is the source of the table? Substance Abuse and Mental Health Services Administration (2000). *Summary of findings from the 1999 National Household Survey on drug abuse.* Rockville, MD: Office of Applied Studies, Substance Abuse and Mental Health Services Administration, Tables G.5–G.9, G.21–G.25.

3. How many categories of drugs are listed in the table? *8* The table lists five specific illicit (illegal) drugs: marijuana, cocaine, crack cocaine, heroin, and hallucinogens. The table also includes a more general label "any illicit drug"; this label includes many other drugs (such as Ecstasy) besides the five types of illicit drugs already listed in the table. In addition, the table lists two types of legal drugs: alcohol and nicotine.

4. What time spans of drug use are tracked in the table? *past year and past month*

   The time measurement is located in the subheading for the age groups and in the column heading for estimated total number of users. Note that the source indicates that the actual year during which the information was gathered was 1999.

5. What are the three age groups the table uses? *12–17, 18–25, and 26 and older*

6. Which drug had the highest total number of users in the past year or past month? *alcohol* More than 138 million people used alcohol in the past year, and more than 104 million did so in the past month.

7. Which drug had the lowest total number of users in the past year or past month? *heroin* In the past year there were 403,000 users; in the past month, there were 208,000.

8. Which age group had the highest level of marijuana use in the past year or past month? *18–25* Twenty-five percent of people aged 18–25 used marijuana in the past year, and 15 percent did so in the past month.

9. Which drug has the highest level of use by the 12- to 17-year-old age group? *alcohol* Of this age group, 35 percent used alcohol in the past year, and 19 percent used it in the past month.

10. Based on the information in the table, which drug is most likely to have the greatest impact on the health of all age groups? *alcohol* Note that the table does not describe the amount or frequency of use. Therefore, it is difficult to make a value judgment about the positive or negative health effects. However, common sense and general knowledge can lead to a reasonable inference that alcohol has a greater impact on the health of users based on the large numbers of total users.

## Three Basic Types of Graphics

Many magazines, newspapers, and textbooks use tables, graphs, and diagrams. These graphics call attention to key concepts. Thus an effective reader takes time to study the ideas within them.

## Tables

Social science, health, and business textbooks often use tables. A **table** is a systematic ordering of facts in rows and columns for easy reference. The purpose of a table is to allow the reader to classify and compare the given facts. Often the facts are given as numbers or statistics. The basic guidelines for reading graphics apply to reading a table. In addition, some tables require that you study the places where columns and rows intersect.

Textbook Skills

**EXAMPLE** Study the accompanying table, taken from the college textbook *Politics in America*, 5th ed. (Dye, p. 192). Based on the data in the table, mark each of the statements that follow **T** if it is true, **F** if it is false, or **DK** if you don't know, based on the given data.

**Sources of Political Campaign News in Presidential Election Years**

Over time network news (ABC, CBS, NBC) has been declining as a major source of campaign news, while cable news (CNN, MSNBC, Fox) has been gaining. The Internet has also gained ground as a source of campaign news, yet it was cited by only 11 percent of Americans as their source of "most news."

| News Sources | 1992 | 1996 | 2000 |
|---|---|---|---|
| Television | 82% | 72% | 70% |
| Cable | 29 | 21 | 36 |
| Network | 55 | 36 | 22 |
| Local | 29 | 23 | 21 |
| Newspapers | 57 | 60 | 39 |
| Radio | 12 | 19 | 15 |
| Internet | — | 3 | 11 |
| Magazines | 9 | 11 | 4 |

Note: Respondents were asked, "How did you get most of your news about the presidential election campaign? From television, from newspapers, from radio, from magazines, or from the Internet?" Television users were then asked, "Did you get most of your news about the presidential campaign from network TV news, from local TV news, or from cable news networks such as CNN or MSNBC?" Respondents could name two sources.

Original source: Pew Research Center for the People and the Press data from a telephone survey of 1,113 voters, November 10–12, 2000, http://www.people-press.org/post00que.htm.

_____ **1.** The source of this table is a reliable source.

_____ **2.** This table charts the voting patterns in presidential elections.

_____ **3.** This information was gathered by interviewing over 1,000 people by telephone.

_____ **4.** The percentage of people using the newspaper as a source of political campaign news declined from 1996 to 2000.

_____ **5.** The people who use cable television as a source of information are more likely to vote than people who use the Internet.

**EXPLANATION** Compare your answers to the ones given here.

**1.** T: This table is based on information gathered by the Pew Research Center for the People and the Press. This organization is well respected by serious journalists and news agencies. In addition, the table was published in a college government textbook.

**2.** F: The title of this table clearly states that it gives data concerning *sources* of political campaign news in presidential election years. The table has nothing to do with how people voted, only where they gathered information.

**3.** T: The source information at the bottom of the table states this.

**4.** T: You can check this way. First, begin in the row labeled "Newspapers"; follow that row over to the column for 1996. Note that 60 percent of people used newspapers in 1996. Continue to follow the newspaper row over to the 2000 column. Note that the data indicate that a smaller number, 39 percent, used newspapers in 2000. Subtracting 39 from 60, you can see that the percentage of people using newspapers as a source for political campaign news declined by 21 percent from 1996 to 2000.

**5.** DK: This table does not give us any information about how people vote, nor does it give any information about the relationship between where people gather information and their voting patterns.

## PRACTICE 1

Study the following table, from the college textbook *Health Styles,* 2nd ed. (Pruitt & Stein, p. 154). Based on the data in the table, mark each numbered statement **T** if it is true, **F** if it is false, or **DK** if you don't know, based on the given data.

**Who Likes to Run, Walk, or Swim: Exercise Participation by Sex and Age**
Percentage of adults aged 18+ years reporting participation in selected common physical activities in the prior 2 weeks.

| Activity Category | Males 18–29 | Males All | Females 18–29 | Females All | All ages and sexes |
|---|---|---|---|---|---|
| Walking for exercise | 32.8 | 39.4 | 47.4 | 48.3 | 44.1 |
| Gardening or yard work | 22.2 | 34.2 | 15.4 | 25.1 | 29.4 |
| Stretching exercises | 32.1 | 25.0 | 32.5 | 26.0 | 25.5 |
| Weight lifting or other exercise to increase muscle strength | 33.6 | 20.0 | 14.5 | 8.8 | 14.1 |
| Jogging or running | 22.6 | 12.8 | 11.6 | 5.7 | 9.1 |
| Aerobics or aerobic dance | 3.4 | 2.8 | 19.3 | 11.1 | 7.1 |
| Riding a bicycle or exercise bike | 18.7 | 16.2 | 17.4 | 14.6 | 15.4 |
| Stair climbing | 10.5 | 9.9 | 14.6 | 11.6 | 10.8 |
| Swimming for exercise | 10.1 | 6.9 | 8.0 | 6.2 | 6.5 |
| Tennis | 5.7 | 3.5 | 3.1 | 2.0 | 2.7 |
| Bowling | 7.0 | 4.7 | 4.8 | 3.6 | 4.1 |
| Golf | 7.9 | 8.2 | 1.4 | 1.8 | 4.9 |
| Baseball or softball | 11.0 | 5.8 | 3.2 | 1.4 | 3.5 |
| Handball, racquetball, or squash | 5.2 | 2.7 | 1.0 | 0.5 | 1.6 |
| Skiing | 1.5 | 0.9 | 0.9 | 0.5 | 0.7 |
| Cross-country skiing | 0.1 | 0.4 | 0.3 | 0.4 | 0.4 |
| Water skiing | 1.5 | 0.7 | 0.7 | 0.4 | 0.5 |
| Basketball | 24.2 | 10.5 | 3.1 | 1.5 | 5.8 |
| Volleyball | 6.8 | 3.1 | 4.4 | 1.8 | 2.5 |
| Soccer | 3.3 | 1.4 | 0.9 | 0.4 | 0.9 |
| Football | 7.6 | 2.7 | 0.7 | 0.3 | 1.5 |
| Other sports | 8.6 | 7.3 | 4.5 | 4.1 | 5.7 |

Original source: *Physical Activity and Health: A Report of the Surgeon General,* 1996.

_____ **1.** Walking is the most frequently used form of exercise for all ages and sexes.

_____ **2.** Females do more stretching exercises than males do.

_____ **3.** Females do more strengthening activities, including weightlifting, than males do.

_____ **4.** This table tracks lifelong exercise behaviors.

_____ **5.** Soccer is the sport least liked by both males and females.

## Graphs

**Graphs** show the relationship between two or more sets of ideas. The most common types of graphs you will come across in your reading are line graphs, bar graphs, and pie graphs.

### Line Graphs

A line graph plots two or more sets of facts on vertical and horizontal axes. The vertical axis sets out a scale to measure one set of data, and the horizontal axis provides another scale to measure the other set of data. These features make a line graph ideal to show the curves, shifts, or trends in data. As the information varies, the line changes to show dips and surges. If the information does not change, the line remains steady. Remember to use the guidelines for reading graphs on pages 775–777, and pay special attention to the labels on the vertical and horizontal axes.

**EXAMPLE** Study the following line graph, from the college textbook *Government in America: People, Politics, and Policy,* 5th ed. (Edwards et al., p. 341). Based on the data in the graph, mark each numbered statement **T** if it is true, **F** if it is false, or **DK** if you don't know, based on the given data.

**Growth in Government Employees**

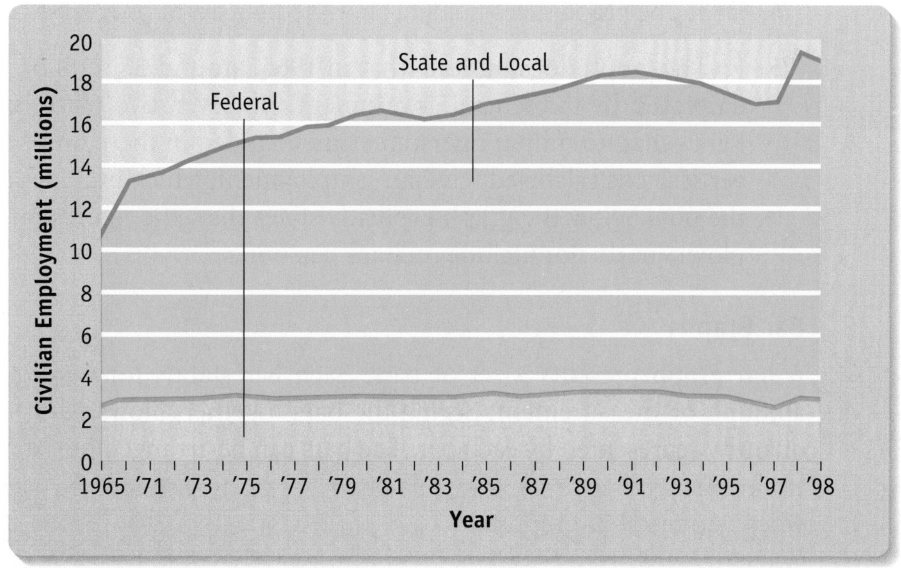


Note: The figures for federal employment do not include military personnel.

Original source: *Budget of the United States Government, Fiscal Year 2000: Historical Tables* (Washington, DC: U.S. Government Printing Office, 1999), Table 17-5.

_____ **1.** The horizontal axis plots the timeline of employment in ten-year periods.

_____ **2.** The vertical axis plots the number of civilian employees in millions.

_____ **3.** The number of people employed by state and local government nearly doubled from 1965 to 1998.

_____ **4.** Many state and local employees and programs are supported by the federal government through grants.

_____ **5.** In 1965, around 2.5 million people, including the military, were employed by the federal government.

**EXPLANATION** Compare your answers to the ones given here.

**1.** F: The horizontal axis plots the timeline of employment in two-year periods, except at the first and last years given.

**2.** T: The vertical axis does plot the number of civilian employees in millions. The numbers are marked off in groups of 2 million.

**3.** T: The number of people employed by state and local government nearly doubled from 1965 to 1998. In 1965, a little over 10 million people were employed by state and local government. By 1998, that number had grown to nearly 20 million.

**4.** DK: The graph gives no data about federal grant programs.

**5.** F: The graph does indicate that in 1965, around 2.5 million people were employed by the federal government. However, two places on the graph tell us that no military personnel are included in these numbers. First, the vertical axis is labeled "civilian" employment, which excludes military, and the note below the graph explicitly states that "the figures for federal employment do not include military personnel."

## Bar Graphs

A **bar graph** presents a set of bars. Each bar stands for a specific quantity, amount, or measurement. Seeing the bars together allows us to compare the quantity represented by each bar. The bars can be arranged horizontally or vertically. Remember to use the guidelines for reading graphics (pages 775–777) when you read bar graphs.

Textbook Skills

**EXAMPLE** Study the following bar graph, from the college health textbook *Total Fitness and Wellness,* 3rd ed. (Powers & Dodd, p. 200). Based on the data in the graph, mark each numbered statement **T** if it is true, **F** if it is false, or **DK** if you don't know, based on the given data.

**Fat Loss from Different Areas of the Body in Women**

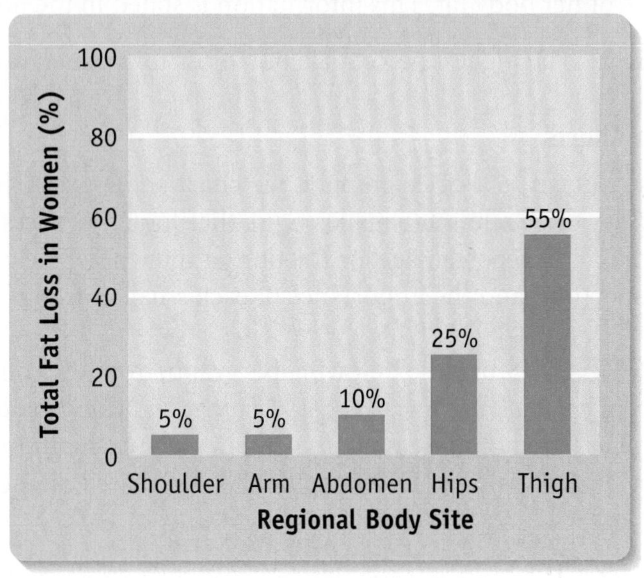


Note: Data based on study of obese women who completed a 14-week weight loss program that resulted in each participant losing approximately 20 pounds of fat.

Source: Data from King & Katch, Changes in Body Density, Fatfolds, and Girths at 2.3 kg Increments of Weight Loss, *Human Biology* 58:709, 1986.

_____ **1.** The horizontal axis measures the fat loss in specific regions of the body.

_____ **2.** The vertical axis measures fat loss by percentages.

_____ **3.** Four regions of the body were measured for fat loss in this study.

_____ **4.** Each woman in the study lost approximately 20 percent of her body fat.

_____ **5.** The highest percentage of fat loss for women occurred in the thighs.

**EXPLANATION**

**1.** T: The horizontal axis measures the fat loss in specific regions of the body. The graph labels this axis "Regional Body Site."

**2.** T: The vertical axis measures fat loss by percentages. The numbers are marked off in 20 percent intervals.

3. F: Five regions of the body were measured for fat loss in this study: shoulder, arm, abdomen, hips, and thigh.

4. F: Each woman in the study lost approximately 20 pounds, not 20 percent of her body fat. This information is stated in the note below the graph.

5. T: The highest percentage of fat loss for women occurred in the thighs.

## Pie Charts

Also known as a circle graph, a **pie chart** shows a whole group as a circle and divides the circle into smaller units that look like slices of a pie. Each smaller slice is a part, percentage, or fraction of the whole. Pie graphs are used to show proportions and the importance of each smaller unit to the whole.

Textbook Skills

**EXAMPLE** Study the following pie graph, from the college sociology textbook *Marriages and Families: Changes, Choices, and Constraints,* 4th ed. (Benokraitis, p. 195). Based on the data in the graph, mark each numbered statement **T** if it is true, **F** if it is false, or **DK** if you don't know, based on the given data.

**Why We Marry**

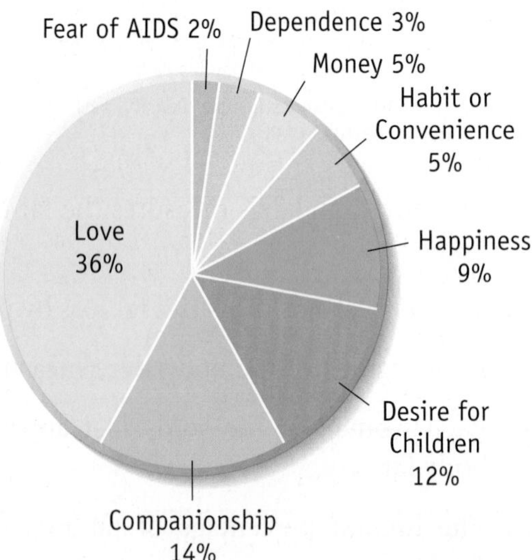


Source: Patterson, J., and P. Kim. 1991. *The Day America Told the Truth: What People Really Believe about Everything That Really Matters.* Upper Saddle River, NJ: Prentice Hall.

_____ **1.** The pie chart is divided into eight parts.

_____ **2.** Fear of AIDS is a major reason for marrying.

_____ **3.** People marry for companionship as often as they marry for love.

_____ **4.** Over a third of the people in this sample said they married for love.

_____ **5.** The people in this sample said that an unplanned pregnancy is one of the reasons they married.

**EXPLANATION** Compare your answers to the ones given here.

1. T: The pie chart is divided into the following eight parts: love, companionship, desire for children, happiness, habit or convenience, money, dependence, and fear of AIDS.
2. F: At 2 percent, fear of AIDS does not rank as a major reason. The slice of the pie that represents fear of AIDS is the smallest section.
3. F: People do not marry for companionship as often as they marry for love. More than twice as many marry for love than for companionship.
4. T: Some 36 percent of the people in this sample said they married for love.
5. F: Unplanned pregnancies are not addressed in this pie chart.

## PRACTICE 2

Textbook Skills

**A.** Study the following graphic, from the college textbook, *The Interpersonal Communication Book*. Based on the data in the graph, mark each numbered statement **T** if it is true, **F** if it is false, or **DK** if you don't know, based on the given data.

### Excuses in Romantic and Workplace Relationships

Here are the five intended messages along with some specific examples. As you read this table visualize a specific situation in which you recently made an excuse. Can what you said (or should have said) be organized into this five-step plan?

| Intended Message | In Romantic Relationships | At Work |
|---|---|---|
| **1.** I see. | I should have asked you first; you have a right to be angry. | I understand that we lost the client because of this. |
| **2.** I did it. | I was totally responsible. | I should have acted differently. |
| **3.** I'm sorry. | I'm sorry that I didn't ask you first. | I'm sorry I didn't familiarize myself with the client's objections to our last offer. |
| **4.** Forgive me. | Forgive me? | I'd really like another chance. |
| **5.** I'll do better. | I'll never loan anyone money without first discussing it with you. | This will never happen again. |

Source: DeVito, Joseph, *The Interpersonal Communication Book*, 10th ed. (p. 230). Published by Allyn & Bacon, Boston, MA. 

_____ **1.** The graphic is a bar graph.

_____ **2.** The graphic presents a five-step process involved in making an excuse in a romantic relationship or at the workplace.

_____ **3.** Bad excuse makers rely on excuses too often.

_____ **4.** A good excuse takes responsibility for wrongdoing.

_____ **5.** The intended message of step 5 suggests that a good excuse is based on changing one's behavior.

**B.** Study the following graph, from the college sociology textbook *Drugs, Behavior, and Modern Society,* 3rd ed. (Levinthal, p. 243). Based on the data in the graph, mark each numbered statement **T** if it is true, **F** if it is false, or **DK** if you don't know, based on the given data.

**Deaths and Cigarette Smoking**

Distribution of the approximately 430,000 U.S. deaths attributed each year to cigarette smoking.

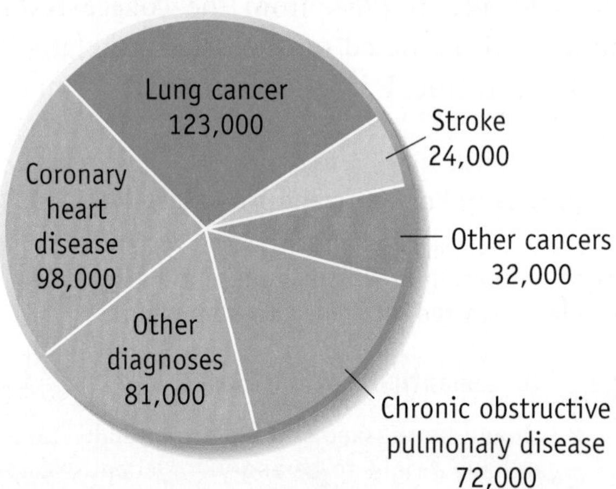


Original source: Centers for Disease Control and Prevention. (1999, March 3). *Morbidity and Mortality Weekly Report.* Atlanta: Centers for Disease Control and Prevention.

_____ **6.** This graph is based on information gathered from the approximately 430,000 U.S. deaths linked to cigarette smoking each year.

_____ **7.** Coronary heart disease is the leading cause of deaths attributed to cigarette smoking.

_____ **8.** Other than the rare cases of genetic defects, cigarette smoking is the only cause of chronic obstructive pulmonary disease.

_____ **9.** This graph is a type of line graph.

_____ **10.** Lung cancer is a major cause of deaths attributed to cigarette smoking.

## Diagrams

A **diagram** is a graphic that explains in detail the relationships between the parts of an idea to the whole idea. Diagrams include flowcharts, pictograms, and drawings.

### Flowcharts

A **flowchart** is a diagram that shows a step-by-step process. Each step or phase of the process is typically shown in a box or circle, and the shapes are connected with lines and arrows to show the proper order or flow of the steps. Flowcharts are used in a number of subject areas including social sciences, science, history, and English.

**EXAMPLE** Study the following flowchart, from the college textbook *Psychology: The Brain, the Person, the World.* Based on the data in the diagram, mark each numbered statement **T** if it is true, **F** if it is false, or **DK** if you don't know, based on the given information.

**Stages of Creative Thought**

The four stages of creative thought proposed by Wallas (1926).

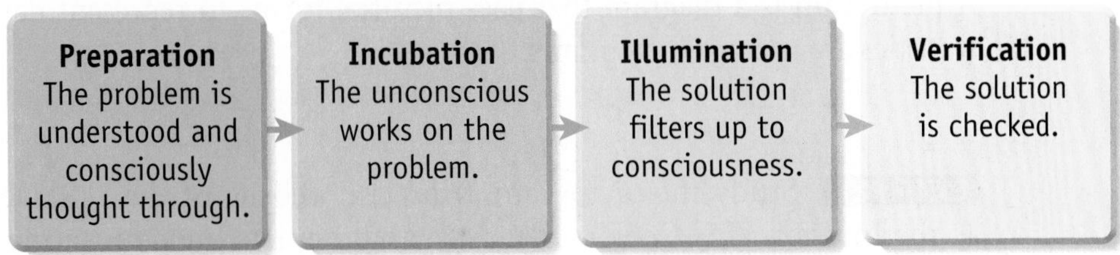


Note: Creativity is defined as the ability to produce something original of high quality or to devise effective new ways of solving a problem.

Source: From Stephen M. Kosslyn & Robin S. Rosenberg, *Psychology: The Brain, the Person, the World* © 2001. Published by Allyn and Bacon, Boston, MA. Copyright © 2001 by Pearson Education. Reprinted/adapted by permission of the publisher.

_____ **1.** The flowchart illustrates four stages of creative thought.

_____ **2.** Creativity focuses only on the ability to produce something original.

_____ **3.** The creative process takes place mainly on a conscious level of thought.

_____ **4.** Incubation occurs before illumination.

_____ **5.** Creativity is a learned behavior.

**EXPLANATION** Compare your answers to the ones given here.

1. T: The flowchart illustrates four stages of creative thought.
2. F: Creativity does focus on the ability to produce something original. However, the definition in the footnote also states that creativity devises effective ways of solving a problem. Thus creativity includes both the ability to create a poem or painting and the practical ability to raise funds.
3. F: The flowchart explicitly states that during incubation, the creative process takes place mainly on an unconscious level of thought and filters into consciousness during the third stage, illumination.
4. T: According to this flowchart, incubation occurs before illumination.
5. DK: The flowchart reveals the creative process, but it does not address the question of whether or not creativity is a learned behavior.

### Pictograms

A **pictogram** is a diagram that uses pictorial forms to represent data. Usually statistics are used in pictograms.

**EXAMPLE** Study the pictogram, from the website of the U.S. Department of the Interior, U.S. Geological Survey that depicts the devastating sequence of the eruption of Mount St. Helens. Based on the data in the pictogram, mark each numbered statement **T** if it is true, **F** it is false, or **DK** if you don't know based on the given information.

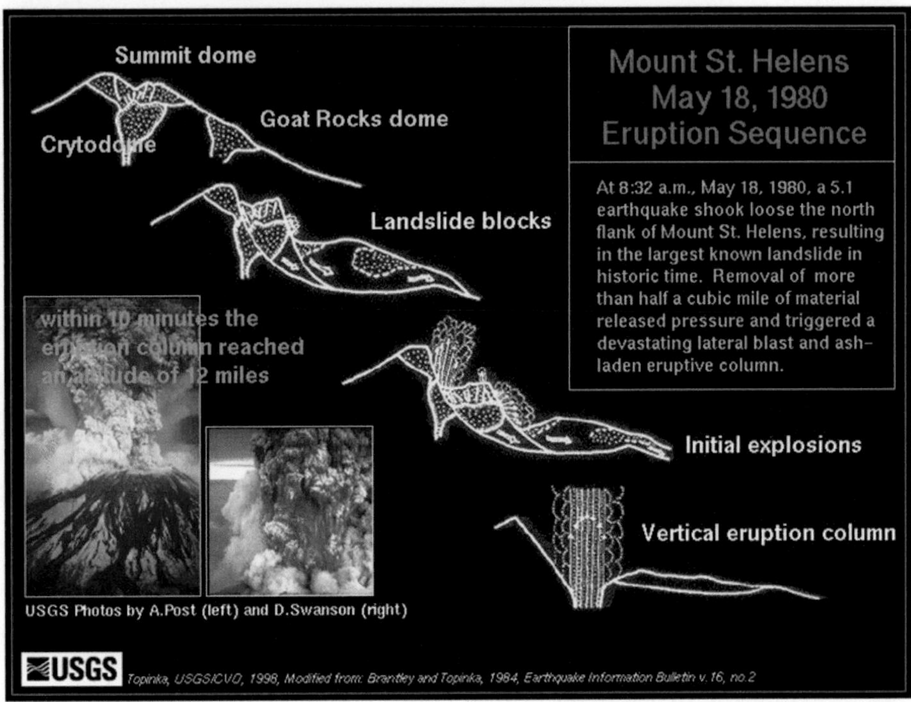


*Source:* http//vulcan.wr.usgs.gov/Photo/Pictograms/May18_sequence.html

_____ **1.** An earthquake caused the 1980 eruption of Mount St. Helens.

_____ **2.** The earthquake caused a landslide that released trapped pressure within Mount St. Helens.

_____ **3.** Within ten minutes Mount St. Helens was leveled to its base.

_____ **4.** A thick column of ash quickly rose to a height of twelve feet.

_____ **5.** Mount St. Helens will erupt again.

**EXPLANATION**

1. T: The caption beneath the pictogram's title states this fact.
2. T: The same caption states "removal of more than a cubic mile of material released pressure and triggered devastating lateral blast." We can logically infer that the earthquake caused this removal of material.
3. F: Within ten minutes a column of tall ash developed. The pictogram clearly depicts that part of Mount St. Helens remains standing.
4. DK: Though logic implies that Mount St. Helens will erupt again, this pictogram offers no evidence that it will do so. The purpose of this pictogram is to depict an historical event.

## Drawing

A **drawing** is an artist's illustration of a process or idea. The drawing shows the relationships among all the details in the picture. Often these drawings are dependent on the accompanying text, and an effective reader must move back and forth between the drawing and text for full understanding.

**EXAMPLE** Study the following drawing, from the college textbook *Health: The Basics.* Based on the data in the diagram, mark each numbered statement **T** if it is true, **F** if it is false, or **DK** if you don't know, based on the given information.

Textbook Skills

______ **1.** During an isometric exercise, the muscle does not lengthen or shorten.

______ **2.** A concentric contraction shortens the muscle.

______ **3.** During an eccentric contraction, the muscle does not move.

______ **4.** Eccentric contractions occur when movement is in the same direction as gravity.

______ **5.** During an isometric contraction, the joint does not move.

**EXPLANATION**

1. T: During an isometric exercise, the muscle does not lengthen or shorten.

**Isometric, Concentric, and Eccentric Muscle Actions**

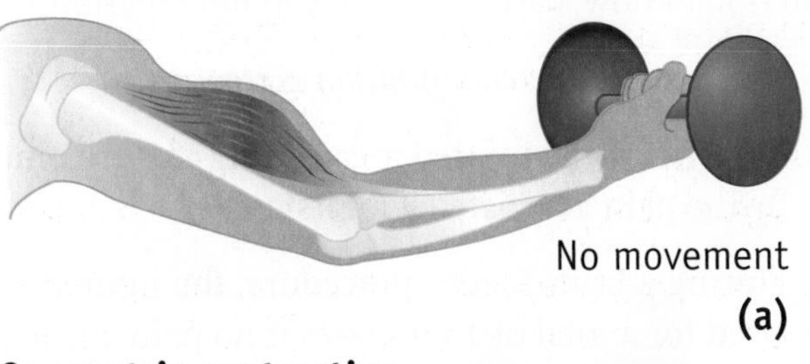


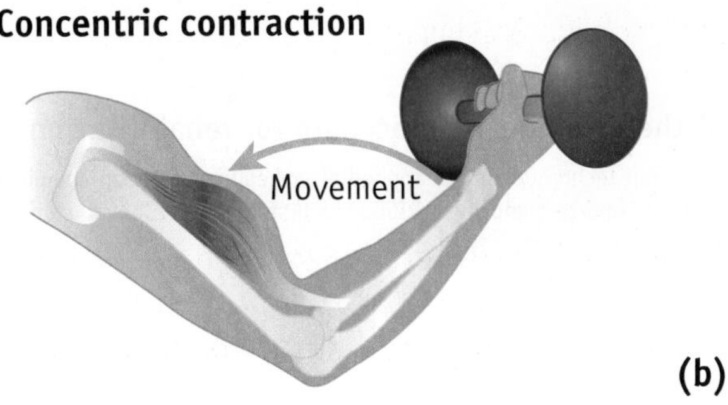


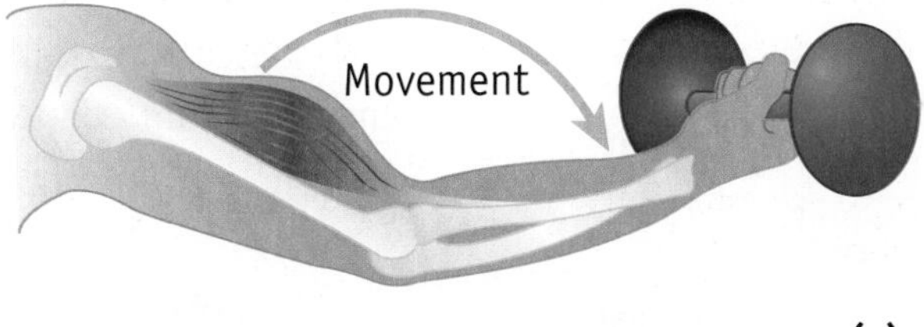


Source: Powers, S., and E. Howley, *Executive Physiology*. Copyright © 1997. Published by Brown and Benchmark, Madison, WI. Reprinted by permission. The McGraw-Hill Companies.

2. T: A concentric contraction shortens the muscle.
3. F: During an eccentric contraction, the muscle lengthens.
4. T: Eccentric contractions occur when movement is in the same direction as gravity. The arrow points in a downward arc, representing downward motion, which is the same direction as gravity.
5. T: During an isometric contraction, the joint does not move.

## PRACTICE 3

Based on the ideas in the following graphic, from the college textbook *Total Fitness and Wellness*, mark each numbered statement **T** if it is true, **F** if it is false, or **DK** if you don't know, based on the given information.

_____ **1.** A synonym for *rehabilitation* is *treatment.*

_____ **2.** Exercise of the injured area during this treatment must be guided by the pain associated with its use.

_____ **3.** During a cryokinetics procedure, the injured area should be exercised for a total of 15 minutes if no pain occurs.

**The steps of the cryokinetics procedure for rehabilitating injuries**

Cryokinetics is a fairly new rehabilitation technique that is applied after healing has been completed. It uses alternating periods of treatment using ice, exercise, and rest known as RICE, which stands for *rest, ice, compression, elevation.*

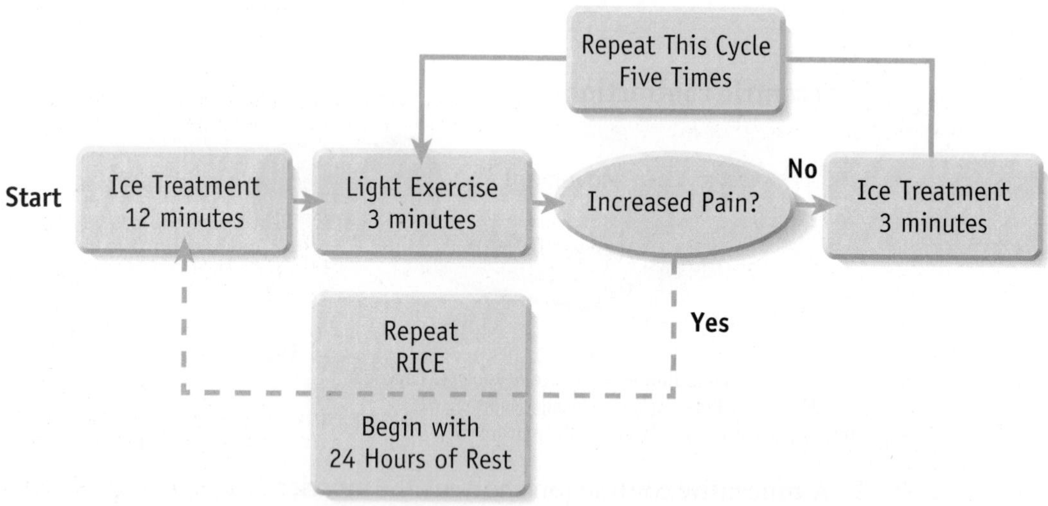


Source: Reprinted from Fig. 13.8, Scott K. Powers, *Total Fitness and Wellness*, 3rd ed., pp. 295, 296.

_____ **4.** RICE stands for the elements of a proper diet to promote healing.

_____ **5.** Ice is used during the procedure to reduce pain.

# REVIEW Test 1

**A.** Study the following graphic from the college textbook *Biology: Concepts and Connections*. Then mark each numbered statement **T** if it is true, **F** if it is false, or **DK** if you don't know, based on the given information.

On the basis of several features, **angiosperms**, flowering plants, can be divided into two groups called monocots and dicots. The names monocot and dicot refer to the first leaves that appear on the plant embryo. These embryonic leaves are called seed leaves or *cotyledons*. The following chart illustrates a comparison of monocots and dicots.

_____ **1.** The graphic is a pictogram.

_____ **2.** A monocot embryo has one seed leaf.

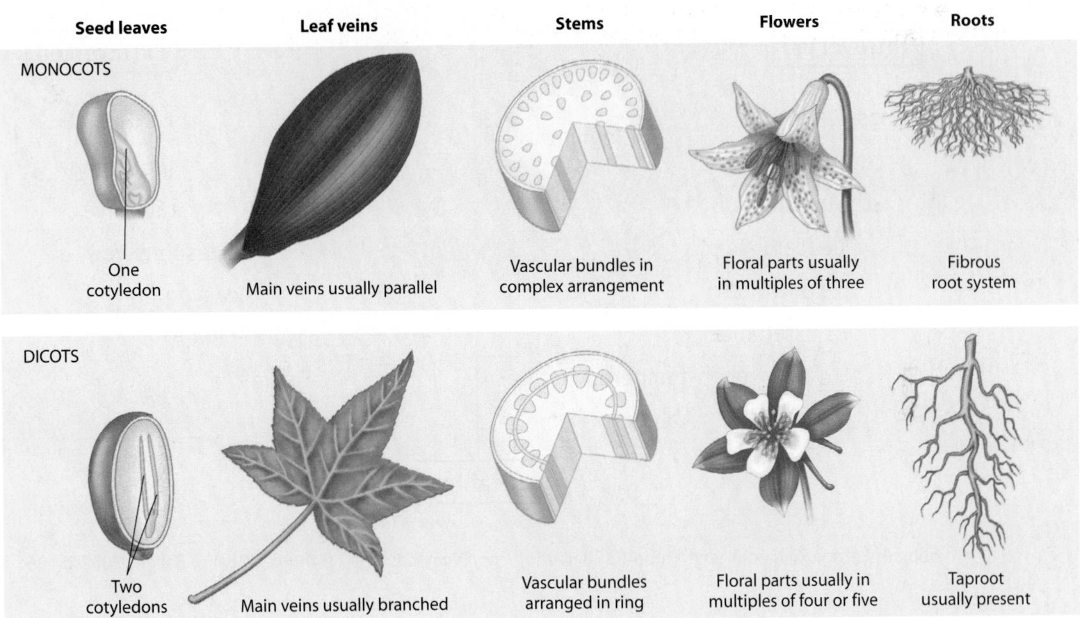


Source: *Biology: Concepts and Connections, 5th ed.* Campbell, Neil and Jane B. Reece, Martha Taylor, and Eric J. Simon. Benjamin Cummings, 2005 p. 625.

_____ **3.** A dicot has two seed leaves.

_____ **4.** The terms *monocot* and *dicot* refer to the number of floral parts.

_____ **5.** The root system of a dicot is fibrous.

**B.** Based on the ideas in the following graphic from *Psychology and Life*, mark each numbered statement **T** if it is true, **F** if it is false, or **DK** if you don't know, based on the given information.

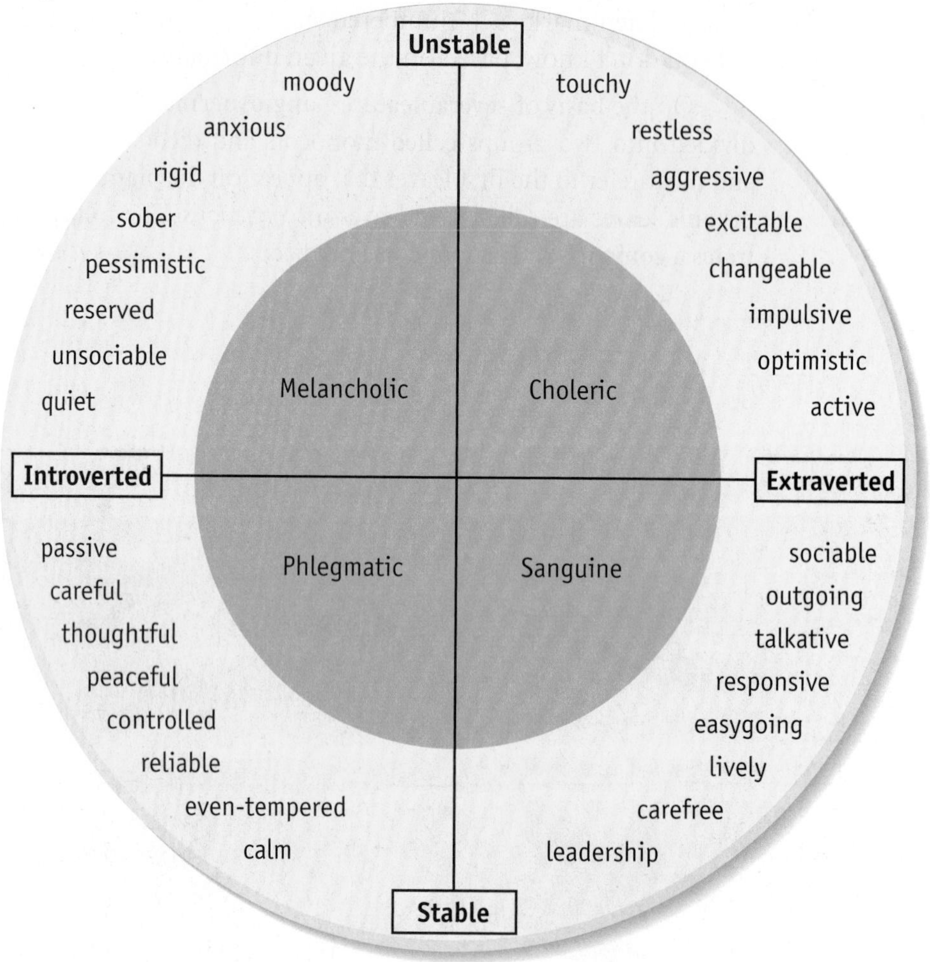

**Unstable**

moody
anxious
rigid
sober
pessimistic
reserved
unsociable
quiet

touchy
restless
aggressive
excitable
changeable
impulsive
optimistic
active

Melancholic
Choleric

**Introverted**
**Extraverted**

Phlegmatic
Sanguine

passive
careful
thoughtful
peaceful
controlled
reliable
even-tempered
calm

sociable
outgoing
talkative
responsive
easygoing
lively
carefree
leadership

**Stable**

Source: Gerrig, Richard J. and Philip G. Zimbardo, *Psychology and Life,* 16th ed., Allyn & Bacon, 2002 p.435.

_____ **6.** This graphic is a bar graph.

_____ **7.** The ideas in this graphic have been scientifically verified.

_____ **8.** A choleric personality type is restless and aggressive.

_____ **9.** A person with a choleric personality type is a less moral person than a person with a phlegmatic personality.

_____ **10.** Melancholic and phlegmatic types are withdrawn.

# REVIEW Test 2

**A.** Based on the ideas in the following graphic, from the college textbook *Messages: Building Interpersonal Communication Skills*, 4th ed. (DeVito, p. 27), mark each numbered statement **T** if it is true, **F** if it is false, or **DK** if you don't know, based on the given information.

**Why You Engage in Interpersonal Communication**

This figure illustrates three aspects of interpersonal communication: your purpose, your motivations, and the results you want to achieve. The innermost circle contains the general purposes, the middle circle the motivations, and the outer circle the results you might hope to achieve by engaging in interpersonal communication.

Guidance, direction, attitude, and behavior adjustment
Need to console, help, befriend, feel needed, gain satisfaction
To help: minister to needs of others, console
Increased knowledge of oneself, and the world; skill acquisition
Need to know, acquire knowledge, learn
To learn: acquire knowledge of oneself, others, the world; acquire skills
Relationship formation and maintenance, friendships, love relationships
Need to form relationships, relate to others, interact
To relate: establish/maintain interpersonal relationships
Influence, power, control compliance, agreement
Need to control, influence, gain compliance, secure agreement
To influence: control, manipulate, direct
Enjoyment, pleasure, satisfaction, gratification
Need for diversion, pleasure sensory gratification
To play: escape from work, enjoy oneself
General purposes
Motivations
Results

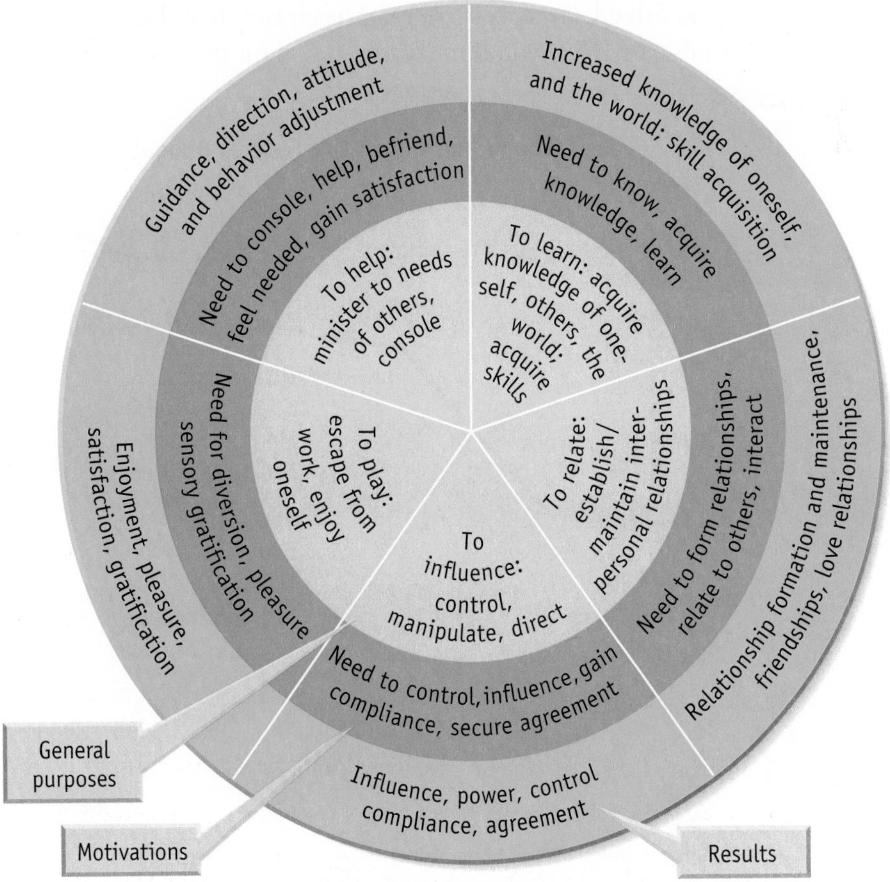

Source: From Joseph A. DeVito, *Messages: Building Interpersonal Communication Skills*, 4th ed. Published by Allyn & Bacon, Boston, MA. Copyright © 1999 by Pearson Education. Adapted by permission of the publisher.

_____ **1.** This graphic is a flowchart.

_____ **2.** The figure illustrates five purposes for engaging in interpersonal communication.

_____ **3.** The general purpose "to influence" is motivated by the need to secure agreement and results in friendship.

_____ **4.** An attitude and behavior adjustment is the result of the need to minister to the needs of others.

_____ **5.** A person who determines to escape from work is often motivated by stress.

**B.** Based on the ideas in the following graphic, from the college textbook *Politics in America,* 5th ed. (Dye, p. 315), mark each numbered statement **T** if it is true, **F** if it is false, or **DK** if you don't know, based on the given information.

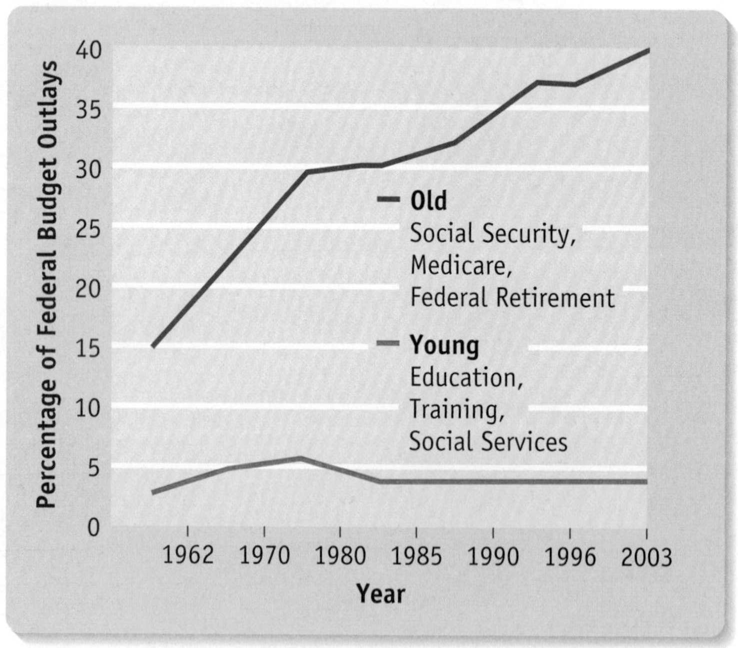


Original source: Budget of the United States Government, 2003.

_____ **6.** This graphic is a line graph.

_____ **7.** The source of this information is not reliable.

_____ **8.** The federal government spends more money on senior citizens than on younger citizens.

_____ **9.** The amount spent on younger citizens has steadily declined since the mid 1980s.

_____ **10.** The federal government spends more money on senior citizens because they are much more likely to vote, which gives them more power with politicians.

# Text Credits


Administration on Aging. "Older Volunteers Leading the Way." U.S. Department of Health and Human Services, 2003. http://www.aoa.gov/press/oam/May_2003/media/fact_sheets/OlderVolunteers.pdf

Agee, Warren K., Phillip H. Ault, and Edwin Emery. *Introduction to Mass Communications*, 12th ed. Published by Allyn and Bacon, Boston, MA. Copyright © 1997 by Pearson Education. Adapted by permission of the publisher.

American Wind Energy Association. "What Is Green Power?" 2003. http://www.awea.org/greenpower/gp_what.html

American Wind Energy Association. "Why Should I Buy Green Power?" 2003. http://www.awea.org/greenpower/gp_why1.html

Asfahani, Magdoline. "Time to Look and Listen" from *Newsweek*, Dec. 2, 1996. All rights reserved. Reprinted by permission.

Aulette, Judy Root. *Changing American Families.* Boston: Allyn and Bacon, 2002.

Barker, Larry L., and Deborah Roach Gaut. *Communication*, 8th ed. Copyright © 2002, 1996, 1993, 1990, 1987, 1984, 1981, 1978 by Pearson Education. Reprinted/adapted by permission of the publisher.

Barry, Dave. "Build Yourself a Killer Bod with Killer Bees" from *Dave Barry Is Not Taking This Sitting Down*! Copyright © 2000 by Dave Barry. Published by Crown Publishers, a division of Random House, Inc.

Benokraitis, Nijole, V. *Marriages and Families: Changes, Choices, and Constraints*, 4th ed. Copyright © 2002, 1999, 1996, 1993 by Pearson Education, Inc. Reprinted by permission of Pearson Education, Inc., Upper Saddle River, NJ.

Bernard, Hannah. "Humpback Whales." Hawaiian Islands Humpback Whale National Marine Sanctuaries, March 2003.

Biden, Joseph, Jr. "Theft of American Intellectual Property: Fighting Crime Abroad and at Home." U.S. Senate Judiciary Subcommittee on Crime and Drugs, Feb. 12, 2002. http://biden.senate.gov/IPREPORT.pdf

Bittinger, Marvin L., and Judith A. Beecher. *Introductory and Intermediate Algebra,* 2nd ed. Copyright © 2003 Pearson Education, Inc. Reprinted by permission of Pearson Education, Inc. Publishing as Pearson Addison Wesley.

Britt, Suzanne. "Neat People vs. Sloppy People." Reprinted by permission of the author.

Brownell, Judi. *Listening: Attitudes, Principles, and Skills*, 2nd ed. Published by Allyn and Bacon, Boston, MA. Copyright © 2002 by Pearson Education. Adapted by permission of the publisher.

Bynum, Jack, and William Thompson. *Juvenile Delinquency: A Sociological Approach*, 5th ed. Published by Allyn and Bacon, Boston, MA. Copyright © 2002, 1999, 1996, 1992, 1989 by Pearson Education. Adapted by permission of the publisher.

Bytwerk, Randall. "How They Lie: Must the Politician Lie?" © 2000 by Randall Bytwerk.

Caldwell, Alicia A. "Tough Talk, Very Little Action." *The Daytona Beach News-Journal*, April 8, 2007, p. 9A. Used with permission of the Associated Press. Copyright © 2007. All rights reserved.

Califano, Jr. Joseph A. "Forward and Accompanying Statement." *No Safe Haven: Children of Substance-Abusing Parents.* National Center on Addiction and Substance Abuse (CASA) at Columbia University, Jan. 1999. http://www.casacolumbia.org. Reprinted by permission.

Campbell, Neil A., Lawrence G. Mitchell, and Jane B. Reece. *Biology: Concepts & Connections*, 5th ed. Copyright © 1994, 1997, 2000, 2002, 2005 by Benjamin Cummings, an imprint of Addison Wesley Longman, Inc. Reprinted/adapted by permission of Pearson Education, Inc.

Campbell, Neil A., Jane B. Reece, and Eric J. Simon. *Essential Biology,* 2nd Ed. Copyright © 2004 by Benjamin Cummings, an imprint of Addison Wesley Longman, Inc.

Carlson, Neil R., and William Buskist. *Psychology: The Science of Behavior*, 5th ed., © 1994. Published by Allyn and Bacon, Boston, MA. Copyright © 1997 by Pearson Education. Reprinted by permission of the publisher.

Carnes, Mark C., and John A. Garraty. *The American Nation: A History of the United States to 1877*, Vol. 1, 10th ed. Copyright © 2000 by John A. Garraty. Reprinted by permission of Pearson Education, Inc.

Carnes, Mark C., and John A. Garraty. *The American Nation: A History of the United States from 1865*, Vol. 2, 10th ed. Copyright © 2000 by John A. Garraty. Reprinted by permission of Pearson Education, Inc.

Carnes, Mark C., and John A. Garraty. *The American Nation: A History of the United States*, 11th ed. Copyright © 2003 by John A. Garraty. Reprinted by permission of Pearson Education, Inc.

Caruso, David B. "Study Urges Ephedra Restrictions." *Orlando Sentinel*, Feb. 4, 2003, p. A11.

"College Binge Drinking, Pill Abuse Intensify," from MSNBC, online, Mar. 17, 2007. Used with permission of The Associated Press. Copyright © 2007. All rights reserved.

Condon, John C. *With Respect to the Japanese: A Guide for Americans*. Yarmouth, ME: Intercultural Press, 1984. Reprinted with permission.

"Consumer Adult Book Purchasing," from 1999 Consumer Research Study on Book Purchasing, *American Booksellers Association,* Book Industry Study Group, 2000. Reprinted by permission of the Book Industry Study Group.

De Vito, Joseph A. *Essentials of Human Communication*, 4th ed. Published by Allyn and Bacon, Boston, MA. Copyright © 2002 by Pearson Education. Reprinted/adapted by permission of the publisher.

De Vito, Joseph A. *The Interpersonal Communication Book*, 10th ed. Published by Allyn and Bacon, Boston, MA. Copyright © 2004, 2001 by Pearson Education. Adapted by permission of the publisher.

De Vito, Joseph. *Messages: Building Interpersonal Communication Skills*, 4th ed. Published by Allyn and Bacon, Boston, MA. Copyright © 1999 by Pearson Education. Reprinted/adapted by permission of the publisher.

DeCarlo, Pamela. "Educating for Sexual Responsibility," Center for AIDS Prevention Studies, University of California, San Francisco. Reprinted from *The San Diego Tribune*, Aug. 18, 1995. http://www.caps.ucsf.edu/sexed.html. Reprinted by permission.

Deckers, Lambert. *Motivation: Biological, Psychological, and Environmental.* Published by Allyn and Bacon, Boston, MA. Copyright © 2001 by Pearson Education. Adapted by permission of the publisher.

DeGeneres, Betty. Excerpt from "Pass Christian, Mississippi" (pp. 1–7) from *Love, Ellen*. Copyright © 1999 by Betty DeGeneres. Reprinted by permission of HarperCollins Publishers.

"Depression: Seasonal Affective Disorder" from the National Mental Health Association. Copyrighted and published by the National Mental Health Association, no part of this document may be reproduced without written consent. Adapted by permission.

Deutsch, Nancy. "A Slave to Routine?" from *HealthDay News*. Copyright © 2002. Reprinted by permission of HealthDay.

"Distribution of Composite IQs of 1937 Standardization Group" from *the Stanford-Binet Manual for the Third Revision*. Copyright © 1973 by Houghton Mifflin Company. Reprinted by permission of The Riverside Publishing Company. All rights reserved.

Divine, Robert A. *The American Story.* Copyright © 2002 by Addison-Wesley Educational Publishers Inc. Reprinted by permission of Pearson Education, Inc.

DiYanni, Robert (ed.). *One Hundred Great Essays.* New York: Longman, 2002.

DiYanni, Robert, and Pat C. Hoy II. *The Scribner Handbook for Writers*, 3rd ed. Copyright © 2001, 1998, 1995 by Allyn and Bacon. Reprinted by permission of Pearson Education, Inc.

Donatelle, Rebecca J. *Access to Health*, 7th ed. Copyright © 2002 Pearson Education, Inc., publishing as Benjamin Cummings. Reprinted by permission of Pearson Education, Inc.

Donatelle, Rebecca J. *Health: The Basics*, 5th ed. Copyright © 2003 by Pearson Education, Inc., publishing as Benjamin Cummings. Reprinted by permission of Pearson Education, Inc.

Drozdowski, Ted. Interview with BB King from *Guitar World*. www.guitarworld.com. Copyright © 2000, Harris Publications, Inc.

Dye, Thomas R. *Politics In America*, 5th ed. Copyright © 2003, 2001, 1999, 1997, 1994 by Pearson Education, Inc. Adapted by permission of Pearson Education, Inc., Upper Saddle River, NJ.

Edwards III, George C., Martin P. Wattenberg, and Robert L. Lineberry. *Government in America: People, Politics, and Policy*, Brief version, 5th ed. Copyright © 2000 by Addison-Wesley Educational Publishers Inc. Reprinted by permission of Pearson Education, Inc.

Federal Emergency Management Agency. "How Do You Rescue a Horse?" FEMA for Kids. 2003. http://www.fema.gov/kids/horse_rescue.htm

Fishbein, Diana H., and Susan E. Pease. *The Dynamics of Drug Abuse*. Published by Allyn and Bacon, Boston, MA. Copyright © 1996 by Allyn and Bacon. Reprinted/ adapted by permission of the publisher.

Folkerts, Jean, and Stephen Lacy. *The Media in Your Life: An Introduction to Mass Communication*, 2nd ed. Published by Allyn and Bacon, Boston, MA. Copyright © 2001, 1998 by Pearson Education. Adapted by permission of the publisher.

"Frequently Asked Questions: Cleaning Your Teeth and Gums (Oral Hygiene)" from ADA.org: American Dental Association, Apr. 14, 1998. Reprinted with permission.

Fritz, Sara (Times Washington Bureau Chief). "Curbing College Drinking Starts with a Change in Attitude," from *St. Petersburg Times*, Apr. 15, 2002. Copyright © *St. Petersburg Times* 2002. Reprinted by permission.

Galvin, Kathleen M., and Bernard J. Brommel. *Family Communication: Cohesion and Change*, 5th ed. Published by Allyn and Bacon, Boston, MA. Copyright © 2000 by Pearson Education. Reprinted by permission of the publisher.

Gamble, Teri Kwal, and Michael W. Gamble. *The Gender Communication Connection.* Boston, Houghton Mifflin. Copyright 2002. Reprinted with permission.

"Garden Banks." National Marine Sanctuaries, 2004.

Gerrig, Richard J., and Philip G. Zimbardo. *Psychology and Life*, 16th ed. Published by Allyn and Bacon, Boston, MA. Copyright © 2002 by Pearson Education. Reprinted/adapted by permission of the publisher.

Girdano, Daniel A., Dorothy E. Dusek ,and George S. Everly, Jr. *Controlling Stress and Tension*, 6th ed. Copyright © 2001, 1997,1993, 1990, 1986 by Allyn and Bacon. Reprinted by permission of Pearson Education, Inc.

Grunwald, Michael. "A Small Nation's Big Effort Against AIDS" from *The Washington Post Foreign Service*, Dec. 2, 2002. Copyright © 2002, *The Washington Post.* Reprinted with permission.

Haines, Valerie J., George M. Diekhoff, Emily E. LaBeff, and Robert E. Clark. "College Students' Top Ten Reasons for Cheating." *Research in Higher Education*, Vol. 25, No. 4. Copyright © 1986 Agathon Press, Inc. Reprinted with kind permission of Springer Science and Business Media.

Harris, Thomas E., and John C. Sherblom. *Small Groups and Team Communication*, 2nd ed. Published by Allyn and Bacon, Boston, MA. Copyright © 2002, 1999 by Allyn and Bacon. Reprinted by permission of the publisher.

Hellmich, Nanci. "Legislators Try to Outlaw Soft Drinks, Sugary Snacks at Schools" from *USA Today*, Feb. 13, 2003. Copyright © 2003, *USA Today*. Reprinted with permission.

"It Gets Around: Mysterious Invention Moves People" from ABCNews.com homepage, Dec. 4, 2001. Reprinted by courtesy of ABCNEWS.com.

Jaffe, Michael L. *Understanding Parenting*, 2nd ed. Published by Allyn and Bacon, Boston, MA. Copyright © 1997 by Pearson Education. Adapted by permission of the publisher.

Johnson, Mark I. "Shark Attacks Decline Globally, Stay the Same in Area," from *The Daytona Beach News-Journal*, Feb. 7, 2003. Reprinted with permission.

Kafka, Franz. "The Metamorphosis" from *Franz Kafka: The Compete Stories* by Franz Kafka, edited by Nahum N. Glatzer, translated by Willa and Edwin Muir. Copyright© 1946, 1947, 1948, 1949, 1954, 1958, 1971 by Schocken Books, a division of Random House, Inc.

Keillor, Garrison. "How the Crab Apple Grew" from *Leaving Home*. Copyright © 1988. New York: Viking Penguin. Reprinted with permission.

Keller, Helen. "The Day Language Came into My Life." In *The Story of My Life.* 1902.

Kelly, Marylin. Communication @ Work. Published by Allyn and Bacon, Boston, MA. Copyright © 2006 by Pearson Education. Reprinted by permission of the publisher.

Kelly, William J., and Lawton, Deborah L. Discovery: An Introduction to Writing, 2nd ed. Copyright © 2003 by Pearson Education.

Kennedy, X. J., and Dana Gioia. *Literature: An Introduction to Fiction, Poetry, and Drama*, 8th ed., Interactive Edition. Copyright © 2002 by X. J. Kennedy and Dana Gioia. Reprinted by permission of Pearson Education, Inc.

King Jr., Martin Luther. "Letter from Birmingham Jail." Copyright 1963 Dr. Martin Luther King Jr., copyright renewed 1991 by Coretta Scott King. Reprinted by arrangement with the Heirs to the Estate of Martin Luther King Jr., c/o Writers House as agent for the proprietor, New York, NY.

Kosslyn, Stephen M., and Robin S. Rosenberg. *Psychology: The Brain, The Person, The World.* Published by Allyn and Bacon, Boston, MA. Copyright © 2001 by Pearson Education. Reprinted by permission of the publisher.

Krents, Harold. "Darkness at Noon" from *The New York Times*, May 26, 1976. Copyright © 1976 by the New York Times Co. Reprinted by permission.

Lee, Jeffrey A. *The Scientific Endeavor: A Primer on Scientific Principles and Practice.* Copyright © 2000 by Addison Wesley Longman, publishing under the Benjamin Cummings imprint. Adapted by permission of the publisher.

Levinthal, Charles F. *Drugs, Behavior, and Modern Society*, 3rd ed. Published by Allyn and Bacon, Boston, MA. Copyright © 2002 by Pearson Education. Reprinted by permission of the publisher.

"Low Ground Waters Can Lead to Sinkholes" from *Streamlines*, Fall 2000. Used by permission of the St. Johns River Water Management District.

Lubar, Steven, and Kathleen Kendrick. "Looking at Artifacts, Thinking About History." Smithsonian Center for Education and Museum Studies. Copyright © 2003 Smithsonian Institution. Reprinted by permission.

Lundestad, Geir. "The Nobel Peace Prize 1901–2000" from *The Nobel Prize, The First 100 Years* (eds. A. Wallin Levinovitz and N. Ringertz). Published by Imperial College Press and World Scientific Publishing. Reprinted by permission of the publisher.

Madura, Jeff. *Personal Finance*, 2nd ed. Adapted from pp. 1, 5, 37, 40, 125, 160, 186–187, 196, 235, 403. Copyright © 2004 by Pearson Education, Inc, publishing as Pearson Addison Wesley. Reprinted by permission of Pearson Education, Inc.

Maier, Richard. *Comparative Animal Behavior: An Evolutionary and Ecological Approach.* Published by Allyn and Bacon, Boston, MA. Copyright © 1998 by Pearson Education. Reprinted by permission of the publisher.

Mansfield, Duncan. "Last Recognized Widow of a Union Veteran in Civil War Dies at 93." Copyright © 2002 News-Journal Corporation. Reprinted with permission of The Associated Press.

Martin, James Kirby, et al. *America and Its Peoples: A Mosaic in the Making*, 3rd ed. Copyright © 1997 by James Kirby Martin, Randy Roberts, Steven Mintz, Linda O. McMurry, and James H. Jones. Adapted by permission of Pearson Education, Inc.

McCafferty, Dennis. "How Long Will You Live?" Originally appeared in the March 2, 2007 issue of USA WEEKEND. Reprinted with permission.

McGuigan, Frank J. *Encyclopedia of Stress.* Published by Allyn and Bacon. Copyright © 1999 by Allyn and Bacon. Adapted by permission of Pearson Education.

Menard, Valerie. *The Latino Holiday Book: From Cinco de Mayo to dia de Los Muertos.* Copyright © 2000 by Valerie Menard. Reprinted by permission of Da Capo/Marlowe & Co., a member of Perseus Books Group.

Motion Picture Association of America. "The Movie Rating System." Copyright © the Motion Picture Association of America, Inc. www.filmratings.com Reprinted by permission.

"Native American Sports Mascots." *Issues and Controversies*, Apr. 12, 2002. FACTS.com. http://www.2facts.com. Reprinted with permission.

Neergaard , Laura. "Doctors Go To Source to Treat Pain from Surgery." Copyright © 2003 The Associated Press.

"No, You're Not Paranoid" from *CQ Researcher*, June 15, 2001, Vol. II, No. 23. Reprinted with permission.

Novak, Mark A. *Issues in Aging: An Introduction to Gerontology.* Published by Allyn and Bacon, Boston, MA. Copyright © 1998 by Pearson Education. Reprinted by permission of the publisher.

O'Connor, Flannery. "Revelation" from *The Complete Stories.* Copyright © 1971 by the Estate of Mary Flannery O'Connor. Reprinted by permission of Farrar, Straus and Giroux, LLC.

O'Connor, Karen, and Larry J. Sabato. *American Government: Continuity and Change.* Copyright © 2000 by Pearson Education, Inc. Adapted by Permission of Pearson Education.

O'Connor, Karen, Larry J. Sabato, Stefan D. Haag, and Gary A. Keith. *American Government: Continuity and Change, 2004 Texas Edition.* Copyright © 2004 by Pearson Education, Inc. Adapted by permission of Pearson Education.

Parish, Ramona. "Messages from a Welfare Mom" from *Newsweek*, Feb. 23, 2003.

Patterson, James, and Peter Kim. *The Day America Told the Truth.* Copyright © 1991 by James Patterson and Peter Kim. Reprinted with the permission of Simon & Schuster Adult Publishing Group.

Pew Research Center. "Sources of Political Campaign News in Presidential Elections Years," November 10-12, 2000. Copyright © 2000 Pew Research Center. Reprinted by permission.

Plutchik, Robert. *Emotion.* Published by Allyn and Bacon, Boston, MA. Copyright © 1980 by Pearson Education. Adapted by permission of the publisher.

Powers, S., and E. Howley. *Exercise Physiology.* Copyright © 1997. Published by Brown and Benchmark, Madison, WI. Reprinted by permission of The McGraw-Hill Companies.

Powers, Scott K., and Stephen L. Dodd. *Total Fitness and Wellness*, 3rd ed. Copyright © 2003 Pearson Education, Inc., publishing as Benjamin Cummings. Reprinted/adapted by permission of Pearson Education, Inc.

"Prevention and Cessation of Cigarette Smoking." U.S. National Cancer Institute, 2003.

Pruitt, B.E., and Jane J. Stein. *Health Styles: Decisions for Living Well*, 2nd ed. Copyright © 1999 by Allyn and Bacon. Reprinted by permission of Pearson Education, Inc.

"Questions and Answers about Cigar Smoking and Cancer," US National Cancer Institute.

"Reviews Luxury Sedans, Lexus LS 430" from *Kelley Blue Book: The Trusted Resource*, Feb. 2003. http://www.kbb.com. Reprinted with permission.

Roesch , Roberta. "How to Take a Bite Out of Criticism" as appeared in *Relationships Today*, August 1988. Copyright © 1988 by Roberta Roesch. Reprinted by permission of the author.

Sanabria, Harry. *The Anthropology of Latin America and the Caribbean.* Published by Allyn and Bacon, Boston, MA. Copyright © 2007 by Pearson Education. Adapted by permission of the publisher.

Sandburg, Carl. "Fog" from *Chicago Poems.* Copyright 1916 by Holt Rinehart and Winston and renewed 1944 by Carl Sandburg. Reprinted by permission of Harcourt, Inc.

"Should Cell Phones Be Banned in Cars?" from *CQ Researcher* Mar. 16, 2001, Vol. II, No. 10. Reprinted with permission.

Sills, Judith. "Co-Parenting Adult Children" sidebar. Copyright © 2003 by Judith Sills. Reprinted by permission of William Morris Agency, Inc. on behalf of the author. Originally appeared in *Family Circle,* May 13, 2003.

Smith, Robert L., and Thomas M. Smith. *Elements of Ecology,* 4th ed. Copyright © 2000 by Addison Wesley Longman, Inc., publishing under the Benjamin Cummings imprint. Reprinted by permission of Pearson Education, Inc.

Soto, Gary. "How Things Work." Copyright © 1985 by Gary Soto. Reprinted by permission of the author.

Sporre, Dennis J. *The Creative Impulse,* 6th ed. Copyright © 2003, 2000, 1996, 1993, 1990, 1987 by Prentice Hall Inc. Adapted by permissions of Pearson Education, Inc., Upper Saddle River, NJ.

"Structure of Skeletal Muscle," SEER Program, U.S. National Cancer Institute, 2004.

Sullivan, Bob. "ID Theft Victims Get Little Help" from MSNBC, online, Feb. 10, 2003. http://www.msnbc.com. Reprinted with permission from MSNBC Interactive L.L.C.

Tannen, Deborah. "Different Words, Different Worlds" from *You Just Don't Understand.* Copyright © 1990 by Deborah Tannen. Reprinted by permission of HarperCollins Publishers, Inc.

"The Disorder Named AD/HD – CHADD Fact Sheet #1." CHADD: Children and Adults with Attention-Deficit/Hyperactivity Disorder, copyright 2004. http://www.chadd.org/fs/fsl.htm. Reprinted by permission.

Troyka, Lynn Quitman. *Simon & Schuster Workbook for Writers,* 6th ed. Published by Pearson Education, Inc. Copyright © 2002, 1999, 1996, 1993, 1990, 1987 by Lynn Quitman Troyka. Reprinted by permission of Pearson Education, Inc., Upper Saddle River, NJ.

"Unfasten Your Seat Belt!" from *Prevention,* July 2003. Reprinted by permission of *Prevention* Magazine. Copyright © 2003 Rodale Inc. All rights reserved.

U.S. Geological Survey. "Cool Earthquake Facts." 2002. http://earthquake.usgs.gov/4kids/facts.html

U.S. Geological Survey. "Types of Volcanic Eruptions." 1997. http://pubs.usgs.gov/gip/volc/eruptions.html

U.S. Geological Survey. "USGS Wildland Fire Research." 1998.
http://www.usgs.gov/themes/Wildfire/fire.html

U.S. Senate Committee on the Judiciary. "The Effect of Violence in the Media." Adapted from Children, Violence, and the Media. September 15, 2007

Wallas, Mary Graham. "The Four Stages of Creative Thought" from *The Art of Thought.* Copyright 1926 by Harcourt, Inc., and renewed 1954 by Mary Graham Wallas. Reprinted by permission of the publisher.

Wanderman, Richard. "One Person's Path to Literacy." Copyright © 2000 by Richard Wanderman.
http://www.ldresources.com/articles/path_to_literacy.html. Reprinted by permission of the author.

Washington, Booker T. *Up From Slavery: An Autobiography.* New York: Random House, Inc., 1901.

Weeks, Dustin. *Batteries and Bottled Water* by Dustin Weeks. Reprinted by permission of the author.

"What Do Users Do on the Internet?" from *The Internet Study.* Stanford Institute for the Quantitative Study of Society. Stanford University, CA. Reprinted by permission.

Wilen, William, Richard Kindsvatter, and Margaret Ishler. *Dynamics of Effective Teaching,* 4th ed.. Published by Allyn and Bacon, Boston, MA. Copyright © 2000 by Pearson Education. Reprinted by permission of the publisher.

Wollstadt, Loyd, MD. "Research Shows Potential Benefits, Risks of Wine" from *To Your Health,* May 6, 2003. University of Illinois College of Medicine at Rockford.
http://rockford.uic.edu/toyourhealth/wine.htm. Reprinted by permission of the author.

Woolfolk, Anita. *Educational Psychology,* 8th ed. Published by Allyn and Bacon, Boston, MA. Copyright © 2001 by Pearson Education. Adapted by permission of the publisher.

"Would you say the government is pretty much run by a few big interests looking out for themselves or that it is run for the benefit of the people?" Copyright © 2000 The Gallup Organization. All rights reserved. Reprinted with permission from www.gallup.com and the poll conducted July 6-9, 2000.

# Photo Credits

P. 24, Bill Bachmann/Bruce Coleman; p. 27, Chris Hondros/Getty Images; p. 31, Lori Adamski Peek/Getty Images; p. 46, Corbis; p. 50, top, Art Wolfe/Getty Images; bottom, Raymond Gehman/Corbis; p. 76, Adey Bryant/ Cartoon Stock; p. 89, AP/Wide World Photos; p. 115, Mike Simons/Getty Images; p. 120, BIOS/Peter Arnold; p. 158, Punchstock; p. 164, Flip Nicklin/Minden Pictures; p. 176, David Sieren/Visuals Unlimited; p. 196, Romilly Lockyer/ Getty Images; p. 204, Punchstock; p. 221, Jim Brandenburg/ Minden Pictures; p. 245, Joanna McCarthy/ Getty Images; p. 255, Strauss/Curtis/Corbis; p. 267, David Weintraub/ Photo Researchers, Inc.; p. 277, Ingo Arndt/Foto Natura/ Minden Pictures; p. 289, Sara Gray/Getty Images; p. 308, Robert Galbraith/Reuters/Corbis; p. 318, James H. Robinson/Photo Researchers, Inc.; p. 359, Bob Daemmrich/ The Image Works; p. 379, ML Harris/Getty Images; p. 409, Noah Graham/Getty Images; p. 411, Mort Walker/King Features Syndicate; p. 415, AP/Wide World Photos; p. 418, Hulton Archive/Getty Images; p. 422, Cumberland County Historical Society, Carlisle, PA; p. 438, Mike Watson Images/Superstock; p. 455, Spencer Rowell/ Getty Images; p. 460, Victoria & Albert Museum/Art Resource, NY; p. 461, left, Reuters/Corbis; middle, AP/Wide World Photos; right, Will & Deni McIntyre/Corbis; p. 467, Jim Brandenburg/ Minden Pictures; p. 475, Zits/King Features Syndicate; p. 480, John Cole/Political Cartoons/ Cagle Cartoons; p. 499, Brown Brothers; p. 503, Gary D. Landsman/Corbis; p. 507, TempSport/Corbis; p. 509, Randy Glasbergen, www.glasbergen.com; p. 515, Bill Bachmann/ PhotoEdit Inc.; p. 521, DILBERT reprinted by permission of United Features Syndicate, Inc.; p. 524, Reprinted with Special Permission of King Features Syndicate; p. 542, Geostock/ Getty Images; p. 549, The New Yorker Collection 1991, Donald Reilly from cartoonbank.com. All rights reserved.; p. 555, Larry Wright © 2002, The Detroit News/Cagle Cartoons; p. 561, National Milk Processor Promotion Board/Lowe Worldwide; p. 564, Eising Food Photography/ Stock Food; p. 575, Zogbaum/Stock Food; p. 577, Peter Willott/St. Augustine Record; p. 582, left, Stockbyte/ Superstock; right, Tom Prettyman/PhotoEdit Inc.; p. 620, National Archives; p. 623, National Archives; p. 633, Library of Congress; p. 648, US Department of Health and Human Services; p. 650, Picture History; p. 671, Mike Powell/Getty Images; p. 687, Steve Mason/Getty Images; p. 694, AP/Wide World Photos; p. 742, Rescue Critters, LLC; p. 751, Reuters/Corbis; p. 769, Jupiter Images

# Index